Forging the Past

FORGING THE PAST

Invented Histories in Counter-Reformation Spain

Katrina B. Olds

Yale
UNIVERSITY
PRESS
New Haven & London

Published with assistance from the foundation established in memory of Oliver Baty Cunningham of the Class of 1917, Yale College.

Copyright © 2015 by Yale University.

All rights reserved.
This book may not be reproduced, in whole or in part, including illustrations, in any form (beyond that copying permitted by Sections 107 and 108 of the U.S. Copyright Law and except by reviewers for the public press), without written permission from the publishers.

Yale University Press books may be purchased in quantity for educational, business, or promotional use. For information, please e-mail sales.press@yale.edu (U.S. office) or sales@yaleup.co.uk (U.K. office).

Set in PostScript Electra and Trajan types by Tseng Information Systems, Inc.
Printed in the United States of America.

Library of Congress Control Number: 2015931444
ISBN: 978-0-300-18522-5 (cloth : alk. paper)

A catalogue record for this book is available from the British Library.

This paper meets the requirements of ANSI/NISO Z39.48-1992 (Permanence of Paper).

10 9 8 7 6 5 4 3 2 1

Let it cause no disquiet if any of those things which are written here are found stated differently elsewhere, since even histories, in the diversity of events, are found to be mutually contradictory; yet they are serviceable for the single fruit of utility and moral worth. I do not care to run the risk of formulating truth; my intention is merely to share ungrudgingly for the utility of my readers what I have read in different writers. For even the Apostle does not say "whatever is written is true" but "whatever is written is written for our instruction."

—John of Salisbury, *Policraticus*

What is verisimilitude but a representation that commands our assent despite our skepticism about human deceitfulness? We sit back and enjoy the show, despite our awareness of the theatrical machinery. We acquiesce in the mystification and embrace the simulacrum.

—Denis Vrain-Lucas, letter from Maison Centrale de Poissy prison, Paris, 1872

Contents

Acknowledgments ix

A Note on Translations and Orthography xiii

Maps xv

An Introduction to History and Myth in Early Modern Spain 1

PART I CREATION

ONE The Forger between Friends and Enemies in Toledo 29

TWO The Jesuits, the Inquisition, and History 63

THREE How to Forge a History:
The Authentic Sources of the False Chronicles 99

FOUR Jews, Arabic-Speakers, and New Saints:
The False Chronicles and Controversy 126

FIVE The Debut of the Chronicles:
Higuera's Republic of Sacred Letters 144

SIX In Defense of Local Saints: Higuera versus Rome 163

PART II: RECEPTION

SEVEN Flawed Texts and the Negotiation of Authenticity 201

EIGHT The *Cronicones* in Local Religion: *Historia Sacra* Writ Small   234

NINE The Politics of the *Cronicones* in Madrid and Rome   260

TEN From Apocrypha to Forgery   286

Conclusion: New Saints, New Histories in Modern Spain   309

List of Abbreviations   315

Notes   317

Bibliography   361

Index   405

Acknowledgments

> It is a laborious madness and an impoverishing one, the madness of composing vast books—setting out in five hundred pages an idea that can be perfectly related orally in five minutes. The better way to go about it is to pretend that those books already exist, and offer a summary, a commentary on them.
> —Borges, "The Garden of Forking Paths"

Not a few times I wished that my forger and his garrulous acolytes had taken Borges's advice, and simply distilled their main points into a breezy summary. This might have made the book easier to write, but then again it might have also eliminated its reason for existing in the first place. Now that I'm emerging from the labyrinth, I am very pleased to acknowledge those who shared their kindness, encouragement, and wisdom during this project's gestation. First thanks should go to Nicolás Antonio and José Godoy Alcántara, without whose long-ago labors this book could not have been written—at least not in a single lifetime. In the course of sorting out the various threads of this story, I often fell into their enjoyable, beguiling, and indispensable warrens of scholarship, only to emerge, days later, with answers to questions I didn't even know I had.

In the realm of the living, I am very lucky to have benefited from the guidance and encouragement of Anthony Grafton and Kenneth Mills. Each in his own way has been the model of consummate professionalism, collegiality, and intellectual rigor to which I will always aspire. In addition to their unflagging enthusiasm, high standards, and generosity, I am grateful for the prodding questions and pregnant suggestions with which they have always managed to enrich my own perspective. I also thank Richard L. Kagan for his crucial interventions, including timely advice on the shape of this project, which he kindly shared over coffee in New York City a number of years ago. For their wisdom, wit, and humanity, I am indebted to Molly Greene, William Chester Jordan, Jim Laine, and Cal Roetzel, as well as to the late Juanita Garciagodoy.

The research and writing of this book never would have been possible without the financial support of Princeton University's Graduate School and History Department, as well as its Association of Graduate Alumni, Center for the Study of Religion, Council on Regional Studies, Program in Latin American Studies, and Shelby Cullom Davis Center. Crucial support came in the form of a J. William Fulbright Foundation research fellowship, and a Charlotte W. Newcombe Dissertation Fellowship from the Woodrow Wilson Foundation. Most recently, I have benefited from the support of the Office of the Dean of Arts and Sciences at the University of San Francisco, and, most of all, from the unstintingly generous assistance of the University of San Francisco's Faculty Development Fund, which, like the forty-hour workweek, we owe to organized labor (in this case, the USF Faculty Association, which is Local 4269 of the AFL-CIO).

The archivists, librarians, and staff at several institutions welcomed me warmly and facilitated my research in countless ways. In Jaén, my thanks to Juan Francisco Martínez Rojas of the Archivo Histórico Diocesano de Jaén, Juan del Arco Moya at the Archivo Histórico Provincial de Jaén, as well as the Instituto de Estudios Giennenses and the Biblioteca Pública Provincial de Jaén. In Madrid, the Biblioteca Nacional and the Real Academia de la Historia furnished essential texts and services efficiently. In Rome, I benefited from courteous and orderly assistance in the Bibliotheca Apostolica Vaticana, Archivio Segreto Vaticano, and the Archivum Romanum Societatis Iesu. In an early stage, I was also lucky to consult the collections of the Archivo General de las Indias and the Escuela de Estudios Hispanoamericanos in Seville, and, in Granada, the Biblioteca Universitaria de la Universidad de Granada and the intimate Archivo Histórico de la Provincia de Andalucía SI. The Hispanic Society of America, New York Public Library's Rare Books and Wertheim Rooms, and Princeton's Firestone Library provided vital materials and workspace over a number of years. At the University of San Francisco, Joseph Campi of Interlibrary Loans, and John Hawk, Librarian and Head of Special Collections at Gleeson Library, have offered cheerful assistance in response to an avalanche of requests.

This book has also benefited from suggestions from audiences at Berkeley's Early Modern Sodality, the California Spanish History Symposium at the University of California at San Diego, the Center for the History of Emotions at Berlin's Max Planck Institute for Human Development, the Early Modern Research Cluster at the University of California at Davis, Princeton University's Center for the Study of Religion, Stanford University's Center for Medieval and

Early Modern Studies, as well as annual meetings of the Association for Spanish and Portuguese Historical Studies, the Renaissance Society of America, the Sixteenth Century Studies Conference, and the Social History Society (UK). A very special *köszönöm* is owed to conveners and participants of "The Vision Thing: Studying Divine Intervention," a National Humanities Center SIAS Summer Institute sponsored by the Andrew W. Mellon Foundation and the Alexander von Humboldt Foundation in 2007–2008, which was hosted by the Center for Advanced Study in Behavioral Sciences in Stanford, and by the Collegium Budapest Institute for Advanced Study.

For scholarly references, timely critiques, encouragement, writing companionship, and more, I am profoundly indebted to Bonifacio Bartolomé, Paula Birnbaum, Liam Brockey, Sarah Buck, Andrea Campetella, Marty Claussen, Karoline Cook, Cheryl Czekala, Dennis Darling, Candice Harrison, Heather Hoag, Katie Holt, Gábor Klaniczay, María Amparo López Arandia, Lois Lorentzen, Kate Lusheck, Ruth MacKay, Julio and Monica Moreno, Tania Munz, Kathy Nasstrom, Marjolein Oele, Rosa Pinzón, Gretchen Starr-LeBeau, Patricio Torres Hermida, Karin Vélez, Taymiya Zaman, and San Francisco's Cafe la Flore. I must also extend my gratitude to those who critiqued early versions of my work, or shared their scholarship, sometimes before they thought it was ready, including Susan Boynton, William A. Christian, Jr., Simon Ditchfield, Freddy Domínguez, María Mercedes García-Arenal, A. Katie Harris, Maria Rosario Hernando Sobrino, Antoine Mazurek, Erin K. Rowe, María Tausiet, Katherine Elliot Van Liere, and Amanda Wunder. Special thanks to Annie Burson-Ryan, Nicole López-Hagan, and Michael Williams for data compilation, and to the students in my seminar on myths and forgeries, as well as Deborah Bruce-Hostler and the anonymous reviewers for Yale University Press, all of whom helped refine, correct, and enrich my writing. Thank you to Elizabeth Puhl for the beautiful maps.

For their enduring friendship, moral support, creativity, and humor, I thank Jessie Betts, Jamie Bonchu, Rebecca Herman, Clare and Erica Judge, Valerie, Megan, and Kevin McQueeney, Elizabeth Puhl, and Mark and Ruby Shoffner. To my own nuclear family, Cameron, Gabriel, and Malcolm Judge, I owe the most transcendent gratitude. For nourishing me in body and soul, for loving companionship, and, above all, for their mere existence, I am more grateful than I can ever say.

Portions of chapters 3 and 6 were first published in Olds, Katrina B. "The 'False Chronicles,' Cardinal Baronio, and Sacred History in Counter-Reformation Spain." *Catholic Historical Review* 100, no. 1 (2014): 1–26, copyright © 2014 The Catholic University of America Press.

Portions of chapters 7 and 9 appeared in Olds, Katrina B. "The Ambiguities of the Holy: Authenticating Relics in Seventeenth-Century Spain." *Renaissance Quarterly* 65, no. 1 (2012): 135–184.

A Note on Translations and Orthography

All translations are the author's except where noted. In quoting primary sources from the period, nonstandardized spelling and usage have been retained. Personal and place-names have been anglicized when there is a standard English usage, but left in the original when not.

Map 1. Iberian Peninsula, circa 1600

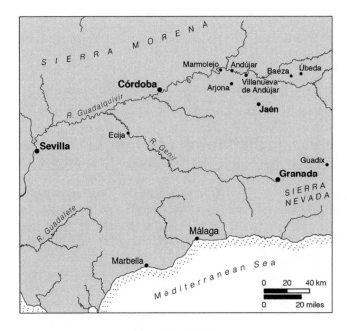

Map 2. Andalusia

An Introduction to History and Myth in Early Modern Spain

At the end of the sixteenth century, the most influential minds of Spain were abuzz with news of an exciting discovery. In 1594, Jerónimo Román de la Higuera, a middle-aged Jesuit priest in Toledo, reported that he had received four long-lost historical texts, the first of which was *The Chronicle of Universal History (Chronicon omnimodae historiae)* by Flavius Lucius Dexter, a contemporary of Saint Jerome and son of a bishop of Barcelona, known in Spanish as Flavio Lucio Dextro. The text, which had been lost in the early Middle Ages, narrated in concise entries the very beginnings of Christianity in Spain and Portugal, and provided details about the epoch of Roman rule in Iberia for which virtually no textual evidence remained. Dexter's narrative was continued by three other authors, Marcus Maximus, Luitprand, and Julián Pérez. Lined up chronologically, these late antique and medieval chronicles provided an unbroken outline of ecclesiastical history from the time of Christ to the twelfth century such as the Iberian Peninsula had never possessed, a cumulative body of historical information that had the potential to alter the way Spanish history was written and imagined.

The texts related a version of Spanish sacred history that was familiar in its broadest outlines, to wit: Roman Hispania was visited by the apostle James the Greater (Santiago), who left a number of disciples behind as bishops of the principal cities, whence Christianity spread quickly. As elsewhere in the Roman Empire, the Christian minority was persecuted until the age of Constantine; after the fall of Rome and various barbarian invasions, Hispania was taken over by Visigoths, who soon converted from the Arian heresy to Catholicism. The Islamic invasion of AD 711 brought renewed persecution and oppression to the Christian majority until the resurgence of northern Christian kingdoms began to chip away at Islamic rule—in what subsequent generations dubbed the Reconquest—beginning with the important victory of Alfonso VI of Castile over Toledo at the end of the eleventh century, with which the fourth and final chronicle closes.

As José Godoy Alcántara, the texts' most influential critic, would explain in his unsurpassed 1868 study of these and other early modern Spanish forgeries, in their coverage of over a millennium of history, Higuera's *cronicones* elucidated an unprecedented wealth of detail regarding the history of Christianity in Spain. They surveyed an eye-popping range of people and places, including "the origin of national [churches], the succession of their prelates, the celebration of councils, heresies that arose and were extirpated, [and] the foundation dates of the old Spanish religious orders." The texts also confirmed a vision of Spanish Christianity that would have been intimately familiar to Catholics in the decades after the Council of Trent (1545–1563). In Higuera's rendition, the beliefs, practices, and traditions of the primitive Church were virtually identical to those of his own: as Godoy explained, according to the chronicles, "since the beginnings of the Church, the authority of prelates was recognized, obedience to the Holy See had been offered, the practice of pilgrimage established, [as well as] the building of temples, the celebration of the mass, the cult of images, and the saints had been favored with the gift of miracles."[1] In other words, early Christianity was fundamentally Counter-Reformation Catholicism as it had evolved after Trent. Moreover, the texts had an impeccable genealogy. According to Higuera, one of his former students, now a Jesuit, had copied them from originals held by a merchant in Worms, who had obtained them from one of the oldest manuscript collections in Europe, namely, that of the Benedictine house of Fulda in the German-speaking territories of the Holy Roman Empire.

If the texts confirmed many received truths about Iberian Christianity, they also introduced scores of new ones. One of the cronicones' most enduring and important contributions was in their enumeration of the names and places of origin of dozens of previously unknown martyrs, saints, and bishops. Oftentimes, this was completely new information to the communities in question; in this way, as Godoy Alcántara pointed out, Higuera tried to "console the places (*pueblos*) that lacked native patron saints," by helping to "uncover those saints who were [hitherto] unknown." Other times, Higuera's texts propped up preexisting traditions in need of some help, as when he "declare[d] as authentic doubtful relics and pious writings that had been rejected as apocryphal."[2]

If the chronicles sounded too good to be true, that is because they were. As late seventeenth- and eighteenth-century critics would eventually determine, the texts were fakes. By the close of the 1700s, learned opinion would turn away from the texts' scintillating historical data. Yet when the cronicones first surfaced at the end of the sixteenth century, this was far from a foregone conclusion. Hernando de Pecha (1567–1659), Higuera's former pupil and a fellow Jesuit, declared that neither Higuera, nor anybody else, could have fabricated the texts. It was simply not possible. In a defense of Higuera, which he wrote sometime between 1640 and 1659, Pecha reasoned that "If one considers the context of these authors, each had his own particular style, stories, events, and lives of different Saints." No one man could have possessed the knowledge, creativity, and skill sufficient to fabricate four distinct authorial voices:

> If the books of Flavius Dexter, Marcus Maximus, Heleca, Walderedus, Luitprand, and Julián Pedro [sic] are false, and were composed by Father Higuera . . . [he] would be the most illustrious man in the world, if he could invent them out of his head, with the chronologies that are in them, with day, month, and year; and with the names of the Emperors, Kings, Prelates, Archbishops, Bishops, Holy Martyrs, Confessors, Virgins, Cities, Villages, and Places of Spain, Italy, and France, and Germany. Such a thing would be incredible.[3]

If the task of ventriloquizing four separate chronicles spanning well over a millennium of history seemed inconceivable to Pecha, it has proven rather less impressive to modern readers, who have worried less about Higuera's techniques as a forger than about his own delusions and inadequacies. In the estimation of Julio Caro Baroja, Higuera was an overly pious albeit prolific crank incapable of achieving very much in terms of conventional scholarship, even by the standards of the time:

> There was, among the Jesuits of Toledo, a father named Jerónimo Román de la Higuera, a man of middling learning, of an obliging nature, curious about antiquities, of unsteady opinions that followed the direction of his impressions, who tended to take part in learned questions with a conciliatory spirit, and who kept busy illustrating ancient geography, writing lives of little-known saints, and the histories of ancient cities, whose dark patches he illuminated and whose gaps he filled with conjectures and infelicitous inductions that many times became received truths. He ended up, like Ulysses, believing in his own fictions.[4]

Thus, Caro Baroja implied, Higuera promulgated his own "Cretan lies." In this way, the Jesuit was like those ancient writers whose excessive fondness for myths had led the Greek geographer Strabo to reject their works as unreliable, and Strabo had lamented "the credulity of the historians and their *philomythia*"— their love of myths.[5] Strabo even declared that on certain historical questions one might be more rightly guided by ancient poets like Homer and Hesiod, rather than by prose historians like Herodotus, Hellanicus of Lesbos, and their ilk.[6]

Yet the stance of the ancients on the relationship between myth and history was more labile and sophisticated than Caro Baroja had allowed. Strabo critiqued writers of history who repeated legends uncritically, yet he also acknowledged that historians and poets alike often found themselves compelled to draw upon legends. This was not necessarily out of an inability to tell truth from fiction, but rather, in order to please the audience, that is, "to gratify the taste for the marvellous and the entertaining."[7] Thus, even as Strabo contrasted history, whose aim was truth, with myth, whose purpose was "to please and to excite amazement," he also acknowledged that legendary material had a place in historical narratives, particularly if it was treated as such. For this reason he praised one historian who "expressly acknowledged the practice" by declaring that he would "narrate myths too in his History." This was in contrast to those like "Herodotus, Ctesias, Hellanicus, and the authors of the Histories of India," who instead inserted the legendary material silently, thereby giving an unwarranted "air of plausibility" to material that they knew full well was apocryphal.[8]

Just as the relationship between myth and fact and between poetry and history was more complex in classical times than Caro Baroja might have imagined, so it was in early modern Spain as well. In the fertile climate of late sixteenth-century Spain, the chronicles' vines grew madly, sprouting long-reaching and elaborate tendrils, such that by the mid-seventeenth century virtually all of Spain's learned men possessed copies of Higuera's chronicles, from Ávila to Zaragoza. At first, manuscript copies radiated out to Higuera's correspondents and remained under the protective mantle of interested patrons. After Higuera's death in 1611, the texts were finally published in a total of seven editions between 1619 and 1651. Now they really did revolutionize Spanish history, as the cronicones fell with a loud splash into the pool of general literate circulation and rippled into the murkier waters beyond.

In contrast to Caro Baroja, who asserted that we must differentiate between deliberate falsifications such as Higuera's texts on one hand, and well-intentioned but apocryphal material such as pious legends, literary "mystifications," and humanist "games" on the other, it is the contention of this book that many early modern texts, in fact, actually resist this categorization. As we shall see, Higuera's texts cannot be segregated from the other forms of historical and hagiographic invention seemingly motivated by well-intentioned "credulity." As *Forging the Past* will suggest, we limit our own comprehension of how these texts came into existence, and why they continued to be important sources of information, if we approach them merely as fakes. Higuera's texts differed in degree, not necessarily in kind, from other works of good-faith scholarship; as such, quarantining them from the broader context of mainstream scholarship in which they were produced prevents us from truly understanding not only the cronicones, but also Spanish historical scholarship and local religion from the sixteenth century to the modern era.

One of the first readers to behold the false chronicles was Higuera's friend and contemporary, the learned bishop of Segorbe, Juan Bautista Pérez. Like the Jesuit, Pérez was intimately familiar with the authentic sources of early Spanish history. When Higuera shared a preliminary version of the chronicles of Dexter and Maximus with him, Pérez remained singularly unimpressed. He related his doubts to Cristóbal Palomares, Toledo's cathedral librarian and a mutual acquaintance, in a 1595 letter: "I wrote these days to Father Higuera telling him that the *Chronicle* of Dexter and Maximus from Fulda, a copy of which I have here, is fake: and I can prove that it is fake with a hundred arguments, but I don't have time to write them."[9] Pérez would react in a similar manner to another discovery that had emerged circa 1595, the lead books (*plomos*) of Granada, a set of forged texts and objects that presented an alternative history in which the earliest Christians in Spain were Arabic-speaking martyrs. Later critics would hail Pérez as a lone voice in a wilderness of credulity, and his critique as a pivotal moment in the history of the chronicles that would cause a sort of crisis of confidence for Higuera.[10]

If Pérez's private objections were an early bump in the road for Higuera, the indomitable Jesuit recovered quickly.[11] In the next few years, Higuera revised the chronicles by significantly augmenting them with entries that touched upon virtually every topic relevant to Spanish religious history. And, as it turned out, Pérez's skepticism remained the minority opinion for the better part of a century. Perhaps it should not surprise us, then, that once the texts entered circulation in print, they inspired the rewriting of Spanish history on a monumental scale, as well as multifarious local and regional enthusiasms. Nearly every seventeenth-century author who treated the late antique and medieval history of Spain felt compelled to reckon with the distinctive historical vision of the cronicones. By the first years of the seventeenth century, references to Higuera's chronicles began to multiply in books on all sorts of matters, including a theological treatise on an early medieval heresy, a saint's life, a municipal history, a history of royal Benedictine monasteries, and a polemical treatise in defense of the tradition that the apostle Santiago was buried in the Iberian Peninsula.

In spite of their popularity, the chronicles were never unproblematic. Their value as historical evidence was contested from the beginning. This was due to the circumstances of the texts' discovery, as well as their several internal weaknesses. First of all, nobody could find the alleged originals in Fulda, nor the merchant in Worms. The trail had gone cold in 1595, when Higuera's former pupil, a Jesuit named Thomas Torralba, died. Moreover, readers complained about the grammatical errors, historical and linguistic anachronisms, and outright chronological mistakes that marred the texts, both in manuscript and print copies. These defects, and the murky details about the texts' origins, led readers to debate their integrity and authenticity over the course of the seventeenth century. Critics were hard pressed to decide: Did the texts' imperfections represent fatal flaws that rendered them useless? Or could some degree of historical information be salvaged from what were essentially authentic texts, but which nevertheless had been corrupted by the imperfect process of manuscript transmission?

As these were difficult questions to resolve, some seventeenth-century readers simply took both positions. At the beginning of his 1615 history of the martyrs of Zaragoza, the jurist and cathedral canon Martín Carrillo seemed to speak directly to critics of Dexter's chronicle when he ventured that in the absence of any sources at all about a remote period, something was better than nothing; and, he reckoned, this particular text was worth reading, especially since it promoted essentially virtuous and worthy aims, such as the commemoration of holy men and women:

> I declare that the work is curious and worthy of regard, especially since no author from our own city has written about these saints [. . .] You should be satisfied that what he writes [. . .] comes from good and authentic authors, is based on valid reasoning, is useful to the people, and provides so many saints to imitate, so that we might admire through them the sovereign marvels of God [. . .] and the memory of so many Bishops—excellent men who, through their works and virtues, planted and disseminated the Holy Gospel in our Kingdom.[12]

Over fifty pages later, Carrillo began to sound significantly less sanguine, as his pragmatic reasons for accepting Dexter's historical witness started to sag under the weight of his own objections to the text. Carrillo noted that although the appearance of the manuscript of the *Chronicon* had been lauded by many people with "great celebration," the text was plagued with "so many improper usages" (*impropriedades*) that he feared "it could lead us to say that [the history] is not [Dexter's], or that it is corrupted, with many things added and subtracted that are not true, and that distort it greatly."[13] Carrillo carefully couched his reservations in the subjunctive tense. Zaragoza was not only home to the cathedral of La Seo, where he was a canon, but also to its traditional rival, the church of Santa María del Pilar, whose canons were some of the earliest and most enthusiastic adopters of the chronicles; in fact, Higuera had sent them an early version of the texts in the first years of the seventeenth century.[14] El Pilar's canons later sponsored what became the first printed joint edition of the Dexter and Maximus chronicles (1619), due in large part to the fact that the texts seemed to support the tradition that their institution was constructed by Santiago on the very spot where the Virgin Mary appeared to him atop a pillar—hence the church's name—centuries before Zaragoza's cathedral.

Remarkably, interest in the chronicles was not limited to the rarified circles of those who could read the Latin texts. Higuera's version of history came to life at the level of lived history and religion as well, as communities embraced new patron saints, regional prelates drew up new liturgical calendars, local scholars wrote new sacred histories, and entire communities began to venerate martyrs that the chronicles had introduced. Like genies let out of so many bottles, Dexter-inspired, revised visions of the ancient Christian past floated through their creator's fingers to become real, and to take on narrative, devotional, and physical existence.

Throughout the 1600s, learned opinion of the chronicles ranged from enthusiasm to skepticism. Although by the close of the century the judgments of a handful of members of the Spanish intellectual elite began to harden into skepticism, this was not a linear or unanimous development. The Sevillian scholar and bibliographer Nicolás Antonio (d. 1684) lambasted the texts in a 1652 manuscript; his appellation for the texts, the "false chronicles" (*falsos cronicones*) persists today, and has been so influential that many authors are under the mistaken impression that the word *cronicón* is itself derogatory when, in fact, it is merely the singular form of the Greek plural *chronica*.[15] Since Antonio wrote at the high tide of Dexter's popularity and influence, his text remained relatively unknown. Two years later, the powerful archbishop of Toledo, Cardinal Baltasar de Moscoso y Sandoval, approved the printing of a comprehensive history of Toledo that cribbed most of its details directly from the false chronicles.[16]

By the time Antonio's critique finally saw print in 1742, Spain was in the early years of the Enlightenment, and the intellectual and cultural climate had shifted significantly. Yet even in this atmosphere of increased skepticism, Antonio's critique did not find an eager audience, and it would not be until the end of the eighteenth century that the Spanish intellectual community at large would agree that the four chronicles were fake. Yet in many ways, it was too late: the texts had already inspired readers to create their own, revised visions of the past, many of which still endure in Spanish memory, myth, and history. To their dismay and irritation, Enlightenment critics and their direct descendants in nineteenth- and twentieth-century academic circles could not undo the fact that during the interval from 1595 to about 1670 the texts had altered the sacred landscape and historical imagination of Spain forever.

Forging the Past examines the social, political, and cultural setting in which Higuera wrote in order to explain how and why these texts made sense. The book traces the texts' trajectory, from creation to circulation to lived experience. It examines the conversations and interpretive acts that made the texts seem real, both to their creator and to their readers, beginning with their "invention" (*inventio*) at the end of the sixteenth century. According to Sebastián de Covarrubias's first comprehensive dictionary of Castilian (1611), *inventar* was to invent a new thing, discover something that already existed, or to fabricate a lie.[17] For Renaissance Italian humanists and artists, *inventio* could possess a somewhat more positive valence, and was often used to denote the emulation of the best models of the past.[18] And, significantly, *invención* could also be employed to describe rediscovery, as in those cases when saints' relics were uncovered anew. Indeed, there were so many relic *invenciones* in the sixteenth century that it must have seemed reasonable to hope that even more would come to light shortly. This, at least, was the conclusion of Don Sancho Dávila Toledo, in his 1611 treatise on the veneration of relics: "We know that there are many other saints in addition to these in particular churches in Spain . . . and many more than the ones already discovered must be those who have not yet been discovered, since the Christians hid them during the general loss of Spain, and they are now in this [Spanish] Church like hidden treasures."[19]

This study approaches the invention of the false chronicles from all of these semantic and historical angles by looking at the social, cultural, and political contexts in which the authenticity of the chronicles was at once created and contested. As we will see, far from outright fabrications, Higuera's texts were fashioned out of an ingenious mix of tradition and invention, of fact and fiction, in a manner characteristic of early modern revisions of the past. As such, the false chronicles are valuable as clues to what was considered "history" in sixteenth-century Spain. They are also works of historiography, that is, purposeful acts of historical imagination and interpretation on the part of their author and readers, in what Alfred Hiatt has called "forgery as a mode of historical writing."[20] For this reason, *Forging the Past* evaluates the texts from two perspectives: first, as what they were supposed to be, namely, late antique and medieval chronicles, and, second, as what they really were, that is, texts written by a late sixteenth-century Jesuit in Toledo. In tracing the twin aspects of the cronicones as both history and historiography, we shall see that the chronicles' more enthusiastic seventeenth-century readers helped construe the texts as reasonably authentic, albeit imperfect; they also conveyed the chronicles' information about the saints to their own communities. Thanks to the reciprocal communication between intellectual-textual communities and the arbiters of local religion, the texts became true among readers and nonreaders alike, and took root in the historical imagination in the long run.

THE FALSE CHRONICLES AND FORGERIES IN HISTORY

Ever since learned opinion turned against the false chronicles, critics have wondered: Why did so many otherwise critical and well-read people believe the texts were real? And why did Higuera forge the texts in the first place? In their authoritative accounts of the false chronicles and other early modern Spanish forgeries, José Godoy Alcántara and Julio Caro Baroja explained the creation and enthusiastic reception of the forgeries as results of excessive religious devotion and a lack of historical sophistication, both of which blinded audiences to the texts' blatant errors and anachronisms, while also motivating the forgers themselves. From this perspective, Higuera was moved to fabricate a comprehensive narrative of the first twelve centuries of Christianity in Spain by a superabundance of piety that induced him to disregard the difference between fact and fiction for the sake of religion. In the imaginative reckoning of one twentieth-century historian, Higuera's religious and scholarly preoccupations were so all-consuming that "in the same way that, in a place in La Mancha, Don Quijote was eager to make the adventures of chivalric novels real, [Higuera], also infected with 'historical Quijotianism,' fell into a craze of inventing historical documentation."[21]

This explanation is unsatisfactory at many levels, for reasons that will be explored at length in this book. First, most fundamentally, as we shall see, neither the texts nor Higuera's claims about them were entirely false. In ways that will become clear from a careful examination of the context of Higuera's own actions, intentions, and methods, he really did discover many ancient texts and inscriptions. The Jesuit was an assiduous hunter of manuscripts and antiquities, and an exceedingly careful historian; as such, Higuera was one of many such men in early modern Spain's learned circles. This is not to say that he was not a forger. Yet it is important to remember that Higuera drew upon actual historical sources, which he used to create new texts that would look and act like authentic chronicles. After all, to create a convincing and successful forgery, one needs to be intimately familiar with the authentic sources of the past.

Moreover, in dismissing the false chronicles as the product of an overly imaginative and pious priest, critics have neglected a rich body of evidence that suggests that neither Higuera nor his readers approached the texts so naively. Through the course of this study it will become clear that for Higuera and many of his readers the lines separating truth and fiction, as well as past and present, were significantly more blurry than they seem for modern historians and their audiences, for reasons that had everything to do with the climate of historical scholarship and religious imagination in early modern Europe. Thus, while it is important to remember that the texts were forgeries, it is also, in some ways, too simple of a characterization. Even Antonio Agustín, the tough sixteenth-century critic who literally wrote the book on how to evaluate numismatic evidence, admitted that there were some spurious specimens that could nevertheless be admitted, due to their high quality. For example, if somebody were to create an inscription that echoed the words of a revered Latin author, that would not be considered a forgery: "if they have made an inscription, nobody can accuse them of being falsifiers, even if it's not true that the words are really from stones, but rather from the papers of Pliny."[22]

In this context, although Higuera was, as far as we know, the individual who created and disseminated the texts, it is far too reductive to dismiss him as an anomalous or unbalanced individual. Recently scholars have moved away from explaining forgeries simply as the product of an individual's intentions. After all, historical forgeries are not merely fake versions of historical narratives. They are also the forger's own commentary on the past, his projection of what should have been, or what, he might hope, was to be. This approach, exemplified in the work of Giles Constable, Anthony Grafton, and Alfred Hiatt, among others, separates the study of forgery from value judgments. Thus, rather than engaging in speculation about the forger's psychological health or deploring his moral turpitude, as historians of early modern Spanish forgeries have done until relatively recently, this study will ask how these texts might be studied fruitfully within the context of mainstream intellectual, cultural, political, and religious history.[23]

This new approach to forgeries has revitalized the study of historiography, as texts previously deemed worthless have provided new insight into the uses of the past. For example, A. Katie Harris has argued that the forged lead books helped contribute to the construction of a new civic and religious identity among the citizens of Granada. From this perspective, the plomos were not simply a religious fraud, possibly perpetrated by disgruntled descendants of former Muslims looking for an entrée into mainstream Catholic history. They also were pieces of textual and material evidence that enabled a city that had been under Islamic rule for most of its recorded history to claim an ancient and prestigious Christian heritage. Other recent studies have also highlighted the extent to which forged or apocryphal sources were part of early modern revisions of religious and civic identity elsewhere in sixteenth- and seventeenth-century Spain.[24]

Although the isolation in which historians have traditionally studied Spanish forgeries would suggest otherwise, the willingness of early modern scholars and clerics to give credence to material artifacts and texts that seem blatantly anachronistic to modern eyes was most certainly not limited to Spain. This is clearly demonstrated by the persistent popularity of the forgeries attributed to a fifteenth-century Italian friar named Giovanni Nanni, also known as Annius da Viterbo. Annius claimed to have been the lucky beneficiary of a recent discovery by a fellow Dominican "in the East" and, like Higuera a century later, he attributed the texts to actual historical personages, including the Egyptian priest Manetho and the Babylonian priest Berosus. Annius's texts, first published in 1498, combined biblical and classical narratives to endow several European dynasties with impressively ancient origin myths.[25] His wildly ambitious literary forgeries included eleven chronicles attributed to eleven separate authors, in what one scholar has called "the most elaborate complex of authorial pseudo-identities the world had seen."[26]

Since Annius was in the service of the Castilian ambassador at the papal court, he naturally dedicated a special place in his imagined history to the reigning Trastámara dynasty of Castile. The inventive Dominican also endowed Spain with cultural primacy over the ancients: according to his Berosus, not only had Spain enjoyed a rich body of literature eight centuries before the Greeks, but its monarchy had predated that of Troy by an astounding six hundred years. Annius had not been the first to endow the Castilian monarchs with an illustrious genealogy that was at once biblical and classical. Several medieval chroniclers, including Rodrigo Ximénez de Rada and Alfonso X of Castile, had claimed that Noah's grandson Tubal as well as Hercules were the Iberian Peninsula's first settlers.[27] Thus, Annius mixed familiar legends, such as the Trojan origins of the Franks, with novel details of his own invention, which helped make his texts immensely appealing for historians elsewhere in Europe. German, French, Italian, and English authors alike drew on his forgeries to illuminate the continuity between their pre-Roman and contemporary "national" histories, as well as to clarify complicated questions of historical chronology. Long after Annius's critics, such as Melchor Cano, Juan Luis Vives, and many others, demonstrated to their satisfaction that the texts were spurious, the commentaries of Manetho and Berosus continued to find their way into historical narratives and imagery throughout Western Europe.[28]

That otherwise spurious texts continued to find traction among the learned public has boggled the minds of many a modern scholar; yet it is important to remember that not all that was forgery was new. If Annius—or Higuera—had not cloaked his texts in recognizably antique raiments, they would have found a distinctly less welcome reception. This is illustrated by the case of Johannes Trithemius, an abbot from the Rhineland, who in the last years of the fifteenth century published a group of spurious texts that stretched from prehistoric times to the Middle Ages. Among other things, the texts supported the long-standing myth that the Franks had descended from the Trojans. This in and of itself was unremarkable, and, indeed, as one recent observer has noted, "Had Trithemius restricted himself only to known myths, his fiction would probably have become a standard reference-work," as did his 1494 catalogue of ecclesiastical authors.[29] Yet by attributing his texts to several hitherto-unknown authors, Trithemius overreached, and made the mistake of introducing more novelty than his audience could countenance.[30]

In evaluating early modern forgeries, it is also essential to keep in mind the long medieval history of falsification and interpolation, which, of course, was not limited to the Iberian Peninsula. Medieval chroniclers often inserted mythological or spurious material into otherwise authentic texts in order to promote specific institutional interests. The Le Mans forgeries are a good example. This collection of documents included a mix of fraudulent and authentic materials of historical and hagiographic import, such as a biography of a ninth-century bishop, a history of the bishops of the city of Le Mans, various saints' lives (*vitae*), and a cartulary (a collection of legal documents such as diplomas, charters, and bulls), which were all assembled as a corpus in the ninth century in order to bolster the claims by the French monastery of Saint Calais that it fell under episcopal, rather than royal, jurisdiction.[31] Another example is the *Hitación de Wamba*, a document purported to be a seventh-century delineation of the diocesan boundaries of the Iberian Peninsula by the Visigothic king Wamba or his successors. In fact, the text emerged several centuries later, in the midst of an eleventh-century dispute in which Bishop Pelayo of Oviedo pushed against the archbishop of Toledo's expanding claims of jurisdiction over several dioceses of Old Castile. Unsurprisingly, modern scholars attribute at least some of the interpolated passages in the *Hitación* to the bishop's circles in Oviedo.[32]

This type of subterfuge was far from uncommon. As Giles Constable observed, "If the intrusion of any fictional element into a document is considered the defining characteristic of forgery, then indeed an enormous number of medieval charters can be said to have been forged." According to one estimate, two-thirds of ecclesiastical documents issued before 1100 were "wholly or partially forged."[33] This has led some scholars to propose that strong distinctions between true and false documents may not serve us well when approaching medieval history. Forgeries were not, at least from the perspective of their perpetrators, outright lies; they were, rather, a recovery of a deeper, more essential truth that had been waylaid somehow. By introducing an invented passage in an otherwise authentic text, for example, the forger would be recovering "accidentally misplaced facts" that confirmed his particular vision of a contested past.[34] Even if we heed those who have criticized this relativistic view of medieval forgery, pointing out that "pious fraud" was not an officially acceptable pretext for falsification, even for the Church, the fact remains that the first instinct of the medieval reader would not necessarily be to rebut a forged or interpolated passage.[35] Rather, it would be to fabricate his own countertext.

This is not one more affliction that can be blamed on what is popularly imagined as the "medieval mind." Well into the Renaissance, the line between true and false texts, objects, and narratives remained unclear, even in the works of scholars who vaunted their own ability to root out apocryphal or patently false texts. As several scholars of forgery have emphasized, in an intellectual context in which speculation, imagination, and creativity were often integral to the act of creating a historical narrative, the "rediscovery" of textual and material evidence quite often bled into outright falsification. Yet while the medieval forger may have been more likely to fabricate an actual physical specimen, in what Walter Stephens dubs "diplomatic forgery," Renaissance and early modern forgers were more given to "literary forgery," in which they claimed to have discovered a later copy of an authoritative but long-lost text.[36] Erasmus of Rotterdam provides an intriguing example of this maneuver. Erasmus is well known for his critical edition of the works of Saint Jerome, and for having debunked various pious legends, such as the apocryphal letters between Seneca the Younger and the apostle Paul, which dated back to the fourth century. Yet the Dutch humanist was also guilty of his own historical fabrication. Into an edition of the works of Saint Cyprian, he inserted a text in praise of martyrdom, unattested by any other ancient authority, that seemed to support the broad, spiritual sense of martyrdom that Erasmus preferred.[37] Other respected scholars of the sixteenth century, such as the Italian humanist Carlo Sigonio, also strategically falsified the occasional document, coin, or inscription while simultaneously decrying forgery or the Spanish moralist Friar Antonio Guevara (d. 1545), who forged a work by the Roman emperor Marcus Aurelius.[38] When Pirro Ligorio, a prominent architect and antiquarian in sixteenth-century Rome, could not find the apposite inscription, he created it simply by repurposing an old one. In this manner, he invented a great many inscriptions.[39] And the fabrication of coins was believed to be so common that Antonio Agustín dedicated an entire section of his *Dialogue on Coins* (1587) to the problem of discerning forged specimens from authentic ones.[40]

It sometimes seems that Renaissance-era scholars did nearly as much to perpetuate and create myths as to dispel them. Even as Erasmus was disproving the legendary correspondence between Seneca and Paul, the related but separate myth that Seneca had been a Christian was gaining traction in learned treatises.

The story itself was of relatively late vintage; it seems to have originated no earlier than the fourteenth century and was repeated well into the seventeenth.[41] Nor can we blame medieval monks for the elaborate legend that Santiago and his disciples, known as the Seven Apostles (*los Siete Varones Apostólicos*), had established the first-century Church in Spain. It was, as Katherine Elliot Van Liere has suggested, humanist historians who animated this legend. Chief among them was the renowned antiquarian scholar Ambrosio de Morales, who detailed the Seven Apostles' comings and goings in his mid-sixteenth-century treatises on the history of Spain.[42]

THE USES OF THE PAST IN EARLY MODERN SPAIN

Was forgery, then, only in the eye of the beholder? For many Golden Age Spanish authors, who had great fun toying with the literary conventions of forgery, the answer was in the affirmative. Narrators of chivalric novels such as *Amadis of Gaul* claimed that their texts were authentic histories generated from manuscripts discovered in exotic, distant locales. They disingenuously contrasted their own entirely "genuine" accounts with other purportedly spurious tales. The narrator of *Amadis* assured his readers that the first three books—featuring the eponymous hero vanquishing dragons and other fantastic foes—had only survived in "corrupt and defective" versions that he had corrected and translated from an unspecified foreign language. The fourth volume, however, had only recently been salvaged from an underground chamber in Constantinople by a Hungarian merchant, who then brought it to Spain.[43]

The problem is that the lost parchment discovered in a distant but prestigious repository, written in a classical or oriental language poorly rendered by medieval scribes and transmitted thence by an untraceable broker, really did exist, at least sometimes. Ever since Renaissance humanists such as Poggio Bracciolini raided the rich manuscript collections of central European monasteries in the mid-fifteenth century, scholars really had been unearthing forgotten codices.[44] In Spain, the murky centuries of Islamic rule provided particularly fruitful territory for historical inventions, at least from the perspective of Christians, both new and old. In the last years of the sixteenth century, just as the first of many lead books were being unearthed successively in Granada, Miguel de Luna, a Christian of Muslim extraction (*morisco*) presented the first part of his fanciful history, the *True History of King Don Rodrigo* (1592). Luna claimed to have discovered the original Arabic text, written by one Abulcacim Tarif Abentarique, in the royal library of the Escorial where his acquaintance Alonso de Castillo worked cataloguing Arabic manuscripts.[45] In the first part of *Don Quijote* (1605), Miguel de

Cervantes parodied this "found text" convention as Cervantes-as-narrator recalls having purchased a manuscript on the street in Toledo. Since the manuscript, *The History of Don Quijote of La Mancha, Written by the Arabic Historian Cide Hamete Benegeli*, was written in Arabic characters, Cervantes-narrator contracts a local morisco to translate it for him.[46] Scholars have speculated that this incident was a sly allusion on the part of Cervantes to Granada's lead books, Luna's *True History*, and perhaps a commentary on the precarious status of moriscos in Spain before the expulsion of 1609.[47]

Early modern forgeries shared the topos of the found text—as well as the motif that they had been discovered in a place "so distant as to discourage verification and so exotic as to compel belief"—with the chivalric novels and other pseudohistories that Cervantes parodied.[48] Perhaps for this reason, early chroniclers of the Spanish discovery and conquests in the New World who transmitted seemingly incredible details about the peoples and customs of the Americas felt obliged to defend their own authorial credibility by asserting that they were writing "true histories," as opposed to novels or fabulous histories.[49] Of course, what made truth and fiction so difficult to disentangle in early modern histories and pseudohistorical novels alike was that the topoi that forgers invoked to underwrite the authenticity of their discoveries were, ever since the Renaissance, also employed by authors of "authentic" histories as well. We now know that the authors of forgeries constructed their texts with a profound understanding of what true histories really looked like, and, moreover, that the techniques of forgers contributed to the critical apparatus of scholars. In his study of early modern Italian histories, Eric Cochrane described forgery as an almost natural outgrowth of the enthusiasm among scholars in the burgeoning field of antiquarian studies, which sometimes induced them to fabricate tangible confirmation of their particular vision of the past. This was a particularly tempting path for ecclesiastical historians. For, as Protestants and Catholics accused the other of having strayed from the original spirit of Jesus and the first Christians, the single most important criteria of truth became that of continuity with the primeval Church. As Cochrane noted, the Catholic position codified in the Council of Trent, namely, "that what was done in the first five centuries of the Christian era ought also to be done in the sixteenth century," was a natural incentive to antiquarian research, to efforts to find material and textual artifacts, and, occasionally, to the fabrication of one's own pseudoantiquarian evidence: "Such, indeed, was the excitement aroused by the new appreciation of ancient archaeological remains that some antiquarians were tempted into anticipating future discoveries."[50] In this sense, learned forgers were mostly guilty of pride in their own mastery of historical and archaeological knowledge.

With this intellectual context in mind scholars have argued that Annius of Viterbo himself employed several recognizably modern principles of historical criticism—such as the distinction between primary and secondary sources, and a sensitivity to historical distance and anachronism. In other words, Annius consciously drew on emerging early modern ideas about what constituted authentic historical evidence to make his forged histories seem verisimilar. As Anthony Grafton has suggested, cases such as these demonstrate that modern historical criticism and techniques of forgery developed in tandem. In order to create a convincing fake, after all, an author had to be aware of what his contemporaries considered *not* fake. Thus, the history of history, as it were, can also be charted from this other, less familiar perspective, from which pseudo-Berosus, Manetho, the lead books, and Dexter look less like aberrations and more like important contributions to early modern conversations about what constituted valid evidence of the past.[51]

In this context, early modern readers often evinced a stunning proclivity to overlook flaws and uncertainties in the sources, particularly when they were reading in the service of devotion and local patriotism. This tendency was not limited to partisans of the false chronicles, nor indeed to Counter-Reformation Spain. Suffridus Petri, a local historian-*cum*-antiquarian of seventeenth-century Friesland, reasoned that in the writing of ancient history, "Antiquities are one thing, the fables mixed up with them another. A good historian should not simply abandon the antiquities because of the fables, but should cleanse the fables for the sake of the antiquities."[52] Here Petri was defending the seemingly fabulous details that peppered his own history of Friesland by suggesting that they may have been remnants of authentic oral traditions, expressed in lost ancient Roman and Germanic songs; and he insisted that even if those sources were not necessarily trustworthy, they were worthy of scholarly preservation nonetheless. While Petri was writing in a different context, his assertion that legendary elements had a place in the writing of the history and antiquities of the North Sea region of Friesland shows that careful consideration of one's sources, and what looks, in retrospect, like "credulity," were not seen as mutually incompatible by the scholars who wrote sacred history in the late sixteenth and seventeenth centuries. Since history, like religion, possessed moral content, one's perception of what, exactly, constituted the correct interpretation of the past was necessarily colored by one's own interests, as well as by local rivalries, factional politics, and the search for patronage. These and other factors would condition responses to the cronicones for centuries.

THE REVOLUTION OF ECCLESIASTICAL HISTORY

In this period the question of how to determine the authenticity of historical evidence was still open, and second only to the question of how to write history. The broader story of the evolution of "modern" historical method has been shaped by Arnaldo Momigliano, whose influential 1950 essay "Ancient History and the Antiquarian" prompted a dramatic shift in the history of ideas. Before Momigliano, a distinctive "Renaissance sense of the past"—the recognition of distance between current and ancient times—had been attributed to fifteenth-century Italian humanists such as Leonardo Bruni and Lorenzo Valla. Momigliano argued, however, that Renaissance historians and authors of treatises on the *artes historicae* were more concerned with proper rhetorical form than with the philological and historical critique of sources that is usually cited as the hallmark of modern historical method.[53]

For Momigliano, the critical assessment of historical sources really only took shape in the late seventeenth century, as inter-European religious conflicts prompted scholars to hammer out "safe historical rules"—in other words, guidelines on how to determine the reliability of evidence, and how to interpret sources—that would elevate historical discourse above confessional or political affiliation. Momigliano argued that the efforts of antiquarians, those long-reviled amateur historians of the Renaissance and early modern period who collected coins, inscriptions, and other artifacts, helped develop rules for evaluating traditions, witnesses, and material objects. Before the integration of antiquarian methods into the writing of history, historians had regarded antiquities as disjointed, incoherent remnants of the past that—as Francis Bacon remarked—had "casually escaped the shipwreck of time."[54] Yet by the seventeenth century, material evidence such as that found in coins, inscriptions, and archaeological excavations had been integrated into the mainstream of historical writing, including ecclesiastical history, which was itself deeply informed by the skills and practices developed by antiquarians—including a preference for primary sources, integration of nonliterary evidence, and the development of criteria for evaluating the reliability of sources. Although earlier figures such as Cyriac of Ancona and Antonio Agustín had professed an appreciation for nonliterary sources over "tradition" as transmitted by eyewitnesses, Momigliano believed that such an attitude—which he dubbed "historical Pyrrhonism"—did not become generalized until the late seventeenth century.

Since Momigliano wrote over half a century ago, scholars have antedated this revolution in historical research and methods to the second half of the sixteenth century.[55] They have also applied his insights to understanding the early modern study of texts, as well as that of coins and inscriptions, and they have challenged his stark distinction between "rhetorical" and "antiquarian" scholarship.⁵⁶ Most importantly for the present study, they have brought attention to the fact that ecclesiastical historians and humanist hagiographers were also central in developing what contemporaries considered more reliable guidelines to determine the authenticity of historical texts, and that they applied these principles in trying to render historical and hagiographic texts more accurate.⁵⁷ The work of Simon Ditchfield, in particular, has highlighted the importance of sacred history—in a broad sense that includes the revision of ecclesiastical histories, liturgical texts, and saints' lives—to the larger project of Catholic reform, particularly in the wake of the Council of Trent.⁵⁸ As a result, we now understand that ecclesiastical historians in the sixteenth and seventeenth centuries were participants, and occasionally forerunners, in the revolution in historical method, as scholars such as Cardinal Cesare Baronio applied their insights and considerable erudition to excising what they saw as the weaker strands in Catholic history and hagiography.

Yet Baronio and other humanist-trained antiquarian scholars helped document, codify, and even create new legends. The persistence of mythmaking, and the willingness to indulge one's own interests, even when they were unsupported or contradicted by the evidence, were not solely Iberian propensities. In the *Ecclesiastical History of the Scottish Nation* (1627), Thomas Dempster, a Scottish antiquarian in the service of James I, proudly claimed several English, Frankish, and Irish saints as Scots.⁵⁹ Nor were such maneuvers limited to Catholics. As Euan Cameron has noted, the "dogmatic stance" of the sixteenth-century Lutheran authors of the polemical history known as the *Magdeburg Centuries* often "overwhelmed their critical faculties," such that "spurious evidence was accepted if it portrayed the papacy or the hierarchy in a bad light," and "inconvenient evidence" was often "explained away."⁶⁰ These tendencies would continue their slow and agonizing demise well into modern times, among ecclesiastical historians of all stripes.⁶¹

The present study builds on the insights of this scholarship to argue that the false chronicles were central to early modern imaginings of the past in Spain, and also to discussions about the nature of historical truth in this period. A strong body of scholarship has detailed how English antiquarians' concern for the details of the local, regional, and national past helped augur the modern interest in "heritage."⁶² Much about these erudite circles, particularly in Spain and Portugal, remains to be illuminated.⁶³ The present study does not pretend to offer a comprehensive guide to ecclesiastical antiquarianism in Spain, although it will certainly suggest that the authors of local sacred histories—Higuera, for one, but also his many readers—were important conduits between learned culture and local religion. Thus, the emphasis here falls less on the place of the cronicones in the development of modern historical consciousness, and more on the social, cultural, and religious contexts within which the texts were created, interpreted, and put to use. In this sense, this project also draws on recent work by Daniel Woolf on the "social circulation of the past," which shows how antiquarian research in early modern England inspired new histories, in the broadest sense of the word, including new historical texts, objects, and oral traditions.[64]

This is not a point of merely theoretical importance. The writing and reading of history was serious business in early modern Spain, and the distant past informed a variety of pursuits, such as architecture, urban planning, fine art, and genealogy.[65] With the end of Islamic rule in Spain, expansion into the Americas, and the rise of Spain as a major power in the fifteenth and sixteenth centuries, interpretations of the past assumed sharper political, cultural, and religious implications. So, too, did the need for a comprehensive history of Spain increase, particularly one that would provide a satisfactory account of the new nation's Catholic origins and identity. The widespread perception that this history was yet to be written, combined with a real lack of sources for the earlier periods, created an urgent demand for historical texts and narratives—which persisted in spite of the efforts of Renaissance-era scholars, including Lucius Marineus Siculus, Pere Antoni Beuter, and Johannes Vasaeus, to document Spanish history.[66] Emperor Charles V's chronicler, Florián Ocampo (1513–1590), attempted to write a complete history of the Spanish kingdoms from antiquity to the present, but the result had fallen short: Ocampo never completed the book, which stopped with the arrival of the Romans in the second century before Christ. Moreover, Ocampo made generous use of Annius of Viterbo's apocryphal material, which enabled him to flesh out the periods for which there was no textual evidence with a continuous line of (legendary) Castilian monarchs for the several centuries after the biblical Flood.[67]

As Spain rose to greater prominence as a world power over the course of the sixteenth century, the perceived lack of decent historical narratives became a sore point. The royal chronicler Ambrosio de Morales claimed that he had been moved to write by an embarrassing encounter with the Italian ambassadors at the royal court, who asked the proud Castilian why nobody had written a comprehensive history of Spain. Their words wounded Morales, since, as he admitted in the prologue to his chronicle, there was no such work, at least not one that was worthy of being read.[68] Morales attempted to address this deficiency with his *General Chronicle of Spain* (published in three parts in 1574, 1577, and 1586), which began where Ocampo left off, but with a markedly more critical spirit, with extensive reliance upon what we now refer to as primary sources and archaeological evidence. It was this chronicle, together with its companion volume, the *Antiquities of Spain*, that helped inaugurate a new era in Spanish history writing.

Indeed, the protagonists of *Forging the Past* were all immensely in debt to this mid-sixteenth-century chronicler and antiquarian. Higuera, like all other enthusiasts of the past of his generation, took seriously the challenges and opportunities that Morales had identified. Throughout his considerable corpus, Higuera wrote in an imagined dialogue with Morales, drawing on the great antiquarian for evidence, and sometimes correcting or supplementing his narrative with sources that Higuera had discovered, authentic and otherwise. The relative lack of sources, particularly for the earliest centuries of Spanish Christian history, created the ideal opportunity for an enterprising scholar to invent his own sources, insert them into circulation, and thus influence the shape of historical and religious opinion. Yet even historical discoveries of relatively plausible authenticity were dangerous. In a context in which new sources and narratives were heavy with contemporary significance, historical claims and revelations were met with divided opinion. Nobody knew this better than Higuera, who dove into this hotly contested territory with apparent glee, again and again.

The book begins by introducing readers to Jerónimo Román de la Higuera as an eccentric multifaceted character whose controversial interpretations of the past were just as likely to invite admiration as disparagement, even before the false chronicles. This was because, as *Forging the Past* contends, Higuera was not operating in isolation: he played an integral albeit contested role in the mainstream of Spanish intellectual life in the late sixteenth century. This becomes clear as we surprise Higuera in mid-*inventio*, in Toledo, where he was not only perfecting the false chronicles, but also writing historical narratives in his own name, often with the sponsorship of learned patrons (chapter 1). As we shall see, Higuera's tweaking of local factional and religious interests helped make his scholarship controversial, even when its content was, in fact, remarkably anodyne. We learn how Higuera tried to bring his vision of the sacred past to life by means of direct advocacy and archaeological subterfuge in the infamous incident of the "discovery" of the temple of Saint Thyrsus (San Tirso) in Toledo in 1594. The resulting controversy divided learned opinion in Toledo. It also brought Higuera to the attention of Jesuit superiors all the way to Rome. Higuera's woes with the Jesuits were not unique, nor were his appeals for help to the Spanish Inquisition (chapter 2). Why did Higuera's bona fide historical endeavors—that is, excepting the false chronicles, which he had not yet disseminated—antagonize Jesuit superiors so, and how did they feed into festering tensions in the Jesuit order about the enterprise of history writing in general? The answer, surprisingly, has nothing to do with the spurious nature of Higuera's texts, as will become clear once we see that the same tensions had also ensnared more prominent and respected figures, such as the eminent historian Juan de Mariana.

Subsequent chapters argue that the forgeries were hardly flights of whimsy, but rather carefully constructed texts that reflected the Jesuit's diligent research and scholarly communication with other enthusiasts of history in Spain and Catholic Europe. Through his intimate familiarity with late antique and medieval Spanish chronicles, saints' lives, liturgical texts, and antiquities, Higuera was able to mold the false chronicles in close imitation of ancient and early medieval models to create the illusion of verisimilitude (chapter 3). It was precisely Higuera's acute awareness of evolving standards of historical criticism that enabled him to mold the texts to the expectations of his audience, and to address several controversial questions of the time, including the role of Jews and their descendants in Spanish history, the authenticity of the plomos of Granada, and the relative value of apocryphal texts (chapter 4). Moreover, Higuera's conversations with other learned men and his unique place in the Spanish Republic of Letters help explain not only the genesis of his project, but also its success, as his friends became the texts' first proponents (chapter 5).

Yet Higuera had his sights upon even higher interlocutors. He wrote in an imagined dialogue with the Roman scholars who were excising many questionable religious traditions from Catholic liturgical and historical texts. In this effort, Higuera buttressed many devotions popular among early modern Spaniards—such as the veneration of Santiago—that seemed to have been undermined by the critiques of figures such as Baronio. Higuera's efforts to preserve local legends by enshrining them in the "history" of the false chronicles also help explain the texts' immediate and dramatic effects on the ground in many communities throughout seventeenth-century Spain. A closer look at the chronicles in the context of Higuera's other texts, including the histories he wrote under his name and his correspondence, reveals that he culled many details for the chronicles from his friends and other members of his extended epistolary network. He also relied upon traditions that had never before found a place in the written sources of sacred history, in what seems to have been a conscious decision to embrace oral traditions over and above historical erudition. After all, as Higuera explained in a letter to a fellow Jesuit, *vox populi, vox Dei*—the voice of the people is the voice of God (chapter 6).

The popularity of the false chronicles was not a foregone conclusion; once they entered print in the decades after Higuera's death in 1611, many readers attacked the texts as deeply flawed, plagued with egregious errors that, for some, marked the cronicones as forgeries. Proponents, in turn, defended the texts by arguing that such flaws were but minor motes that should not detract from the deeper truth the texts conveyed about the special relationship between Spain, its saints, and God. This rather generous hermeneutic also guided local responses to the chronicles, as in the dozens of communities where new saints were discovered thanks to the information provided by the texts (chapter 7).

These responses also included the writing of sacred history (*historia sacra*) by local scholars, particularly in the Andalusian dioceses of Seville and Jaén. While most studies of Spanish antiquarians still focus on the more visible luminaries of the epoch, such as Ambrosio de Morales, Antonio Agustín, or Jerónimo Zurita, chapter 8 examines how provincial historians integrated textual, material, and visual evidence with the false chronicles to intervene in local religious devotion. It also points toward the importance of their reliance on regional intellectual and social networks for collecting this evidence, and argues that a vibrant early modern Republic of Letters—which is quite familiar to students of seventeenth- and eighteenth-century French and English history—may have also been part of the regional intellectual life of early modern Spanish antiquaries. Indeed, as the careers of these historians suggest, a plethora of woefully underacknowledged connections bound such regional Spanish scholars not only to "popular" religion in their own communities, but also to mainstream intellectual culture in early modern Europe.

The cronicones also mattered in two of the most powerful places in the early modern world: Madrid and Rome (chapter 9). As we shall see, royal courtiers and other high religio-political actors of the seventeenth century were prominent in transmitting, publishing, and arguing about the texts among themselves, and also with other European readers. The question of the texts' authenticity posed broader implications, including the nature of apocryphal texts and whether holy objects and texts should be judged with rigorous empiricism, as Roman theologians, critics of the chronicles, Protestants, and scientific thinkers such as Galileo were suggesting, or whether, when it came to divine matters, it was better to err on the side of pious affection for the sake of a deeper, supernatural truth. This same fundamental dilemma troubled proponents and critics alike in the eighteenth and nineteenth centuries, as the debate about the chronicles became increasingly pointed and extended to broader questions regarding the relevance of Enlightenment theories and, by extension, the very nature of historical and religious truth, until the final descent of the cronicones into scholarly ignominy (chapter 10).

Yet, in spite of the derision with which modern scholars have come to regard the false chronicles, their indelible mark on local history and religion remains. The fact that saints that Higuera fabricated still form the basis of heritage and local identity in many locations throughout the Iberian Peninsula suggests that in confusing truths with fictions so completely that scholars into the twenty-first century were still attempting to sort them out, the crafty Jesuit ultimately succeeded in reshaping the past, present, and future (Conclusion). In this sense, the story of the creation, reception, scholarly rejection, and endurance of the false chronicles is also about the development of Spanish national identity, as Iberian scholars have been forced to come to terms with modernity and the convoluted history of their own history.

Before addressing the historical context of Higuera and his forgeries, we may wish to get a taste of the chronicles themselves. Here, in a typically laconic passage, Flavius Lucius Dexter relates the outstanding events of the years 115–116:

> In Osuna in Betica province, Saint Leo and his companions are martyred.
> Trajan makes Armenia, Assyria, and Mesopotamia into [Roman] provinces.
> An earthquake almost ruins the entire city of Antioch.
> The Jews in Lybia fight each other.
> Saint Marcus Bolanus Florentius, son of Rusticus Bolanus, a Spanish consul, and disciple of the holy apostles who had converted in Tyle (now known as Syla), martyred in Seville on October 27.
> The letters from the Virgin Mary to Saint Ignatius are celebrated.[69]

The passage is entirely typical of the first of the four chronicles: the staccato prose relates an unrelentingly chronological and episodic succession of events. As a narrator, Dexter is a consummate annalist but an incomplete historical character: he lists events in simple Latin prose, rarely inserts himself into the text, and provides no broader context or analysis whatsoever. He chronicles a range of events, from the principal events of early Christianity to the lives of the Roman emperors and the itineraries of early bishops and evangelizers, across the geographical range of the Roman Empire. Yet, with the progression of time, the author tilts ever more heavily in an Iberian and Christian direction, until, by the end of the text, in 430, we are squarely in the arena of Roman Hispania and its Church.

As opposed to the fuller treatment of a long-form narrative history, such as one would find in classical historians such as Thucydides or Tacitus, Higuera's annals, like their medieval counterparts, lacked main characters, dramatic tension, sweeping conclusions, and overarching narratives; there was no reflection upon cause and effect, no attempt to reconcile loose ends, no accounting of one's sources, no attempt to explain the broader significance of events. In this, Higuera convincingly emulated the style and content of medieval chronicles.

This should not be a surprise; like other successful forgers, Higuera mostly "authorized, expanded, or reconciled known facts," as José Godoy Alcántara noted over a century and a half ago.[70] In fact, Higuera composed the earliest draft of the chronicles of Dexter and Maximus by literally piecing together excerpts from authentic annals. In this way, he attempted to strike a balance between innovation and tradition. He furthered this effect by attributing three of his four texts to historically verifiable personages whose existence had been confirmed by trustworthy patristic and medieval witnesses, such as Saint Jerome and Saint Isidore of Seville. And since Higuera folded his fabricated historical details into an otherwise unremarkable body of authentic chronicle material, it is hardly surprising that the cronicones seemed to many—but not all—contemporary readers as convincing facsimiles of what they purported to be.

When these reasonable likenesses of medieval annals entered print in the decades following Higuera's death, they benefited from the additional support of paratextual material seeded with conspicuous markers of "antiquity" that made them seem even more convincing to readers in Counter-Reformation Spain. For example, all three editions of Dexter—one in 1619 and two in 1627—were accompanied by explanatory prefaces and purportedly authentic bonus material meant to buttress the texts' rather wobbly authority. These additional items included, for example, a letter from Dexter himself to Orosius, an actual late antique Spanish priest and respected annalist in his own right. In the letter, Higuera qua Dexter provided a number of expository details that filled out the rather lean biography of this fifth-century contemporary of Jerome. The epistle not only served as an important historical source for its intended audience, but also as a de facto argument for the authenticity of the chronicle itself.[71]

In other words, like most other successful forgers, our Jesuit—and his seventeenth-century editors—made the texts convincing to an audience by shaping them according to contemporary biases and expectations regarding historical evidence. In addition to sharing the form, appearance, and content of their purported peers, the chronicles were further linked, via their author, to the world of historical learning in early modern Spain, as we shall see. Thanks to Higuera's education, research, and connections—with what Jesuit superiors referred to with suspicion as "third parties" in Toledo and elsewhere—he had amassed a considerable collection of historical sources, acquired an intimate knowledge of early Christian and Iberian history, and accumulated dozens of correspondents with similar interests and expertise, with whom he shared sources, information, and debate. Higuera's assiduous research, as well as his privileged location in Toledo among the men who were disinterring, collating, and editing some of the oldest Iberian historical texts for the very first time, helped make him intimately familiar with authentic sources of Spanish history. In other words, Higuera's texts were convincing simulacra because they were not constructed ex nihilo; their attribution, content, and format were profoundly indebted to actual late antique and medieval sources, many of which Higuera's peers in Toledo were bringing out of obscurity in the last years of the sixteenth century. This enabled Higuera, like the best forgers, to seed his documents with verifiable details, to anchor them in a recognizable textual tradition, and to endow them with a suitably prestigious intellectual genealogy, as lost manuscripts recovered from the venerable monastic library of Fulda.

Higuera extended his emulation of the medieval chronicler to his own working methods. Like many of his august predecessors, Higuera reworked and updated mostly conventional material according to his own biases, while mixing in invented and apocryphal details in support of his own interpretations of the past and present. If, as Giles Constable has noted, medieval documents contained "an indefinite number of stages between an absolutely genuine record and one that is sheer forgery," so, too, in Higuera's chronicles we shall detect a range of positions, from outright fabrication in some cases, to direct (albeit uncredited) copying of authentic histories.[72] Thus, like so many other medieval (and some early modern) authors, Higuera fabricated documents, artifacts, and other items of historical significance, not for private gain, but to buttress his own interpretation of the past, particularly—but not exclusively—when it came to those topics for which he had shown special concern in his other writings, including the importance of Jews and Mozarabs in Toledo's early history, as well as the Spanish apostleship of Santiago. By examining Higuera's use and manipulation of authentic sources to confect his false histories, we shall begin to understand better his notion of truth, in which exemplarity seems to have taken precedence over factual accuracy *sensu stricto*. This, in turn, will leave us better equipped to understand Higuera's motives, not to mention the success that the chronicles enjoyed after his death.

Part I

CREATION

1

THE FORGER BETWEEN FRIENDS AND ENEMIES IN TOLEDO

> No one is to be considered a liar who says something which is false, but which he believes to be true, because, as far as he himself is concerned, he does not deceive but is the victim of deception. So the person who, without exercising sufficient caution, trusts false statements and regards them as true, should not be accused of lying but sometimes of rashness.
> —St. Augustine, Enchiridion

Well before the false chronicles propelled Jerónimo Román de la Higuera into infamy, the intrepid Jesuit was already known in his native Toledo for using his historical expertise to make controversial claims about Spain's sacred past. Higuera's complex role as a respected yet divisive man of learning and religion is well illustrated by a little-known debate that erupted over two discoveries in Toledo, one bibliographic, and the other archaeological, at the end of the sixteenth century. The first find had been unremarkable: sometime in the 1580s, as Higuera was poring through the rich trove of manuscripts in Toledo's cathedral library, he came across an eighth-century letter from King Silo of Asturias that described an early medieval church dedicated to an early Christian martyr named Saint Thyrsus (San Tirso). The significance of the letter would not become clear to Higuera until the second discovery, which occurred in August, 1594, when workers excavating a site in the Plaza Mayor alongside the cathedral uncovered a cluster of ruins and archaeological artifacts. Suddenly it was clear: the letter, Higuera claimed, made it plain that the Plaza Mayor ruins belonged to the early medieval chapel erected for the Christians living under Islamic rule — known as Mozarabs — in honor of Tirso. The city should immediately adopt Tirso as a patron saint and reconstruct his chapel on that very site.

To modern ears, this might sound like an unremarkable gesture of Counter-Reformation piety. After all, in early modern Spain, the veneration of early Christian martyrs was standard fare. Yet in the powder keg of Toledan religious and intellectual politics, this seemingly anodyne suggestion was an explosive provocation. In the days after Higuera aired his claims, a veritable maelstrom arose among learned Toledans, as the members of the local civic and ecclesiastical elite fought bitterly about the alleged ruins of the church of San Tirso, the letter from King Silo, and Higuera's reliability. The controversy soon divided Toledo's elite, just as the false chronicles would later divide Spain's men of letters. Like that latter debate, the discussion of San Tirso would focus primarily on questions of historical research, including, but not limited to, the authenticity of Higuera's historical sources.

In this sense, the conflagration over San Tirso among the members of Toledo's civic and religious elite parallels the long-term controversy over the *cronicones*. On one side were Higuera's supporters, who admired his scholarship in spite of its flaws and shared Higuera's vision of the past. On the other end of the spectrum were the doubters, those who regarded the Jesuit's texts and promotion of certain religious and historical causes as inherently untrustworthy and who accused him of scholarly malfeasance and forgery. For generations, this divergence of opinions was easy to explain: early doubters were exceptional minds, men of uncommon perspicacity who could see through Higuera's pious pretenses. Believers, unsurprisingly, came out somewhat worse for the wear, as credulous patriots and religious enthusiasts who were more concerned about their own pet religious causes—such as the ecclesiastical primacy of Toledo, the Santiago creed, or the lead books of Granada—than with historical truth and scholarly integrity.

Yet the virulent reactions that Higuera and his texts prompted among his contemporaries in Toledo and beyond cannot simply be equated with the defense of truth against falsehood; as a closer examination of questions of urban renewal, historical erudition, and Mozarabic history in late sixteenth-century Toledo will reveal, at question was not so much the integrity of Higuera's scholarship as his vision of Toledo's past, present, and future. As Higuera knew quite well, to make claims about the history of a single saint was, in essence, to make a claim about the early history of Christianity in Toledo, of its families, and of the nature of its religious identity. In attempting to bring the Mozarabic cult of this saint back to life, Higuera intervened aggressively in ongoing discussions about the nature of Toledo's sacred history and squared off with many of Toledo's other learned men, who, like Higuera, took the city's history quite seriously. His superiors in the Society of Jesus were quite irritated by the ignominy of being dragged into the ensuing public debate which, they feared, might threaten the Society's interests. The intrigue, in which Higuera was accused of forging the letter of Silo, eventually would extend all the way to the royal palace in Madrid and to the head of the entire Jesuit order in Rome, Claudio Acquaviva, thus jeopardizing Higuera's already tenuous standing in his own religious order.

The incident, with its mix of forgery, history, hagiography, and politics, is a fitting introduction to Higuera as a complicated character who prompted a range of reactions among his contemporaries. Higuera's determined advocacy for San Tirso exemplifies the complex methods, motives, and alliances that animated him in his various pursuits. It is thus a particularly revealing moment in Higuera's long career, one that allows us to view, among other things, the ways in which he drew upon archaeological, documentary, and hagiographical traditions in order to formulate a vision of the past that was as seductive to some as it was repellent to others. We also get a vivid sense of why and how Higuera's works created such an uproar, not only while he was alive, but also for centuries after his death. The San Tirso incident also helps underline the often ignored fact about the controversial Jesuit, namely, that he was a central figure in Toledan intellectual, religious, and cultural life of the late sixteenth century.

DISCOVERING SAN TIRSO

In itself, the discovery of human and architectural remains in Toledo was not particularly surprising. The densely settled city perched atop the high, rocky banks of the River Tajo had been populated continuously for over a millennium. As any Toledan would have known, a short stroll to the fields north of the city walls would bring one to the open-air ruins of a Roman circus. In the latter years of the sixteenth century, efforts to open Toledo's tight warren of crooked streets into a more "modern" cityscape led to many major excavations and thus, discoveries, in a ground larded with flagstones, coins, bones, and other relics of ancient and medieval populations.[1] Higuera's intrigue had its roots in the fortuitous archaeological find by laborers digging several feet below street level behind the cathedral for a complex construction project. A royal hospital for the incurably ill was due to be erected upon the site, and workers had just started to excavate its foundations when they hit stone. They soon found that the stones were part of a larger complex of what seemed to be the ruins of a building. Along with several large building stones and the ruins of a vault, they unearthed a cache of archaeological treasures, including human bones, Roman and Castilian coins, and a copper disk (figures 1.1 and 1.2).

Yet this discovery was different. The cathedral's head architect (*maestro de*

Figure 1.1. "The letter of King Silo was false, and the invention of a certain priest [margin: 'this was Father Geronymo Roman de la Higuera, Jesuit'] who, tempted by the devil, invented [it], and he fooled the abovementioned Don Alonso de Cárcamo, who was a secular and unlearned man." In 1754, a cathedral canon named Francisco Xavier de Santiago Palomares copied this "Warning to the Reader" by Canons Palomares and Carvajal into this copy of the *Traslado de la carta y relacion qve embio a sv Magestad . . . a cerca del Templo que en ella se ha hallado del señor San Tyrso* (Madrid, 1595) © Biblioteca Nacional de España, R/8499, 1r.

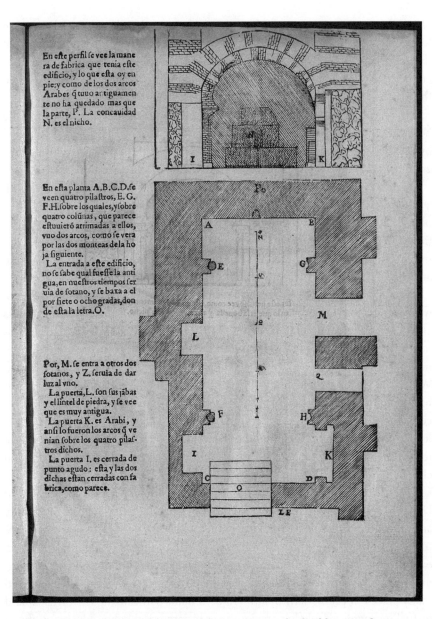

Figure 1.2. "The ancient location of the entrance to this building is unknown; in our times it served as a basement, and one reaches it by descending seven or eight steps, where marked by the letter O." Here Cárcamo/Higuera mixed past and present in order to imagine the ruins in their former state, as the Church of San Tirso. *Traslado de la carta . . .* (Madrid, 1595)
© Biblioteca Nacional de España, R/8499.

obras), Maestro Juan Bautista Monegro, soon noted that the stone slabs seemed to belong to the intact foundations of a significant building. He wondered about the presence of so many human remains, and, above all, about the curious copper disk. Monegro's field experience made him something of an expert on the physical remnants of Toledo's various stages of history, and he quickly identified the building stones as the foundations of a ruined chapel or temple, and the bones as the remains of an old Christian cemetery. Nonetheless, he was stumped by the medal, which after being cleaned by a coppersmith revealed a mysterious engraving upon its face: a crown above the letters C and S (figure 1.3).

What was this strange object, and what did it mean? For contemporaries with a keen interest in Toledo's history, the answer would be anything but trivial. In a place that many considered to be the oldest and most prestigious seat of Christianity in the Iberian Peninsula, which nevertheless had been under Islamic dominion for nearly four hundred years in the Middle Ages, patron saints were an important part of the early modern period's program of recovery and re-Christianization. Thanks to Toledo's history as the capital of Visigothic Spain, whose rulers were unseated by the Islamic invaders in 711, the city and its saints also possessed special significance for the Hapsburg monarchy, whose court was nearby in Madrid. King Philip II himself sponsored the recovery and reenshrinement of the relics of two early Toledan saints in the latter half of the century. With royal patronage, the body of Eugenius, Toledo's legendary first bishop, was recovered from the monastery of Saint Denis of Paris in 1565. The relics of fourth-century Spanish martyr Santa Leocadia were translated with great fanfare by the Jesuit Miguel Hernández Hernández, from Flanders to Toledo, where they were received in 1587 by Don Pedro Carvajal Girón de Loaysa, dean of the cathedral chapter (*cabildo*) under whose stewardship her cult remained thereafter.[2]

When Monegro realized that these were no ordinary ruins he appealed to Higuera, a Toledan native known for his encyclopedic knowledge of the history and archaeology of the city and its environs, where the vestiges of successive centuries of Roman, Visigothic, Islamic, and Castilian rule were literally piled atop each other—not neatly stratified, as in geological layers, but messily overlapping, in the ongoing cycle of architectural and cultural interaction that characterized many places in premodern Spain. Higuera made scrutinizing the physical and textual remnants of Toledo's previous lives his preferred hobby, like many aficionados of local history who, aside from a handful of secular men of learning, came mostly from the ranks of the clergy. Higuera's peers included cathedral canons, professors at the university, and members of the religious orders who dedicated themselves to disinterring every possible fragment of manuscript or material evi-

el nueuo templo ciertos vasos,y entre otros vn aguamanil,con el nõbre del Arçobispo,y el suyo,por cifra,con vna corona real, y estas letras,C.S.que parece dizen,a Cixila Silo:el qual era muy amigo destas agudezas y cifras:y assi puso vn letrero a la puerta de san Iuan de Prauia,donde yaze,q̃ se lee dozientas y sesenta vezes esto, Silo princeps fecit.La tapa deste aguamanil,q̃ seruia de dar la comunion de la sangre a los fieles,es la q̃ con esta va,y se hallo en las mesmas ruynas,por dõde mas se comprueua ser aquel el sitio del tẽplo,y se tiene por cierto.Pareciome cosa digna de q̃ V.M.passasse los ojos por ella,y supiesse lo demas que va dicho:en cuyos bienauenturados dias nuestro Señor ha querido ofrecer tãtas ocasiones à V.M. en q̃ mostrasse el santo y religioso zelo que tiene en amplificar la religion y culto de los santos,a quien deue esta ciudad los cuerpos de san Eugenio,y santa Leocadia.Y la misma obligaciõ tienen las yglesias de Alcala, Ebora, Guadix,y Murcia,y otras,a las quales V.M. ha restituydo las reliquias de sus patronos,santos,y naturales.Y assi parece q̃ en estos mismos tiempos ha sido nuestro Señor seruido se hallassen las ruynas del tẽplo de san Tyrso martyr,y natural desta ciudad,que parece(como los demas santos,se han querido seruir de V.M.)tãbien este gloriosissimo martyr quiere hazer lo mismo, aparejandole silla en el cielo por los muchos seruicios q̃ tantos santos han recebido de V.M. en la tierra. Y si V.M.fuere seruido se embie mas larga relacion desto,se harà.

El tapador del aguamanil
que se hallo,es en esta manera.

Figure 1.3. "The cover of the ewer that was discovered"; picturing the medal "To Cixila from Silo" in *Traslado de la carta* . . . (Madrid, 1595) © Biblioteca Nacional de España, R/8499.

dence in order to reconstruct Toledo's storied past, beginning with its legendary foundation by Hercules.

In this endeavor, Higuera and other researchers spent many hours poring through the cathedral's rich manuscript collection, copying rare hagiographical and liturgical texts, medieval chronicles, royal privileges, and anything else they could find that would help illuminate the darker corners of Toledo's ancient and medieval past. They also relied upon contacts in the field, such as Maestro Monegro, to keep them apprised of notable discoveries.[3] After all, according to the prevailing wisdom among early modern students of the past, material remains—coins, inscriptions, and other physical clues that could be found underneath the city's plazas, streets, and buildings—were as important as the written record, if not superior.[4] Higuera and his peers were particularly interested in pivotal moments and figures in Toledo's history, such as its first settlers, evangelizers, and Christian reconquerors. Certain questions pertaining to these early centuries preoccupied learned Toledo. Where, for example, was the legendary cave where Hercules lived after he established his pillars at the Strait of Gibraltar? Had an apostle brought Christianity to Toledo and, if so, was it Santiago, or Saint Peter, or Saint Paul? Where was Saint Ildefonso born, and where was the lost monastery—known as El Agaliense—where he was abbot in the seventh century?[5]

While Higuera and his peers drank from the same pool of historical sources, they often parted company in the answers to these questions, and publicly debated the reliability of each other's sources and interpretations, particularly in the decades around 1600. As among modern academics, many of their intellectual disagreements were also colored by factional politics, interpersonal conflicts, and, above all, the desire to defend one's intellectual territory. Not only were many of Higuera's interlocutors as well versed in history, hagiography, and antiquities as he; they were also just as invested, on a personal and professional level, in the past. For these men, Toledo's history and antiquities were a serious matter, with profound implications. The inextricable entanglement of Toledo's past with its present meant that new discoveries would be seized upon by the city's arbiters of historical matters in order to forward their particular visions of the past. Thus, when Higuera declared that the letter from Silo was the crucial piece of evidence that would explain the Plaza Mayor discovery, and more about Toledo's medieval history, he had to have known that he was entering dangerous and highly charged territory, the tense and productive space where Toledan politics intersected with religion and history. In this context, a completely new source or interpretation could prompt a volley of attacks on one's character, methods, and integrity.

This is precisely what happened when Higuera publicized his discovery. On its face, the letter was not particularly remarkable. It was addressed to Archbishop Cixila of Toledo from King Silo of Asturias and dated AD 777, which put it a little over fifty years after Visigothic rulers of Hispania were overthrown by North African forces under Arab command. Both the sender and recipient of the letter were actual historical figures: as the standard sources of medieval Castilian history confirmed, Silo presided over the northern Christian territory of Asturias in the eighth century, and Cixila occupied the See of Toledo at approximately the same time, at least as far as the sometimes incoherent chronologies of existing medieval histories would allow.[6] The text opened with Silo's rather conventional lament for the ills that Toledo's Christians suffered under their Islamic masters:

> It pains me that you are living so miserably there, and I have much pity on you, because you suffer so many ills under those Moors, who were born for a bad death; not content with swarming over you, they impose outrageous exactions, and everyday they strive for your deaths.[7]

King Silo continued by reviewing the events that led up to his letter—events that, it must be noted, would have been abundantly familiar to the letter's recipient, Archbishop Cixila of Toledo:

> And there your lives have been in great danger, because you began to build a church to the martyr San Tirso, near the main mosque, and Bailiff Zuleima Yusef Aben-Abdil, who rules Toledo, wanted to kill you, but, appealing to the judge Muhammad Ibn Rahman, he ordered that you be freed, and he gave you permission to build it, thanks to the money you gave him.[8]

This information about the recent travails of the Toledan flock, complete with the names and titles of the key actors, might have provided helpful background for the sixteenth-century reader. Yet to modern ears, the detailed exposition sounds suspiciously superfluous, rather like the due diligence of a conscientious and garrulous forger. King Silo continued by summarizing his recent petitions to the Moorish ruler on behalf of Toledo's Mozarabs, thanking Cixila for a recent gift of relics and detailing the gifts he was sending in return. These included liturgical ornaments for the celebration of the Mass, including a silver chalice to hold the consecrated wine, a paten, which is the plate where the consecrated communion wafer is placed, and, finally, a basin in which the officiating priest would wash his hands. As Silo explained, the round metal lid of the basin bore the insignia of the crown of Asturias, as well as the letters C and S in an abbreviation of their respective names. In Higuera's gloss, then, the medal said "[a] C[ixila] S[ilo]," that is, "To Cixila from Silo."[9] In short, the letter did not make any startling revelations about Toledo; to the contrary, it confirmed conventional wisdom among early modern Catholics about the rough state of affairs that Spain's Christians confronted during the many centuries of Islamic rule.

If the letter's content was relatively uncontroversial, the claims that Higuera forwarded for it were not, as far as many supporters of Toledo's existing patron saints were concerned. Higuera interpreted the letter as solid evidence that the large stones uncovered at the site were part of the Mozarab-era chapel to San Tirso, while the skeletons must have been later, perhaps the remains of Christian soldiers who died during the reconquest of the city in 1085. According to Higuera's interpretation, then, the letter confirmed the identity of the ruins; and, in a characteristic bit of circular logic, the copper lid inscribed with C and S was, in turn, evidence of the authenticity of the letter. If Higuera was correct on either count, the ruins would be an unprecedented piece of evidence for the endurance of Christianity in Islamic Toledo, as well as confirmation of a previously unknown patron saint and martyr for Toledo's Mozarabic community. Controversy erupted by Christmas of 1594 as Higuera and his allies, including the city's *corregidor* (royal governor), began to marshal a new interpretation of Toledo's religious history, one that put a new saint at the center of the city's sacred geography.

HISTORICAL ERUDITION IN TOLEDO

How and why did Higuera's opinion matter? As a native and longtime resident, Higuera was a familiar presence among the city's learned elite. He was born, along with a twin brother named Hernando, to Toledan parents in 1537 or 1538.[10] Of the following seventy-four years he spent on earth, Higuera would pass nearly forty in Toledo. His education kept him close to the principal institutions of learning and religious patronage in the city, namely, the cathedral and its affiliate, the University of Toledo, founded as the Colegio de Santa Catalina in the late fifteenth century for the purpose of educating poor boys to become future diocesan clergy.[11] During his studies in arts and theology in the 1550s and 1560s, Higuera gained some knowledge of Greek and Hebrew, in addition to his mastery of Latin. Higuera became a Jesuit novice in 1562 as a young man of twenty-four, after he graduated from the university—possibly with a doctorate in theology.[12] For his first twenty years as a Jesuit he taught at the Society's *colegios* throughout Castile, as the young and growing order soon put him to work as a Latin instructor in its rapidly expanding network of schools, including those of Madrid, Ocaña, Plasencia, and Toledo.[13] In 1578 he was asked to issue a theological approval of a treatise on rhetoric, and in 1584 he was put in charge of supervising instruction at the new Jesuit colegio of San Eugenio in Toledo, as the school's first prefect of Latin studies.[14] In Ocaña in 1590 he took the fourth and final vow (of special obedience to the pope) to become one of the few full-fledged members of the Society, a *profeso*, and later that same year he issued an approval for a treatise on the theological mystery of the Mass.[15] The bulk of the Society's members were not invited to take the final vow; the fourth vow marked Higuera as one of a select few.[16] Yet during his several years in the Jesuit colegio of Ocaña, Higuera's fortunes in the Society declined, and in 1594, shortly before the San Tirso discovery, he was sent back to Toledo against his will to become prefect of studies.[17]

Although he was forced to reside elsewhere in Castile for long stretches of his career, Higuera maintained strong connections with Toledo, his *patria chica*. He did so in part through regular correspondence with members of the city's intelligentsia, and through his ongoing research on Toledo's saints, prelates, and liturgy. Higuera's long experience as a Jesuit, as well as his prodigious appetite for historical research, acquainted him with some of the most illustrious men of learning in sixteenth-century Spain. If Toledo was not as active or important a center for scholarly activity as it had been during the time of the famous school of translators under Alfonso X of Castile in the thirteenth century, it was still home to one of the richest intellectual environments in early modern Spain, with a small but significant body of wealthy patrons of scholarship and visual art, particularly among the members of the high clergy. Although it had not hosted the imperial court since the Hapsburgs moved to Madrid in 1561, Toledo remained the cultural, intellectual, and religious capital of Spain, and with a population of nearly sixty thousand at the end of the sixteenth century, one of Spain's largest cities.[18] The city had a large and prosperous merchant class, thanks to textile manufacturing. As the titular head of the Spanish church, the archbishop collected a tremendous amount of tribute, giving him a higher income than most of Spain's top nobles. The cathedral was the see of the wealthiest and most powerful archdiocese in Spain, and its canons were some of the most erudite men in Spain.[19]

A number of the learned men who congregated in the archbishop's palace and cathedral also taught at the University of Toledo, under the auspices of the cathedral chapter. These were Higuera's teachers, models, and peers; and, like him, they were engaged in researching, rewriting, and reimagining Toledan (and Spanish) sacred history, conscious of their place in one of the preeminent spaces of knowledge in early modern Spain.[20] While Spanish humanist scholarship in the Erasmian vein had declined in the second half of the sixteenth century thanks to its perceived association with Protestant tendencies, Spanish thinkers did continue to write, research, and seek manuscript sources for the past.[21] The most prominent and respected member of these circles during Higuera's lifetime was Antonio Agustín (1516–1586), who had returned to Spain in the 1560s to reside in Catalonia as the archbishop of Tarragona after spending almost thirty years in Italy. In Spain, Agustín communicated with a large network of other aficionados of Spanish history and antiquities, including Jerónimo de Zurita, the Aragonese royal chronicler, the humanist scholar Juan Ginés de Sepúlveda, and the jurist Diego de Covarrubias.[22] While Agustín is best known for his *Dialogue on Coins*, he also enjoyed a reputation for expertise on matters of ecclesiastical antiquity, of which Higuera—like any self-respecting learned man of the late sixteenth century—was well aware.

One can imagine that many young and ambitious men of learning must have consulted Agustín on difficult historical questions, just as Higuera himself did in 1576. While teaching at the Jesuit colegio in Madrid, Higuera wrote to ask Agustín's opinion about an early medieval church practice whereby the bishop of Rome would distribute pieces of the consecrated host to the priests of the other churches within the city. Higuera was doubtlessly already engaged in the careful and painstaking research into ecclesiastical antiquities that would occupy him for the rest of his life, and he wondered, among other things, whether the practice—first described explicitly in a fifth-century letter from Pope Innocent I—could be traced further back to apostolic origins. Agustín responded with his perceptive doubts about the reliability of the passage ascribed to Innocent, which modern critics now regard as the product of a later writer.[23]

During Higuera's intellectual formation, both as a student and Jesuit in Toledo, he rubbed elbows in the university and the cathedral library with assiduous students of Spanish history. Toledo remained an important center for philological and historical scholarship in the late sixteenth and early seventeenth centuries, thanks in part to the cathedral's considerable collection of books and manuscripts.[24] And while Toledo's university could never compete with those of Salamanca and Alcalá de Henares for scholarly prestige, it was able to attract a handful of scholars of international stature, possibly due to its proximity to the royal court. Among Higuera's mentors and peers in Toledo was Álvar Gómez de Castro (d. 1580), who in addition to being a collector of inscriptions, editor of historical documents, and historian, is best known for his status as a distinguished Hellenist at a time when one could enumerate the number of Spaniards proficient in Greek on one or two hands. He had come to Toledo from Alcalá to occupy the chair of Rhetoric and Greek at the relatively new university mid-century, and ended up staying for just over three decades.[25] It would be surprising if the determined Higuera had not made the acquaintance of Gómez and his many learned peers, including Ambrosio de Morales, the royal historian Florián Ocampo, and the Vergara brothers, Juan and Francisco. Higuera's unpublished history of Toledo contains a remembrance of Gómez so detailed that it suggests he was, at the very least, acquainted with the great Hellenist, and perhaps had even studied with him.[26]

After his death in 1580, Gómez de Castro was replaced by André Schott, another accomplished Hellenist, philologist, and antiquarian scholar (whose name is often Latinized as Andreas Schottus). Schott, a Flemish Jesuit who had come to Spain in 1579 in the service of Antonio Agustín, from 1583 chaired Greek and Rhetoric at the new university of Zaragoza. Before leaving Spain in 1594, Schott made sure to raid its rich manuscript collections to produce what would eventually become a four-volume compilation of historical sources on Spain and its empire, the *Hispania illustrata* (Frankfurt, 1603–1608). This well-connected scholar of international standing corresponded with scholars throughout Europe, such as Justus Lipsius and Isaac Casaubon, and went on to teach elsewhere before his death in Antwerp in 1629.[27]

Schott was just one of the learned men connected with the university who also frequented the Toledan library and with whom Higuera would have regular contact. The cathedral was another important milieu for those involved in editing the sources of Iberian history, such as Antonio de Covarrubias y Leyvas, *maestrescuela* of the Toledo cathedral and an important patron and practitioner of historical and philological scholarship, who, among other commissions—including an appearance at the Council of Trent—had helped collect books and manuscripts for Philip II's repository at El Escorial.[28] Like Agustín and Schott, Covarrubias was regarded as exceptionally knowledgeable in all things historical, and, like his peers, he recognized the value of both documents and historical artifacts for this purpose, which explains why he cited numismatic evidence when he was consulted by the royal secretary on the correct spelling of the name of a Visigothic king. Covarrubias was also a central figure in Toledo's civic and cultural life. For example, when the city received the relics of the martyr Santa Leocadia in 1587, he helped write the inscriptions that would embellish the triumphal arches. When Archbishop Gaspar de Quiroga y Vela died in 1595, the cathedral chapter asked Covarrubias to review the funeral oration and to compose the inscription under the archbishop's portrait in the cathedral; Antonio was commemorated in three paintings by his friend El Greco.[29] It should not surprise us to discover that this well-respected civic and intellectual figure was an ally of Higuera. As one of the Jesuit's contacts, Covarrubias would put Higuera in contact with other learned men, such as Jerónimo Blancas, the Aragonese royal chronicler and fellow enthusiast of ecclesiastical antiquities, and he would also be one of the very few cathedral canons to take Higuera's side during the San Tirso controversy.

In other words, Higuera was working within an identifiable intellectual community. This is not to say that his interpretation of the past was not idiosyncratic. But his posthumous reputation should not blind us to the fact that Higuera was an integral member of the intellectual community centered on the Toledo cathedral in the second half of the sixteenth century. By the 1590s, thanks to his communication with scholars such as Covarrubias, Blancas, and others, Higuera, who was now in his sixties, began to reap the results of his lifelong commitment to learning. He had accumulated a significant collection of historical manuscripts and books, and drew upon them in several ongoing research and writing projects. These included an ecclesiastical history of Toledo, an edition of the *Itinerary* of Antoninus Pius, and the early version of the chronicles of Dexter and Maximus, all of which he would attempt, unsuccessfully, to see into print.

Higuera was not, however, one to slip into the obscurity of an early retirement. In 1594, almost immediately upon his return to Toledo, Higuera began to come to the attention of Toledo's learned men and his Jesuit superiors for a number of pursuits that, as he himself complained, made him a pariah among many of his peers. The San Tirso debacle was just one. In order to understand the conundrums that Higuera created for himself in the last years of the sixteenth century, it is necessary to ask: What did this saint and his Mozarabic-era cult mean to Higuera? Why was he willing to jeopardize his career as a Jesuit to promote San Tirso, and what did he believe was at stake? To answer these questions, let us return to the scene.

URBAN RENEWAL AND THE POLITICS OF SACRED HISTORY IN TOLEDO

Part of the answer to questions about Higuera's motives can be found in the shifting geography of Toledo. In the second half of the sixteenth century, members of Toledo's elite had been trying to reshape the city and, in the process, restore what they believed was its essential Christian identity while also imparting a more modern and magnificent luster on the wealthy city. In the last third of the century, successive archbishops, royal governors, municipal officials, cathedral canons, noble families, and wealthy merchants, who usually found themselves at odds with one another when it came to political and economic matters, nonetheless united in an effort to reshape Toledo. The renovations were part of ongoing efforts on the part of civic and religious leaders to erase—or at least soften—the Islamic tinge in the city's architecture and public spaces. The chronicler Francisco de Pisa articulated the conviction that the city's decrepitude was an unwelcome relic of its non-Christian past when he complained about Toledo's "narrow and Moorish streets" in his 1605 *Description of the Imperial City of Toledo*.[30] In this view, the widening of plazas and streets, introduction of Italian-style palaces and facades, construction of sewers, and promulgation of new regulations to clean up the streets—including a prohibition on allowing pigs to wander loose—were all part of an ongoing endeavor to modernize the city.[31]

The recuperation of Toledo's lost glory became even more urgent as Castile gained greater political and economic prominence. Even after 1561, when the Hapsburg court opted to remain in Madrid, rather than in Toledo, this onetime imperial capital of medieval Castile remained an important seat of power in a new age of Iberian, Catholic global expansion. In this context, the discovery of archaeological remains would necessarily come to possess rather pointed significance for the many powerful arbiters of matters historical, religious, and artistic. Among the most influential of these were the cathedral canons, whose chapter had embarked on an expansion in the 1590s. The Hospital del Rey—the royal hospital for the incurably ill—that was located directly behind the cathedral's east wall, abutting the Plaza Mayor, was to vacate the premises, enabling the space to be transformed into an annex of the cathedral. Here the wealthy church would expand its *sagrario*, "a complex of rooms containing chapels, a sacristy, vestiary, and a treasury to store the cathedral's incomparable collection of jewels, relics, and other precious objects."[32] The hospital would be relocated to a new building to be erected quite close by, just north of where it used to be on the west side of the Plaza Mayor. In August 1594 under Maestro Monegro's supervision workers had demolished the older buildings on the site and were digging the new foundations when they found the archaeological ruins that would become the object of so much controversy.

ACCUSATIONS AND ALLIANCES

In a short letter written around Christmas of 1594, Alonso de Cárcamo, corregidor of Toledo, alerted King Philip II to the discoveries. Cárcamo's account, which was almost certainly ghostwritten by his friend and ally Higuera, presented a brief but cogent summary of the historical evidence in favor of identifying the ruins as those of the Mozarabic-era church of San Tirso. The corregidor also included the pivotal documentary evidence, the letter of Silo, both in Latin and in Spanish translation. In support of the letter, Cárcamo-Higuera cited a line of the Mozarabic hymnal proving that Tirso had been commemorated in early medieval Toledo. The hymn opened with a direct appeal to Tirso, which Higuera interpreted as confirmation that the saint was remembered as a native of Toledo: "Oh martyr, with tears, oh *vernule*, we entreat you." As Higuera explained, *vernule* could mean "slave," or, more commonly, "native," as in "slave born in the master's house," and the very same word was used in the hymnal to refer to Toledo's recently enshrined patron Saint Leocadia, where it was interpreted as indicating that she was a native of the city. Thus, the passage proved that Tirso was also a native of Toledo.[33]

Higuera-as-Cárcamo pressed his point further, arguing that the king had a special responsibility to this saint in particular and that it was incumbent upon him to honor supernatural guardians of the nation. If the corregidor was duty-bound to serve the saint as well as the well-being of the city, so much more so the king. This would best be achieved by rebuilding Tirso's temple and restoring the saint to his home. In exchange, the saint might feel moved to intercede on behalf of his native city and the monarchy. Yet to do nothing would mean allowing the saint's opponents to "exile him from his native land and his natural origin."[34] This awareness of the importance of the cult of the saints for the common good, combined with the desire to foment local devotion to new saints, appealed to Philip II, well-known as an enthusiast for saints and their relics. According to a later account by Higuera, the king responded positively to Cárcamo's communications; reportedly he had the Infanta Isabel read Cárcamo's *Memorial* aloud at court, and even promised to come visit the ruins himself.[35] At the same time, the entire memorandum was made public in a version printed surreptitiously in Toledo around New Year's Eve.[36]

This use of the Mozarabic hymnal as a proof-text was an astute move, as it gave Higuera's argument a respectability that the letter from Silo alone could not provide. The Mozarabic liturgy, whose major texts included a missal, hymnal, and breviary, was venerated by contemporaries as a uniquely Iberian guide to historic Catholic rituals. The texts' rich poetic, musical, and hagiographic content made them obligatory references for anybody interested in the history of early Iberian Christianity.[37] Since the texts were believed to have originated with the apostle Santiago, to then take their definitive shape under the Visigothic bishop Saint Isidore of Seville, they were consulted as a reliable guide to a plurality of early Hispanic saints, many of whom were still lost in the mists of pre-Islamic Spanish history. The liturgy was particularly significant in Toledo, where it had endured in the city's six historically Mozarabic parishes, even after having been put to trial by fire and replaced everywhere else with the Roman rite in the eleventh century.[38] The liturgy had fallen into disuse by the turn of the fifteenth century, when the humanist cardinal-archbishop of Toledo Francisco Ximénez Cisneros had its extant texts collated, emended, and copied in new editions. Cisneros also revived the practice of having the liturgy recited in the Toledo cathedral, where he endowed a Mozarabic chaplaincy precisely for this purpose.[39] In this sense, then, Higuera was drawing upon an unimpeachable and quintessentially Toledan source to promote this Toledan saint.

Higuera's advocacy for San Tirso attracted significant support among the city's secular elite—with the exception of one notable foe, the *alcalde mayor* (chief magistrate) of Toledo, Juan Gómez de Silva—while deeply antagonizing several members of Toledo's religious hierarchy, and, in the process, the superiors of his own religious order. Like some other Castilian cities, Toledo's municipal government consisted of two overlapping bodies: the *ayuntamiento*, headed by the *corregidor* and staffed by *regidores* (councilmen), and the *cabildo* (municipal council), staffed by *jurados* (nonvoting aldermen) with various administrative responsibilities and functions. Proponents of San Tirso included the corregidor and several regidores, who soon began to generate popular support for the nascent cult. During Holy Week of 1596, while the king was in town, Toledo's regidores arranged for the formation of a religious confraternity in San Tirso's honor, and the city's Augustinian canons agreed to host the group in their church.[40] At the same time, several regidores petitioned the king to sponsor reconstruction of the historical church.[41] In addition, Cárcamo commissioned the Golden Age playwright Lope Félix de Vega Carpio (usually referred to simply as Lope de Vega) to write a tragedy about the saint's martyrdom. Higuera later remembered the play rather extravagantly as "comparable to those by the illustrious ancients, Sophocles and Euripides."[42]

Whether Higuera's enthusiastic appraisal was hyperbole or not, Toledo was never to discover. Lope de Vega's play was never published, nor did it ever grace the stage. Higuera and Cárcamo's advocacy for this new patron saint had seriously irked the cathedral canons, who were, after all, the principal sponsors of the construction project that had revealed the would-be ruin of San Tirso's church. Moreover, Toledo's cathedral already possessed the relics of the city's patron saints, Eugenius and Leocadia, whose stewards were the cathedral canons. If the corregidor's efforts to introduce a new patron saint threatened to undermine their own stewardship of Toledo's devotions, it also jeopardized the cathedral's plans for the Plaza Mayor project. If Higuera and his supporters were ultimately successful in converting the site to a church, where else could the canons build in a city already crowded with antiquities? Particularly irksome was the interference of Corregidor Cárcamo, a temporary royal appointee in a rotating position whose influence was disputed and circumscribed by the notoriously cantankerous cathedral chapter.

The cathedral was the largest employer in Toledo and the diocese was, by far, the wealthiest in Spain, with annual rents exceeding two hundred thousand ducados.[43] The cabildo's members were among the most powerful clerics in Spain. Moreover, since cathedral canonries tended to be occupied by blocks of individuals from the same family for several generations, they often enjoyed family ties to fellow canons past and present, as well as to other prominent citizens in Toledo and to the royal court.[44] For example, the dean of the cabildo, Don Pedro Carvajal Girón de Loaysa, was the brother of another canon, Don Álvaro de Carvajal, who held the high post (*dignidad*) of abbot of Santa Leocadia and served as royal almoner (*limosnero*). In addition to being the head of this massive and wealthy corporation, Dean Carvajal was also the nephew of García de Loaysa Girón (1534–1599), who at the time of the discovery of the temple of San Tirso was the acting governor of the archdiocese under the absentee archbishop Archduke Albrecht of Austria, and would go on to occupy the see himself for six months before his death in 1599.[45]

Whereas corregidores were purposefully chosen from outside and regularly rotated to different posts so that they could govern without vested interest, the cathedral cabildo was there to stay, and canons were not shy about reminding the temporary royal appointee of his proper place. For example, in 1596, the cathedral chapter took Cárcamo and the ayuntamiento to court over a dispute over ceremonial precedence. Apparently they felt affronted by the corregidor's request that the dean and cabildo hand him a velvet cushion upon which to kneel when the city went in a rogatory procession to the sagrario. The legal dispute was resolved in the corregidor's favor.[46] Higuera and Cárcamo had to have known that in this context, where far less contentious matters often ended in litigation, their hopes for San Tirso would not be met as neutral suggestions.

If we are to believe Higuera's own rather self-serving account of events, which he recorded in a manuscript from the first years of the seventeenth century, these factional politics were entirely to blame for the San Tirso debacle; it was not, as Higuera's foes would allege, that they stood in principled opposition to Silo's letter, which they believed the Jesuit had forged himself. From Higuera's perspective, it was, to the contrary, a matter of simple political one-upmanship. Namely, Dean Carvajal was irritated that he had been beaten to the chase by the corregidor. In Higuera's account, the Jesuit himself had been the object of intense lobbying on the part of representatives from the civic and ecclesiastical elite; both hoped to recruit him to compose an account of the momentous discoveries relating to San Tirso, so that they could be the first to alert the king to the news. Higuera describes a tense period right around the New Year, 1594. On one side was Doctor Don Alonso de Narbona, a prominent jurist, professor of law at the University of Toledo and literary figure, who was sent by the corregidor.[47] On the other was the canon-librarian Maestro Cristóbal Palomares, who lobbied for the dean of the cathedral chapter and even set up a secret meeting with Higuera and Dean Carvajal, during which the two tried to convince the Jesuit to withhold his draft memorial from the corregidor for one more day; in the meantime, they asked, perhaps he might compose an even longer one for them? Higuera agreed and drew up a document for Dean Carvajal the very next day. Yet, according to Higuera, Carvajal acted too slowly. The dean waited to forward the news to Madrid until after Three Kings Day in January, but was outdone by the corregidor, who sent Higuera's memorial and the "C S" disk to the king. The corregidor's faction also had Higuera's memorial printed, which Dean Carvajal and friends misinterpreted as gloating, "to thumb one's nose, as they say," at the losing party.[48]

While it is hard to believe that Higuera could have remained so innocent of the maneuvering that he so astutely chronicled, certain details of his account ring true. As a powerful jurist and parish representative, it is plausible that Narbona would have served as go-between for the corregidor. It is also true that Palomares and Higuera had a strong working relationship, which could have made the secret meeting with Dean Carvajal possible. Moreover, it also seems believable that those parties interested in Toledo's saints, history, and urban renewal, including both the cathedral chapter and the corregidor, would have sought to recruit Higuera, the individual who, it must be remembered, was in possession of the letter and the medal, key pieces of evidence that would explain a monumental discovery to be set before the king.

Motivated by these implicit territorial and political considerations, and perhaps miffed at their momentary eclipse in the eyes of the king, a core group of cathedral *capitulares*, led by the chapter's powerful dean, explicitly objected to the San Tirso project in historical terms. By March 1595, they launched a pointed and vicious attack on Higuera and his evidence. Foes of the project managed to have the printer of Cárcamo's *Memorial* jailed briefly, since he had printed it surreptitiously, without the required royal privilege or inquisitorial censorship.[49] They soon responded with their own printed attack on Higuera and his chief piece of historical evidence, the letter to Silo.⁵⁰ In this peculiar war of pamphlets, Higuera and his interlocutors lobbed not libelous screeds, but passages from liturgical texts, decrees from obscure ecclesiastical councils, rival interpretations of Latin grammar and morphology, and complicated calculations of historical chronology.

The most strident voice of opposition was that of Doctor Pedro Salazar de Mendoza (1549–1629), a wealthy and powerful cleric best known to historians as one of the patrons of El Greco. Although he would later join the cathedral as *canónigo penitenciario*, at the time he was the administrator of the Hospital de San Juan Bautista, also known as the Hospital de Tavera and, as a member of the Governing Council of the archdiocese, "among the most influential churchmen in Toledo."⁵¹ In addition to being one of El Greco's first Toledan supporters, Salazar was a learned man who was fascinated by history and genealogy, and had been a student of Higuera's at the Jesuit colegio of Ocaña.⁵² Like Higuera, he was composing a historical catalogue of the prelates of Toledo, among several other projects, and upon his death he left behind a remarkable private library consisting of more than thirteen hundred books.⁵³

In March 1595, with the support of Dean Carvajal and under the cover of anonymity, Salazar printed a pamphlet entitled *Difficulties with, and Objections against, the Opinion that the Blessed Martyr Saint Thyrsus was a Native of Toledo*, attacking the letter to Silo and Higuera's assertions about San Tirso on several points.⁵⁴ Here Salazar objected that Tirso could not have been a native of Toledo, because, according to Saint Simeon Metaphrastes—the compiler of the *Menology*, an early medieval Byzantine collection of early saints' lives much consulted by later hagiographers—the martyr was actually a native of Caesarea, in Bithynia. Besides, if Tirso had been from Toledo, Salazar reasoned, some traces of his memory would have endured in the region over the centuries. Salazar disputed Higuera's interpretation of the line about Tirso in the Mozarabic hymnal, and posited that a spelling error misled Higuera to interpret the word as the vocative case, *vernule*, which should instead read *vernulae*; this would change its case in Latin, so that the line would read "Oh martyr, we who were born slaves in our own homes (*vernulae*), we entreat you with tears," rather than Higuera's "Oh martyr, with tears, oh *vernule*, we entreat you."⁵⁵ In other words, the hymnal did nothing to support the notion that Tirso was a native of Toledo.

Salazar also attacked the argument for the ruins. Although he conceded that two lines in Toledo's Mozarabic breviary indicated that Archbishop Cixila had built a church, they did not specify that it had been in Tirso's honor. Salazar claimed to have consulted several architects who deemed the alleged "ruins" to be simply piles of architectural debris, probably remnants of other building projects dumped there over the centuries. Nor was the "C S" disk convincing. As Salazar noted, it was too finely worked to have been made by the Visigoths who, as everybody knew, were shoddy craftsmen. Finally, Salazar assaulted the linchpin of Higuera's argument, the letter from King Silo, which turned out to be quite vulnerable to critique. He noted that the letter suffered from a serious chronological flaw: King Silo's rule in Oviedo began in 797, but the letter was dated 777, before he was king. Nor, according to Salazar, was Cixila archbishop: he died circa 750, twenty-seven years before he supposedly received the letter.[56]

If pressed, Salazar would have been forced to acknowledge that questions of chronological and historical detail often plagued even authentic documents, as the method for determining dates remained a matter of debate in the early modern period. In fact, modern scholars disagree with his reckoning, and suggest instead that Cixila occupied the see from 774 to 783.[57] Yet even if one could discount Salazar's critiques on that chronological point, the letter from Silo was hobbled by a more serious handicap. The simple fact was that although Higuera claimed to have copied the text from an original written in "Gothic" hand— from the Visigothic period—that he had encountered in the cathedral library, nobody could find the alleged original. Here Salazar delivered what he clearly intended to be the death blow to this questionable document, citing a fundamental principle of canon law, from the decretals of Gregory IX: "If we do not see the authentic document, we cannot be satisfied with copies."[58]

In a pamphlet responding to these and other objections, Higuera-Cárcamo agreed that according to canon law, original documents were required in legal procedures. Yet he countered that history had a somewhat more capacious category for truth than did law:

> In judicial acts, all the evidence must be conclusive. But in historical matters, like the one at hand, anything can be evidence, even a conjecture, without worrying about the subtleties of the law.[59]

While many histories drew upon authentic legal documents, such as royal privileges and other archival sources, it would be impossible to actually write history if it required the same level of proof as did the law. By this overly exacting standard, most written histories would fail.[60] In the realm of hagiography, uncertainty was especially common. Since martyrologies usually did not record martyrs' place of birth, disputes between cities about saints were to be expected. Just as various cities claimed Saint Vincent, for example, the place of birth of San Tirso was a matter of dispute. Such disputes were actually a positive development for the pious Catholic: they helped inflame devotion. Besides, even if it turned out that Higuera was wrong and San Tirso was not a native of Toledo, what harm would it have done to venerate him?

> Because what disadvantage results if San Tirso is from Toledo? Or what damage to the faith results? What prejudice [does it have on] good customs? Even if there were some sort of mistake, it would not be a prejudicial one.[61]

This is why learned men often opted not to dig too deeply into such questions. After all, the veneration of the people for their saints was the higher good, one that the challengers to San Tirso would be wise to preserve, and which they unwittingly undermined by airing their objections in printed treatises where unlearned eyes might apprehend and misinterpret them.

Higuera recruited venerable allies to join him in answering Salazar's volley of attacks, including the former royal chronicler, Esteban de Garibay (1533–1599), and Alonso de Villegas (1535–1603), *racionero* of the Toledo cathedral and author of a widely read collection of saints' lives (*flos sanctorum*). At first, Garibay endorsed San Tirso in a short letter to Philip II, but by October 1595, upon discovering that the original letter of Silo could not be found, he reversed himself and even recommended that the king have the Inquisition look into the matter.[62] Villegas, in contrast, wrote his own vita of Tirso, and, based on a manuscript he found in the Franciscan monastery of Toledo, responded to Salazar's objections with a line of reasoning consonant with Higuera's own somewhat capacious hermeneutic principles. As was perhaps to be expected from a man whose preferred form of expression was the homily, Villegas—a fellow graduate of the University of Toledo—opened with a homey anecdote in which he disparaged the foes of San Tirso by comparing them to the proverbial peasant who complained to his wife that nobody knew his name in his village's municipal council. She advised him to object to whatever they proposed so that they would have to notice him.[63] Villegas also echoed many of Higuera's arguments about the historical and liturgical evidence. He declared that the Mozarabic missal and breviary clearly referred to Tirso as a native of Toledo, regardless of what Salazar had asserted. If Simeon Metaphrastes seemed to indicate otherwise, this was probably a mistake, for even saints could err; Saint Augustine himself once published an entire book of retractions and corrections. Villegas alluded here somewhat incorrectly to Augustine's *Retractions*, which was actually a rereading and reconsideration by the older Augustine of the works he had written as a younger man.[64] Either way, Villegas argued, even if the *Menology* was correct and Tirso was a native of Caesarea, it was quite plausible that Tirso would have fled from Caesarea to escape persecution and ended up in Toledo. This was like the Toledan saint Leocadia, who was forced to flee Flanders during first-century persecutions.

Villegas also confronted the accusation that Higuera had forged the letter to Silo. He admitted that the letter might contain some errors, but objected that this did not completely void its currency as historical evidence. Many documents—and even inscriptions—could contain scribal errors, but that did not mean that they were all apocryphal. Besides, Villegas posited, these were just inconsequential details (*menudencias*), not nearly sufficient to invalidate the essential truth of the letter's historical witness. As the Italian humanist Giovanni Pico della Mirandola said in reference to the writings of Origen, sometimes it was better to accept the heart of the document and disregard its infelicities; and, Villegas continued,

> This must be done for histories that are so ancient, because whoever goes around looking for and finding trifles will fall into difficulties that he will not know how to escape. The life of San Tirso in Metaphrastes, and the letter of Silo, should be accepted as they are, such that their essences are looked at, and will be found to be certain: and trifles will cause confusion.[65]

It was more important that early Christian martyrs, such as Tirso, be rediscovered and properly venerated, than to quibble over insignificant details that did nothing to detract from the fundamental message for Toledo of San Tirso's model of endurance in his faith at a time of persecution.

This hopeful hermeneutic, which privileged an exemplary narrative over punctilious attention to detail, would be employed repeatedly not only by Higuera but also by readers of the cronicones in the following century, with varying results. In this case, the arguments of Higuera and Villegas were not enough to detract from the objections to King Silo's letter, especially as raised by the guardian of the cathedral collection, Higuera's friend, the librarian Maestro Cristóbal Palomares. In the midst of this flurry of polemical treatises, Palomares had been searching furiously for the manuscript from which Higuera claimed to have copied the letter.[66] Lo and behold, sometime in the second half of 1595, the librarian found a letter from King Silo in a bound volume of manuscripts in the cathedral collection, just as Higuera had contended. Yet he concluded that it was a later interpolation, a forgery, and not the "original" Higuera had cited. For one, the bishop of Segorbe, Juan Bautista Pérez, who assembled the volume in 1582 while a cathedral canon in Toledo, had no recollection of it, as he explained in a January 1595 letter to Palomares.[67] This led Palomares and Dean Carvajal to append a stern "Warning to the Reader" to the cathedral manuscript, warning future readers that the document was apocryphal, a fraud (*dolus malus*) perpetrated by a certain person who had inserted it into the codex without the librarian's knowledge.[68]

In his marginal comments in the cathedral library's copy of the printed *Memorial*, Palomares was even more frank. He warned readers that the text contained information about San Tirso that was "false, and the invention of a certain priest who, tempted by the devil, invented the letter of Silo" (see figure 1.1). Moreover, Palomares implied that Higuera had taken advantage of the corregidor's lack of sophistication in order to fool the "secular and unlearned man." Naturally, Higuera was not able to deceive Palomares, who had sniffed out the interpolated letter. Once it came out that San Tirso was not really a native of Toledo, Palomares feared, it might redound upon the authentic patron saints of Toledo, "lest it be thought that those who are truly patrons and natives of Toledo" had been introduced with "the same lack of gravity" as San Tirso. He explained that he would allow the *Memorial* to remain in the cathedral library "so that if some time this is discussed [in the future], the truth will be known."[69]

These accusations did not remain in the margins, and Higuera's opponents were not shy about assigning blame in public. Salazar, Palomares, and Carvajal formally accused Higuera of forgery, trying, unsuccessfully, to bring the matter before the Inquisition.[70] Naturally Higuera's Jesuit superiors, all the way up to General Claudio Acquaviva in Rome, were alarmed. That Higuera had now attracted the enmity of powerful members of the cathedral chapter sent the Jesuit superiors into a panic. In October 1595, Hernando Valdés, rector of Toledo's colegio, alerted Acquaviva. As he detailed the accusations against Higuera, Valdés also tried to shield himself from Acquaviva's possible censure, explaining that he had tried to control Higuera, but to no effect. Experience had shown that prohibiting Higuera from getting involved in such matters was as futile as "putting doors on the countryside":

> The worst thing is that, while he is here, he will not stop interfering with these matters and inflaming them more, either on his own or through third parties, even though he has been ordered not to. If he had not made a fuss, we would have made sure from the beginning that this would be buried; but he is of a restless temperament, and he never stops, but rather he is always causing a stir.[71]

No matter what Valdés or others mandated, Higuera persisted in "fidgeting with these matters and inflaming them," either on his own or through third parties, such as the corregidor of Toledo, even though he had been ordered not to do so. "What is to be feared," Valdés warned, "is that the whole fraud [*maraña*] will be exposed, which will discredit the Father [Higuera], and the Society gains nothing."[72]

The head of the Jesuit province of Toledo at the time was Francisco de Porres, whom Acquaviva had already entrusted with several other sensitive tasks, such as improving relations with the Dominican order, and with enacting the reforms of the Jesuit Fifth General Council in 1594.[73] The cautious and diplomatic Porres attempted to avert a public scandal by conducting his own internal investigation of the Higuera affair, the results of which he described in a long letter to General Acquaviva in December of 1595. When questioned, Higuera produced a bizarre and muddled story in which misunderstandings, unhappy coincidences, and his own clumsiness were to blame, not a desire to forge documents. Higuera affirmed that he had consulted a copy of the letter to Silo in a "book of histories and letters" commissioned by Juan Bautista Pérez; this would have been sometime before 1591, when the canon left Toledo to become bishop of Segorbe. It was in this volume where many other habitués of the Toledo library, including Loaysa Girón, also had seen the letter about ten or eleven years previously. This detail was corroborated by Loaysa Girón himself, whose notarized testimony to this effect survives in Toledo's archive of notarial protocols, and was also corroborated by three additional witnesses: "Jerónimo," a monk from the extramural Toledan monastery of Sisla, Maestro Monegro, the architect of the cathedral project, and Luis Pérez de Zayas, the administrator of the royal hospital.[74] In other words, there *had* been a "Gothic" original of King Silo's letter in the cathedral library. Unfortunately, it disappeared when the papers of the previous librarian went to his heirs upon his death in 1589.[75]

It does seem possible that Higuera could have been telling the truth about this. After all, Loaysa Girón was no naïf when it came to historical documents. The governor of the archdiocese was an accomplished scholar in his own right, who in addition to having served as a canon of Toledo's cathedral as well as royal almoner, chaplain, and tutor of the heir to the throne, was a noted collector of manuscripts and patron of Greek learning. He was intimately familiar with Toledo's cathedral library: it was there that he had collected and collated scores of manuscripts in preparing his 1592 edition of the church councils of Spain, and it was also where he had pored through volumes of manuscripts in preparing his 1593 edition of Isidore's works.[76] Further evidence included the textual alibi of Higuera's own manuscripts. During his relatively long tenure in Ocaña, Higuera had been hard at work on an ecclesiastical history of Spain, which, as his fellow Jesuits attested, contained a copy of the letter in question.[77] It could not have been inserted at a later date, Porres reasoned, since it dated to a time before

Higuera came to Toledo, and it was bound in the intact volume of his notebook, written on the same type of paper, and with the same ink, as the manuscript text.

Provincial Porres was persuaded by this and other evidence that the letter was not a forgery—or at least not a recent forgery that could be pinned on Higuera. In any other circumstances, this evidence, along with the testimony of a political and intellectual heavyweight like Loaysa Girón, would have meant exoneration and triumph for Higuera. Yet, as in so many other arenas of his life, Higuera was to make matters rather difficult for himself. For, as he finally had to admit to Porres, there was no original letter to Silo, or at least not anymore, for he himself had destroyed it several years ago, by accident. Palomares was right when he accused Higuera of interpolating a later copy into the volume and passing it off as ancient. But Higuera insisted this was not a case of forgery; rather, he chalked it up to a tragicomic incident. One January, Higuera explained, he borrowed the volume from the library, with the permission of the treasurer of the cathedral. While at home paging through the volume, the brazier at his side suddenly overturned. The burning embers singed the text of the letter and stained the rest of the page. Since it was the winter rainy season, the paper was damp and the ashes soaked right into the page itself, such that he could not scrape them off. Higuera panicked, knowing that the ill-tempered Palomares would be infuriated. Alonso de Narbona agreed, and advised him to clean off the stains.[78] So Higuera asked a copyist to transfer the text of the letter to the following page, which just happened to be blank. Then Higuera himself scratched the ink off the other, damaged page. Higuera denied that any purposeful fraud had been at work, and, in his manuscript account of the events, protested that he had acted naively, "as a man who knew little about trickiness and legal cleverness," never suspecting "that they would raise such a commotion about it."[79]

Porres concluded that Higuera was not guilty of forgery. Nevertheless, thanks to his colossally foolish actions, not to mention his impolitic dealings with his own superiors, the Jesuit provincial contemplated exiling him from Toledo. Several prominent members of the Toledan Jesuit community pushed for this solution, including Juan de Mariana and Rector Valdés of Madrid. Others disagreed, including Gil González Dávila and Pedro de Ribadeneira, believing that the events did not even warrant minor punishment, such as penitence, "since there was enough material to defend him." Porres put his weight behind this more lenient position, and advised Acquaviva that it would be unwise to risk alienating the corregidor by ejecting Higuera from Toledo. Instead, Porres recommended letting the matter die, but he also kept the option of exile in reserve: "After a few months, and after things have calmed down, if it seems that there is some objection to keeping him in Toledo, his superiors can move him without offense."

(This is what transpired a mere three years later, when Higuera once again provoked his superiors' wrath, as we shall see.) Loaysa Girón imposed silence on all the parties involved, and ordered both sides to stop publishing texts about the matter.[80] In this way, the flare-up subsided, and the opposition to San Tirso effectively triumphed by default.

GENEALOGY AND THE POLITICS OF MOZARABIC IDENTITY IN TOLEDO

Why did Higuera insist so stubbornly upon the authenticity of the Silo letter and, for that matter, upon Tirso's Toledan ancestry? Why did he risk his standing in the Jesuit order by antagonizing so many powerful individuals in Toledo, just to resurrect the memory of a relatively obscure early Christian martyr who, as even he seemed to admit, may not have even been from Toledo?

Part of the answer lies in Higuera's belief that a rebuilt church to San Tirso, cheek-by-jowl with the cathedral's sagrario on the Plaza Mayor, would have given the city's historic Mozarabs a renewed visual and physical presence at the center of Toledo, just as the proposed confraternity in the saint's honor would have enabled its members to claim a spiritual and cultic continuity with their Mozarabic ancestors. Although other cities, such as Cordoba, were famous for their Mozarabic populations, Toledo was believed to have hosted the largest and longest-lasting Christian community during the Islamic period. Thus, at a time when this historic population no longer had a discernible social identity, when Toledo's Mozarabs existed only, it seems, in their distinctive liturgy, a restored temple to San Tirso would have reanimated the spirit of a specifically Toledan brand of medieval Christianity.

This was of particular interest to Higuera, who claimed to be descended from those Toledan Mozarabs who had persevered under Islamic rule. By looking more closely at how imagination, invention, and historical sources intersected in Higuera's own account of his family history, it will become clear that in this context Mozarabic history conducted a potent charge for the Jesuit, particularly in light of lingering doubts about the purity of blood of his extended family. In a time and place where statutes regulating purity of blood (*limpieza de sangre*) had been instituted by many civic and ecclesiastical institutions, and inquisitorial persecution of "new" Christian descendants of Muslims and Jews (*conversos*) was in full swing, historical and genealogical research were effective weapons. Learned men such as Higuera—as well as his onetime student and foe, Pedro Salazar de Mendoza—might attempt to document their own familial origins in a preemptive or defensive attempt to establish their limpieza as "old" Christians.

Was Higuera promoting San Tirso to put his own family, imagined as Old Christians, quite literally at the center of Toledo? This might have been the case if Higuera's claims, or the early modern significance of "Mozarabs," were so straightforward. Yet, as we will often find during our examination of Higuera and his texts, seeming certainties tend to crumble under our touch. While Higuera's genealogical claims help make his determined advocacy for San Tirso more understandable, it would be a misreading of the context to reduce this interest to crass personal motives, for reasons that will become clear from a closer look at the contested significance of Mozarabs in the sixteenth century.

For one, Higuera's Mozarabs were not quite the unimpeachably Old Christians they seemed to be. In the reckoning of the cronicones of Flavius Lucius Dexter and Julián Pérez, Toledo's Mozarabs were descended from the first Jews of Toledo who had arrived from Jerusalem centuries before the Crucifixion, during the Babylonian Captivity. When Toledo's first-century Jews heard from their cousins in Jerusalem about the persecution of Jesus and his followers, they objected most vociferously. They also requested instruction in the faith directly from the apostles, who obliged by sending Santiago to preach the Gospel in Spain. As a result, many Toledan Jews converted, and Christianity took root in Spain before anywhere else in the West, even Rome. The Christian descendants of the Spanish Jews, then, engendered the indigenous class of Toledans who resided in the city before, during, and after Islamic rule. In other words, Toledo's Mozarabs were the oldest Christians in Spain, even though they were also descended from conversos, and thus, technically, new Christians.[81]

Higuera's complex vision of the Mozarabs' religious and cultural identity was part of a broader ambivalence among early modern Toledans about the long coexistence of the city's Christians with predominantly Muslim and Arabic-speaking rulers and neighbors. Since the Mozarabs no longer seemed to exist as a distinct population, but more as a genealogical construction, retroactively claimed as illustrious ancestors, their identity was a matter of inconclusive discussion: Had they been the oldest Christians in Spain, descendants of the Visigoths and Romans? Were they perhaps descended from Jews? Or were they unholy hybrids, Arabic-speaking Christians who had been sullied by their prolonged social and religious contact with their Islamic neighbors and overlords?[82]

Joining Higuera in a more positive view were individuals such as Pedro de Alcocer, an early sixteenth-century historian of Toledo, and Francisco de Pisa, who celebrated the Mozarabs as progenitors of the Toledan nobility.[83] On the other hand were those who denigrated the Mozarabs as somehow corrupted. According to one etymology popular at the time, "Mozarab" derived from the Latin *mixti Arabes* (mixed with Arabs) which had since morphed into the vernacular *mistarabes*. The implication was that like the moriscos, Mozarabs lacked limpieza, if not in their blood, then in their suspect cultural and linguistic affinities.[84] This sentiment was echoed by Fray Agustín Salucio in his treatise "On the Origins of the Peasants They Call Old Christians." Salucio's larger argument was with what he believed was the twisted and unfair logic of limpieza statutes, which restricted conversos and moriscos from holding office due to the corruption of their blood by their respective Jewish and Muslim ancestors. Salucio countered that at least new Christians knew their own origins, whereas the Old Christian nobility's ancestry was shrouded in oblivion. The most likely explanation, Salucio slyly offered, was that Old Christian knights were descended from Mozarabs, vile and low-born descendants of cowards who capitulated to the Muslims.[85]

Salucio's treatise helps illustrate that the very definition of "Mozarab" was contested. In this climate, when Higuera and his allies publicized the letter from Silo, promoted the Mozarabic cult to San Tirso, and put Mozarabic Christianity at the center of the city, they were taking a definitive stance on a controversial question. At stake in the San Tirso affair, then, was not just Higuera's vision of his own religious and cultural origins, but those of the entire community. It was this constellation of historical, religious, and political interests that attracted the attention of many prominent authorities, including the corregidor and the king. It was also this mix that proved distasteful to a powerful faction of Toledo's ecclesiastical elite.

WAS HIGUERA A CONVERSO?

It is worth returning to the question of Higuera's own interests in these matters. Higuera sprinkled clues about himself and his origins, real and imagined, throughout the many texts he wrote in his own name. Yet he reserved his most extensive exposition for his manuscript "Treatise of the Lineage of the Higueras and also of the Last Names Peña, Romano, and others, and also an Account of the Mozarabs of Toledo." Here, Higuera granted himself ancient and illustrious origins, which, like the past lives of those reincarnated as modern celebrities, were never dull nor obscure. He traced his paternal last name back to the Garden of Eden, relying on a mix of legendary and authentic material characteristic of this inherently untrustworthy genre. Thus, we are told that the Latin "Ficulnus," of which Higuera was a vernacular derivation, could be traced back virtually to Creation; after all, the *ficus* (fig tree) was, according to some interpreters, the tree of the knowledge of good and evil from which Adam and Eve had eaten.[86] The long presence of the Higueras in the Iberian Peninsula was also confirmed by epigraphic evidence collected by none other than Antonio Agustín, who, it seems, found *ficus* and its variations in many Roman place names and inscriptions. Higuera boasted that Agustín's word was golden, since he was "the most reluctant" of all people to assert things that "could not be strongly defended."[87] In other words, Higuera's historical evidence was trustworthy via proxy.

It would be unfair to single out Higuera for his more far-fetched genealogical claims. The search for legitimizing familial origins and the use of rather dubious sources characterized early modern genealogy as it was mobilized in historical arguments, iconography, and political discourse throughout Europe.[88] Indeed, making bold and unconfirmable arguments about the illustrious origins of one's distant ancestors seems to have been an occupational hazard for genealogists, and, it must be emphasized, not only among those writing in the service of conversos.[89] Pedro Salazar de Mendoza, the most outspoken foe of Higuera's claims about San Tirso, helped himself to a plethora of details drawn from the forgeries of Annius of Viterbo in his magnum opus, a history of the Spanish nobility in which he followed a well-established but uncritical medieval precedent by beginning with the biblical Flood and then tracing Toledo's foundation to one of Noah's sons.[90] Salazar's lost history of the Toledan archbishops relied heavily upon Higuera's false chronicles, as did a biography of his ancestor, the fifteenth-century archbishop of Toledo, Cardinal Pedro González de Mendoza, in which he showcased the four false chronicles as particularly valuable sources.[91] One scholar has hypothesized that this text was actually an attempt on the part of Salazar to obscure his own converso origins.[92] Nor was Salazar a stranger to the principle that was implicitly endorsed by Higuera in defense of San Tirso, namely, that some degree of mythmaking was acceptable if it was in the service of a greater good. In addition to retroactively improving his own pedigree, he altered many of the lineages in his treatise on the Castilian nobility by making conversos into descendants of Old Christian reconquerors of Toledo. Salazar was even accused by one contemporary of being a *linajudo*, a genealogist for hire, who along with his "gang" had "tyrannized" Toledo with their willingness to give false testimony of converso lineage.[93]

Higuera moved to only slightly more solid ground to argue that the Higueras had been among the original Mozarabic families of Toledo who, in turn, were the progenitors of the Visigoths. Yet in a genre notorious even at the time for its mythologizations and sleight of hand, Higuera relied on a remarkable amount of actual archival evidence to support the history of his more recent relations, including, for example, royal charters and diplomas (*escrituras del archivo*) documenting property and privileges granted to members of the family for their service in the pivotal Reconquest battle of Las Navas de Tolosa in 1212.[94] Higuera also cited documents from the archive of Don Pedro de Rivera, the feudal lord of the "villa of Saint Martin"—possibly the extramural Toledan parish of Saint Martin de Tours—that recorded the public service of various members of his family. He also drew upon documents he had obtained in correspondence with a lateral relation from the synonymous Figueroa (or Figuera) family in Braga, Portugal.[95] For good measure, he also cited the false chronicle attributed to Julián Pérez, which, unsurprisingly, confirmed Higuera's vision of his own ancestry, including the illustrious deeds of several members of the Ficulnus family during Toledo's reconquest.[96]

As he moved closer to his own time, Higuera put less emphasis on Mozarabs, whose distinctive cultural and linguistic identity seems to have faded in the fourteenth and fifteenth centuries, and instead traced the careers of various forebears who had ascended socially and politically through royal and public service. Among his more distinguished paternal relatives, Higuera claimed, was a great-great-great grandfather named Sancho de la Peña, who was a knight (*caballero*) and corregidor of Jaén in the mid-fifteenth century. His son, Antonio de la Peña, became a regidor of Toledo in the last few decades of the century.[97] Another notable fifteenth-century ancestor was Fernán García de la Higuera, secretary to kings Juan II and Enrique IV of Castile, as well as to Don Diego López Pacheco, the Marquis of Villena. Fernán García's loyalty was his undoing, as he followed his lord in his ill-fated rebellion against Ferdinand and Isabel, and had his family property confiscated in punishment. One of his sons—Lope Fernández de la Figuera—moved to Braga, where his descendants may have included two successive sixteenth-century deans of the cathedral, Diogo Figueira and his nephew, Pedro da Rocha Figueira.[98] More recently, Higuera's maternal grandfather, Joan Álvarez Romano, was a secretary for the Inquisition, as well as an *alguacil mayor* (chief justice or constable).[99]

The professional trajectory of these fifteenth-century ancestors is familiar to scholars of late medieval converso families in Toledo, which was home to a large and relatively prosperous Jewish population before the mass conversions of the later Middle Ages and the 1492 expulsion officially ended the Jewish presence in Castile. After converting, many members of such families were able to ascend to greater respectability—and sometimes nobility—through various paths, including royal service, enlisting with a religious order, or by becoming the member of an educated profession, such as the legal or notarial service. The preponderance of conversos among Toledo's fifteenth- and sixteenth-century population became proverbial, such that one derogatory nickname for Toledans was "aubergine-eaters," since the eggplant was believed to be a prototypically Jewish food.[100]

Higuera was quite aware of the circumstantial evidence that seemed to suggest that he was descended from conversos, and that his more recent, sixteenth-century relations—who included at least one attorney and possibly a notary—were of less exalted status than those illustrious fifteenth-century gentlemen. Others were downright problematic, at least in terms of limpieza. Perhaps since the legal and notarial professions were believed to be occupied by conversos, rumors of impure blood dogged many of those who shared his last names, particularly among his maternal relatives. In the treatise, Higuera conceded that an individual who shared one of his mother's last names had been punished by the Inquisition over a century before. This may have been a matter of public knowledge, since, as Higuera noted, the penitential garment (*sambenito*) of the individual in question was still hanging in the parish church of Saint Román. Yet, he countered, "it is known from the Inquisition," that this Garçia de Cuellar "was a foreigner and without descendants."[101] In other words, he was, rather conveniently for Higuera, a rootless, childless individual, whose lack of limpieza could not be used to impugn the reputation of anybody in the past, present, or future.

Yet more recent and persistent doubts surrounded Higuera's first cousin, Pedro de la Higuera, who was married to Higuera's maternal aunt (and the father of an eponymous cousin, Licenciado Hierónimo de la Higuera, an attorney who should not be confused with our protagonist).[102] While he was alive, Pedro was so dogged by rumors about his limpieza that he requested two official confirmations (*probanzas*) of his status as an Old Christian. The first was conducted in the archiepiscopal court under Cardinal-Archbishop Juan Martínez Siliceo, the instigator of the midcentury purity of blood statutes in the Toledan cathedral; the second, in 1568, was heard by the city's corregidor.[103] Decades later, Pedro's cloudy reputation continued to hover over his seven children, and, apparently, his lateral relations, including Higuera's sister Ysabel, who joined Pedro's children in requesting yet another probanza before Toledo's royal governor in 1598. The testimony, elicited from a cluster of artisans, civil servants, and low-level clerics, including two familiars of the Inquisition, a notary public, and an *alguacil*, revealed that Pedro was quite a character who attended a regular card game at the houses of two Toledan notaries. His peculiar habit of calling out "Here comes my Jew" when he received a card that he considered unlucky—the Golden Horse, roughly the equivalent of the jack of diamonds in an Anglo-French deck—seems to have raised doubts about his limpieza.[104] One witness, a Toledan jurado whose father was one of the regular hosts of the card game, explained that Pedro's saying was simply about cards: he feared the Golden Horse as a harbinger of bad luck, for he lost every time he was dealt it. For this reason, he would sometimes resort to tearing it in half. As another witness explained, it was quite common for players to have a superstitious aversion to one particular card, which they would receive with "irritation." Perhaps for this reason, Pedro's impassioned ejaculation had become idiomatic among cardplayers meeting with ill luck.[105]

In other words, "Here comes my Jew" was the irritated, anti-Semitic outburst of an unlucky gambler, not some sort of coded affirmation of Jewish heritage or belief. It might seem surprising that such a trivial matter could raise doubts about one's limpieza, and it could be that other issues that were unmentioned in the probanzas had muddied Pedro's reputation. In this case, in emphasizing this story about the card game, the petitioners may have been acting preemptively, trying to distract from other, more pressing evidence. Yet, in a society in which perception was perhaps more important than reality—in which actual understanding of the tenets and practices of Judaism was remarkably thin, even among those in charge of prosecuting "Judaizers"—the word "Jew" was itself dangerous. Moreover, in this context in which public perception was the measure of limpieza, Jewish or Muslim heritage might be imagined or even invented by one's foes; genealogical blackmail was not uncommon, at least if we are to trust contemporary complaints about linajudos such as Salazar de Mendoza, who would supplement their income by exacting payment in exchange for withholding damning evidence about one's lineage, or by falsifying documents.[106]

If limpieza rested upon the slippery sands of what contemporaries referred to as "public voice and fame" (*pública voz y fama*), historians would be well advised to exercise considerable caution before making confident assertions of Higuera's converso status. Even many contemporaries acknowledged that the probanzas de limpieza were deeply flawed, since they might rest upon falsified genealogical proofs, or be prompted by nothing more than gossip. This has led one historian to conclude that the very category of limpieza was highly unstable, even "farcical."[107] If inquisitorial persecution and limpieza de sangre statutes created an incentive to falsify or improve one's lineage, gave rise to an entire profession of genealogists for hire, and left behind a hall of mirrors for the historian, perhaps the best one can do in such matters is to cite circumstantial evidence, while affording it the weight that it deserves.

Although Higuera's posthumous reputation as a forger has led observers to imagine that the battle over San Tirso was waged by the partisans of truth against falsehood, we have seen that matters were significantly more complex. As Higuera was well aware, he forwarded his argument for a new patron saint among men of considerable power and, in many cases, of high intellectual caliber. The members of this small community of interconnected individuals shared a keen interest in the past and present of Toledo, and many of them knew the contents of that cathedral library just as well, or better, than he did. In sum, if anybody was qualified to discount and demolish Higuera's interpretation, it was his peers, who in addition to drawing on the same liturgical, hagiographic, and annalistic manuscripts were also competing with Higuera to write the new, authoritative history of Toledo. Yet as we have seen, battles over Toledo's past were not purely academic, and the lines in the sand kept shifting with interpersonal and local politics. So, while Salazar de Mendoza might have been the outraged voice of punctilious concern for historical accuracy in the context of the San Tirso debacle, one looks in vain for a similar concern in his own works.

Higuera himself was well aware of the complex nature of genealogical knowledge in early modern Spain, as we have seen from his treatise on his own ancestors, where he combined unconfirmable claims about an illustrious ancestry with the levelheaded use of archival documents he had collected from obscure repositories in Castile and from relatives in Portugal. In the short term, then, it was not so much a question of prima facie flaws in his historical scholarship that incited local opposition to San Tirso as the fact that Higuera was unable or unwilling to navigate tactfully the contentious and crowded religio-political waters of late sixteenth-century Toledo. Whether this was out of bravura or remarkable obliviousness is impossible to determine at this distance. Yet it meant that in life—as in death—Higuera and his scholarly religious activities occupied an often uncomfortable ground, where they alternately provoked scorn or acclaim, but rarely indifference. The same difficulties would characterize Higuera's relationship with the members of his own religious order, and would hinder his attempts to translate his long labors in the archives into publications, as the following chapter will detail.

2

The Jesuits, the Inquisition, and History

Higuera's abiding interest in creating a Hispanocentric early Church, closely tethered to the landscape, monuments, and geography of the Iberian Peninsula, brought him into contact with the ancient sources of Spanish history in his scholarly research, and it also prompted him to advocate for the past in a number of other treatises that argued quite strenuously for the introduction of new and forgotten saints to the attention of local communities, in Toledo and beyond. These efforts also necessarily involved reinterpreting the local history of places throughout the Iberian Peninsula. Ironically, it was these projects, and not the false chronicles, that were to prove most controversial during Higuera's lifetime.

While Higuera corresponded with dozens of learned men in Spain and Portugal, with whom he exchanged texts, inscriptions, and arguments about Iberian saints and history, it was among the Toledan municipal elite that he would find his most earnest and receptive audience. As we have seen, this was due to the fact that Higuera's assertions about the past touched quite directly on local sacred and identity politics. In this, Higuera found an enthusiastic audience among a cluster of Toledo's jurados and regidores; thus it was that a number of these mostly aristocratic members of the city's government, most of whom were not university graduates, joined Corregidor Cárcamo in supporting Higuera's schemes for the San Tirso site.[1]

It was also among the Toledan municipal elite that Higuera was to find persistent supporters of his magnum opus, the massive *Ecclesiastical History of Toledo*, which Toledo's jurados apparently believed would be an appropriately formidable and erudite monument to the city's past and present glories. In early 1595, just as the San Tirso pamphlet wars were about to burst into the public eye, these allies of Higuera began to petition Jesuit superiors for permission to have the ambitious (and rather unwieldy) work printed with municipal sponsorship. Yet even after repeated petitions by Higuera and Toledan officials to Jesuit superiors, permission was not forthcoming. In light of the potential for claims about the past to inflame local passions, and in view of Higuera's difficult relations with his own religious order circa 1595, his repeated failure to procure permission to publish this, or any other of his treatises, is not entirely surprising. Yet as we shall see, this was not due to the perceived quality of his scholarship. In fact, even by the high standards of his day, Higuera's texts were carefully documented, learned, and extremely ambitious. They suggest that in erudition he was a worthy rival of any other scholar of his generation. Yet if Higuera's learning was not in question, why did the Jesuits refuse to allow *Toledo* to be printed, even under another's name? For many modern interpreters, the answer has been clear: since Higuera forged the false chronicles, his other works must have been forged as well. Moreover, due to his reputation, Higuera would have been mistrusted by his contemporaries, hence the Jesuits' refusal to let the text reach print.[2]

This argument has several weaknesses. The first is that, although Higuera might have been considered untrustworthy by some of his peers, this was for reasons that had little, if anything, to do with the nature of his historical scholarship. To assume otherwise is to commit the error of mistaking forgery for a symptom of an underlying pathology, rather than a recognizable and not uncommon medieval and early modern scholarly tactic. Therefore, we will need to look elsewhere to understand the fate of *Toledo*, and Higuera's fortunes in general. As we shall see, the answer, like many things regarding the enigmatic and multifaceted Higuera, is much more complex than it might appear at first blush, and pursuing it will plunge us into tensions swirling around the heart of Spanish culture, politics, and religion.

In point of fact, Higuera's mammoth work was not a spurious text at all. Far from a forgery, as a comparison of *Toledo* with its closest peers will suggest, the text was a rather critical survey of the city's past that adhered closely to contemporary norms of historical scholarship. Thus, Higuera's failure here and elsewhere had more to do with his own personality, and with the political valence of Spanish sacred history in general, than with any perceived deficiencies in his scholarly methods. In order to understand this point and to address why Higuera's manuscripts remained unpublished in toto, in spite of his ongoing efforts to see them into print, we must look to a confluence of factors, the first of which was the contentious internal struggles afflicting the Jesuit order in the second half of the sixteenth century. The ensuing debates generated tensions between Castilian Jesuits and their Roman leaders on one hand, and between the leadership of the Society of Jesus and the Spanish monarchy on the other. In this ongoing conflict, the Spanish Inquisition played a particularly sensitive role, a fact which, as we shall see, Higuera was not at all shy about exploiting in his own struggles. Yet Higuera's pugnacious personality and Jesuit politics were only part of the problem. As an examination of the broader context will reveal, Higuera was caught in yet another tangled web, this one not of his own making: namely, a broader debate about the proper role of Jesuits in the writing of sacred and secular history.

HIGUERA THE AUTHOR

Although Higuera was remembered posthumously as a forger, in life he was known as a learned man. At the same time, he came to occupy a risky position as a vocal dissenter in matters of the governance of the Society of Jesus, and as a close ally of certain individuals among the Toledan governing elite. In all of these pursuits, Higuera combined a forceful advocacy for renewing Spanish religious history and devotion with a determined sense of the exemplary role of sacred history as an idealized template for the past, present, and future of Spanish Catholicism.

In this sense, Higuera was not altogether different from erudite peers in the Society of Jesus and beyond, such as Juan de Mariana (1536–1624), who also sought to recover the sources of Spanish holy history. Mariana was only a couple of years older than Higuera, but he outlived him by thirteen, and he was much more accomplished as a historian and scholar. Mariana was also a prominent member of the Toledan Jesuit community, trusted by its leaders with sensitive tasks—such as contemplating the punishment that Higuera should undergo for his part in the San Tirso controversy. In this capacity, Mariana had been privy to many of Higuera's missteps over the years. As the perspicacious historian observed in a 1616 letter to a mutual acquaintance, Higuera was "a person who undertook many projects but did not finish any of them, as far as I know."[3]

Mariana could be forgiven for mistaking Higuera's lack of publishing success for the product of an ambitious but desultory mind. Mariana's own ambitions as an author were more fully realized. He is still remembered fondly in the annals of Spanish scholarship for his *General History of Spain* (*Historiae de rebus Hispaniae*), which had reached three Latin and four Spanish editions by his death in 1624. Mariana's crisp narrative and relatively dispassionate authorial voice earned him the posthumous sobriquet of "the Spanish Livy," and his relatively critical approach is often contrasted with Higuera's seemingly more credulous stance.[4] Baltasar Porreño (1569–1639), Higuera's former student and a Cuencan cleric, seems to have had a clearer picture of Higuera's ambitions, if not his achievements, when he ventured that the Jesuit's "great gifts and erudition are known to the entire world," and predicted that "they will be even more so when God sees to it that his works—upon which he spent the best years of his life—are published."[5] Porreño would have been surprised to find that posterity has almost entirely overlooked Higuera's erudition, thanks to the fact that subsequent critics have been more eager to malign him for forging the false chronicles than to examine the quality of the works he wrote in his own name. Porreño would also have been disappointed about the ultimate destiny of these manuscripts, which, for the past four centuries, have languished successively in monastic, aristocratic, and state repositories not far from Higuera's native Toledo.

Yet as his surviving manuscripts make plain, Higuera was an omnivorous reader and researcher who did not limit himself to surveying ancient authors, inscriptions, or archival documents, but collected tidbits from them all, at the same time, from everywhere possible. One manuscript includes lists of English monarchs, excerpts from Pliny the Elder's *Natural History*, a Visigothic inscription in Toledo, and an inscription he found in the works of the Italian antiquarian Onofrio Panvinio.[6] He channeled the results of this research into his ongoing writing projects, which included a survey of Spanish ecclesiastical history, a massive history of Toledo, several genealogies, lives of saints, scriptural commentaries, hagiographical hymns, historical editions of Latin classics, a six-hundred-verse elegy for Saint Torpete of Pisa, and even a poetic epic on the reconquest of Cuenca in dactylic hexameter.[7] Judging from this voluminous output, Higuera must have been immersed simultaneously in at least two or three major projects at a time, many of which stretched on for decades. Upon his death, he left behind finished and rough drafts on a bewildering variety of topics. These included approximately twenty texts dealing with historical and hagiographical matters that Higuera wrote in his own name. In addition to the "Treatise of the Lineage of the Higueras," he finished three additional studies of the history and genealogy of several of Toledo's noble families, as well as a history of the Jesuit colegio of Plasencia; an account of the rebellion of the Granadan moriscos in 1568; an edition of the *Itinerary* of Antoninus Pius; and a handful of scriptural commentaries.[8] Among the projects left incomplete at the time of his death in 1611 were the ecclesiastical history of Spain, a massive Spanish martyrology, and a treatise on Toledo's ecclesiastical primacy.[9] Additional texts, now lost, included surveys of the antiquities of Badajoz and Lusitania; treatises in defense of the relics of Sacromonte and of Santiago; histories of the cities of Braga, Caravaca, Cuenca, and Mérida; commentaries on the works of Martial; a history of Charlemagne; vitae of Saints Narciso and Mancio; a brief account of the foundation of Madrid; and treatises on *The Descent of Our Lady to the Holy Church of Toledo* and *On the Mountains and Rivers of Spain*. This does not include the four false chronicles which, of course, he presented as authentic historical texts, and a cluster of minor but spurious texts that Higuera claimed to have discovered, such as the various *Fragments* attributed to a Saint Athanasius of Zaragoza and the *Epitome temporal* by Isidore of Beja.[10]

As an examination of *Toledo* will demonstrate, Higuera poured an astounding amount of information into his treatises, the product of his wide-ranging and careful readings in the areas in which one would expect a Latin professor to be proficient: Greek and Latin classics, sacred scripture and biblical commentaries, patristic and medieval history and theology. These he supplemented with his own archival research. In addition, Higuera was an assiduous student of antiquities; like his counterparts, such as Cesare Baronio in Rome, he believed that recapturing the spirit of the early Church would require integrating what we would call archaeological evidence with the testimony of the venerable Christian witnesses preserved in liturgical and hagiographic texts. This helps account for the scores of inscriptions that Higuera included in *Toledo* and his other works.

Yet even if Higuera's range of interests was typical of an antiquarian age in which historical scholarship was increasingly infused with protoarchaeological research, his prodigious output and ambitions for *Toledo* were not. This massive, bombastic book, it was hoped, would be the first history worthy of Toledo, this most ancient and venerable imperial capital of Spain, and the first to chronicle in loving detail the ancient glories and modern promise of the erstwhile home of the Hapsburg monarchs, who had abandoned it for Madrid in 1561. A wildly ambitious work of monstrous length, in which the author chronicled over three millennia of Toledan history, *Toledo* was Higuera's most accomplished piece. It was also his longest; in one copy, the manuscript surpasses five thousand pages.[11] In a meandering narrative interrupted at every turn by an astounding number of erudite asides and primary sources, Higuera traced the fortunes of Toledo from its settlement by the descendants of Noah up through the turn of the seventeenth century. While modern readers might find this an odd vantage point, this was very much in keeping with medieval and early modern expectations, in which the narrative of local history was inextricable from the biblical record of divine interventions in the course of human events. In the process, Higuera showcased his own formidable knowledge of biblical, classical, medieval, and contemporary sources, drawing upon his own recollections and local knowledge of the city to draft the exasperatingly lengthy text. That his most exhaustive and labor-intensive work was never published must have been a terrible blow to the longtime Jesuit, who was never granted permission to publish any of the other treatises he wrote in his own name, either. In order to understand why, it is worth returning to the autumn of 1594.

"HE USES SCHEMES AND CUNNING TO GET WHAT HE WANTS"

At this point, Higuera had just been moved from the Jesuit house of Ocaña, where, after having arrived circa 1589, he had become an unwelcome presence.[12] When he left for Toledo in 1594, his relieved superior wrote to thank General Acquaviva: Higuera had been "one of those who used to cause the most trouble in this house," and now that he was gone, there was peace.[13] Higuera was moved back to the Toledan colegio of San Eugenio, where he was to reside, along with approximately fourteen other members of the Society of Jesus, for the next four years, until he was once again moved against his wishes.[14]

It was in this context, in which one member of a small community was emanating waves of discontent, that the Toledan provincial, Francisco Porres, granted Higuera permission to work on an account of the history of Toledo. This proved to be a misstep. As Porres would later explain in an exculpatory letter to Acquaviva, he had only done so because two Toledan jurados had appealed to him personally to allow it.[15] Yet, as Porres later protested, he never imagined it would see the light of day: "I assumed that it would . . . take years," due to Higuera's "lengthiness in all things." Yet, as it turned out, Porres remarked bitterly, "he already had [the whole thing] written," and, it dawned on the provincial that it had been Higuera's doing—a "maneuver of his"—to have the jurados intervene on his behalf.[16] In other words, Higuera had manipulated him.

Higuera had calculated, correctly, that due to his previous difficulties and now in the midst of his current, public conflict with the Toledan cathedral chapter, the patience of his superiors would be thin indeed. So he brought in a third party. In what his superiors considered a characteristically sly maneuver on his part, the crafty Higuera had members of the city's government appeal directly to Porres, thinking that the Jesuits would go out of their way not to alienate any significant portion of the religious or civic elite. Yet Higuera was wrong. His superiors saw through the scheme, and, over the next four years, his repeated requests for permission to publish *Toledo*, at least under his own name, were to be denied repeatedly.

At issue was not the perceived quality of Higuera's historical scholarship. For decades, he had been permitted to write and research, and to accumulate a large collection of books and manuscripts, in his various posts within the Society, for all of his ongoing projects. Yet his timing was exquisitely poor. By February of 1595, Higuera's ghostwritten *memorial* in favor of San Tirso had been circulating publicly for over two months, and, as Porres must have known, the opposing faction in the cathedral chapter was preparing to launch its own public attack on the corregidor and his Jesuit accomplice. Higuera's history of troublemaking, and of pulling third parties into internal Jesuit matters, most recently in Ocaña, also worked against him. As Francisco Valdés, the rector of Toledo's colegio, observed about his charge, "[Higuera] uses schemes and cunning to get what he wants," namely, by convincing prominent "outsiders" to lobby his superiors.[17]

The sense that Higuera was attempting to manipulate them irritated Jesuit superiors, judging from the repeated exchanges among Higuera, Porres, and Acquaviva regarding the proposed project. Later in 1595, and again in 1598, Higuera's municipal sponsors continued to petition the Society to allow the history to be published.[18] Yet if they thought that Acquaviva would relent based on their demands, they were sorely mistaken. For it was precisely the involvement of local municipal interests in the project that concerned the Jesuits. As we have seen, improving upon local history, even in the interest of the greater glory of Toledo, was never a purely neutral move in a time and place where the past was electric with political and religious significance. And as the San Tirso debacle was making clear, Higuera was not one to be trusted to navigate these waters with subtlety or discretion.

For Acquaviva, the overseer of a religious order with a truly global presence, it was paramount to the Society's success to keep its members from becoming entangled in local political squabbles. Of particular concern was the opening that local controversy could create for the Society's enemies, including other civic and ecclesiastical entities keen to interfere in Jesuit internal affairs. This is why, instead, in a 1595 letter to Porres, he averred that "in such matters, even if they are good, since they are profane, they are not for us," an impression that, as Acquaviva reminded the provincial, had been confirmed by "costly experience." As a compromise, he offered, the city could have the work printed, but under somebody else's name.[19]

With the publication of the first Latin edition of Mariana's *General History of Spain* (1592), Acquaviva had discovered the sparks that even a relatively anodyne account of the past could generate among local notables, who were perennially sensitive to any perceived slight, no matter how incidental.[20] Even in limited circulation, the text managed to raise hackles, thanks in part to its extensive and detailed treatment of Spanish political history. In January 1594, Acquaviva found himself writing an apology to the Marchioness of Camarasa, Ana Félix de

Guzmán, for a passage about her husband's ancestors that she had found offensive. The marchioness was the daughter of Pedro Pérez de Guzmán y Zúñiga, the first Count of Olivares and a member of a cadet branch of the powerful Medina Sidonia clan. Her husband, Francisco Manuel de los Cobos, was the second Marquis of Camarasa and a member of one of Spain's most powerful grandee families.[21]

The marchioness objected specifically to the phrase *ex infimo loco* ("from the lowest rank") that Mariana had used to refer to the origins of her husband's grandfather, Francisco de Cobos y Molina (d. 1547), the famous secretary of state and counselor to Emperor Charles V. In an aside during a discussion of medieval reconquest campaigns, Mariana mentioned that a territory in the Jaén region known as the Adelantamiento of Cazorla had been under the feudal domain of the archbishop of Toledo until the archbishop granted it to Francisco de Cobos in the first half of the sixteenth century. This honor had been at the behest of the emperor, by whose "select favor and grace" the marquis had thus been "lifted up from the lowest rank" to a position of great authority.[22] Although service to the monarchy was a relatively common route for advancement to noble status in early modern Spain, Mariana's characterization was too close to the bone for the sensitive Marchioness of Camarasa, as it probably would have been for any Spanish blueblood. In response to her objections, Acquaviva temporarily halted sales of the book until the passage in question could be removed, and, in the subsequent Spanish editions, Mariana softened his wording to remove the implication of low birth.[23]

Objections to Mariana's history would increase exponentially in 1595 with the appearance of the first Spanish edition. The most sustained attack was by Pedro Mantuano, secretary to Juan de Velasco, the Constable of Castile, and an ardent defender of Santiago; he alleged that Mariana had not commemorated the apostle's Spanish mission with the necessary exuberance. In fact, in light of the sustained battles waged around the turn of the century by supporters of Santiago to substantiate the history of his preeminence against challenges by Roman reformers, on one hand, and by supporters of Teresa of Ávila, on the other, it is somewhat jarring, even now, to read the disclaimer with which Mariana concluded his discussion of the apostle: "The great antiquity of these and other similar matters, together with the lack of books, means that we cannot affirm with certainty any of these opinions, nor discover the truth with certainty. The reader's judgment will remain free in this part."[24]

Judging from their internal correspondence, Higuera's superiors were concerned that his *Toledo* could generate even greater fallout, thanks to its rather detailed treatment of many of the city's most prominent families, and, it must be said, Higuera's less steady hand. Indeed, even in manuscript, Higuera's vision of Toledan history was already proving controversial. Just how this could have been the case for an unpublished and, from the Jesuit perspective, unauthorized text is not entirely clear, although it seems that Higuera must have been allowing his Toledan allies to copy portions of the work-in-progress. Rector Valdés fretted in an October 1595 letter to Acquaviva that this history would present "more difficulties than with any other that has come out until now," since, although Higuera had called it an ecclesiastical history, "it deals with lineages and similar matters than cannot but help to offend many." As Valdés informed Acquaviva, certain prominent families had already taken umbrage at the fact that Higuera had made "other people the heads of their houses."[25]

Valdés may have been referring Higuera's revisionist take on the ancestry of the prominent Toledo family that traced its origins to Count Pedro Paleologus, the third son of the Byzantine emperor, whose descendants included the dukes of Alba, the marquises of Villafranca, and the counts of both Oropesa and Orgaz.[26] The two most influential early modern historians of Toledo, Pedro de Alcocer and Francisco de Pisa, had repeated the standard line on this family: the Byzantine prince Pedro, like so many other foreign soldiers—including French, Catalan, Flemish, and others—had come to Castile in response to Alfonso VI's call for assistance in taking Toledo from its Islamic rulers circa 1080.[27] His greatgrandson was believed to have been Don Esteban Illán (ca. 1151–1208), Toledo's heroic medieval alcalde, who in addition to having played an important role in the city's history was also the progenitor of a long line of Toledan *alcaldes mayores*. These magnificent achievements over several centuries, and the central place of the clan in the history and reconquest of Toledo, were commemorated in the vault of the cathedral, where Pedro Paleologus himself was depicted on horseback.[28]

Higuera was not the first to express skepticism about these rather grandiose claims. After recounting the principal elements of the legend, Pisa admitted that not everybody agreed with this version of the family's history: "however, others say that neither this gentleman [Esteban Illán] nor those of his lineage and descent were Greek in nationality, but rather [they were] descendants of Old Christians of this city, called Mozarabs." Pisa reasoned that this would not have been such an ignominious ancestry since, from his perspective, the Mozarabs had persevered in the faith "without having been contaminated by the sect of the Moors."[29] As was his wont, Higuera dispensed with disclaimers and simply demoted several lines of Toledan aristocracy from Greek royalty to run-of-the-mill Mozarabs: instead of Don Pedro the Byzantine prince, Esteban Illán was descended from a much more distant relative, a "most noble Gothic knight," named Don Esteban who, as it happened, was also the father of the seventh-century Archbishop Saint Ildefonso of Toledo. Higuera agreed that Esteban Illán had been particularly loyal and heroic during Toledo's twelfth century, as a "very prominent gentleman of this city, loyal, prudent, and very rooted here."[30] Higuera added new details to the career of this alcalde mayor, including that during the minority of Alfonso VIII of Castile he led the attack against a recalcitrant nobility who had seized Toledo's castles and city gates for King Ferdinand I of León. Esteban Illán was rewarded with land in the parish of San Juan Bautista; it later became the property of the counts of Orgaz and, during Higuera's lifetime, the Jesuit *casa profesa*, which he believed had also been the birthplace of Ildefonso. Here, as usual, Higuera was combining archival research with his own hagiographic agenda to create something new. As Higuera confided in a letter to a fellow Jesuit, he had concluded that Don Esteban had been, like the other medieval residents of the city, a Mozarab, based on Arabic documents that mentioned him as a native of the city's parish of San Román, as well as the lack of medieval documents—"privileges and instruments" that would attest to Esteban Illán's Greek origins.[31]

In his repeated refusals to even consider granting a Jesuit imprimatur to the work, Acquaviva alluded to past incidents in which the Company had been damaged by a secular history, and warned about the potential of such histories to offend. In a direct letter to Higuera in 1596, Acquaviva enjoined him, "as a person who loves the good name of the Company," to desist, "since it is good if nothing leaves our hands that can offend and damage the Order itself." At the same time, Acquaviva asked Francisco de Valdés, Toledo's rector, to have the text itself sent to Rome for review.[32] In 1598, Acquaviva wrote to the city of Toledo and floated a compromise: why not have the city print the history under somebody else's name?[33] That way, he reasoned, "we will save ourselves the annoyances and notice" stirred up by other histories that had come out with Jesuit sponsorship. After all, as experience had shown, Acquaviva underlined in a letter to Luis de Guzmán, who had replaced Porres as provincial, "this is not an occupation for Religious men."[34]

Yet Valdés did not send the history to Rome, Higuera did not stop working on it, and (as far as we know) nobody sneaked into Higuera's quarters to make a copy of the text in secret, a rather extreme measure that Acquaviva suggested to Provincial Guzmán on one occasion in 1597, with the rationale that this would enable a review of the text by "the appropriate fathers."[35] In fact, it seems that Higuera's Jesuit superiors never even read *Toledo*, at least while he was alive. This does not mean that the actual content of the history was inconsequential, but it certainly gives the lie to any suggestion that the Jesuits were concerned about the relative authenticity of the text, or of the sources that Higuera used in order to write it. What did preoccupy Jesuit superiors was the city's interest. In fact, by 1598, Acquaviva had begun to worry that Higuera's Toledan patrons might not be trustworthy stewards, even for a ghostwritten history: they seemed to be too beholden to Higuera himself. He urged Guzmán to withhold permission for an edition, even under the name of another author, unless it became clear that the city would have the book examined carefully by "very intelligent people" who would excise potentially offensive passages. Acquaviva was particularly concerned about wounding the sensibilities of the members of the cathedral chapter, Higuera's historic foes since the San Tirso incident, when, as Acquaviva noted, certain "gentlemen" (*señores*) had agitated to have Higuera exiled from Toledo. It was thanks in part to his powerful ally, Corregidor Cárcamo, that Higuera had been left where he was. Now, three years later, Acquaviva concluded that the time had come to remove the problematic father from Toledo: "The months that he has been in Toledo will have satisfied the former corregidor." Yet the astute Acquaviva, ever-alert to the need to prevent political tensions, instructed the provincial to dissimulate: tell the former corregidor "that there are other reasons which compel [us] to make this move." In the meantime, "Your Reverence should believe that, as long as that Father is there he will always be stirring things up."[36] Now he instructed Guzmán, "remove him, and put him in a remote colegio, where he does not put himself, or us, in similar difficulties."[37]

Thus it was that by November of 1598, Higuera found himself in the high plains of La Mancha, residing in Belmonte, a small town over a hundred miles from Toledo and about sixty miles from the sleepy regional capital of Cuenca. For Higuera, this was a woeful exile indeed. For his Jesuit superiors, it was the perfect solution, as it had the virtue of removing Higuera from the orbit of his allies in Madrid and Toledo. From La Mancha, Higuera could, however, continue to importune General Acquaviva in correspondence, which he did. In July 1599, Higuera petitioned for permission to work on an unspecified ecclesiastical history and to have one of his philological projects published: this was his edition of the Antonine *Itinerary*, a list of Roman mile markers attributed to the second-century Roman emperor Antoninus Pius, which, in addition to being a popular tool for antiquarian research, was also politically innocuous.

Acquaviva nipped Higuera's aspirations in the bud, while, true to form, remaining attentive to the delicate balance of compassion and discipline required in matters of personnel. In his correspondence with the provincial Hernando de Lucero, Acquaviva allowed that it might be a good idea to allow Higuera to work on the ecclesiastical history in question, particularly if he lacked any other occupation, which seems to have been the case. Yet Acquaviva reiterated that Higuera should be given to understand that "it does not suit us to write or publish histories, since experience has shown us that they do not make us win, rather, we lose." He warned against allowing Higuera to harbor any illusions about the ultimate fate of the text, for, to allow him to believe that there would be hope for eventual publication "[would be] pure condescension, and later he would be upset." Regarding the *Itinerary*, the cautious Acquaviva reasoned, "if it is a secular matter, I do not see why it should be published; if it is ecclesiastical, it can form part of what he has been working on."[38]

A few months later, in October 1599, Higuera wrote to Rome to complain about his exile in La Mancha. Once again, Acquaviva attempted to assuage Higuera's discontent without directly addressing his underlying anxiety about his standing in the Society:

> Although I feel, with the requisite compassion, your affliction and labor, I hope that by now it will have passed. You should not think that Father Hojeda moved you for the reason that you say, but rather because you did not do as well in Toledo as where you are now. May you be consoled by the fact that these are things with which God tests his subjects, and teaches them to better themselves in his service.[39]

Higuera's unease and his suspicion that he was being deceived only multiplied in the ensuing five years, as he was shuffled from colegio to colegio. After Belmonte, Higuera was sent to Plasencia, then Ocaña, then back to Belmonte again by 1607. In the last year or two of his life, Higuera lived in Madrid, and, finally Toledo, where he died in 1611.[40]

THE CONTROVERSIAL *TOLEDO*

Historians have long assumed that Higuera's history of Toledo remained in manuscript because it was considered to be less reliable than other such texts, larded with references to spurious documents of Higuera's invention. The false chronicles do make the occasional appearance in the *Toledo*, but as we have seen, the Jesuits did not object to the text out of the belief that it was a forgery or that it relied upon forged texts. This is a point that bears some emphasis, for these notions continue to gain traction in spite of the fact that they were disproven by Nicolás Antonio over three hundred years ago, in what remains the most considered treatment of the cronicones, the *Censure of Fabulous Histories*. The heart of Antonio's treatise was a point-by-point comparison of Higuera's account of Toledan history in the false chronicles and the *Toledo*, respectively.[41] Antonio concluded that Higuera did *not* draw upon the chronicles at several key moments in the history of Toledo, such as in his account of the city's foundation. Moreover, Antonio identified several pivotal passages when the two parallel narratives contradicted each other. For example, the chronicles of Dexter and Julián Pérez followed earlier authors, including Arias Montano and Esteban Garibay, in attributing the city's foundation to the Jews of the Babylonian Captivity, who had been forced out of Jerusalem during its destruction in 586 BC by the Babylonian emperor Nebuchadnezzar II. The emperor was in fact defeated in Egypt, yet postbiblical legend extended his exploits further west, to Libya, Spain, and many points in between, where he was supposed to have been assisted by the captive Jews. In *Toledo*, however, Higuera flatly rejected this notion with a rejoinder that, it must be admitted, he would have done well to apply to his own work:

> This would be very well put if it had any grounds for truth or were based on anything but conjectures... It would be reasonable for anyone taking on the task of great history to look and consider if what he puts his name to really is history and not more legend or fabrication than anything else; and it is outrageous to write about uncertain things, which have little foundation, with the freedom and confidence of someone writing up the conclusions or mathematical demonstrations of Euclid.[42]

Yet if *Toledo* was not a forgery, why did the Jesuits refuse to allow it to be published? After all, Higuera's text did not differ radically in scope, substance, or style from the other histories of Toledo written in his lifetime, which included Pedro de Alcocer's influential *History, or Description of the Imperial City of Toledo* (1554) and the *Description of the Imperial City of Toledo, and History of Its Antiquities* (1605), by Francisco de Pisa, the Toledan chaplain.[43] As even a cursory examination of the work reveals, far from being a "fraudulent history," in comparison with its two closest contemporaries Higuera's *Toledo* is longer, more erudite, and better researched, thanks in large part to its incorporation of historical documents into the text itself.[44] In terms of approach, Higuera was arguably in the middle of the spectrum, less credulous about the sources than Alcocer, and more forgiving of legendary detail than Pisa.

Like these other contemporary histories of Toledo, Higuera's text consisted of a detailed narration of the city's history up to the contemporary age, a survey of its pagan and Christian antiquities, and a praise of its nobility, fertility, and native sons. Higuera, like Alcocer and Pisa, surveyed events of religious and political significance, while also providing hagiographical accounts of Toledo's illustrious rulers, martyrs, and bishops across the ages. All three authors shared with medieval chroniclers a notion of local history that was also universal history, in which small-scale events were inextricable from the biblical record of divine interventions in the world. Thus, Toledan history began at the very beginning, when Noah's descendants were repopulating the earth in the wake of the Flood. After these auspicious beginnings, Alcocer, Higuera, and Pisa all traced a broadly recognizable narrative arc, anchored by the same historical milestones, including the foundation of Toledo by Tubal, Noah's grandson, followed by centuries of legendary monarchs with eponymous topographical names like Iberus and Hispanus. This era was brought to an end by the successive waves of invaders: Greeks, Carthaginians, Romans, Germanic tribes, and Arab and Berber forces all took a turn at Toledo's helm, until they finally yielded to the dominion of Castilian reconquerors in the High Middle Ages. Finally, all three authors brought their histories of the city up to the very recent past, with surveys of the prominent political and religious figures of the sixteenth and seventeenth centuries.

Like Alcocer and Pisa, Higuera approached the fearsome task of summing up over three thousand years of the city's history by employing the narrative conventions of Renaissance chorography, a heterogeneous historical genre quite popular in early modern Spain.[45] And like Alcocer and Pisa, but at considerably greater length, Higuera surveyed Toledo's ancient foundations, documented the antiquity of its Christianity, and traced the continuity of these origins across the centuries, as well as offering a plethora of information about local geography and history in a variety of narrative registers, including the classically informed humanist conventions of the *laus* and *descriptio urbis*, and the more typically Christian narrative devices of miracle stories and episcopal catalogues.[46]

Yet if the broad outlines of Higuera's *History* would have been familiar to his readers, his text differed from those of his peers in a number of important ways. The most striking is that, in comparison to its peers, it is gargantuan. This is due to another significant difference: in contrast to the comparatively lean and succinct narratives of Alcocer and Pisa, Higuera's text is interrupted constantly by what we would refer to as primary sources, most of which he claimed to have collected himself, such as medieval documents, as well as Latin (and occasionally Greek, Arabic, and Hebrew) inscriptions along with complete translations into Castilian.[47] Higuera did this to showcase the fruits of his research, as well as to establish his bona fides as an author and researcher. By including entire sources, many of which are no longer extant, Higuera also provided a valuable service for future scholars, who have only recently begun to uncover the many documentary and epigraphic treasures concealed within the history of Toledo and its sister text, the *Ecclesiastical History of Spain*.[48] Yet while the inclusion of entire documents, as well as dozens of inscriptions, was a strong and significant methodological statement itself in favor of the value of primary sources for the early modern historian, Higuera's lengthy documentary detours, combined with seemingly endless digressions on various topics only sometimes germane to the narrative, also have the unintended effect of making *Toledo* a laborious and often exasperating read, even by the standards of Baroque historiography.

Since Higuera was an unrestrained and undisciplined narrator, it is easy to miss the fact that he was also a relatively sophisticated and careful reader who reflected upon the value of his sources. Higuera's ability to provide cogent explanations in which he drew upon his own archaeological sleuthing, textual and historical knowledge, and vivid historical imagination is revealed by comparing his discussion of the cave of Hercules with Alcocer and Pisa's account of the same topic. This fabled cavern under the parish church of San Ginés was an area of productive tension for any chronicler of Toledo, as we see in Alcocer's rich mythological imaginings, whereby the cave was a magical place that gave Toledo its fabled mystery. According to Alcocer, a Greek necromancer and astrologer named Ferecio had discovered the large and scary cavern when he came to Toledo as its second founder (after Tubal). Ferecio encountered a serpent and a dragon inside, both of whom he domesticated with his knowledge; he then dedicated the cave to Hercules who, he deduced, must have sent the serpent to Toledo in order to predict the future. Thereafter Ferecio imparted his knowledge of the supernatural to the first settlers of the city, whom he instructed in making sacrifices to the gods, particularly Hercules. It is Ferecio's legacy, Alcocer reasoned, that gave Toledans their natural inclination for astrology and magic, which, he informed the reader, the French call the "Toledan art." Later, the Christian Visigoths locked the cave in an attempt to eradicate the superstitions connected with it. The cave remained sealed until the last Visigothic king, Rodrigo, violated the sanctuary in search of treasure. This act prompted God to punish Spain with the fall of the Visigoths and the subsequent Islamic invasion in the early eighth century. As Alcocer reminded readers, when Rodrigo broke the locks on the cave—which in other versions of the story was a palace instead—he found not the treasure he had been seeking, but rather a premonitory panel upon which were depicted several figures in Arab dress, with the message: When this painting is seen, the people who are depicted here will enter Spain and take it over.[49]

The comparatively sober Pisa chose a markedly less fantastic take in his brief discussion of the cave. Pisa rejected the notion that the cave had been made by Hercules and dedicated as a temple to the gods. For Pisa, the cave, like all natural things, had been created by God. The fact that there were architectural elements within the cave, such as pillars and walls, was not evidence that it was an ancient temple; rather, these were the traces of attempts by humans to alter and refine the cave for their purposes. Here Pisa concluded that the most likely explanation was that Toledans of old, like wild beasts before them, would have found the cave to be a welcome refuge from the elements, or from long military sieges.[50]

In contrast to the relative concision of Alcocer and Pisa, Higuera's account of the cave of Hercules was a departure point for a lengthy and rambling section that reads like the miscellany of a classical encyclopedist like Pliny the Elder crossed with a medieval scholastic, shot through with Higuera's characteristic mix of erudition, pedantry, and wit. In this set piece, Higuera rejected Ferecio, the serpent, and the dragon, and moved instead directly to the most cogent explanation, and, remarkably, the one closest to modern interpretations—namely, that the cave might have been part of a well-engineered subterranean sewer system constructed by the Romans. Yet, in forwarding this first hypothesis, Higuera unloosed a concatenation of facts and antiquarian tidbits about Roman sewers, such that the thread of the argument is nearly lost. After citing the Roman architect Vitruvius at length in order to explain how the Romans constructed the *cloacae*, he regaled the reader with a disquisition on the Roman cult to Cloacina, the goddess who supervised the sewers. Higuera traced the history of the important position of sewer supervisor and explained that Romans would often come from elsewhere in order to occupy the post; for good measure, to support this point he marshaled a number of inscriptions honoring prominent *cloacarii*. After exploring other tangential points about Roman sewers, including the fact that the Romans used to throw the bodies of Christians into them, Higuera reached the anticlimactic conclusion that the cave of Hercules was not a sewer after all, due to its size and the nature of its construction.[51]

Higuera repeated this characteristically scholastic maneuver, in which he presented an opinion only to decide that it was not entirely satisfactory, for the length of his discussion of the cave. Thus, in a chapter on "The Opinions of Other Learned Men on the Abovementioned Cave and the Reasons That They Have," followed by several other chapters on the same topic, the reader is treated to a meandering rumination on whether the cave had served as a place where magic and other diabolical arts were taught, as legend (and Alcocer) had it; or if it was, perhaps, a Greek temple or a Christian cemetery. In the process, we also follow many digressions related to necromancy, including the tale of a magical head that would scream "there's a Jew in Tavera!" until any Jew unlucky enough to enter the city of Tavera left (this went on for a long time, until the fed-up citizens of the city destroyed it); a discussion of a university in Islamic Seville where the future pope Sylvester II reportedly studied magic in the tenth century; the story of a young man en route to study in Paris who, waylaid by a demon, ended up studying magic in a cave in Toledo instead; what befell the soldiers in the service of a medieval king of Castile who, while debating who was more brave—Achilles or Hector—were suddenly frightened by a ghost from among Hector's followers who asked who would now dare to doubt who was braver, itself a tangent to a discussion of the alleged magical powers of Don Enrique de Villena (d. 1434), a famous scholar and descendant of the royal family of Aragon; and, finally, a detailed account of the doomed 1546 expedition into the cave of Hercules sponsored by Archbishop Juan Martínez Siliceo, which ended with a sudden flood, a dramatic escape, and, if we are to believe Higuera, the premature deaths of several of the participants shortly thereafter.[52] After considering whether the cave was a place of hiding for Christians, a cemetery for martyrs, or a refuge from war, Higuera concluded with the equivocating bottom line that it could have been all of these things in succession. Why, then, the lengthy narrative? As Higuera clarified in an exculpatory aside, he had gone on so long in order to prove the larger point that Toledo was already equipped with natural defenses long before the Romans came along, thanks to its privileged physical location.[53]

In the process of trying to follow the wandering and compulsively documented argument, which, as Higuera recognizes, might have tested the reader's patience, it is easy to forget that the narrator has presented a number of rather plausible explanations for the cave, none of which involved a dragon. Higuera's miscellany on the cave of Hercules proved so informative—and, it must be said, entertaining—that even his erstwhile foe, the Toledan scholar Pedro Salazar de Mendoza, felt compelled to plagiarize it. This he did, silently, in a brief account of Toledo's history, where he followed Higuera nearly point-by-point: here, in radically shortened form, are the cave as a Roman sewer; a brief excursus on the history of Roman sewer construction; a quick rundown of the cave as a center for necromancy, the "Toledan art"; and, finally, a close paraphrase of Higuera's account of the 1546 expedition and its ill-fated participants.[54]

A final characteristic of note differentiated Higuera's *Toledo* from its peers. Unlike Alcocer or Pisa, Higuera reflected consciously on the difficulties of his sources, and on the methodological dilemmas that confronted any would-be historian of ancient Spain, particularly for the centuries before Christ. For example, regarding the years after Tubal, when Toledo was first settled, Higuera ruminated, one could not be sure of much of anything, "since we do not know the names of the settlers, and not even the language that they used then." We can be sure, he reasoned, that Tubal would have introduced good customs, "but this is all so full of darkness that almost nothing can be known with certainty or specificity."[55] Admittedly, a lament about the lack of sources was inevitable in Renaissance histories of Spain. For Alcocer, it was merely a trope: after briefly complaining that the early period was necessarily one of conjectures, he nevertheless enumerated dozens of rulers, such as Ibero, Tago, Luso, and Hispanus, as the successors of Tubal in the centuries before the Phoenicians, thanks in large part to Annius of Viterbo's pseudo-Berosus which, Alcocer affirmed, was indispensable thanks to the wealth of detail it provided about this era. Indeed, thanks to Annius, Alcocer was able to create a historical narrative that combined various strands of mythology with biblical chronology.[56]

Pisa also asserted that the lack of documentation made it almost impossible to write anything about Spain in the centuries before the arrival of the Carthaginians. Since he was significantly more skeptical about the clarity of the ancient period, Pisa's account of these early generations was comparatively lean. Pisa incorporated entire sections from Alcocer's text, yet he was also quick to reject notions that he considered foolish. Pisa began his narrative with the arrival of Tubal in Spain after the Flood, but then expressed his impatience with the survey of the wanderings of this important founding father of Spanish cities, which was customary, not only in Alcocer's book, but also in other contemporary chorographies. Pisa remarked that there was in fact no need to speculate about where Tubal might have set foot. It was likewise moot to recount the legendary monarchs after Tubal in detail, because most of them were fictional. As Pisa reasoned, it was preferable to emulate the restraint that Mariana had evinced in his *History*, by rejecting the "fictions" of "modern historians." (Here Pisa was exaggerating a bit: the sober Mariana had included several Annian kings in his account of those early years of Spain, but he had also rejected many others.)[57] Pisa also declared the futility of attempting to trace place-names from eponymous kings, and bemoaned the tendency to attribute any event of significance to a fictional king of the same name; he objected, for example, that one did not need to posit a king named Ibero to derive the name of the Iberian Peninsula.[58]

Of course, Pisa was still a man of his age, and so we should not be shocked to find that, directly after articulating his objections to the practice, our author recounts that a king named Hispalis gave his name to Seville (*Hispalis*), and a governor named Atlante bestowed his appellation to the ocean. Nor did Pisa refrain from repeating many of Alcocer's details about the other legendary kings, even if he did often preface these tales with a frosty "it is said." Pisa also had his limits when it came to those who might challenge the bundle of legends surrounding Santiago; these skeptics he dismissed as "excessively curious" individuals, who "have wanted to find [. . .] a flaw in such a clear and simple thing, and to know more than it is suitable to know."[59]

Higuera did not share Pisa's aversion to sharing legendary material, and he was even more generous than Alcocer with the colorful anecdote or edifying detail about these ancient rulers, whom he knew were possibly fabulous. The result, from one perspective, is a history that is even more chock full of legendary and speculative material. For example, on the eponymous King Hispanus, whom Pisa dispatched in a few crisp lines, Higuera spilled gobs of ink. First he explored the question of his identity, including whether Hispanus had been a nephew of Hercules, as some asserted; then there was the question of his character, which was edifying: in addition to possessing all of the heroic virtues, the mythical monarch had been "a very select prince, just, gentle, liberal, courageous, and magnanimous." Higuera went on to demythologize the king just a bit, by dismissing as nonsense the notion that it was Hispanus, not the Romans, who built the aqueduct of Segovia; and, after a digression on the location of the famed Iberian temple of Hercules, Higuera calculated when Hispanus died, by comparing and correlating Iberian and biblical chronologies.[60]

In the dedication to the city of Toledo, Higuera discussed the difficulty of establishing clear historical chronologies, particularly in those opaque centuries before Christ. The problem, he said, was that one often needed to fight "tooth and nail with antiquity" in order to get a sense of the ancient period. Antiquity herself was guilty of "disguising her deeds with the crude and ludicrous embellishment of fables, and, hiding them in the darkness of obscurity, making them disappear in the centuries to come." The historian was left in the lurch. Like "those who take chestnuts out of their prickly husks, [and] have to peel off their sharp quills before they can enjoy the pith," the historian is forced to clear away a "mountain of thorns and stinging thistles before he can bring something to light."[61]

Higuera evinced a similar sensitivity to the difficulty of separating legend from fact in his discussion of Annius of Viterbo's Berosus. The matter of how much credit to give to these texts was, he noted, a "hard fought controversy," with critics such as Gaspar Barreiros, Benedicto Pereyra, Juan Vergara, and Juan Luis Vives on one side, and on the other, those who had drawn on the Annian texts, such as Per Antoni Beuter, Florián Ocampo, Juan de Pineda, and Guillaume Postel.[62] In this, Higuera presented himself as a moderate, who was cautiously inclined to accept the Berosian texts as authentic, but with some reservations. Thus, Higuera resolved to draw on Annius's fragments, but only when they did not contradict scripture or the "torrent of grave and accepted authors."[63] In other words, as long as Annius's sources did not contradict the truths of religion and tradition, he would admit them. Indeed, in *Toledo*, Higuera cited the Annian forgeries to document Noah's movements, to support the idea that Ham had been a potion-using necromancer who was also called Zoroaster, and to buttress the assertion that the Spanish, Italians, and Gauls were among the oldest peoples in the world, along with the rather more familiar and fully attested ancient kingdoms of the Babylonians, Egyptians, Assyrians, Ethiopians, and Greeks. Yet on this last point,

Higuera drew a line in the sand, seemingly without a shred of self-consciousness: he was referring here to Annius, but had done so only by abbreviating his "prolix and annoying narration."[64]

It is true that Higuera's reservations about Annius sound suspiciously like the topos of critical rejection, whereby Renaissance authors were wont to demonstrate their skepticism about a source, to demonstrate that they were intelligent, critical readers—only to go ahead and use it anyhow.[65] Yet a related text suggests that Higuera's thoughtfulness about his sources was more than superficial, and that his cautious use of apocryphal texts was a consistent position. In the unfinished *Ecclesiastical History of Spain*, which he dedicated to the future Philip III in 1593, Higuera reflected upon his method and sources in a "Prologue to the Christian Reader." Here he echoed contemporary complaints that the Islamic invasion had put Spain at a disadvantage: if it had not been for these "barbaric" peoples, "enemies of urbanity and literature," Spain would be "as rich as any other nations that are or have ever existed in the world" in sources for the ancient and medieval periods. Instead, Higuera ruefully admitted, "We are forced principally in these first years to beg for some of the things we might say, with the result that the narrative does not seem right on the mark on every point."[66] In his search for sources that would not only shed light upon the arrival of Christianity in Spain with the apostles Santiago, Peter, and Paul, but also on the first few centuries of Iberian bishops, heresies, and councils, Higuera admitted that a tough road was ahead of him. Perhaps this is why, rather than offering the customary *protestatio auctoris* in which the narrator laments that his abilities are not equal to the task, Higuera instead reflected upon himself as a pioneer. In order to write about these sacred matters in a "pure and ecclesiastical style," he would need to draw upon sources of more questionable authenticity than the "grave and ancient authors" upon which one would customarily rely. Borrowing a sentiment first attributed to Pliny the Elder, Higuera reasoned that such sources should not be jettisoned outright simply because they had been deemed apocryphal: "We will not reject or scorn any author," he said, "no matter how modern or little-known, as long as he bases his opinions on good reasoning and arguments." Just as a source that had been given credit since "time immemorial" should only be admitted if it were credible—since "we give more credit to truth than antiquity"—an apocryphal source might also contain truth, a principle tacitly admitted by Pope Gelasius when he allowed Catholics to read portions of certain books by heretics.[67]

Here Higuera was referring to the so-called Gelasian decree (which scholars now attribute to sixth-century Gaul, rather than to the late fifth-century papacy of Gelasius I himself). In fact, the fifth section of the decree, *De libris recipiendis et non recipiendis*, consists of a list of apocryphal works excluded from the scriptural canon. Yet Higuera knew very well that medieval artists, sermon-writers, and liturgists had, for centuries, drawn prodigiously upon these texts, thanks to the picturesque and edifying details that they provided about the lives of the saints and the Holy Family.[68] When he said Gelasius had allowed Christians to read books by heretics, Higuera was probably alluding to the fact that the decree did allow that orthodox Christians could licitly read various extracanonical works by authors such as Eusebius of Caesarea and Origen of Alexandria, in spite of their authors' having erred in rather significant ways; Eusebius had adhered to Arianism, and many of Origen's ideas had been condemned as heretical.

In *Toledo*, Higuera evinced a similar fearlessness about confronting both the possibilities and difficulties of apocryphal sources. Here he considered the relative value of another famous forgery, the *True History of the King Don Rodrigo*, which narrated the familiar story of the Arabic conquest of Spain in the eighth century from the perspective of an eyewitness, one Abulcacim Tarif Abentarique. The royal translator Miguel de Luna, who was also involved in the composition of the lead books of Granada, claimed to have discovered the Arabic manuscript of the *True History* in the royal library of El Escorial. After its initial publication in 1595, the work became quite influential in historical and literary accounts of the Arab conquest; for example, Francisco Pisa and Higuera both cited Luna in order to support their conviction that the cave violated by Rodrigo was not, in fact, the Cave of Hercules under Toledo's church of San Ginés, explored in the ill-fated expedition of 1546, but in fact, a different cavern, located a mile east of Toledo.[69]

Yet if Pisa simply cited Luna's *True History* on this point without comment, Higuera signaled his reservations, noting that the text contained certain "deviations," and "details that do not agree with the good Authors of our history, which are the sources of Spanish history"; these variations, Higuera noted, had led some readers to doubt the text's authenticity. Here Higuera may have been alluding to the fact that Luna's version of the story omitted familiar legendary details such as the "ghastly penance" inflicted by God upon Rodrigo for his sins, consisting of having his genitals devoured by a snake. Instead, Luna's Rodrigo simply disappeared into the Castilian countryside, disguised as a shepherd, without suffering any divine retribution at all. Luna's "deviations" and the doubts they raised led Higuera to conclude that he would use the text, but with "caution."[70]

As we have seen, Higuera did not use apocryphal sources naively. Rather, he signaled clearly to the reader on several occasions, both in *Toledo* and its sister text, the unfinished *Ecclesiastical History of Spain*, that his was a conscious and careful strategy. In this sense, Higuera emerges as neither excessively credulous nor critical, but somewhere in the middle. Higuera did not necessarily evince greater credulity or propensity to mythmaking than his peers. Some may find this a difficult pill to swallow, in light of his posthumous reputation as a forger, and, admittedly, this short *discursus* on method and sources should not be oversold. Yet in comparison with his peers, the narrator of both of these texts demonstrated solid capacity for critical thought; a well-articulated sensitivity to the pitfalls of writing history, particularly for a time that was not well documented, for a place such as ancient Toledo; a prodigious capacity for historical research; and, finally, the conviction that even fallible written sources could be salvaged for useful information. As we shall see later in this story, it was this latter principle that Higuera's readers, in turn, would embrace in their own readings of his chronicles in the following century.

In other words, Higuera shared the ability to demythologize, as well as to use authentic epigraphic and archival sources, with many other scholars at the vanguard of historical method in Spain and beyond, including Italian humanist hagiographers, Gallic legal scholars, and English antiquarians, among others.[71] We should not let his posthumous reputation blind us to the possibility of including Higuera with such esteemed company. Yet it begs the question: if *Toledo* offered a rather conventional vision of local history, why was Acquaviva so apprehensive about its publication? To understand this, we will need to look more closely at Higuera's own troublesome relations with his fellow Jesuits.

"A GOSSIP AND A SOWER OF DISCORD": HIGUERA AND JESUIT DISSENT

As it turned out, 1595 was not the first time that Higuera had caused trouble by involving third parties in what Jesuit superiors considered internal business. While the San Tirso incident certainly created a new level of anxiety among superiors in Toledo and Rome, Higuera's fortunes in the Company had already taken a sharp turn for the worse, judging from a biting assessment by inspector Gil González Dávila in a 1592 report to General Acquaviva:

> [Higuera] has always been inconstant in the past. He made quite a mark and created a scandal. And now his confidence is always suspected of being unreliable. He is a gossip and a sower of discord, and not only among those of the residence. He is also strongly suspected of dealing with outsiders as well. He does nothing to help union and peace.[72]

While the inspector did not specify the nature of the "scandal" that Higuera had caused in the past, his concern about Higuera's trustworthiness suggests that the objections raised by superiors in Toledo—namely, a noxious tendency to bring controversy to the Society's doorstep—had already been of concern during his residence in Ocaña, circa 1589–1594.

What had Higuera done to merit this indictment? His beginnings with the Society had been auspicious. By his own account, Higuera felt a calling to become a Jesuit when he completed the Spiritual Exercises of Ignatius of Loyola while still a student at the University of Toledo, but resisted the vocation until he finished his studies.[73] As a novice in the 1560s, Higuera would have been mentored by some of the very first Jesuits, Loyola's followers, who were still in positions of leadership in those early decades of the Society's existence. As a fixture of Castilian colegios in the last four decades of the sixteenth century, Higuera would have instructed hundreds—perhaps thousands—of young men in arts and letters. In this capacity, as another Jesuit later remembered, Higuera had taught "many of those who are today among the most eminent of this century of human letters, in Greek, Hebrew, and Latin, in prose, and verse," including Lope de Vega, Francisco de Quevedo, and Higuera's Toledan nemesis, Pedro Salazar de Mendoza.[74] Higuera's increasing responsibilities were accompanied by an increasing level of commitment to the Society.

Yet between taking his fourth and final vow in 1589 and his death in Toledo in 1611, Higuera's tenure in the Society became quite rocky. Looking at the broader Jesuit context reveals that Higuera's problems with his superiors were not limited to the waves created by his involvement with members of the Toledan municipal government, nor were they unique to Higuera himself. In fact, by the 1580s, Jesuit superiors were confronting a veritable epidemic of dissent among Spanish Jesuits, particularly in Toledo, as the late sixteenth-century Society of Jesus went through a massive realignment that proved painful for many in Castile. Ever since the order's foundation in 1540, it had been dominated by Spaniards in leadership and membership alike. Yet in the middle decades of the sixteenth century, as the Society grew and became more international, its Roman leadership attempted to make it increasingly centralized. Many Spanish Jesuits resented the fact that the order's center of gravity was shifting to Rome, fearing that they were losing their national autonomy to the increased authority of the general. They were. As part of this effort, in the 1570s, the first non-Iberian general, the Belgian Everard Mercurian, removed most of the Spanish Jesuits from their posts in Rome and sent them to other provinces or back to Spain.[75] The purge continued under Mercurian's successor, the Neapolitan Claudio Acquaviva, a fearless headbuster in this and many other matters, whose tenure began in 1581 and lasted until 1615.

These events sparked an all-out conspiracy among a number of Spanish Jesuits to topple what they perceived as foreign and autocratic Roman rule. This strife erupted into the open in the 1580s. The conflict transcended Jesuit intramural politics, as dissidents attempted to gain support for their cause by appealing to the monarchy and the Inquisition against their own leadership; in other words, by playing Madrid against Rome as part of the broader, ongoing battle for power between the Spanish Hapsburgs and the papacy. By the same token, the Madrid faction—the royal court and members of the Inquisition's Supreme Council— used Jesuit dissidents to assert independence from Rome. In the ensuing controversy, which lasted until the early years of the seventeenth century, seven successive popes, two kings of Spain, and General Acquaviva (who outlived them all) fought over the Society's constitution, name, and privileges. Castile, particularly Toledo and Valladolid, was the heart of the opposition, where dissenters did not hesitate to appeal to Philip II, Philip III, and the Inquisition. Agitators included Higuera, but also many of the most respected and venerable members of the Society, including Juan de Mariana and Pedro de Ribadeneira.[76] In fact, Mariana wrote an entire treatise detailing the ways in which the Society was being mismanaged. However, he had the good sense to keep the text—which later editors gave the inflammatory title of the *Discourse on the Ailments of the Society of Jesus*—hidden in his quarters; it was nonetheless discovered upon his arrest in 1609, when Mariana was imprisoned for his denunciation of Philip III's devaluation of the currency.[77]

In the numerous inflammatory memoranda (*memoriales*) sent, usually anonymously, to the king, the Inquisition, and the pope beginning in the 1580s, dissenters played on anti-Jesuit stereotypes and perpetuated fears about worldwide Jesuit conspiracies. This was not hard to do: Philip II was apprehensive of the Jesuits' autonomy and perceived intimate links to the papacy, and the Dominicans who dominated the Inquisition resented the special privileges and immunities that the Society had secured from the papacy in 1584. Dissenters demanded that the Spanish provinces be supervised by a Spanish overseer (*comisario*) which would, effectively, give their branch of the Society more autonomy; for, as they argued, a foreigner—such as Acquaviva—could not possibly understand or respect the Spanish Inquisition, which was, of course, an arm of the monarchy.[78]

One particular point of tension was a papal privilege that granted Jesuit confessors the right to deal with certain matters of conscience in-house, rather than being required to report their members' minor heretical statements (known as "propositions") or other lesser transgressions to the Inquisition. In a move calculated to inflame the Madrid faction of courtiers and inquisitors, *memorialistas* denounced this as an excessive freedom that reflected the general's lack of respect for this particularly Spanish institution.[79] In order to press this point, in 1586 they went so far as to denounce the provincial of Toledo, Antonio Marcén, for not having reported a fellow Jesuit to the Inquisition. Instead, Marcén had allowed the offender, suspected of solicitation in the confessional and heresy, to be sent to Rome for discipline. Thanks to the memorialistas' agitation, Marcén was jailed (and later released) by inquisitors and, in the long term, the Jesuit constitution and curriculum of study (*ratio studiorum*) became subject to inquisitorial scrutiny. Another provocative memorial raised the specter of what would happen if the general were to become a Protestant. Dionisio Vázquez, a onetime resident of Toledo's casa profesa, stoked these fears in a memorial he sent to the Inquisition in the 1580s:

> If a General of the Society were to decide to deviate from the holy and Catholic doctrine of the Church, he could very quickly inundate the world with errors, merely by removing the good and loyal superiors and preachers, and by replacing them with [their heretical] counterparts.

In this way, Vázquez attempted to provoke Madrid to act against the current Jesuit general, who, he said, subjected his subordinates to an omnipotent and "absolute rule."[80] (And in this sense, memorialista critiques anticipated the accusations that would soon coalesce in anti-Jesuit literature such as the *Monita secreta*, a spurious set of "secret instructions" allegedly followed by the Jesuits in their diabolical conspiracies.)[81]

Another point of tension between Spanish Jesuits and the Roman leadership was the perceived prevalence of conversos in the Society. As Robert Maryks has argued, Acquaviva and others, particularly the Italian and Portuguese Jesuit factions, were convinced that the Castilian dissenters were part of a converso conspiracy to destabilize the Society, and they argued for the need to purge individuals of Jewish ancestry from the order. As a result, at the Fifth General Congregation in 1593, which came at the peak moment of memorialista agitation, as well as a time of increasing pressure on the Society from Rome and Madrid, the Jesuits adopted a decree barring descendants of Muslims and Jews from admittance to the Society, in spite of the objections of a number of prominent Jesuits, including Juan de Mariana, Antonio de Possevino, and Pedro de Ribadeneira. In addition, the Congregation capitulated in the matter of inquisitorial jurisdiction and relinquished the privilege to absolve minor heresies in matters of conscience, which, it was decided, would hereafter be reported to the Inquisition. Finally, the Congregation also censured the memorialistas, a move that would be repeated by the Sixth General Congregation in 1608 as well.[82]

At the same time, Acquaviva strengthened his own position by silencing dissenters at the provincial level and installing loyalists to prominent positions of authority in Spain; thus did Francisco de Porres become provincial of Toledo and Gil González Dávila provincial of Castile. As part of this initiative, Acquaviva asked the latter to conduct a general inspection of the Jesuit houses in the Toledo province in 1592, in the year before the Fifth General Congregation. The inspector had been on the lookout for residents of the colegios who seemed somehow suspicious or nonconformist, with the hope that dissenters could thus be identified, silenced, and, if necessary, isolated, thus preventing the further spread of the contagion of discontent among otherwise loyal members of the Society. In addition to Higuera, sixteen other Jesuits were identified by González Dávila as "subjects who require special governance and consideration."[83] These Castilian troublemakers included Francisco Abreo (or Abreu), who, it was feared, was sharing anti-Jesuit writings with influential members of the royal court, including, worryingly, the royal confessor and members of the Castilian parliament (*Cortes*); he found himself expelled from the order in 1592.[84] Another unruly subject was Bartolomé Sicilia, whose insubordination had gone unchecked due to his powerful outside allies. González Dávila recommended careful actions in a handful of the cases, including that of Higuera's contemporary in Ocaña, Francisco de Portocarrero, an unstable, fragile, and melancholy subject in need of special handling (as we shall see later, Portocarrero was also a noted relic collector and one of the first to mention Higuera's chronicles in print). In the inspector's estimation, Diego de Santa Cruz, who had sent letters of complaint to the Inquisition denouncing many Jesuit practices, including the order's trademark general confession, was "crazy" and should be silenced. The damage may have been done already, as Santa Cruz's writings were taken seriously by inquisitors, who forwarded them to the pope.[85]

Two years after the inspection, in 1594, Higuera was expelled from the Ocaña residence. The Jesuits already suspected that he was dealing with outsiders, including inquisitors, members of the royal court, and other agitators pressing for substantial reductions in Jesuit privileges and autonomy. Thus, it makes sense that in 1595, when Higuera began to rally Toledan regidores and jurados behind the two causes of San Tirso and *Toledo* only months after being sent to Toledo, Jesuit superiors would have reacted with great apprehension.

THE PROBLEM WITH SECULAR HISTORY: GENERAL CLAUDIO ACQUAVIVA

We have already seen that Higuera was part of a broader tide of dissent among Castilian Jesuits. He was also far from the only member of the order to see his written works kept out of publication. The memorialista debacle had vividly demonstrated to Acquaviva the potential dangers that political intrigue, and specifically the involvement of secular powers in internal Jesuit affairs, could pose to the Society as a whole. In the midst of the turmoil that afflicted the Jesuit order in the last decades of the sixteenth century, General Acquaviva grappled with the question of how to handle the many texts produced by historically minded Jesuit scholars, not only in Spain, but also in places such as Central Europe, where religious conflict made political missteps potentially quite dangerous for the relatively new religious order. The interpretation of the past presented real potential pitfalls for the general, whose worldwide presence and close working relationship with many European elites made for a complex diplomatic task. It required balancing the needs of the Jesuits with the various ecclesiastical and secular interests in each territory—many of which were competing with Jesuits and each other for patronage, resources, and influence.

Acquaviva's hesitation about Higuera's history of Toledo arose at the same time that the general was attempting to formulate a coherent approach to Jesuit-authored books. This was not just about Higuera, Toledo, or Spain. We see these growing pains in Acquaviva's peevish responses to more prominent authors, such as Pedro de Ribadeneira, a companion of Ignatius, inaugural member of the Society, and a prolific and respected writer. Acquaviva expressed grave apprehensions about Ribadeneira's 1588 history of the English Reformation since, he said, it contained "things touching affairs of states or kingdoms," that could "offend and are of little use."[86] A Jesuit censor later expressed nearly identical concerns about Mariana's *General History of Spain* before its Latin edition was published in 1592. The anonymous censor in Paris fretted about several potential problems with the manuscript, including the possibility that certain passages might offend French, Portuguese, Neapolitan, and Sicilian interests, as well as specific aristocratic families, some of whom, he noted, were generous donors to the Society.[87] Indeed, we have already seen that highly placed individuals had taken offense at Mariana's characterizations of their ancestors. Yet of larger concern to the censor was the fact that this was secular history: "It is worthy of being considered whether it is acceptable that a religious man, and of the Society, should write a profane history, full of the wars, seditions, treasons, factions, strategems, and frauds of Princes and Kings."[88]

Once Mariana's text was published, matters became even more complicated, particularly in France, where the Jesuits were resented by Catholics and Huguenots alike, as they were regarded as obeying papal and Spanish interests. The 1594 assassination attempt against King Henry IV represented a tipping point: the would-be assassin, Jean Châtel, had attended the Jesuit college of Clermont in Paris, where Mariana taught from 1561 to 1574. This helped give currency to the notion among the Society's foes that its members were "the chief promoters of tyrannicide theory in France."⁸⁹ Tensions flared between the Jesuits and Gallican lawyers, who used the moment to retroactively blame the Jesuits for the 1589 assassination of a previous monarch, Henry III. In the meantime, Châtel's trial ended with his conviction, the execution of one of his former Jesuit teachers, and the expulsion of the Jesuits from France. The king allowed the Jesuits to return in 1603, but the charge of promoting regicide continued to haunt the Society; it did not help that Mariana's 1599 treatise on the education of kings, *De rege et regis institutione*, was perceived to have supported regicide. The text itself was burned and banned in France after a fanatical Catholic successfully dispatched King Henry IV in 1610.⁹⁰

The scale and significance of the French case puts Higuera's San Tirso controversy into perspective as a minor affair. Yet it also helps explain why Acquaviva was so apprehensive about the prospect of any given Jesuit publication to offend secular interests and thereby imperil the sometimes tenuous standing of the Jesuits in any particular locale. This might help explain Acquaviva's crisp response in 1595 to one Diego de Morales, an Ocaña Jesuit who had written a seemingly innocuous text on the sacraments. Morales would not receive permission to print the text, Acquaviva reported, "because this matter of printing has gone so far that it is necessary now to be a little strict about it."⁹¹

Historical scholarship per se was far from objectionable to the politically astute Roman leadership. After all, the Parisian college of Clermont had hosted a cluster of researchers in historical theology and philology in the late sixteenth and early seventeenth centuries, including Mariana himself.⁹² Yet the scope of Jesuit historical research, as imagined by Acquaviva, was tightly circumscribed: history in the Jesuit mold would chronicle the order itself, while avoiding any matters that could ruffle the feathers of political authorities, prominent families, or powerful ecclesiastical institutions. Thus Acquaviva hoped to commission general histories of the Society, written under the close supervision of Jesuit superiors in each of its provinces around the world by suitably grave and learned individuals handpicked by provincials.⁹³ Indeed, several such manuscript histories were produced in the years around 1600, including an account of Madrid's colegio by Francisco de Porres and a history of the province of Andalusia by Martín de Roa. These, in turn, served as raw material for a history of the Society in Spain by Ribadeneira (which remained in manuscript).⁹⁴ A little over two decades later, Acquaviva attempted to give historical research a firmer institutional and academic foundation by drawing up plans to establish "ecclesiastical academies" where historical research would be pursued. While the *academiae* themselves never really came to fruition, Acquaviva did approve a set of statutes in 1612 that give a sense of what sort of work he imagined they would do: research conducted at the academies would be at the service of the entire Society of Jesus, and the resulting texts would be used by Jesuits around the world to explain the faith in their schools, or to confound heretics in debates. In other words, the aim of historical scholarship was the greater glory of God, not the particular interests of any given place or individual.⁹⁵

In the meantime, Acquaviva continued to grapple with how to regulate the Society's many would-be authors. In order to clarify his evolving expectations and concerns, in early 1598, in the midst of his difficulties with Higuera and the Toledan history, Acquaviva devised a set of guidelines intended, it seems, to safeguard the good name of the Company from the "inconveniences" that had arisen of late among authors whose works were being examined by Jesuit censors. In the future, Acquaviva stipulated to the provincials of Spain, all written works would be prescreened by anonymous readers. Each provincial would "secretly give [texts] to those who have to see them," and if they were judged to be unsuitable for publication, prospective authors would be advised of the opinion, fait accompli. The anonymity of the readers would be preserved in order to avoid "unpleasantnesses," and, perhaps more importantly, to remove the opportunity for authors to lobby the readers for a more favorable opinion.⁹⁶

It is unclear when or if this new system was ever put into practice in the four Spanish Jesuit provinces. What is certain is that Acquaviva seemed to have decided rather quickly that the provisional system of censorship was inadequate. In a March 1599 letter to all the provincials of Europe, Acquaviva set forth a new, centralized process for examining works before publication. Instead of the "very different opinions of the different reviewers who are chosen to examine the books," texts would be reviewed by an international council of learned men based in Rome. These trusted counselors would review "all the books that our [members] would print," so that they could "be printed with more security, firmness, and the satisfaction of all."⁹⁷

Yet the holes in this new net of censorship might have been larger than the fish it was supposed to catch. Almost immediately, Acquaviva clarified that "the books that should be sent to us before printing are those about theology and scripture," not history.⁹⁸ And, in spite of his best efforts, individual Jesuits did continue to publish histories that fell far short of the general's ambitions for more neutral ecclesiastical histories. The possible political ramifications of these texts, which chronicled particular territories and were often patronized by secular leaders, continued to preoccupy Jesuit superiors, such that the books in question were allowed to be published only in censored form. For example, Matthäus Rader's ecclesiastical history of Bavaria, commissioned by the Wittelsbach duke Maximilian I, was censored by superiors due to "its pro-Wittelsbach interpretation of the struggle between the fourteenth-century emperor Ludwig the Bavarian and the papacy."[99] Acquaviva expressed similar reservations about projects more specifically concerned with the sacred past, including Christopher Brouwer's history of Trier's antiquities and bishops, which was published only in a heavily censored version in 1626.[100] In short, Higuera was not the only author whose ambitions were stymied by Acquaviva's concerns about the proper role of history-writing. His difficulties were, however, exacerbated by his place among a renegade party of Castilian Jesuits, and by his continued habit of appealing to third parties to interfere in what, from the perspective of Jesuit superiors, were strictly internal matters.

HIGUERA AND THE INQUISITION

A vivid sense of the tensions between Higuera and the reforming faction loyal to Acquaviva, and of Higuera's role in fomenting these tensions, emerges from his testimony before two inquisitorial tribunals in 1603 and 1604.[101] For, unlike other fellow memorialistas, who had the discretion or wisdom to publish their complaints under the blanket of anonymity, or who soon fell into line or faded away quietly, Higuera seems to have been remarkably tone-deaf to the howls of his superiors. By this time, the most vocal memorialistas had been silenced by the reforms and mandates during Acquaviva's reshuffling; yet Higuera, remarkably, persevered in voicing his dissent. And he did so in a manner that seemed calculated to inflict the most damage possible and to irritate his superiors most gratuitously. Indeed, the possible threat that Higuera was believed to pose comes into clearer focus when we remember that the memorialistas had launched their assault on the Roman general and Jesuit governance precisely by appealing to the Inquisition, and to this royal institution's expansive sense of its own power. Higuera was, at this point, one of a small number of recalcitrant, disaffected Castilian dissenters who continued to rail against the changes in Jesuit governance, in spite of the coordinated efforts to extirpate, silence, and discipline them in the last years of the sixteenth century. In his testimony before the Inquisition, Higuera continued to evoke the political and religious grievances of the memorialistas in polemical language. He waged a lonely battle against the perceived restrictions on his freedoms, and against the slights he had suffered at the hands of his peers and superiors thanks to his willingness to denounce them to the Inquisition.

In 1603, Higuera submitted a complaint to the tribunal of Llerena regarding his fellow Jesuits in the residence of Plasencia, in the well-worn memorialista tactic of accusing the Jesuit leadership of shirking its duty to the Inquisition.

As Higuera alleged, "It is common parlance and received wisdom in the Jesuit house of Plasencia that they are not required to declare to the Holy Office, or its deputies, propositions and other things that the Holy Office should know about, and that require censure."[102] Opening with this politically and theologically sensitive accusation was an astute move on Higuera's part, for it guaranteed that he would receive a proper audience with inquisitors, who were reluctant to commit precious resources to would-be denouncers. At first, as the Llerena inquisitor noted in his summary of the 1603 proceedings, the Holy Office had assigned a local agent of the bishop, rather than an actual inquisitor, to hear Higuera's testimony because, as experience had shown, "it sometimes happens that [witnesses appear] to ramble on rather than out of any real necessity."[103] As it turned out, Higuera's accusations were taken seriously, and he was called before the Llerena tribunal itself.

In spite of the official secrecy with which the Inquisition was supposed to operate, as a member of a small religious community, Higuera's comings and goings did not go unnoticed by his peers. If Higuera's reputation for denouncing his fellow Jesuits to the Inquisition did not precede him to Ocaña, where he moved sometime in the nine months following his testimony in Llerena, it would not take long for the news to reach his new peers at the colegio. By May 1604, Higuera was before inquisitors a second time, in the tribunal of Ocaña, where he denounced the colegio's vice-rector and prefect of studies, Pedro de Carvajal, along with many other members of the residence. Higuera once again complained that his fellow Jesuits had failed to show the proper deference to the Inquisition and to respect its jurisdiction over matters of conscience. He alleged that, on one specific occasion, Vice-rector Carvajal had refused, in spite of Higuera's urging, to denounce a Jesuit novice to the Inquisition for making the proposition that it was not a mortal sin to visit a brothel.[104] Although this was an extremely common claim among Spaniards of all stripes, the Inquisition had characterized it as a heretical assertion in 1573; as such, it belonged properly to inquisitorial jurisdiction, and was not a matter for informal correction within a religious house.[105] Jesuit circumvention of the Inquisition possessed an even greater potential charge in 1604, since the Society had already relinquished the privilege of addressing minor matters of conscience via "fraternal correction" in the Fifth General Congregation over ten years before. And this specific charge was also a principal point of contention for one of the very few other memorialistas still vocal at the time, Hernando de Mendoza.

In a lengthy memorandum that he submitted as a supplement to his oral testimony to Ocaña's inquisitors in May, 1604, Higuera complained bitterly about the poor treatment he had received at the hands of his superiors in retaliation for his testimony before the Inquisition, and depicted himself as the victim of unfair persecution. Although Higuera referred to a handful of allies, including a fellow *profeso* in Ocaña, Father Diagómez, and Bartolomé Andrés de Olivenza, a former *consultor* in the colegio of Cuenca and provincial of Sardinia, he was relatively isolated, at least vis-à-vis the Jesuits, even if he still continued to communicate with many of his allies in Toledo.[106] This fact and his continued pugnaciousness explain why he was treated as a pariah in the 1590s and 1600s. Thanks to his dutiful appearance before the Inquisition in 1603, Higuera had, by his own account, found himself transferred from one colegio to another, demoted, and trailed by spies. This was because, as the sexagenarian Jesuit expressed with shock and dismay, ever since he had denounced the Society before various inquisitorial tribunals, he had gotten nothing but grief, even though all he had done was testify about "matters of good governance of the Company."[107] Higuera recalled how, upon returning from testifying in Llerena in 1603, he had been met with taunts, and "everybody from the colegio said that I wanted to destroy the Society." When Higuera complained, Rector Manuel de Arceo responded by threatening him: if Higuera continued to appear before the Inquisition, he would "have a miserable life, which they would give to me, and [Arceo] bragged about this before [another] Father."[108] At the same time, the Castilian provincial removed him from his positions of responsibility within the colegio. Adding insult to injury, on one particularly galling occasion Higuera was denied dinner when he returned from denouncing his colleagues to the Inquisition, even though he had just endured a Lenten fast while on the road. Higuera pointed out that this poor treatment had begun only after he submitted many *memoriales* to the inquisitorial tribunal of Llerena, as well as to the Inquisition's governing body, the Supreme Council, in Toledo. Finally, he accused Jesuit superiors of being more concerned with preserving their own prerogatives than with the secrecy of the inquisitorial tribunal.

Higuera was being extraordinarily naive if he thought that this maneuver of playing one institution against the other would succeed in the long run. Indeed, it did not take long for the game to catch up with him. From his superiors' perspective, by provoking inquisitorial intervention in internal Jesuit affairs, Higuera was jeopardizing more than just his own position within the Society: he was violating the order's hard-earned and fiercely defended autonomy from other secular and religious jurisdictions. For this reason, Jesuit superiors all the way up to General Acquaviva must have been particularly infuriated when, sometime in late 1603 or early 1604, Higuera persuaded the inquisitors of Llerena to command the Jesuit provincial to promote him to the position of Prefect of Studies in Madrid. He should not have been surprised when he arrived in Madrid to find that the new rector, none other than his enemy from Plasencia, Manuel de Arceo, found a pretext to deny him the post. As Higuera explained in his 1604 memorial to Ocaña's inquisitors, Arceo had used subterfuge and espionage to rationalize the move; he said the Jesuits had intercepted a letter from Higuera to the Inquisition in which it was revealed that Higuera was about to denounce Francisco de Benavides, a former confessor to the queen and currently the Society's agent in Rome, to the Inquisition.[109] To prevent this, Higuera said, his superiors punished him. Not only were Jesuit superiors violating the confidentiality and jurisdiction of the Inquisition; they were obstructing the truth.[110]

Higuera alleged that Jesuit superiors' latest attempt to silence and intimidate him had unfolded at a meeting in Madrid in the early months of 1604. Here they resolved to issue a complaint to the Llerena Inquisition that it had overstepped its bounds by essentially ordering the Jesuits to send this maverick profeso to Madrid as Prefect of Studies. His superiors also decided to return Higuera to Ocaña and demand that, as punishment, he donate half the books in his library to the colegio of Madrid.[111] Naturally, Higuera's vexations did not end there. Higuera's appearance before Ocaña inquisitors in 1604 had been precipitated by an even more frightening development: the appearance of his sworn enemy Manuel de Arceo as the new vice-rector of Ocaña. Even more ominous was the fact that his other foe, Francisco de Benavides, was due to return shortly from Rome. This, he explained, had led Higuera to appeal to the Ocaña inquisitors for protection. He was afraid that this well-connected man, who had the ear of General Acquaviva and links to the powerful Duke of Lerma, would conspire with his other enemies to ruin him. Higuera asked the inquisitors to convince Jesuit superiors in Spain and Rome to protect from gossip or scorn those Jesuits who testified before inquisitorial tribunals. Considering that Higuera had gone to the Inquisition to denounce his superiors, and that they were the selfsame individuals exacting many of the retributions he had suffered, it was a woefully ridiculous request.

Perhaps realizing that the Inquisition might feel somewhat disinclined to intervene in the internal backbiting and squabbling among members of this small and self-protective community, in his written memorial Higuera attempted to capture the inquisitors' sympathies by echoing the rhetoric of the memorialistas of the 1580s and 1590s. He suggested that these problems were all due to the fact that the general was a "foreigner" who did not understand the great authority of the Inquisition. Higuera hinted darkly that the Society possessed rather too much power; in other words, the Society might actually be trying to interfere with the jurisdiction of the Holy Office by attacking one of its witnesses, a potentially serious violation of the Inquisition's dignity: "Since it is known that I denounced Padre Benavides, who is powerful in this province, the provinces are full of the news, and the general is very aware of it, and I am very afraid that they are going to destroy me."[112] Thus Higuera implied rather dramatically that the Jesuits' retribution against him might include foul play. He even declared that if something were to befall him, the Ocaña tribunal should consult other inquisitors familiar with the details of his situation, presumably because they would be able to provide leads for any resulting criminal investigation.[113]

Higuera explained to the inquisitors that the Jesuit reputation for excellence in virtue and letters had made its members lose any sense of restraint. The order had become so powerful that they could destroy anybody, even if it meant lying: "[T]he members of the Company are very clever; they know and can make up many things." With an "arrogance that blinds them," the Jesuits have become convinced that their good reputation has protected them; under its shield, they could engage in all sorts of machinations: "they think everything is allowed them."[114] In case the inquisitors were disinclined to worry about Higuera's fate as an individual, he also hinted that these Jesuit maneuvers could very well threaten all of Christendom:

> The Company is a most powerful religious order that has access to all of the ecclesiastical and secular princes in the world; they have won many confidences, and they can destroy. I do not mean me, I'm just a worm, but I mean very powerful people.[115]

In this way Higuera evoked the apocalyptic scenarios proposed by earlier memorialistas, and by Jesuit foes, like Spanish Dominicans, who had stoked speculations that the general could become Protestant and bring down Catholicism worldwide. For example, the vociferous Dominican Fray Alonso de Avendaño had been denounced to the Inquisition in 1594 for preaching that the Jesuits, like the illuminist heretics (*alumbrados*), were "a new people who had risen in Spain in order to destroy it."[116]

Especially galling from the Jesuit perspective was Higuera's strategy of appealing to third parties in what should have been internal matters, as when he had convinced the Llerena Inquisition to grant him a promotion. His personality, as well as local political considerations—and not, it should be emphasized, the perceived quality of his historical scholarship—prevented Higuera from receiving the support and acclaim that he felt he deserved.[117] Even Higuera himself sensed that his agitation had impeded his publishing success. Naturally, he put a somewhat more heroic spin on his position in his account to inquisitors in 1604: he had written "some books that I believe could be of service to God and of some luster for my nation," including the history of Toledo, the *Ecclesiastical History of Spain*, his corrected edition of the *Itinerary* of Antoninus Pius, and "many works on the councils of Spain," but, as Higuera sulked, if he had not "done the duty of a good Christian and a God-fearing religious man," such as denouncing perceived transgressions of his fellow Jesuits to the Inquisition, then the texts would have had a better outcome.[118] Yet the resolute Higuera did not hesitate to antagonize his superiors in these ways time and time again; once more in 1606 he requested permission to publish the manuscripts through a proxy sent to Rome. Not surprisingly, permission was denied.[119]

It is worth emphasizing that, in spite of his difficult relationship with his superiors, Higuera was dedicated to the Society of Jesus. At the very least, he considered it better than the alternatives. In an unpublished history of the Jesuit house of Plasencia, he chronicled the grim fate that awaited those who left the Society, voluntarily or otherwise. Most of the eleven onetime residents of the residence expelled from the Company, he noted, were subsequently dealt a severe punishment by God, and died shortly thereafter. For that reason, he mused, "it is better to suffer and endure any difficulties" than to "throw off the yoke of Religion."[120] In this, Higuera also reflected the sentiments of his peers. For example, Pedro de Ribadeneira wrote an entire dialogue on the severe punishments meted out by God to former Jesuits (although, as one modern scholar notes mordantly, their unfortunate fates might have had more to do with the fact that those who left the Society also lost their entire estates, which they had surrendered upon entrance).[121] Nor was Higuera's rocky relationship with his own order reflected in official Jesuit history. In a late seventeenth-century continuation of Ribadeneira's history of illustrious Jesuits, Higuera was remembered as "a man well deserving and worthy of being regarded among the most learned in Ecclesiastical antiquity in our generation."[122]

Yet, in the long run, Higuera has been remembered as the antithesis, in word and deed, of his fellow Toledan Jesuit Juan de Mariana. Mariana, the so-called Spanish Livy, is usually celebrated as an opponent of the mythical and forged histories of the sixteenth and seventeenth centuries, thanks to his expressed skepticism about the lead books of Granada and the false chronicles, as well as his apparent departure from the approach of his predecessors, such as Florián Ocampo and Esteban Garibay, who integrated mythical material into their histories of Spain.[123] Mariana signaled his skepticism about the sources for the distant past in a discussion of a traditional etymology that derived the name of the Guadalete River from "Lethe," which was, of course, also the name of the legendary river of oblivion in Greek mythology. Mariana threw his hands up: "I transcribe more than I believe, because it would not be easy to either refute that which others write, nor try to prove with arguments what they say without very much probability."[124] Here Mariana was echoing the self-aware disclaimer proffered by Quintus Curtius Rufus, the first-century author of the fable-ridden *History of Alexander the Great*.[125] In the long run, thanks to statements such as these, Mariana has enjoyed a reputation for critical thinking and historical acumen, leading many to cite his as the first "modern" history of Spain. Higuera's works, in contrast, have been dismissed as frauds, and not very convincing ones at that.

Yet the contrast between the sober narrator of the *General History of Spain*, on one hand, and the somewhat more extravagant author of the *Toledo*, on the other, should not be overstated. As his old foe Pedro de Mantuano pointed out, Mariana was not immune to the convenience and allure of apocryphal texts for those murky early years of Spain's history, which he populated with many of the same legendary monarchs that, like Alcocer, Higuera, and Pisa, he found in the Annian forgeries. More incredibly, the 1623 edition of the *General History*, which appeared when Mariana was eighty-seven years old, cited the chronicles of Dexter, Maximus, and Julián Pérez more than a dozen times. Even if we concur with the early twentieth-century Hispanist Georges Cirot in attributing these references to an interpolator—which seems increasingly unlikely—it must be acknowledged that the positions of these two Toledan Jesuits on the value and use of historical sources is much closer than has been acknowledged.[126]

In forging the false chronicles, it is true that Higuera exhibited outrageous nerve. Yet, as this examination of Higuera's own critical acumen has suggested, he was just as conscious of the wobbliness of the sources upon which he relied as his contemporaries, if not more so. While Higuera's deep affection for the saints would never have allowed him to breeze over Santiago with the distinct lack of enthusiasm that Mariana evinced, he was not averse to stripping away miraculous explanations or layers of gratuitous myth when he believed it was necessary. This has been lost in the fog of vituperation that has enveloped Higuera ever since he was identified as the forger of the false chronicles. Often forgotten in the sound and the fury over the *cronicones* is how much profound knowledge, subtle learning, and hard work was necessary to produce them, as well as the texts Higuera wrote in his own name. By looking more closely at this erudition, as well as its social and intellectual context—by looking at *what* Higuera did and *how* he did it—we might come closer to understanding *why*.

3

How to Forge a History: The Authentic Sources of the False Chronicles

Although he had been thwarted many times before, when he died in 1611, Higuera—the perpetual thorn in the side of the Society of Jesus, the frustrated author of histories he could not publish, and the hapless promoter of San Tirso— had achieved partial success in at least one of his scholarly endeavors. This was the introduction of the false chronicles, those four forged historical annals of his own manufacture. In creating these texts, what did Higuera hope to achieve? How did he think these simulacra would be received by his audience? And why did the forgeries fool so many of early modern Spain's readers? In order to address these questions—which are central to understanding the false chronicles, not to mention their endurance in Spanish history, culture, and religion—we shall, in the following chapters, investigate the history of the chronicles themselves, specifically, their real and imagined origins, as well as Higuera's sources and techniques. Only then might we begin to apprehend what Higuera thought he was doing, and for what ends.

To create a convincing forgery, one needs to be intimately familiar with the *authentic* sources of the past. As we shall see, the thematic and stylistic proximity of Higuera's texts to their purported peers helped convince many readers of their authenticity, in spite of enduring uncertainties about their origins and the flawed state of their manuscript copies. In Higuera's scholarship, as in many extant medieval charters, we find a range of positions from faithful reproduction of authentic originals to outright invention and nearly everything in between.[1] This is no accident: Higuera seeded his four chronicles with just enough familiar details and cloaked them in recognizably ancient vestments, such that they seemed plausible, albeit strange and possibly flawed, to those who beheld them. Higuera did not merely try to approximate the rhetorical style and annalistic format of the authentic chronicles that he emulated; he also drew upon many of the same sources and employed the same working methods as the annalist. Like authentic ecclesiastical chronicles, Higuera's texts worked their magic not with grand theses or compelling character development but, like the Annian forgeries, through what Walter Stephens has called "the accumulation of minutiae."[2]

This propensity to build upon authentic material to create an enhanced version of history was no less true of Higuera than it was of any number of other more celebrated scholars, and it helps remind us of the similarities that connected Higuera and other early modern forgers to their medieval counterparts. For these reasons, we would be limiting our own understanding of the cronicones if we regarded them only from the vantage point of the sixteenth century. We must also try to take them seriously as medieval chronicles—or, rather, as a reflection of how Higuera and his peers understood the medieval chronicle tradition and Iberian sacred history in general. To create the texts, Higuera took on the role of the annalist; he also played the antiquarian, the philologist, the critic, and, of course, the intermediary between the texts and their public. This means that the texts can be imagined not merely as forgeries, but also as complex amalgams of the true and the false; of the ancient, medieval, and early modern; and of the purposefully deceitful and the unwittingly misleading. The longer one scrutinizes these curious products of early modern erudition, the harder it becomes to draw a clear line between where the real ends and where the imagined takes over.

DEXTER AND HIS CONTINUATORS: THE CRONICONES AS A CORPUS

Like Annius before him, Higuera cast himself as the rescuer and restorer of texts long believed to have been lost. We can see how he began to construe himself as the texts' sponsor in a 1594 letter to Juan Bautista Pérez in which Higuera described the chain of custody through which the documents had passed: first, he explained, he had come across a printed excerpt of certain annals a number of years before, but they appeared without any identifying information whatsoever. He brought the texts to the attention of a "very learned German" in Madrid, who assured him that these annals were part of a larger text that still survived in Fulda, which chronicled important events in the history of various Spanish churches. Higuera wrote to a contact in Ingolstadt and asked that he procure a copy for his old friend, an effort that bore fruit three years later when the copies that would form the basis for the cronicones arrived from Germany.[3]

Like other successful forgeries, three of the four chronicles were attributed to actual historical figures mentioned in other authoritative texts. In fact, it was entirely plausible, in the sixteenth century, that Dexter, Maximus, and Luitprand had written histories that had been lost, and it was not entirely inconceivable that memory of the fourth—Julián Pérez—could have faded over time. After all, in the mid-fifteenth century the long-lost history of the Germans by the Roman author Tacitus had been rediscovered, after not having been seen since antiquity. Renaissance-era scholars had encountered many other such treasures among the manuscripts of monastic collections throughout Europe; and Fulda, where the cronicones were said to have been hidden, had been a particularly fruitful cache.[4]

The matter of textual alibis for the first three authors was also simple. From Jerome's catalogue *On Illustrious Men*, Higuera plucked "Dexter," son of Bishop Pacianus of Barcelona, and also, crucially, the author of a universal history that Dexter had dedicated to Jerome; nonetheless, Jerome admitted, "I have not yet read [it]."[5] As far as we know, nobody else had either. This late fourth-century reference was the last documented trace of the text until over a thousand years later, when the German abbot (and forger) Johannes Trithemius mentioned Dexter in his 1494 *Liber de scriptoribus ecclesiasticis*.[6] Higuera elaborated upon the slim biographical information from Jerome to create a new and improved Dexter for a sixteenth-century audience. First, he manufactured the chronicle itself, which began in AD 1 with the birth of Christ and ended in the early years of the fifth-century reign of the Visigothic king Theodoric I. Higuera claimed that this was the second half of a much longer text, one that began, like other universal chronicles, with Creation and the biblical past, and ended in the author's own times.

Higuera refashioned Jerome's Dexter into a three-dimensional character by endowing him with a portentous identity. He added two new and quintessentially Roman first names to Dexter's lonesome personal name, and he furnished him with a well-placed position in the imperial administration to match. With these maneuvers, then, "Dexter, son of Pacianus" was transformed with a flourish into "Flavius Lucius Dexter, praetorian prefect." These details were provided in a framing epistle, which Higuera naturally claimed to have received along with the chronicle itself. In the letter, Fl. L. Dexter addressed Orosius, the historian and protégé of Augustine of Hippo. In addition to linking Jerome's Dexter to Higuera's, the letter also helped resolve some of the questions that sixteenth-century readers might have posed: for example, it might have seemed strange that an eminent scholar such as Jerome would not have had occasion to read Dexter's history. Yet as pseudo-Dexter explained, the answer was quite simple: the history was not finished until AD 430, a decade after Jerome died.[7]

The chronicle of Marcus Maximus picked up precisely where its predecessor had left off, spanning from AD 430 to 612. Like Dexter, Maximus had actually existed, according to yet another *Catalogue of Illustrious Men*, this one authored by Isidore of Seville; here Maximus was remembered as a seventh-century bishop of Zaragoza and the author of many works in verse and prose, including a short history of the Gothic era in Spain.[8] Like Dexter's universal history, this last text, along with Maximus's other works, seems to have disappeared into oblivion soon after Isidore wrote of them. This allowed Higuera to neatly transform the short narrative history of the Goths into a simple continuation of Dexter. Since Maximus-via-Isidore presented a rather lean biography, Higuera was compelled to supply many additional details to create the second chronicler as a historical character: thus to the résumé of the bishop of Zaragoza was added a vocation as a Benedictine monk (an anachronistic touch that would later attract criticism).[9]

By attributing his forgeries to authentic authors who had been attested by unimpeachable patristic authorities, and by having each chronicle build its predecessor, Higuera employed the forger's age-old technique, namely, to create an air of "verisimilitude and significance" for his lost texts by citing a list of real or imagined authors who had made reference to them. With these textual alibis, the forger helps ease the text into circulation and, he hopes, ultimately improves the chances for its acceptance.[10] In fact, these particular lost texts had been sought unsuccessfully for centuries (and, indeed, modern scholars continue to seek possible traces of Maximus's lost history of the Goths in particular).[11] Indeed, Higuera was not the first to try the trick of conjuring actual texts from these laconic lines in Jerome and Isidore's works. In the early sixteenth century, two Spanish authors cited histories of Dexter and Maximus as if they had read them. The first was Fray Juan de Rihuerga, in his manuscript history of Spanish antiquities; there he counted "Dextero" and "Maximo" among the authors who could be consulted on early Spain. It is quite likely that Higuera would have encountered Rihuerga's texts, since they formed part of the collection of his friend, the Toledan hagiographer Alonso de Villegas.[12] A much more ambitious, imaginative, and disingenuous effort to resurrect these lost texts was exerted by Don Lorenzo de Padilla (1485–1540), royal chronicler under Charles V, who asserted that Dexter had been a chronicler of ancient dynastic genealogies, much in the mold of Annius's pseudo-Berosus. Thus, in his *Catalogue of the Saints of Spain* (1538), Padilla elaborated on Jerome's terse account to create "Lucio Dextero," a collector of the histories of the ancient kings of Spain all the way from Tubal, Noah's grandson and the first resident of Iberia, up to the fabled "great drought" that afflicted Spain sometime before the arrival of Christianity. Padilla also went on to cite Dexter and Maximus for information about Spain's early, pre-Roman rulers in his later *Chronicle of Spain* (ca. 1570).[13]

These citations of Dexter and Maximus in a list of *auctoritates* were, of course, substantially different from the much more imaginative and substantive efforts of Higuera, who not only reanimated their authors, but also created for the erstwhile chronicles an entire textual universe, including the chronicles themselves, in which were recorded the most important moments of Iberian ecclesiastical history in an interlocking chain of texts, as well as a significant body of paratextual materials. Dexter recorded the birth of Christ, the lives and deaths of Roman emperors, and, most of all, the evangelization, conversions, and martyrdoms of Iberian Christians. Maximus picked up the thread in the fifth century, and in addition to notable bishops and saints, recorded political events, such as the conversion of the ruling Visigothic dynasty from Arian to Catholic Christianity in 587, which marked a pivotal turn toward the mainstream of European Christendom. Also included in some printed editions of Dexter-Maximus were short additions by Braulio and Heleca, who had been actual early medieval bishops of Zaragoza.[14]

With the third and fourth chronicles, Higuera's inventions became more ambitious, and, for that reason, all the more precarious. For one, Higuera had trouble deciding what to call the imputed author of the third chronicle. In early drafts, he was "Eutrand," but later Higuera asserted that he had also been known as "Luitprand." This might at first seem like an unwise vacillation by a forger who had too many different stories to keep straight. Yet upon closer examination, it becomes clear that this was part of Higuera's strategy to anchor his texts in some semblance of historical reality. With this maneuver, Higuera conflated Eutrand, an ecclesiastical author about whom not much was known, with Liutprand or Liudprand, an actual tenth-century bishop of the Lombard city of Cremona. Liutprand had been the Holy Roman Emperor's ambassador to the Byzantine court, and it seems that his authentic works were only just beginning to be rediscovered and published in Higuera's time.[15] Higuera changed the spelling of his name from Liutprand to L*ui*tprand, and fabricated an Iberian stint at the tail end of the Lombard bishop's career by having him leave Cremona for Fulda, where he served as librarian, thence to Spain to become a subdeacon in Toledo's cathedral (where he also read the first two chronicles).[16]

Higuera had Luitprand's own chronicle pick up neatly where Maximus left off, in the early years of the seventh century, and it ended in the mid-tenth century. Luitprand recorded several familiar milestones in Spanish history, including the eighth-century fall of King Rodrigo and the subsequent Islamic invasion. Here Higuera echoed the familar legend that Rodrigo had been undone by his lust for Cava Florinda, whose father, Julian, the Visigothic governor of Ceuta, avenged her rape by inciting Tarik of Tangier to attack Spain in 711. Luitprand described the subsequent invasion and evolution of a "captive" and "miserable" Mozarabic population, particularly in Toledo.[17] The chronicle also parroted the medieval tradition that the "pseudoprophet" Muhammad had preached in Cordoba in AD 615, about seven years before his pivotal migration to Medina, the Hegira.[18] Higuera could not resist having Luitprand weigh in on a few matters of great local interest, such as the location of the fabled Agali monastery, a matter of contention among learned Toledans.[19] And, in a determined poke at the smoldering ashes of the San Tirso controversy, Higuera also had Luitprand confirm the principal details of the letter from King Silo to Bishop Cixila: and so, the pseudo-chronicler dutifully reported, during their years of captivity, the Toledan Mozarabs had indeed been blessed with a new church to San Tirso, erected by Bishop Cixila in 781, just as Higuera's letter said.[20]

As in the previous chronicles, Higuera created the illusion of authenticity by providing an epistolary framework to help establish the narrator's place in time and space, as well as other purportedly medieval paratextual materials. The text of the chronicle itself was followed by miscellaneous excerpts from the chronicle (known as *adversaria*), and by several letters between Luitprand and his contemporary Regimund, bishop of the See of Illiberis in Andalusia, site of an important ecclesiastical council in AD 300.[21] Since the terse narrative conventions of the medieval chronicle did not allow for prolix biographical backstory, the letters gave Higuera space in which to underwrite and more fully explain his inventions; here he explained where the chronicles of Dexter and Maximus had been hiding in the previous three or four hundred years since they were mentioned by Jerome and Isidore, respectively. Luitprand noted that he had consulted Dexter-Maximus in the Fulda collection while serving as its librarian, and he explained that the texts had landed in this Carolingian repository of learning in the wake of the Islamic invasion when Archbishop Elipandus of Toledo sent the texts to Charlemagne for safekeeping. The venerable emperor of the Franks then took it upon himself to send them on to Fulda, which is where Luitprand himself consulted them—in an "an ancient parchment"—about a century later.[22] This was, for early modern readers, a plausible scenario, as many valuable texts and saints' relics were believed to have been spirited north into Carolingian hands for safekeeping, where they would wait out the Reconquest. Thus, like the relics of Santa Leocadia—kept in a Belgian abbey until Philip II recovered them in 1587—Dexter, Maximus, and Luitprand had now, also, come home.[23] To these materials Higuera also added his own commentary, which in the printed versions of the chronicle appeared alongside or just underneath the text. Here Higuera elucidated obscure passages or provided references to authoritative texts that corroborated Luitprand's version of events.

If Higuera brought these texts into the present, he also inserted himself into the past, and conjured a version of Luitprand that bore a startling likeness to how Higuera must have imagined himself. This Luitprand, like his Jesuit reinventor, was a seeker of lost historical treasures, and possessed a keen philological mind. Both Higuera and his historical avatar drew upon historical and philological knowledge in order to correct the *Itinerary* of Antoninus Pius. Higuera also had Luitprand articulate the careful steps that informed his philological work: as the chronicler explained in one of his paratextual epistles, since existing manuscripts of the *Itinerary* were honeycombed with the corruptions and errors of many successive copyists over the centuries, Luitprand had endeavored to address these problems by making a careful comparison of his own personal copy of the text with a manuscript he found in Fulda, in a practice that philologists of Higuera's time and today would recognize as the necessary and laborious practice of collation. After collation came the process of sorting through the textual variants to decide which were interpolations and which were authentic passages; Luitprand had followed with correction.[24]

If Luitprand seems to have been Higuera's predecessor as a rediscoverer of lost sources in Fulda, and an authoritative source on Toledan historical questions of enduring importance, Julián Pérez, the author of the fourth and final chronicle, resembled the Jesuit in another imagined sense, in that he was a descendant of the city's Mozarabs. Julián Pérez's text began with the conquest of Toledo in the eighth century by Arab and Berber armies, and ended with the city's reconquest and resettlement by Christians in the late eleventh century, with an emphasis on the latter period.[25] Here again we see Higuera becoming more and more ambitious. Unlike Dexter, Maximus, and Luitprand, Pérez possessed no existence apart from the forgeries. Higuera seems to have conjured him out of thin air. No previous author had vouched for him, and nobody had been looking for a lost chronicle by this hitherto obscure Toledan. This is probably why Pérez received a somewhat fuller biographical treatment in the chronicle than the other authors. Higuera was astute enough to cloak him in enough recognizable detail to make his existence plausible, and to provide him with impeccably Old Christian credentials.[26]

In addition to belonging to a prominent Mozarab family, Julián Pérez was the archpriest of the parish of Santa Justa as well as a hero of the Reconquest. Like many clerics of the time, the Toledan archpriest participated personally in military campaigns along with his friend and contemporary, El Cid, the Reconquest warrior of fact and legend.[27] Yet Pérez symbolized more than just triumphant Castilian Christianity. Higuera also molded him into a historical character who would embody, and resolve, the tensions that actually arose in eleventh-century

Toledo in connection with the restoration of institutional Christianity. The reconquest of Toledo had brought central Castile into direct contact with Gregory VII's reforming papacy. The pope promptly—and infamously—installed a French archbishop, the Cluniac Bernard Sauvetot, in order to enforce the abolition of the Mozarabic liturgy and the introduction of the Roman rite. The resulting tensions culminated in the inconclusive judicial ordeal in which King Alfonso VI allegedly threw the Roman and Mozarabic breviaries into a fire to see which would prevail.[28]

Here and elsewhere in this admittedly eccentric text, Higuera endeavored to create a sense of authenticity by making sure to connect the text quite closely with its purported peers. If he had followed the model of patristic and medieval ecclesiastical chronicles in composing the chronicles of Dexter, Maximus, and Luitprand, here Higuera turned to the significant corpus of Latin and vernacular chronicles of medieval Castile, many of which were being committed to print for the first time in the mid- and late sixteenth century. In its use of seemingly fabulous or legendary material, for example, this text resembled its putative peers. Again, here Higuera was far from innovative. In his account of the trial between the two liturgies, Higuera, like Francisco de Pisa and Juan de Mariana, echoed Ximénez de Rada, long considered an authoritative source for this era. Thus it should not surprise us to find that in the estimation of one scholar, Julián Pérez's version of the story was "lively but no less credible than chronicles of these events that were written by Toledan historians in the eighteenth century."[29]

However, as we would expect, Higuera's version of medieval Castilian history was not simply Ximénez de Rada or Lucas de Tuy rehashed. The historical character of Julián Pérez also embodied Higuera's characteristic preoccupation with finding middle ground, and with retroactively reconciling seemingly opposing historical categories into a newly harmonious vision of Spanish sacred history. Thus, on one hand, Higuera had the fictional Pérez serve under the French archbishop of Toledo. On the other, he also made him archpriest of one of the few parishes permitted to retain the Mozarabic rite after it was abolished. In other words, Pérez was a symbol of the endurance of a particularly Toledan brand of Christianity, which, Higuera seems to have been arguing, could coexist with the papally directed, French-inflected mainstream Church, even while maintaining its distinctive identity.[30] As we shall see, this attempt to bring the local and the universal into harmony, to negotiate a compromise between uniquely Spanish traditions and Rome's normalizing impulses, ran like a red thread through Higuera's works. In the meantime, as if being a reconquering Mozarabic cleric who served Toledo and the pope were not enough, Higuera also made Julián Pérez, like Luitprand, a seeker of lost manuscripts. In his letters and the chronicle itself, Pérez also explained that he had found many important documents in the cathedral archive, including, for example, the *Dypticon toletano*, a list of Toledo's bishops, as well as more exotic treasures that he translated from the Arabic, Hebrew, and Latin originals. These included letters in which representatives of the Jewish communities of Toledo, Zamora, and Jerusalem debated the teachings and death of Jesus.[31]

In its only printed edition, which appeared in 1628, the chronicle and the accompanying *adversaria* were framed by paratextual materials that helped situate the texts themselves in time and space and create the historical character Julián Pérez. The chronicle was prefaced by a dedicatory letter from Julián Pérez to a contemporary, Abbot Albert of Fulda, which accounted for the origins and subsequent fate of the actual codices of the chronicles, those lost physical specimens whence, one was to believe, Higuera's copies had been derived at a much later date. Here Julián Pérez addressed Abbot Albert as a fellow collector and scholar with whom he exchanged texts and knowledge, and he provided further details to help cement the veracity of the enduring relationship that Higuera had invented between the chroniclers of Spanish history and the library of this illustrious monastery. Thus, in passing, Pérez repeated Luitprand's story about the Castilian embassy to Charlemagne, which had seen a number of valuable codices, including those of Dexter-Maximus, as well as a life of Hierotheo in Greek by Dionysius the Areopagite, the works of Eulogius of Cordoba, and a treatise against iconoclasts by Claudius, bishop of Turin, all transferred for safekeeping to Fulda.[32]

THE CHRONICLES AS PASTICHE

As we have seen, Higuera emulated the authentic and familiar sources of medieval history in format, content, and style. He also reproduced the working method of the medieval annalist in many aspects of his research and writing. By looking more closely at how Higuera acted as a chronicler in his own right, we will begin to see how the notion of "forgery" might prove rather limiting when attempting to understand the cronicones. A remarkable and little-noticed characteristic of the first two chronicles is that they owe a large part of their material to the Eusebius-Jerome corpus of universal and ecclesiastical histories. This was no accident: Higuera worked deliberately to ensure that his texts would interlock almost seamlessly with the long tradition of medieval chronicles written in continuation of these two early annalistic paradigms.

In this, Higuera was being faithful to long-standing tradition. As per Bernard Guenée, when medieval authors wrote about the past, they did so in one of two ways: either as history, in which case they adopted the lengthier narrative style of Eusebius's *Ecclesiastical History*, or as chronicle, for which they drew on the same author's *Chronicle*, also known as the *Chronological Canons*.[33] In the *History*, this fourth-century church father narrated at length the story of the survival of Christianity through persecution to triumph and legalization under the emperor Constantine, and included long excerpts from primary documents.[34] The *Chronicle*, in contrast, related events in concise entries listed in chronological order in parallel columns according to kingdom. This enabled the reader to locate an event in several chronological systems simultaneously, identifying the count in the Hebrew, Roman, and Greek years, for example. As each empire faded, its chronological column was omitted, so that by the end of the *Chronicle* only one column remained, and all history became Roman and Christian.

In the Middle Ages, the *Chronicle* survived only in the Latin translation and expansion by Jerome, who followed Eusebius's annalistic form, universal scope, and imperial chronology. Jerome's rendering, which spanned from the time of Abraham to his own late fourth-century context, inspired continuations by many lesser-known figures in the provinces of the former Roman Empire, each of whom incorporated the Eusebius-via-Jerome material into his own narrative. In Western Christendom, these continuators included, for example, Orosius, Prosper of Aquitaine, Hydatius of Galicia, Victor of Tunnuna, John of Biclarum, and Isidore of Seville. Collectively, they narrated events in the Roman Empire, East and West, from Creation to the early seventh century, with some regional, chronological, and topical variation.

Interest in this type of ecclesiastical chronicle enjoyed something of a revival in the sixteenth century, as Catholic authors such as Cardinals Baronio and Bellarmine answered Protestant critiques with historical scholarship. These universal chronicles were very important sources for those hoping to chart (and claim) the history of early Christianity. Cesare Baronio's magisterial and detailed account of Catholic history, the *Annales ecclesiastici* (1588–1607), forwarded the proposition that the Church had not, as its critics alleged, lost its apostolic mandate, but, in fact, represented a fundamental continuity in the institutions, beliefs, and practices of Christianity across the centuries, from its origins through the first twelve centuries of its existence. Later continuators, including Antonius Pagius, brought the work up to the eighteenth century. The *Annales* probably did little to change Protestant minds, but the work was enormously influential in Catholic Europe, including Spain, where the first few tomes of this twelve-volume juggernaut of erudition arrived just as Higuera was drafting his own texts, in the last years of the sixteenth century and the first years of the seventeenth.[35]

Baronio (often Latinized as Baronius) consciously departed from the eloquent and classically inflected literary style of more recent Renaissance humanist historians in order to create annals in the mold of Eusebius-Jerome. While the Roman reformer incorporated many of the methodological innovations characteristic of Italian humanists, he was disinclined to adopt the more refined narrative style of humanist historiography. Baronio resisted reflecting on the causes of events or on their interrelation, and he often interrupted the narrative unity of his work by including long documents in their entirety or by embarking on long digressions.[36] For Baronio, "history" was associated with elaborate *inventiones* or displays of rhetorical virtuosity, and with particularistic interests, in contrast to "annals," whose "plain" style was more appropriate for universal Catholic history, as suggested in these comments from the *Annales*:

> I will leave to the historians of the nations those narratives that are long winded, round about, and drawn out in a roundabout fashion, and those speeches contrived with the greatest skill and invented and composed according to the opinion of each individual and displayed according to what the author sees fit. I will, therefore, write annals rather than history. And I will follow the kind of speech that is most appropriate to the majesty and dignity of the Church. And I shall narrate the things that have to be discussed in a way that is wholly pure and sincere, and free from any kind of invention or figment, just as they happened, taking them year by year.[37]

Here Baronio drew a series of parallel contrasts that are crucial to understanding how readers such as Higuera emulated his work. Complicated, elaborate narratives, Baronio suggested, are the province of "historians," who write mainly for the sake of their own people, shaping the evidence to fit their narrow rhetorical aims. "Annalists," in contrast, employ a careful and plain style to patiently allow the facts to speak for themselves — facts that, as in the *Annales*, contribute in a constant, stalactitic drip to a bedrock of evidence for the antiquity and authority of the Church. Ambrosio de Morales expressed a similar disdain for eloquence in the prologue to his *General Chronicle of Spain* (1574–1586) when he professed to have been more concerned with truth and diligence than eloquence.[38]

In Baronio's *Annales*, the Church was, already in the first century of its existence, institutionally mature and fundamentally identical to its current shape, *semper eadem* ("always the same").[39] As such, its institutions, practices, and doctrines had never deviated from apostolic models. Baronio demonstrated this by tracing and citing apostolic precedents wherever possible. He proceeded in chronological order, purposefully granting pride of place to that which came first and marshalling every nugget of evidence he could find to describe every conceivable detail of the early Church, including, for example, how the apostles wore their facial hair, the exact place of the Nativity, and what sort of animals were in the barn in Bethlehem. To this end, he tried to establish fixed dates for every important event in church history, while relying on philological and antiquarian methods for collecting and evaluating historical sources. This meant that Baronio often compared sources on the basis of their reliability, like Renaissance humanists, and incorporated coins and inscriptions as evidence. He was also attentive to the emergence of new archaeological evidence, as evinced when he incorporated into a new volume of the *Annales* details from excavations in the Roman catacombs shortly after they happened.[40]

Higuera emulated this Baronian vision of the early Church in a way that would have been very familiar to his contemporaries, since it closely resembled Counter-Reformation ideals: in the cronicones, the Church was always led by bishops, heavily populated with martyrs and other saints, and, in this fantasy scenario, only lightly touched by monasticism and politics. The Immaculate Conception, pilgrimage, the cult of saints and relics, and many other practices that would have been unrecognizable to first-century Christians in reality were, in Higuera's rendering, present in Catholicism from the very beginning.[41]

HIGUERA VERSUS CARDINAL BARONIO

It is significant that Higuera chose the ecclesiastical annal and not hagiography, narrative history, or some other genre to engage in his own conversation with Baronio as both model and foil; he opted, like Baronio, to rewrite Catholic history not in an eloquent historical narrative, but in the chronologically ordered ecclesiastical annal of the type pioneered by Eusebius and continued by Jerome. Yet even Higuera's contemporaries acknowledged that the most signal contribution of the cronicones was not in how they harmonized with Baronio, but, rather, in how they directly countered him. This was, first of all, evident from the fact that for Higuera, the early Church was decidedly Iberian. While the Roman provenance of the earliest bishops and martyrs was undeniable, in Higuera's rendering, Spain gave the oldest see in the Western Church a run for its money.

In addition to shifting the Church's center of gravity to Spain, Higuera's texts attempted to recomplicate the Baronian texts by repopulating them with traditions that had been eliminated in the revisions. Thus, like his peers, Higuera responded vigorously to challenges to beliefs about Santiago, and in Dexter's chronicle, the apostle was depicted in terms that by the late sixteenth century had become traditional: he was the evangelizer of the Iberian Peninsula, who had erected a church in honor of the Virgin in Zaragoza, and who, after his martyrdom in Rome, was brought by boat to be buried in Compostela.[42] Gaspar de Escolano, the author of an early seventeenth-century history of Valencia, acknowledged this important function of the chronicles when he asserted that it must have been God himself who revealed the texts so that Spain could at last defend Santiago from Baronio more effectively.[43]

Higuera was rarely content with merely parroting tradition. So he went even further to make Santiago not simply the apostle to the Spanish, but also the founder of what was, for all intents and purposes, a simulacrum of mature Tridentine Catholicism in first-century Spain. In Higuera's hands, Santiago became much like one of the delegates assembled at the mid-sixteenth-century Council of Trent. He was, for example, sensitive to the importance of bishops for church governance, and so appointed them in a dozen places throughout Roman Hispania, such that the early Iberian Church was fundamentally an episcopal institution in which the bishops and their urban sees were the many points of light in the still predominantly pagan landscape of Hispania.[44] In his role as apostle to Iberia, Santiago encouraged the practice of pilgrimage, converted many Jews, especially near Madrid, and instituted observance of the feast of the Immaculate Conception of the Virgin, reflecting the belief that Mary herself was conceived without the stain of original sin. (In point of fact, this traditional belief, quite popular in sixteenth-century Spain, remained highly controversial well into the nineteenth century; it was finally declared dogma in 1854.)[45]

Higuera often countered Baronio's revisions in the false chronicles, where apocryphal traditions were often brought back to life by Higuera's sleight of hand. He restored traditions that Baronio had rejected outright in the *Annales* and in the revised Roman Martyrology, and he amplified the specifically Iberian origins or flavor of various saints, including the "Seven Apostles." Higuera dutifully elaborated upon the Martyrology's relatively spare account of these legendary first bishops of Spain, and greatly enhanced the significance, duration, and impact of their Iberian itineraries.[46] In this type of effort, Higuera did not merely disregard well-known humanist critiques in order to preserve some questionable traditions, as had Baronio; he went much further, by blatantly constructing new and elaborate details with which to further adorn already apocryphal figures. For example, Higuera pushed against Baronio's efforts to debunk the Renaissance-era legend that the Roman philosopher and statesman Seneca the Younger, a native of Cordoba, had corresponded with the apostle Paul, and that as a result of their epistolary exchange, Seneca had secretly converted to Christianity. Baronio, like Erasmus, rejected both the late antique pseudepigrapha and the Renaissance-era conversion myth, due to historical inaccuracies.[47] Higuera responded by writing the letters into Dexter's chronicle, and by giving the relationship a distinctly Spanish flavor: Seneca had sent many letters to Paul while the apostle was on a visit to the Iberian Peninsula in AD 64, and, for this reason, Dexter noted, "it is believed" that Seneca became Paul's disciple as well as a hidden Christian.[48] Higuera was also purposefully contrary, as when he had Dexter attest to the authenticity of Annius's texts. By the time Higuera wrote, the texts had been rejected by many critics, yet we find a remarkable moment in the chronicle of Dexter: in AD 300 a Spaniard named Lucius Valerus "gathered in five books the fragments of Berosus."[49]

Higuera fused patristic, hagiographic, and historical sources to wildly augment the Iberian role in apostolic and early Christianity. This is exemplified in the case of the Christian centurions. In the Gospels of Mark and Matthew, mention was made of an unnamed centurion who had exclaimed, at the foot of the Cross, that Jesus was truly the Son of God. Jerome identified this centurion as one Cornelius, "from the Italian contingent," who in fulfillment of a biblical prophecy had been among many who had come to see Jesus upon the Cross.[50] In his revisions of the Martyrology, Baronio identified Cornelius the Centurion as being martyred on February 2, having been baptized and made a bishop by the apostle Peter, although Baronio did not specify where.[51]

Here, as elsewhere, Higuera drew upon unimpeachable biblical and patristic traditions in order to create something new and rather less reliable. He reinterpreted Jerome's "Italian contingent" rather broadly to make Cornelius a native of Spain. Higuera further complicated the tradition by splitting one centurion into two: he separated Jerome's Cornelius from the unnamed centurion in the Gospels by making them father and son. Thus, according to Dexter, Caius Oppius, the son of Cornelius, who was also a centurion, was among the first gentiles to believe in Jesus, and he was from Malaga. After preaching to the Jerusalemites with Saint Peter, Caius Oppius returned to his dwelling in Corinth, where he hosted the apostle Paul and gave shelter to Spanish pilgrims en route to the Holy Land. By the year 70 he had decamped to Milan, where he became the city's third bishop, as well as a friend to Emperor Hadrian.[52]

In this way, in marked contrast to some of his more critical peers and predecessors, Higuera exploited the ambiguities and complexities of hagiographical traditions; rather than attempting to clarify or clear away these problem spots, Higuera dove in and, like a magpie, snapped up resplendent details with which to adorn his historical narratives. This was true even of relatively minor figures in early Christian history; for example, he contradicted Baronio to assert that the apocryphal traditions were correct: Saint Peter had a daughter named Petronilla.⁵³ Higuera also had Dexter dutifully record the legendary correspondence between the Virgin Mary and Saint Ignatius of Antioch, as well as the Virgin's letter to the people of Messina, even though he must have known that Baronio dismissed both traditions as apocryphal.⁵⁴ In the year 86, according to Dexter, "Among Messinans, the memory of the Blessed Virgin Mary is celebrated, since she had sent them a sweet letter." In 430, "the Hebrew letter from the Blessed Virgin to the same citizens of Messina was discovered in the Messinan public registry [*tabulario*]."⁵⁵

Higuera also reaffirmed and recomplicated a number of traditions surrounding Pontius Pilate, including the legendary correspondence between the Roman procurator and the emperor Tiberius. In the *Annales*, Baronio had evinced serious doubts about the story that Pilate had written to Tiberius in order to lament his own involvement in Jesus's death. Eusebius, Tertullian, and Orosius all recorded the story, and by the Middle Ages the patristic accounts had sprouted elaborate tendrils, such that the very letter from Pilate to Tiberius inevitably appeared. The document was printed several times in the fifteenth, sixteenth, and seventeenth centuries, as were other letters that had Pilate informing Tiberius of the Resurrection and other miracles, and the emperor asking the Roman Senate to declare Jesus a god.⁵⁶ Baronio was skeptical and commented dismissively, "Whether this be true [. . .] we leave to the judgment of the prudent reader."⁵⁷ Yet Higuera pushed back against this skepticism and wrote two of Pilate's letters into Dexter's chronicle. Here the chronicler reported that Pilate wrote to Tiberius of the miracles and death of Jesus, and, four years later, another letter that prompted Tiberius to commend Jesus to the Senate.⁵⁸

Even while refusing to adhere to the more exacting standards of the best early modern historical and hagiographic research, Higuera also emulated it, selectively. It is no mistake that the cronicones, just like Baronio's *Annales*, anchored the events of sacred history to a fixed chronology—which to many sixteenth-century readers was seriously wanting in traditional liturgy and hagiography—and he also tethered familiar legends to the Iberian landscape. In order to fill in the details of the world of the primitive church, Higuera, like Baronio, drew on Roman literary sources, such as the very popular *Epigrams* of the Roman poet Martial.⁵⁹ In these efforts, Higuera was particularly concerned with saints. Yet these should not be mistaken for the overdetermined saints—those paragons of heroic virtue—that scholars have conditioned us to look for in the Counter-Reformation Church.⁶⁰ Stripped down to the bare minimum of biographical detail, the saints, bishops, and martyrs of the cronicones are not wreathed in Christian virtues, heroic or otherwise. Higuera's martyrs are exemplary only in their implied willingness to die for the faith. Saint Liberata, for example, who Higuera conflated with another female saint, appears in Dexter's *Chronicon* in a single colorless line:

> In AD 138, 889 years since the foundation of Rome, Wilgefort, or Liberata, daughter of the Portuguese King Catellius, suffered in Amphilochius.[61]

Liberata/Wilgefort and all the others are spare, lean saints, placeholders who serve as indexes of Iberian sanctity through the ages. They do not teach or exhort, unlike the saints in Diego de la Vega's *Paradise of the Glory of the Saints* (1602) in which the saints were "mirrors from whose light and example we can compose and adorn our own."[62] Nor do they comport themselves in a risible manner; these hagiographies-cum-chronicles offer virtually nothing for the incredulous Protestant critic to mock. In this limited sense, Higuera outdid Baronio. He configured his texts so that they would not be bogged down with any of the material that Renaissance humanists and church historians had been trying to remove. They are *annales ecclesiastici*, even more spare and unapologetic than the ones that Baronio was writing.

HIGUERA AS ANNALIST AND COMPILER

It may seem to modern readers that Higuera's pastiche of authentic and invented material represents a clear-cut forgery. This has certainly been the verdict of modern scholarship, which has seen in the cronicones very little of enduring value. Yet when we look more closely at the context, here again, the story becomes even more complex. In fact, by distorting the works of his late antique and medieval predecessors in accordance with his own biases, Higuera was actually participating in the long and venerable tradition of the medieval universal chronicle. If an annalist wanted to write universal history—that is, an account of events from Creation up to one's own time and place—he would simply have no other choice than to draw upon the words of his predecessors; in describing the centuries before Christ, he would look to biblical texts; for early Christianity, patristic sources; and, for more recent history, other medieval annals. In other words, the first task of a chronicler was *compilatio*, the gathering of relevant passages from various authorities. The thirteenth-century Dominican Adam of Clermont described his abridgment of Vincent de Beauvais's *Speculum historiale* as having been "compiled . . . from the phrases and sentences of learned men." Yet he characterized his efforts as much more than simply copying: through his judicious selection and reorganization of elegant yet forgotten older sources, the words of the ancients had been rescued from the negligence of posterity.[63] In other words, he created something new, in a process often described in apiological terms: like the bee gathering pollen from a field full of blossoms, the compiler collected relevant material from a variety of sources, then returned to his hive, where he would put the relevant passages (*sententiae*) into chronological and narrative order (*ordinatio*), reconcile internal contradictions among the various sources (*concordia diversarum sententiarum*), and add material from his own time, place, and perspective.[64]

Since, for the medieval author, the genesis of any dependable text was to be found in its reliance upon trusted authorities, copying previous chronicles was not an illicit scholarly act, but the proper way to begin. Thus, practices that might seem to modern readers like plagiarism, interpolation, and piracy were, for a medieval chronicler, trustworthy methods to bind his text to reliable historical authorities. Indeed, as one scholar recently observed, "the idea of intellectual property had little place in ancient or early modern historiography," and condensing, copying, and imitating one's predecessors was "an uncontroversial technique that went back to classical historiography."[65] This helps explain why modern editors of these texts are still sorting out the resulting tangle of authentic with interpolated material in manuscripts that might contain an undifferentiated admixture of authentic, interpolated, plagiarized, and corrupted passages from a variety of hands and times. The situation was not necessarily improved by scholars of Higuera's generation. The dire state of affairs is suggested by a 1615 edition of the chronicle of Hydatius of Galicia prepared by the Cordoban scholar Luis de San Llorente, an edition that, in one recent estimation, provides "a good example of the atrocities that could be committed against a text in the early days of textual criticism: there is unnecessary and gratuitous emendation and substitution of words, expunction (of words, phrases, and whole entries), misreading of the manuscript, and a great number of typographical errors."[66]

The principal historical sources for Roman and Visigothic Spain represented the cumulative product of centuries of recopying, adaptation, and addition. The interlocking nature of these texts, and the difficulty of separating the various textual strands they embodied, is illustrated by their often being collected, copied, and published as a corpus through the early modern period, such that, in one surviving manuscript, we find John of Biclarum's text together with those of Jerome, Prosper, Victor, and Isidore, as well as with the *Ecclesiastical History* of Rufinus.[67] To disentangle these threads to make sense of the text would require active, not passive, reading. In other words, the chronicler's active working method of *compilatio* and *ordinatio* found its logical extension in the reader's own *judicium*. The medieval reader was expected to intervene in the text: he would not simply regard the text as a finished product, as a passive reader, but rather, leave his mark on the manuscript in his own annotations, emendations, and continuations of the text, and in this sense, become a fellow author or composer.[68]

In this context, it is unsurprising that medieval continuators of Eusebius-Jerome saw themselves as part of a shared textual tradition that was always being revised, improved, and supplemented. Yet this has made it difficult for modern editors to separate the strands of authentic material from later interpolations: after all, introducing one's own perspective into a previous text was part of the process of creating a new one.[69] Each of the medieval continuators of Eusebius-Jerome began with the recognizable core of chronologically arranged information from his predecessor. Thus, Prosper of Aquitaine (ca. 390–ca. 465) began his chronicle with an epitome of Eusebius-Jerome, including a summary of some of the highlights of biblical history. To this, Prosper added a more detailed account of events all the way to his own time, the mid-fifth century, and centered in his place, which was Gaul. Likewise, Hydatius of Galicia (ca. 400–ca. 474) imagined his chronicle as a continuation of Eusebius-Jerome, such that the two texts were supposed to be read in the context of each other. Hydatius picked up precisely where Jerome left off, and his narrative brought the cumulative record of events in this remote corner of the Roman Empire up into the mid-fifth century. Like Prosper, he focused on the Goths, who were then invading Galicia and Lusitania.[70] In the mid-sixth century, Victor of Tunnuna continued Prosper's chronicle, as well as his tradition of organizing the entries according to the chronology of Roman consuls, as he described events in the eastern and western halves of the empire from the mid-fifth to mid-sixth centuries.[71] When John of Biclarum (ca. 592–ca. 614), a monk from Santarem (Portugal) returned from studying in Constantinople, he brought a copy of Victor of Tunnuna's chronicle back with him. He drew upon the text in his own continuation of the Eusebius-Jerome tradition.[72] John situated his narrative within the wider context of the Roman Empire, as reflected in the dual chronology according to which he organized events, in both the regnal years of Roman emperors as well as in reference to the succession of Visigothic rulers in Iberia, whom he depicted as strong, legitimate rulers (no easy task for the tumultuous sixth century).[73]

John of Biclarum's most immediate influence was on Isidore of Seville (ca. 560–636), the famed early medieval author of the encyclopedic survey of knowledge known as the *Etymologies*. In his chronicle, Isidore drew upon his predecessors' texts as starter dough: into the mix went Victor and John's continuations of Prosper-Hydatius, as well as Paulus Orosius's *Seven Books of History against the Pagans*, which chronicled the movement of Alans, Sueves, and Vandals into Spain at the beginning of the fifth century.[74] Since Isidore wrote in the wake of the conversion of the Visigothic monarchy from Arianism to Catholicism, a conversion in which he and his family had been instrumental, it is perhaps unsurprising that the chronicle depicted the reigning Visigoths as more united and Catholic than perhaps they really were. Regardless, Isidore's chronicle, alongside his *History of the Goths*, later became fundamental to the early modern revival of Gothic heritage, which coincided with Higuera's lifetime. The relics of Isidore and his three siblings Leander, Fulgentius, and Florentina were discovered near Cáceres in the second half of the sixteenth century, and Philip II and Bishop Sancho Dávila Toledo of Jaén took some relics for their own collections. In the wake of these discoveries, Fulgentius was adopted as the patron saint of the diocese of Cartagena in 1594. And according to at least one seventeenth-century interpreter, Isidore's family, and, with him, the Hapsburg dynasty, was descended from King Reccared, whose conversion to Catholicism had extirpated the Arian heresy from the Iberian Peninsula.[75]

If Higuera emulated the style and substance of the medieval chronicle, he also seems to have followed the chronicler's working method, which was to build solidly upon the texts of his predecessors. The net effect is that the four chronicles form an interlocking and self-referential corpus. Higuera wrote Dexter and Maximus just as his predecessors had written their annals: the first step was compilatio, then ordinatio, followed by the intercalation of his own material, which was, in large part, bent toward his own time, place, and biases. Dexter and Maximus seem to have begun as extracts of these earlier texts, which Higuera sprinkled with passages of his own, as the seventeenth-century critic Nicolás Antonio first noticed. Antonio identified over three-quarters of the material in an early draft of Dexter-Maximus that dates from circa 1594—and which may have even belonged to Juan Bautista Pérez—as having derived from Prosper of Aquitaine's fifth-century epitome of Jerome's chronicle (which was itself a continuation of Eusebius); likewise for Maximus, for which Higuera drew heavily upon Prosper. When he ran out of this material, he turned to Hydatius of Galicia. Of the remaining entries that were not part of the existing chronicle tradition, few represent outright innovation on Higuera's part. In fact, most of this material is entirely conventional: for example, in the first century, Higuera introduced fixed dates for familiar events, such as the arrival of Santiago, which, he said, occurred in the year 36. Higuera also intervened in order to grant a handful of Iberian sees a firm claim for apostolic succession, as he recorded that Santiago had named bishops in a number of cities, including Braga, Zaragoza, Barcelona, and Toledo. It is worth noting that Higuera did not provide an unequivocal support for Toledan claims to primacy; in fact, in this version of Dexter, the very first bishops Santiago was supposed to have appointed were in Braga and Zaragoza, in the year 45, and not in Toledo, which did not receive its first prelate until fifty years later.⁷⁶ Of course, in subsequent drafts, the texts metastasized considerably, as Higuera pumped a wealth of new material into Dexter and Maximus, such that if the first hundred years of this early Dexter contained thirty distinct entries, there were over five times as many in the same chronological bracket in one 1627 edition of the text, thanks to Higuera's additions.⁷⁷

One particularly agile practitioner of the technique of compilatio, ordinatio, and concordia was Lucas de Tuy, whose thirteenth-century *Chronicon mundi* began as an appendix to Isidore of Seville's *Chronicon*. Lucas began by combining information from other Latin chronicles going back to the earliest days, and added and subtracted entries as he saw fit. Lucas also remolded previous texts in order to write history from a distinctly Castilian-centric perspective, and most pointedly, for his own diocese, by "systematically and deliberately tampering with his sources in order to promote the interests of his beloved church of León against those of its rival, the primatial see of Toledo."⁷⁸ This inclination could lead Lucas to make some rather outlandish moves, such as when he suggested that Aristotle had actually been Spanish.⁷⁹ Significantly, Lucas also enriched his narrative by drawing upon new sources, such as epic poetry, hagiographical sources, and historical romances. The net effect was that certain traditions that had only circulated in legendary form — such as the intrigues of the chivalric hero Bernardo del Carpio — became part of the canon of historical, rather than fictional, literature, and, as such, were subsequently transmitted as historical fact by Lucas's continuators, such as Ximénez de Rada.⁸⁰

In his willingness to draw upon sources that may have been disregarded by previous chroniclers, Lucas de Tuy was typical of other thirteenth-century Latin chroniclers, many of whom began to cite legendary sources as historical evidence for the first time. This meant a new appreciation of scriptural apocrypha — noncanonical texts of the Old and New Testaments — as well as of "apocrypha" in the broader sense of texts of uncertain authorship and authenticity. It is not that medieval historians lacked the ability to sort out internal contradictions, anachronisms, or errors, nor that they did not know the difference between apocryphal and canonical material, or between texts deemed either legendary or historical. As Sicard of Cremona explained in a preface to his chronicle of universal history, "less authentic" texts that illuminated the childhood of Christ were nonetheless useful, since they "are agreeable to the ears and increase devotion."⁸¹ In other words, texts that were not necessarily trustworthy in their historical detail could nevertheless fulfill important devotional and pastoral functions for the preacher, historian, or exegete. In this way, a medieval chronicler such as Lucas de Tuy shared with the biblical exegete and sermon-writer the tendency to enrich his narrative with colorful and edifying details for the sake of the larger good;

and, to this end, when faced with conflicting accounts of the same incident, for example, he would often keep them both rather than reject one, preferring to "harmonize conflicting accounts rather than decide which were reliable or not."[82] In the medieval chronicle, as in Higuera's pseudomedievalia, this method could lead to the proliferation of mutually contradictory details, to narrative incoherence, and an overflow of detail, not all of it relevant. This explains why, in Dexter's text, when Higuera recorded the apocryphal tale of the conversion and miraculous healing of Pilate's wife, he refused to choose between the two separate traditions that identified her alternately as Claudia or Procula, and instead kept them both, making her "Claudia Procula."[83]

Like the late antique and early medieval chronicles that were the chronicles' putative peers, Higuera's texts were also supposed to have been in conversation with one another over the centuries. Yet, whereas the attention of many of the Eusebian continuators had been focused on the battle for power on the part of "barbarian" rulers in the western half of the Roman Empire, Higuera's chronicles focused on ecclesiastical history, like Eusebius's *Ecclesiastical History*, which narrated the story of the martyred and embattled Greek Christian community and its guardian, Constantine the Great. Higuera's chronicles likewise focused on matters ecclesiastical, but in this case, the bishops, martyrs, heretics, and councils chronicled were overwhelmingly located in the Roman provinces of Hispania. Higuera cannot be said to have been writing national history. His texts did not concern themselves with the dynastic history of Spain and Portugal, which, for most of his lifetime, were united during the union of the crowns under the Hapsburgs, from 1580 until the ultimately successful Portuguese revolt in 1640. Rather, Higuera emulated Eusebius-Jerome in representing Iberian territories as part of Rome, in which Roman emperors and governors, as well as Roman geographic names, were essential points of reference. Yet Higuera's Hispania was, in comparison, remarkably apolitical, populated by apostles, saints, and bishops, with the occasional provincial governor or imperial decree having an impact at the local level through the martyrdom or persecution of Christians. And, like Lucas de Tuy, Higuera often brought new details under his narrative umbrella as part of his larger aim of Iberianizing sacred history.

This bundling of legendary detail with known facts is exemplified in Higuera's treatment of Dionysius the Areopagite. The historical Dionysius was an Athenian convert of the apostle Paul, mentioned in Acts 17:34, who over time had become confused with Saint Denis of France, the first bishop and patron saint of Paris. In the Middle Ages, these two distinct figures were further conflated and merged with a third, the pseudonymous author of the group of late antique and Neoplatonic texts known as the Dionysian corpus. Ambrosio de Morales had echoed this medieval equation of three distinct individuals, while also giving the legend a distinctly Spanish twist by furnishing the proverbial apostle to the French with an Iberian itinerary, as well as Spanish disciples, whom he installed as bishops during his second-century travels. The first of the Dionysian apostles was Hierotheo, whom Dionysius had dubbed "divine," according to another earlier tradition.[84] Higuera, perhaps aware that the very existence of Dionysius, and of affiliates such as Hierotheo, had been vigorously rejected by scholars such as Joseph Scaliger, mounted a concerted defense via chronicle, and depicted Hierotheo as foundational in the history of Spanish Christianity.[85] As in so many other matters, Higuera was elaborating here upon Morales, who had made Hierotheo one of the converts from the apostle Paul's legendary Spanish sojourn.[86] In Higuera's further rendering, Hierotheo became a native of Segovia—and not, as his name and associations might have suggested, of a Greek-speaking region—who returned to his city to occupy its see after his better-known stint as bishop of Athens. This was not an uncontroversial claim, since it directly challenged a tradition that identified Saint Fructuosus (also referred to as San Fructos or Frutos), Segovia's patron saint, as its first prelate: this prompted a polemic that would last well into the seventeenth century.[87] The second of Dionysius's Spanish disciples was, according to tradition, Eugenius, the first bishop of Toledo. Higuera's innovation here seems to have been to link him explicitly to Hierotheo, to furnish him with a second given name—Marcellus—and to identify him as a Roman from the imperial family.[88]

AUTHENTIC SOURCES OF THE FALSE CHRONICLES: HAGIOGRAPHY AND LITURGY

This was just one of many such moves that Higuera made in order to write Spain into the early history of Christianity, often in direct opposition to more recent assessments by respected scholars in Rome and elsewhere. For information about the early saints, Higuera drew rather uncritically upon the heterogeneous range of extrabiblical texts that modern scholars refer to as "hagiography," including literary and liturgical sources, late antique and early medieval historical martyrologies, and anecdotal narrations of saints' lives (vitae).[89] In Higuera's period, authors such as Alonso de Villegas and Pedro de Ribadeneira were giving the genre of saints' lives a new lease on life, in updated, amplified, and relatively uncritical collections known as *flos sanctorum*. Whereas in some quarters of late medieval and Counter-Reformation Europe these hagiographical traditions were being scrutinized from a newly critical perspective, hagiographers such as Villegas and Ribadeneira seem to have disregarded these new developments in scholarship almost completely. In their late sixteenth- and early seventeenth-century collections of saints' lives, they accumulated legendary, apocryphal, and conventional material in a manner that would have been recognizable to their medieval forebears, such as Jacobus de Voragine, the compiler of the *Golden Legend*.[90]

Of special interest were the early Christian martyrs, those who had been put to death in the four centuries before Christianity was legalized in the Roman Empire, and who served as compelling symbols of forbearance and piety for early modern Catholics (and Protestants, for that matter). In the search for the most trustworthy and antique sources of information about the early Christian martyrs, the poems of Aurelius Clemens Prudentius (d. 413) were crucial. This late antique poet from Hispania eulogized several martyrs of the Great Persecution (303–311) in Rome and its Spanish provinces in the fourteen poems that made up his *Liber peristephanon* ("The Book of the Martyrs' Crowns"). While modern historians are uncertain whether the fourth and final edict of the persecution, which would require Christians to offer a sacrifice to the Roman gods, was even enforced in Spain, the conviction that this had been a time of tremendous persecution and suffering had been central to Spanish Christianity since at least the time of Prudentius.[91] Among the martyrs whose gruesome deaths were chronicled by the poet were Saint Vincent and his eighteen anonymous companions from Zaragoza; Fructuosus and his two deacons in Tarragona; Justo and Pastor in Alcalá de Henares; Acisclo, Zoilo, and Victoria in Cordoba; Saints Emeterius and Chelidonius in Calahorra; and Saint Eulalia in Mérida. These fifth-century poetic texts became part of the Mozarabic liturgy, where they were rendered as hymns (*carmina*).[92] They were also copied separately into the *Pasionario hispánico*, a collection of liturgical readings on the saints that started out in the seventh century with a core of Prudentius-era martyrs and then grew over time, such that its eleventh-century recension included these and eight other Spanish martyrs: Leocadia in Toledo; Justa and Rufina in Seville; Vincent, Sabina, and Cristeta in Ávila; and Servando and Germán in Mérida.[93]

After having fallen out of circulation in the Middle Ages, manuscripts of Prudentius's *Peristephanon* were rediscovered by fifteenth-century Italian humanists; printed editions began to appear in the early sixteenth century, beginning with a Venetian edition from Aldus Manutius (which was bound with Prosper of Aquitaine's chronicle), followed by several Spanish editions in the sixteenth century. This crucial early Christian source was eagerly plumbed by those who, like Higuera, were hungry for details about the pre-Nicene Church. Antonio Gallonio, author of a late sixteenth-century treatise on the modes of martyrdom, drew liberally on the text. So, too, did his fellow Oratorian Cardinal Baronio, who "ransacked" Prudentius in his revision of the Roman Martyrology and for the *Annales ecclesiastici*, as part of what Simon Ditchfield has called the "paleo-Christian revival" of the late sixteenth century.[94] In a short excursus on historical method in his *Coronica general*, Morales also identified Prudentius as a reliable source, in spite of his writing in the inherently untrustworthy genre of poetry. As Morales reasoned, it "should not disturb anybody that this author is a poet, nor should they think that he might have faked something," even though, as everybody knew, poets were free to do so thanks to the capaciousness of their genre. Yet "because he was such a good Christian," Prudentius approached the story of the saints as a "historian, and not a poet," such that his poems could be read as history, without any fear that they might contain fiction.[95] Morales also looked to the liturgy for information about the early history of Spanish Christianity. It was this research, in fact, that led him, like others, to weave many contested threads of the Santiago legend into his own serious works of historical scholarship.[96]

Higuera took Morales at his word, and, like these and many other early modern Catholic scholars, drew upon Prudentius's poems as straight historical sources. Since Higuera was especially fond of Diocletian-era martyrs, he found a rich source in the *Peristephanon*'s sundry details about those put to death under Dacian, the Roman *prases* (governor) of Hispania, a favorite topic of hagiographers. The Dacian persecutions were particularly poignant since they came just a decade before Constantine the Great's legalization of Christianity, which ended the persecutions. Yet, from the perspective of modern scholarship, faith in Prudentius was misplaced. Archaeological evidence—including the absence of "martyrial epitaphs"—suggests that far fewer Christians were put to death in the West during the Great Persecution than literary sources such as the *Peristephanon* would seem to indicate.[97] In a technique that would be unwittingly emulated by his avid sixteenth-century Jesuit reader, as well as many other hagiographers, Prudentius had multiplied the ranks by converting legendary martyrs into historical ones. Like several other late antique and early medieval hagiographers, Prudentius composed "passions for past martyrs, creating a literary drapery with which to cover up the absence of reliable historical facts."[98] He did this by bringing a number of preexisting hagiographic legends under the umbrella of the Diocletianic persecution, and specifically linked them to Dacian.

Prudentius's own rather generous attitude toward historical accuracy, combined with his preference for Iberian martyrs, made his poems particularly well suited for later repurposing and amplification. And thus, Higuera followed suit. In the cronicones, he included all of the Prudentian martyrs, and added many more for good measure. Thus, if Prudentius commemorated merely twenty-two Iberian martyrs, in Dexter's chronicle, where Higuera dates the Great Persecution to 300–308, we find six times as many, for a total of 132. This, Dexter informs us, did not include the additional martyrs of indeterminate number whose names had been lost to time.[99] In addition to amplifying the Prudentian martyrs, Higuera also paid tribute to the poet's manner of commemorating them by including a number of *carmina* in the chronicles, which he attributed to the various chroniclers, but which were probably of his own manufacture.[100]

Here, again, Higuera adhered to a mainstream vision of early Christian history. When Dexter's chronicle filled in the blanks by peopling the fourth century with scores of martyrs, some familiar, others obscure, the text answered a perceived need. The problem was that for Spain the historical record of martyrdom was rather scant. For early modern interpreters, the martyrs commemorated by Prudentius were the exceptions. What of those who had not been so lucky, whose memory had been obliterated by time, whose relics had disappeared, and whose sacrifice had left no trace in the historical sources, let alone in the communities where they had been born or put to death? That many martyrs languished in such oblivion was a conviction shared by most conscientious scholars of early Christianity in Spain. How else might one explain the relative paucity of information about what were believed to be a nearly infinite number of martyrs under Diocletian? Such a lamentable fate had almost befallen the "innumerable martyrs" of Zaragoza, an anonymous cohort of victims of the Great Persecution whose names, like those of so many others, had been lost, but whose relics had been recovered thanks to a miracle. When the Romans incinerated the bodies of the martyrs so that the Christians could not venerate them, God intervened, and allowed their ashes to sprinkle down to the ground in a rain of white powder. There the martyrs' infinitesimal relics were promptly collected by devotees, and then deposited for safety into a crypt in the Zaragozan church of Santa Engracia, known, after its contents, as "Santas Masas."[101]

In order to restore the memory of what were believed to be many such forgotten martyrs, Higuera, like Prudentius, "exercise[d] the poet's freedom to alter not only details, but also basic elements and even identities," particularly by "conflating the legends of people who [bore] the same name," even when he knew they "belong[ed] to entirely separate traditions" and had "nothing in common except their names."[102] Just as Prudentius had invented many biographical details to grant specific martyrs starring roles in the drama of the Great Persecution, Higuera seems to have located many saints who lacked specifics or identifying details in extant historical sources, and, drawing on his own extensive knowledge of patristic texts and medieval chronicles, provided them with a fixed place in the narrative of Spanish sacred history. The difference, of course, was that Prudentius had done so in the somewhat more elastic genre of poetic verse, rather than in the form of a historical annal. Yet, over the course of the Middle Ages, many readers and successors of Prudentius had performed the same feat in their own texts, as they integrated and improved upon his material in their own respective liturgical, literary, or historical sources.

HISTORY AND FABLE, TRUTH AND VERISIMILITUDE

By resurrecting forgotten martyrs through the medium of the ersatz medieval chronicle, Higuera—like Prudentius—obeyed a deeper mandate, one that followed the logic of poetry rather than history. From this perspective, it was arguably the former, not the latter, that possessed a greater claim upon truth. As Aristotle had argued in the *Poetics*,

> It is not the function of the poet to relate what has happened, but the *kinds* of things that might occur and are possible in terms of probability or necessity. The difference between the historian and the poet is not that between using verse or prose; Herodotus' work could be versified and would be just as much a kind of history in verse as in prose. No, the difference is this: that the one relates actual events, the other the kinds of things that might occur. Consequently, poetry is more philosophical and more elevated than history, since poetry relates more of the universal, while history relates the particulars.[103]

Higuera's chronicles were, like Prudentius's *carmina*, written from two perspectives, which to some but not all early modern scholars seemed distinct: on one hand, they were history—the province of verifiable fact—and, on the other, they also obeyed the laws of poetic verisimilitude, in the Aristotelian sense of "what is possible according to the law of probability or necessity."[104]

From this angle, Higuera looks less like a historical forger, and more like the late antique poet upon whose material he drew so liberally. The enduring truth was that many Christians had been martyred. For the pious, this central fact was more important than these easily forgotten, mundane details, the particulars, such as the names of the martyrs, or their precise places of birth or death. Here again we see Higuera as part of a much longer tradition in which history, hagiography, and liturgy intersected, overlapped, and bled into one another, and refused to separate themselves out into distinct genres. In this tradition, the highest good could be served by any and all, whose poetic conventions were not separated by rigid considerations of genre. Classical rhetoricians had been aware of this sometimes complex relationship among, and sometimes fluid boundaries between, poetry and history, fables and facts. As one scholar explains, this led Quintilian and others, such as Abelard and John of Salisbury, for example, to conclude that poetic fables could serve an important function; from this perspective, "provided it is a virtuous individual who is doing it, the act of lying is permissible if it serves the truth, secures a higher good, or produces what is generally advantageous."[105]

Even as many other practitioners of historical scholarship in early modern Europe were attempting to extricate the apocryphal from the historically verifiable elements of sacred traditions—in other words, separating "poetry" from "history"—the long tradition of relying upon legends and noncanonical texts for additional information about holy history continued in the work of Higuera, and many others; as we have seen, solid precedent existed for this in the Latin chronicle tradition, particularly beginning in the thirteenth century. In this, Higuera also fell in behind Prudentius and later medieval liturgists who had drawn upon hagiographic sources of uncertain authorship, such as the collection of apocryphal apostolic Acts known as the pseudo-Abdias, in composing individual readings for the Mass. If early liturgists often "domesticated"—and validated—apocryphal traditions in this manner by incorporating them into the liturgy, so, too, did Higuera codify many strands of hagiographic legend by reshaping them into annals.[106] In his poetics, then, Higuera was, once again, a typical Jesuit professor of Latin and letters. As a good student of classical and medieval rhetoric, Higuera knew that "poetic fables" could, if used properly and with good intention, possess moral utility. In his texts, Higuera sought not to trick or confuse the reader, but to explain, clarify, justify, and elaborate. His histories possessed a normative, moral function; even if the texts could not always be confirmed beyond a doubt or by human means—at least at the level of detail—they nonetheless spoke to a deeper truth, one that was particularly important for the purposes of instructing and edifying the faithful during difficult and contentious times. In this sense, Higuera privileged the appearance of truth over particular truths. He used "fables" to move his audience toward the greatest good, the ultimate truth, namely, the veneration of God and the saints.[107]

4

JEWS, ARABIC-SPEAKERS, AND NEW SAINTS: THE FALSE CHRONICLES AND CONTROVERSY

As we have seen, Higuera parted company with many—although certainly not all—of his contemporaries, not in his desire to recover the oldest sources of Spanish history and holiness, but, rather, in his willingness to supplement them with texts that he fabricated or manipulated himself. This was in spite of the fact that Renaissance philology and historiography, along with enduring interconfessional conflicts in the wake of the Reformation, brought new demands for historical accuracy and philological precision, even among Catholic scholars, as Higuera was well aware. How, then, can we understand Higuera's disregard for these evolving higher standards of historical and hagiographic research? To put it bluntly, if Higuera was capable of accurately transmitting, as well as critically assessing, authentic historical texts, why did he resort to forgery? To get a better sense of what was behind his selective blindness to higher critical principles, we shall focus on those historical matters that Higuera manipulated most notably in the false chronicles. It is in Higuera's wild multiplication of the number of martyrs in Roman Hispania, as well as in his imaginative rendition of the roles of Jews and of Arabic-speakers in Spanish sacred history, that we see most clearly the creative interplay between tradition and innovation that characterized Higuera's working method in the chronicles and elsewhere; not coincidentally, these were topics of great interest and controversy among Higuera's peers and readers.

THE GRANADAN FORGERIES, 1588–1599

Thanks to their plethora of details regarding early Christian martyrs, there were, for devoted students of Iberian sacred history, few sources that could rival the false chronicles. Remarkably, such an exceptional cluster of texts did emerge, the so-called plomos of Granada. This group of texts and relics unearthed in the last years of the sixteenth century are often compared to Higuera's chronicles, since both sets of texts generated tremendous controversy and informed Spanish learned discourse for many years to come. The discovery of the lead books was preceded by a prophetic parchment written in Castilian, Arabic, and Latin, discovered in 1588 in the rubble of Granada's old minaret along with a number of relics that included a piece of the Virgin's handkerchief and a bone of the protomartyr Saint Steven; the former was sent to King Phillip II at El Escorial, where it was placed in the reliquary next to the Altar Mayor. Subsequently, from 1595 to 1599, twenty-two circular lead disks engraved in Arabic, as well as relics and ashes believed to be calcified human remains in cremation pits, were unearthed atop the hillside known as the Sacromonte ("sacred hill"). Most of the texts were attributed to Saint Cecilio, the legendary first bishop of Granada and one of the Seven Apostles, who were believed to be Santiago's disciples and the first bishops and evangelizers in the Iberian Peninsula. According to the lead books' unique interpretation of these figures, Cecilio and his brother, Thesiphon, were actually Arabic-speakers from the Arabian Peninsula who had been martyred on the Sacromonte along with several other disciples of Santiago.[1]

The texts posed vexing problems of interpretation, not the least of which was the so-called Salomonic script in which they were engraved, indecipherable even to seasoned Arabic translators. An additional dilemma was presented by the books' idiosyncratic theological and historical content. At a time when moriscos were reviled by the Old Christian mainstream as patent threats to the religious and genetic integrity of the Spanish body politic, the plomos' suggestion that the very first Christians in the Iberian Peninsula had been a group of Arabic-speakers, and that Granada's first bishop was himself an Arab, represented a rather bold recasting of history.[2] Equally audacious were the plomos' claims that God demonstrated a continued preference for Arabic, and, by extension, for the moriscos themselves, as the privileged media for his communications.

Yet the books' more unconventional theological and historical details proved irrelevant for proponents in Granada, who mostly ignored the plomos' implicit exaltation of the moriscos to a providential role in Spanish history. As the committee of translators assembled by Archbishop Pedro de Castro, the plomos' most fervent patron and defender, slowly deciphered the texts, tantalizing evidence of the ancient history of Christianity in Granada emerged. The texts also endorsed a number of devotions and doctrinal positions of special local and national interest with a historical basis in the earliest Iberian Church—exactly as Higuera's chronicles had. For Granadans, the plomos seemed to promise an unbroken history of Christian faith and practice, which allowed proponents of the texts to overlook some of their more idiosyncratic characteristics—such as their having been written in Arabic six hundred years before the language was spoken in Spain. As A. Katie Harris has argued, in the hands of local historians, Granada, which had been Muslim for most of its recorded history, was suddenly endowed with a solidly Christian civic identity and antiquity, a prestigious genealogy of faith and practice dating right back to the first-century martyrs and, via Santiago, the apostles themselves.[3]

By providing historical evidence for the Immaculate Conception of the Virgin Mary, the primacy of the Granadan see, Santiago's Spanish mission, and, more broadly, the veneration of relics and martyrs, the plomos, like the false chronicles, appealed to local pride, Counter-Reformation zeal, and Spanish patriotism simultaneously. In contrast, Rome's reaction to the discoveries was marked by initial caution, which soon morphed into outright antagonism, particularly as Archbishop Castro ignored repeated requests to forward the plomos themselves to Rome for scrutiny. Not surprisingly, Castro's efforts to defend what he considered Granada's spiritual patrimony against papal—and, increasingly, royal—opposition earned him little goodwill outside Granada. The tug-of-war continued even after Castro's death until, finally, in 1632, King Philip IV (1605–1665) ordered the lead books seized from the lockbox in the abbey of Sacromonte, which Castro had established in honor of the discoveries. In the meantime, the Roman and Spanish Inquisitions also prohibited translations of the plomos from circulating publicly.[4] Finally, the question of the texts' authenticity was resolved definitively—at least from the papacy's perspective—in 1682, when Pope Innocent XI condemned the plomos as heretical, Islamic-flavored "human fictions, fabricated for the ruin of the Catholic faith."[5]

This was certainly not the outcome that Archbishop Castro had foreseen when, almost immediately after the first lead book was discovered in 1595, he began to consult many of Spain's most distinguished scholars for their assistance in deciphering the texts, including Benito Arias Montano, Pedro de Valencia, Juan Bautista Pérez, Juan de Mariana, Antonio de Covarrubias—and Jerónimo Román de la Higuera. Of these, only the last two expressed any enthusiasm whatsoever. Covarrubias wrote in support of the prophetic parchment in 1594. Yet his endorsement was perhaps not exactly what Archbishop Castro had hoped, as Covarrubias professed to be unable to read the Salomonic characters.[6] For Arias Montano, an esteemed scholar who had edited the multilingual edition of the Bible known as the Antwerp Polyglot (1572), the coincidence of so many "novelties" was rather less compelling. In a 1595 letter, Arias Montano archly advised Castro to resist popular pressure to authorize questionable artifacts and thus risk giving ammunition to Protestant critics.

Jews, Arabic-Speakers, and New Saints

It has been a year of similar occurrences, because in these lands there have been found many stones, marbles, bricks, tiles engraved with various letter forms, some of which have been Arabic, which have been brought to me by clerics, friars, and laymen who are of the excited opinion that these are treasures. The adversaries of our Church, having seen that in some places credit is given to miracles that are not well examined . . . take the occasion to affirm that this is how it used to happen in past times. On the other hand, the common people, who are well disposed to novelties and gossip, want these things to be authorized, more so that they have something to talk about than in order to improve their lives.[7]

Montano's student, the humanist Pedro de Valencia, concluded that the texts were a fraud perpetrated by unlettered men, and Juan Bautista Pérez wrote a fifteen-point rebuttal of the plomos objecting to their blatant historical inaccuracies, linguistic errors, and internal inconsistencies.[8] Especially irritating to Pérez had been the so-called Salomonic script, which he believed was simply a slightly altered version of the Latin alphabet. He disparaged the forger's lack of imagination, asking why, if the forger of the lead books had really wanted to invent a new and strange script, he had not bothered to make a more concerted effort by writing in code, for example, or by adopting characters from Hebrew, Arabic, Armenian, "Chaldean" (Babylonian), Ethiopian, or Indian alphabets—all of which were available in print in Spain, as Pérez could attest, since he possessed several dictionaries of these languages himself.[9]

HIGUERA AND THE ARCHBISHOP OF GRANADA

Unlike many of his learned peers, Higuera responded enthusiastically to the discoveries and even offered to come to Granada to personally assist the archbishop in defending the authenticity of the texts and relics. In return, Castro seems to have considered Higuera a trusted advisor, from whom he solicited and accepted advice on how to publicize and defend the discoveries from critics. Over the following five years, the archbishop communicated news about the ongoing discoveries with Higuera and sent him passages from the texts as they were deciphered. For example, in 1596 Castro forwarded a passage in translation from one of the lead books, as well as a cluster of material from the texts, which Higuera—in characteristic fashion—digested by integrating into his treatise in their defense.[10] The following year, Castro sent Higuera an update on the discoveries, which, as he promised, was supplemented by a personal visit from Castro's secretary and messenger, Jerónimo de Herrera. Castro commented on

Higuera's being in a privileged position, for, "I have not given such a specific account to anybody anywhere else." This, he reasoned, was appropriate in light of how much Higuera had labored on behalf of the discoveries. The archbishop also forwarded preliminary drafts of treatises in defense of the plomos so that Higuera might correct and supplement them before they reached publication. There may have been an ulterior motive here, as Castro also encouraged Higuera to share the texts with his fellow Toledan Jesuit Juan de Mariana, whose distinct lack of enthusiasm about the discoveries was, as Castro ventured optimistically, probably just because he was not well informed about their progress.[11]

In addition to sending Higuera detailed lists of items to research and respond to—which Higuera did, with his customary prolixity—Castro invited him to the relics' official authentication ceremony in 1600. Higuera's superiors actually granted him permission to go, but word arrived too late.[12] Then, after the ceremony, Castro took the trouble to send Higuera a copy of a printed text certifying the authentication of the relics. In return, Higuera begged for updates about the construction of the abbey of Sacromonte, on the content of the liturgical readings (*officia propria*) for these martyrs, and on the process of translating the lead books. Higuera repeatedly peppered Castro and his secretary Herrera with requests for any relevant material from the plomos that might support traditional beliefs about Santiago—which many Spaniards felt were being undermined by the critiques of Roman cardinals such as Baronio and Robert Bellarmine. Higuera was preparing yet another treatise on the matter, which he eventually sent to Rome.[13] Archbishop Castro seems to have reciprocated and to have taken Higuera's advice on various matters, including, for example, strategies for defending the plomos in writing.[14]

In light of this evidence of continued and friendly communication between Higuera and the archbishop of Granada, it is necessary to respectfully disagree with the long-standing interpretation that Castro distrusted and disdained the Jesuit. This body of correspondence simply does not support one historian's colorful and influential assertion that Castro "treated this embarrassing ally coldly," nor does it substantiate speculation that Higuera was a risky contact for Castro due to the false chronicles; nor, for that matter, that Higuera ever importuned the archbishop for money.[15] Here, as in so many other areas of scholarship on the cronicones, the image we receive of Higuera has been distorted mightily by the knowledge of his subsequent infamy when, in fact, as we have seen, Higuera's public reputation does not seem to have been in question during his lifetime. Even if he clashed with his Jesuit superiors before, during, and after the San Tirso debacle of 1594–1595, Higuera remained in good standing with the broader community of like-minded scholars, as evidenced by his continued communication and collaboration with contacts in Toledo and beyond. In this context, it seems quite difficult to understand why Castro would have disdained Higuera, particularly since he seemed to have been perfectly happy to communicate with him on various detailed questions regarding the plomos and their fate. To assert otherwise would seem to attribute to the archbishop a rather preternatural sense of premonition, as well as a capacity for historical and philological critique that he simply does not seem to have possessed.

In any case, as part of his ongoing assistance to Archbishop Castro, Higuera contemplated how to best address the objections that, by 1596, when barely any of the lead books had been translated and not all of them had even been discovered yet, were already being registered by gimlet-eyed observers such as Juan Bautista Pérez. Higuera professed to be unperturbed by the prospect of addressing Pérez's critiques, since, as he said of his friend, "it is his nature to try to scrutinize and even contradict everything."[16] Besides, Higuera counseled Castro, in such matters it was preferable to keep in mind a generous spirit that surpassed human law and history, and looked instead to the criteria of divine truth. Indeed, this was the approach that he had recommended in conversation with another Toledan luminary who looked unfavorably upon the Granada discoveries, García de Loaysa Girón.

> I begged him to let himself be guided by, and walk toward, pious affection, without which one ends up at many precipices: and [I said] that nobody should reject something that requires so much consideration and study on account of a few difficulties, even if they are considerable.[17]

In other words, miraculous matters required a special sort of consideration, motivated more by a pious and generous spirit than by hermeneutical rigidity. In his manuscript history of Toledo, Higuera had recommended the same approach — one informed by "pious affection" — toward Toledo's relics of Santa Leocadia, and it is a principle that seems to have motivated his own work, as we have seen.[18] Even so, Higuera reasoned, doubts such as Loaysa Girón's stimulated debate which, in turn, could only help reveal the truth more fully: "I believe that it has been for the greater glory of God that some people, with considerable zeal, have presented such great resistance and opposition, so that in this way the truth will be more settled."[19] In this effort, historical evidence of course would be important, but even more so were miracles — such as those that had accompanied and followed the discoveries — which Higuera advised, constituted the strongest argument in the plomos' favor.

Higuera may have been pious, but he was not so naive as to believe that miracles alone would be enough to convince skeptics of the plomos' authenticity, so he also spilled much ink in an attempt to help Castro address those questions that pertained to the realm of human history as well. And this is the point at which the collaboration between the Toledan Jesuit and the archbishop began to fray. For, as Higuera methodically worked to anticipate and address the many objections to the plomos—including that there seemed to be no other record of the first-century persecution that killed the martyrs of Granada—he took recourse to an explanation that, for Castro, was simply beyond the pale. "I have stopped to think many times," Higuera remarked in a letter to Castro, "how no memory at all of these martyrdoms and of the destruction of the Church in Spain remained in the [texts of the] Sacred Writers."[20] Yet in Higuera's capable hands, this was only an apparent dilemma, for as he reported to Castro, one very important trace of the event was right under the noses of every God-fearing Christian: in the New Testament itself. The key passage appeared in Paul's Epistle to the Hebrews (10:32), where the apostle enjoined his audience to "remember those days in which you were enlightened" after they had suffered. According to Higuera, this passage had been misinterpreted by biblical exegetes over the ages. Paul was not writing to Jewish converts to Christianity in Jerusalem, but, rather, to the Jews of Spain who had converted. With this matter clarified, so too was the true historical significance of the passage; for if Paul were writing to *Spanish* Jewish converts, the "suffering" to which he referred must have been none other than this otherwise unattested late first-century persecution in Granada—unattested everywhere, that is, except in the plomos.[21]

In this instance, however, Castro was singularly ungrateful for Higuera's heuristic gymnastics, and he responded with outright irritation at the implication that Granada's first Christians had practiced Judaism: "And you say next that these saints were Hebrews; there is no reason to talk about this, Sir: they were not of the Hebrew nationality, they never received the law of Moses, nor were they ever circumcised." After all, if Granada's martyrs had once been Jews, from the perspective of an early modern Old Christian such as Castro, they had been *conversos*, and if *limpieza de sangre* was a prerequisite for the highest secular and ecclesiastical offices in early modern Spain, it most certainly would have been required of an office that was higher still, that of Granada's patron saint.[22]

Nor did Castro evince any interest whatsoever in Higuera's other pet projects, such as the purported remains of the temple of San Tirso. As he plainly admitted to Higuera, who had undoubtedly written to him regarding the discovery with enthusiasm, "I did not pay much attention to it, since it did not concern me," but, he elaborated, he was not inclined to give the notion much credit, for "what was discovered in Toledo does not seem to have much foundation."[23] Here the contrast between Higuera and the patron of the plomos is stark: it is hard to imagine the Jesuit regarding any discovery of potentially great historical and religious significance with such indifference, no matter where in the Iberian Peninsula it had occurred. And this disjunction between Castro and Higuera parallels a broader disconnect, that is, between the respective fates of the two sets of texts in the long term. Although the plomos and the cronicones emerged around the same time, attracted some of the same foes and proponents, and informed debates about the shape of Spain's sacred past for centuries afterward, an analogy between the two has serious limits. For one, Higuera's texts were read much more widely than the lead books, which were disseminated only in selected passages in translation. The chronicles were never banned, and, indeed, once in print, they circulated easily and widely in several editions. In contrast to the lead books, which were written in barely recognizable Arabic rendered in "Salomonic" characters, the false chronicles were, in their entirety, theologically accessible and culturally legible. As we have seen, Higuera's texts adhered to the familiar and conventional generic form of the annal, as opposed to the theologically risky mix of prophetic and scriptural address employed by the narrators of the plomos.[24] The false chronicles were squarely orthodox in their theology; in fact, the texts avoided theological matters almost entirely in preference for content of historical and hagiographical significance. It is true that the plomos were also infused with plenty of Old Christian traditions and informed by contemporary theological and ecclesiological notions.[25] Yet they were also sufficiently controversial in style, content, and presentation to lead to early restrictions on the circulation of their translations, and, ultimately, to earn them the opprobrium of the 1682 papal commission. In contrast, the false chronicles were completely anodyne in terms of orthodoxy, stylistically unremarkable, and culturally mainstream.

THE FALSE CHRONICLES AND THE SPANISH JEWS

In spite of these significant differences, Higuera's placing such an emphasis on the pivotal role of the Spanish Jews in early Christianity and on the antiquity of their presence in the Iberian Peninsula has also led subsequent observers to conflate his texts with the lead books. Indeed, in both the *History of Toledo* and the false chronicles, Higuera did depict Hebrew-speakers as precocious converts to Christianity, particularly in first-century Granada and Toledo. As Higuera explained in *Toledo*, early Jewish converts were the ancestors of the city's native inhabitants, the Mozarabs. With this devious logic, Higuera effectively endowed Toledo's Mozarabs with Jewish ancestry while also making them the "oldest" Christians in Spain. This has led some interpreters to posit that Higuera used the chronicles, like his invented genealogies, to rehabilitate the conversos from which he seems to have been descended. From this perspective, both the plomos and the cronicones were forged, in part, to legitimize the descendants of non-Christians in a Spain that was increasingly hostile to them.[26]

However, whereas the lead books were unprecedented in their advocacy for Arabic-speakers and their latter-day descendants, the false chronicles' version of Jewish history was, in fact, not wholly distinctive; nor was it entirely positive. Aside from his assertion that the Mozarabs were the descendants of Toledan Jews, Higuera made relatively few new claims for Spanish Jews and conversos. In point of fact, Higuera's reinterpretation of early Christian history as having involved actual Jews was not as novel as Archbishop Castro—and many subsequent scholars—thought. The Toledan Jesuit was just one of several other sixteenth-century authors who drew directly or indirectly upon late medieval rabbinical traditions to write the Jews into mainstream Spanish history. For example, Higuera echoed Pedro de Alcocer in identifying the Jews, along with the Greeks, Carthaginians, and other distant ancestors of Tubal, as some of the first documented populators of the Iberian Peninsula. According to this narrative, the Spanish Jews could be traced back to a specific contingent of Hebrews who were led directly from their Babylonian captivity to the Iberian Peninsula by Pyrrhus, a nephew of King Hispanus, who was entrusted with the task by Nebuchadnezzar. Once ensconced in their new home, the Toledan Jews became particularly important, as testified by the magnificent synagogue, second only to the temple in Jerusalem; this, as Alcocer explained, effectively removed the Iberian Jews from the jurisdiction of Jerusalem.[27] Higuera pursued this notion to its logical conclusion by having Julián Pérez assert that all the Jews in the West had paid tribute to the synagogue of Toledo, not Jerusalem, in a manner that rather neatly anticipated the jurisdictional primacy the Toledan cathedral would later claim over the other Iberian sees.[28]

By the last decades of the sixteenth century, the distinct role of the Iberian Jews was familiar to learned men of Higuera's generation, thanks to Benito Arias Montano, the accomplished Hebraist and biblical scholar who in his scriptural commentaries echoed these medieval Sephardic notions about the ultimate origin of the Spanish Jews, and to Esteban de Garibay, the Basque royal chronicler who had rejected them. Arias Montano elaborated upon the historical importance of Toledo's Jewish population by tracing the origin of the city's name to a Hebrew word.[29] Thus, when Higuera asserted in the chronicle of Julián Pérez, as well as in his own *History of Toledo*, that the Iberian Peninsula was the location of the biblical realm of Tarsis, one of King Solomon's Mediterranean trading partners, he was in fact merely appropriating a late medieval rabbinical tradition.[30] Even the rather bizarre idea that Paul had written not to Jerusalem but to Spanish Jews, which so irritated Archbishop Castro, was not new with Higuera, but had already been recorded by the Latin chronicler Per Antoni Beuter (1490–1554); he in turn had culled the tale from a fourteenth-century anti-Jewish summa.[31]

Another persistent tradition given new life by Higuera was that the Iberian Jews had played no role whatsoever in the Crucifixion, and that they had explicitly disavowed the actions of their correligionists in a long letter.[32] This notion first emerged in converso and rabbinic circles in the fifteenth century, in the wake of widespread anti-converso violence in Castile. Pedro de Alcocer picked up this tradition to assert that, since the Jews had come to Spain long before the unfortunate events, "neither they, nor their ambassadors in Jerusalem," could have consented to the Crucifixion.[33] Higuera, never content to merely parrot his predecessors, produced the actual letters—three of them—in which the Jews of Toledo not only vociferously objected to the Crucifixion, but also, remarkably, evinced interest in Christianity itself. Higuera had Julián Pérez report that the letters had been discovered in his own time, when Alfonso VI of Castile first took possession of reconquered Toledo.[34] In one, a Toledan rabbi named Eleazar wrote home from Jerusalem with news of Jesus, including an account of his miracles and virtuous character. In another, the leaders of the Jerusalem community asked their Spanish counterparts to endorse their condemnation of Jesus, and to refuse entry to anybody connected with Jesus, such as charlatan missionaries. To all of this, the sensible Toledan Jews responded with a defiant request for instruction in the new faith from the apostles Peter and James (Santiago). According to Julián Pérez, Eleazar later converted to Christianity and was martyred in Lyons. By the by, Toledo's Jews also informed their correspondents that their Toledan ancestors had translated the Hebrew Bible into Greek at the behest of the Hellenistic ruler of Alexandria. Thus, from Spanish Jewry had not only emerged the very first Christians in the West, but also the Septuagint.[35]

Higuera included the text of one of Eleazar's letters in his *Toledo*; he claimed to have found the letter not in the cathedral archive—where Julián Pérez was supposed to have left it in the eleventh century—but, rather, among the papers of Pedro de Alcocer. In what could be interpreted as a disingenuous and conspicuous display of his own critical acumen—an instance of the topos of critical rejection—Higuera warned that although the letter had circulated among learned men, he was in no position to verify its trustworthiness: "Since I have not seen the original, I remit it to the reader." The Toledan archives possessed many hidden treasures, yet to be discovered: "There is an immense jungle of papers in the archive of this imperial city," and, as a complete inventory of those papers had not been completed, "its truth has not been determined."[36] In fact, as we have seen, Higuera had put great stock in the letter, both in the *History of Toledo*, where he cited it as evidence for the history of Spanish Jews, and also in the chronicle of Julián Pérez, where it appeared as one more scholarly achievement in the remarkable manuscript-hunting career of Higuera's eleventh-century Mozarabic alter ego.³⁷

Just as there was a limit to the depths of Toledo's archival fonts, there was a limit to Higuera's preferential treatment of the Jews. And thus his writings also include defamatory images of the Jews as perfidious betrayers of Christ, a motif that would have been abundantly familiar to his readers. In another letter to Pedro de Castro, Higuera noted that the Jews' refusal to convert to Christianity was the flaw for which they were rightly detested as "abominable."³⁸ In the chronicle of Dexter, we find the medieval commonplace that it was the Jews' "envy" that led to the Crucifixion.³⁹ In Julián Pérez, Higuera transmitted the tradition that the Toledan Jews were to blame for the Islamic conquest, since they had willingly opened the city gates to the North African invaders; this example of prototypically "Jewish" treachery was cited by many others, including, notably, Pedro Sarmiento, the fifteenth-century proponent of the limpieza de sangre statutes in Toledo.⁴⁰ Nor did Higuera shy away from the more inflammatory charges of blood libel, as in a 1589 letter in which he encouraged Cardinal Baronio to grant universal, Church-wide veneration to a would-be martyr, the "Holy Child of La Guardia." This small boy was supposed to have been crucified by Jews and conversos in the Toledan town of La Guardia in 1490. The resulting trials and executions resulted in the virtual elimination of the town's Jewish and converso community; the child had been venerated locally as a martyr ever since.⁴¹

THE LETTER FROM HEAVEN

That Higuera could have combined this sort of reflexive anti-Semitism with what looks to us like a relatively more tolerant attitude seems very puzzling, particularly if we are looking for a consistent attempt on his part to advocate for Jews and conversos, which, according to many modern critics, was one of his animating aims in fabricating the chronicles. Yet, in fact, it is far too simple, and anachronistic to boot, to see Higuera as a crusader for a persecuted minority to which he may have belonged. Higuera was not writing pro-Jewish or pro-converso polemic; he was collecting material for his version of Spanish sacred history, an endeavor that did have its own polemical aims, but which was also by definition cumulative, ecumenical, and, above all, messy. Higuera did repeat, and silently improve upon, several legends that depicted the Jews and their descendants in a somewhat more positive fashion. But, as in his scholarship more generally, Higuera was not consistent. He did not necessarily reconcile what might seem like contradictory positions on complex matters, including the history of Iberian Jewry, within one particular opus or across his various treatises, manuscripts, and letters.

A single document exemplifies this point. While teaching in Cuenca in 1591, Higuera found a letter in an "old book." He lent it to an acquaintance, who in turn copied the letter, along with an epistle from the legendary Prester John, into his own manuscript, now held by the Spanish Biblioteca Nacional.[42] According to its short preface, the letter had been found seven leagues outside of Ávila, at Santa María la Blanca, after having fallen from heaven. The presence of this letter among Higuera's papers discomfited the venerable scholar of Spanish history, Julio Caro Baroja, who remarked mordantly that "the man who starts with such a discovery can find anything."[43] Yet, as it turns out, this particular letter from heaven—often referred to by its Latin title, *Epistola Jesu de die dominica*—was in fact a very popular document, the most widespread of several such heavenly epistles to circulate in the Middle Ages. In one scholar's estimation, the text was "known by Christians from the coast of Malabar all the way to Iceland"; Higuera's particular recension belonged to a Provençal strain of the tradition. The text survives in Latin and all the Romance languages; it exists in both prose and verse versions, and in Greek, Armenian, Arabic, Celtic, Ethiopian, Germanic, Hungarian, Slavic, and Syriac renditions. The letter, which first surfaced in the sixth century, enjoins people to observe the Sabbath, pay tithes and first fruits, and help the needy, or face a variety of gruesome punishments. Such was the wide appeal of the epistle that it even surfaced in a Hebrew version in order to scold one particular Jewish population about its moral shortcomings.[44]

Thus, the letter from heaven was completely conventional material; that Higuera copied it was not, *pace* Caro Baroja, a particularly significant measure of his critical faculties, nor lack thereof. After all, as we have seen, the simple fact of copying an apocryphal text did not mean that one necessarily believed in it. To complicate matters further, we should note that one of Higuera's own chronicles registered an outright condemnation of this selfsame letter from heaven. We find this material in a group of letters appended to the chronicle of Luitprand, which included a letter from Licinianus, an actual sixth-century bishop of Cartagena, to Vincent, a bishop of Ibiza. Licinianus ridiculed Vincent, who apparently had read the *Epistola Jesu de die dominica* from the pulpit. The bishop of Cartagena called such letters "diabolical figments," and explained that the only written missives God had ever sent down from heaven were the Ten Commandments. Further letters had been made unnecessary by the Incarnation: Christ "did not need to send the Apostles letters from heaven" because he "filled their hearts with the Holy Spirit" instead. Licinianus pushed the analogy further to accuse those who disseminated these letters of "Judaizing." After all, if written communiqués like the *Epistola Jesu* were more characteristic of a time before Christ, then, in the post-Incarnation world, they were perilous throwbacks that would seem to "compel us to Judaize," both in their insistence upon the external observance of the law—in the Sabbath—and in their appearance as the written word, rather than as spiritual inspiration. In other words, the letters, like Judaism as a whole, privileged the law over the spirit, and thereby were a dangerous temptation for Christians.[45]

The juxtaposition of the *Epistola Jesu* with the letter from Licinianus might prompt us to ask a number of questions regarding Higuera's intentions, such as whether he too saw a Judaic threat in the *Epistola Jesu*, and whether he agreed with the supercessionist logic expressed by Licinianus. Yet this is to get ahead of ourselves by a long shot. Higuera did not forge the letter from Licinianus, just as he had not forged the letter from heaven. In fact, scholars consider this letter and four others found in the chronicle of Luitprand as authentic specimens. Licinianus's negative opinion of this epistolary genre had been echoed by others, including Charlemagne himself, who issued a 789 decree calling the *Epistola Jesu* "most false and utterly bad."[46]

As we have seen, the ecclesiastical chronicle was a genre given to accumulation, accretion, and multiplication of detail, much like a notebook or commonplace book; in such texts, one searches in vain for sustained analysis of cause and effect, coherent narrative, or indeed, internal consistency. The manuscripts into which Higuera copied these texts were part of the enterprise of his research, in which accumulation—and not the principle of careful selection—was paramount.[47] Thus, if we look for a consistent and coherent position on these heavenly epistles—or on the role of Jews and conversos in Iberian sacred history—we are bound to be confounded, just as if we attempt to discern a clear line separating false from authentic material in Higuera's writings. Higuera did not construct a coherent authorial voice, either in the texts he wrote in his own name, or in his forgeries. He was, among other things, a compiler, who never reduced his material when he could expand it, who never streamlined when he could elaborate. For this reason, Higuera presents an ambiguous record on these hot-button issues which, like the question of his limpieza de sangre, cannot be squared neatly with modern categories. This points to the complexity of Higuera's position as author, compiler, and forger. It also reminds us that Higuera, like his fellow historian Juan de Mariana, probably transcribed more than he believed.

If we envision Higuera as a collector of oral traditions and learned legends, as well as archival and epigraphic evidence, all of which he hoped to use for pious causes, the nature of his disagreements with Archbishop Castro becomes clearer. For, in spite of his interest in first-century Granada, the archbishop of Granada did not share Higuera's omnivorous appetite for historical knowledge. Pedro de Castro was concerned more narrowly with filling in the blanks of Granada's ecclesiastical history to supplant the narrative of Muslim dominance with one of Christian endurance under difficult circumstances. It is from this perspective that we might understand Castro's irritation at the suggestion that Granada's first Christians had been Jews; and it also helps explain his distinct lack of interest in news about the temple of San Tirso, to which he did not feel moved to extend the courtesy of pious affection.

THE CHRONICLES AND NEW SAINTS

Yet Higuera and Archbishop Castro did share the conviction that the newly discovered lead books should have real-world effects. For his part, the archbishop established an abbey in the martyrs' honor at Sacromonte and sponsored several scholarly projects, including translations of the plomos and the composition of new histories of Granada. Higuera seemed to have hoped that local arbiters of the sacred would likewise use his chronicles to rediscover and embrace lost and forgotten local saints. In this, too, Higuera was largely successful. This was no accident. Higuera had engineered the texts carefully by singling out preexisting traditions that were, for lack of historical detail or documentation, in danger of collapsing. He retrofitted these wobbly hagiographical structures so that they might withstand more bracing winds to come. And he performed this maneuver dozens of times in order to endow communities throughout Spain with more complete and illustrious sacred genealogies. Thus to the towns of Osuna and Utrera, in the archdiocese of Seville, he introduced eighteen hitherto-unknown martyrs from the era of Diocletian's Great Persecution. Via Dexter, he furnished Segovia with its first bishop, the aforementioned Hierotheo, a move that would greatly displease partisans of Saint Fructuosus, Segovia's *other* first bishop.[48] As we will see in chapter 6, for the Valencian Dominicans, who had discovered a small pile of anonymous relics, he fashioned one Anglina, a Diocletian-era virgin-martyr. To Tobarra la Vieja, in the Albacete region, he granted the pious Roman virgin Victoria. An earlier tradition, recorded in the revised Roman Martyrology, had it that Victoria suffered martyrdom under Dacian after having fled a betrothal to the pagan Eugenius; she then went on to attract a number of likeminded virgin followers and performed many miracles.[49] In Higuera's version of the story, which appeared in the chronicle of Luitprand, the pious virgin was, as in the Martyrology, afflicted with scruples about marriage and sacrifices to the gods, with the crucial difference that here she escaped her engagement by fleeing Rome for "a city called Turbula in Spain." There she established a convent and was subsequently martyred. As Luitprand noted, the ravages of the Moorish invasion unfortunately meant that Victoria's memory had been forgotten over time, as had the original name of the town, which, having been "corrupted by the Saracens," was now "Tovarra."[50] Remarkably, in order to bring this saint back home, as it were, Higuera took the additional step of writing directly to the parish priest of this community known today as Tobarra la Vieja, to alert him to these details, and to encourage him to adopt Victoria as the local patron saint.[51]

Higuera similarly introduced a new saint to Yepes, near Ocaña. This was made possible with the assistance of Francisco de Portocarrero, a fellow *memorialista* and Jesuit troublemaker, who upon his return from Rome to Ocaña in 1591 brought a significant haul of catacomb relics, with papal permission.[52] Among the more than eighty saints whose remains Portocarrero kept in a secure trunk in his cell in the Ocaña Jesuit residence was Percellius, whose broken skeleton seemed to suggest a rather violent death. Saint Percellius apparently already enjoyed local veneration in the town of Yepes, although his absence from the Roman Martyrology meant that he was not yet an official martyr of the universal Catholic Church. When local officials discovered that the martyr's remains were in the region, they successfully petitioned the king to grant them to the town. As Portocarrero shared his spoils, Higuera dutifully wrote Percellius into the chronicle of Luitprand as an early Christian martyr and native of Yepes, which could have made it possible for the town to argue for the antiquity and legitimacy of the cult.[53]

Matchmaking efforts such as these were made possible not only by Higuera's connections to enterprising relic-collectors such as Portocarrero; more important, perhaps, was his own knowledge of Roman-era Iberian place-names, as well as his research into local hagiographic traditions. This helps explain why he spent so much time trying to establish the correct text of the Antonine *Itinerary*: doing so gave him a rich resource with which to realign the terrain of early Christian martyrdom. Higuera did this by drawing upon the rather shaky principle of speculative etymology, in which phonetic similarities acted as historical argument. Saint Percellius, for example, surfaced in Luitprand as a native of "Hipponis," which was a plausible—although hardly certain—Latin name for the modern town of Yepes. Higuera made sure to address a possible source of confusion by preemptively identifying Percellius's native "Hipponis" as a place in the Hispanic region of Carpetania, not to be confused with its homonymic city in North Africa, the home of Saint Augustine.

Yet Higuera's most spectacular legacy would be in Arjona, in the Andalusian diocese of Jaén. Dexter's chronicle identified the town as the place where Saints

Bonosus and Maximianus had been martyred. Baronio had included the names of these two saints in the Roman Martyrology, but without any other information; in a marginal note, he recorded that their acts had been lost. In other words, all that was known was that Bonosus and Maximianus had been martyred somewhere on August 21, but not when, where, why, or how.[54] Higuera had Dexter redress this problem, albeit imperfectly: he provided the martyrs with not one, but two dates and places of death. First he included them as mid-second-century martyrs of Barcelona (*Blanes*); then, over a century later, they appeared again, in AD 308, this time as martyrs in "Urgabonae in Baetica."[55] Drawing on the Antonine *Itinerary*, sixteenth-century scholars had concluded that the latter location was Arjona. And this is precisely where the relics of Bonosus and Maximianus were subsequently unearthed, thanks in part to an attentive local reader of the chronicles, a theology professor at the University of Baeza named Francisco Háñez de Herrera, who brought the relevant passage in Dexter's chronicle to the attention of the municipal and ecclesiastical authorities in 1628.

Háñez's felicitous appraisal of the text set in motion a series of events; the participation of several hundred Arjona residents, the active intervention of the cardinal-bishop of Jaén, and a remarkable archaeological coincidence helped transform the medieval (and possibly Islamic-era) castle complex at the town's center into a holy place. Upon discovering the news that the town had been the place of death for illustrious early Christian martyrs, Arjona's secular and sacred authorities petitioned Bishop Baltasar de Moscoso y Sandoval for permission to venerate them as patron saints; after permission was granted and an August festival celebrated in their honor, Arjona's residents began to congregate at the crumbling castle at the center of town in the hopes of receiving a hint from God about where, precisely, the martyrs might be buried. According to contemporary testimony, those present experienced a variety of signs that confirmed the benevolent presence of martyrs: ghostly apparitions of Roman soldiers, bright orbs of light bobbing around the castle's many towers, the tolling of heavenly bells, and sweet, celestial aromas. Residents began to dig, both with and without episcopal approval, in a rather chaotic process; Arjona was soon rewarded for its efforts with two skulls, a pile of human bones and ashes, as well as what seemed to have been instruments of martyrdom, including nails, shackles, and fragments of a steel blade.[56] Further digging revealed an astounding number of purported relics; accumulated discoveries came to include several additional skulls, countless bone fragments, many piles of ash, and a winch that, it was believed, the Roman governor had used to drag Bonosus and Maximianus up and down the side of the castle before ultimately murdering them. Under the supervision of Friar Manuel Tamayo, head of the Granada province of Franciscans and theological consultant to the Cordoba tribunal of the Inquisition, continuing excavations uncovered new relics and artifacts into the 1630s.

In nearby Baeza, a scattering of relics, inspired by a few lines in the chronicle of Julián Pérez identifying nine martyrs of Baeza—Bishop Victor of Baeza and his companions, Alexander, Marianus, Justus, Abundius, Straton, Rufinus, Rufinianus, and Faustus—would also come to light, beginning in 1629.[57] At the same time, under Moscoso's sponsorship, construction of a new sanctuary in honor of Bonosus and Maximianus proceeded, beginning with the demolition of Arjona's old castle walls, which were replaced with a new foundation in 1635. By mid-century, thanks to the financial sponsorship of the cardinal-bishop of Jaén, it had become a proper church and sanctuary in honor of Bonosus and Maximianus.[58] The Arjona shrine became a magnet for relic-hungry pilgrims from the greater region, who in turn shared their bounty with friends, relatives, patrons, and clients. Some pilgrims came from further away, such as from the Canary Islands and northern Spain, so that by the mid-seventeenth century, Arjona's relics could be found far afield.[59]

This was particularly significant in Jaén, which even after its thirteenth-century reconquest had been an arena of endless border skirmishes between—and among—rival Christian and Islamic powers. Few traces of pre-Reconquest history existed in literary sources and, as the excavations in Arjona revealed ashes, bones, and apparent tools of torture and martyrdom, residents and pilgrims created a new history and geography, mapping a local sacred topography through their devotions. With the help of the cardinal-bishop, who sponsored research, excavations, publications, and new liturgical offices in honor of dozens of saints discovered to have had a connection with Jaén, the local sense of religious history was transformed. The public cult to the Arjona relics would still face significant obstacles, as we shall see in chapter 8. Yet, when one beholds the enthusiastic public veneration of the saints that these discoveries prompted in the diocese of Jaén, one cannot help but imagine that this is precisely what Higuera had in mind.

As we have seen, Higuera's interests were not limited to his own local *patria* of Toledo, but encompassed a territory coterminous with that of Hapsburg Spain, which also included Portugal during the union of the crowns from 1588 to 1640. Even in his universal perspective, Higuera did not neglect the particular. This is exemplified not only by his concerted efforts to document, resurrect, and glorify Toledo's past, but also by his generous sprinkling of new or forgotten saints, martyrs, bishops, and church councils into all corners of the Iberian Peninsula through the cronicones. In this sense, Higuera seemed to be drawing more on the old Roman sense of "Hispania" than early modern ideas of a nascent Spanish nation or empire based on dynastic claims.[60] It is worth noting that Higuera, unlike some of his contemporaries within and outside the Society of Jesus, did not see much value in Spain's other possessions in the Americas, Europe, or Asia. It is the Hispanic, peninsular context that we need to keep in mind when reading the chronicles. And, as I have argued, we must resist the temptation to see them as solely one thing or another; they were not solely a product of Higuera's preoccupations with Toledo, nor with the Jews and conversos, nor only with Spain itself. If anything, Higuera's ambitions for the chronicles seemed to encompass much more than his own beloved religious traditions — beyond the primacy of the Toledan see, the antiquity of Toledan Mozarabs and conversos, and beyond, even, the *venida de Santiago* — if the texts' proximate effects throughout Spain in the following years are any indication.

5

THE DEBUT OF THE CHRONICLES: HIGUERA'S REPUBLIC OF SACRED LETTERS

In September 1611, Father Jerónimo Román de la Higuera lay dying. Thanks to the seventeenth-century Jesuit historian who described Higuera's last days in a history of the *collegium* of Alcalá de Henares, we can conjure the scene: our protagonist, a now-feeble seventy-four-year-old man, was receiving visitors at his deathbed, and those in attendance, probably fellow residents of the Jesuit house, asked the learned and pious priest to commend their souls to the care of the saints once he crossed over into the other world. Although this was a customary request from the living to the moribund in premodern Europe, it was particularly appropriate in this case, since, as the historian reminds us,

> [Father Higuera's] entire object of study was the lives of Saints, with a particular inclination and devotion toward giving information about those who were not so well known in Spain. To [these saints] he affectionately entrusted himself, as he recognized on various occasions he had himself received singular favors from them. And he kept them very much in the forefront of his mind in the last days of his life.

Yet apparently Higuera could be an insufferable pedant, even in his reduced state, and so:

> When he was barely able to speak, and those who were present were naming saints to which he might recommend them [in heaven], he corrected them on the saints' names, and told them about others which they did not know.[1]

Higuera's visitors were treated to what we can imagine was a characteristically prolix and exacting lesson from this lifelong teacher and scholar, a man whose encyclopedic knowledge of Spanish history and hagiography remained intact even at death's door, where he summoned his waning breath to expound upon the lives, deeds, and memory of Spain's many forgotten saints.

While the contemporary Jesuit historian probably intended the story to serve as a pious remembrance of a fallen brother for his Jesuit readers, this remarkable moment, in which a feeble, hoarse Higuera enjoined those who surrounded him to recall obscure martyrs and saints down to the correct rendering of their names, is a rather fitting distillation of Higuera's methods, motivations, and aims. Here we can see that for Higuera the remembrance of the saints was an urgent necessity, a heroic task in which personal devotion, scholarly punctiliousness, and a concern for the next generation were intertwined. Even as he focused on distinctly Iberian concerns, Higuera remained alert to contemporary debates about the evolving shape of history, hagiography, and liturgy among his fellow Spanish interpreters of the sacred past as well as between them and their Roman counterparts. Just as he did on his deathbed, so too during his life did Higuera encourage those around him—in physical proximity or in textual community—to remember the saints. In this, as we shall see, Higuera seems to have had a higher good in mind, one that answered to the deeper moral callings of Catholic piety.

Yet this mise-en-scène of Higuera as the dedicated yet lonely hagiographer on a quixotic quest to revive the memory of the saints has its limits as a metaphor for his life and work. For, as it turns out, even if Higuera was the architect of the cronicones, he was far from being their lone author. We have seen that his coauthors included Eusebius and Jerome as well as Prosper of Aquitaine, Lucas de Tuy, and Rodrigo Ximénez de Rada. His unwitting collaborators were not limited to the long-deceased chroniclers whose works he pillaged and repurposed. As Higuera's own Jesuit superiors complained, he had a persistent predilection for communicating with third parties beyond the walls of the collegium. If this tendency irritated his higher-ups in the Society, it is also what connected Higuera with a broader community that transcended his religious order as well as the borders of Castile; these connections with fellow enthusiasts of the sacred past will complete our understanding of the origins of the cronicones.

We find in Higuera's papers many saints, images, and pious traditions that had escaped the notice of more prominent historians and hagiographers, and which Higuera was able to accumulate thanks to his correspondents. By looking more closely at the texture of these connections, we will be able to see the fine ligaments binding the false chronicles to other, less familiar sources of historical and hagiographic information. As this and the following chapter will suggest, the role of Higuera's friends, acquaintances, and other learned correspondents in providing historical information, apocryphal and otherwise, makes his chronicles a record of scholarly collaboration and correspondence, and not simply the record of one man's overheated religious imagination. The importance of a broader Republic of Sacred Letters for the false chronicles—and for early modern Spanish historical scholarship—has gone virtually unnoticed, as scholars have preferred to ask how Higuera's texts dovetailed with his own interests or how his version of sacred history echoed peculiarly Spanish religio-political concerns.[2] In fact, Higuera's learned networks help reveal his methods and sources; they also point toward Higuera's own understanding of what he was doing, and why.

ORIGINS

The chronicles had their gradual and tentative debut in the last years of the sixteenth century and early years of the seventeenth, as Higuera began to share brief excerpts from the four texts with his learned acquaintances, even as he continued to revise and expand the texts in light of his own interests and those of his correspondents. If, as we have already seen, like many other forgers past and present, Higuera endeavored to insert his texts "neatly into the ordered ranks of other sources, real, fake, and ambiguous, which readers may be expected to know," we have not yet witnessed how Higuera resolved the problem of lending his texts a plausible tale of origin.[3] Higuera was drawing upon the chronicles of Prosper and Hydatius at the same time, and in the very same place, that they were being discovered, corrected, and published, often for the first time, by men with whom he enjoyed significant personal and occupational connections. In this context, Higuera could scarcely afford to be careless. If they were to win acceptance among his more exacting peers, the cronicones would need to occupy a recognizable place among authoritative and traditional texts. Yet we have also seen that Higuera was not always a disciplined storyteller, and that the multiplication of contradictory detail that characterized the texts themselves sometimes also complicated the stories surrounding them. The effect could be disorienting, as we see in the contradictory stories that arose to explain the texts' origins. Like other *inventores* such as Annius of Viterbo (or, in a very different time and place, Joseph Smith), Higuera claimed to have received his texts from a mysterious contact who, by the time the chronicles emerged, could no longer be found. Somewhat unexpectedly, readers of the cronicones contributed to the intrigue by attesting to other, parallel copies that seemed to antedate the Fulda recension, and the texts soon accumulated alibis, afterlives, and backstories independent of Higuera himself.

We can reconstruct this early history thanks to the first citations of the chronicles around 1600 by several of Higuera's contacts, including Cardinal Juan Salazar, the Spanish Jesuit Gabriel Vázquez, the royal chronicler Prudencio de

Sandoval, and Bishop Sancho Dávila Toledo. These early adopters introduced the chronicles as pivotal evidence in a number of treatises on controversial historico-religious themes, which also helped cloak the texts in respectability. These appearances helped foment interest in Higuera's chronicles for several years before he allowed full copies of the texts to enter circulation in manuscript. Conscious or not, Higuera's strategy of initially sharing only fragments of the cronicones, and only with trusted correspondents, not only helped stoke demand, but also built up vested interest on the part of proponents—such as Prudencio de Sandoval or the canons of Zaragoza's church of El Pilar—in defending the texts' authenticity. This guaranteed that the cronicones would outlive Higuera himself, and, after he died, finally see their way into print.

From about 1605 until well into the 1620s, manuscript copies of the texts of widely varying quality began to circulate among the interested. The chronicles came with an impressive pedigree that helped many readers overlook their many serious flaws. As the Franciscan Juan de Calderón would explain in a preface to his 1619 edition of Dexter-Maximus, he prepared the text by consulting "an old codex" in the monastic library of Fulda that had been sent to Higuera ("a most diligent hunter of ancient matters") by Thomas Torralba (1554–1595), a Jesuit and one of Higuera's former pupils in grammar in the Society's Ocaña collegium.[4] Little is known about Torralba, a native of Ocaña, except that he had gone to Germany as a layman in the 1570s as part of the retinue of the Spanish ambassador to the Holy Roman Emperor, entered the Society of Jesus in 1574, and went on to serve in various leadership roles, including procurator and consultor, in Czech, Hungarian, and Slovakian houses. At the time that he was supposed to have sent Higuera the texts from Fulda, Torralba was serving among the Jesuits in central and eastern Europe. Yet, by the time Torralba's name began to be mentioned in the origin accounts of the cronicones, he had been dead for a good six years.[5]

The sudden appearance of "impressive books" with "mysterious but impressive origin stories" is, as Anthony Grafton reminds us, just one of the many tactics employed by forgers ever since antiquity. By linking newly discovered texts with a venerable repository such as Fulda, Higuera, like other forgers, created the illusion that "what might seem an individual's free invention had in fact been preserved for uninterrupted centuries in an inviolable archive."[6] Yet while the Fulda story furnished the chronicles with a distant yet prestigious origin, it also possessed the distinct disadvantage of being confirmable, and therefore rebuttable. This would become clear later in the seventeenth century, as the texts' more diligent and well-connected readers would try, and fail, to track down the purported original manuscripts in Fulda, or anywhere else. Perhaps for this reason, in the years around 1600, the early adopters of the chronicles tergiversated and claimed the texts had also been preserved in other manuscript collections in Spain and elsewhere. Francisco de Portocarrero was the first to print rumors about parallel manuscript traditions. In the foreword to his 1616 treatise on the miraculous appearance of the Virgin Mary to Saint Ildefonso in Toledo, Portocarrero piled on textual alibis for the chronicles and echoed the Fulda story by affirming that he had seen the very letter in which Torralba told Higuera of his discovery. In case this was not enough, Portocarrero testified to other codices that, it was implied, predated the Fulda exemplars. These included a manuscript formerly held by the Hieronymite monastery of Santa María de La Sisla outside Toledo, which was later obtained by the Toledan humanist Juan de Vergara (1492–1557). This copy was no longer extant, Portocarrero explained, as Vergara's papers had been scattered after his death. Portocarrero also claimed to have seen, among the papers of the scholarly bishop Antonio Agustín, a copy of the chronicle of Julián Pérez that was old (and presumably authentic) enough to have borne the annotations of the late medieval courtier and chronicler Fray Juan Gil de Zamora. Finally, Portocarrero recounted a variant of the Fulda story, according to which Torralba had not actually copied the text in Fulda, but procured a copy from a merchant in Worms who had obtained it on good authority from the famed repository.[7] Other authors would later attest to other rumors, such as one that placed a copy of Dexter in the manuscript collection of a fourteenth-century bishop of Jaén or, even more tantalizing, among the papers of the venerable Vercelli library in northern Italy, home to an international collection of medieval manuscripts.[8]

HIGUERA'S INTELLECTUAL MILIEU

Higuera was working within an identifiable intellectual sphere, and he fashioned his texts in accordance with what he perceived as the norms and practices of historical scholarship. Thanks to these connections—and, of course, through his Jesuit education—Higuera was heir to many of the best practices of Renaissance philological scholarship. This is not to say that his interpretation of the past was not idiosyncratic. It was. Yet in terms of personal connections as well as scholarly approach, Higuera was in the same universe as some of the most assiduous students of Spanish history in the late sixteenth century, with access to one of the richest repositories of historical documents in Spain, not to mention indirect contact with Jesuits further afield engaged in similar research, such as the intellectual heirs of Peter Canisius at the University of Ingolstadt.[9] Like many of his peers, Higuera was participating in a project just as important to Spanish intellectual and cultural life as the better-known endeavors of contemporaries Juan de Mariana and Antonio Agustín: namely, finding, correcting, and publishing historical sources, itself part of the broader attention to original sources in scholarly research characteristic of the early modern period.

In this context, in which archival spelunking went hand-in-hand with historical and philological scholarship, it was not implausible to scholars of Higuera's generation that long-lost historical texts were as yet undiscovered. During Higuera's lifetime his peers in Toledo, including Juan de Mariana and García de Loaysa Girón, engaged in an ultimately unsuccessful effort to collect, correct, and publish all of Isidore of Seville's scattered works.[10] At the same time, lesser-known historical sources emerged from obscurity, such as the chronicles of Hydatius, Victor of Tunnuna, and John of Biclarum. In these efforts, Mariana and Loaysa Girón were joined by André Schott and Higuera's friend and colleague Juan Bautista Pérez (1537–1597), the bishop of Segorbe. Pérez, an avid collector of manuscripts, shared Higuera's interest in uncovering sources of early Spanish ecclesiastical history; their activities overlapped in Toledo in the 1570s and 1580s. The bishop's highly placed connections, as well as his knowledge of Arabic, Greek, and Hebrew, made him a scholar of a superior order to the rather less distinguished Higuera. As the Latin secretary to the cardinal-archbishop of Toledo, Gaspar de Quiroga, Pérez served the cathedral in various capacities, including as canon and librarian. In this way, Pérez gained direct and intimate acquaintance with a number of important manuscript collections and with some of the most learned men of the time; for example, in Antonio Agustín's effort to collate surviving manuscripts of Spanish ecclesiastical councils with their published versions in the 1570s, the antiquarian-bishop contacted Pérez in Toledo.[11]

In handling the fundamental texts of ecclesiastical history in Toledo's collection, Pérez collected and emended several sources for the history of Visigothic and Muslim Iberia. One of his manuscripts, which survived long enough to be inventoried in the nineteenth century, enables us to glimpse the nature of his collecting and scholarly methods. Among the two dozen works copied into the manuscript, which modern scholars have dubbed the Segorbe Codex, were an undated Latin vita of the "Seven Apostles" (*los Siete Varones Apostólicos*), the legendary first bishops of Spain, as well as the hitherto-lost chronicles of Victor of Tunnuna and John of Biclarum.[12] The Segorbe Codex not only reveals that Pérez was one of the first to uncover lost and important sources for Spanish history, but it also enables us to witness Higuera's colleague in the process of employing recognizably modern philological methods to collate and emend his manuscript. For example, he drew on three separate exemplars to prepare his corrected version of Victor of Tunnuna and John of Biclarum's chronicles and, in the margins, made a note of alternate readings and emendations. Such was the integrity of Pérez's labors that his corrected manuscript formed the basis for what were, until recently, the only modern editions of these two chronicles.[13] Pérez left the Segorbe Codex and other texts in the cathedral library of Toledo when he left to occupy the Valencian see of Segorbe in 1591.[14] A quick look at the subsequent fate of the codex after Pérez left Toledo reveals the extent to which this relatively unknown figure helped shape scholarly inquiry in his immediate environs and beyond. A few years later, André Schott dusted off the Segorbe Codex in order to prepare an edition of the chronicles of Victor of Tunnuna and John of Biclarum. At the same time, he also sent a manuscript copy to a contact named Markus Weber, who in turn made copies for the Calvinist polymath Joseph Scaliger, an eager collector of early chronicles due to his interest in historical chronology.[15] Schott also sent the texts to Ingolstadt, where Henry Canisius, a learned canon lawyer and nephew of Peter Canisius, would use them to prepare the first printed edition of the chronicles of Victor of Tunnuna and John of Biclarum in 1600.[16] Schott drew upon Pérez's codex as the basis for his own edition of the two chronicles, which appeared in his *Hispania illustrata* (1603–1608).[17]

The fortunes of the Segorbe Codex confirm that through Pérez and in the Toledan cathedral library itself, Higuera had access to important bundles of historical texts at a time when they were still unknown to most early modern readers. In this milieu, the task of discerning authentic from interpolated material was central. Here again, Higuera was quite typical of his age in that he possessed a selective sensitivity that enabled him—like most of his contemporaries—to be a savage critic at one moment and to sanction seemingly apocryphal sources the next. In this, he was also a good student of Ambrosio de Morales.

HIGUERA AND MORALES

Like any other self-respecting ecclesiastical historian of the time, Higuera learned how to approach texts with the new, more rigorous reading strategies pioneered by humanistic critics in the Renaissance, such as Lorenzo Valla and Erasmus of Rotterdam, and emulated by peers such as Juan Bautista Pérez. These techniques including a heightened sensitivity to anachronism in language, style, and detail; careful attention to possible corruptions of the text in manuscript, particularly due to sloppy copyists; and the ability to correct a text's language in light of possible variant readings in the context of the document and its times.[18] Higuera was also conversant in the emerging norms of antiquarian scholarship, which had evolved as a parallel to the textual humanism of Valla or Erasmus. In Spain, this strand of scholarship was most fully developed by Ambrosio de Morales, whose two-volume *Antiquities of the Cities of Spain* formed an essential guide for any serious student of ancient Spanish history in Higuera's time and beyond. Morales, who served as royal chronicler under Philip II, is best known for his *General Chronicle of Spain*, which was a continuation of the chronicle written by Florián Ocampo, Charles V's chronicler. Ocampo had intended to write the history of Spain from ancient times to the present, but only reached the arrival of the Romans. Morales picked up the thread in the late third century before Christ, while eschewing some of the more apocryphal elements that had led many to criticize Ocampo, including the latter's inclusion of many of the legendary monarchs that Annius da Viterbo had recorded in his pseudo-Berosian texts. Morales's critical stance and masterful treatment made *La coronica general de España* an obligatory reference for anybody writing on the history of Spain for centuries. His relatively indulgent treatment of a number of legendary elements in Spanish religious history provided an influential template for Higuera. Morales, like Higuera after him, adduced local liturgical traditions and the evidence of local relic cults in order to buttress the historicity of Santiago and his Seven Apostles, as well as other early figures such as Pedro of Braga and Hierotheo.[19]

Yet for Higuera—and his subsequent readers in the seventeenth century—Morales's survey of antiquities, *Las antigüedades de las ciudades de España*, was perhaps even more influential. Morales intended the *Antigüedades* (1575) to be a companion piece to the chronicle, and, in fact, the books were often bound together. While the aim of the latter text was to narrate the great events of Roman and Gothic Spain, the *Antigüedades* was written without the tug of a chronological narrative. Like other contemporary European treatises on antiquities, Morales's volume was meant to convey information for its own sake: in this case, to establish the names and locations of the ancient places discussed in the *Coronica*. In the preface, Morales explained that this aim necessitated a very different sort of argument, which, he admitted, also would require prolixity. Since "our Spaniards really want to know" not only the names and locations of ancient cities, but also the complete line of reasoning and evidence leading to the conclusions, "it was necessary not to fold it into the rest, but rather to reserve it for this space, where it can be dealt at great length freely and without fear of any impediment."[20]

Yet while the *Antigüedades* did address these questions with frightening exhaustiveness, it was not merely a catalogue. It was also intended as an exemplar of antiquarian method. As Morales explained, he hoped it would become a guide for Spanish antiquarians, who had been deprived by "certain Italians" of their great knowledge about antiquities, which they "have always kept to themselves, and refused to share with everybody publicly."[21] To help remedy this situation, to bring this knowledge to the Spanish audience—and, in the process, incidentally highlight his own intellectual versatility and diligence—Morales opened the book with an introductory "General Discourse on the Antiquities of Spain," a methodological treatise on the sources upon which the study of antiquities rests, and an explanation of how to interpret ancient inscriptions. Whereas many antiquarians were known for collecting coins and inscriptions for the sake of illuminating ancient customs, Morales was most interested in locating and identifying the modern location of ancient Roman settlements. In the "Discourse," he outlined the principal sources of "antiquities" that would aid in this effort, divided into thirteen overlapping categories, including archaeological, textual, and oral sources. The list merits some examination, for it essentially served as a how-to manual for Higuera's generation and for the local ecclesiastical historians of the seventeenth century and beyond who would form the principal audience for his cronicones.

When looking for an ancient place, Morales began, the first important sources of information were "signs and traces of antiquity," such as ancient receptacles, pottery shards, coins, statues, foundations, and stones that might hint at an ancient settlement. He noted that coins and inscriptions were especially important as remnants of antiquity. Ptolemy's list of places according to latitude and longitude could also be extremely helpful in correlating ancient and modern places, except for the unfortunate fact that modern copies of his work had been corrupted by errors of copying and translation. Morales also gave pride of place to the *Itinerary* of Antoninus Pius, a manuscript list of routes used by soldiers and Roman officials, with places and distances along the way, which like Ptolemy's text was still being revised and corrected by Morales and his peers according to the principles of philological criticism; as we have seen, these efforts continued into Higuera's day and beyond. Other Greek and Latin geographers, such as Pliny, Strabo, and Pomponius Mela, also provided specific locations. The works of Greek, Latin, and some Spanish historians, as well as classical poets such as Martial and Prudentius, could also be scanned for passing references to places. Among textual authorities, Morales also included Spanish church councils and the lives and legends of saints, especially readings (*lectiones*) from the Roman Breviary. He also pointed to modern place-names as historical sources, noting that an ancient name could sometimes be inferred, especially if the name had not changed much. Morales deemed the "authority of credible people" to be useful; in contrast, popular opinion (*comun opinion* [sic]) could be valuable only if it was "in line with reason," or else it could prove useless.[22]

Some of these categories were better developed than others; for example, the reader who looked forward to learning about Morales's approach to "ancient coins, or medals" would be disappointed, for Morales had virtually nothing to say on the topic and he included no coins in the body of his text. Yet his discussion of inscriptions in the "Discourse" reads like a student workbook. Morales explained that Roman monuments came in four major forms: sarcophagi (*cippos*), mile markers, altar stones, and dedications. He cited numerous examples of each type of monument and explained how to interpret them in what could have been practice exercises. The hypothetical student-reader might have followed along as Morales sketched the monument and transcribed the inscription—expanding the abbreviations and filling in lacunae—then translated it into Castilian and discussed its significance.

In his approach to inscriptions as primarily sources of historical data and not as aesthetic or romantic objects, Morales reflected an emerging consensus in the latter half of the sixteenth century among antiquarian scholars.[23] Yet Morales made no claims to absolute certainty. It might seem somewhat surprising that the author of the paradigmatic collection of Spanish antiquities, which remained the standard reference for centuries until members of the Royal Academy of History began their own surveys in the eighteenth century, claimed no monopoly on the truth of his claims. Like Higuera after him, as well as many authors of local sacred histories in the following century, Morales acknowledged that identifications of ancient names and places were notoriously difficult to prove. In this, he could only offer the most plausible readings:

> Nobody should expect that I have the material to prove what I say with firm and authoritative reasons that would provide complete certainty, and ascertain the truth entirely. Rather, if I am able to offer good conjectures that make what I say seem probable, that is a lot. Because in this subject one cannot go any further than demonstrating that something is verisimilar and probable, since none of the reasons that can be offered can do more than provide some good probability.[24]

In admitting the immense uncertainty and difficulty involved in addressing questions so remote in time, Morales seemed to be leaving the door open for precisely the sort of reinterpretations and challenges to which his text would be subjected by later readers, including Higuera and his peers, who seemed to have looked to the *Antigüedades* both as a methodological treatise to be emulated and as an encyclopedia to be plundered—and assessed critically when in the wrong.

HIGUERA THE CRITIC

Morales himself had studied the works of many cutting-edge Italian antiquarians of the sixteenth century, and, as his reader, Higuera became an unwitting heir to the methodological insights of these figures. These included, for example, the prevailing wisdom among late sixteenth-century historians that numismatic and epigraphic evidence was comparable—or even superior—to narrative or documentary sources. In this sense, Higuera was completely "modern." This led him, on occasion, to disparage certain scholarly techniques as antiquated or specious. For example, in his manuscript history of Toledo, Higuera dismissed as ridiculous the arguments of those—such as Benito Arias Montano and Esteban de Garibay—who traced the name of the Toledan village of Escalona back to a homonym in Hebrew, "Ascalon," in spite of the fact that he often used this same type of specious etymology for his own aims, as we have seen.[25] In a rejoinder that might well have been lifted directly from the pages of Agustín's *Dialogues on Medals, Inscriptions, and Other Antiquities*—a benchmark of critical numismatics and epigraphic studies—Higuera countered that "written documents, inscriptions, and coins are good witnesses, since they reveal the locations of ancient settlements better than the nonsense of the similarities of words."[26] Yet there were no Hebrew inscriptions or Roman coins in Escalona, nor did written documents help. Higuera himself unearthed evidence in the archives: a royal privilege from Alfonso VI of Castile attested that the Escalona area was unpopulated in the eleventh century. When Toledo was reconquered, the village did not yet exist, so it could not have existed in biblical times.[27]

In light of his posthumous reputation, it might seem ironic that Higuera of all people would challenge a source that perhaps under different circumstances, he probably would have used to adorn the ornate hagiographical embroidery of the false chronicles with yet another new saint. Yet attacking the reliability of another scholar's sources was part and parcel of early modern intellectual exchange, and who better to detect a fabrication than one so intimately familiar with the sources himself? We see Higuera's rather ambiguous place in these scholarly social networks through his correspondence with other erudite gentlemen, such as Jerónimo Blancas (d. 1590), the royal chronicler of Aragon. As Higuera prepared the edition of the Antonine *Itinerary* that General Acquaviva later refused to let him print, the Toledan canon Antonio de Covarrubias put Higuera into contact with Blancas. This was logical, since Blancas was well acquainted with the *Itinerary*: he had used the Roman list of mile markers to identify many ancient place-names in his extensive *Commentary* on the *Annals of the Crown of Aragon*, written by his predecessor as Aragonese chronicler, Jerónimo Zurita. Like Higuera, Blancas had an omnivorous historical imagination and produced a monumental amount of work on a variety of topics, including a history of the bishops of Zaragoza, a defense of Santiago, and a number of treatises on the pageantry, protocol, and history of the Aragonese monarchy. In his works, much like Higuera, Blancas preferred the edifying story over the more mundane truth; as such, he cited legendary monarchs to give Aragon a historical origin independent of neighboring Navarre, and allegedly fabricated a set of medieval legal privileges (*fueros*) in order to grant the office of the Justicia de Aragón a suitably ancient origin.[28]

Remarkably, however, Higuera evinced a distinctly critical perspective in his correspondence with Blancas, showing that he could be a tough critic when he wanted to be. In a 1589 letter, after the customary praise of his correspondent's learning and intelligence, Higuera quizzed Blancas closely about a discrepancy between their respective interpretations of the *Itinerary*. Higuera (and Florián Ocampo before him) reckoned that the place that Antoninus Pius referred to as "Calagurrus Julia Nasica" was probably the city called "Naja" by the Romans, but Blancas identified it as Loharre, in Aragon (modern scholars reckon that "Calagurrus" is modern Calahorra). This was an important question, since the late antique poet Prudentius was believed to have been born in Calagurrus. Higuera entreated Blancas to reveal the evidence that led him to this decision, including, for example, inscriptions.[29]

More pointedly, Higuera inquired about a peculiar document that Blancas had adduced in support of this position in his *Commentaries* on Zurita; this was a canonical letter from the monastery of San Pedro de Taberna (sometimes spelled Tabernas), in the Ribagorza region of Aragon. Higuera challenged its veracity, or at least its integrity, by pointing out a fundamental chronological error: the letter recorded the martyrdom of Saints Nunilo and Alodia shortly after the Moorish invasion of 711. Yet other, more established sources, such as a well-known document from the archives of the Navarran monastery of Leyre, where the martyrs' relics were kept, dated their death over a century later, to the mid-ninth century. In response to this challenge, Blancas rather weakly retorted that Higuera's opinion about the identity of the city of Naja was novel, and therefore wrong; thus, there was no reason to privilege it over the more venerable and verifiable documents to which Blancas had access.[30] Yet modern critics concur with Higuera (and his source, Ambrosio de Morales) in considering the San Pedro canonical letter a forgery, although they do not agree on the culprit, identified variously as either the monks of San Pedro de Taberna, who wanted to counter a rival monastery's claim to the relic of Saint Pedro's arm, or Blancas himself.[31]

Due to Higuera's notoriety as a forger, this selective ability to demonstrate critical acumen has gone almost entirely unnoticed. Nor do most scholars realize that among his papers and even in the chronicles themselves, Higuera preserved many authentic historical texts that he inevitably encountered in the course of his meticulous research in the rich fonts of the Toledan library, or obtained through his correspondence. A recent study of the sixty inscriptions that appear in Higuera's unpublished ecclesiastical history of Spain concludes that fewer than half—approximately twenty-four—were false, and that of those forgeries, only four could be attributed to Higuera with any certainty.[32] In other words, Higuera preserved more authentic inscriptions than forgeries. Admittedly, his renditions contained misreadings, faulty transcriptions, and other minor distortions, but the inscriptions themselves, it seems, were genuine. In contrast, absolutely none of the inscriptions that the fifteenth-century humanist and antiquarian Cyriac of Ancona recorded for the Iberian Peninsula were authentic, according to a recent assessment of his mixed legacy for Spanish antiquities.[33]

Higuera's epigraphic acumen was sharp. His rendering of architectural details was so accurate that modern archaeologists have been able to draw on his sketches in order to locate most of his inscriptions in situ and compare them with modern renditions. In several instances, Higuera was the first and only person to record the inscription until the modern age, when scholars were able to verify his transcriptions. In one case—a cluster of Roman inscriptions from the Extremaduran municipality of Ibahernando—Higuera's information represents "the oldest systematic epigraphic record."[34]

What makes Higuera's transcriptions of documents or inscriptions such a complicated matter, however, is his tendency to silently improve the texts through inspired misreadings or other editorial interventions. Where modern scholars have been able to identify the discrepancies between the actual inscription and Higuera's version, it has often emerged that the Jesuit tampered with the names, in particular, to make them sound more Roman; in one case, he changed a Gothic-sounding patronym into a more patently Latin one.[35] We see the same principle at work in another authentic source, an anonymous chronicle of the Benedictine monastery of Sahagún, which the enterprising Jesuit attempted to improve, as was his wont, by furnishing it with an author dubbed "Alberto."[36]

Higuera's efforts have made it difficult for scholars to sort out the authentic from the spurious. The hall-of-mirrors effect is multiplied when we turn from Higuera's autograph manuscripts to the false chronicles themselves, into which he also copied authentic sources. As we have seen, the 1640 edition of Luitprand included eight letters from early medieval Spanish church fathers, five of which modern scholars consider to have been transcribed from authentic sources, albeit with several misreadings.[37] Higuera also transcribed important and seemingly authentic documents from the archive of his alma mater, Toledo's University of Santa Catalina, regarding the late fifteenth-century condemnation of the *maestrescuela* of the Toledo cathedral—a relative of the royal secretary Hernán Álvarez de Toledo—by the Inquisition. "Had Higuera not recorded these facts," mused one recent scholar, "we would know nothing of them today since most of the original Inquisition records [of Toledo] have been lost."[38] Further scrutiny of the false chronicles, as well as of Higuera's voluminous manuscripts, will doubtlessly reveal more problematic yet promising scholarly treasures.

EARLY MODERN SOURCE CRITICISM

In sorting through the sources he was gathering, the critical assessment of sources was essential, and, of Higuera's peers, few were as well practiced, nimble, and uncompromising in this task as Juan Bautista Pérez. This is probably why Higuera sent the earliest version of Dexter-Maximus to his friend circa 1594–1595. As we know, the bishop of Segorbe dismissed the text out of hand, just as he had the plomos and the letter from San Tirso. For this formidable scholar and discerning reader — a historically minded critic attuned to anachronism and a philologically aware reader sensitive to textual error and contradictions — it was rather simple. These newly discovered texts were, like the forgeries of Annius of Viterbo, discredited by their own deep historical and philological flaws.[39]

Although Pérez's critique of the chronicles has not survived, we can reconstruct its contours from summaries by later authors, such as Gaspar de Escolano. They included the objection that "Flavius Lucius Dexter" was not one individual, but rather two separate men with the patronym Dexter fused into one.[40] It was impossible that the Dexter mentioned by Jerome could really have been the author of the text, since the real Dexter would never have gotten the name of his father's predecessor as bishop of Barcelona wrong, as had Higuera's pseudo-Dexter. The texts contained serious errors of chronology, as when Santiago was recorded as consecrating bishops in Spain in AD 45, by which time he had already died. Finally, the texts contained many mistaken names and dates for the prelates of Toledo.[41]

Pérez's critique is usually cited as the death blow to this shorter, preliminary version of Dexter-Maximus. In the estimation of José Godoy Alcántara, "Higuera understood that it was critically wounded, and he abstained from giving anybody else a copy."[42] Wounded by the accusation that the texts were fake, and afraid of being unmasked as the forger, Higuera retreated, licked his wounds, and spent the next four years improving the texts, biding his time until his old friend died in 1598, at which time he revised and relaunched them. Yet in discussions of this supposedly pivotal moment for the chronicles, the most egregious omission has been the broader context of historical and philological critique in which Pérez's comments were offered. The sharing of new textual discoveries was part and parcel of the conventions that governed scholarly communication in early modern Europe.⁴³ It is in this context that we can best understand Higuera's desire to share the texts with Pérez in the first place. In light of his rather well-known endeavors to correct medieval manuscripts, it seems unlikely that Higuera would have expected him not to critique the texts. After all, Pérez's critique of Dexter-Maximus was part of a broader discourse in which authenticity and inauthenticity were tightly bound to each other, in a textual universe in which one was not necessarily surprised to encounter spurious material intercalated with the authentic. It was simply a step in the process of philologically informed scholarship to separate the two, or, when this was not completely possible or desirable, to record one's reservations for the use of future scholars.

This is precisely what Pérez himself had done. While copying Isidore's *History of the Goths, Vandals, and Sueves* into the Segorbe Codex, Pérez had become aware of a significant corruption in the text's prologue, known as the *Dedicatio ad Sisenandum* after its dedicatee, King Sisnandus. Thanks to his collation with other manuscripts, Pérez identified the prologue, which traced "Hispania" back to Noah's grandson, the eponymous King Hispanus, as a later interpolation because the prologue was not attested in earlier manuscripts; in this, incidentally, modern scholars have concurred with Pérez.⁴⁴ Pérez was intimately acquainted with the occupational hazards that the corrector of medieval manuscripts would confront. A careful reader would need to discern corruptions, misattributions, and falsifications, remaining alert to the possibility that the authenticity of the manuscript may not be airtight. He knew, too, that the sources for Spanish history were shaky, and that the earlier the source, the more likely it would contain a significant interpolation or other serious flaw. In the end, Pérez did not tear up the *Dedicatio ad Sisenandum* and discard it; rather, he preserved it in his collection of historically significant texts, but with the requisite cautionary notes for readers who would encounter the manuscript after him.⁴⁵

Perhaps these exacting standards are what prompted Higuera to consult Pérez in the first place. Either way, Higuera arguably would have expected Pérez to submit Dexter-Maximus to the same careful textual, philological, and historical critiques that he had brought to his other scholarly endeavors. In this context, it seems quite unlikely that Pérez would have concluded that Higuera had forged the texts outright. Pérez was aware that becoming the unwitting transmitter of a flawed or forged manuscript was simply one of many pitfalls that awaited a collector of manuscripts. When he declared that the manuscript of Dexter-Maximus was "fake," and that he could prove it with "a hundred arguments," Pérez was not suggesting that Higuera was the perpetrator, but, rather, that he had received a flawed copy that medieval hands had confected. And he may have been suggesting that Higuera had simply failed to perform philological due diligence, and passed along a text that, based on his expertise, he should have been able to discern as false. After all, from Pérez's perspective, what separated the conscientious philologist from his somewhat less scrupulous friend was the willingness to disregard spurious material, such as the *Dedicatio ad Sisenandum*, even if it proved useful or appealing. Nonetheless, we know that Pérez continued to hold Higuera in good will, and that their intellectual relationship continued. In his last will and testament of 1597, Pérez left Higuera a thick volume of information on the lives of the early archbishops of Toledo, "because he is writing about this topic, and it will benefit him greatly."[46]

HIGUERA'S REPUBLIC OF LETTERS

The interactions of these Iberian men of sacred letters were conducted according to the norms familiar from recent scholarship on the Republic of Letters, which, as Anne Goldgar has noted for a later period, was a "community of obligation," in which an ethic of cooperation induced participants to engage in "reciprocal service."[47] This included, for example, the collegial practice of bringing one's own learned acquaintances into contact with each other through letters of introduction.[48] These polite norms and his own extended epistolary network enabled Higuera, like many other members of the Republic of Letters, to conduct much of his research via proxy; even when away from Toledo, Higuera was able to importune his friends, such as the chaplain of the papal nuncio or the librarian Cristóbal Palomares, to procure documents for him.[49]

Yet Higuera's community was not quite the idyllic, egalitarian, or interconfessional Republic of Letters that many scholars, following Jürgen Habermas, have identified as a precursor to modernity, an emerging public sphere that would cross religious and territorial boundaries to become an important site of public debate in the modern era, particularly in anglophone and francophone Europe. Higuera's circles did not constitute a progressive, urbane, and mobile community of scholars. Nor was it, as in seventeenth-century England, a realm of civic antiquaries, where barristers, notaries, and country clerks communicated about antiquities, heraldry, and genealogy.[50] Rather, this was a mostly ecclesiastical community, an informal association, whose aims were not the disinterested exchange of ideas, but, instead, the sharing of texts and information that would help illuminate Iberian antiquities and history for fellow Catholic scholars in Hapsburg territories.[51] In this sense, Higuera was a member of one of those "local communities of savants" that dotted the intellectual landscape of early modern Europe whose interests and labors presaged the "antlike industry" of ecclesiastical antiquarians of the later seventeenth century.[52]

Thanks to Higuera's surviving papers, as well as references within his own texts, the broad outlines of this intellectual community can be discerned, as can approximately sixty of his correspondents. In addition to high-level clerics, such as the archbishop of Granada, Pedro de Castro y Quiñones, and Prudencio de Sandoval, the cousin of Philip III's royal favorite, the Duke of Lerma, many more correspondents are conspicuous for their lack of distinction: these included local parish priests, some fellow Jesuits, as well as other miscellaneous clerics, such as the cathedral canons who must have furnished Higuera with the list of information regarding the benefices and bells of Toledo's cathedral.[53] More far-flung contacts with whom Higuera exchanged texts and information included Gaspar Álvares de Lousada Machado (1554–1634) and his employer, the archbishop of Braga, Fray Agostinho de Jesus; Bartolomé Andrés de Olivenza, the Jesuit provincial of Sardinia; Vicente Justiniano Antist, the prior of the Dominican monastery of Valencia; Doctor Don Luis de Castilla, the Toledan archdean and cathedral canon; and Don Pedro González de Acevedo, the bishop of Plasencia.[54]

The letters include scant personal information and instead focus on quite narrow questions of historical and hagiographic interest. For example, in response to a request, one Antonio Sánchez sent Higuera a copy of the letter from the sixth-century Saint Toribius of Astorga condemning the reading of apocryphal scriptures, with little by way of personal comment.[55] A notable exception was the brief lament that the priest Juan Amador de Don Diego appended to his 1586 report on the antiquities of Cazorla, in the mountains outside Jaén. Amador bemoaned the fact that he had already been in exile from Toledo for three months, and specified the ways that Higuera might help him gain his return, specifically, by appealing to a highly placed cleric in Toledo, whose ear, he hoped, Higuera might bend.[56] Another rare detail about real-life circumstances and relationships appeared at the end of a 1600 letter from the Seville Jesuit Juan de Soria. After having discussed various ancient place-names in Roman Britannia, the defense of Spain's patron saint, Santiago, and a handful of obscure saints, Soria wrapped up his letter with a friendly nudge: Higuera should finish his works-in-progress soon, because, as Soria heard, another author—Don Fernando de Mendoza— had already been working on an ecclesiastical history of Spain for five years, and "I would not want somebody else to be first."[57]

Higuera was a voluble correspondent who shared documents, inscriptions, and exhaustive commentary with his friends and received the same in return. He and his interlocutors debated questions of historical and hagiographic import, usually with a singular focus on matters of linguistic, chronological, or philological detail. Higuera's considerations of various questions occupy several hundred folios, including, for example, more than seventy densely written pages on the primacy of the Toledan see; thoughts on the precise year in which Saint Hermenegild died; and a long consideration of "The Two Saint Millans and Three Columbas" and of the two saints by the name of Syncletice.[58] One regular correspondent, the antiquarian bishop of Plasencia, Don Pedro González de Acevedo (1534–1609), sent Higuera several genuine inscriptions from the region, which the Jesuit duly copied into the histories he was writing under his own name.[59] A canon in Tarragona, who Higuera characterized as a "person of much learning and goodness," sent an inscription that ended up in Higuera's manuscript *History of Toledo*.[60] A Baeza physician sent a text regarding Saint Pedro de Baeza, and still other correspondents forwarded detailed narratives regarding the history, geography, and religious devotions of a variety of locales, ranging from Burgos in the north, Cádiz in the south, Valencia in the east, and, nearly thirteen hundred miles to the southwest, Tenerife in the Canary Islands; much of this Higuera used to enrich the false chronicles.[61] If Higuera relied on his contacts to share their discoveries with him, he also drew upon their specialized linguistic expertise to help in his own research. While the Jesuit professor could read and write Greek and Hebrew, he did not know Arabic, and so he asked his contacts to decipher Islamic-era inscriptions that he encountered in his research.[62] These contacts included the royal interpreter Diego de Urrea, the Granadan morisco Alonso de Castillo, and the morisco Jesuit Ignacio de las Casas, all of whom had helped translate the lead books of Granada at various points in time, and one of whom—Castillo—may have helped forge them.[63]

As we have seen, Higuera drew upon his intimate knowledge of Spanish antiquities and historical texts to replicate the form, function, and content of authentic chronicles. By fulfilling contemporary expectations about how forgotten historical texts might have reappeared after centuries of oblivion, as well as how such texts might look and what they should contain, the false chronicles gained acceptance among many learned readers. Yet if they had merely been a pastiche of authentic sources and if Higuera had limited himself to echoing familiar themes of Spanish sacred history, his texts would not have exerted such enduring and pervasive influence on the religious and intellectual landscape in early modern Spain. Rather, the texts themselves seem to have functioned for their readers much as other apocryphal texts did: just as the New Testament apocrypha filled in gaps in the account of the life of Jesus in the synoptic Gospels, the cronicones supplied lively detail to fill in blank or foggy areas of the Roman and Visigothic past in Spain. At a time when learned interpreters did not agree on which books and traditions were apocryphal, nor about the relative historical and theological value of those texts, the latitudinarian end of the scale was represented by scholars such as Higuera (and arguably Morales), who admitted texts, even those of uncertain authorship, for the information they could provide about the past.[64] This helps explain how, in spite of their many flaws, the chronicles came to be regarded as useful sources of historical information in the late sixteenth and seventeenth centuries. In this sense, Higuera worked in the interstices between what we would call medieval and modern views of history, and created a vision of the past that would prove alternately appealing and vexing for his readers.

6

IN DEFENSE OF LOCAL SAINTS: HIGUERA VERSUS ROME

We can trace the reciprocal relationship between Higuera and his interlocutors in the example of Anglina, a new saint Higuera created for Valencia. In 1588, the friars of Saint Dominic in Valencia discovered what seemed to be a long-hidden reliquary. Workers renovating an old funerary chapel came across a tiny box in the hollow of a wall that contained several bones, a small cloth, and a powdery, spice-like substance. Since the box was decorated with what looked like a scene of martyrdom and was accompanied by a small slip of paper bearing the word "Anglina," the logical conclusion was that it contained the relics of a martyr of the same name. As the monastery's prior, Vicente Justiniano Antist, related in his short Latin treatise, *On the Discovery of the Holy Body of Saint Anglina, Martyr*, upon surveying the monastery's most elderly friars, he was able to determine that there had been a cult to a martyr named Anglina long ago, but his informants could offer little additional information about her identity or the subsequent ebbing of her cult. And while Antist was too discreet to mention this, the saint presented a rather serious problem for her would-be hagiographer: she did not appear in the official Roman Martyrology, nor in previous historical martyrologies.[1] This led Antist to issue an appeal:

> Therefore, again and again I beseech and implore each of those learned men who might find his way to this narrative, that whatever material about the life, martyrdom, and translation of the body of this martyr that he may come upon in the books that he reads, please send it to us, the sooner the better. For his assistance, he will receive a great prize from God.[2]

Like any conscientious scholar, Antist—the author of several works of scholastic theology and hagiography—also wrote directly to those better informed than he, among them Jerónimo Román de la Higuera.³ Father Higuera was happy to oblige in the search for information about the mysterious Anglina, but perhaps not exactly in the manner that Antist had anticipated. The Toledan Jesuit must have encountered the same documentary void as Antist, and yet Higuera was not one to suffer such difficulties idly. From Antist's mention of a long-forgotten cult among Saint Dominic's elderly friars, Higuera fashioned a more fully articulated—and yet verisimilar—historical and hagiographic construction. He quickly set to fabricating the information that Antist had been seeking, drawing upon his own knowledge of Catholic historical, hagiographic, and liturgical traditions in order to reverse-engineer "Anglina from Valencia" into existence. This he achieved by writing the saint into the chronicles attributed to Luitprand and Julián Pérez; in the latter, for example, Anglina was memorialized in the third century:

> At this time was the martyrdom in Edetanis in Valencia of Saint Anglina, and of her female companions in martyrdom, who, due to their confession of the Faith, triumphed in a virile manner; the annual celebration of these martyrs in Valencia is on October 21.⁴

Thus, from a box of bones and wispy memories, thanks to a few pen strokes, Anglina became one of the multitudes of martyrs put to death during the Great Persecution of Diocletian and an established martyr of Valencia.

It is unlikely that Antist ever had the chance to appreciate Higuera's efforts on his behalf; he died in 1595, before the false chronicles entered wide circulation. Yet Higuera's maneuvers proved decisive, and his chronicles would become the baseline for further elaboration upon Anglina's vita in the centuries thereafter, as they would be for so many other new and reinvented saints. After his texts entered print in the first decades of the seventeenth century, one reader of the chronicle of Julián Pérez—the aspiring hagiographer Pedro de San Cecilio, a Mercedarian friar of Valencia—discovered the information Higuera had placed there, which he took to be new and important information about Anglina. And so several decades after Antist's entreaty for information, the Valencia Dominicans finally received a response in the form of San Cecilio's letter, into which he dutifully copied lines from Higuera's chronicles about Anglina; the new prior of Saint Dominic sent thanks for this "happy news" about the monastery's resident virgin-martyr.⁵ The seeds planted by Higuera continued to sprout new tendrils in successive decades through the exertions of the chronicles' more enthusiastic readers, some of whom even went so far as to further elaborate on Higuera's forgeries with new ones of their own. In the 1660s, an enterprising Benedictine monk named Gregorio de Argaíz included Anglina in two of his false chronicles, which he characterized as continuations of Higuera's chronicle of Marcus Maximus. Here Anglina was further embroidered, such that her anonymous female co-martyrs became nuns, and Anglina herself, the formidable abbess of an entire Carmelite convent.[6] In this guise she was remembered well into the nineteenth century, as one of the saints whose relics were held by the Valencian Dominicans, and, by Carmelites, as one of many "glories" of the order.[7]

Anglina the Carmelite abbess, the fourth-century martyr, and longtime denizen of Saint Dominic, was confected in large part through the correspondence between Antist and Higuera; in this, Anglina is not an isolated example. As we have seen, Higuera's own deep familiarity with authentic historical, hagiographic, and liturgical sources enabled him to transform information about local religious traditions into something resembling historical fact in the false chronicles. Indeed, Higuera's correspondence was crucial to this work. As a regular correspondent of several dozen fellow learned men with whom he found common cause in an enthusiasm for ancient texts and artifacts, Higuera was connected through historical, philological, and protoarchaeological debate and conversations to a sort of Republic of Sacred Letters. Higuera's friends and contacts, such as Prior Antist in Valencia, became virtual coauthors, collaborators in the forgery, sometimes unwitting, and maybe sometimes not. Higuera's extensive correspondence with these relatively obscure clerics helps explain the astounding level of local detail for places throughout Spain in the false chronicles. It also reveals a little-known regional dimension to historical and hagiographic research in this period, which is better known for the efforts of Roman worthies such as Cardinal Baronio and his collaborators to collect information about Catholic traditions from their counterparts throughout western Europe, and for the pioneering efforts of Heribert Rosweyde and his Bollandist successors to collect and publish a comprehensive record of the saints' acts and passions.[8]

Higuera focused on hyperlocal saints and holy traditions, not merely in order to embroider hagiographic fantasies for his friends and contacts, but also as part of an attempt to counter the increasingly critical manner in which the sources and narratives of the sacred past were being evaluated and reshaped by the late sixteenth- and early seventeenth-century Roman reformers. Higuera's texts appeared at a pivotal moment when antiquarian and philological erudition was being put to the service of Tridentine reform. In Rome, Cardinal Baronio and others were rewriting Catholic liturgy, history, and hagiography, and, in the process, effectively encouraging the efflorescence of sacred history as a genre, as regional scholars responded to their enquiries in kind.[9] Like many of his counterparts in Italy, Higuera wrote in dialogue—part real, part imagined—with Baronio, as we will see in a remarkable and little-noticed document, a 1589 letter from Higuera to the Roman reformer himself, in which, just as in the false chronicles, Higuera simultaneously emulated and countered Baronian visions of the sacred past. By seeing the letter and the chronicles as part of this broader Counter-Reformation context, Higuera's motives and methods will become more clear, as will the larger question of the chronicles' enduring presence in Iberian *historiae sacrae*.

BARONIO AND THE REFORM OF THE SACRED PAST

The interpretation of the past was of intense importance for early modern European scholars of all confessional stripes, thanks in part to the religious controversies of the sixteenth century, in which history was an important polemical weapon. As Protestants attempted to claim the mantle of the apostles by tracing a continuous chain of witnesses to the truth, they were countered by Catholic scholars, most notably Cardinal Baronio, in his magisterial and detailed *Annales ecclesiastici*. Historical research of this sort was also an important dimension of reform within the Roman Church, as was the case with the less familiar but equally important scholarly endeavors undertaken by Baronio, Cardinal Robert Bellarmine, and other members of the Sacred Congregation of Rites in the late sixteenth and early seventeenth centuries. As part of the comprehensive liturgical reform that Pius V initiated in the 1560s and 1570s—which would continue under successive popes well into the seventeenth century—single, Roman versions were created of texts that previously existed in a multiplicity of forms. Thus, local variations in the breviary, martyrology, and missal, which with their prescribed readings and calendar of the feasts of saints and martyrs structured the cultic calendar, were now suppressed unless they could demonstrate that they had been in uninterrupted use for two hundred years. Local breviaries were replaced with the standard Roman version, such as the revised Roman Breviary of 1568, which was to determine the shape of the liturgical year and the remembrance of saints and martyrs on a universal level.[10]

In the process, the hagiographic readings of the revised Roman Breviary were reduced in number, as was the level of anecdotal detail. In the revised readings, the saints appeared as exemplars of virtue and piety, moving away from the more idiosyncratic depictions characteristic of medieval hagiography and apocrypha. In order to render internally consistent the liturgical readings devoted to saints and make them historically accurate and theologically appropriate, revisers often expunged questionable or apocryphal material, corrected errors of fact or chronology, and, on occasion, incorporated information from non-Roman liturgical texts, such as breviaries from elsewhere in Italy and beyond. To achieve this higher standard for the Martyrology, Roman scholars struggled to reconcile the often contradictory accounts of the place, date, and manner of the martyrs' deaths given in their principal sources, such as the late antique and medieval Latin martyrologies of Bede, Ado, and Usuard.[11] The end result was that many saints were eliminated from the revised Roman Martyrology altogether, excluded by default, as their local liturgical observations were effectively done away with by the imposition of the new Roman liturgical books. In revising these central texts of Catholic liturgy, reformers were making a direct impact on the cult of saints, and, by extension, upon local history and identity. Before the late medieval and Counter-Reformation papacy reformed and centralized the canonization of saints, the making of saints was a much more local and informal process; for many centuries, a regional reputation for sanctity was enough to secure one's place in the local pantheon. With the centralization and reform of the liturgical books in the decades after Trent, however, many of these local saints were doomed to oblivion, at least on the official level of ecclesiastical observance.

The fear of losing a beloved saint to the reformers' knife was to haunt many partisans of local saints throughout Catholic Europe. As in Italy, so, too, in Spain, the cults of small-scale, obscure saints, venerated only in particular communities and not by the national or universal Church, were most seriously jeopardized by Roman reforms.[12] Unless a saint attained the level of universal commemoration by the entire Church, the arrival of the new Roman Breviary in the 1570s meant the suppression of the *officia propria*, the liturgical readings dedicated to that particular saint on their feast day, which were often printed separately from the Breviary by individual dioceses or religious congregations. The papal bull that preceded the 1568 revised Breviary requiring two hundred years of continuous observance was to become a formidable challenge to the individual cult of saints who enjoyed merely local or regional fame. And it was, for this reason, absolutely central in shaping, and possibly even inspiring, Higuera's hagiographic research and forgeries.

Yet if Baronio rejected many traditions, in the estimation of the most discerning philological minds of the seventeenth century, his revisions were not nearly as complete as they could have been. Baronio's critics included Isaac Casaubon and Joseph Scaliger, who lambasted the cardinal for what they believed was an overly indulgent stance on apocryphal traditions.[13] And at least one seventeenth-century critic accused him of having added rather too many saints to the Martyrology.[14] Baronio's unwillingness to excise legendary overgrowth is exemplified in the Martyrology's treatment of Dionysius the Areopagite. Although Lorenzo Valla and other humanist critics in the fifteenth and sixteenth centuries challenged the conflation of the biblical Dionysius with both Saint Denis of France and the pseudonymous author of the group of late antique and Neoplatonic texts known as the Dionysian corpus, Baronio retained the composite figure of Denis-Dionysius as a Parisian martyr and Neoplatonic author in the revised Martyrology.[15] While some regarded Baronio as insufficiently rigorous on these and other questions, he was widely despised in Spain for having wielded his critical knife rather too liberally, as when he attacked the Spanish Hapsburgs' claims to Sicily in volume eleven of the *Annales*, which led King Philip III to ban the tome in 1605.[16] Yet there was little room in Baronio's scheme for regional or national patriotisms; rather, he aimed to adopt a universal perspective removed from local interests. In the *Annales*, for example, in reference to the Milanese church's claims that it possessed apostolic origins, Baronio stated frostily, "tracing the history of single churches is not our concern."[17]

Particularly galling for those of Higuera's generation was the 1602 edition of the Roman Breviary, which characterized the apostle Santiago's evangelization of Iberia as a provincial tradition. Spanish readers reacted as if the apostolic mission had been demoted from fact to fiction. Anxiety was stirred up even before the Breviary was published; in a 1595 letter to Archbishop Castro, Higuera fretted about the attacks of "foreigners" on Santiago, and five years later he sent a defense of the historicity of the apostle's Spanish mission to Baronio.[18] Once the Breviary was printed, proponents all the way up to the king were disappointed and outraged. Baronio and his collaborator Bellarmine omitted the qualification in subsequent editions, although this was hardly relevant to many wounded Spanish partisans, who continued to publish refutations of Baronio for decades afterward.[19]

Cardinal Bellarmine had anticipated the dangers that an excessively rigorous approach to revising the Roman liturgical books would pose, and he recognized that this would need to be moderated by taking into account the importance of long-standing tradition as well. To this end, Bellarmine developed a number of guidelines for revisions that would respect scripture and tradition, while also heeding the more stringent criteria of early modern philological and historical scholarship. As Simon Ditchfield explains, Bellarmine otherwise envisioned "drastic consequences," including "the near emptying of the [Martyrology] and the correspondingly drastic reduction of the *Proprium sanctorum* in the [Breviary]."[20] This is precisely what the Discalced Carmelite historian Francisco de Santa María (1567–1649) believed that Baronio had already done, as he mused angrily in a now-lost manuscript history of Arjona. Santa María, who had been named historian of his order in 1625, noted that Baronio at first added many new saints to the Martyrology, but then, in successive editions, he removed more than he added. "In the month of January alone," Santa María estimated, were 138 erstwhile saints who, "along with many companions, had been dislodged" from their rightful places among the holy. The Spanish Carmelite compared Cardinal Baronio to an unscrupulous, eviction-happy landlord: "The liberty [that he took] seems all the worse to me, because to knock a saint out of the place and tenancy that he already possessed in the Church raises qualms."[21]

Santa María was not alone in his sense of bereavement and outrage over Baronio's perceived predations on the territory of Hispanic sanctity. Yet he does seem to have represented the far end of a spectrum, at least in terms of his willingness to air such complaints publicly and repeatedly, in spite of inquisitorial censure. This was made clear in the debacle surrounding Santa María's 1630 *General Prophetic History of the Order of Our Lady of the Carmen*, which he wrote in his capacity as the official chronicler of the Discalced Carmelites. Here Santa María claimed that the prophet Elias, whom Carmelites regarded as the founder of their order, had been "more holy" than the apostles. He also implicitly challenged the Church's authority by asserting that the order had been established directly by God (*de iure divino*).[22] At a time when Protestant claims made the Roman Church sensitive about apparent attempts to circumvent papal authority, this was not a wise move, and inquisitors were unamused. In response to inquisitorial censure, the work was reissued in 1641 with several changes: the phrase *de iure divino* disappeared, and Elias became "*as* holy as the apostles," not "more."[23] Yet Santa María was obstinate. In a 1643 *Defense of the First Volume of the General Prophetic History*, ostensibly written to demonstrate that he was in conformity with the Inquisition's objections, incredibly, Santa María again asserted that Elias was "more holy" than the apostles.[24]

Another thorn in Santa María's side was that Baronio had stripped Bishop John of Jerusalem of his traditional title of saint. After all, according to Carmelite lore, John of Jerusalem gave a monastic Rule to the hermits living in Mount Carmel, thereby endowing the Carmelites with their first institutional shape. Thus, when Santa María referred to John as a "saint" in the 1630 edition of the *General History*, it was a deliberate provocation. He knew Baronio's position already. This is made clear in another passage from the lost history of Arjona, where Santa María grumbled:

> I am not surprised that he stripped John of Jerusalem of the title of "Saint"—which he always held until Baronio. After all, he also took the honor away from so many other Saints who used to be in the Martyrologies.[25]

In the 1643 *Defense*, Santa María again backed down in appearance only, probably in response to inquisitorial objections. He amended his previous opinion, admitting that he had been wrong to call John of Jerusalem a saint. Yet he doubled back, postulating wishfully that if only Baronio had been able to read his text he would have changed his mind about John and let him retain the title of saint. After all, as Santa María noted, he was not the only person to find fault with Baronio. In his epitome and continuation of the *Annales*, Henricus Spondanus expressed a similar sentiment, noting that if Baronio had seen what Spanish scholars had written in Santiago's defense he might have decided to maintain his initial opinion that Santiago had come to Spain.[26]

Santa María might have been alone in the virulence and bluntness of his attack of Baronio, but he was far from alone in chafing at the seemingly corrosive effect of Baronio's historically minded revisions. In an undated and unsigned letter, Vicente Antist—the same Dominican who had discovered Anglina's relics—reflected upon one of Baronio's evictions: "It's true that, as an Italian, this author has taken this saint away from us through a frivolous and obvious evasion." To make matters worse, Antist noted, Baronio had denied that several saints were Spanish, including Hierotheo, Damasus, and Lorenzo. But "what bothers me the most is that he reduces the business of the coming of Santiago to Spain to a mere tradition, and I've seen more than a hundred witnesses to it, and some of them are from more than a thousand years ago." In the end, the Valencian Dominican attributed Baronio's maneuvers to Italian jealousy of Spanish holy treasures.[27]

These angry and patriotic reactions to Baronio's relatively minor revisions are less familiar to scholars than the more notorious hubbub that arose due to the 1602 Breviary's treatment of Santiago, led, notably, by the crown. Yet these objections were arguably just as important, for they reflect a deep anxiety that liturgical reform would usher in a widescale displacement of legitimate and long-term—albeit underdocumented—saints from their rightful quarters. Between 1591 and 1594, the Jesuit Juan de Soria wrote three punctilious letters to Baronio in which he detailed several errors and omissions, including a number of saints and pious traditions which, according to Soria, had been left out of the revised Roman Martyrology without good reason. Soria, who served as a preacher in Seville and Granada, shared Higuera's preoccupation with the perceived narrowing of the halls of holiness. "Why, truly," he asked Baronio, "are there not enumerated in the holy records several [saints] whose holiness is attested by everybody?"[28] Among the Iberian saints who, he felt, had been neglected in the shortsighted revisions were the child-martyr of La Guardia, whose 1490 murder had prompted the widescale persecution of the Jewish and converso community in that Toledan town, and more long-standing figures such as Spain's Seven Apostles, the Mozarabic child-martyr Pelagius of Cordoba, and Acisclo, Victoria, and Zoilo, whose relics had been discovered in Cordoba in 1575. As Soria noted bitingly, the cardinal would have found plentiful evidence for the holiness of many of these saints in the chronicle of Ambrosio de Morales, had he bothered to consult it.[29]

BARONIO VERSUS SPAIN

This less familiar aspect of Spanish reactions to Baronio is evident in Higuera's own texts, which seem to have been engineered precisely in order to counter many of these reforms. And while scholars have recently argued that the introduction of liturgical reform was not a simple top-down process, and that the Breviary and Martyrology, for example, were living texts, shaped through ongoing conversations between individual churches and Rome, this was certainly not how matters looked from Spain. It is true that the representatives of many dioceses, particularly in Italy, wrote to the cardinals of the newly established Sacred Congregation of Rites after 1588 to petition for permission to maintain their local liturgical observances, and that, contrary to the rather drastic fears expressed by Spanish partisans, Roman revisers retained most pious traditions while only excising the more dubious from the Martyrology and Breviary. If Baronian revisions sometimes fell short of the standards of his toughest critics, they provoked a rather different reaction among regional clerics. As the reformers applied the higher critical standards evolving in learned European circles to local cultic texts and histories, scholars such as Pietro Maria de Campi, in the Italian see of Piacenza, responded in kind and attempted to demonstrate that their particular visions of the sacred past—and of their own religious traditions—possessed the requisite antiquity increasingly required by the universal Church. In this reciprocal—albeit unequal—process, which Simon Ditchfield has characterized as the universalizing of the particular and the particularizing of the universal, Spain was at a distinct disadvantage. Relatively little evidence existed to support many traditions about the first centuries of Iberian Christianity, such as the *venida de Santiago* and the apostle's appointment of the Seven Apostles of Spain. This situation had not necessarily improved, even with the efforts of Renaissance-era scholars, including Lucius Marineus Siculus, Pere Antoni Beuter, and Johannes Vasaeus, to chronicle the early saints and bishops of Roman Hispania. In their efforts to more fully elucidate the opaque early history of Iberian Christianity, sixteenth-century authors ended up integrating into their historical treatments many legends that formerly existed only in nonhistorical sources, such as liturgical and hagiographic texts.[30]

Higuera, like Bellarmine and Francisco de Santa María, sensed the danger implicit in the Roman revisions, and his chronicles are in many ways an extended effort to fasten jeopardized saints' cults to the bedrock of history. While many dioceses and religious orders were able to retain their officia propria, many other local liturgical traditions simply did not possess documentation of continuity for the required two hundred years, and their saints disappeared in the new Roman liturgical and martyrological texts.³¹ This could happen for a variety of reasons: some may have enjoyed a robust and well-documented public cult that had nonetheless declined of late; others may only have been recorded in an obscure liturgical manuscript languishing in an uncatalogued monastic library or cathedral archive. Some were, in fact, named in the revised Roman Martyrology, but with a different, non-Iberian place of birth or death; others were merely listed by name, without any specific biographical indicators to link them to Spain or Portugal; still others, such as the child-martyr of La Guardia, were not in the Martyrology at all, and so were unrecognized by the Church Universal.

Higuera was abetted in his effort to rescue these saints by the remarkable privilege granted to Iberian churches by Pope Gregory XIII in his 1573 brief, entitled *Pastoralis officii*, which stipulated that a saint not included in the Roman Breviary could still be commemorated with an officium proprium if he were a native or patron saint of the diocese, or if his body, or "notable" relics thereof, rested in the diocese.³² This remarkable privilege, which awaits its historian, seems likely to have been a product of Spanish dominance of the papacy in the late sixteenth century.³³ The loophole proved of immense interest to Higuera, who seems to have combed through local breviaries from throughout the Iberian Peninsula—but particularly in Castile—in search of saints whose officia propria might be saved, thanks to the terms of *Pastoralis officii*. Higuera apparently hoped that his efforts would in many cases prompt the faithful to grant these saints the devotion they demanded and deserved. As we have seen, however, if saints were commemorated merely on a local level, then the survival (or rebirth) of their cults—specifically, their officia propria—would depend upon Roman recognition of the tradition.

PRESERVING LOCAL SAINTS

In the second half of the sixteenth century, the dilemma of Church rejection confronted the Castilian city of Sigüenza, which claimed to have possessed the relics of Saint Liberata since the fourteenth century. Sigüenza's difficulties arose in 1568, when the publication of the new Roman Breviary effectively suppressed the medieval officium in the saint's honor, at least until the cathedral chapter could prove that her cult dated back at least two hundred years.³⁴ Higuera intervened in the midst of a decades-long effort on the part of Sigüenza's civic and religious authorities to rescue Liberata's officium. A cluster of mid-sixteenth-century hagiographical texts regarding Liberata and the 1569 translation of a rib-bone from Sigüenza to her native Bubáguena suggest that local advocates were attempting to renew and document the history of the cult in the wake of its suspension.[35] In an anonymous midcentury pamphlet, *The Life and Martyrdom of the Fortunate Saint Liberata*, the outlines of her life and death were recounted with a wealth of colorful detail, just as she had been depicted in the medieval officium, as one of the female nonuplets born to the wife of the ruler of Lusitania. Out of shame, as the story went, the queen ordered her midwife to have the newborns drowned, because nine offspring was "monstrous, even in pigs or other animals," let alone in a woman of high birth. The sympathetic Christian midwife took pity on the infants and raised them as her own. All nine emulated their foster mother's piety and continence; as a result, they were all ultimately beheaded due to their refusal to recant their faith.[36]

Higuera selected elements from this traditional version of Liberata with other threads regarding a separate virgin-martyr named Wilgefort to link the two, both in the false chronicles and in his correspondence with Baronio himself. In a 1589 letter, five years before the first draft of the false chronicles, Higuera wrote to Baronio about Liberata and four other saints who, he believed, had been unjustly neglected in the recent Martyrology. Higuera urged Baronio and his fellow "grave and learned men" to restore or alter the entries on these martyrs that, he believed, were mistaken in the text's most recent recension. In addition to Liberata were Constantine's daughter Constantia (also known as Constance), who Higuera believed should be remembered not merely as a pious virgin, but also as a martyr; Obdulia, who, Higuera argued, was one of Ursula's eleven thousand companions in martyrdom (known by two other homonymic names, Oddilia and Ottilia), whose relics were held by Toledo; Seculina, an obscure Ávilan martyr whose liturgical office Higuera found in a parchment breviary in Ávila; and, finally, the child-martyr Christopher, the alleged victim of ritual murder at the hands of the Jewish community of La Guardia in 1490.

Higuera's most ingenious and influential efforts, in the letter and beyond, were on behalf of Liberata, linking her to the martyr Saint Wilgefort.[37] The two were commemorated on separate days as different saints, Liberata on January 18 as a virgin from Como (Italy), and Wilgefort on July 20 as a Portuguese martyr (known in French as Ontcommer, in German as Ontcommera) who, "for the love of chastity and the Christian faith," had been crucified.[38] In the Roman Martyrology, Baronio had declined to include a number of colorful details about Wilgefort, such as the legend that in answer to her prayers asking that she be made unattractive to repel the fiancé to whom she was promised, she grew a beard; this is how she was depicted in many late medieval northern European visual representations, as a bearded, crucified woman, with a fiddler—a poor devotee—at her feet.[39]

Higuera reminded Baronio that according to tradition, Liberata was the daughter of a Portuguese ruler who was descended from the Roman imperial line. Higuera also alerted Baronio that Liberata's relics were kept in a magnificent mausoleum "honored with the frequent reverence of the faithful"—in other words, that her cult in Sigüenza was active and continuous. Although Higuera juxtaposed this Liberata—and not the one from Como, who was already in the text—with Wilgefort, he made no mention whatsoever of the would-be suitor, the beard, the fiddler, or any other elements of the Wilgefort tradition.[40] Higuera was not one to leave matters to chance, and so he also wrote the composite figure of Liberata-Wilgefort into his chronicles. The chronicles of Dexter and Julián Pérez commemorated "Wilgefort, or Liberata, daughter of the Portuguese King Catellius," as one of nine sisters who all resisted marriage and died as martyrs. She was not only beheaded, as in the Liberata tradition, but for good measure, crucified as well, like Wilgefort. Higuera wisely omitted the unseemly detail about the beard, possibly cognizant that it was precisely the sort of risible anecdote that reformers were suppressing in their revisions. Instead, he displaced the beard onto yet another saint, Paula of Ávila, also known as "Barbata," who was mentioned by Gregory of Tours and other medieval authors.[41]

It was not Higuera's innovation to link Liberata with Wilgefort; the Flemish theologian Johannes Molanus equated them in his 1568 edition of Usuard's martyrology, although he reversed his position in subsequent editions.[42] Yet Higuera's efforts were the most influential, probably because they came at a crucial moment when historical evidence for the antiquity of Liberata's cult was desperately needed in Sigüenza. In the early 1600s, the cathedral and municipal councils of Sigüenza appealed to the Congregation of Rites for approval of the medieval officium. The first petition was denied in 1605. The adjudicating cardinal explained that the liturgical readings submitted by Sigüenza on Liberata's behalf "seemed apocryphal."[43] In response, Sigüenza revised and shortened the officium and, for the first time, merged her with Wilgefort. This second petition was unsatisfactory to Cardinal Bellarmine, who noted in his 1621 denial that the two saints were not commemorated on the same day in the Martyrology. Nor, Bellarmine pointed out correctly, did any liturgical or historical document seem to contain any information whatsoever about the specifics of Liberata's life and death. Since the acts of martyrdom were not preserved, all that was certain was that she was a nonuplet, born to gentiles, and was crucified in Lusitania—when this happened, or who had instructed her in the faith, was unknown.[44]

Baronio was similarly unpersuaded by Higuera's entreaties, and in the 1597

Martyrology the entries for Liberata, Wilgefort, and Obdulia remained the same. Nor did Baronio deign to add any of the other missing martyrs that Higuera signaled in his letter to the ranks of martyrs of the universal Church. Yet, in the long run, Higuera's efforts on behalf of Liberata were successful. In 1625, Sigüenza submitted a third petition for the officium proprium, now enriched with details from the false chronicles. The petitioners also sent Prudencio de Sandoval's 1610 treatise on the history of Tuy, which followed Higuera's account of the nine sisters.[45] The Congregation of Rites approved the petition, and the new *officium cum octava* bearing the name of both saints and describing Liberata as crucified—like Wilgefort—was printed the next year. After having voted down similar proposals on at least three previous occasions, Sigüenza's cathedral chapter also moved her feast day from her customary day in January to Wilgefort's day, July 20.[46]

Future research will be necessary to clarify whether Higuera's texts were decisive, or whether the Congregation of 1625 was well disposed to the third petition for the officium proprium for other reasons, such as the replacement of Cardinal Bellarmine, who died in 1621, with a former papal legate to Spain.[47] Regardless, Liberata was thereafter intertwined with Wilgefort, in Sigüenza and elsewhere. The prophylactic beard was not mentioned in the new office; nor did it appear in Liberata's chapel in Sigüenza, which was renovated in 1694.[48] Yet it sprouted in other visual representations, beginning with the first and only edition of Julián Pérez's chronicle, prepared by the royal courtier Lorenzo Ramírez de Prado and printed in Paris in 1628. The text's *Adversaria* included an engraving of a bearded, crucified "St. Wilgefort, alias Liberata, who the Belgians . . . call Ontcommera," with a fiddler at her feet, just as in the parallel medieval northern European iconography of Wilgefort. This was not an isolated case, for, as Ramírez indicated in a handwritten note below the image in one copy of the text, he had beheld similar images in Madrid and Zaragoza while traveling with the royal court.[49]

Higuera was so successful in linking Liberata-the-Iberian-nonuplet to Wilgefort-the-bearded-virgin-martyr that in the eighteenth century, after his texts were revealed to have been forgeries, the beneficiaries of his efforts were put in an awkward position, hard-pressed to find verification that their beloved local cults did not rely upon the historical testimony of Higuera's texts. This is what prompted the dean of Sigüenza's cathedral, Diego Eugenio González Chantos y Ullauri, to write an 1806 *Vindication* in which he argued strenuously—and sometimes speciously—for the great antiquity of Liberata's cult.[50] For one modern bishop, the associations with the false chronicles seemed insuperable, and so he simply changed Sigüenza's patron saint to the Virgin Mary in 1962. Yet the bishop's decision was opposed by the cathedral chapter, whose members successfully reversed it in 1967.[51]

This is just one example of how Higuera intervened in local cultic politics through his writings, which he seems to have composed while keeping one eye on Rome and the other on the Iberian religious landscape. It is also one of several instances in which modern historians of the sacred have since attempted to disentangle their holy traditions from the false chronicles, and, by extension, from Higuera's reverse engineering—which, ironically, might have been what saved them for posterity in the first place. For, as we shall see, Higuera's resolve to reinforce jeopardized local saints made his texts irresistible fonts of information for seventeenth-century sacred histories, local patriots, and other students of the sacred past.

Higuera went beyond buttressing and Iberianizing apocryphal figures and traditions to purposefully and systematically reinvent obscure early Christian martyrs for the sake of specific communities. In his texts, Higuera retained or introduced many saints who had been canonized by tradition, but who were not necessarily documented in historical sources or who were mentioned in manuscripts of limited circulation, which meant that they certainly had not come to the attention of, say, Roman reformers. Higuera adopted these orphaned martyrs by furnishing them with a place of death or birth in the cronicones. By locating these stray saints in a specific point in time and space, Higuera grounded them in something that seemed like historical reality, filling the hole in the sacred tradition with the ballast of a history of his own making.

THE REPUBLIC IN THE DEBUT OF THE CHRONICLES

Higuera did not work alone. In the same sort of circular process at work in the creation of Liberata-Wilgefort or Anglina of Valencia, Higuera drew upon information he received from his friends and contacts to populate the false chronicles with particular details; then he would send those portions of the chronicles to his contacts for their use. This dialogic process is evident in the earliest appearances of Higuera's texts in a variety of Latin and vernacular texts around the turn of the sixteenth century. The very first to cite Higuera's *spuria* in print was the Jesuit theologian Gabriel Vázquez, who used a letter from Eutrand (an early version of the name for Luitprand), as pivotal evidence in his 1594 defense of the cult of saints, images, and relics against heresies past and present, *De cultu adorationis libri tres*.[52] In the treatise, Vázquez posed a series of objections to the Spanish heresy of adoptionism, according to which Jesus had become the son of God by virtue of adoption. In the process, Vázquez also vindicated its most prominent and obdurate defender, Elipandus, the eighth-century archbishop of Toledo. The problem for sixteenth-century Spaniards like Vázquez, Higuera, and others was that in citing the Mozarabic liturgy in support of his Christology and by refusing to recant, even when importuned by Charlemagne himself, Elipandus made the distinctive Toledan liturgy a source of ignominy. From the perspective of his critics, Elipandus's adoptionism was a variation of Nestorianism, according to which Christ's human and divine natures were distinct. In this way, by deemphasizing Christ's divinity in favor of his human nature, Elipandus and his fellow Mozarabs had been guilty of making a theological concession to Islamic critiques of the doctrine of the Trinity.[53] The accusation resurfaced in the eleventh century, when the Christian reconquest of Toledo brought renewed scrutiny upon the city's large Mozarabic population and their liturgy; it took on a particularly pointed valence in the sixteenth century, when, as Vázquez contended, an analogous threat to the adoration of Christ's human nature was presented by iconoclasts such as John Calvin, who attacked the adoration of the Host or of the Cross or crucifix.[54]

There was no denying that Elipandus had been an important part of Toledan and Mozarabic history. Yet his stubborn defense of heresy—and the doubts this had cast upon Mozarabic Christianity—made the Toledan archbishop an object of concern for Spanish theologians and historians—not just Higuera—well into the early modern period. In an attempt to repair the damage, Juan de Mariana had suggested that it was likely that the archbishop actually had recanted, although there was not a shred of evidence to confirm Elipandus had wavered—in fact, his obstinate letters to Charlemagne suggested quite the opposite.[55]

Into this charged territory Vázquez entered boldly by presenting evidence in the closing paragraphs of his treatise that confirmed what Mariana had only dared to hope: namely, Elipandus had recanted, been reconciled, and then went on to have a fruitful career as a member of the emperor's cortege. The key piece of evidence was a letter attributed to Luitprand that Higuera furnished to Vázquez along with extracts from the false chronicles. The letter referred in passing to Elipandus's having, indeed, "repented seriously and truly of his error about the adoption of Christ."[56] Were the letter authentic, it would have been a startling and absolutely central contribution to medieval Spanish history. In vindicating Elipandus, for example, the letter might have cleared away the lingering stigma connected with the liturgy, legal privileges, and historical identity of Toledo's Mozarabs, by providing ammunition with which to fight the persistent accusation that the Mozarabs had been tainted theologically and by blood by virtue of their long coexistence with Muslims.[57] Perhaps this is why Higuera did not stop with the letter, and also wrote Elipandus into the chronicle of Luitprand as a repentant and orthodox character, who, after having tearfully renounced his heretical views in a synod at Toledo in 795 at the behest of Charlemagne, also sent the emperor "many books written in Gothic script."[58] He then also served as archdeacon in Toledo under Archbishop Cixila, who sheltered the Mozarabic community during Islamic rule.[59] Thus Higuera converted Elipandus from a pertinacious heretic into one in a line of orthodox prelates of Toledo, and, in a characteristic compromise, he became a faithful servant of the Carolingian emperor, while also championing the Mozarabic resistance—which, historically, was not just to Islamicization, but also to Carolingian reform.

Higuera generously bestowed these sorts of inventions upon many of his friends in accordance with their shared interests. This is exemplified in the works of Prudencio de Sandoval (1553–1620), a Benedictine monk, onetime royal chronicler, and bishop of the Galician see of Tuy who, like his Jesuit friend, was an assiduous researcher and discoverer of ancient sources, some genuine and some perhaps not.[60] Sandoval's historical career was jump-started by his appointment as royal chronicler under Philip III in 1599, obtained through the patronage of his cousin the Duke of Lerma, the royal favorite.[61] At a time when the false chronicles were still only in limited, manuscript circulation, Higuera's texts made a conspicuous and crucial appearance in Sandoval's works. The chronicle attributed to Marcus Maximus, whom Higuera had reimagined as a Benedictine monk, proved fundamental for Sandoval's 1601 history of the Benedictine order, where he cited the text in support of his claims for the apostolic origins of monasticism, as well as for the Benedictine order's venerable antiquity in Spain. The chronicles of Dexter and Julián Pérez, in turn, served as load-bearing posts for Sandoval's expansive vision of the holy history of Tuy, published in 1610. Without Higuera's texts, Sandoval would have had scant material for the early years of Christianity in the region, or for his contention that Saint Liberata and her eight sisters belonged to Galicia, and not Portugal. In the course of researching his book, Sandoval requested historical information from Higuera, who obligingly sent along fragments of writings by Saint Athanasius (the purported first bishop of Zaragoza), which, as far as can be surmised from this distance, were of rather more recent vintage, although whether Higuera forged them or not remains unclear.[62] In return, Sandoval helped Higuera; for example, even after the Jesuit's position on San Tirso had been discredited, Sandoval endorsed Higuera's claims in his published 1615 collection of medieval histories.[63]

Higuera's hand can be discerned likewise in the *Life of Saint Vitalis* (1601) by Sancho Dávila Toledo (1546–1625), the well-connected son of the Marquis of Velada and bishop of Cartagena who received the entire body of Vitalis from the Roman catacombs as a gift from Pope Clement VIII in 1594. While this significant relic was to take pride of place in the bishop's already considerable collection, virtually nothing was actually known about the life, death, or biography of Vitalis himself.⁶⁴ Higuera, undeterred by the hagiographic vacuum, furnished Dávila with a purportedly medieval Latin vita identifying the saint as a native of Athens, a companion of Dionysius the Areopagite, and an archdeacon of Toledo. For good measure, he also had Julián Pérez provide corroborating evidence of the authenticity of the vita in his chronicle. Unsurprisingly, Higuera's documents would prove central to Dávila's account of the life and death of Vitalis, published a few years later during his stint as bishop of Jaén.⁶⁵ Thus, thanks in large part to Higuera, Dávila's nearly anonymous skeleton became a venerable martyr and important link in the chain of Iberian sacred history, as well as the centerpiece of the bishop's relic collection, which was praised in verse by the Golden Age poets Francisco Gómez de Quevedo and Lope de Vega.⁶⁶

Higuera's texts proved similarly fundamental for the canons of El Pilar in Zaragoza, probably since they presented a possible solution to an immediate problem for partisans of the church of Nuestra Señora del Pilar. According to a twelfth-century tradition, the Virgin appeared in the flesh to Santiago on the banks of the river Ebro, atop a pillar (hence "El Pilar") transported by angels. At the Virgin's request, Santiago later constructed a church on that very site. Based on this legend, the church of El Pilar had long contested the ecclesiastical primacy of Zaragoza's cathedral, known as "La Seo," which had become a cathedralic see upon the city's twelfth-century reconquest. Since the early sixteenth century, the Pilar canons had been waging a pitched battle to supersede La Seo as metropolitan see.⁶⁷ For this, they needed evidence to substantiate their claims of greater antiquity.

Once again, Higuera's texts proved pivotal in furnishing a preexisting yet vague tradition with precise chronological and historical coordinates. According to Dexter, Santiago himself established the church in AD 37, which provided de facto acknowledgment of El Pilar's primacy.⁶⁸ In 1607, Higuera sent a copy of the first two cronicones to two of El Pilar's canons: these were Bartolomé Llorente y García (ca. 1540–1614), an Augustinian canon serving in the Aragonese *diputación general*, who in 1613 would become chronicler of the crown of Aragon, and Bartolomé Morlanes y Malo, a well-trained humanist who corresponded with some of Europe's most discerning scholars, such as the Flemish Justus Lipsius.⁶⁹ Llorente, who had already drafted a number of petitions to the papal tribunal of the Sacra Rota regarding Pilar's primacy and even visited the Rota in person as El Pilar's agent in 1583, was excited to have this new evidence. Yet he was also an astute scholar, and in letters to Higuera he noted several serious errors and contradictions in the manuscript and requested "a more correct copy," which Higuera sent in 1608.⁷⁰

With the new information provided by Dexter and armed with a somewhat more trustworthy copy of the text, Llorente requested a formal opinion from the Rota on whether El Pilar had been the location of Zaragoza's cathedral before La Seo. In the end, the Roman tribunal decided in El Pilar's favor, and in a 1630 decision cited the chronicles, among many other sources, as important evidence of El Pilar's "greater antiquity." Several times the auditors cited Francisco de Bivar's 1627 Lyons edition of Dexter-Maximus; yet they also acknowledged that critics, such as the Augustinian canon Gabriele Pennotto, had objected strenuously to the texts. Ultimately, the Roman auditors noted, the question of whether those texts merited approval or rejection would be left to God.[71] At the same time, a cluster of new works of Zaragozan history and hagiography appeared in the early decades of the seventeenth century, taking full advantage of the mother lode of information about El Pilar and other Zaragoza saints provided by the false chronicles.[72]

AUTHENTIC SOURCES, INVENTED SAINTS

To create the false chronicles, Higuera pulled information from obscure hagiographic and liturgical texts—such as breviaries, *santorales*, martyrologies, and hymnals—that he discovered in Toledo and elsewhere. This means that the information he supplied to his friends may not have been completely fabricated; when it came to Elipandus, Vitalis, El Pilar, and others, Higuera may very well have drawn upon sources that, by the measure of his own times, were relatively trustworthy. Moreover, the collaboration between Higuera and his friends went in both directions, and the Toledan Jesuit drew upon documents that he received from afar. One significant contact was Gaspar Álvares de Lousada Machado (1554–1634), secretary to Archbishop Fray Agostinho de Jesus of Braga (1537–1609) and archivist of the royal repository of Torre do Tombo in Portugal. Higuera and Álvares shared the same constellation of historical interests and pursuits and, like his Toledan contact, Álvares is considered somewhat less than reliable as a historical source by modern scholars.[73] The two corresponded on many matters of mutual interest, such as the contentious question of whether Santa Liberata and her eight sisters belonged properly to Spain or Portugal.[74] Álvares and Higuera shared mutual acquaintances, such as Prudencio de Sandoval and the Toledan canon Alonso de Villegas. These four men exchanged many texts, including copies of the false chronicles, which Higuera sent to Braga at the request of Álvares and the archbishop in 1602, as they were researching the history of Braga's early bishops.[75] For his part, Villegas had been one of the few cathedral clergy to support Higuera in the San Tirso affair. Villegas even wrote his own treatise on San Tirso, which he shared with Álvares de Lousada. Shared interests did not preclude the learned friends from disagreeing, as is seen in Álvares's careful and pointed response to Villegas in which he argued that the Portuguese cult to Tirso predated the Toledan one.[76] Higuera, in turn, contested Álvares's position that Liberata was Portuguese by adducing evidence from his own false chronicles—those of Dexter and Julián Pérez—as well as a section of a lectionary from the diocese of Sigüenza, the city that claimed to possess her relics.[77]

It may have been in response to Álvares and his patron that Higuera was able to write Saint Pedro de Rates, the legendary first bishop of Braga, into his chronicles. Although the first bishop of Braga had been commemorated by previous historians, in Dexter's account his existence was given chronological precision: here Pedro de Rates is remembered as having been appointed by Santiago as Braga's prelate in AD 37.[78] The cult to Pedro de Rates dated back to the ninth century, and the saint had been included in the mid-sixteenth-century chronicles of Johannes Vasaeus and Ambrosio de Morales as a disciple of Santiago.[79] Álvares had sent Higuera a vita and an account of the translation of the relics of the saint; it is impossible to determine whether the secretary or the archbishop of Braga were aware that Higuera would use the information he sent to pad the chronicles with new details about Pedro de Rates.[80] But it is important to note that in this case, as in many others, it is just as likely that Higuera was the recipient of a forged text as its originator. Perhaps Álvares had encountered an authentic vita of Pedro de Rates in the Portuguese royal archives; perhaps he had not. Either way, Pedro de Rates attained his particular shape through ongoing conversations among Higuera, Álvares, and the archbishop of Braga, and like so many other figures in the false chronicles, Braga's first bishop seems to owe his existence to a mix of solid historical research as well as outright invention. Here, as elsewhere, where to draw the line between one and the other is not immediately clear.

In reviewing other instances in which Higuera's friends drew upon his spurious sources in their own published books, it becomes difficult, and sometimes simply impossible, to identify causality, assign blame, or trace the vectors of influence. Higuera asked his correspondents for information about specific saints and other pious traditions; he responded to many requests for the same. In attempting to sort out which came first—the vested interest or the invented document—and who was responsible for the fabrication, one begins to experience the slightly nauseating sense of stumbling through a circus hall of mirrors. Such is the case with Chirinos, a Mozarabic monk and a key figure in the history of the miraculous Cross of Caravaca, as well as a player in Higuera's own version of his Mozarabic ancestry. In 1610, presbyter Juan Robles Corvalán published an account of the heavenly origins and subsequent fame of the cross, held in the parish church of Caravaca, in the diocese of Cartagena. According to Licenciado

Robles, the cross had been delivered by angels to a monk named Chirinos, who was at that time in the captivity of the Moorish king of Caravaca. Chirinos was granted permission to say Mass in the royal presence, but, to his dismay, found himself without a cross. Luckily, angels appeared at that very moment, bearing a crucifix in their hands—which, as it turned out, they had just ripped from the chest of the patriarch of Jerusalem. Amazed by the miracle, the Moorish king converted, and, Robles affirmed, the cross had been venerated in Caravaca ever since.[81]

In support of this account of the history and miracles of the Cross of Caravaca, Robles, a former student of Higuera's from a Jesuit collegium, cited the customary ecclesiastical and historical texts, as well as a number of less familiar sources, including miracle tales preserved in the parish archive, as well as medieval miracle paintings and Arabic inscriptions in the church itself. To decipher the latter, Presbyter Robles requested the assistance of Miguel de Luna, the Granadan morisco who had helped translate—and possibly forge—the lead books, another set of late sixteenth-century forgeries. According to Luna, these inscriptions confirmed the legend of the angelic *translatio crucis*. In addition, Robles received from Higuera an old manuscript from Toledo and fragments of the chronicle of Julián Pérez, which further illuminated the life of Chirinos the monk.[82]

In this effort, Higuera was not only aiding a former student. He was also elaborating on his own genealogical fictions for, according to his manuscript "Treatise on the Lineage of the Higueras," his family was descended from the bloodline of the pious Mozarabic monk.[83] Did Higuera invent Chirinos, as scholars have suggested, or might he have come across the figure in his research, or in a letter from one of his correspondents? Or might it have been the case that Luna or Robles encountered "Chirinos" in one of the Caravaca inscriptions, and that Higuera simply elaborated upon the information they had given him? It is not clear. The point is that in the Caravaca case as in so many others, the variety of actors and interests involved means that the invention cannot always be blamed on Higuera alone.

In his ongoing conversations about the sacred past, many contested questions were addressed through historical and philological debate, which often gave rise to exaggerations, falsifications, and even outright subterfuge. Sometimes the guilty party was Higuera. Other times it was another enthusiastic student of the past who took it upon himself to enhance the historical record. Moreover, in several discrete instances, some evidence suggests that Higuera was not fabricating or forging so much as bringing a particular manuscript tradition out of obscurity, albeit with his characteristic tendency to enhance the truth. The case of Santa Victoria of Tobarra suggests how Higuera brought together various strands of epigraphic, liturgical, and hagiographic evidence in order to construct a new and improved saint. Around the turn of the century, he wrote to Doctor Ginés Gómez, the parish priest of Tobarra in the diocese of Cartagena, urging him to adopt Victoria as a patron. Although all known martyrologies identified the virgin-martyr as Roman, Higuera reasoned that the texts did not explicitly state that she died in Rome, or even in Italy. In fact, as he informed Ginés Gómez, Baronio described Victoria in the revised Roman Martyrology as having been put to death in a place called Trebula.[84] Since, as Higuera acknowledged, at least three different places could be identified as Trebula, including two in Italy, he turned to epigraphic evidence to deduce that this was the "Turbula" that Ptolemy had identified as a city in Hispania, modern Tobarra, as he concluded thanks to a dubious argument from etymology: "And looking at the allusion of the word, there is a great proximity between Turbula and Tobarra." To further sway the hand of Tobarra's parish priest—who he hoped would introduce local veneration of Victoria as a hometown martyr—Higuera marshaled corroborating evidence from three of his own cronicones, a fourteenth-century martyrology from Plasencia, and an inscription found in the Talavera home of the sixteenth-century chronicler Doctor Bartolomé Frías de Albornoz, a prolific correspondent on inscriptions (best known to modern scholars for a 1573 treatise on contracts in which he denounced chattel slavery of Africans).

Although it is tempting to assume that Higuera, in a deus ex machina maneuver, fabricated these and other sources in order to help his friends, here, as elsewhere, matters simply may not have been so simple. In looking at the sources that Higuera cited in his letter to the parish priest of Tobarra, traces of his actual historical research emerge and the legend of Victoria—as commemorated in the false chronicles—begins, upon closer inspection, to look as if it were erected upon solid historical ground. In the chronicle of Luitprand, Higuera cited a relatively straightforward inscription, attesting to a vow made by a citizen of Tobarra in honor of Victoria, which "Luitprand" himself remembered having seen in Cartagena. Luitprand also noted, for good measure, that the memory of Victoria and her sisters had been lost with the arrival of the Moors. The inscription Higuera claimed to have seen in the collection of Frías de Albornoz presented further (plausible) evidence of a long-standing local cult to Victoria: with an equestrian statue, the "Republic of Tobarra" thanked one Marcus Aurelius Maximianus who, through his prayers to Santa Victoria, had chased a "colossal dragon" from the town. Finally, Higuera alluded to the Plasencia martyrology, which described Victoria in terms almost identical to the description in the chronicles of Luitprand and Julián Pérez. Higuera's conclusion to Ginés Gómez was that, based on this preponderance of evidence, Victoria could—and should—be rendered public veneration, based on the antiquity of her cult. Higuera's efforts eventually bore fruit; his correspondent Francisco de Cascales, an accomplished Latinist and the author of various historical and poetic texts, identified Victoria as a native of Tobarra in his 1598 *Discurso de la historia de Cartagena*.[85] It is not clear whether the town embraced the new saint, although she was remembered as a native of Tobarra by at least one author in the eighteenth century in terms that come directly from the account in Luitprand.[86]

Another example of Higuera's use of plausibly authentic and antique sources to rewrite history is that of Saints Vicente (Vincent) and Leto, Spanish martyrs whose place of death had been left unspecified in the revised Roman Martyrology. In his chronicles, Higuera forged a connection between the saints and a specific time and place: according to Dexter and Julián Pérez, Vicente and Leto were twin brothers put to death in Roman "Libisosa," an ancient settlement near Lezuza, in La Mancha. For good measure, the martyrs were also mentioned in the letter from Silo to Cixila of Toledo. The letter had been widely publicized in the pamphlet ghostwritten by Higuera for Toledo's corregidor, and it was there that Bernardo de Rojas y Sandoval, the influential cardinal-archbishop of Toledo, noticed the detail about the Lezuza saints. He had the pamphlet sent to the town's authorities in 1595 and, in response, Lezuza's citizens took a vow to celebrate the twin martyrs' sacrifice every year thereafter with a public festival and procession. As it turned out, this version of Vicente and Leto's death was corroborated by two manuscript breviaries in Seville and possibly by an old Portuguese santoral printed in 1513 that seventeenth-century readers later encountered in their research.[87] In other words, all of these pieces of epigraphic and documentary evidence—even the ones cited by pseudo-Luitprand—seem to have been actual specimens Higuera collected through research and correspondence.

HIGUERA'S SURVEY OF THE SACRED PAST

In these efforts, Higuera often made use of a creative reading of ancient geographical sources, such as the Antonine *Itinerary* or Ptolemy's *Geography*, in order to endow non-Iberian saints with unimpeachably Spanish or Portuguese places of birth, death, or both. Yet he also drew on sources unknown to Baronio, including local religious traditions that he learned about through his social networks—which extended to low-level clerics and antiquarians, many of whom posterity has forgotten save in these isolated traces in Higuera's papers. In these efforts, Higuera engaged in a sort of survey of sacred antiquities in Castile and beyond. The contours of this project can be discerned by examining Higuera's own papers, which include dozens of letters regarding matters of local history, religion, and antiquities from correspondents from throughout Hapsburg Spain, with a preponderance from the region around Toledo, and, more broadly, in Old and New Castile. In Higuera's correspondence, we glimpse a world still poorly understood by scholars, a sort of subnational Republic of Letters in which regional erudites such as Higuera hobnobbed with both the prominent and the obscure, small-scale as well as highly placed ecclesiastics, from illustrious cardinals, archbishops, and cathedral canons at the center of Spanish religious life to the now-anonymous presbyters, licentiates, and notaries at the cultural and political peripheries. His contacts far and wide responded with a wealth of information about sacred antiquities, including the memory of relics, saints, and apparitions. While many of these letters were addressed by name to Father Higuera, the identity of their authors is not always discernible. Yet the geographical and topical range of his contacts is suggestive of the scope and aims of Higuera's project. From the Canary Islands, for example, he received a nine-folio account of the discovery of three miraculous images of the Virgin in Tenerife, and, from another correspondent, a list of the relics in the village of Torrejón de Ardoz, not far from Madrid, which included the caul that covered the infant Jesus when he emerged from his mother's womb.[88] From the mountains of Toledo came a cluster of reports, including an account of the hermitage, mines, castle, and churches of the village of El Molinillo, and a 1596 letter to Higuera's ally, the corregidor of Toledo, detailing the antiquities of Mala Moneda, today an active archaeological site with ruins dating back to the Roman period.[89] Among Higuera's papers we find a wealth of such documentation, such as the history of the foundation of a Dominican *beaterio* in Toledo; the origins of a miraculous image from Santa María del Prado in the Zaragoza region; and a collection of sources on the history of Plasencia, including royal privileges, papal bulls, epitaphs, and more.[90]

Like antiquarians in subsequent centuries who scoured the countryside for popular memory of forgotten monuments and inscriptions in oral traditions, Higuera sought local remembrances that he could use in his historical research.[91] Yet the most immediate antecedent and an important model for Higuera's effort seems to have been the *Relaciones geográficas*, the systematic survey of Castilian geography and history that agents of Philip II conducted in the 1570s and 1580s throughout Spanish Hapsburg territories, including the Americas. His agents asked respondents to address forty-five questions about the location, geographic features, governance, and history of their respective localities. The questionnaire also asked specifically about any local antiquities—including ruined buildings and inscriptions—as well as about the history of local relics, hermitages, and miracles.[92]

The resemblance of Higuera's inquiries, and the responses he received, to the

Relaciones geográficas may have been by design. Several of the letter-writers shaped their correspondence to its template, perhaps in response to Higuera's prompting. Higuera's contact in Tendilla told him outright that his response was simply a copy of the relevant portions of the village's 1580 response to Philip II.[93] A writer in the Extremaduran locality of Montanchez wrote his report as a response to a series of questions about the town's antiquities, remarkable relics, and legal privileges and, as in many responses to the *Relaciones geográficas*, the author included a vivid account of how the town had been reconquered; in this case, crafty local Christians concealed themselves in goatskins in order to get close enough to slaughter the Moorish sentries guarding the castle.[94] Higuera received a similar report from a Cartagena friar named Geronymo Hurtado, who sent a wealth of information regarding the city's topography, agricultural products, prominent families, and ecclesiastical institutions. Hurtado also included a hand-drawn map of the city, a prominent feature of many of the *relaciones*, particularly from the Indies. Higuera also received a lengthy report from Juan Amador de Don Diego, the priest who had written regarding the antiquities of Cazorla while also complaining about his exile from Toledo.[95]

Higuera's extensive correspondence with these relatively obscure clerics helps explain the astounding level of local detail in the false chronicles. Much like Ambrosio de Morales, who drew on the *Relaciones geográficas* as a source of information about Roman-era antiquities, Higuera duly incorporated the information he received from his correspondents into the false chronicles.[96] In the process, he often transformed what we would call oral tradition into "history" proper. One example is found in the chronicle of Luitprand, which in the year 744 records a dramatic tale about the fate of a convent in Roman Carpetania, a region of the southern Meseta between the Guadarrama mountains and the Tajo River, during the Islamic conquest. According to Luitprand,

> At the limits of Carpetania [the Madrid region], many Benedictine virgins urged God to absorb them into the earth so that they would not be violated by the Moors; and a certain bell is [now] heard regularly at the hour of the day as a summons, just as when they used to come together for prayers.[97]

Even underground, the convent's church bell continued to ring, summoning the faithful to pray several times a day in memory of the brave virgins. In his *History of Toledo*, Higuera added another picturesque detail: when the bells sounded, they seemed to be saying "Quiteria," the name of one of Saint Liberata's eight sisters and the patron saint of Ajofrín, nearby in the Toledo mountains.[98]

Far from a fanciful invention on Higuera's part, the tale of the buried convent was lore in the mountains southwest of Toledo that he had learned from one of his correspondents. In a 1596 letter from Ajofrín, Licenciado Pedro Gómez Molero answered Higuera's request for information on the town's annual pilgrimage to the nearby monastery of San Pablo de los Montes, in the Toledan mountains. He explained that in order to properly answer Higuera's queries on the topic, he had surveyed elderly villagers, including his own grandparents, to conclude that the pilgrimage had begun with an apparition of the Virgin during a tough Reconquest-era drought, when Mary commanded the local faithful to construct a hermitage on the spot which many—but not all—believed was the location of the monastery of San Pablo. Ever since, the inhabitants of Ajofrín made a pilgrimage to the site every May.[99] Yet Gómez Molero, contending with the plasticity of popular memory, admitted that there was some uncertainty as to the exact location of the Virgin's apparition. Some believed that it was on the hill where the friary of San Pablo was now located; others asserted that it was at a holy fountain; and still others, atop a former convent whose precise location was also a matter of debate, but which some believed was near San Pablo. Here Gómez explained to Higuera that the convent in question had disappeared suddenly in a dramatic series of events during the eighth-century Islamic invasion. When the nuns discovered that the treacherous Count Don Julian had offered the region to the Muslim ruler of Toledo out of greed, they threw themselves into prayer, full of despair. The Virgin then interceded on their behalf by burying the entire convent underground, including its inhabitants, for safety. The friars of nearby San Pablo reported that they could hear the bells of the convent still dutifully marking the hours from beneath the earth.[100]

In collecting this information, Higuera, like other conscientious hagiographers of his time, struggled with the tendency for disparate saints and their legends to become intertwined in a thick tangle of undergrowth. And like Baronio and, later, the Bollandists, the Jesuit sought specific and verifiable information that would help clarify matters. We can see this in Higuera's attempts to determine where Quiteria had been martyred. According to Doctor Pablo León de Zamora, Quiteria had been put to death in Marjaliza (also spelled Margeliza), in the Toledan mountains, not far from Ajofrín. In their correspondence Higuera honed in on a number of apparent contradictions between the oral traditions that León had shared with him and the written accounts Higuera had consulted: whereas León said Quiteria was supposed to have perished at the site known as the "Holy Fountain" in Marjaliza, according to a manuscript history of Quiteria, Higuera countered, the saint was martyred upon "Monte Columbino," whence her body was carried for safekeeping to the hermitage of San Pedro. León explained that this was only an apparent contradiction, because, in fact, "since time immemorial," the mountain upon which Marjaliza was located had been known as "Columbino," in honor of the droves of doves (*columbas*) that were wont to congregate there, and nearby, he informed Higuera, was the very old hermitage of San Pedro. In other words, their seemingly disparate stories were, in fact, in harmony.[101] Higuera wanted to stabilize this wobbly hagiographic edifice by committing it to written form. So he asked Doctor León to have official testimony of these legends taken among the residents of Marjaliza and nearby Casalgordo. This meant confirming the information "juridically," that is, by having testimony about Quiteria ratified in the presence of a notary, the legal gold standard from the legalistic perspective of early modern Spain. With the notarized testimony in the works, then, Higuera felt comfortable including the information in his *History of Toledo*, where he concluded that the people of Marjaliza had good reason to have adopted Quiteria as their patron and to "believe piously with not a little verisimilitude" that she was martyred there.[102]

VOX POPULI, VOX DEI

In corralling and confirming relatively obscure legends from the Castilian countryside, Higuera did much more than simply engineer a set of texts that would represent his own interests and those of his friends. His aims were broader, and seem to have been motivated by a conviction that letting local traditions wither on the vine would be to impoverish Spanish religious life. For Higuera, the collective devotion of a community—as preserved in its oral traditions or in its liturgical manuscripts—possessed an authority and legitimacy that outweighed that of a Baronio or a Morales, or even an Higuera. He explained this position in an undated letter to a fellow Jesuit, Hernando de Ávila. The letter concerned the question of where Ildefonso, a patron of Toledo, had been born. According to one tradition, the seventh-century bishop arrived to this world in the very house where Higuera resided, the casa profesa of the Toledo Jesuits, which had previously belonged to the Counts of Orgaz; before that, it was the property of Toledo's thirteenth-century alcalde, Don Esteban Illán.

To support this relatively uncontroversial assertion, Higuera cited the remembrances of his grandmother, Teresa de la Higuera, who had died twenty years before, at the age of 105: "[She] told me that she had heard from her parents and grandparents that Saint Ildefonso was born in that house, which has been attested for over 200 years." Then he explained his rationale for accepting her testimony, in a remarkable defense of the value of local memory:

> This is not a new thing, but old common knowledge from a long time ago. I say this so that it is understood that this is not a tradition from 30 or 40 years ago

but rather from time immemorial, and such traditions are more authoritative than some historians. That is because this is the opinion of many who say the same thing, not only in this time period, but in many, and for that reason it has more authority than the assertion of four or five historians, who, although they may be very authoritative, [represent] the opinions of not more than four or five witnesses. In contrast, tradition contains the sayings of a city, which agree with each other by common consent, without contestation, contradiction, or variety in opinions, and for this reason I know it has been said, *vox populi vox dei* (the voice of the people is the voice of God).[103]

This type of wisdom, Higuera waxed, was like a spring that instead of bursting forth with clear water, continually produced something that, for a historian, was just as valuable: "people who testify the same thing." In other words, popular tradition emerged in a perfect state of nature, which is why, Higuera emphasized, even learned men such as Álvar Gómez, Ambrosio de Morales, and Juan de Mariana imbibed it; like Higuera's grandmother, they, too, identified the Jesuit casa profesa as the birthplace of the saint.[104]

In valorizing common consensus as a key criterion for determining the validity of hagiographical traditions, and in citing over two hundred years of oral tradition as "time immemorial," Higuera sounded like an unwitting prophet of post-Tridentine reforms. "Time immemorial," after all, was the period of time—later changed to the more specific period of one hundred years or more—that a diocese needed to document in order to be able to receive papal authorization for a public veneration of an uncanonized saint in the wake of the canonization reforms in the late sixteenth and seventeenth centuries.[105] Yet in his rather sanguine declaration of the value of vox populi, Higuera also articulated a position that was becoming increasingly unpopular in his own times. *Vox populi, vox Dei* had possessed an ambiguous valence ever since its first appearance in a 798 letter by Charlemagne's courtier, Alcuin of York, who warned that, in matters of episcopal appointments, "we must not listen to those who are wont to say *vox populi, vox Dei*, for the confusion of the mob is always very close to insanity." After all, "the people in accordance with divine law are to be led, not followed. And when witnesses are needed, men of position are to be preferred."[106] At a time when the consent of "the people" was believed to be necessary for a legitimate selection of religious and political authorities, Alcuin's counsel was observed mostly in the breach, as medieval chroniclers continued to cite the dictates of vox populi when describing political decisions that, in truth, were made by a rather limited circle of political and religious elites. For example, bishops were often said to have been chosen "by the election of the clergy and the people (*populi*)," where the *populus* was actually made up of "those fellow clerics who were responsible for the acclamation of bishops."[107] In other words, *vox populi, vox Dei* was "not a cry of the common people themselves, but rather . . . of their leaders."[108]

Yet by the sixteenth and seventeenth centuries, the political and religious value of popular acclaim was on the wane, and Alcuin's rather less favorable estimation seems to have been on the ascendant, at least if we are to judge by (the admittedly anomalous) Montaigne, for whom vox populi was "too often the mother of ignorance, injustice, and inconstancy."[109] A similar disdain was evidenced by Golden Age playwrights such as Lope de Vega, who bemoaned the rowdiness and general uncouthness of the "common people" (*vulgo*), even while drawing upon their distinctive idioms for colorful literary detail.[110] For Tridentine Catholicism, the question of the value of popular traditions was rather more complex. To Protestant accusations that its many nonscriptural traditions demonstrated that the Church had departed from apostolic models, Catholic theologians before and after the Council of Trent countered with the notion of the insufficiency of the Bible. In its most expansive form, the idea was that scripture needed to be interpreted and supported by Church tradition, as preserved in the writings of the Greek and Latin fathers, conciliar decrees, and papal pronouncements. The Tridentine fathers had affirmed this value of tradition as a source of authority alongside scripture, and specified that by virtue of their direct succession from the apostles the papacy and the Roman Church possessed the authority to serve as guardians and arbiters of tradition in perpetuity.[111]

While the authority of specifically apostolic tradition was an uncontroversial matter among Catholic thinkers, the value of other, later historical, hagiographic, and liturgical traditions remained a matter of some dispute. At one end of the spectrum, for example, the Dominican theologian Melchor Cano explicitly rejected traditions based only on vox populi. In his consideration of the relative value of history as a source for theology in his posthumous *De locis theologicis libri XII* (Salamanca, 1563), Cano criticized those authors—such as Jacobus de Voragine, the compiler of the *Golden Legend*—who included such testimony in their texts, particularly if the traditions seemed questionable or false. As Cano reasoned, "common opinion is generally false," and an author who limited himself to repeating it would merely be reporting an opinion about the facts, not the facts themselves.[112] Such was the case, for example, with the popular notion that John the Baptist had really been the Messiah, which, since it was simply wrong, Cano recommended the conscientious historian to simply pass over in silence. In some cases, however, common opinions were not fundamentally false, but simply mistaken to a lesser degree: the details were wrong, but the essence was true. For example, in a strict, biological sense, Joseph was not the father of Jesus, yet he had raised the boy, and was married to his mother. In this way, it was not entirely false when, in popular discourse—and in a few scriptural passages, as Cano noted—Joseph was referred to as such. In these situations, Cano counseled, the historian should record the common opinion, although he should also explain why it was erroneous.[113]

The danger, of course, was that, in giving credence to popular testimony—like the musings of grandmothers—these sorts of misconceptions would worm their way into histories of the saints and of the Church. Cano singled out the *Golden Legend* for scrutiny on this count, echoing Juan Luis Vives's barb that the Dominican hagiographer had an iron tongue, a heart of lead, and a mind that was neither rigorous nor alert.[114] If Vives the consummate Latinist was exercised by de Voragine's ineloquence, Cano was rather more worried about the undue influence that the active imagination of the common people had been allowed in this and other works of sacred letters. As Cano pointed out, it was not the ignorant who were at fault, but, rather, learned men like de Voragine, who should have known better: "serious and grave men do not go out hunting for the idle talk of the common people." The historian who would like to be taken seriously by theologians, Cano says, does not collect "little slips of paper" unworthy of being read, "nor adjust his work to the fable-telling of old ladies."[115] The vulgar tendency to believe in miracles and marvels too readily made this particularly ill-advised. Roman reformers in the half century following Trent had been busily trying to extirpate from Church tradition those elements of popular wisdom that, from their perspective, had been allowed to sully the record. Yet Cano, who had been in attendance at Trent, was distinctly aware of the dangers of following this line of reasoning to the other extreme, and he warned his readers not to make the Protestant mistake of rejecting all of the Church's traditions just because of a handful of false ones, such as the errors that had crept into some passages of the liturgy.[116]

In sum, by affirming vox populi as an authoritative source of hagiographic and historical information, Higuera was standing in opposition to the prevailing winds coming out of Rome and the centers of theological inquiry in Spain, such as Cano's Salamanca. And yet, here as elsewhere, Higuera's position bore more than just a passing resemblance to that of his influential model, Ambrosio de Morales, who had been Cano's student. Morales did not share his teacher's instinctive distrust of the lives of saints, and, a decade after the end of Trent, he took a more latitudinarian approach in explaining his method of writing about saints in the first part of his *General Chronicle of Spain*. "Although the history of saints must be like other histories in having great certainty and authority," Morales reasoned, its aims and methods remained distinct from other histories that dealt merely with the mundane realm of humanity. The histories of saints "are written for other ends that are higher than those to which [human] history usually aspires. And thus the manner of writing them must be very different in order to achieve [those high ends]." This is how, Morales believed, Isidore of Seville had approached the task of writing about the saints in the Mozarabic missal and breviary: not in a cold and overly demanding manner, but with an approach informed by his piety and love of God.[117]

Morales expanded upon these thoughts in an excursus in which he surveyed the varieties of hagiographic sources. Here he privileged the most trustworthy, the so-called acts (*acta*), those original judicial processes of martyrs' deaths, or later accounts of the same processes, known as passions (*passiones*). Morales's list of other acceptable sources bears a remarkable resemblance to what we might imagine as Higuera's bibliography: it included the writings of "grave and very authoritative writers," such as Prudentius, or the authors of historical martyrologies, including Bede, Adon, and Usuard; lives of saints; liturgical texts, particularly in matins readings about saints from the Mozarabic liturgy; old santorales; and, finally, "the common consent of the majority of the Christian church, and tradition."[118]

By "common consent," Morales was referring specifically to liturgical sources, such as the Mozarabic liturgy, which had been accepted by the Church for centuries. One should not contradict or reject these texts lightly, without a very compelling reason, since they had been received and believed for so long.[119] For example, just because a liturgical life of a saint might lack an author's name did not mean it should be rejected out of hand: that the church had admitted the text and others like it into its readings meant that such texts possessed good faith. In this, the universal consent and tradition of ecclesiastical usage would and should significantly outweigh other deficiencies. Thus, Morales counseled, one should be reverent and approach the texts of the Mozarabic missal and breviary with "obeisance" (*acatamiento*) lest one offend God by handling such sacred matters too roughly. The weight of common consent was such that one would have to be virtually insane to reject, for example, the celebration of a festival in a saint's honor: "If somebody were so evil and debauched as to deny that this were true ... this would be a great insanity and utter nonsense, worthy of punishment. Because with Christian humility we should believe that if the Church has decided ... to institute a festivity, that it must have been due to considerable consideration and certainty, and without that, such a solemn and celebrated demonstration would not have been allowed."[120]

PIOUS AFFECTION:
HIGUERA AND BARONIO REVISITED

Morales's conviction that cumulative weight of tradition or "common consent" should outweigh other, lesser considerations, particularly when it came to the veneration of the saints, was shared by many of his successors in sacred scholarship. For example, in defense of the lead books of Granada, the Cordoban scholar Bernardo de Aldrete asserted that "matters concerning saints should not be judged by ordinary rules," since God could do things that defied ordinary human understanding.[121] Nor was the notion that sacred matters should be handled somewhat more gingerly, rather than scrutinized in the unforgiving light of reason, limited to early modern Spain. The idea of pious affection can, in some ways, be traced to a broader premodern notion that truth itself possessed moral content. In this universe, that which promoted piety was true; that which detracted from good religion, false.[122] From this perspective, which Higuera shared with many of his medieval forebears, intent was paramount, such that "the same deed might be either good or evil depending on whether it was performed with good or bad intent."[123] Thus, in the estimation of the thirteenth-century canon lawyer Henry of Susa, the bishop of Ostia (Hostienses), the prayers offered to an individual believed to be a saint would be considered by God, even if the person was uncanonized. As Giles Constable has argued, "by this standard, a forgery designed to promote truth and justice would not be considered a forgery, in the pejorative sense, at all."[124] It was, rather, the restoration of the proper order of things: in this way, "[medieval] forgeries . . . brought order into the confusions and deficiencies of the present."[125] Forgeries, then, "represented an effort to establish order, and the forgers were thus asserting and protecting rather than deforming truth and justice."[126] Higuera likewise seems to have believed that his texts were preserving or restoring the correct order of things. Baronio and the reformers were disordering a previously intact world of holiness, and there were saints who needed saving. With holiness at stake, the means were justified by these higher ends. And the means—recycling, altering, and fabricating historical evidence—were themselves shaped by the newly critical age in which Higuera, like Baronio, was educated. In this, it must be emphasized, Higuera was not alone. The notion that religious and historical truths needed to obey a deeper moral purpose had not disappeared after the Middle Ages; rather, it still held sway among ecclesiastical polemicists of varying stripes well into the early modern period. For that matter, it guided the writing of confessional history in some circles well into the twentieth century.[127]

While it might seem that in giving credence to vox populi Higuera was once again working in opposition to his Roman nemesis, the illustrious Cardinal Baronio, matters are not quite so simple. The two scholars of the sacred shared an appreciation of the potential hagiographic and historical value of local oral and written traditions—vox populi—such as those that Higuera repeatedly drew upon to write the false chronicles. Baronio and his collaborators had revised the Martyrology with the help of many Higuera-like figures throughout the Italian peninsula, such as parish priests and other enthusiasts of sacred history, who sent old breviaries and other documentation in support of their local history and saints. While Baronio certainly had little compunction in rejecting traditions for which he felt there was insufficient evidence, he also could be rather generous in his approach to local cults. Thus, when the commission revising the Martyrology decided that a lack of "positive historical proof of the saint's historicity and sanctity could be overlooked in deference to the strong tradition among the faithful and supporting divine signs like miracles," Baronio and his companions were, like Morales, deferring to "common consent" with "obeisance."[128] In this, they heeded the witness of historical breviaries, martyrologies, santorales, and missals, as well as something that bears a striking resemblance to Higuera's vox populi.

A remarkable—and admittedly anomalous—example is found in the case of Saint Cesidio of Trasacco, from the hometown of Baronio's mother. This otherwise obscure martyr and his anonymous companions were included in the revised Roman Martyrology on August 31, which Baronio justified briefly in his marginal commentary: "[Cesidio] is celebrated for the many daily miracles; I am talking about the things witnessed and experienced, since it is my mother's birthplace."[129] Unlike other martyrs, who were attested by previous martyrologies or parallel manuscript traditions, Cesidio was authorized by popular testimony with which Baronio was personally familiar. We see here a very different Baronio from the one envisioned by Spain's wounded partisans of Santiago, one sensitive to the value of local devotions, particularly when they were supported by communal tradition. This Baronio seems to differ from the Spanish Jesuit in degree, not in kind.

Another similarity between Baronio and his Toledan counterpart is that they both possessed the ability to demythologize, if not a consistent desire to do so. The cardinal's reluctance to challenge the *Donation of Constantine*, a forgery that was already notorious when Lorenzo Valla excoriated it in a late fifteenth-century treatise, has caused critics to scratch their heads for centuries. By Baronio's time, any conscientious scholar knew of Valla's stinging critiques of the *Donation*, which recorded Constantine's historically implausible gift of the entire western half of the Roman Empire to Pope Sylvester I. Yet, as Baronio reasoned in his treatment of the topic in the *Annales*, it would have been "inconceivable" if the emperor had *not* rendered such a special gift to the head of the Church, thus, "the truth of Christ urges us" to accept it as true. In other words, faith and the weight of the accepted tradition of papal supremacy ceded to historical or critical judgment. These deeper truths would, by necessity, be defended from the more fickle imperatives of historical or philological critics. So convinced was Baronio of the need to preserve the authority of this tradition, particularly at a time when papal supremacy was being challenged, that—as Glen Bowersock has suggested—he went so far as to transmit a blatant falsehood about a recent archaeological discovery in order to grant legitimacy to the *Donation*. In a note to his treatment of the topic in the *Annales*, Baronio mentioned that recent excavations of Saint Peter's had revealed bricks inscribed with the name of Constantine. This would have meant that, just as the *Donation* claimed, Constantine had erected the basilica in honor of Saint Peter and that archaeological evidence supported the *Donation*'s endorsement of the primacy and sovereignty of the Roman papacy.[130]

Far from the pitiless demoter of long-standing saints imagined by Higuera and his peers, here emerges a rather different Baronio, one who was sensitive to the value of local devotions, political considerations, and the integrity of the Church in the face of its critics. Like Higuera and many other early modern ecclesiastical scholars, Baronio knew how to mobilize the tools of historical criticism "onesidedly, as an instrument to explode adverse claims," but opted out of doing so when it meant scrutinizing traditions dear to his own interests.[131] This is where good faith scholarship and forgeries seem to have overlapped. For Higuera, pious affection entailed caring so much about a tradition that one might nudge it from the somewhat dubious arena of unconfirmable legend into the more solid one of truth. Of course, we should not make the mistake of collapsing the differences between the Toledan Jesuit and the Roman cardinal. Whereas Baronio preserved preexisting traditions such as the *Donation* or Saint Cesidio in a sort of hagiographical grandfather clause, Higuera went much further. He did not simply enshrine the sacred and preserve the particular; he also augmented the sacred to create new, improved narratives.

That said, it is worth pausing at one particularly surprising moment in which Higuera, who spent his entire life trying to document and resurrect forgotten martyrs, disavowed a miraculous explanation outright, with a critical attitude almost completely missing in the false chronicles. As we have seen, credulity and criticism were not mutually exclusive, even in the works of our Toledan forger, and like many other early modern antiquarian scholars, Higuera tended to record the totality of what he collected, even if he did not necessarily believe it all himself. We see this dynamic at work in a remarkable passage in Higuera's *Toledo* in which he provided a rather different take on the story of the miraculously tolling bells of the underground convent—the one he had codified in the chronicle of Luitprand, thanks to his correspondent in Ajofrín. During one of Higuera's many entertaining digressions on the cave of Hercules, he mentioned a cave in England, which—according to the late antique church father Clement of Alexandria—produced a sound like the clashing of cymbals when the wind passed through it. Higuera added that he had also heard from "trustworthy individuals" of a similar phenomenon in the hills outside Toledo, and that this was the very location where a convent had sunk into the ground during the Moorish invasion, to protect its inhabitants from violation. Like the English cave, the buried convent was believed to produce the noise of tolling bells at regular intervals, almost as if it were still marking the monastic hours. Yet Higuera rejected the notion that the tolling was miraculous. Instead, he offered a remarkably reasoned and naturalistic explanation. The cavity where the convent was located, like Clement's English cave, made a distinctive sound when the wind passed through it, from natural causes. This was clear via deductive reasoning: "Since, if they have the same causes, the same effects necessarily follow." Moreover, "I believe that [the people] exaggerate when they say that [the bells ring] at certain hours and a certain number of times a day, and it could be that the wind rushes in sometimes at those times, and it produces those effects. This, for somebody who does not know natural philosophy, would seem like a great miracle."[132] In just a few brutal lines, Higuera demolished vox populi in favor of something like cold rationality.

Yet, in the end, it was not Higuera's command of natural philosophy that made him an infamous yet obligatory reference in Spanish history. It was instead his dogged efforts to grant saints like Vitalis, Liberata, and others a permanent place in Catholic history and liturgy, a determined and flawed undertaking that earned him enduring infamy. Higuera's texts seem to have been custom-made specifically to help devotions meet the more stringent criteria of historicity emerging in Counter-Reformation Rome. They were also militant statements in favor of what scholars, following William Christian Jr., now call "local religion," that is, those sometimes idiosyncratic devotions rooted in local memory and landscapes. In these efforts to write local saints back into history, Higuera drew on a number of sources unknown and simply unavailable to Baronio and his researchers, including local inscriptions, obscure manuscript and early print liturgical books, and local pious legends and traditions, which Higuera seems to have considered it a duty to preserve. As we have seen, the "authentic" played a much more significant role in the genesis of the cronicones than scholars have sufficiently acknowledged, as did Higuera's place in a broader intellectual community. The saints he preserved were not all of recent vintage, nor were they all invented, by any means. The legends Higuera culled from his correspondents were both new and old; sometimes they were produced by local consensus, at other times, they seem to have come out of almost complete obscurity, such as a single medieval manuscript. Some were the subject of large-scale local devotions, and others the province of a select few. Some were documented in ancient manuscripts, others circulated only in what could be called oral tradition.

By taking pains to preserve as many local traditions and saints as possible, Higuera seems to have felt that he was working in direct opposition to Baronio, who was in a Rome that must have seemed very distant to Higuera, who had never left Spain. The cronicones embodied what Spain could never actually recover: a continuous textual record of Catholic Christianity from the time of Christ. In this sense, Higuera created a history that was at once counter-Protestant and counter-Baronio.[133] To counter Protestant critics, he documented the origins of Tridentine Catholicism to the primitive apostolic church; against Roman claims to greater antiquity of the faith, he moved the primary sphere of apostolic action from Rome to Spain. The notion of Spain as a new Rome resonated far and wide in Spanish culture and politics, and was certainly not limited to the cronicones.[134] Ecclesiastical independence from Rome was not complete, but it is true that Spain effectively had a national church in the early modern period. The Hapsburgs had inherited control over it thanks to the terms of the *Patronato Real*, a privilege that Ferdinand and Isabel had obtained from a compliant papacy, meaning that it operated effectively as a national church, much like the sort created by Henry VIII in the 1530s.

It was, in part, a function of Spanish ecclesiastical autonomy that Higuera's efforts were so successful. While the desire to buttress sacred history with details of questionable reliability was not uniquely Spanish, the terms of *Pastoralis officii* were unique to Spain. The scale of Higuera's efforts and his research methods suggest that he had in mind not a trivial addition to history, but meant to bring about new devotions or reinforce preexisting ones, particularly with the help of this remarkable papal privilege whose terms he astutely and repeatedly exploited in the name of popular wisdom. This would not have been possible anywhere else in the Catholic world. Many other tangible effects of Higuera's texts on local religion and historical scholarship elsewhere in Spain and Portugal await more detailed study. It is to those early effects, and critical responses to the chronicles, that we now turn.

Part II

Reception

7

Flawed Texts and the Negotiation of Authenticity

> Let her avoid all apocryphal writings, and if she is led to read such not by the truth of the doctrines but out of respect for the miracles contained in them; let her understand that they are not really written by those to whom they are ascribed, that many faulty elements have been introduced into them, and that it requries infinite discretion to look for gold in the midst of dirt.
> —Jerome, Letter to Laeta

If Higuera fabricated his chronicles in response to his friends' desiderata, what made him think that the sources he received in return were not similarly faked? And did the men in Higuera's circles—such as Gabriel Vázquez, Prudencio de Sandoval, and Sancho Dávila—suspect that the historical documents they received might not be trustworthy? Were they simply naive victims of Higuera's ploys, or might they have guided his hand, perhaps by suggesting the types of documents that they would need in their research, or the type of information they would like to have discovered? And, finally, why would Higuera's readers continue to perpetuate the illusion that these texts—which, as even proponents acknowledged, contained many blatant errors and anachronisms—were authentic? In the midst of so much uncertainty, how and why did Higuera, his friends, and his audience forge ahead? The answers to these intertwined questions lie in the particular context in which the cronicones debuted, and in the rather ambiguous nature of historical and religious truth in early modern Spain.

THE VALUE OF THE CHRONICLES

Tantalizing references to Higuera's chronicles by early adopters, combined with the fact that the texts themselves were still only circulating in partial copies among Higuera's friends until the end of the first decade of the seventeenth century, whet the interest of the learned and the curious, of serious scholars and dilettante collectors alike. Yet the demand for reliable copies of the chronicles outstripped supply, such that aspiring collectors went to great lengths to procure a copy for themselves. If we can believe Tomás Tamayo de Vargas—who, as a determined defender of the cronicones, was hardly a disinterested observer—one man in Seville was so desperate to lay his hands upon Dexter's text that he offered the whopping sum of five thousand ducats for a manuscript copy, enough to build a palace, or furnish a respectable dowry for five prospective nuns.[1] Tamayo de Vargas related this anecdote in his widely read summary and defense of Dexter's text, the *Ancient Novelties of Spain* (1624), in which the future royal chronicler of Castile paid particular attention to those details that illuminated the "antiquity of the Christian religion in the Kingdom of Toledo," as well as the "truth of the doctrine of Flavius Lucius Dexter." Naturally, Tamayo de Vargas regarded five thousand ducats as a reasonable reflection of the real value of Dexter for Spain. This included having provided historical proof for "the first foundation of her Churches, the antiquity of the Faith she preserves and of the Prelates who governed her, the saints who defend her, the learned men who impart luster upon her, the Councils that make her glorious, and the observation of the Apostolic Traditions that make her venerable." In all of these senses, Dexter's text was "a unique adornment of the Church against the Heretics."[2]

As Higuera's friends and correspondents began to cite and share their manuscript copies of Dexter-Maximus, the chronicles entered the pool of general circulation with a loud and conspicuous splash, as Spain's most influential readers sought copies for themselves. Even if not all those who collected the chronicles in manuscript actually read them, the texts spread quickly, such that by 1608–1609, Archbishop Pedro de Castro in Granada, Bishop Prudencio de Sandoval in Pamplona, Bishop Sancho Dávila in Jaén, and Archbishop Agostinho de Jesus in Braga all possessed copies, as did the prelates of Palencia, Santiago, Seville, and Sigüenza, the cathedral chapters of Seville and Valencia, the Jesuit colegio of Plasencia, and other notable individuals, including the constable of Castile, Juan de Velasco, and the Duke of Alcalá, Don Fernando Afán de Ribera, a prominent collector of books and art.[3] To meet demand, Higuera tried but failed, through no fault of his own, to get the chronicles printed. As he explained in a 1607 letter to Canon Bartolomé Morlanes of Zaragoza, unfortunately the ship conveying the manuscripts for printing in Flanders sank, and, as it turned out, so did Higuera's hopes of seeing the cronicones in print during his lifetime.[4] Yet once the texts entered print in the 1610s and 1620s, they spread like billowy pollen in springtime, insinuating themselves into nearly every intellectual nook and cranny on the peninsula.

Proponents of Iberian pious traditions embraced the cronicones as useful weapons in several larger and ongoing battles, and many defenders of the texts, like Tamayo de Vargas, framed their advocacy as part of a broader imperative to protect Santiago, Spain, or Catholicism itself from foreign and heretical enemies alike. By attesting to many of the traditions and beliefs central to Catholic and Spanish identity in the annalistic format of late antique chronicles, in a spare style believed to be more verisimilar than the florid details of medieval hagiographic texts, the cronicones seemed not only a fitting riposte to Protestant critics, but also the ideal foil to Cardinal Baronio's reforms. As we shall see, the texts found particularly enthusiastic proponents among partisans of Santiago, who cited Dexter-Maximus alongside other venerable witnesses to the antiquity of this tradition. They were also cited in defense of the controversial doctrine of the Immaculate Conception, in support of the ecclesiastical primacy of Toledo over the other Spanish sees, in favor of the antiquity of El Pilar in Zaragoza, and both for *and* against Saint Teresa of Ávila's appointment as copatron saint of Spain.

Yet the texts were never, even for rabid proponents, unproblematic, and seventeenth-century Spain was gripped by ongoing controversy about their relative value for Iberian history and religion. Critics were hard-pressed to decide: Did the texts' imperfections represent fatal flaws that rendered them useless? Or could some degree of historical information be salvaged from what were essentially authentic texts that nevertheless had been corrupted by the imperfect process of manuscript transmission? Readers of the chronicles did not decide—as we might—whether the texts were real or fake; they lingered in the considerably broad gray area that, for a premodern reader, existed between these two poles. Thus, even those who harbored serious doubts about the texts' integrity or authenticity nevertheless felt free to draw upon them for particular causes, and, from their perspective, in good faith.

READING WITH DOUBT

We have already seen that the early modern Spanish scholar, like his Renaissance humanist forebears, was fluent in the basic tenets of philological method. This included, for example, the axiomatic conviction that ignorant and unscrupulous medieval scribes made the process of manuscript transmission fundamentally flawed. From this perspective, it behooved the knowledgeable reader to remain vigilant for inevitable errors, lacunae, and interpolations. It was also generally accepted that the best manner for smoothing over these rough patches was by comparing and correcting one manuscript copy with another, preferably older and more pristine. In this, the reader of the cronicones in manuscript circulation circa 1600 was at a distinct disadvantage. The multiple copies of each chronicle shared serious problems: they were riddled with significant historical and linguistic anachronisms, suffered from notable errors of fact, chronology, and detail, and, most seriously, they varied sometimes quite drastically from one another in length and content. Without the medieval original, or any sense of which copies were the most reliable, the reader of the chronicles was at sea. He could not perform the most fundamental task of the conscientious scholar, which was to collate his own manuscript with other, more reliable copies, and to correct his own accordingly, thereby producing a third, improved exemplar.

The genesis of these many difficulties was, of course, the unusual provenance of the manuscripts themselves. According to the story, they had been sent to Spain as partial copies, rendered by unknown hands, in an unknown time and place, from originals that could not be found. In the first decades of the seventeenth century, three non-Spanish Jesuits—Christoph Brouwer, Melchior Inchofer, and Cornelio a Lapide—searched in vain for the originals. Inquiries were made at the Benedictine abbey of Fulda itself, and among the Jesuits of Fulda and Worms. Nobody remembered ever having seen the chronicles among the many manuscripts of the collection at Fulda. Nor, indeed, did anybody recall Thomas Torralba, who was supposed to have transmitted the texts to Higuera. To Inchofer's queries regarding Torralba, the rector of the Jesuit house of Fulda professed ignorance; the Jesuit in question, he suggested, must have since "moved to another place." In this, the rector was entirely correct, as Father Torralba had moved on to the next world in 1595.[5]

For the extremely skeptical reader, blatant anachronisms such as Dexter's unprecedented two first names—Flavius Lucius—marked the texts as spurious. Juan Bautista Pérez proclaimed that he had never encountered dual given names in his perusal of ancient Latin sources.[6] Juan de Mariana's critique was founded in a similar suspicion of novelty, although it appears to have been based on hearsay rather than firsthand knowledge. Mariana confided his doubts in a 1614 letter to Heribert Rosweyde, the Flemish Jesuit who edited the first volumes of the *Acta sanctorum*. Mariana remarked, "About Dexter, what can I say? I have not seen it, but based on the accounts from others, I suspect that it is similar to the Berosus of Viterbo."[7] It seems that the Spanish Jesuit had not even deemed it necessary to read the text himself to know that Dexter's chronicle was, as he remarked in another letter, like the Annian texts, "fake and worthless."[8]

While Pérez and Mariana might have considered themselves critical voices crying in a wilderness of credulity, the texts' proponents, in turn, regarded their skepticism as excessive, dangerous, and bordering on heretical. Thus Gaspar Escolano (1560–1619), the Valencian royal chronicler, drew on Dexter in his 1610 history of Valencia—with some reservations, as we shall see—to counter recent critics of Santiago's historical mission to Spain. Among this reprehensible number, Escolano included Baronio, naturally, but he also singled out Mariana, citing the "ill-founded and ardent suspicion which, in this century, [Baronio and Mariana] have tried to raise against such a well-researched truth."[9] It should be noted that Mariana had published a treatise in *defense* of Santiago just one year before the publication of Escolano's *First Decade*.[10] However, Escolano felt that Mariana's close and critical reading of the early medieval sources had done more damage than good, particularly since the Jesuit critiqued the work of Seville's own Saint Isidore, whose *Ortu et orbitu patrum* was often cited by defenders of Santiago as a pivotal proof-text. Like some modern scholars, Baronio and Mariana expressed doubts about whether the text was really the work of Isidore, or if, in fact, it was merely written by a later author under his name.[11] Escolano regarded these propositions as scandalous. He attributed Baronio's excessive scruples to what he imagined must have been the Roman reformer's special hatred for Spain, and he rebuked Mariana for evincing only lukewarm enthusiasm for this most central pillar of Spanish Catholicism. In being "too cautious" in his reading of the sources, Mariana had hurt Santiago—and, by extension, Spain itself.[12]

According to Escolano, a similar excess of scruples led Juan Bautista Pérez to reject Dexter and Maximus's writings outright in 1595, and, in Escolano's lightly mocking depiction, to react to the texts as if they were ghosts or demons:

> The modern censors of antiquity, as if some ghosts from the next world had appeared to them, have begun to express wonder at the resurrection of these two books, and to conjure them to find out if they really are them, or if they are fantastic items, imagined by some prankster.[13]

For Escolano, the dilemma presented by the manuscripts circulating under Dexter's name was more complicated. Admittedly the text contained errors. Yet, as he reasoned, this was a function of the circumstances: Dexter's chronicle had not reemerged from oblivion whole, but in fragments trickling out of Fulda like "relics of venerable antiquity," which were then patched together by Higuera. The end result, Escolano admitted, left much to be desired, particularly since the manuscripts' variation from one another made it difficult to know which copy was more authoritative. At the same time, Escolano admitted that the chronicle may not have been written by the actual Dexter himself, the historical praetorian prefect immortalized by Jerome. It was possible, Escolano conceded, that somebody in the Middle Ages could have penned a chronicle under Dexter's name. In this scenario, the modern *Chronicon* would have been, at worse, a pseudo-Dexter. This did not, however, diminish its importance.

Unlike those "modern censors of antiquity" like Pérez, Baronio, and Mariana, who foolishly rejected a text with so many flaws as unsalvageable, Escolano, like most of his peers, was convinced that even apocryphal texts possessed value, and that the errors in the codices of the cronicones had to be corrected and the flawed texts rendered useful. The flawed state of existing manuscripts was not a theoretical matter for Escolano, whose own copy of Dexter was missing a crucial passage for the Valencian historian. This was the line in which Dexter affirmed that Santiago had visited Valencia and appointed a disciple named Eusebius as the city's first bishop. When he noticed the omission, as Escolano later remembered, he wrote Higuera to request a better copy of the chronicle. The Jesuit soon obliged, and further explained that Escolano's manuscript was an "epitome" (*defloratio*) in which the scribe had only included certain passages of interest to the person commissioning the copy.[14]

In other words, while Dexter's chronicle was not perfect, this did not mean that one should reject it completely. For example, in one early version of the chronicle, Dexter committed the rather egregious error of misidentifying his father's successor—Saint Severus—as the current bishop of Barcelona, during his own lifetime; in fact, however, Severus preceded Pacianus. Juan Bautista Pérez singled this out as another reason why the text should be regarded as spurious. Escolano, in contrast, reasoned that this was just as plausibly the error of a sloppy copyist or later interpolator. To judge otherwise was to be guilty of excessive scruples:

> When one discovers a small defect in the work of a historian, it is overly harsh to then put his work to the test, and deny that it is his. None of these [chroniclers] write evangelical history, nor do they have the freedom to deceive and lie, not even in the events of their own times.[15]

One could not just jettison every book that contained errors. Like the old soldier who stabbed the page and shouted "you lie, you lie," every time he came across an objectionable passage in Paolo Giovio's account of Charles V's military campaigns in Italy, the reader of the cronicones may need to intervene in the text itself to salvage what was useful.[16] A similar rationale was articulated by the Zaragoza Franciscan Diego Murillo, who, in his 1616 treatise in defense of El Pilar, explained that since the highest good was to promote faith and good customs, it was always better to affirm sacred traditions than to subject them to intensive scrutiny. For this reason, "one must flee as if from the plague from the men who, with arrogant and subtle cunning raise scruples about ancient traditions, asking for new testimony to confirm them, as if well-founded tradition were not the most effective."[17] It was better to embrace the exemplary story, particularly when it came to sacred matters.

As Ambrosio de Morales and Higuera had both noted, a certain degree of uncertainty was admittedly unavoidable for the historian who wished to address ancient history. Due to the obscurity of the ancient past, embracing flawed sources was sometimes the only way to recover a portion of the truth. Martín de Roa, an Andalusian Jesuit who incorporated the cronicones into several of his local histories of the Seville region in the first decades of the seventeenth century, compared the process of recovering ancient Iberian place-names to trying to find one's way in the dark:

> The distance from antiquity in this matter, more than any other in history, casts as much of a shadow, and obscures the truth, as much as the darkness of nighttime does to the eyes. We suffer as much in the former as we do in the latter: when, following a tiny light in middle of a great darkness, and straining the eyes to recognize what is there . . . and some things look like something else, and a lot of time nothing is what it seems . . . This is why we feel our way around in ignorance and darkness, following the thread of ancient matters, most of the time with more effort than results.[18]

For authors like Roa, writing ancient history, like discerning shapes in a dark room, was an inexact science. Just as the nighttime prowler would be grateful for a ray of light, readers such as Roa embraced the cronicones with gratitude for their flawed yet indispensable contribution to Spanish sacred history.

IMPERFECT TRUTHS:
THE CHRONICLES AS USEFUL APOCRYPHA

Judging from the number of authors who drew on the Higuera corpus of texts and the heuristic agility with which they explained away the flaws, most early seventeenth-century readers agreed with Escolano, Murillo, and Roa's assessment that the imperfect state of the cronicones was well within the range of normal. Thus, when Dexter had Santiago appointing bishops in Spain in the years after he had died, the apologist could reason that this was simply a slip of the pen, or a misprint; either way, a chronological error could be corrected by a conscientious editor. Seventeenth-century readers apprehended their manuscript or printed copies of the chronicle of Dexter, or of Julián Pérez, for example, with a certain set of expectations. They knew that the authorship was not certain, they knew the texts' origins were somewhat foggy, and they knew that the copy in their hands might not be identical to any other. They nevertheless expected to find useful material.

In this, readers of the chronicles were participating in a much older hermeneutic tradition going back to the early centuries of Christianity. As François Bovon has argued, for many early Christian interpreters, extracanonical texts and apocryphal traditions formed a middle category, of "useful" or "profitable" books. Many authors of medieval hagiographical and liturgical texts likewise took a rather pragmatic approach to the theological problems posed by texts of uncertain authorship, and concluded that even if these "useful books" may not have possessed apostolic authority, they nevertheless provided exemplary tales for pious edification, which could, for example, be incorporated into sermons.[19] As Alfred Hiatt explains, "for medieval authorities confronted with a possible forgery . . . the task was not (as it was for humanist criticism of documents) to determine the inherent truth or falsity of a document, but rather to determine its degree of validity. And it is important to emphasise that a text would on occasion validate itself through the potency—the credibility and acceptability—of its narrative."[20] This middle way endured, even as a relatively more rigorous humanist discourse around true and false documents evolved during the Renaissance.

In the early modern period, this notion of truth simply took its place alongside the newer and more rigorous tools of philological and historical critique. When the mid-fifteenth-century theologian Nicholas of Cusa critiqued the *Donation of Constantine*, he characterized it as an apocryphal text—one whose author was unknown or unconfirmed, but which could still be read licitly.[21] In contrast, Cusa's contemporary, the Italian humanist Lorenzo Valla, cited the *Donation*'s anachronistic language and implausible historical details to conclude that it was an outright forgery, and, as such, should be rejected and extirpated from the tradition. While Valla is celebrated by modern scholars as heralding a new, more critical age, it was arguably Cusa's hermeneutic, not Valla's, that would prevail among their fifteenth-century contemporaries; as Hiatt has argued, "If the Middle Ages came to an end with the works of Valla [and others], no one seems to have noticed."[22] Indeed, like many of their medieval and Renaissance predecessors, early modern readers plotted the truth value of texts within an interpretive matrix that admitted a range of possibilities and measured the truth of their texts in degrees rather than absolutes.

Yet if active reading was the key to using apocrypha correctly, it was not for the ignorant or faint of heart. Defenders of the chronicles depicted their labors as essential services for Spanish history and holiness, in which they heroically separated the authentic wheat from the more apocryphal chaff. From this perspective, critics such as Mariana were simply unwilling to engage in the tough philological, historical, and linguistic work required to make the false chronicles useful. Proponents such as Escolano were well aware that it would be essential to conduct this act of critical reconstruction carefully, so as not to provide more ammunition to domestic and foreign critics of Spanish sacred traditions. Yet it was clearly worth the effort. At stake were several highly contentious and complex religio-political issues. Thanks to the perceived double threat posed in the late sixteenth and early seventeenth centuries to Spain's patron saint, Santiago, by tough critics such as Baronio, Mariana, and their ilk, and by domestic proponents of making the recently canonized Saint Teresa of Ávila copatron of Spain, the texts were eagerly sought, scrutinized, and put to immediate use by partisans on both sides, as the copatronage controversy gripped learned, ecclesiastical, and courtly circles in the first decades of the seventeenth century. For foes of copatronage, such as representatives of the guardians of the apostle's relics, namely, the cathedral chapter of Santiago de Compostela, Dexter's chronicle was particularly useful in that it attested to the entire bundle of traditions, including Santiago's Spanish apostolate, his appointment of the Seven Apostles, his foundation and construction of the church of the Virgin of El Pilar, and his eventual burial in Compostela.[23] In contrast, *Teresianos* somehow found evidence in the chronicles that Santiago's apostolate had not been continuously remembered in days of yore, as the Seville cathedral canon Francisco Morovelli de Puebla argued in a 1628 treatise.[24] More generally, the cronicones were believed to safeguard the integrity of Spanish Catholicism itself. The cult of the saints needed to be protected from extreme critics, such as Protestants, but to a lesser extent it also needed to be protected from fellow Catholic scholars who were insufficiently cautious in their critiques, such as Baronio and Mariana. After all, as Murillo warned in his treatise on El Pilar, to doubt the miraculous establishment of the church of El Pilar by Santiago would be to "open the door to the audaciousness of the heretics who deny traditions."[25]

With the integrity of the faith at stake, proponents of the chronicles surmised that the discovery of the texts circa 1594 had been anything but accidental. Gaspar Escolano suggested that God had chosen this pivotal moment to reveal the texts after they had been lost for over a thousand years during the "general flood" of Moors throughout the land. God sent forth the cronicones to combat heretics as well as those "modern censors of antiquity" such as Baronio and Mariana.[26] Like the Hebrew prophets Enoch and Elijah, who according to biblical and patristic tradition would return to earth to prefigure the Second Coming and face the anti-Christ in battle, the cronicones had emerged "during this final judgment" to vanquish those who seemed to threaten fundamental notions like Santiago's special relationship with Spain. In this eschatological scenario, divine light revealed these texts, as well as the lead books of Granada, and God provided them with powerful "godfathers"—human sponsors—"for greater confirmation of the truth."[27]

With the very shape of religion, politics, and society arguably at stake—not to mention concerns about Santiago and the Virgin of El Pilar—it could be difficult for those who took a rather less indulgent stance vis-à-vis the chronicles. This was particularly true in Zaragoza, where the canons of El Pilar constituted a vocal and influential block of support for the texts. This is what Martín Carrillo (1561–1630) was to discover. In his history of the diocese, Carrillo, who was rector of the cathedral-run University of Zaragoza and abbot of the monastery of Montearagón, made a point of excluding those early bishops attested only by Dexter. This move, as he later noted ruefully, earned him the opprobrium of his peers, and Carrillo felt obliged to address the value of Dexter's text for his arguments in his following book, the 1615 *History of the Glorious Saint Valero . . . with a Catalogue of all the Prelates, Bishops, Archbishops, and Abbots of the Kingdom of Aragon*. Carrillo had good reason to regard Dexter's text as less than trustworthy: it did not mention Saint Valero from Zaragoza, the saint who was, after all, the topic of his treatise. "This," he explained, "just gives me a greater suspicion that this history of Dexter is deformed, or not true, or something has been removed from it."[28] He granted that if the original in Fulda—or even a reliable medieval copy—could be tracked down, then at the very least a proper edition could be issued and the text evaluated fairly on its merits. In the present state of affairs this was scarcely possible: each circulating manuscript was crowded with additions, corrections, and commentary, not by a single authoritative editor but according to the individual whims of each and every reader through whose hands the texts passed. This, Carrillo conceded, was not the fate of Dexter's text alone. It was true for most of the surviving sources regarding Aragonese history, which, like Dexter's, "circulate in manuscript, and they are so defective, that if their authors saw them today, they would not recognize them."[29]

As Carrillo was to find, in the first two decades of the seventeenth century, even a moderate skepticism about the chronicles was extraordinarily difficult to sustain in a Zaragoza where El Pilar was the ascendant party, and reference to Dexter was de rigueur. Yet we should not mistake Carrillo for a neo-Pyrrhonist. Even if he disdained the cronicones for their implicit support of El Pilar, he hoped like any other local patriot to accrue more religious and historical glory for his favorite causes, which he promoted with the same questionable scholarly tactics and expansive sense of pride as his peers. Carrillo was also a canon at El Pilar's traditional rival, Zaragoza's cathedral, which was known as La Seo. As a partisan of La Seo, Carrillo attacked El Pilar's claims so relentlessly that his 1615 *History* became controversial before it was even published: the royal printing license stipulated that the book be bound and sold with an additional pamphlet in which the author would address a number of objections to his arguments. These included Carrillo's controversial assertions that Santiago had not built El Pilar, but rather Zaragoza's church of the Savior, and that La Seo had existed in its present location long before the church of El Pilar was constructed. Carrillo also needed to answer for having claimed martyrs for the city who, according to received wisdom, were actually natives of other places.[30]

We can witness a similar oscillation between credulity and skepticism in a 1624 treatise on historical chronology by the Dominican Alonso de Maldonado, who did not reject the cronicones. In contrast, he spent so much space considering the false chronicles—as well as the forgeries of Annius of Viterbo and the lead books of Granada—that he ended up neglecting the main purpose of his text, which was to outline a universal system of historical chronology. Yet, in the course of anticipating and addressing the critiques of the chronicles—which, in true scholastic fashion, he did in a twenty-four-point argument—he inadvertently exposed the texts' weak flank to a wide audience, one made even wider by his having written in the vernacular. For example, Maldonado argued that as an author, Dexter did not exhibit a particularly high level of critical thought, and that, in fact, his "simplicity" (*llaneza*) seemed to suggest rather middling learning.[31] This, and not a desire to falsify the past, was why Dexter had failed to perform the fundamental tasks of the historian, such as reconciling conflicting accounts or assessing the reliability of his sources. While Maldonado conceded that Dexter's methods as a historian would not stand up to scrutiny, they did not preclude his chronicle from being a valuable source for information about what was believed among "ancient Spaniards."[32] Dexter was a collector, not a scholar; in this sense, the chronicle was not proper history, but a repository of traditions and beliefs that had been general among his peers. This meant sometimes discounting Dexter's rather grandiose claims for the Spanish contribution to early Christian history, such as when Dexter identified the unnamed Greeks who importuned the apostle Philip to introduce them to Jesus on Palm Sunday in John 12:20–21 as Spaniards, and characterized this incident as "a clear portent of the fact that the Spanish would become the first among the Gentiles to be worthy of having [the Gospel] preached to them."[33] Maldonado dismissed this as just one of many examples of Dexter's misguided attempts to claim for the Spanish "everything that did not have a known owner."[34]

In spite of his rather critical assessment of Dexter's text, Maldonado concluded that notwithstanding many apparent slips of the pen and what for a sixteenth-century Dominican were unforgivable errors—such as the text's claim that the Immaculate Conception had been observed since apostolic times—readers should use Dexter as an important historical source, which "deserves the same credit as the histories by serious authors."[35] Maldonado even extended this latitudinarian attitude to Annius of Viterbo, whose forgeries had long before been condemned in the court of learned European opinion. Following the same logic that he had applied to Dexter, Maldonado defended his fellow Dominican from accusations of forgery: Annius had merely transmitted texts that may have been forged by others, such as ancient rabbis; as such, his only fault was to have believed the learned Dominicans who furnished the text from somewhere in the Orient. Far from accusing Annius of forgery, he reasoned, we should thank God for preserving the texts, when so many others had been lost forever.[36]

The rather forgiving hermeneutic with which readers such as Maldonado approached texts of apocryphal status also helped eliminate many of the seemingly serious problems with the texts in the first place. In this circular logic, the chronicles were apocryphal because they were of uncertain authorship; and nobody could prove that Dexter or Maximus or the others had actually written the texts because they were also of uncertain transmission. It was feared that they could have been tampered with, altered, or corrupted, perhaps even by heretics. This is why a judicious editor and extensive *ilustraciones*—illuminating commentary to guide the reader—were desperately needed to render the rough and flawed prose coherent and complete.

THE CHRONICLES IN PRINT:
THE DISASTROUS 1619 EDITION

The perceived need to correct and stabilize the texts, combined with the patronage of partisans of El Pilar, Santiago, and other causes, helped usher the chronicles into print. Between 1619 and 1651, each of the four chronicles was printed at least once, and some twice, in a total of seven editions, each of which varied widely in terms of length, quality, and expense. As we have seen, proponents and foes alike recognized that the authorship of the cronicones was not confirmable beyond a shadow of a doubt. What this meant as far as their historical value was a matter of contention. Attitudes toward apocrypha were in transition, and like so many other texts and traditions, works of uncertain authorship were subjected to increased scrutiny. The texts' patrons and supporters were aware that in this contentious atmosphere their historical value would need to be defended tooth and nail. Thus, the printed editions of the chronicles would need to support, defend, and elucidate, much more than would be customary for a run-of-the-mill historical text.

Each edition included the requisite royal permissions, licenses, and theological approvals that would have accompanied any other licitly printed work at the time. Yet the editors of the cronicones made an extra effort to pad the text with material that would help establish the bona fides of the purported authors as well as their own. In this effort, the "rhetoric of typography and textual configuration" would prove crucial, just as it had for editions of Annius of Viterbo's pseudoantique chronicles.[37] So, too, would the paratext, namely, the supplementary material, including prefaces, dedications, epistles, authorial commentary, lists of authorities, and other such items which exist, per Gérard Genette, at the "fringe of the printed text," and yet "which in reality control one's whole reading of the text."[38]

The first edition was printed in Zaragoza in 1619 and included Dexter and Maximus, as well as other texts copied from Higuera, including short continuations of the chronicles by Heleca and Braulio (actual bishops of Zaragoza), and poems penned by Maximus in honor of Saint Hermenegild and the Virgin of El Pilar (figure 7.1).[39] In a preface, the text's editor, the Zaragoza Franciscan Juan de Calderón, furnished a brief biography of Dexter, addressed possible objections and doubts about the text and its author, and directed readers to the oldest authorities he could find on Dexter himself, particularly the early Latin church father Jerome. Calderón also explained the mechanics of how he had assembled his edition by consulting multiple manuscript copies circulating in and around Zaragoza. Calderón addressed other pressing issues, such as the provenance of the original manuscripts of the cronicones, which was explained paratextually in a letter from Luitprand recounting his own discovery of the texts in Fulda. The epistle also recounted how these Spanish texts had ended up in a central European monastery in the first place (namely, Charlemagne sent several texts to Fulda for safekeeping, where Luitprand consulted them). In addition, Calderón directed the edition to notable and sympathetic dedicatees, including Don Pedro de Molina, a vicar who served the archbishop of Zaragoza, and Pedro González de Mendoza, a cathedral canon in Granada. The text was also dedicated to the Virgin of El Pilar, "conceived without sin," the kingdom of Aragon, and the city of Zaragoza.

Those who hoped that the text of Dexter-Maximus would be corrected and the uncertainties of the many contradictory manuscripts resolved once it entered

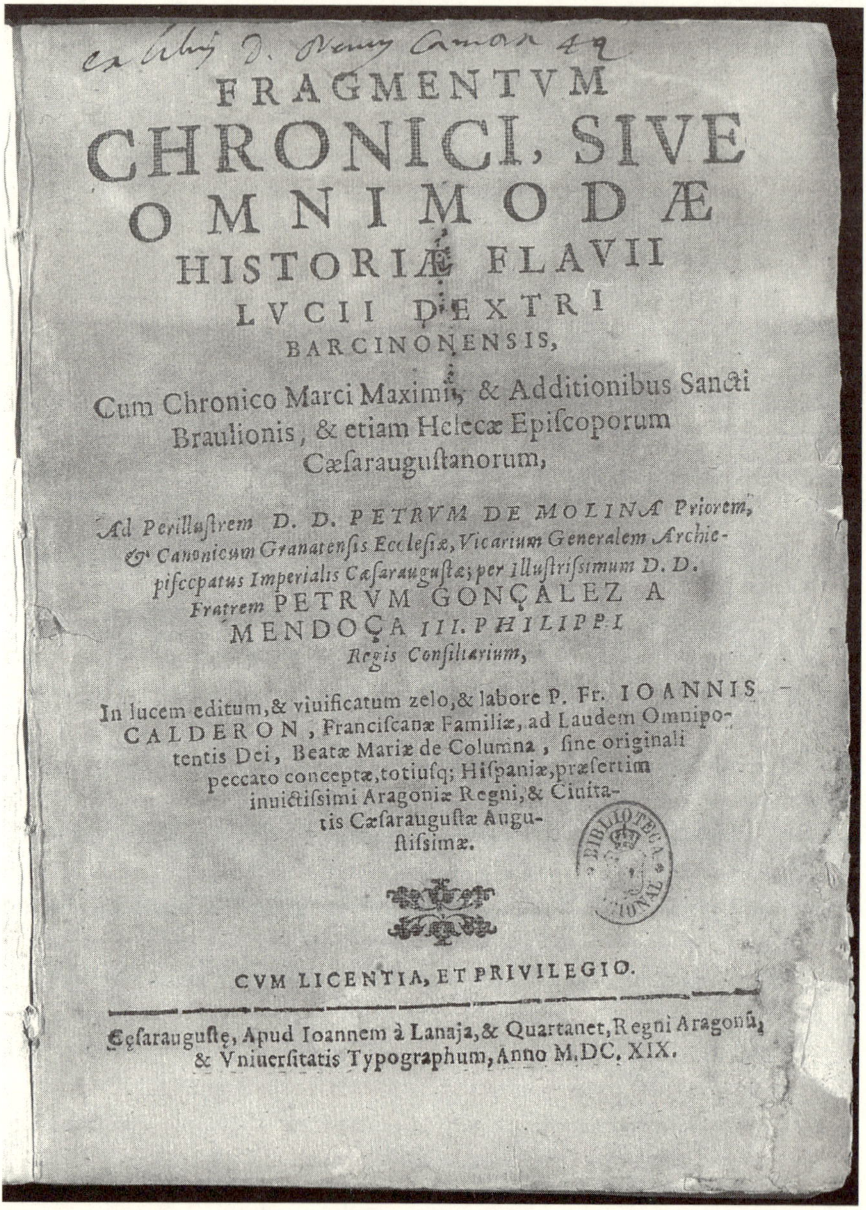

FRAGMENTVM CHRONICI, SIVE OMNIMODÆ HISTORIÆ FLAVII LVCII DEXTRI BARCINONENSIS,

Cum Chronico Marci Maximi, & Additionibus Sancti Braulionis, & etiam Helecæ Episcoporum Cæsaraugustanorum,

Ad Perillustrem D. D. PETRVM DE MOLINA Priorem, & Canonicum Granatensis Ecclesiæ, Vicarium Generalem Archiepiscopatus Imperialis Cæsaraugustæ, per illustrissimum D. D. Fratrem PETRVM GONÇALEZ A MENDOÇA III. PHILIPPI *Regis Consiliarium,*

In lucem editum, & viuificatum zelo, & labore P. Fr. IOANNIS CALDERON, Franciscanæ Familiæ, ad Laudem Omnipotentis Dei, Beatæ Mariæ de Columna, sine originali peccato conceptæ, totiusq; Hispaniæ, præsertim inuictissimi Aragoniæ Regni, & Ciuitatis Cæsaraugustæ Augustissimæ.

CVM LICENTIA, ET PRIVILEGIO.

Cæsaraugustę, Apud Ioannem à Lanaja, & Quartanet, Regni Aragonũ, & Vniuersitatis Typographum, Anno M.DC.XIX.

Figure 7.1. The disastrous 1619 edition. Juan de Calderón, ed., *Fragmentum Chronici, siue Omnimodae Historiae Flavii Lucii Dextri* (Zaragoza, 1619) © Biblioteca Nacional de España, R/3570.

Table 7.1. Surviving print copies of Higuera's cronicones in Spanish libraries

Chronicle	Editor	Place And Date Of Edition	Surviving Copies In Spanish Libraries
Dexter-Maximus	Juan de Calderón	Zaragoza, 1619	39
Dexter-Maximus	Rodrigo Caro	Seville, 1627	32
Dexter-Maximus	Francisco Bivar	Lyons, 1627	56
Marcus Maximus	Francisco Bivar	Madrid, 1654	72
Luitprand	Tomás Tamayo de Vargas	Madrid, 1635	41
Luitprand	Lorenzo Ramírez de Prado	Paris, 1640	20
Julián Pérez	Lorenzo Ramírez de Prado	Paris, 1628	23
Total			283

Sources: Catalogue of the Biblioteca Nacional, Madrid, and the Catálogo Colectivo del Patrimonio Bibliográfico, maintained by Spain's Comunidades Autónomas and the Spanish Ministerio de Cultura's Dirección General del Libro, Archivos y Bibliotecas.

The relatively poor rate of survival for early printed works makes it quite likely that the total circulation of the cronicones was even greater than suggested by these preliminary figures, which do not include the many copies held in Portuguese, Italian, and other European libraries, not to mention collections in the Western Hemisphere.

print were to be sorely disappointed by the 1619 edition, which was popular but widely panned (table 7.1). For many of his contemporaries, Calderón fell short as an editor. In rendering the various manuscripts of Dexter-Maximus into print, Calderón could have opted for one of two critical approaches: the first would have been to choose the manuscript that seemed most trustworthy, and silently smooth out errors and textual variations in order to render a clean and correct copy. Alternatively, a more conscientious scholar might have opted to recreate an exact replica of the best manuscript, while also pointing out variations among the manuscripts and leaving grammatical or orthographic errors in place, noting when the hand changed, and retaining *homoeoteleuta*—errors on the part of the scribe, such as when he might inadvertently miss a line of copy, which was particularly common when two lines in a row ended with the same words.[40] Calderón did not smooth out the errors, nor did he point them out. This did not seem to have been a deliberate choice, as it was, for example, for Calderón's contemporary, the Flemish hagiographer Heribert Rosweyde, who believed that retaining the errors in medieval hagiographic texts was an act of devotion.[41] At least as it seemed to Calderón's critics, he failed to adopt any particular critical stance at all. The edition was simply sloppy. As the Cordoban antiquary Pedro Díaz de Ribas noted, not only had Calderón done nothing to clean up the manuscripts but he had even committed new and unpardonable mistakes, such as inadvertently including marginal comments in the body of the text.[42]

A more critical and careful commentator was needed, somebody who would save the reputation of the texts before it was too late. In his 1624 treatise in defense of Dexter, Tamayo de Vargas declared that the poor state of Calderón's edition had prompted him to write this three-part offensive in Castilian: for the first hundred pages, in the *Ancient Novelties of Spain: Flavius Lucius Dexter Defended*, Tamayo de Vargas answered recent critiques of the texts; next he enumerated the *Antiquity of the Christian Religion in Toledo, in Demonstration of the Truth of the Doctrine of Flavius Lucius Dexter*, which included a vigorous defense of Toledo's claims to ecclesiastical primacy, supported by the ancient authority of Dexter; and, finally, he concluded with a miscellaneous assortment of other items of interest in an *Ascertainment of Some of the Illustrious Memories of Ecclesiastical History for Spain*, all derived, naturally, from the chronicles. Tamayo de Vargas worried that the damage wreaked by Calderón's careless editing may have soured some readers on the texts altogether, and he resolved that it would have been better if Calderón had not printed the text at all rather than expose it to the general reading public before it was ready. After all, the text had reached the seventeenth century in such a "poor state" (*mal trage*) that it required careful reconstruction, as well as extensive commentary. Instead, Calderón had jumped the gun, "hurrying to publish" and thus "exposing it to the shame and judgment of all, without any qualms." As a result, the text received an unenthusiastic welcome and was even deemed "unintelligible or mendacious" by critics. This would be resolved shortly, Tamayo de Vargas assured his readers, by his own edition of Dexter-Maximus in which he would "smooth out the difficulties" with learned commentary written in Latin, the "language of learning," the only adornment worthy of such a text.[43] This edition was never to see the light of day.

In the meantime, Tamayo de Vargas tried to turn the discrepancies among the various copies of Dexter from a liability into an advantage. He noted that "the transcriptions of this work, which are in learned (*curiosas*) libraries, are so different from each other," that it was simply not possible that they could have been the product of a single mind. This sort of diversity could only be produced by many scribes working their destructive magic upon the codices over many centuries.[44] In contrast, he reasoned, if one person had forged the texts then all the extant manuscripts would have looked the same.

Tamayo de Vargas also tried another tack, to grant Dexter legitimacy by associating the text with other prominent courtiers and historians who, he assured the reader, were, like him, toiling away on a suitable set of comments to support the texts. This was such a monumental task that for some, like Higuera and Catalonia's Fray Francisco Diago, it had been cut short by death. Other eruditos reportedly working on Dexter included the Jesuit Francisco Portocarrero, as well as Higuera's nemesis, the Toledan canon Pedro Salazar de Mendoza. Tamayo de Vargas also listed Juan Fonseca i Figueroa, the royal librarian and close friend of the royal favorite, Gaspar de Guzmán, the Count-Duke of Olivares; Miguel Martínez del Villar, member of a prominent Aragonese family and regent in the Aragonese royal council; a Jesuit named Paulo Albiniano de Rajas; and the Discalced Carmelite historian Fray Francisco de Santa María. Tamayo de Vargas also assured the reader that prominent courtiers in the circles of the Count-Duke of Olivares had been engaged in the search for the texts' originals, including Don Balthasar de Zúñiga, the uncle and intimate of the count-duke, and Don Luis Lasso de la Vega y Guzmán, the Count of Añover.[45]

Although we have no way of confirming that all of these prominent men of learning and politics were, as Tamayo de Vargas asserted, actually engaged in protecting, defending, and seeking better manuscripts of the false chronicles, he was correct that the texts had become the object of curiosity in these circles. As a postulant for the patronage of the count-duke, Tamayo de Vargas was in a position to know: he dedicated his 1624 treatise to a highly placed cleric in the Olivares family's private funerary chapel, and solicited odes and other prefatory materials from a number of prominent individuals, including Juan Fonseca i Figueroa and the royal chaplain and preacher Francisco Sánchez de Villanueva.

BAROQUE EDITIONS AND PARATEXT AS POLEMIC

The use of paratextual material to ground the chronicles in a confirmable time and place, to link them with familiar historical characters and to sprinkle them with authentic-sounding details, attained new heights in printed editions of the chronicles after 1619. The tendency toward increasingly extravagant and elaborate editions is exemplified in the two separate 1627 editions of Dexter-Maximus prepared (without knowledge of each other) by Rodrigo Caro, the Seville antiquary, and Francisco de Bivar, a Cistercian abbot; it would continue with the successive print versions of each of the four chronicles published from 1628 to 1651. In contrast to Calderón's relatively lean, 130-page book (figure 7.2), Caro and Bivar's editions each surpass five hundred pages, as each respective editor wrapped the annalistic core in layer upon layer of supplementary material in truly baroque displays of their scholarly exertions (figure 7.3). Much of this para-

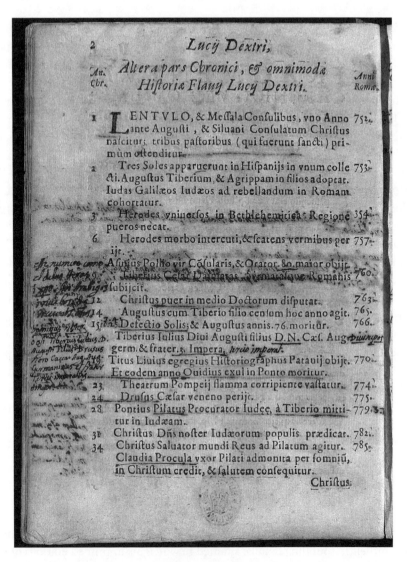

Figure 7.2. The first page of Calderón's edition of Dexter's chronicle, beginning with the coming of Christ. The top of each page includes dual chronological columns: on the left, a count of years since the Incarnation, and on the right, since the foundation of Rome. Period annotations in the left-hand column point out that the Anno Domini chronology is anachronistic, and also supply a passage missing from this edition, which the reader evidently discovered when collating this printed copy with another manuscript of the cronicón. Juan de Calderón, ed., *Fragmentum Chronici* (Zaragoza, 1619) © Biblioteca Nacional de España, R/3570, 2r.

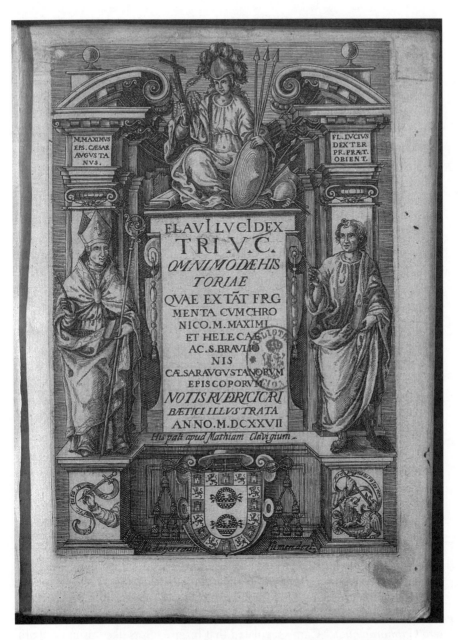

Figure 7.3. Caro's 1627 edition. Rodrigo Caro, ed., *Flavi Luci Dextri V.C. omnimodae historiae quae extant fragmenta cum chronico M. Maximi et Helecae ac S. Braulionis caesaraugustanorum episcoporum* (Seville, 1627) © Biblioteca Nacional de España, R/12758.

textual padding was customary. Caro's text was preceded by poetic odes in praise of the wisdom of Dexter and of Caro himself, which pivoted upon clunky puns on both of their names. In addition, Caro drew up an extensive catalogue of patristic and medieval authors who had attested to Dexter's existence, including venerable authorities such as Antonio Agustín and Cardinal Baronio; this was so much sound and fury for, as it turned out, Agustín and Baronio, like many before them, had merely mentioned the lost history of Dexter and certainly had not endorsed the authenticity of its early modern manifestation, as Caro craftily implied.

In Caro's *ilustraciones*, which were printed directly after the passages in question, he folded in all manner of detail to help elucidate the text's significance and to help prove its authenticity (figure 7.4). In this sense, Caro, who is best known to modern scholars for his *Canción a las ruinas de Itálica*, a Petrarchan celebration of the erstwhile Roman city just outside Seville, continued in the tradition of medieval scholastic commentary by creating a parallel text replete with explanations and citations, which would be read alongside the original as a guide to correct comprehension.[46] For example, Caro included many inscriptions—either from his own collection, or, more often than not, from Ambrosio de Morales—that he believed would help vouch for Dexter's version of history. He also larded the commentary with corroborating or contradictory details—depending on the passage at hand—from Morales and Baronio, ancient martyrologies, and other trustworthy and familiar classical, patristic, and medieval authorities. The volume concluded with a cluster of appendixes and finding aids, such as topographical and topical indexes, as well as a list of common epigraphic abbreviations, since perhaps even an accomplished Latinist would have needed some help to know that QBFQS denoted *quod bonum faustumque sit* ("which may be a favorable omen").[47]

Yet the first task of the conscientious editor was to establish a trustworthy text by correcting it as common sense or historical knowledge might mandate. In this task Calderón had failed spectacularly; Caro boasted that he had worked quite hard to redress these flaws and shore up the text through extensive reworking. In the commentary, Caro pointed to one particularly egregious error in a passage in AD 100. Here the 1619 edition described the martyr Antima Maximilla as having married a man named "Caius Fonterus of the Cattles' Fodder" (*C. Fontero Capitorumque*).[48] Caro speculated that bizarre errors like this in the Latin were perhaps because neither Calderón nor his copyist could actually read the "Gothic" handwriting of the Fulda original. Caro corrected the paleographical error with an alternate reading that, it must be said, did not so much clarify the obscure idiom as bring it only slightly closer to the realm of plausibility. Thus, in

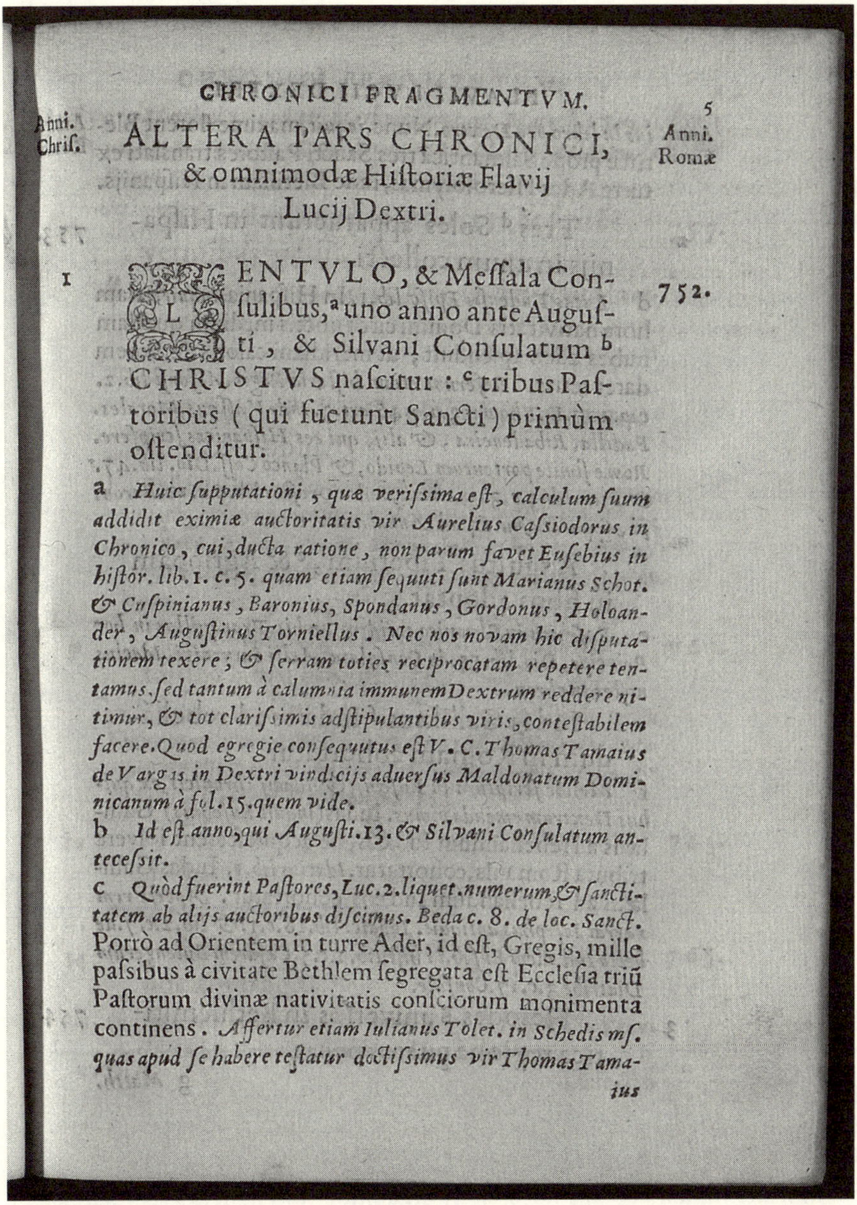

CHRONICI FRAGMENTVM.

Anni. Chrif.

ALTERA PARS CHRONICI,
& omnimodæ Hiſtoriæ Flavij
Lucij Dextri.

Anni. Romæ

1
LENTVLO, & Meſſala Conſulibus,[a] uno anno ante Auguſti, & Silvani Conſulatum [b] CHRISTVS naſcitur : [c] tribus Paſtoribus (qui fuerunt Sancti) primùm oſtenditur.

752.

[a] *Huic ſupputationi, quæ veriſsima eſt, calculum ſuum addidit eximiæ auctoritatis vir Aurelius Caſsiodorus in Chronico, cui, ducta ratione, non parum favet Euſebius in hiſtor. lib. 1. c. 5. quam etiam ſequuti ſunt Marianus Schot. & Cuſpinianus, Baronius, Spondanus, Gordonus, Holoander, Auguſtinus Torniellus. Nec nos novam hic diſputationem texere; & ſerram toties reciprocatam repetere tentamus, ſed tantum à calumnia immunem Dextrum reddere nitimur, & tot clariſsimis adſtipulantibus viris, conteſtabilem facere. Quod egregie conſequutus eſt V. C. Thomas Tamaius de Vargas in Dextri vindicijs aduerſus Maldonatum Dominicanum à fol. 15. quem vide.*

[b] *Id eſt anno, qui Auguſti. 13. & Silvani Conſulatum anteceſsit.*

[c] *Quòd fuerint Paſtores, Luc. 2. liquet. numerum & ſanctitatem ab alijs auctoribus diſcimus. Beda c. 8. de loc. Sanct. Porrò ad Orientem in turre Ader, id eſt, Gregis, mille paſsibus à civitate Bethlem ſegregata eſt Eccleſia triũ Paſtorum divinæ nativitatis conſciorum monimenta continens. Aſſertur etiam Iulianus Tolet. in Schedis mſ. quas apud ſe habere teſtatur doctiſsimus vir Thomas Tamaius*

Figure 7.4. The first page of Caro's edition of Dexter's chronicle, beginning with the coming of Christ. Only the first eight lines belong to the text of the chronicle proper; the bottom two-thirds of the page are Caro's annotations (marked as footnotes a, b, c). Rodrigo Caro, ed., *Flavi Luci Dextri . . . omnimodae historiae* (Seville, 1627) © Biblioteca Nacional de España, R/12758.

Caro's Dexter, the martyr instead married a man known as "Caius Fonteius Big Head" (*C. Fonteio Capitoni*). In light of this awkward rendition, it seems that Caro was rather overstating the case when, in a mordant aside, he boasted of having restored this "wretchedly mutilated passage" to "pristine elegance," much as Erasmus of Rotterdam described his own heroic efforts to edit the letters of Jerome: "I have slain with daggers the spurious and interpolated passages, while I have elucidated the obscure parts in my notes."[49]

If Caro's notes were flying buttresses intended to fortify the text, the elaborate observations that adorned the other 1627 edition of Dexter-Maximus formed a veritable cathedral of commentary (figure 7.5). In this, Bivar's Lyons edition is perhaps a fitting metaphor for the life of Bivar (1584–1635), in which avid and sometimes polemical scholarship met fervid devotion. While living in Rome as the Cistercian agent (*procurador*) to the papal curia from circa 1620 to 1626, Bivar prepared his own annotated Dexter-Maximus.[50] In the process, he also leapt into what seems to have been the first extended dispute about the authenticity of the cronicones to occur outside of Spain. He padded his edition with extensive prefatory material, including letters from various learned men in praise of his edition; a short vita of Dexter the historical figure; and not one but two short treatises in defense of the text's authenticity. On each page, Bivar's commentary appeared under the text of the chronicles; like Caro's, it formed an arsenal of cross-references, citations, and polemic. While to call it a narrative would be to overstate its coherence, this material forms a virtual parallel book, in which the author embarks on extended discussions of the annalistic entry at hand, forwards apologetics on one aspect or another, and pours out heaps of evidence from his own research to support his arguments, including inscriptions, coins, and documents. Bivar folded entire documents into his copious notes, some authentic, and others of rather more recent confection. In this sense, he emulated the printed rhetoric of Annius's pseudo-Berosus, whose editions included supporting documents that the Italian Dominican claimed to have discovered himself. Just as in these texts, so, too, in Bivar's edition "the paratextual presentation of the texts, and their explicit intertextual references among themselves, create[d] a maze within which naive or credulous readers could lose their bearings."[51]

Bivar's commentary was not merely an adjunct to Higuera's spare annals: it forms a veritable dialogue with the text itself. As dialogues go, it is a rather meandering and dry one indeed. In this, Bivar participated in the prevailing style among seventeenth-century ecclesiastical antiquaries of all confessional stripes. By heaping mounds of documentary, epigraphic, and other historical evidence into his pages, he hoped to create solid bases of erudition to prop up an imperfect

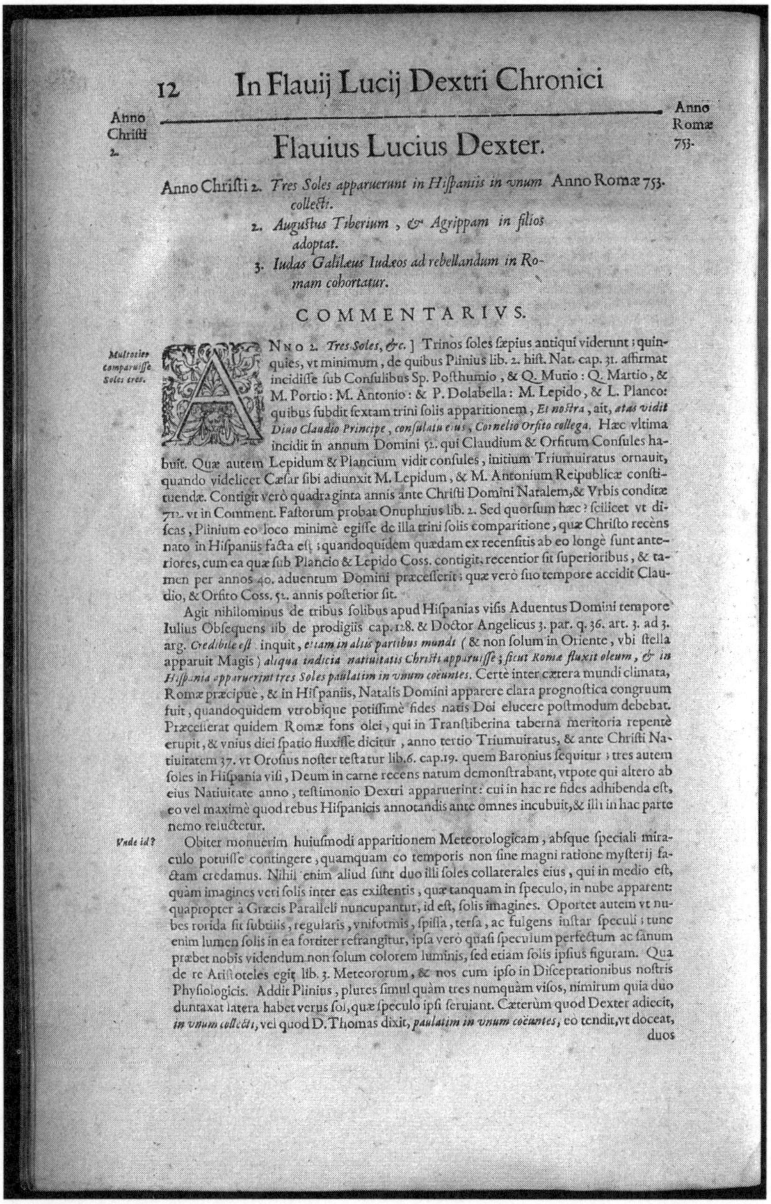

12 In Flauij Lucij Dextri Chronici

Anno Chriſti 2. | Anno Romæ 753.

Flauius Lucius Dexter.

Anno Chriſti 2. *Tres Soles apparuerunt in Hiſpaniis in vnum collecti.* Anno Romæ 753.

2. *Auguſtus Tiberium, & Agrippam in filios adoptat.*

3. *Iudas Galilæus Iudæos ad rebellandum in Romam cohortatur.*

COMMENTARIVS.

Multoties comparuiſſe Soles tres.

ANNO 2. *Tres Soles, &c.*] Trinos ſoles ſæpius antiqui viderunt; quinquies, vt minimum, de quibus Plinius lib. 2. hiſt. Nat. cap. 31. affirmat incidiſſe ſub Conſulibus Sp. Poſthumio, & Q. Mutio: Q. Martio, & M. Portio: M. Antonio: & P. Dolabella: M. Lepido, & L. Planco: quibus ſubdit ſextam trini ſolis apparitionem, *Et noſtra*, ait, *ætas vidit Diuo Claudio Principe, conſulatu eius, Cornelio Orſito collega.* Hæc vltima incidit in annum Domini 52. qui Claudium & Orſitum Conſules habuit. Quæ autem Lepidum & Plancium vidit conſules, initium Triumuiratus ornauit, quando videlicet Cæſar ſibi adiunxit M. Lepidum, & M. Antonium Reipublicæ conſtituendæ. Contigit verò quadraginta annis ante Chriſti Domini Natalem, & Vrbis conditæ 712. vt in Comment. Faſtorum probat Onuphrius lib. 2. Sed quorſum hæc? ſcilicet vt diſcas, Plinium eo loco minimè egiſſe de illa trini ſolis comparitione, quæ Chriſto recèns nato in Hiſpaniis facta eſt; quandoquidem quædam ex recenſitis ab eo longè ſunt anteriores, cum ea quæ ſub Plancio & Lepido Coſs. contigit, recentior ſit ſuperioribus, & tamen per annos 40. aduentum Domini præceſſerit; quæ verò ſuo tempore accidit Claudio, & Orſito Coſs. 52. annis poſterior ſit.

Agit nihilominus de tribus ſolibus apud Hiſpanias viſis Aduentus Domini tempore Iulius Obſequens lib de prodigiis cap. 128. & Doctor Angelicus 3. par. q. 36. art. 3. ad 3. arg. *Credibile eſt* inquit, *etiam in aliis partibus mundi* (& non ſolum in Oriente, vbi ſtella apparuit Magis) *aliqua indicia natiuitatis Chriſti apparuiſſe; ſicut Romæ fluxit oleum, & in Hiſpania apparuerint tres Soles paulatim in vnum coëuntes.* Certè inter cætera mundi climata, Romæ præcipuè, & in Hiſpaniis, Natalis Domini apparere clara prognoſtica congruum fuit, quandoquidem vtrobique potiſſimè fides natis Dei elucere poſtmodum debebat. Præceſſerat quidem Romæ fons olei, qui in Tranſtiberina taberna meritoria repentè erupit, & vnius diei ſpatio fluxiſſe dicitur, anno tertio Triumuiratus, & ante Chriſti Natiuitatem 37. vt Oroſius noſter teſtatur lib. 6. cap. 19. quem Baronius ſequitur; tres autem ſoles in Hiſpania viſi, Deum in carne recens natum demonſtrabant, vtpote qui altero ab eius Natiuitate anno, teſtimonio Dextri apparuerint: cui in hac re fides adhibenda eſt, eo vel maximè quod rebus Hiſpanicis annotandis ante omnes incubuit, & illi in hac parte nemo reluctetur.

Vnde id?

Obiter monuerim huiuſmodi apparitionem Meteorologicam, abſque ſpeciali miraculo potuiſſe contingere, quamquam eo temporis non ſine magni ratione myſterij factam credamus. Nihil enim aliud ſunt duo illi ſoles collaterales eius, qui in medio eſt, quàm imagines veri ſolis inter eas exiſtentis, quæ tanquam in ſpeculo, in nube apparent: quapropter à Græcis Paralleli nuncupantur, id eſt, ſolis imagines. Oportet autem vt nubes rorida ſit ſubtilis, regularis, vniformis, ſpiſſa, terſa, ac fulgens inſtar ſpeculi; tunc enim lumen ſolis in ea fortiter refrangitur, ipſa verò quaſi ſpeculum perfectum ac ſanum præbet nobis videndum non ſolum colorem luminis, ſed etiam ſolis ipſius figuram. Qua de re Ariſtoteles egit lib. 3. Meteororum, & nos cum ipſo in Diſceptationibus noſtris Phyſiologicis. Addit Plinius, plures ſimul quàm tres numquàm viſos, nimirum quia duo duntaxat latera habet verus ſol, quæ ſpeculo ipſi ſeruiant. Cæterùm quod Dexter adiecit, *in vnum collecti*, vel quod D. Thomas dixit, *paulatim in vnum coëuntes*, eo tendit, vt doceat, duos

Figure 7.5. Bivar's 1627 edition of Dexter. Bivar's commentary occupies most of this first page of Dexter's chronicle. Francisco de Bivar, ed., *Fl. Lucii Dextri . . . Chronicon omnimodae historiae . . . nunc demum . . . commentariis apodictis illustratum* (Lyons, 1627) © Biblioteca Nacional de España, 1/12556, 12r.

text.⁵² By providing further documentary evidence for pious traditions that had been forgotten, or rejected outright by later critics, Bivar's commentary amplified and extended Higuera's own efforts. This is visible in Bivar's machinations on behalf of the apocryphal tradition that the Virgin Mary had corresponded with Saint Ignatius of Antioch. Skeptics, including Baronio, disputed the authenticity of the tradition (as have many modern critics), based on the absence of the texts in Jerome's list of Ignatius's writings. Higuera recorded it as history in Dexter.⁵³ Bivar went even further: he copied two of the letters in toto in his commentary even while acknowledging that "among many, their letters are considered suspect."⁵⁴ He also used paratext to support the much-debated letter from the Virgin Mary to the people of Messina, Sicily; to Dexter's brief account of the tradition, Bivar again appended the text in question, a copy of which he claimed to have discovered in the library of the Cistercian Abbey of the Santa Espina in central Castile. To support El Pilar's claims of apostolic antiquity, he cited not only the apocryphal vita of Pedro de Braga, but also archival sources that he had encountered in various collections, including, for example, a bull of Calixtus III, a pre-Tridentine Zaragozan missal, and two royal diplomas.⁵⁵

In these ways the paratextual material, particularly the discursive commentary, underwrote Bivar's particular interpretation of a given passage, and, more generally, the authenticity of the chronicle itself. Without these *ilustraciones*, the text was naked and vulnerable to attack, as in Calderón's slipshod edition. This was articulated more fully in the two apologetic treatises that bookended the edition. In the first, "Defense of this Chronicle for the Reader," Bivar outlined in great detail the labors he had undertaken in order to prepare his edition. As one who was never inclined to wear his erudition lightly, he included a verbose (and, in light of his intended readership, rather superfluous) account of all the ancient and modern authorities he had consulted in order to complete his heroic task, which, with a conspicuous lack of modesty, he compared to that undertaken by Jerome in his effort to render the *Chronological Canons* of Eusebius into coherent Latin.⁵⁶ In this light, the flawed state of modern copies of Dexter was not, as it had been for critics, fatal. Rather, Bivar turned this into a testament to his own scholarly grit. If recent scribes had helped clear away some errors, they nevertheless introduced new ones as well. This meant the texts were in need of serious salvage work, which Bivar had undertaken with his sleeves rolled up. The errors were so many: "Who," he exclaimed rhetorically, "could count all of the shifting clauses, the duplications, the mutilations?" All of this, Bivar reported, he had "trimmed away," and thus "restored [the text] to pristine purity" by consulting documents and books in a number of libraries, including El Escorial, and, in Rome, the libraries of the Vatican, the Jesuit Collegio Romano, the Benedictine Collegio Gregoriano, and the Oratorians' Vallicelliana, the last of which, he noted, was well known as the place where Cardinal Baronio had pursued his scholarly labors.[57]

The second defense, *An Apologetic for Dexter against a Recent Attacker*, appeared as an appendix to the edition. Here Bivar specifically addressed the objections of one of the text's first European critics, Gabriele Pennotto, an Umbrian abbot of the Lateran Congregation of Augustinian Canons. Pennotto first encountered a citation of Dexter's chronicle in a 1618 history of the Augustinian Hermits by Joan Márquez (1565–1621), a royal preacher and chair of theology at Salamanca. Since at least the fourteenth century, Pennotto's Order of Augustinian Canons had jousted with the Order of Augustinian Hermits over which of the rival orders possessed greater antiquity and a link to Saint Augustine of Hippo. Pennotto and his fellow Canons claimed that the Order of Hermits was a later innovation, and that the Canons' own manner of life originated, in contrast, from Christ and the apostles, later ratified and codified by Augustine himself in a fifth-century rule. Thus, when Márquez, citing Dexter, asserted that the first Augustinian had been a Spanish hermit named Leporius (a fifth-century bishop of the Andalusian diocese of Utica), and that one of Spain's oldest monasteries—Toledo's La Sisla—had actually been an Augustinian hermitage, he was engaging in a bit of deliberate provocation.[58]

Pennotto took the bait. He was singularly unamused by Márquez's claims, to which he objected strenuously in a *Three-Part History of the Entire General Order of the Sacred Order of Clerical Canons* (1624). As part of his broader counteroffensive, Pennotto attacked the textual authorities that Márquez had adduced for his argument, including Dexter's chronicle. Here he echoed a number of complaints common among Dexter-skeptics, including that the various manuscript copies and printed editions failed to agree with each other. Upon consulting Calderón's 1619 edition, which he obtained from a Zaragozan canon in Rome, Pennotto found that the two long passages cited by Márquez regarding the foundation of Sisla were completely missing. Pennotto asked how somebody could rely on such an unsteady text to make any historical argument all; if one compared the printed edition with whatever manuscript Márquez had drawn upon, he fumed, "Either you will laugh, or maybe you will grow red hot [with anger]."[59]

To assail Márquez's credibility even further, Pennotto made note of a rumor that had reached him in Rome: heretics, he warned darkly, may very well have tampered with the texts in Fulda. Pennotto averred that Higuera's friend Gaspar Álvares de Lousada had voiced these same fears in a (now lost) treatise regarding Santa Liberata. Pennotto quoted Álvares:

They could have been corrupted by Magdeburg heretics, [a possibility] that the most learned Father Jerónimo de Higuera called to my mind on more than one occasion: for, in fact, [the texts] truly do possess manifest contradictions. For example, in the proper names of the cities and the saints, the texts have been added to and corrupted by individuals not a little distant from those ancient centuries.[60]

Bivar responded angrily to Pennotto's objections, which he dismissed not with reasoned arguments so much as various lines of ad hominem attack, as was his wont. In what was doubtlessly a well-worn scholarly cliché even in his time, Bivar accused Pennotto of having written his text carelessly over the course of a single evening. Bivar did concede it was possible for heretics to have altered the text—for example, by duplicating entries and altering place-names, sometimes beyond recognition—yet he also affirmed resolutely that the text bore absolutely no trace of heretical theology. He also attacked Calderón's edition, and lamented that this was the text that Pennotto had the misfortune to consult. For, as Bivar boasted, unlike Calderón, who seemed to have relied upon a single, incomplete, and flawed manuscript, Bivar himself had gone to great lengths to make Dexter reliable, principally by using good philological method: he collated the 1619 edition with not one but two manuscripts, one of which was Higuera's own autograph copy in the collection of Don Pedro de Rojas, the Count of Mora; the other was in the pristine royal library at El Escorial.[61]

LOCAL SAINTS AND THE CHRONICLES: FRANCISCO DE BIVAR AND ARJONA

While it is clear that Pennotto's objections to Dexter owed much to the perceived threat that the text posed to the claims of his own Order of Canons, at first glance it is somewhat more difficult to identify what was at stake for Bivar, besides his own honor as a scholar. Yet when we look more closely, it becomes clear that the Cistercian was motivated by a combination of intellectual and religious interest. In addition to defending his own scholarly bona fides against the calumnies of critics an international, Latin-reading audience, Bivar was deeply invested in the authenticity of the texts, thanks to a cluster of recent relic discoveries. The first was in 1625, when the abbot of Santa María de Villaverde de Sandoval, a Cistercian monastery in León, discovered a skull which, thanks to Dexter's chronicle, he identified as a relic of Hierotheo. As we have seen, according to the *cronicón*, Hierotheo—the legendary disciple of Dionysius the Areopagite—had enjoyed a stint as Segovia's first bishop. By claiming to have found a relic of Hierotheo, and in publishing an account of the *inventio* shortly thereafter, the Leonese Cistercians were issuing a challenge to the partisans of Segovia's *other* first bishop, Saint Fructuosus, as part of an ongoing rivalry. The partisans of Fructuosus had already objected in 1621, when an inscription in honor of Hierotheo was mounted in Segovia's cathedral. The 1625 discovery was just the latest volley in a battle that would continue throughout the seventeenth century. Bivar entered the fray in his commentary to the 1627 edition of Dexter-Maximus, where he cited the discovery of the relic and Dexter's testimony to affirm that Hierotheo should thus be venerated by Segovians as their local saint and first bishop.[62]

In the years that followed, Bivar's interest in the cronicones deepened, thanks to the second, much more significant set of relic discoveries in the diocese of Jaén, particularly in the town of Arjona. As we have seen, Dexter's chronicle identified Roman "Urgabone"—modern Arjona—as one of the places where saints named Bonosus and Maximianus had been martyred, and there the relics were unearthed, beginning in 1628. After returning from Rome in 1626, Bivar entered the service of Melchor de Moscoso y Sandoval (d. 1632), the bishop of Segovia, as a chaplain; he also became an important advisor to the bishop's brother, Baltasar de Moscoso y Sandoval, the cardinal-bishop of Jaén.[63] The Cistercian's efforts were to be crucial in the process of helping to legitimize the Arjona relics, and in the continuing defense of their chief proof-text, Dexter's chronicle. Although Bivar would also prepare treatises on a variety of other historical and theological topics—including the Immaculate Conception, saintly Cistercians, and Aristotelian logic, physics, and metaphysics—the new saints in Jaén, and the texts that underwrote them, would attract the bulk of his efforts from the 1620s until his death in 1635.

After the initial discoveries in 1628, Moscoso y Sandoval authorized the creation of a public cult to the martyrs; in the meantime, he continued to engage scholars such as Bivar in the hopes of finding additional historical evidence that the martyrs had met their end in Arjona. The difficulty was that while the revised Roman Martyrology affirmed that Bonosus and Maximianus had existed, and had been martyred on August 21, it did not identify their place of birth or death. In his commentary, Baronio noted that although the early hagiographer Usuard referred to their acts of martyrdom, the document itself seemed to have been lost.[64] This meant that the sole source attesting to the martyrs' place of birth or death was the single line of Dexter's chronicle that the Baeza theology professor Francisco Háñez de Herrera had cited when he alerted Arjona to the relics in May of 1628. Making matters somewhat more complicated was the fact that the relics uncovered in Arjona did not bear any prima facie evidence that they belonged to the martyrs identified by Dexter's *Chronicon*, nor, for that matter, was there any material evidence that the bones and ashes were even the physical remains of saints at all.

Thus, in order to legitimize the emerging public cult to Bonosus and Maximianus in Arjona, the cardinal-bishop needed that missing evidence, the martyrs' acts or *passio*, both of which he directed his advisors to seek high and low among libraries in Spain and Rome.⁶⁵ Here, as at other points in the sinuous story of the Arjona relics, Bivar's intervention would prove instrumental. In the notes to his edition of Dexter, Bivar enumerated the previous hagiographers — including Usuard, Equilinus, and Galesinus — who had consulted the saints' acts. He repeated Baronio's lament about their absence, and then dropped a tantalizing clue: "We trust that God will at some time reveal those acts."⁶⁶ Bivar seems to have made good on the implied promise; in 1629, word reached Moscoso that the Cistercian was in possession of the missing document, "*Passio Bonosi et Maximiani*," which Bivar claimed to have discovered in a prestigious manuscript collection. Soon thereafter, the Baeza Carmelite Francisco de Santa María — a relative of the cardinal-bishop — brokered a deal with Bivar: in exchange for the acts, Moscoso would give the Cistercian "a large relic of the saints and some of their blood." Although the cardinal-bishop reflected privately to Santa María that he "would not want to commit simony," he nevertheless accepted the offer, promising to divide the most significant relics discovered in Arjona "from now on" with Bivar in exchange for the document.⁶⁷

Yet, as it turned out, the missing link, the document that Moscoso coveted so greatly that he was even willing to tread dangerously close to the sin of buying and selling things belonging to the spiritual realm, was hardly perfect. When the promised document arrived in Baeza two months later, in the summer of 1629, Santa María wrote to Moscoso with some disappointment that although it would "illuminate things that we did not know," it would not, however, fulfill "all of our expectations."⁶⁸ A particular sticking point seems to have been the question of the document's provenance, which Bivar had never clarified, and which Moscoso and Santa María seem to have misunderstood (perhaps willfully) as the Vatican Library. When pushed, Bivar defensively repeated his protestation that he had copied it from a trustworthy source, but admitted that he had no idea where the original could be found:

> I wish I could affirm that [the acts] were in the Vatican Library or in another of equal authority. But when I wrote to tell Your Paternity that I had them, I did not affirm that I had gotten them from there; rather, I only said that I had them. And now I assure Your Paternity, on my word as a priest, that I believe they are

legitimate. And if this is not enough for those *señores* to believe in them, then I will I have fulfilled my devotion, and as long as the Holy Martyrs receive [my devotion], I will be content.[69]

Six years later, Bivar's story shifted, and he suddenly remembered having discovered the acts among a number of papers belonging to the late Cistercian historian Bernabé de Montalbo.[70]

Yet in 1629, Bivar merely asserted that the document was trustworthy, and that he should be believed. One reason for his defensiveness, and for Moscoso's concern, was that a member of another religious order had sent the cardinal-bishop a different version of the acts. Bivar's unnamed rival possessed an apparent advantage: his document, he averred, had been discovered in the Vatican collections.[71] Thus Bivar was forced to address the natural question: in the absence of any solid evidence about either document's provenance, which one was trustworthy? In letters to both Moscoso and Santa María, Bivar revealed a convoluted tale behind the acts' discovery and transmission that suggests that he was not the only cleric resorting to historical research verging on subterfuge in search of an illustrious patron in the cardinal-bishop of Jaén. Bivar resorted to specious arguments and ad hominem attacks to defend himself. Rather than specifically address the discrepancies between his acts and this second version, Bivar impugned the character of the unnamed document broker. He explained that he was well acquainted with this untrustworthy character, and that he had firsthand knowledge of his deceitful character, since they had worked together before. On one occasion, they were both reading in the library of the Count of Gondomar, Don Diego Sarmiento de Acuña (1567–1626), the ambassador to England best known for having negotiated the seventeenth-century Spanish Match, which would have wed Charles Stuart, the Prince of Wales, to the Spanish infanta, Doña María de Austria. During his time in London, Gondomar had gathered so many books (as well as the relics of English Catholic martyrs) that his residence in Valladolid hosted "the largest private library in Spain."[72]

It was there, as Bivar told Moscoso, that the Cistercian found an unknown and ancient manuscript history of the Cistercian order. The upshot, according to Bivar, was that the rival priest later took credit for the discovery himself, even though he never even looked at the document, and thus could not be trusted. Bivar also declared that his three years of study in Rome allowed him to state categorically that neither the acts of Bonosus and Maximianus, nor Dexter's *Chronicon*, were in the Vatican libraries. He had personally reviewed all of the manuscripts of saints' lives while preparing his edition of Dexter, and he would have seen the acts of Arjona if they had been there. And, as Bivar pointed out, the Vatican was simply the last of three different stories the unsavory document broker had used to explain the origins of the Arjona acts. The first was that he found it in the abbey of Fulda, along with the original of Dexter's text. Bivar protested that neither the acts, nor Dexter's *Chronicon*, had been in Fulda at any time in living memory, for Bivar himself had come up short in a search he had commissioned while in Rome. Next, the broker indicated a monastery in France. Bivar shrugged off this claim as well: "I do not know if [the *Chronicon*] is there or not, with or without the acts, because I have not seen it," but it was unlikely, since short chronicles such as Dexter's did not usually incorporate short saints' lives, and were usually bound separately. Bivar ended his diatribe against his rival with a somewhat vacillating defense of the authenticity of his own copy of the acts, ultimately insisting that it was only due to Santa María's urging that he had passed the acts along to the bishop in the first place. Thus, Bivar washed his hands of the responsibility of affirming the ultimate origin of the acts, while simultaneously professing his faith in their "sincerity and truth."[73]

We can get a sense of the personal and intellectual interests that Bivar felt were at stake in the matter of the acts—and, by extension, in the related questions about the authenticity of the Arjona saints and of Dexter's chronicle—from another 1629 letter to Santa María in which he confessed that he felt compelled to alert the cardinal-bishop to his rival's machinations to make sure that the "mischief" and "intrigue" of his "so-called acts" would not "obscure the glory of God in his Martyrs."[74] If the existence of a rival set of acts seemed to threaten Bivar's reputation, they could do even more serious damage to the nascent cult of the Arjona saints in particular, and to the cult of saints in general. Yet just as damaging as the false acts, Bivar worried, were the uses to which the martyrs' relics might be put by overly credulous devotees, as in the case of a seemingly spectacular series of marvels that occurred in Marmolejo, a small village northwest of Jaén. In the autumn of 1629, María Blanca, a servant in an aristocratic Marmolejo household, claimed that whenever a small packet of relics from Arjona were applied to her body, they began to bleed. The young woman soon became a major attraction in the village, and the house became a veritable circus, as María's masters, other members of her household, various members of the clergy, and neighbors all applied small bundles of relics to the girl's body several times a day, hoping to reproduce the miracle of the bleeding relics with their own hands.[75]

By November, Marmolejo's parish priest expressed serious reservations about the alleged miracles, and urged the cardinal-bishop to have María Blanca removed from the house and from the influence of her fellow servant-girls, so that she might be examined "by a learned person."[76] News soon reached Bivar in his Leonese monastery and he urged the bishop and his advisor to put an end to the debacle. Bivar sounded a remarkably self-centered note as he endeavored to communicate to Santa María the depth of the anxiety that this incident had spurred in his mind. The Cistercian reflected upon the love and devotion he felt for the Arjona saints, in part due to a "known miracle" that relics from the shrine had already worked in his own monastery earlier that year. Bivar cautioned that the bishop should proceed carefully, if only for Bivar's own sake:

> Know that I have more vested in the Saints of Arjona than anybody thinks [...] I love and revere them, and more would happen to me than I can emphasize if, by means of such a pious pretext, their glory were obscured. Until now, things have gone prudently; let's not lose it all over something that is neither here nor there.[77]

He concluded his warning with a strikingly defiant phrase, as if he were inviting Santa María to a challenge: "and of course I say to Your Paternity, don't touch my relics, I love them very much . . . "[78] Here we see that it was desperately important to Bivar that the saints of Arjona, and, by extension, Dexter's chronicle, not be undermined—not by the rival claims of the "fake" acts of Bonosus and Maximianus, not by excessive scruples about the acts' provenance, and certainly not by dubious miracles performed by a suggestible servant girl in a small town in Jaén. His bluster suggests the extent to which he believed that his own reputation was intertwined with that of the Arjona relics, and with the text that had revealed them, Dexter's chronicle.

In spite of Bivar's tergiversations and the bishop's lingering uncertainties about the document's provenance, before the end of 1629, his version of the acts had become an important element in the emerging narrative of the history and discovery of Arjona's saints. Bivar's document was disseminated by Moscoso to the scholars in his service, who, in turn, communicated their details to members of Andalusia's learned community almost immediately. In the summer or early autumn of 1629, the *Passio*, in Latin and in Spanish translation, debuted in an elegiac pamphlet by Juan de Aguilar, a teacher of letters and humanities in Antequera. The acts were, as Aguilar said, "a jewel which (as far as I know) [Bivar] found in the Vatican Library."[79] Aguilar penned a second pamphlet that celebrated the discovery of the Arjona relics in prose and poetry, also printed in 1629; the same year, a third, anonymous text appeared in Jaén, in which "a devotee" of the saints related the wondrous events, including heavenly lights and other miracles, that had accompanied the discoveries.[80]

These publications were not merely meant to attract attention—and pilgrims—to Arjona, although that certainly was one effect. They were also, it seems, indirect requests for help. With their classicizing images and epideictic rhetoric, the pamphlets spoke not only to miracles, but also to the importance of scholarship. They were arguably aimed at Andalusia's reading audience of *letrados* who, it seems, the cardinal-bishop hoped would respond with an additional piece of evidence to help substantiate Bivar's document. Perhaps an inscription kept in a private collection, or a coin uncovered along the river's edge, would illuminate this dark period in Jaén's history, and help substantiate the emerging narrative of a hitherto unknown fourth-century persecution in Arjona. And indeed, such relics of antiquity were flushed out in short order, as we shall see in the following chapter. In 1630, the relics, Bivar's reputation, and Dexter's chronicle would all be put to the test once again, but this time in Rome, where the stakes were significantly higher than in Marmolejo or even Madrid.

Thanks to continued excavations and the discovery of mounds of ash, by the 1630s and 1640s, the Arjona relics were becoming unmanageable. While the most valuable and significant finds, such as skulls and other identifiably human remains, were guarded under lock and key by an agent of the cardinal-bishop, the ash was simply uncontainable. Not only was it infinitely partible, it was also eminently portable, especially when baked into the "little martyrs' rolls" produced for pilgrims by enterprising locals.[81] In addition to posing difficulties for would-be regulators of local religion, such as the bishop's vicars and the guards attempting to keep pilgrims from sleeping in the shrine—efforts that do not seem to have been particularly determined or efficacious—the proliferation of relics posed a serious mathematical difficulty. Dexter had only mentioned two Arjona martyrs, yet the volume of purported relics far exceeded the number of martyrs.[82]

Thus the cardinal-bishop's scholars scrambled to find additional martyrs in the historical record. Along these lines, in 1634, the Discalced Carmelite Jerónimo Pancorbo argued that five hundred additional Christians had met their ends in Arjona during the Great Persecution under Diocletian, although he was forced to concede that their names had since been lost.[83] The continuing uncertainty about the identity of the martyrs did not inhibit local enthusiasm. Several *arjoneros* remembered the saints in the pious bequests of their last testaments, even if they were not always certain who those saints actually were. In 1629, Antona Sánchez de Amor set aside the modest sum of six *reales* for what she referred to somewhat imprecisely as "the house that will be made for the holy martyrs who have been discovered in this town."[84] Two years later, this murkiness remained in the testament of the relatively wealthy Doña Catalina Panduro, whose goods included luxury textiles and leather-covered furnishings. She directed that of the sixty masses that should be said in her honor, two should be dedicated to the "holy martyrs who have appeared in this village." More humble devotees, such as the widow Ana de Quesada, offered two masses to Bonosus and Maximianus by name in 1629, but also to their unnamed "companions" in martyrdom, whose very existence was still merely a working hypothesis for Moscoso's scholars.[85]

In spite of a long career defending, promoting, and annotating the cronicones, Tamayo de Vargas began to sound a somewhat more sour note midcentury due to the fact that he disagreed with several passages in the chronicles of Luitprand and Julián Pérez that identified the Roman-era municipality of Complutum as Guadalajara—and not, as he would have had it, Alcalá de Henares. This led him to argue that these passages had been added by the first person to have encountered the original manuscripts—that is, they were Higuera's interpolations.[86] Thus we see that Tamayo de Vargas, like Bivar, Caro, Calderón, and Higuera himself, shared the conviction that historical truth was necessarily accessed through imperfect channels. In addition to operating with a different set of assumptions about the nature of truth, these men apprehended the challenges and opportunities posed by the false chronicles from within their own situational contexts. Indeed, debates about the false chronicles, like conversations about ecclesiastical history and antiquities elsewhere in early modern Europe, were not conducted in scientific sterility. Protestations of disinterestedness aside, most readers were simply not engaged in a search for objective, disembodied truth. While modern critics would conclude, based on the clearly interpolated nature of much of the material, that these texts were entirely untrustworthy and should have been disregarded outright, the majority of seventeenth-century Spanish readers leaned toward a more generous hermeneutic, in which particular portions could be salvaged, rehabilitated, and cited as authoritative, even while others might be jettisoned as unreliable.

8

The *Cronicones* in Local Religion: *Historia Sacra* Writ Small

> Every day countless Histories of Cities, Churches, Religious Orders, and Kingdoms are born, which treat almost nothing except fabulous origins, Apostles, and supposed Preachers of the Faith, Martyrs carried from distant lands to falsely ennoble places that were not their motherlands, and badly invented or ridiculous Antiquities. If these books were cleansed of these Fables, they would end up reduced to very few pages indeed.
> — Nicolás Antonio

Thus the critic, bibliographer, and jurisconsult Nicolás Antonio wrote in the late seventeenth century in the opening pages of his *Censure of Fabulous Histories*, the first systematic critique of the false chronicles. "There is no place in Spain," Antonio continued, "no matter how small or obscure, that is not thinking of writing its own history now with the material it finds in this recently discovered mine, which is most abundant in oddities and novelties."[1] Antonio was correct to point to the pervasive influence of the texts on the writing of Spanish history; after all, it was arguably on this microlevel of peripheral or otherwise unremarkable places that Higuera's forgeries were to have their most tangible and enduring effects. In the first decades of the seventeenth century, enthusiastic partisans of the chronicles began to cite the texts in support of the introduction of new saints and to write new versions of local sacred history. This was particularly—but not exclusively—true in Andalusia, where the false chronicles helped create local cults to new martyrs, such as Bonosus and Maximianus in Arjona. As in Arjona, so, too, in the archdiocese of Seville the chronicles underwrote new patron saints who were subsequently introduced into the diocesan liturgical prayers, and, finally, became important points of reference in new works of sacred history.

Yet parochialisms and "fables" are, for our purposes, hardly the whole story, if only for the simple reason that the pervasive influence of the chronicles on local religion has been much bemoaned, but little studied. For those in search of the antecedents of modern historical or archaeological method, the religious "credulity" of the early modern intellectuals who wrote works of local sacred history is profoundly troubling. One scholar put it bluntly when he wondered at the "infantile" religiosity that would lead a learned man such as Rodrigo Caro to record a number of miracles of the Virgin of Consolation in Utrera, as he did in a 1622 treatise.[2] There is an interesting and compelling narrative to be told about the evolution of historical criticism in Spain—and, more broadly, Europe—at the time. After all, the efflorescence of local histories inspired by the chronicles was part of an array of responses to the post-Tridentine context in which history, hagiography, and liturgy were being revised according to new, stricter standards of evidence, as we have seen. These revisions, particularly as spearheaded by Cardinal Baronio, and, by the mid-seventeenth century, the Jesuit hagiographers in Flanders known as the Bollandists, were, in turn, informed by fundamental changes in the nature of historical thought and practice, particularly with the integration of antiquarian methods and interests, which brought new types of evidence into the creation of "history."

The efflorescence of new local sacred histories was particularly rich in Andalusia, where inhabitants of territories long ruled by Muslims sought concrete details about those early centuries of Christianity that had preceded what many regarded as "the destruction of Spain," that is, the Islamic invasion and subsequent hegemony. This could mean proving that an apostle had planted the first seeds of the faith, that the place had been home to early Christian martyrs, or that it had been an important diocesan see in those early days. The ideal *historia sacra* would support all of these claims. Now, with the information provided by the cronicones, these communities could write the book, as it were, on their ancient Christian foundations and piety. Hence, Dexter's version of history enabled places like Jaén that in reality had been shaped fundamentally by Arab-Islamic culture—in everything from agricultural technology to architecture, urban design, and place-names—to take a historiographical shortcut to an antiquity that was unimpeachably Christian.

An examination of works of sacred history and their authors cannot afford to neglect lived religion, nor can it neglect those lesser intellects who have been largely forgotten by posterity. The authors of these texts were, more often than not, amateur history enthusiasts—middling clerics and other *letrados* who spent their free time digging up Roman coins, exploring medieval ruins, and collecting information about their local saints, relics, and churches. These men, who staffed churches and monasteries in regional capitals and small towns throughout Spain, are still poorly understood by historians. It was precisely these antiquarians who, having milked Higuera's texts for details about the history of their own respective localities, communicated the information to local audiences and sought to enshrine these new visions of the past in civic and religious tradition. In Andalusia we find an extensive but largely unfamiliar network of these individuals, in a variety of social and occupational roles, who gathered physical remnants of the ancient and medieval past in their homes, notebooks, and letters, and who adhered to the latest European norms in collecting, recording, and evaluating antiquities. They did so with the same beguiling combination of credulity and criticism that characterized the work of so many other earlier antiquaries. Like their counterparts elsewhere in Europe, men such as Rodrigo Caro, Antonio de Quintanadueñas, and Martín de Roa, inter alii, collected antiquities, critiqued texts, and exchanged ideas and objects as part of a wider Republic of Letters. By surveying a sample of these local sacred histories, we shall see that the uses to which authors put the cronicones were anything but "odd" or "novel," *pace* Antonio; rather, they helped authors find solutions to some of the most vexing historical and theological questions of the time, in books that, while admittedly parochial in scope, nonetheless possessed broad resonance in early modern Spain, and that reveal hitherto neglected links between the culture of scholarship and local religion.

LOCAL SAINTS AND THE CHRONICLES: SEVILLE

In Seville, the introduction of new saints to the liturgy precipitated a strenuous debate, suggesting that when it came to the false chronicles and local religion, matters were never simple. Here we see that even accomplished scholars like Rodrigo Caro, a proponent of the new saints, wrote with eminently practical aims in mind, including that of intervening in local cultic politics. Several years before his edition of Dexter-Maximus would see the light, Caro was already attempting to connect local communities with lost native sons and daughters. In the cronicones, Caro had discovered at least eighteen Diocletian-era martyrs who were natives of the archdiocese of Seville. The first beneficiary of Caro's efforts was his own place of birth, Utrera, a municipality just southeast of Seville which, according to Dexter, was the place of birth and death of five early Christian martyrs.[3] With the support of Utrera's municipal and ecclesiastical authorities, Archbishop Pedro de Castro (formerly of Granada) added three of the martyrs, Straton, Rufinus, and Rufinianus, to the diocese's liturgy; two others were not given an official public cult because they were listed only in the noncanonical Greek Menology.⁴ Caro wrote a short work to support his claims for Utrera's formidable antiquity and holiness and, more pointedly, to validate the recent decision of Utrera to adopt the martyrs as patron saints. The first half of the book documented the ancient origins and miraculousness of the image of the Virgin at a sanctuary in Caro's hometown. In addition to being an antiquarian scholar with humanist aspirations, Caro was a Counter-Reformation Catholic, and thus it should not be surprising to find that he was a devotee of the Virgin of Utrera, as he attested in a dramatic eyewitness account of a 1605 miracle when she interceded to make it rain. The second half of the treatise, a "Relation of the Inscriptions and Antiquity of the Village of Utrera," was dedicated to Fernando Enríquez Afán de Ribera, the Duke of Alcalá, himself a well-known collector of art and antiquities. Caro did not marshal these Roman inscriptions only to show off his collecting acumen to his patron, but also to establish that Utrera was the place referred to in Dexter's chronicle as "Betis" and "Utriculo," and where those five martyrs had been put to death during the Great Persecution under Emperor Diocletian in AD 308.⁵ (Based on the apparent phonological similarity between "Betis" and "Baeza," some of the same saints would also be claimed by that city in the diocese of Jaén.)

The problem, as Caro ruefully admitted, was that he had been unable to confirm the Roman name of Utrera with epigraphic evidence. None of the familiar classical geographical authorities—such as Strabo, Pliny, or Antoninus Pius's *Itinerary*—mentioned Utrera. Nor had Caro found any "ancient marbles," "ruins," or even "tithe records" that attested to the Roman-era name(s) of Utrera. To resolve the gaping hole in the epigraphic record, Caro presented in a rather unconventional manner the passage in Dexter's chronicle suggesting Utrera had been called both "Utriculo" and "Betis" by the Romans: in the treatise, he had the line typeset as if it were an inscription, centered on the page, printed all in capital letters, with the full justification and irregular spacing that usually represented the text of a monument, albeit with the punctuation that an inscription would lack (figure 8.1).⁶

LOCAL SACRED POLITICS

That the preeminent antiquarian of seventeenth-century Andalusia would resort to this sleight of hand may seem remarkable. Yet in view of the charged context in which local saints' cults were debated, it is hardly surprising. Caro was deeply involved in an effort to bring new, cronicones-informed saints to local communities in Seville, which he had to have known would spark opposition. This is precisely what had occurred in the recent past during the time

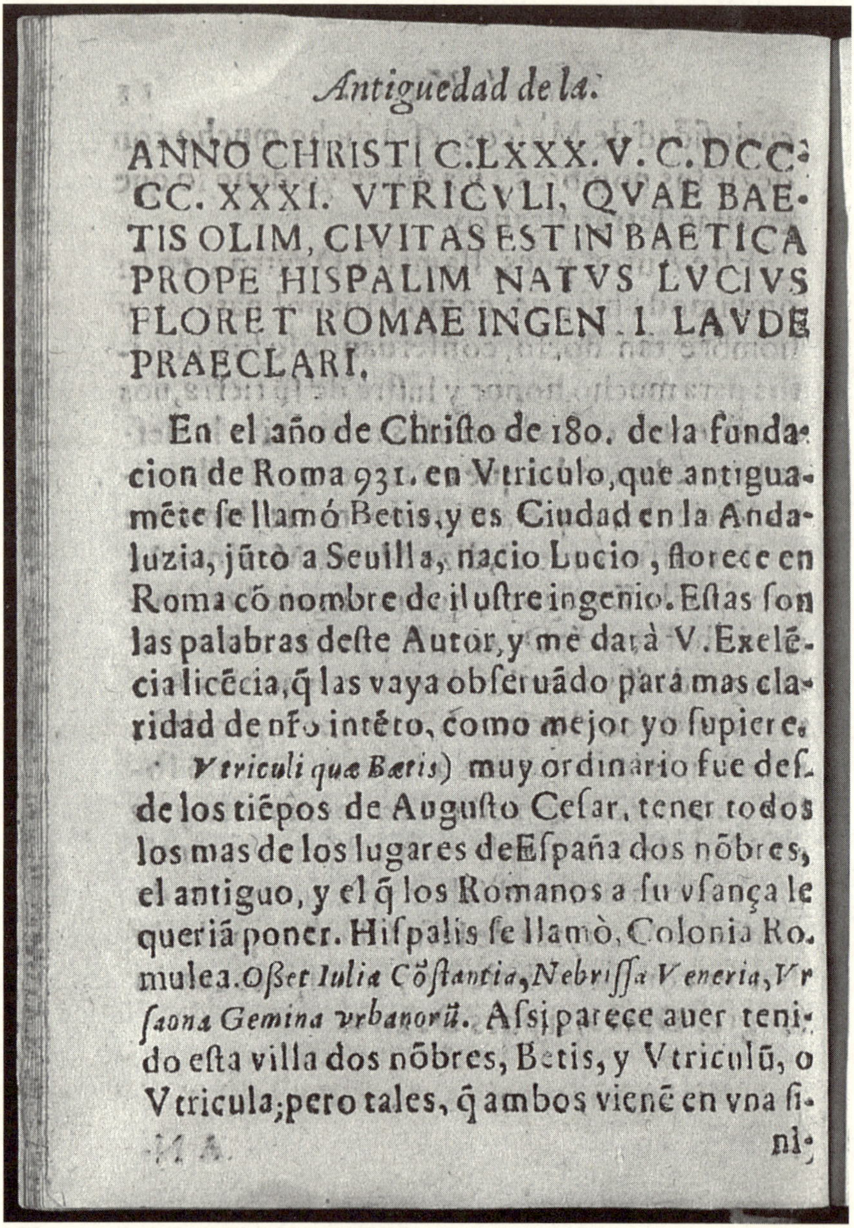

Antigüedad de la:

ANNO CHRISTI C.LXXX. V. C. DCC-
CC. XXXI. VTRICVLI, QVAE BAE-
TIS OLIM, CIVITAS EST IN BAETICA
PROPE HISPALIM NATVS LVCIVS
FLORET ROMAE INGEN. I. LAVDE
PRAECLARI,

En el año de Christo de 180. de la fundacion de Roma 931. en Vtriculo, que antigua-
mēte se llamó Betis, y es Ciudad en la Anda-
luzia, jūto a Seuilla, nacio Lucio, florece en
Roma cō nombre de ilustre ingenio. Estas son
las palabras deste Autor, y me dara V. Exelē-
cia licēcia, q̃ las vaya observādo para mas cla-
ridad de nr̃o intēto, como mejor yo supiere.

Vtriculi quæ Bætis) muy ordinario fue desde los tiēpos de Augusto Cesar, tener todos
los mas de los lugares de España dos nōbres,
el antiguo, y el q̃ los Romanos a su usança le
queriā poner. Hispalis se llamò, Colonia Ro-
mulea. *Ossec Iulia Cōstantia, Nebrissa Veneria, Vr-
saona Gemina vrbanorū.* Assi parece auer teni-
do esta villa dos nōbres, Betis, y Vtriculū, o
Vtricula; pero tales, q̃ ambos vienē en vna si-
nl-

Figure 8.1. Dexter's text rendered as an inscription. In Rodrigo Caro, ed., *Relacion de las inscripciones y antigüedad de la Villa de Utrera* (Osuna, 1622) © Biblioteca Nacional de España, R/2896, 11v.

when members of the cathedral chapter had been attempting—unsuccessfully, since the 1590s—to introduce a new officium proprium in honor of Saint Laureano. The effort had been given a new impetus in 1601 with the discovery of the saint's relics, even as many, including members of the municipal *cabildo*, openly doubted their authenticity. Another opponent was Martín de Añaya Maldonado, a canon at Seville's Royal Convent of the Sword of Santiago, who, in a treatise that is no longer extant, disparaged the addition of Laureano to the liturgy.[7]

Notwithstanding these fault lines, Caro forged ahead with his ambitions to introduce new saints to the diocese. At his prompting, Archbishop Castro had begun to investigate yet another set of new saints, this time in Osuna, the town sixty miles southeast of Seville where Caro had initiated his university studies in the 1590s.[8] Within a year of the archbishop's death in 1623, the cathedral chapter, acting in his stead in *sede vacante*, voted to authorize the addition of thirteen new saints to the liturgy in Osuna. This was once again thanks to Dexter's text, which identified Arcadio, Leon, Donato, Nicephoro, Abundancio, and his eight companions as natives of the municipality.[9] The decision was not supported by all the members of Seville's cathedral chapter, and a fierce controversy ensued. Opposition centered on divergent interpretations of the prelate's authority as well as the historical value of the cronicones. In the ensuing debate, local religion, liturgical revisions, and antiquarian scholarship collided. In 1626, Seville's cathedral canon Alonso de la Serna attacked the introduction of new prayers to the diocese's officia propria, arguing that neither the prelate nor his proxies possessed the authority to alter the liturgical calendar. This, Serna argued, belonged solely to the high pontiff of the Church, or his delegates, such as the cardinals of the Roman Sacred Congregation of Rites. In March of 1628, Serna received external confirmation of his opinion from several theologians from the University of Salamanca.[10]

In a testament to the decentralized nature of many ecclesiastical procedures, as well as the lack of unanimity on these and other questions of how to regulate the veneration of the saints, the Congregation of Rites forwarded the completely opposite interpretation later that same year. We know this because the cardinal-bishop of Jaén, probably with the conflagration in Seville in mind, had appealed directly to Rome to clarify the procedures for introducing officia propria of new saints. By the fall of 1628, Saints Bonosus and Maximianus had already been acclaimed as Arjona's patrons and celebrated with public processions. By December, their relics were venerated publicly at the open-air shrine and pilgrimage site that Arjona's castle had since become.[11] Baltasar de Moscoso y Sandoval, the cardinal-bishop of Jaén, had not yet introduced a prayer in their honor to Jaén's liturgical calendar. He hesitated due to *Quod a nobis*, the bull that prefaced the 1568 Roman Breviary and specifically prohibited any changes to the liturgy without special permission from Rome. Yet, as we have seen, Gregory XIII's subsequent brief, *Pastoralis officii* (1573), seemed to permit such changes, as Moscoso noted. The cardinal-bishop asked the Congregation of Rites to resolve this apparent contradiction. In its December 1628 opinion, the Congregation responded to Moscoso's satisfaction that although *Quod a nobis* stated that the Breviary could not be altered in any way, this prohibition was superseded by Gregory XIII's brief, which did indeed allow Spanish prelates to institute new officia propria to saints who were natives or patrons of the diocese, or whose relics were located therein.[12]

If the plain sense of *Pastoralis officii* quite clearly granted Spanish prelates the right to add new saints to local liturgies without papal approval, so long as the saint was a patron of the locality, or if a significant relic was held in a church therein, why did Moscoso feel the need to consult Rome, and why would Serna and the Salamanca theologians have challenged Castro's decision to add new saints to Seville's liturgy in the first place? As we have seen, part of the answer is that opinions on these and other matters were evolving, in Rome and beyond. Yet once again, local cultic politics also contributed. In questioning the procedural propriety of Castro's decision, Serna and the others were also issuing a challenge to his sole source, Dexter's *Chronicon*. In an anonymous treatise dating from circa 1630–1632, Serna charged that even if the archbishop possessed the right to alter the liturgy, he should not have done so based solely on Dexter's historical witness, which was faulty. Due to the text's errors, the uncertain circumstances of its discovery, and the lack of originals, Serna deemed the text apocryphal in the sense of a text of uncertain authorship. While early modern Catholic scholars possessed a range of opinions about the relative value of apocryphal texts, very few took such a radical stance as Serna, who posited here that they were instruments of Satan.[13]

In defense, Caro asserted that the archbishop—and the cathedral chapter in his stead—had acted correctly, since "the testimony of authentic histories, to which all learned men give credit" had proven that the saints in question had been natives of the diocese.[14] Caro was correct in arguing that prelates of the Church possessed the jurisdictional authority to add new saints; yet, as he knew very well, the only "authentic history" that placed the new saints in Utrera and Osuna was Dexter's chronicle. And Caro was also acutely aware that learned opinion on the text was hardly unanimous. In 1628, one of his Madrid contacts had already warned Caro that Serna had joined forces with the royal courtier Francisco de Rioja in order to "destroy Dexter."[15] So, just to be safe, Caro also appealed to the even higher considerations of honor and piety. He argued that to rescind the prelate's approval and remove the prayers, images, and altars already in the possession of devotees in Utrera and Osuna would be wrong, not to mention prejudicial to the authority of the office of archbishop and to the dignity of the cult of saints. It would be better to "tolerate and conceal a pious error," rather than damage the reputation of Archbishop Castro and his advisors, who would be made to look like "ignorant, easy, and foolhardy men" for having thrown themselves into something that they did not understand. A rescission would throw the faithful into confusion and dismay, and lead them to question Catholic truths, since, "if in such a grave matter there is no stability, then there is stability nowhere, not even in ecclesiastical matters."[16]

In the meantime, the cult to the new saints of Seville continued to gain ground in spite of the opposition as Caro and his allies kept up their efforts. In 1632, Antonio de Quintanadueñas, a Jesuit based in Seville, published a short treatise on *The Glorious Martyrs of Osuna* on commission from Osuna's principal church, and dedicated it to the feudal lord of the town, the Marquis of Peñafiel. By this time construction had already begun on a new church to the martyrs, and Quintanadueñas expressed hopes that the saints' relics would be revealed as a result of these devotional and historical efforts. In the text, he even suggested where to start digging.[17] Five years later, Quintanadueñas's *Saints of Seville* was published, with a dedication to the dean and chapter of the city's cathedral and a theological approval by Rodrigo Caro. Quintanadueñas reaffirmed the right of the bishop to adjudicate these matters, defended the authority of the cronicones on these and other questions, and introduced several new saints, many of whom were supported by the cronicones.[18] Quintanadueñas's vision of the new hagiographic, historical, and liturgical order in the diocese was then attacked by Añaya Maldonado of Seville, who disparaged the introduction of so many Dexter-inspired saints to the liturgy—many of whom, he alleged, were not saints, nor were they from Seville. Caro responded on Quintanadueñas's behalf with a point-by-point defense.[19]

It is significant that the first sustained public debate about the relative value of the false chronicles as historical evidence erupted, in the context of local sacred politics, among the arbiters and custodians of Seville's scholarly and religious precincts. Yet there is still another dimension to opposition to new saints and cults, beyond the cronicones. At this moment, Seville's various canons and clerics were also embroiled in a parallel dispute regarding Teresa of Ávila's proposed copatronage, with Santiago, of Spain. The contours of this polemic did not overlap neatly with the debate about the saints of Osuna and Utrera; nor, more broadly, did doubters of the cronicones come down evenly on one side or another. In this instance, Añaya Maldonado and Serna joined the new archbishop of Seville, Diego de Guzmán, in opposing copatronage.[20] As Erin Rowe points out in her pioneering study, a range of motivations can be imputed to the combatants on either side of the copatronage debate, including, but not limited to, the search for patronage, "personal animosity, financial gain, . . . literary notoriety or competition," religious devotion, and, of course, the ever-shifting relationship between local and national politics of the sacred.[21] In this sense, the Seville case provides a suggestive example of the scholarly and political maneuvers that accompanied the making of new saints, as well as a hint of some of the theological and intellectual issues at stake for both proponents and foes of the false chronicles in the seventeenth century. Just as local interests could help create a more favorable climate for reception of the chronicles—as had been the case among the partisans of Zaragoza's church of El Pilar—they could also work against the texts. Either way, these conflagrations should not be mistaken for disinterested debates about the nature of truth. They were deeply embedded in and formed by local animosities and tensions between and among different ecclesiastical and secular factions. These and other factors conditioned reception of the texts, as they would continue to do in the following centuries.

SACRED HISTORY ON THE SMALL SCALE: THE CRONICONES IN ANDALUSIAN HISTORIAE SACRAE

It is worth looking more closely at the individuals who, usually at the request of a patron, connected the cronicones to the local sacred landscape with their works of sacred history. The authors were usually clerics of considerable learning but with perhaps more modest career prospects, such as Francisco de Háñez de Herrera, the Baeza professor who communicated the news about the Arjona martyrs to that community in 1628. We might imagine them as "regional" eruditos. These were not the most prestigious or well-known scholars of Spain, but they were of a type: industrious and antiquities-minded specialists in all things past, always on the hunt for an inscription, an unearthed Roman coin, or a bit of local lore.[22] The better connected, such as Caro, had ambitions that reached further afield, to Madrid or possibly Rome; but the less prominent, such as Jaén's Francisco de Rus Puerta (ca. 1598–ca. 1653), worked in relative isolation from high political circles, in the service of a local prelate, but nonetheless as part of a broader community of like-minded individuals who shared textual, social, and cultural points of reference. In many ways, these seventeenth-century authors were fruits of the same intellectual tree as Higuera: they looked to the same core of classical, patristic, and modern authorities, and above all, to Morales and Baronio, as the progenitors of sacred history as it was written in Spain. These spelunkers of arcane treasures dug up every bit of historical evidence relating to their locality they could muster, including textual and material remains: this included even the most sidelong reference by classical or patristic authorities, as well as epigraphic or numismatic evidence, archival documents, and local oral traditions. Most authors did not hesitate to cite these data secondhand, and in this, they were especially prone to plunder Morales's texts, and, of course, the cronicones, to fill in the many chronological and geographical gaps left by this aggregate body of mostly written tradition.

Local sacred history was not an entirely new genre, nor was it only a Spanish preoccupation. Claims of Christian antiquity and constancy had gained a new urgency throughout Europe in the century following the Council of Trent, as the Catholic Church waged a pitched battle to defend its claims of apostolic authority against Protestant challenges. Simon Ditchfield has also traced the ways in which the efforts of Roman reformers like Baronio prompted local religious figures, such as Pietro Maria Campi of Piacenza, to revise their own ecclesiastical traditions according to stricter standards of historicity. Ironically, even as these "local Baronios," as Ditchfield dubs them, emulated Rome's historiographical model, their intensely local perspectives often contributed to an almost anti-Baronian narrative of particularity, in a centrifugal movement pulling them away from Rome's universalism.[23]

Rus Puerta, a parish prior in the small Jaén town of Bailén, might have been more prolix and punctilious than most Spanish sacred historians when he promised that his 1634 *Ecclesiastical History of the Kingdom and Bishopric of Jaén* would chart the region's *Beginnings, and Progress in the Christian Religion*, starting with *The Preaching of the Holy Apostles Jacob, Peter, Paul*, spanning *From the First Century of the Christian Church to the Twelfth*; that it would catalogue *The Bishops about Whom Memory Remains, The Location of Ancient Places*, and *Other Antiquities Worthy of Being Known* in the diocese; and, finally, that it would relate *The History, Tradition, and Antiquity of the Holy Veil of Veronica*, as well as of *The Saints and Martyrs of Arjona and Baeza, and of Other Places*[24] (figure 8.2). Yet most seventeenth-century local historians shared with Rus Puerta the desire to collect as much information as possible about the origins and persistence of Christianity in their respective regions. This meant harvesting every conceivable detail from a wide range of sources, including the cronicones or the lead books of Granada, but also previous chronicles, hagiographies, and Roman antiquities. In this effort, the chronological net was cast wide. Thus, books whose titles seemed to promise a straightforward hagiographic treatment, such as Quintanadueñas's *Glorious Martyrs of Osuna*, or to treat a more strictly secular theme, like a 1629 *History of the Antiquity, Nobility, and Gran-*

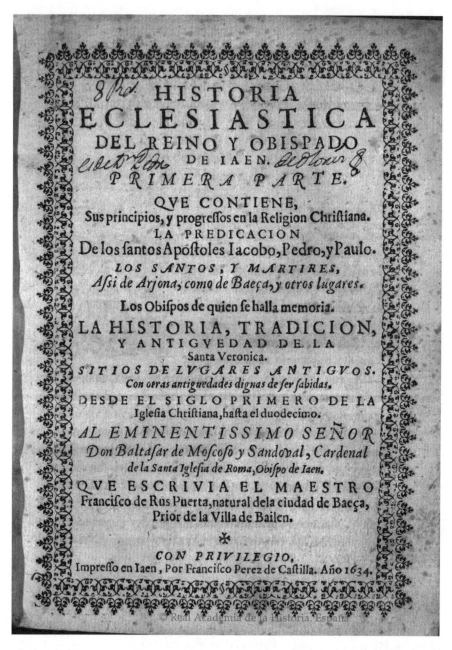

Figure 8.2. Francisco de Rus Puerta, *Historia eclesiastica del reino y obispado de Iaen* (Jaén, 1634) © Reproducción, Real Academia de la Historia, 14/7023.

deur [of Madrid], unfailingly combined sacred and secular, ancient and modern, in what might be dubbed local historia sacra.²⁵ At its base were the twin pillars of religious history and antiquarianism, neatly encompassed in the title of Caro's 1622 treatise on *The Sanctuary of Our Lady of the Consolation and the Antiquity of the Village of Utrera*.²⁶

In addition to surveying their city's ancient foundations, praising its fertility and nobility, documenting the antiquity of its Christianity, and tracing the continuity of these origins across the centuries, many of the authors of these local histories also attempted to record the inscriptions, coins, and other signs of antiquity that they had encountered in their ramblings through the countryside. These chorographies were not merely focused on "the smallest places conceivable"; rather, they were surveys of the sacred geography of the many discrete places that made up the diocese as a whole—of the type contained in *visitatio liminis* reports sent to Rome—crossed with a substantial collection of inscriptions and other antiquities.²⁷ For these authors, the sacred was intertwined with civic and political history. Rus Puerta followed his *Ecclesiastical History of Jaén* with *The Bishops of Jaén, and Second Part of the Ecclesiastical History . . . with Additions . . . and the Ancient and Modern Chorography of the Same Diocese and Kingdom* in 1646, which remained in manuscript. Rus Puerta intended the *Chorography* to be read alongside the *History*, just like Morales's treatise on antiquities was to accompany his chronicle. Rus Puerta's treatise was appended to the ecclesiastical history, but it was distinct, in that it also enabled the reader to identify the places mentioned in the history, and it served as a survey of the diocese's major religious institutions, whether Roman, medieval, or modern. It was at once an episcopal catalogue, a list of local martyrs, a survey of antiquities, and an exhaustive record of the region's major political and religious milestones.²⁸

In the search for evidence to prove that Christianity had been introduced during the time of the apostles and had persisted across the centuries in spite of several centuries of Islamic rule, the cronicones were absolutely fundamental to these authors, and proved especially useful in their vexed attempt to establish historical toponyms. In *Ecija: Its Saints, and Ecclesiastical and Secular Antiquity* (1629), the Jesuit Martín de Roa juggled conflicting pieces of evidence that suggested a variety of different ancient names for Ecija, a town northeast of Seville. He tackled the problem of a place-name that even many contemporaries believed was derived from the Arabic for "skillet," an etymology that has prevailed in the modern idiom. Roa angrily dismissed this as a mere "popular fable" (*fábula verdaderamente vulgar*), and asked incredulously why the first settlers would have named the town after the misery caused by Ecija's notoriously fierce heat.²⁹ Instead, Roa cited a number of Roman-era inscriptions to argue that Ecija was the

Roman "Astigi," but that its name originated from the Greek, and its existence actually predated the Roman presence. Roa concluded that changes in pronunciation over time, and not Arabic linguistic influences, had corrupted "Astigi" into "Ecija." Implicit in Roa's etymological maneuvers is the assumption that for a seventeenth-century Catholic historian, Muslim origins would hardly have been proper in the sort of exemplary Christian foundational account that Roa was writing. Roa's aversion to the Arabic heritage extended to his own scholarship; whereas an earlier generation of Jesuits in Andalusia had been schooled in Arabic in order to help convert Muslims, Roa had not, judging from the fact that he was forced to ask a Granadan morisco to translate the Arabic inscription on a tomb found in a friend's house.[30]

Roa had taken up the question of Ecija's name in order to establish that it had been a site of martyrdom. According to Dexter's chronicle, one Saint Crispinus—a disciple of Santiago—had been put to death in "Astigi" during the Neronic persecutions.[31] Roa was able to catalogue Ecija's Roman antiquities, as well as its loyalty to the king from the time of the Reconquest, from familiar late antique and medieval sources. Yet without the information provided by the chronicles of Dexter and Julián Pérez, he would have had virtually nothing to say about ancient Christianity in the town. Indeed, as the authors of historiae sacrae repeatedly lamented, in a trope that antedated them by many centuries, few written records had survived what they believed to have been centuries of constant persecution of Christians by Roman and Islamic rulers. In spite of these problems, and the often tortuous logic needed to reconcile the cronicones with the known historical record, authors of local sacred histories relied on the texts as fundamental aids to bring ancient Christianity back to life. They applied their erudition and local knowledge not just to showcase their command of the sources, nor to summon romantic images of antiquity. Rather, as we have seen, they aimed to reanimate the early martyrs, bishops, and saints, and to inspire their communities to hail them as prominent features of the religious landscape, sometimes in the face of considerable opposition at home. It was this focus on learning for a specific end that most clearly distinguished local sacred history from purely antiquarian scholarship that studied the ancient world for its own sake.[32] For example, even before writing the book, Roa participated in efforts aimed to "awake the memory and veneration of the Holy Martyr [Crispinus] in the hearts of the citizens," including composing the inscriptions on two triumphal arches to the martyr commissioned by the city. Judging from this context, Roa was probably echoing the aspirations of his civic sponsors when he speculated that perhaps the historical research and devotional energies being directed toward Crispinus might inspire God to reveal his relics to the village.[33] Higuera would have been proud.

ANDALUSIAN ANTIQUARIANISM AND LOCAL RELIGION AFTER BARONIO

These conversations about history and holiness were conducted within a broader community of learning that was in some ways intensely provincial in scope and interests. Unlike the lay antiquarians in early modern England described by Daniel Woolf, many of whom were lawyers and physicians, the most prominent collectors of antiquities in Spain seem to have been either local gentry or members of the clergy.[34] Although lay collectors were not unknown, ecclesiastical interests remained central to the pursuit of knowledge in Andalusia, where the four main centers of learning and patronage were, in declining order of prestige and wealth, the sees of Seville, Cordoba, Granada, and Jaén-Baeza. In Seville, learned men tended to work for the archbishop, or at the Jesuit colegio of San Hermenegildo. Rodrigo Caro had moved to Seville in 1596 to complete his studies, which he had begun in Osuna; at the latter university, many other men preoccupied with sacred antiquities had also studied, including Bernardo de Aldrete and his brother José, Alonso de la Serna, and Martín de Roa—and, earlier, Pedro Salazar de Mendoza, Higuera's old foe.[35] In Seville, Caro combined his study of antiquities with his duties as a diocesan inspector and advisor (*letrado de cámara*) for Archbishop Pedro de Castro, and moved in the same learned circles in Seville as Juan de Robles and the painter Francisco Pacheco; and, as we have seen, Caro also worked closely with Quintanadueñas, who resided in Seville's Jesuit house.

These authors were linked by more than shared patrons. They also participated in the same conversations. We can get a sense of the ties that bound these men to the archbishop of Seville, to each other, and to learned men in Toledo and Madrid, in one noteworthy moment in June 1628. In the midst of the controversy sparked by Serna's 1626 challenge to the new officia propria for the archdiocese, Caro received a letter from his contact in Madrid, the royal cosmographer Antonio Moreno. Moreno related that Archbishop Guzmán had enlisted a squadron of pens for hire to write the officia for the new saints; the list included not only several well-known partisans of the cronicones—including Roa, Tamayo de Vargas, and Bernardo de Aldrete—but also remarkably, eventual foes of the texts, Alonso de la Serna, Francisco de la Rioja and, incidentally, Pedro Salazar de Mendoza.[36]

The cluster of scholars in service to the archbishops of Seville and Granada overlapped with the less prominent but regionally important diocese of Jaén. The 1628 relic discoveries in Arjona had raised the profile of the region, which also included the university and cathedral of Baeza, and was stewarded for twenty-eight years by Cardinal-Bishop Moscoso y Sandoval, nephew of the former royal favorite, the Duke of Lerma. The cardinal-bishop's career enables us to witness the central role that historical scholarship came to occupy in the post-Baronian church, even in a relatively peripheral diocese such as Jaén. For Moscoso, as for many other post-Tridentine prelates, promoting and regulating local religion were two sides of the same coin. Of particular interest are Moscoso's attempts to subject new and existing local devotions to more rigorous examination and regulation, which, happily for modern historians, had the effect of producing an unprecedented flourishing of historical scholarship in seventeenth-century Jaén. In the ongoing effort to promote and historicize the new saints and other local devotions, the cardinal-bishop engaged several scholars, including Rus Puerta and his younger contemporary, Martín de Ximena Jurado (1615–ca. 1660).[37] Moscoso's contacts also extended to clerics prominent in Andalusia at large: in Seville, these included Rodrigo Caro, the Jesuits Juan de Pineda and Antonio de Quintanadueñas, and the Discalced Carmelite preacher Jerónimo de Pancorbo in Seville; in Córdoba, Bernardo de Aldrete; and in Granada, the Sacromonte canon Martín Vázquez Siruela (1600–1664), a staunch supporter of the lead books, the cronicones, and the new Arjona relics.[38] Finally, the cardinal-bishop also corresponded with scholars in northern and central Spain, at the royal court and beyond, such as Tamayo de Vargas, Francisco de Bivar, the Valencian antiquarian Vicente Mariner, and the Jesuit Bernardino de Villegas, a professor of theology at Alcalá de Henares.[39]

In addition to commissioning research on the Arjona saints, the cardinal-bishop reevaluated existing legends, such as the story that the Virgin Mary, accompanied by Saint Ildefonso, had descended from heaven to proceed through the streets of Jaén before astonished observers in 1430.[40] He also sponsored research into the preexisting cult to Saint Eufrasio, the first bishop of Iliturgi, which some believed was the modern city of Andújar, where his relics had been rediscovered at the end of the sixteenth century.[41] Other local devotions that received their first extensive historical treatment during Moscoso's tenure as bishop included the "Holy Face" of Jaén's cathedral, believed to have been part of the same cloth known popularly as Veronica's veil, chronicled in loving detail by the local enthusiast Juan Acuña del Adarve, and the cults of Pedro Pascual, a Reconquest-era bishop of Jaén, and of Valencia, taken captive and martyred by the Moors.[42]

Finally, there were the martyrs of Baeza, whose relics, much like those of Arjona, emerged thanks to an alert reader of the cronicones. In mid-1629, Francisco Bilches, the rector of Baeza's Jesuit colegio, notified the city that the text of Julián Pérez made reference to several previously unknown local martyrs. They included Victor, an eighth-century bishop of Baeza, his companions Alexander and Marianus, as well as third-century martyrs Justus and Abundius, all of whom were recorded in the Roman Martyrology, but without a place of death. Thenceforth, events unfolded much as they had in Arjona. The theology faculty of the university of Baeza issued its recommendations: notwithstanding a few possible objections that might be raised about the historicity of the martyrs (including that an old martyrology had them dying in Rome, not Baeza), the cardinal-bishop should spare no expense in encouraging devotion to the new martyrs, particularly at a time when, as the Baeza theologians bemoaned in the perennial plaint of the guardians of piety, Catholic faith had become so lukewarm. By August of 1629, the martyrs were adopted as patron saints of Baeza; the bishop encouraged a general procession, votive masses, and fasting in their honor; miraculous lights began to appear around the site of Baeza's old alcazar; and the faithful began to dig. As in Arjona, various "censures and penalties" issued by ecclesiastical authorities failed to prevent the assembled devotees from digging without supervision: the frantic and unauthorized excavations only halted after a wall collapsed and blocked access to the hole where their attentions had been focused.[43]

Moscoso's policy of enshrining new saints while investigating their authenticity yielded contradictory results, and these new cults often seem to have possessed a rather improvised and sometimes precarious quality. In spite of some lingering doubts, including rival claims from Guadix's town of Baza, the cardinal-bishop ended up adding a total of twelve new Baeza martyrs to the diocesan liturgical calendar in 1640; in addition to the five whose relics were discovered in 1629, he also introduced prayers to Saints Faustus and the aforementioned Straton, Rufinus, and Rufinianus (notwithstanding rival claims from Seville), as well as three others that the lead books of Granada had identified as natives of Baeza.[44] In the case of Eufrasio as well, the cardinal-bishop considered, and then disregarded, rival claims by other dioceses, or contrary evidence raised by his own scholars. This was also true for Potenciana, a would-be saint whose tomb and relics were discovered in a derelict hermitage on the banks of the Guadalquivir River in Villanueva de Andújar where, according to local tradition, the holy virgin had lived and died a few centuries previously. In April 1628, Moscoso personally opened Potenciana's tomb with great fanfare, accompanied by an entourage of local nobles and clerics; Ximena Jurado included a sketch of the site in his manuscript collection of local antiquities (figure 8.3). In consonance with the diocesan *Constitutions* he had recently promulgated, the cardinal-bishop then attempted to restore the "decency" of Potenciana's cult by translating her remains from the decrepit tomb in which she was buried to a new chapel he had endowed. Yet Potenciana's fate oscillated in the ensuing decades, in part because she was not an

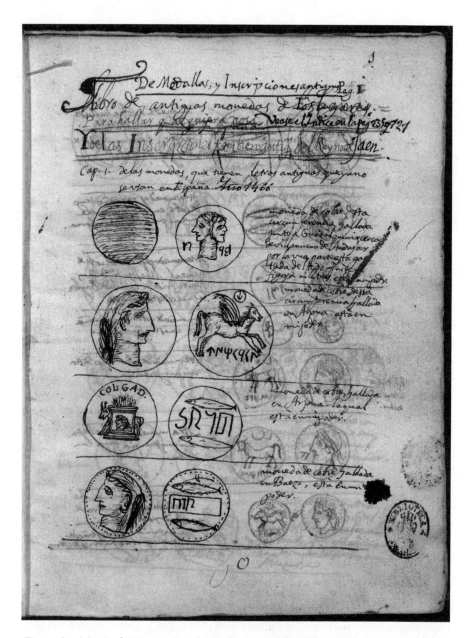

Figure 8.3. Martín de Ximena Jurado's collection of "Medals and Inscriptions: Book of ancient coins from places in Spain. And also the ancient inscriptions of the Kingdom of Jaen." The first page begins with "Chapter One. The coins that bear ancient characters (*letras*) that are no longer used in Spain." In Martín de Ximena Jurado, *Antigüedades del reino de Jaén* (ca. 1639) © Biblioteca Nacional de España, Ms. 1180, 1r.

official saint. She was not commemorated in any of the universal Catholic liturgical books, such as the Roman Breviary or the revised Roman Martyrology. Thus it would be essential to find evidence of a continuous cult so that she could be grandfathered into sanctity as a *casus exceptus*: this special category of exception granted sanctity to those holy individuals who had never been canonized formally, but who had been venerated locally or regionally since "time immemorial," which, in 1624, Urban VIII had defined as one hundred years or more.[45]

In 1640, a dozen years after the discovery of her tomb, the shrine and the research were finally complete, and Moscoso prepared to give this long-standing devotion a proper place in the official life of the church. Yet as other learned clerics began to investigate the would-be saint in preparation for adding Potenciana to the diocesan liturgical calendar, the historical foundations beneath her began to give way. Sacromonte's Vázquez Siruela seems to have been the first to start chipping away at the arguments in her favor; to his objections, local booster Acuña del Adarve responded with pious indignation, and more than a hint of menace: "Keep in mind," he warned, "the saints are good friends; you would not want to have them angry with you, and especially not my saint."[46] Yet Vázquez Siruela's critiques were echoed by the Cordoban scholar Pedro Díaz de Ribas, who pointed out that no historical evidence placed Potenciana in the region, and that some traditions identified her as a native of Rome.[47] Yet, in the end, swayed perhaps by Acuña's determined advocacy, Moscoso opted to enshrine the saint's relics in a new chapel, commission Vázquez Siruela to prepare a petition to Rome for the *casus exceptus* and, in 1644, add a liturgical feast (an octave) in her honor to the revised diocesan calendar.[48]

Moscoso often chose the path of lesser caution in such debates, even when significant disagreements divided Andalusia's scholars. This is exemplified in the case of Hierotheo who, as we have seen, Dexter had identified as a native of Spain and bishop of Segovia. Francisco de Rus Puerta argued that while Hierotheo had been Segovia's bishop, the cronicones also made it possible that he had been a native of Arjona. Moscoso agreed, and also included Hierotheo in the new liturgical calendar of 1644.[49] Another example is in the three saints Isacio, Croton, and Apolo, who, according to Dexter, had died in "Alba." In their editions of Dexter, Bivar and Caro argued that "Alba" was Arjona which, as Pliny the Elder had attested, had been known by the two Latin names of "Alba" and "Urgabona."[50] Detractors, including Rus Puerta, Roa, Tamayo de Vargas, and Adán de Centurión, the Marquis of Estepa, contended that "Alba" was a mistranscription for "Abla," the town in the diocese of Guadix.[51] In spite of these dissenting opinions, Moscoso opted to claim the martyrs for his diocese. The three martyrs were added to the revised liturgical calendar of 1644, along with thirty-seven others, including Saint Eufrasio, Pedro Pascual, Potenciana, Arjona's Bonosus and Maximianus, and new Baeza martyrs which now numbered fourteen.[52]

As for many scholars of the distant past elsewhere in early modern Europe, in the attempt to find acceptable evidence, Rus Puerta, Ximena Jurado, and their contemporaries often butted up against its absence. This is the most probable explanation for the Arjona coin, a remarkable specimen certified by Ximena Jurado. In his books and manuscripts, which included surveys of the history and antiquity of the diocese of Jaén, Ximena Jurado combined material, visual, and textual evidence in a manner that connects him to similar, more prominent figures in Italy, England, and elsewhere (figure 8.3).[53] Thus, in 1637, when the printer Pedro de la Cuesta unearthed a coin while strolling along a lane leading to the Guadalquivir River, he sent the small and corroded copper specimen directly to Ximena Jurado, who was known in the area to be "an aficionado of collecting ancient coins." On its face was an imperial portrait of the fourth-century emperor Maximian, who ruled the western half of the empire during the Great Persecution, and on the back, the words "In the Municipality of Alba Urgabone the Christian Superstition Was Destroyed." For Ximena Jurado, who sketched and described the coin for the cardinal-bishop, the significance of the find was clear: the fourth-century Romans had the coin minted in commemoration of a massive persecution that had rid the town of Christians; in thanks, they had raised a temple in Maximian's honor and pledged to offer a burnt sacrifice and wine upon its altar.[54] In other words, the find provided independent verification—in numismatic form—of the persecution during which Arjona martyrs had perished, which had not been recorded by a single ancient author with the exception of Dexter (figure 8.4).

The coin was precisely the sort of seemingly unimpeachable evidence that Moscoso and his clerics had been seeking. As Ximena Jurado pointed out to the bishop:

> The matter of this coin is so great that, in a question of antiquity, it cannot be greater. Because the authority that inscriptions in stone and coins have is so much, that the law mandates that more faith and credit should be given to such epigraphs than to the testimony of many witnesses.[55]

Ximena Jurado echoed the convictions of scholars of antiquities throughout Europe, for whom coins (as with inscriptions) were believed to be more trustworthy than texts; coins were produced by official mints, and thus more difficult to forge. The cardinal-bishop apparently agreed, as did the town of Arjona, which celebrated the discovery in November 1639 with a religious festival. The

Figure 8.4. The numismatic evidence for the Arjona martyrdoms: "Explication of an ancient coin of Arjona. And on how worthy it may be to persuade us that in this Village, which used to be called MUNICIPIO ALBENSE URGAVONENSE, an almost infinite number of martyrs suffered in the time of the emperors Diocletian and Maximian in whose honor was struck this very curious copper coin that I possess." In Martín de Ximena Jurado, *Antigüedades del reino de Jaén* (ca. 1639) © Biblioteca Nacional de España, Ms. 1180, 296r.

following year, Ximena Jurado personally presented the coin to the municipal council of Arjona.[56]

THE CRONICONES AND LOCAL MEMORY

In addition to documenting the physical, documentary, and supernatural evidence for these and other saints' cults, Rus Puerta, Ximena Jurado, and other scholars in the cardinal-bishop's service also became the first to document Jaén's sacred history and traditions. Like Caro, Roa, or indeed the cluster of Zaragoza historians who wrote about El Pilar, these local sacred historians, like Higuera himself, were shaping vox populi even as they sought to preserve it. And while to modern audiences, local sacred histories, with their tortuous excurses and speculative etymologies, might read like rarified treatises destined to collect dust, to contemporaries, these were not abstract texts isolated from action. Admittedly, their authors applied their antiquarian erudition to intensely parochial concerns. Yet they were also in conversation with one another, with local and sometimes national audiences. We can get a glimpse of this broader audience from many of the books collected in the private libraries of the canons of Toledo's cathedral, including Quintanadueñas's *Saints of the Imperial City of Toledo* of 1651 and Ximena Jurado's *Catalogue of the Bishops of Jaén* of 1654 (figure 8.5).[57]

Yet the audience for these works of local sacred history was not limited to the literate urban elites who could afford to purchase them; as Richard Kagan has pointed out, their information about local saints, for example, would also make rich fodder for sermons, and, in effect, "instruct the inhabitants of a particular place how to think about the community in which they lived."[58] The example of Jaén once again proves particularly instructive. By penning their respective histories of the diocese and acting as collectors of specimens from throughout the region, both Rus Puerta and Ximena Jurado became known as authorities on the past, and they were consulted as such when historical information was needed, both in person while alive and through their texts when they were gone. In this way, these local antiquarians connected the dominion of popular memory with texts written about the past, and vice versa. We can witness this mutual communication in one particular moment later in the seventeenth century, when Salvador Medina, a scribe and head treasurer (*contador mayor*) of Jaén, testified in the *casus exceptus* petition for Pedro Pascual, still under way in 1662. The aim was to establish that a public cult to the saint had been continuously active for at least a century. When questioned about how he knew the contours of the saint's biography, Medina answered, significantly, that he had heard Rus Puerta recount the martyrdom of the saint in Moorish captivity, and that he had also read about the later discovery of the martyr's remains in the works of Quintanadueñas and Ximena Jurado.⁵⁹

Like the cronicones that informed them, these works of historia sacra shaped local religion all over Spain. In the mid-seventeenth century, Rodrigo Caro called to mind some of the other places where, in the approximately fifty years since the texts were discovered, saints had been recovered from obscurity. Thanks to information from Dexter, Caro boasted, Alcalá de Henares, Arjona, Baeza, Carmona, Ecija, Jaén, Niebla, Seville, Sigüenza, Tocina, Utrera, and Xérez de la Frontera all "had the good luck to have discovered in Dexter or Maximus that they were the native lands of martyrs."⁶⁰ To Caro's list we may well add several more examples, some in well-known places, and others more obscure and scarcely noticed by scholars. In the latter category are Saints Vicente and Leto, who were identified as natives of Lezuza, in the Albacete region in the mid-seventeenth century, thanks to Alonso de Requena Aragón, a *bachiller* and native of Lezuza, who first encountered the relevant details in the cronicones.⁶¹ Another relatively unknown example of the cronicones' local effects was in Lerma, where in 1613 an Augustinian friar named Luis de los Ángeles appeared before an apostolic notary public to report that he had discovered in the chronicle of Julián Pérez, as well as in a manuscript found among Higuera's Toledan papers, that the village of Lerma had taken its name from "Lerama," the family name of one Saint Caliopa, a Roman-era martyr.⁶² In support of this novel assertion, the friar had the relevant passages copied into the testimony, where they remained unnoticed for over a century—as far as we know—until a local schoolteacher penned a 1716 account of Saint Caliopa's life and death in Lerma, drawing prodigiously upon the cronicones.⁶³

Few landscapes of the sacred were transformed as sensationally as in the diocese of Jaén, yet the widespread emergence of new saints and devotions throughout Spain in the seventeenth century suggests that the residents of Arjona and Baeza were not anomalous in their intense interest in, and receptivity to, news from the false chronicles. In sacred histories of Mérida, Segovia, and Toledo, the cronicones were cited as crucial evidence for new or revised saints' cults, sometimes in the face of local opposition.⁶⁴ In a manuscript treatise dedicated to the sixth Marquis of Tarifa, Fernando Enríquez Afán de Ribera, the Cordoban antiquary Díaz de Ribas argued that according to the cronicones and the lead books of Granada, Saint Hiscio, one of the Seven Apostles, had been the first bishop of Tarifa— and not, as others claimed, of Gibraltar. In response, it seems, the city adopted him as a patron saint and requested a relic of Hiscio from Archbishop Castro of Seville, which he granted in 1620.⁶⁵ In Madrid, the chronicles helped provide hagiographers with information on the new farmer-saint Isidore and his wife

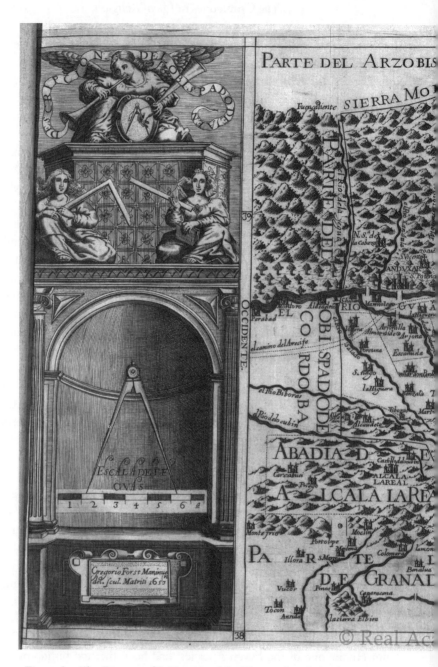

Figure 8.5. The Diocese of Jaén mapped for Ximena Jurado by the engraver Gregorio Forstman y Medina, signed in the corner "Gregorio Forst Man." The works of seventeenth-century antiquaries such as Francisco de Rus Puerta and Martín de Ximena Jurado in Jaén provided the first

comprehensive guides to local history, and, like this map, are still important guides to the past, in spite of their distortions. In Martín de Ximena Jurado, *Catálogo de los obispos . . . de Jaén* (Madrid, 1654) © Reproducción, Real Academia de la Historia, 5/407.

María, and Julián Pérez's chronicle was the source for another saint included in Madrid's civic iconography in the early seventeenth century.[66] In books on Huesca, Palencia, Valencia, and Zaragoza, the chronicles were cited matter-of-factly, without comment on their relative merits, itself a significant indication that for some mid-seventeenth-century authors, the chronicles had become just one of many acceptable textual authorities.[67]

Of course, the effects on local religion were not always welcome. The suggestion that Segovia's first bishop had been Hierotheo and not Saint Fructuosus sparked a fierce seventeenth-century polemic, as we shall see. Well into the eighteenth century, local controversies raged over details from the false chronicles. In Sigüenza, the disagreement centered on one crucial line in Julián Pérez, which seemed to suggest that an anonymous relic in the cathedral belonged to a seventh-century bishop of the French diocese of Limoges. Opponents contended that this detail must have been a pious fabrication, inserted by the cronicón's editor out of a misguided desire to help Sigüenza identify its relic, and that, in fact, the relic belonged instead to the city's twelfth-century bishop, Martín Muñoz de Hinojosa, known as the Holy Priest.[68] And, in the late eighteenth century, Zaragozans were still arguing about whether Saint Athanasius had been its first bishop, as the cronicones alleged.[69]

These widespread local dimensions of Higuera's influence are just beginning to come into focus. Yet if, even after surveying the influence of the cronicones on Spanish historia sacra, we are still tempted to dismiss the chronicles and their influence as a minor and regrettable eruption of credulity that can be separated neatly from mainstream Spanish history, we may wish to pause to consider the diligent research of those nineteenth-century scholars who resolved to catalogue the complete effects of the cronicones on history, liturgy, and hagiography. In his indispensable 1853 guide to Enrique Flórez's *España sagrada*, Pedro Sainz de Baranda listed all the officia propria of the Spanish liturgical year, and he signaled twenty-two *rezos* that had been introduced thanks to Higuera's texts.[70] However, this was clearly a low estimate, for, as we have seen, the cardinal-bishop of Jaén alone authorized at least that many cronicones-inspired officia in his 1644 reform of the Jaén liturgy. A similar desire to cleanse the historical record prompted Tomás Múñoz y Romero to make careful note, in his *Bibliographic-Historic Dictionary of the Old Kingdoms, Provinces, Cities, Villages, Churches, and Sanctuaries of Spain* (1858), of which local histories had been marred by a reliance upon the *cronicones*. The appearance of these texts, he lamented, was a "sad and shameful event" that had made the otherwise rich historical genre of local history "the most contemptible of all."[71]

These detailed denunciations, combined with the evidence of the manuscript and printed histories surviving in modern collections, enable us to estimate that from circa 1600 to circa 1800, at least 164 works of sacred history cited the cronicones.[72] In other words, it now seems clear that Higuera's texts—much more than the lead books, for example, whose significance was relatively limited to Granadan local history, and only somewhat more broadly, to the burgeoning field of Spanish orientalism—were absolutely central to evolving visions of the past in early modern Spain.[73] Well into the seventeenth and eighteenth centuries, thanks to the dovetailing of the chronicles with particular political, religious, and local interests, even those who decided that the cumulative effect of the cronicones' flaws made them unreliable as historical sources often found it impossible to relinquish the texts entirely. In such instances, their perceived benefit for the sake of a deeper truth made the chronicles incredibly compelling. As we shall see in the following chapter, not even the men at the very centers of Spanish intellectual and cultural life in Toledo and Madrid were immune to the tantalizing mine of detail provided by the cronicones, and it was thanks in part to their patronage of luxurious editions of the texts of Dexter, Maximus, Luitprand, and Julián Pérez that the works of these ersatz chroniclers enjoyed a remarkable longevity, even among those who may have known better.

9

The Politics of the *Cronicones* in Madrid and Rome

While the most enthusiastic and enduring proponents of the texts were regional historians of the sacred like Francisco de Rus Puerta of Jaén, their evolving fortunes would be shaped to a much greater degree by influential arbiters of all things religio-political, at home and abroad. In the 1630s and 1640s, it would be at the royal court in Madrid, and more specifically, in the circles around the royal favorite, Don Gaspar de Guzmán, the Count-Duke of Olivares—an avid collector and generous patron of learning—where the texts would be prepared, critiqued, and published. If we find the most prominent supporters of the cronicones among well-connected courtiers, it was from those same circles that their most vociferous foes emerged. That men on both sides belonged to the same social and political networks should not come as a surprise: defending or publishing the chronicles was one path to attracting attention at court; so, too, was attacking them. Both reactions are unwitting testaments to the central place that the false chronicles would occupy in Spanish intellectual life of the seventeenth century and beyond. In the meantime, the cronicones would fare considerably worse in the wider realm of learned Catholic opinion, particularly in papal Rome, where the ongoing controversy over the lead books of Granada, as well as the ascendance of French interests, negatively conditioned reactions. There the cronicones and their supporters would, with a handful of significant exceptions, be met with outright skepticism.

THE CHRONICLES AT THE ROYAL COURT

The first readers of the chronicles were interested prelates, cathedral chapters, and a handful of antiquarian-minded aristocrats, but by the 1620s and 1630s the texts had spread much further, such that royal courtiers and more prominent clerics would now become their principal editors, sponsors, and readers. The confluence of patronage and genuine interest in the texts means that by the middle decades of the seventeenth century, rare was the well-informed courtier or scholar who did not have a copy of at least one of the chronicles in his collection.[1] In this, as in so many other matters of state, religion, and scholarship, the Count-Duke of Olivares—the *valido*, or favorite, of King Philip IV from 1621 to 1643—played a prominent and complex role. Olivares was a generous and active patron whose nepotism in political and ecclesiastical appointments helped attract a steady stream of postulants, among whom we find both enthusiastic proponents and determined foes of the cronicones. Even while some of the count-duke's intimates would dedicate reams of expensive paper stock to publishing the chronicles with elaborate commentary, others, such as his librarian Francisco de Rioja, would attack them without mercy. In order to understand both positions, it is important to recognize that by the time of Olivares's ascendancy, the false chronicles had made their way into the heart of Spanish intellectual and political life, such that collecting, elucidating, defending, and attacking the chronicles, like participating in literary controversies, became simply one more dimension of courtly politics. Of the six succeeding editions of the texts published between 1627 and 1651, five were sponsored by royal courtiers, prominent prelates, or both. The count-duke's rich book and manuscript collection—which he had accumulated thanks to a generous royal privilege whose terms essentially allowed him to raid monastic and cathedral libraries—was the genesis of at least two of these editions. In this context, collecting, correcting, editing, and preparing the chronicles for publication were tools of scholarly and courtly ambition.[2]

We can witness this type of jostling for political favor in the respective careers of Tomás Tamayo de Vargas, Rodrigo Caro, Lorenzo Ramírez de Prado, and Francisco Bivar, the four men who prepared editions of the cronicones in the decades after Calderón's widely disparaged 1619 edition. Over the more than two decades of Olivares's career as *valido*, they attempted to curry favor through their editions of the cronicones, as well as in public responses to critiques of the texts, which often came from within Olivares's circles. The political valence of scholarly work helps explain why Tamayo de Vargas dedicated his 1624 *Defense* of Dexter to Don Francisco Fernández Bertrán, the *abad mayor* of the Olivares family chapel, as well as to the powerful dean and cathedral chapter of Toledo. Although many details of Tamayo de Vargas's career remain to be illuminated, it seems that this and other endeavors succeeded in bringing him favor at court, judging from the fact that he procured the coveted sinecure of Castilian royal chronicler by 1626.[3] Of course, one's fortunes were never certain at court, particularly for somebody like Tamayo de Vargas, who languished just outside Olivares's circles.

Perhaps this is why in the *Defense* Tamayo trumpeted the fact that his next effort would be to produce a learned and well-annotated edition of Dexter-Maximus. If he hoped that this would help him attract continued patronage while also warding off the competition, he was to be bitterly disappointed on both counts. A year after becoming royal chronicler, just as his own edition was (allegedly) nearly ready for the press, Tamayo de Vargas discovered that Caro had him beat, and that the Seville antiquary's Dexter-Maximus was about to be printed. The chronicler exploded with anger. Tamayo de Vargas's own efforts were to be superseded by Caro's 1627 edition, to which he had contributed no small part. As he wrote to Caro, "the deception does not bother me, as others have assumed; rather it is the time that I wasted, because I assume that, if this work was in your hands, you won't have left me even any crumbs." In a backhanded attempt to shame his former friend into acknowledging his own efforts, he added, "I am certain that you, being who you are, will honor me in your book. It would behoove you to make a note of that which I gathered up, and observed first, which it would be an act of gratefulness to repeat."[4] Tamayo's name is conspicuous for its absence in Caro's edition.[5]

Caro was in the midst of his own decades-long and ultimately fruitless attempt to attract courtly patronage, and he probably calculated that the damage to his friendship with Tamayo de Vargas would be worth the risk. In any case, Tamayo de Vargas evidently stopped working on Dexter-Maximus, and instead started to prepare editions of the other two chronicles, those of Luitprand and Julián Pérez, neither of which had entered print yet. The royal chronicler had been able to consult these manuscripts in the count-duke's well-stocked library, but, unfortunately, he was not the only learned courtier pinning his hopes on impressing Olivares with the first edition of a cronicón. A year later in 1628 Tamayo de Vargas was once again blindsided, this time by Lorenzo Ramírez de Prado's edition of Julián Pérez, which the courtier had printed while serving as royal emissary in Paris (figure 9.1). Tamayo de Vargas was furious. As he fulminated in a letter to a friend, he had been the first to encounter the manuscript in Olivares's library. After improving the text with his own handwritten amendments and marginal notes, he (unwisely) lent the text to Ramírez de Prado, who then went on to have it printed under his own name, without consulting Tamayo de Vargas, in a clear "violation of the rules of friendship."[6]

Tamayo de Vargas must have thought that he was finally rising to the challenge of this bare-knuckle scholarly environment in 1635, when he debuted the first printed edition of Luitprand. Yet in spite of the fact that he was the royal chroni-

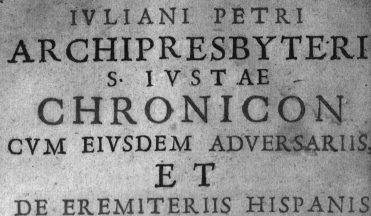

Figure 9.1. The only edition of the chronicle of Julián Pérez, prepared by the courtier Lorenzo Ramírez de Prado. As indicated by the annotation at the center left of the page, this copy was "corrected by Don Martín Jimena." Lorenzo Ramírez de Prado, *Iuliani Petri Archipresbyteri Santae Iustae Chronicon* (Paris, 1628) © Reproducción, Real Academia de la Historia, 5/460.

cler, and that he had prepared the edition from an exemplar in the count-duke's library, Tamayo de Vargas failed to attract any courtly patronage for the edition, which was dedicated not to any well-placed courtiers, but to Andalusian erudite Adán de la Centurión, the Marquis of Estepa, the assiduous advocate for the lead books of Granada and patron of regional scholarship. The royal librarian Juan Beltrán did contribute a guide to Tamayo's notes, but the balance of the accompanying material—which consisted of an index and poems in praise of Tamayo—was penned by relative unknowns.[7]

In 1640, Tamayo de Vargas was soon outmaneuvered once again by Ramírez de Prado, who prepared a lavishly annotated and illustrated edition of Luitprand, which he introduced, in a notable swipe at the royal chronicler, as "now having been printed for the first time" (figure 9.2). The volume opened with an engraved reproduction of the 1626 portrait of the count-duke by the Flemish artist Peter Paul Rubens (figure 9.3) and included other reproductions of documents and antiquities. It also included epistles, endorsements, and elaborate Latin *elogia* from prominent intellectuals at court, including the Jesuit Juan Eusebio Nieremberg, the historian Luis de Tribaldo, and the royal librarian and Hellenist, Vincent Mariner. Ramírez de Prado not only outdid Tamayo de Vargas in courtly appurtenances, but also in the substance of the text itself. Whereas the 1635 edition included only Luitprand's chronicle, *adversaria*, and editorial annotations, Ramírez de Prado's bombastic volume boasted even more extensive commentary, as well as other (genuine) texts by Liutprand of Cremona, such as his history of the deeds of emperors and kings of Europe, his "Embassy," which had only been published once before (by Henry Canisius in Ingolstadt), and a book of the lives of the popes, which Ramírez de Prado claimed to have prepared by collating old "parchment manuscripts" with a 1602 Mainz edition.[8]

The central place of scholarshop on the cronicones in the search for patronage is also confirmed by Caro's career, which was characterized by an ultimately unsuccessful search for courtly favor in the 1620s, 1630s, and 1640s. In one of his first jaunts for patronage, Caro dedicated his 1627 Dexter-Maximus to the count-duke's relative Don Alonso Pérez Guzmán, the brother of the eighth Duke of Medina Sidonia.[9] The following year, at the urging of his friend Antonio Moreno Vilches, the royal cosmographer, Caro reconsidered this strategy and attempted to curry favor with Ramírez de Prado instead. Yet Moreno does not seem to have been particularly well informed: when he expressed optimism that Caro's notes to Julián Pérez would, like his edition of Dexter-Maximus, bring him to the court's attention, he was unaware that Ramírez de Prado's own edition of the same chronicle was about to enter print.[10] Although Caro, like Tamayo de Vargas, was to be outmaneuvered by Ramírez de Prado, the scholar from Seville was

Figure 9.2. Lorenzo Ramírez de Prado, *Luitprandi subdiaconi toletani* [. . .] *Opera quae extant* (Antwerp, 1640) © Reproducción, Real Academia de la Historia, 3/1267.

Figure 9.3. Portrait of the Count-Duke of Olivares, after Peter Paul Rubens. In Ramírez de Prado, *Luitprandi subdiaconi toletani [. . .] Opera quae extant* (Antwerp, 1640) © Reproducción, Real Academia de la Historia, 3/1267.

no babe in the woods. That deception and double-dealing were not confined to hardnosed courtly circles is suggested by the fact that Caro was having a work of history ghostwritten for him at the very same time. In a 1628 letter, Moreno reported that the book, which was being written by the "parish priest of Los Palacios," was nearly finished and that it had the "foundations" to which Caro would now add the "decoration and luster" that "your works should have."[11]

In 1631, Caro once again appealed for the count-duke's patronage, this time through Francisco Morovelli de Puebla, a pertinacious foe of Saint Teresa's co-patronage who was in Olivares's favor at the time. Yet Caro never managed to ingratiate himself with any of Olivares's advisors. Notable among these was Francisco de Rioja (ca. 1583–1659), who had known Caro ever since his days as a cathedral canon in Seville. As members of the small but active circles of learned men in the Andalusian city in the early part of the seventeenth century, they had shared texts and friends; indeed, Caro had obtained his first copy of the cronicones from Rioja.[12] In those early days, Rioja was still sanguine about the texts, and he even cited them favorably in a treatise on behalf of the Immaculate Conception.[13] Yet by 1628 Rioja had become a determined foe of the texts, such that he and the Seville canon Alonso de la Serna, as we have seen, decided to "destroy Dexter." Rioja did not actually strike against Dexter and Caro in print until 1640, when he penned an anonymous treatise that would renew their rivalry, and the long-simmering tensions between the rivals would erupt into a public debate about the false chronicles that one scholar has characterized as an "open war."[14] In 1628, Caro's friend Moreno wrote of this anti-Dexter conspiracy in terms that doubtlessly echoed his friend's own sentiments: "I consider those who bastardize these matters of Homeland and Nation"—in other words, those, like Rioja, who critiqued the cronicones—"to be bastard Spaniards."[15]

If, in terms of their success in gaining political capital from their work on the cronicones, Ramírez de Prado was at one end of the spectrum and Tamayo de Vargas and Caro at the other, Francisco de Bivar fell somewhere in the middle. At first, the Cistercian's connections were more monastic than royal. His Dexter-Maximus was printed not in Spain, but in Lyons, where it appeared with the royal imprimatur of King Louis XIII. At this point, Bivar was still laboring in relative obscurity; rather than dedicating the edition to a courtier in a more advantageous position, he named a cardinal who was, at the time, out of favor. Cardinal Gabriel Trejo Paniagua had been in the circle of the former royal favorite, the Duke of Lerma, so after the rise of Olivares his position at court became rather untenable, at least until 1627, when he was unexpectedly chosen by the count-duke to become president of the Council of Castile.[16] By 1631, Bivar's fortunes had changed somewhat for the better, judging from the fact that he was asked to contribute an *encomium* to Ramírez de Prado for that well-placed courtier's 1640 edition of Luitprand.[17] Bivar continued to enjoy increasing patronage in the following decades; in 1651, his edition of Marcus Maximus was issued in a luxurious printing under the sponsorship of the now-archbishop of Toledo, Baltasar de Moscoso y Sandoval. Unfortunately, Bivar was unable to enjoy this posthumous edition.[18]

THE CHRONICLES IN DANGER: ROME, CIRCA 1630

Beyond Spain, the texts were provoking a much more marked lack of sympathy; by 1630, with three editions of Dexter-Maximus in circulation, as well as one edition of Julián Pérez, the texts had become objects of curiosity in Rome. The third decade of the century would become a moment of high tension for those concerned with the fate of Dexter's chronicle, including not only Caro, but also Bivar and, by extension, his patron and protector, the cardinal-bishop of Jaén. As we have seen, Moscoso had supervised the introduction of a number of new saints in his diocese underwritten by the false chronicles, and commissioned several scholars to document, research, and defend the discoveries, which included the particularly spectacular series of relic *inventiones* in the town of Arjona. Yet in 1630, just as the cardinal-bishop was preparing a trip to Rome as part of a royal entourage, he received news from his Roman contacts that the papal Congregation of the Index of Prohibited Books was scrutinizing a text that relied heavily upon Dexter—and, more specifically, upon Bivar's reading of Dexter. In other words, the cronicones (and possibly their defenders) were in jeopardy.

The book under scrutiny had been written by a regular correspondent of Bivar's, Melchior Inchofer (1585–1649), a Jesuit better known to historians as the author of a 1633 condemnation of Galileo.[19] His *Vindication of the Truth of the Letter of the Blessed Virgin Mary to the Messinans* (1629) was a Latin defense of the legend that the Virgin Mary had delivered a letter from heaven to the people of Messina in Sicily, a tradition that had already been challenged by critics including Baronio. Inchofer's lengthy explication of the tradition, which included an edition of the epistle itself, may have been guilty of nothing more serious than offending the powerful archbishop of Palermo, who seems to have feared that the Jesuit's prominent patronage of Messina's "Virgine della lettera" would overshadow his city's patron, Saint Rosalia, whose own epistle had only recently been rediscovered.[20] Inchofer's superiors, fearful of entangling the Society of Jesus in a broader political battle with the archbishop and his Spanish protectors, immediately recalled the Jesuit to Rome. They also persuaded him to soften his claims, which he did, in a 1632 edition in which he allowed that it was merely *prob-*

able, rather than certain, that the Virgin had bestowed a heavenly letter upon the lucky Messinans; a year later, the Congregation of the Index prohibited the first, unexpurgated edition of the text.[21] Another sticking point may have been that the letter from the Virgin, like the cronicones and Granada's plomos, affirmed the tradition of the Immaculate Conception, a controversial cause near and dear to the Spanish monarchy. Thanks in part to the rising political fortunes of the French, Urban VIII's Rome was increasingly hostile to Spanish Hapsburg interests. This has led some scholars to posit that antipathy to Inchofer's treatise (and to the lead books) was due, at least in part, to their defense of this quintessentially Spanish devotion.[22]

In 1630, the cardinal-bishop of Jaén and his scholars fretted that doubts about Inchofer's text, and about the lead books of Granada, had now begun to spread to the authenticity of the chronicles and the Arjona relics. Supporters worried that the Congregation's scrutiny of Inchofer's text, as well as continued Roman objections to the plomos, might land one or both sets of texts on the list of prohibited works. The discoveries, of course, shared thematic, chronological, and religious overlap. And they shared defenders. For example, Dexter had memorialized the Messina tradition with a brief but straightforward confirmation that in the year 86, "Among Messinans the memory of the Virgin Mary is famous, a kind letter having been sent to them by her." In the fifth century, according to Dexter, the letter had been rediscovered in Messina's public records.[23] Inchofer cited these passages as the principal evidence for the authenticity of the Virgin's letter. So crucial was this testimony to Inchofer's argument that he spent twenty-five pages in the treatise detailing the many reasons why the chronicle was not apocryphal and could, in fact, be trusted on this question and many others.[24]

The potentially negative implications of this mutual association were made plain in an internal memorandum composed between 1634 and 1639 by Cardinal Desiderio Scaglia (1567–1639), a Roman inquisitor who also served as one of Galileo's judges. The cardinal of Cremona's assessment survives in a dossier of material on the plomos prepared by the Roman Inquisition. Scaglia noted that in the voluminous commentary that Bivar included in his edition of Dexter's chronicle, the Cistercian not only cross-referenced the plomos and Dexter's testimony in order to assert the authenticity of both, but Bivar also asserted erroneously that the antiquity and authenticity of the lead books had been established by Archbishop Castro acting in the capacity of "apostolic judge." (In fact, in the offending passage, Bivar referred not to the lead books themselves, but to the parchment found in Granada's Torre Turpiana, which predated the appearance of the lead books.)[25] More worrying for Scaglia was that the misinformation propagated by Bivar was no longer confined to "printed books," but had now been inscribed in stone—literally. The cardinal described a long inscription referring to the plomos in Sacromonte that had been penned by Bernardo de Aldrete; this Cordoban antiquary, we will recall, had not only defended the plomos, but he had also written two treatises on the Arjona relics.[26] For the cardinal of Cremona, it was simply too much to countenance that "the proposition that these sheets [of lead] are true and Catholic is consecrated in marble for immortality"; as he suggested to the inquisitors, "it is necessary to seize upon an energetic remedy," which he left unspecified.[27]

These concerns were shared by other Roman critics of the lead books, among whom were the influential cardinals Baronio and Bellarmine. At the very same time, the papal nuncio was losing patience in the decades-long attempt to procure the lead books from the zealous guardians at Granada's abbey of Sacromonte. In a concession to Roman pressure, the Spanish Inquisition banned dissemination of all translations of the plomos and required the surrender of those in private possession in 1631. A year later, Philip IV took even more drastic measures, and ordered the lead books seized from the lockbox in the abbey of Sacromonte and brought to Madrid.[28] In this charged context, at least in retrospect, it might have seemed unwise for Bivar to continue to suggest, as he did in the 1627 *Dexter*, that the respective fates of the lead books and the cronicones were conjoined, and that God revealed them to Spain within a year of each other so that skeptics could see that the details of one confirmed the other.[29] Yet this is precisely what he did in the 1630 *Apologetic and Suppliant Petition for Dexter*, a short treatise sponsored by the cardinal-bishop of Jaén, who brought a copy with him to Rome in 1630 in hopes that it might help persuade Rome to withhold any possible censures of the text.

Here Bivar argued that since Dexter's text contained nothing contrary to the faith, the Congregation of the Index had no legitimate reason to limit its circulation among Catholics. On this point, Bivar was on relatively solid ground: none of the cronicones treated matters of doctrine in any detail, and, even in passing, Higuera had hewn closely to mainstream Counter-Reformation theology. And, as Bivar pointed out, Dexter's text belonged squarely to the realm of human history. The author named bishops and indicated where martyrs died: he had not pronounced on matters of doctrine, nor had he claimed apostolic authority. As pious—not doctrinal—material, the chronicle was subject to a broader margin of error and a lower bar of proof.[30] Here Bivar was echoing medieval theologians, who had long made a distinction between matters of doctrine and matters of piety: the former were the concern of theologians and the latter were usually left alone, unless they impinged upon orthodoxy.[31] Thus, Bivar concluded, not without reason, that Dexter's text was not heretical: "On the contrary, nothing in it is against good morals, nor would offend Aristarchus [of Samothrace, the proverbial critic] himself."[32]

What, then, of the possible objection that Dexter's chronicle was apocryphal? Here Bivar found himself in a somewhat more delicate situation. First was the problem that the apocrypha were defined in a variety of ways. Bivar contended that the text in question did not conform to one common definition, that of a text of unknowable or unconfirmable authorship. He conceded that the question of authorship was perhaps complicated somewhat by the possibility that extant copies might contain interpolations or adulterations from later copyists. Nonetheless, Dexter's text should not be censored or banned on that account. Nor did the chronicle meet another definition of apocrypha, namely, a text claiming divine inspiration but clearly lacking it, such as the apocryphal Gospel of Barnabas which, among others, had been prohibited by the Gelasian Decree. Since Dexter's text had no claims on having been divinely inspired or instructed, his chronicle simply could not be classified among these types of apocrypha. Even so, Bivar pointed out, many of the works that Gelasius condemned, such as the letters between Christ and King Agbar of Edessa, circulated freely among Catholics. Moreover, Dexter's text was certainly harmless compared to the "fables" propagated by Annius's discredited texts which, as Bivar pointed out, the Church continued to allow to be reprinted willy-nilly, such that they "pointlessly occupy the hands of many [Catholics]," even with their considerable flaws. In contrast, Dexter's chronicle was "lacking all blemish and suspicion."[33]

Even while denying that Dexter's text was apocryphal in any sense, Bivar tacitly admitted that the cronicón did, in one limited sense, resemble those extracanonical texts and traditions that had been allowed to inform and inspire the devotion of the faithful throughout the Middle Ages. Even if the authenticity of Dexter's text could not be confirmed beyond a doubt, like many apocryphal traditions the work was useful for increasing piety—which was, on balance, the highest good. Along these lines, Bivar asserted that even if not all of the chronicles' details about martyrs throughout Roman Hispania could be vouchsafed, "he who might accept [the text] as true does not deviate at all from the Catholic Faith or from good morals and piety, or the Christian religion, because truly they were killed either here or there, [and so] it does not interfere with faith or piety."[34] In other words, the martyrs that Dexter commemorated had died somewhere. It was immaterial if Dexter were mistaken about some of the places of martyrdom, because the text still possessed pious value: encouraging the veneration of the saints, no matter where they died, was fundamentally good—a quintessentially Higueran sentiment.

Yet Bivar was convinced that even if the text was technically a product of human effort and not divine inspiration, it did, in fact, possess providential significance. God knew that the cult of saints was jeopardized by Protestant critics and other threats, and he wanted Spain to have the text and the plomos so that veneration of the martyrs might be reinvigorated in this time of need. This was clear from the coincidence of numerous portents around the time that both sets of texts were discovered, including the identification of the relics of the Granada martyrs, the discovery of the head of Hierotheo in 1625, and the unearthing of the Arjona relics, all of which were "many lights shining in the foggy night to illuminate the authority of Dexter's text."[35]

Finally, with an eye toward the international audience at the papal court, Bivar also addressed the critiques of Matthäus Rader (1561–1634), a Tyrolean Jesuit who had come across Bivar's edition of Dexter while preparing his 1627 edition of Martial's *Epigrams*. In a companion *Commentary* (1628), Rader mercilessly attacked both the chronicles and Bivar himself. This is not surprising: Rader shared none of the pious affection for Iberian sacred history that colored many Iberian readers' view of the text. To Rader, a formidable historian in his own right, the chronicles' reiteration of Hispanocentric pious legends, many of which already had been discredited by Baronio and humanist scholars before him, as well as its exaltation of Hispania as the privileged locus of apostolic Christianity, seemed ridiculous. In prefatory remarks, Rader quoted an anonymous Jesuit who likened Dexter's text to medieval legends, a "hodgepodge of fables" in which "the Spanish have their Annius of Viterbo."[36] Rader himself poked fun at Dexter's assertion—and Bivar's enthusiastic endorsement—of the late medieval notion that Seneca the Younger had been a secret Christian: "Therefore what type of Christian? I say a hidden one. Truly so hidden, I reckon, that not even Seneca himself knew that he was a Christian."[37]

Bivar contested the claims of this well-connected Jesuit not by means of direct rebuttal, but, rather limply, by showcasing his own connections to Roman circles of learning and power, and, specifically, by highlighting his epistolary friendship with Inchofer—who by this time had found a comfortable place in Rome among the circles around the papal nephew, Cardinal Francesco Barberini. Inchofer soon found himself serving as consultant to the selfsame Congregation of the Index that had censured the first edition of his Messina treatise. Bivar tried to cash in on this admittedly tenuous connection to Barberini circles by including an appendix to the 1630 treatise that consisted of a letter from Inchofer. Here the Jesuit praised Bivar's erudite edition of Dexter, the very same edition that had come in for such a pummeling by Rader. Bivar introduced the letter, rather triumphantly, as a riposte by one learned German Jesuit—by which he meant Inchofer—to another, namely, Rader.[38] Yet as was so often the case, Bivar's claim was wildly inflated. In fact, Inchofer's letter did absolutely nothing to rebut Rader's charges against Dexter and his commentator. Rather, its significance seems to have been more tactical than substantive, signaling that Bivar's friends and protectors included this consultant to the Index, the same Congregation that, it was feared, was on the verge of banning or censoring Bivar's edition and related texts. (In the long run, the glory of Bivar's ally was short-lived: Inchofer fell afoul of the Jesuit order after writing a parody of the order, *The Monarchy of the Solipsists* of 1645, for which he was sentenced to life imprisonment in a Jesuit residence; he died not long afterward.)[39]

Although Rader's reaction to this counterattack is unknown, Bivar's short treatise did succeed in attracting the attention of another old foe, the Augustinian Canon Gabriele Pennotto, who quickly drew up a lengthy and detailed critique of Bivar, which he included in a 1630 treatise on the seemingly unrelated topic of sermons on the eremitic life that many, including cardinals Baronio and Bellarmine, had attributed to Augustine. Pennotto sharply disagreed with this attribution, chiefly because it would implicitly contradict the Augustinian Canons' own vision of their origins and history. In a digression, Pennotto singled out Bivar's 1630 treatise for its defense of Santiago, and likened him to those defenders of Santiago who wrongly privilege the traditions of local, particular churches over and against those of the Church Universal.[40] While this astute critique may well have been lodged against many of the partisans of Hispanic holy traditions, it also could have been directed back at those, like Pennotto, who wrote in defense of their own religious order's idiosyncratic interpretation of the past. In any case, Pennotto's arguments were even more specious than Bivar's characteristically flimsy attacks, and consisted mostly of a sensationalized critique of the circumstances of the publication of Bivar's *Petition for Dexter*, rather than its substance: thus, Pennotto noted, the pamphlet had appeared without the requisite theological approvals, without inquisitorial censure, and without the author's disclaimer required by the Council of Trent, all of which, Pennotto concluded dramatically, would make one suspect that the book was "not legitimate but rather originated from a clandestine and secretive place."[41]

In the end, after all of these various sallies in the battle for and against Dexter and his latter-day defenders, the concerns of Bivar and his patron came to naught. When Moscoso arrived in Rome in the summer of 1630, hoping to resolve the disquieting questions surrounding the fate of Dexter's chronicle, he soon found that his anxiety had been unwarranted, at least in this arena. In August he wrote, relieved, to Bivar:

I have not found that which we feared in Spain. Here Dexter is not being discussed, as I found out from the Secretaries of the Congregations themselves, and from other people who can inform me. (Since the lead books of the Sacromonte of Granada were requested [by the papal nuncio], you know what was feared.)[42]

Rather than being banned by the Roman Inquisition, Dexter's chronicle soon made an appearance among papal scholars, as when, also in 1630, the Roman tribunal of the Sacra Rota affirmed the church of El Pilar's claims to greater antiquity over Zaragoza's La Seo cathedral. Its written decision cited Dexter, albeit with some reservations.[43]

The text and its most visible non-Spanish booster (Inchofer) had evaded suspicions, but Moscoso's Arjona relics would encounter a dead end in Rome, even as they continued to attract devotees at home. We know that at some point during his Roman sojourn in the early 1630s Moscoso appealed in person to Urban VIII for guidance on the question of how to formally evaluate the Arjona relics. This was partly because he hoped to attract Roman patronage of the discoveries, for which purpose he presented Bivar's treatise to the pope himself, with two other texts on Arjona: these were the *Relation and Memorial of the Investigations that Have Been Conducted into the Prodigies and Marvels That Have Been Seen . . . in Arjona*, in which two of his vicars had summarized the testimony of over six hundred witnesses to the various wonders and miracles at Arjona's shrine, and Bernardo de Aldrete's *The Phenomena or the Flashing Lights, and the Sign of the Triumphant Cross of the Holy Martyrs of Albens Urgavo, Bonosus and Maximianus, and of Others Dressed in Purple with Blood*, which outlined the evidence, chiefly from Dexter's chronicle and the *acts* of Bonosus and Maximianus, arguing for the Arjona martyrs' historical existence. Aldrete also enumerated the supernatural signs that seemed to confirm the authenticity of the manifold relics that had emerged at the site.[44]

Although the theological and procedural guidelines for the canonization of saints had been the subject of ongoing reform over the sixteenth and seventeenth centuries, particularly during the Barberini papacy, Moscoso was soon to discover that the "canonization" of relics was, in comparison, virtually uncharted territory. When he asked Urban directly how he should proceed in the matter of Arjona, the cardinal-bishop was met with a markedly indifferent and inscrutable retort. According to a later account by one of the bishop's advisors, Urban responded simply: "the Bishop of Jaén should perform his duty." In other words, Moscoso should go home and judge the matter himself.[45]

In the absence of definitive guidance from Rome on how exactly this should be done, Moscoso allowed the local Arjona cult to flourish and spread. In the 1620s and 1630s, pilgrims—as well as the cardinal-bishop's sponsored publications regarding the relics—spread the Arjona devotion, as did tiny pieces of the saints themselves, well beyond Jaén to Castile and even the royal court itself. Here Moscoso's own connections were crucial. His father, Don Lope de Moscoso y Ossorio, the sixth Count of Altamira, returned from the shrine in 1628 and brought a relic to Luisa de la Ascensión, known as La Monja de Carrión. Among the many natural and supernatural remedies this Clarisan abbess offered her clients (among whom were many highly placed men and women, such as the Count of Altamira and the Countess of Monterrey) was a relic from Arjona, which, as she suggested on one occasion, would relieve diabolical possession.[46] Other courtly collectors of Arjona relics included the Count of Ricla and the Count of Palma del Río, whose grandson was healed by the relics. News of the relics' healing properties also reached a Toledo cathedral canon named Felipe de Centurión, son of the Marquis of Estepa. Thanks to a poultice made from fragments of the relics, Felipe found relief from a gruesome testicular infection which prevented him from walking. In thanks, he donated silver ornaments to the Arjona shrine, which he visited in person.[47]

THE SCAFFOLDING OF COMMENTARY: "TREAT DEXTER MORE GENTLY"

If the relics netted by Higuera's texts were accepted rather readily into pious circulation in the 1620s and 1630s, the fortunes of the cronicones and their proponents became decidedly more mixed in the 1640s. When the 1641 death of Tamayo de Vargas left vacant the post of chronicler of the Indies, his peer and sometime-rival Rodrigo Caro calculated that his hour had arrived at long last, and renewed his effort to attract courtly patronage. The scholar from Seville was stymied by the fact that his Madrid contact could not gain access to Olivares, nor to Rioja, who proved to be a particularly determined gatekeeper.[48] It was at this juncture that Rioja realized that the time was opportune to finally make good on his earlier threat to "destroy Dexter," or at least to land a glancing blow upon Caro and this text that was so dear to him. Rioja was handed this opportunity in 1640 by an unrelated series of events unfolding in Catalonia, where the count-duke's oppressive policies had provoked open rebellion; known as the Catalan Revolt, the conflict would last until 1652, outliving Olivares himself. Shortly after the conflagration erupted, the city councilors of Barcelona had a treatise printed in their name, the *Catholic Proclamation* (1640), ghostwritten by an Augustinian friar. In the text, the magistrates protested the count-duke's violation of their traditional legal privileges, while also professing their loyalty to the crown and arguing for the antiquity of the faith in Catalonia. Among the sources they cited to support the latter claim was Dexter, who had repeated Jerome's assertion that a Barcelona priest named Vigilantius had disseminated heresy in early Christian Spain. In his commentary, Bivar clarified that according to another patristic author, Gennadius of Massilia, the heretic had actually been *"natione Gallus."* That this ignominious heretic had been French, not Catalan, was welcome news for the author of the *Catholic Proclamation*, as was Bivar's praise of Barcelona as a land of many illustrious martyrs, both of which were cited in the treatise.[49]

In response, Rioja, who, along with Adán de la Parra and José Pellicer, had just been recruited as a hired pen for Olivares's own ad hoc *junta de cronistas*, went on the offensive with a short screed called *Aristarchus, or Censure of the Catholic Proclamation of the Catalans*, printed anonymously later in 1640.[50] Rioja adopted the role of Aristarchus, the Greek critic and grammarian proverbial for his erudition and critical thinking, and attempted to undermine the credibility of the restive Catalans by comparing their erroneous and hypocritical ways to that of the proverbially untrustworthy Jews. Along these lines, Rioja accused the Catalans of bad faith. How else could one account for their use of Dexter's chronicle, whose forger was such an ignoramus that he had not even been able to create a convincing fake. Instead, like Annius of Viterbo in an earlier century, the creator of this and the other cronicones had undermined the good name of those actual authors to whom he had attributed his works. Rioja noted damningly that such willful blindness to the flaws of one's source was among the tactics rarely scrutinized when employed in the name of religion, and he concluded that "the only ones who support Dexter are those who do not mind if the places where they were born are honored with follies."[51]

Although Rioja did not mention Caro by name, he had to have known that the Utrera native had cited Dexter extensively in his own 1622 treatise on the city's antiquities, and the zinger stung. In response to the scant twenty-three lines in Rioja's *Aristarchus* regarding the cronicones, Caro countered with a 132-page manuscript, *In Defense of the Writings of Flavius Lucius Dexter, by an Anonymous Author* (ca. 1641–1646). Here he conceded to "Aristarchus" that the received text of Dexter was not perfect, and that "insolent hands" could well have inserted glosses or phrases not in the original. Yet he protested that the errors actually made the texts more believable: it was completely absurd to think that after having exerted so much effort to invent the texts, a hypothetical forger would then have neglected to expend the small amount of additional effort to correct his text and polish his prose. In this way, the flaws actually helped prove the texts' authenticity. They were not the unfortunate oversights of a careless and sloppy forger. They were the scars born by any authentic medieval manuscript. Like all ancient manuscripts, those of Dexter and Maximus had been distorted by the passing of time. If other long-lost Latin texts had been mangled by monastic copyists until they were restored by conscientious Renaissance editors, it should hardly be surprising that the cronicones, which had disappeared without a trace, should likewise require careful and extensive reconstruction. For this reason, it fell to scholars such as Caro to smooth over the rough patches and to separate inadvertent interpolations, later additions, and outright errors from the authentic core of the text. Caro's own efforts in this respect were exemplary: so damaged was the text of Dexter-Maximus, he reported, that in preparing his 1627 edition he had been compelled to make substantive corrections on nearly every page.[52]

Yet the larger principle in question was whether a text should be rejected outright due to its flaws. Unsurprisingly, Caro argued that this was unacceptable on several counts. From the legal perspective, one was not permitted to punish the truth because of lies, nor to allow the useful to be corrupted by the useless. By the same logic, one would never consign a sick person to the grave because of a simple wound; neither, then, should a text be rejected because of a handful of errors because, in spite of all of its flaws, Dexter's text retained a core of truth. Indeed, the *Chronicon* was rather like Odysseus, who, returning home after his lengthy odyssey, was so changed that his wife Penelope did not recognize him. As the story went, the hero was known by his nurse, Eurycleia, who recognized the distinctive scar Odysseus had received in battle with a wild boar long before. Likewise, although the passage of twelve hundred years had disfigured the texts of Dexter and Maximus, astute readers could detect signs (*señales*) of their essential identity. In order to do so, they would need a perceptive guide who could note and correct corrupt passages and illuminate obscure ones. Readers of the cronicones, like Penelope, would need a Eurycleia to point them beyond the sometimes sloppy external appearance of the texts toward their true value.

By this logic, Calderón's 1619 edition was guilty not only of being careless, but also of leaving its readers alone in a textual jungle without a guide. In the case of texts so profoundly damaged by the passage of time, careless scribes, and possibly unscrupulous compilers, learned commentary was not just an optional accessory. It was the skeleton that kept the text upright. The commentator did not just smooth over textual irregularities and elucidate obscure passages; his annotations also presented external evidence—which Caro called "alibis"—that would enable readers to see the truth of the text itself. These included cross-references to other, familiar authorities, but also, more importantly, evidence that was only just coming to light in the decades since the texts' discovery, such as the plomos, the relics of Arjona, and other recent archaeological finds. Caro cited as an example a coin unearthed in 1641 by Jerónimo Pancorbo, the Cordoban Carmelite, that confirmed there had been Neronian martyrs in Roman Betica, something that no historical witness—save Dexter—had recorded.[53]

Rioja or another skeptic would have responded that nobody knew about Neronian martyrs in Andalusia because there hadn't been any in the first place: for philosophers, such arguments from silence are logical fallacies. But Caro turned the silence of the sources to his favor by invoking that all-important escape clause of the early modern Spanish historian of the sacred: the centuries of warfare that were believed to have all but decimated much of the textual and material evidence of early Spanish history. And this is why God had waited so long, until it was safe, to reveal these texts and other manifold clues of Spain's illustrious Christian past, so that they might serve as ammunition in the present confessional battles, while also helping to edify the faithful.[54] This is where a learned commentator became so desperately important, for only he could construct a bridge between the chronicles and their readers; only he could elucidate the evidence that could contextualize and verify the texts. A skilled editor would build a defense into the very structure of the text and, it was hoped, help soften the resistance of the skeptical reader. Without this support, the texts could not—should not—be read or evaluated.

Caro's conviction that the commentary was just as important as the chronicle itself was confirmed in practice by seventeenth-century readers, many of whom cited the commentaries rather than the chronicles themselves. This had been the case with the authors of the *Catholic Proclamation*, who cited Bivar's commentary in confirmation of their vision of the Catalan sacred past. It was true, also, of Caro's ally Antonio de Quintanadueñas, author of *The Glorious Martyrs of Osuna* (1632), who cited the ancillary material provided by Bivar and Caro in their respective commentaries rather than the texts themselves.[55] Many readers did not even bother to consult the Latin originals, and instead cited Tamayo de Vargas's popular Castilian *Defense*.[56]

Yet, as Caro was well aware, the complementary relationship between commentary and text would be particularly crucial when the texts left Spain and entered the hands of well-connected men of learning throughout Europe, who would be naturally less sympathetic to Iberian concerns; without the all-important buttressing that editors such as Caro and Bivar had provided, the fragile edifice of Dexter-Maximus might collapse. We can see Caro developing this logic over a decade before his confrontation with Rioja, in a 1629 letter in which he tried to puzzle out why Matthäus Rader had "resolved to mistreat Dexter, without realizing that he offends the Spanish Nation in this action." Caro had caught wind of Rader's misgivings about the chronicle, and although he only knew of them secondhand, he asked his unnamed correspondent, who may have been a Jesuit, to contact Rader and urge him to "treat Dexter more gently."[57] Caro reasoned that Rader must have consulted "a copy naked of comments," when, in fact, as we have seen, Rader had actually lambasted Bivar's heavily annotated edition. Caro also fretted about how the censure of this German Jesuit would redound upon his own chances of attracting patronage in Madrid. In a letter to Antonio Moreno, Caro expressed hope that, with any luck, his foe Rioja would not find out about Rader's challenge. Otherwise, "it would be the best day of his life: I will not give him such good news, nor will I tell anybody else about it, so that he will not find out about it; otherwise I'm sure he would put up posters on all the street corners." To console his own woes, Caro dished about Rioja's age ("They tell me that he toils in studying how to discredit Dexter, and it has taken a toll on his face, which seems to have been picked at by the years") and predicted that his foe would fail spectacularly: "I think that he is going to meet with disillusionment [*desengaño*], if it is possible for any light of reason to make its way to a man so impassioned by his cause."[58]

ACTIVE READERS: RENDERING THE FLAWED TEXT USEFUL

In light of the sinuous history of anti- and pro-Dexter polemic, one may well wonder whether anybody, apart from the protagonists of these ongoing battles over their authenticity, was actually reading the cronicones at all. We know that they were being collected and published at the highest courtly levels, but were they being read? As always in the history of reading, the answers are partial and provisional, but not for this any less significant. There are hints that many courtiers and prominent ecclesiastics in Madrid read the texts, and not merely to debunk them. For example, in the 1635 edition of his *History of the Most Strange Nature*, a Pliny-esque miscellany of marvels, wonders, and miracles from throughout the natural world, the courtly Jesuit Juan Eusebio Nieremberg cited the chronicle of Julián Pérez in support of the legendary account of Santa Liberata/Wilgefort and her beard. He also discussed other holy marvels, such as the Cross of Caravaca, and the Arjona relics; the latter, Nieremberg related, had a propensity to bleed in the hands of pilgrims returning from the shrine.[59]

Yet, aside from those whose personal, professional, and devotional interests were intertwined with the chronicles, did any other readers of the chronicles extend such an indulgent attitude to the texts? Or were most, like Pennotto, Rader, and Rioja, less forgiving? Again, the answers are mixed and incomplete. While most non-Iberian readers seem to have been decidedly unimpressed, we find one significant exception in the Flemish Jesuit Cornelio a Lapide, professor of sacred letters at Louvain, who adopted a cautious middle path in his 1647 *Commentary* on the Acts of the Apostles. Lapide raided the texts for useful details, such as the precise year in which the apostle Matthew died (which, according to Dexter, was AD 66). At the same time, Lapide also expressed concern since, even as many learned men had cited the text avidly, many others had expressed serious doubts about its verisimilitude. On balance, Lapide resolved to rely upon Dexter's chronicle only when it concurred with other, more grave authors, but he avoided making a definitive pronouncement on the text's authenticity one way or the other. This may have been a pragmatic stance more than a matter of principle; after all, the book had been printed in Antwerp, in the Spanish Netherlands, with royal license from Philip IV.[60]

Another sample of reader responses can be found in the most vivid and immediate piece of evidence that a reader could provide: his own manuscript annotations. For example, in Ramírez de Prado's very own copy of his edition of Julián Pérez, we find a Latin annotation under the print of Wilgefort/Liberata: "In the parish of San Antón in Zaragoza this image of Saint Barbata exists . . . I saw and observed it in the year 1642 when I was on a royal expedition."[61] In the front flyleaf of another exemplar of Julián Pérez, we find a handwritten dedication from Ramírez de Prado to Gregorio López de Madera, a well-known jurist and defender of the lead books of Granada; this proves that the volume was given as a gift, but not necessarily that it was read.[62]

In a few cases, however, we find more extensive marginalia that enable us to glimpse over the shoulders of several contemporary readers who, in some cases, darkened nearly every page of the text with their ink, and for whom reading the chronicles was a contact sport. One particularly vigorous annotator, emender, and exciser was Martín de Ximena Jurado (see figure 9.1). While serving as secretary to the cardinal-bishop, who had been made the archbishop of Toledo in 1646, Ximena Jurado conducted extensive research in the city's rich manuscript collections, compiling material for the ecclesiastical history of Jaén that he would publish in 1654. In the process, he left his mark in a copy of the 1628 edition of Julián Pérez, which he collated and corrected in consultation with a manuscript from the collection of the Count of Mora, and another vellum copy from the Toledo cathedral.[63] (Ximena Jurado may not have realized that the Count of Mora's manuscript was made from Olivares's copy, the same that Ramírez de Prado had used to prepare his edition in the first place.)[64] In addition to correcting the text, in the margins he also made a note of archival documents from the Toledan fonts that seemed to corroborate details in Julián Pérez, such as an ecclesiastical council whose decrees were signed by a priest named Julián: proof, perhaps, of the chronicler's historical existence.[65] Ximena Jurado's notations were not the stray marks of the vaguely interested reader. Through his efforts, Ximena Jurado literally transformed his copy of the printed text into a new and improved edition, which must have been the aim: perhaps Ximena Jurado was contemplating his own edition of Julián Pérez, to supplant Ramírez de Prado's faulty effort. Or perhaps he had already finished, and the annotations were the whole point: having corrected the text, it was ready to be used in his own histories. Either way, further research will doubtlessly reveal additional examples of active readers rewriting their texts in this and perhaps other ways.[66]

For a sympathetic reader, the texts' many typographical and chronological errors were superable barriers. This was also the case for another seventeenth-century reader of the same chronicle who, like Ximena Jurado, collated the printed copy with another, superior manuscript, and also cross-referenced this chronicle with the others, including that of Marcus Maximus.[67] On several pages, this reader added sentences and crossed out entire passages, in what looks like an attempt to bring the printed text into line with what he considered the more accurate manuscript he had before him.[68] For example, he amended Visigothic names that appeared in the printed edition as "Humesendlus" and "Lupus Fideus" to read (only somewhat more plausibly) as "Gumesindum" and "Lupum Ficuleum." Elsewhere, next to a mention of a bishop of Braga named "Epitatius," he wrote, "it should read Idatius or Itatices."[69] In the process, he also corrected obvious errors of typography and layout, such as in one passage where he united a group of errant words with their orphaned clause, or another in which he introduced a paragraph break[70] (figure 9.4). This was a rather considerable undertaking, since, judging from the egregious errors in the Latin—such as a persistent misspelling of the papal letters known as encyclicals as "endyticas"—the typesetters and press that Ramírez de Prado had engaged employed appallingly poor paleographers, never mind Latinists.[71]

Yet this sort of active use of the text could also just as easily shade into abuse and even attack. We can witness this in two sets of rival marginalia left by readers of different generations in the pages of a heavily annotated copy of Julián Pérez held in the library of Spain's Archivo Histórico Nacional. The earlier set of comments dates to the 1640s, and the reader left behind clues as to his identity. In one passage, Julián Pérez referred to a letter from King Alfonso VI that invoked the heavenly "patrons of all of Spain" including Facundo and Quiteria and her eight sisters, but not Santiago. The annotator noticed the omission, and wrote in the margin: "Make a note of this for the defense of the Patronage of Saint Teresa of Jesus, which I wrote about and printed in 1628."[72] This helps identify the reader as Don Francisco Morovelli de Puebla, author of a 1628 treatise in defense

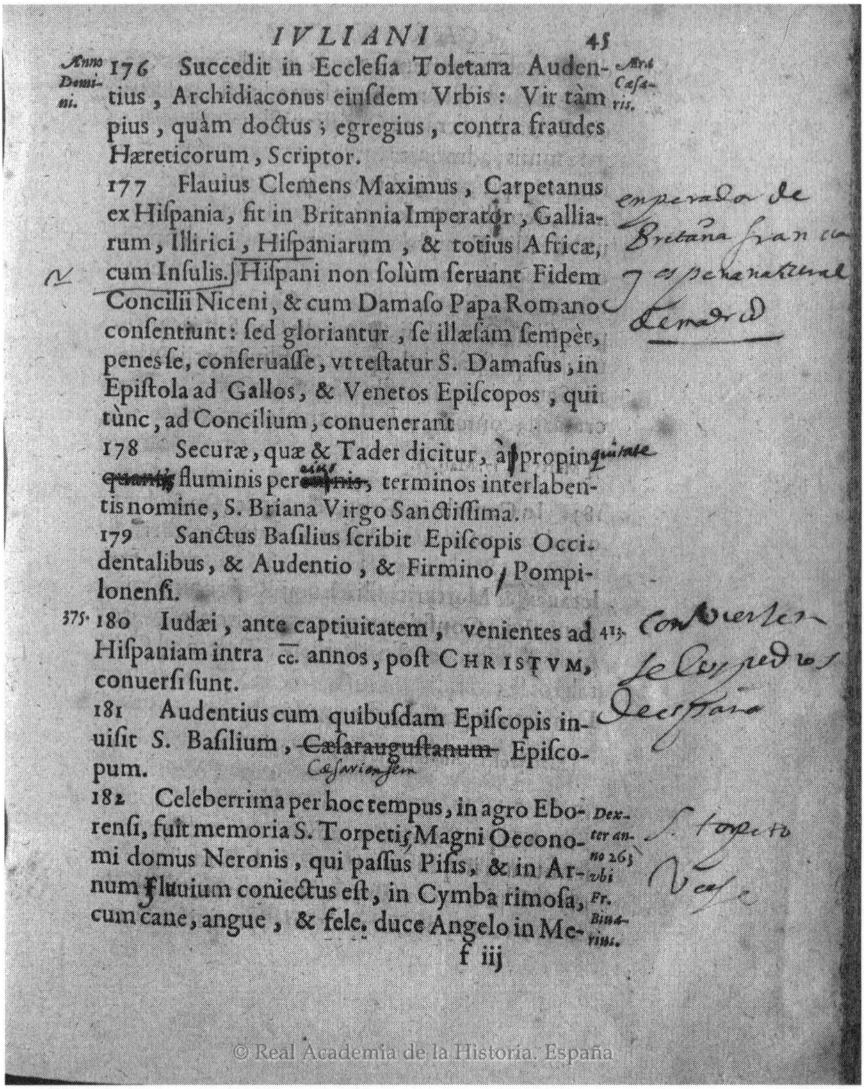

IVLIANI 45

Anno Domini. 176 Succedit in Ecclesia Toletana Audentius, Archidiaconus eiusdem Vrbis: Vir tàm pius, quàm doctus; egregius, contra fraudes Hæreticorum, Scriptor. *Alia Cafaris.*

177 Flauius Clemens Maximus, Carpetanus ex Hispania, fit in Britannia Imperator, Galliarum, Illirici, Hispaniarum, & totius Africæ, cum Insulis. Hispani non solùm seruant Fidem Concilii Niceni, & cum Damaso Papa Romano consentiunt: sed gloriantur, se illæsam semper, penes se, conseruasse, vt testatur S. Damasus, in Epistola ad Gallos, & Venetos Episcopos, qui tunc, ad Concilium, conuenerant

178 Securæ, quæ & Tader dicitur, appropinquante quantis fluminis perennis, terminos interlabentis nomine, S. Briana Virgo Sanctissima.

179 Sanctus Basilius scribit Episcopis Occidentalibus, & Audentio, & Firmino Pompilonensi.

375. 180 Iudæi, ante captiuitatem, venientes ad Hispaniam intra cc̄. annos, post CHRISTVM, conuersi sunt. 413.

181 Audentius cum quibusdam Episcopis inuisit S. Basilium, Cæsaraugustanum Episcopum. *Cæsariensem*

182 Celeberrima per hoc tempus, in agro Eborensi, fuit memoria S. Torpetis Magni Oeconomi domus Neronis, qui passus Pisis, & in Arnum fluuium coniectus est, in Cymba rimosa, cum cane, angue, & fele, duce Angelo in Mef iij

Dexter anno 263 vbi Fr. Bina rius.

Figure 9.4. Correcting the Chronicle. Ramírez de Prado, *Iuliani Petri . . . Chronicon*
© Reproducción, Real Academia de la Historia, 5/1639, 45.

of Teresa's copatronage, in which he cited Dexter as one of several authorities to support his contention that Santiago had not been the first to spread Christianity in Spain.[73] In addition to marking items for future use, Morovelli, like Ximena Jurado, emended the text by drawing on his own conversations with the editor of the chronicle himself. In one passage, Morovelli corrected what was a clear typographical error, where Ramírez de Prado had erroneously rendered Saint Victor of Baeza as "of Braga." And he made a note: "It should say from Baeza. That this is 'from Baeza' is inferred from Father Higuera's copy [. . .] and Don Lorenzo Ramírez acknowledged this when I was at the court this year of 1639."[74]

This reader was joined by another, who, judging from the hand, made his notes in the late seventeenth or early eighteenth century. This second reader took a decidedly more critical stance, as when he made merciless fun of the pretensions of Julián Pérez to grant venerable antiquity to the order of the Benedictines. A passage in the short treatise "A Description of the Hermitages in Spain," which followed the *Adversaria*, assured readers that a certain hermitage was said to have been endowed by Helen, after her son, the emperor Constantine, legalized Christianity in the fourth century. To this, the incredulous reader retorted: "Where will it all end? That the order of Saint Benedict is older than Constantine the Great? This seems to be for idiots and that's all."[75]

This type of critique was not limited to the later period, as we can see in the marginalia made by one early seventeenth-century reader of Calderón's 1619 edition. The reader was irritated by the text's imbecilities, which he noted early and often. Under a line in the chronicle of Maximus that begins, "I, Marcus Maximus, who write this, lived for many days in the See of Santa María del Pilar," the reader made snide note of this bald-faced attempt on the part of the forger at confirming his own existence: "So that we will know his name he puts these words as if they were a prognostication of the incredulity that we would have about the author of these writings. Dexter says the same thing [. . .] and for this reason I think it's all flour ground by the same mill."[76] The reader pointed out anachronisms in language ("people did not talk in that way at that time") as well as repetitions ("one would think that the author would not have included this twice"); and expressed general skepticism regarding pseudo-Maximus: "He is the one from this book [as opposed to the historical Maximus of Zaragoza] and is not worth anything."[77]

As recent scholarship has emphasized, the perceived instability of texts did not come to a heroic end with the emergence of the printing press. To the contrary, the new technology introduced another level of uncertainty and insecurity around questions of authenticity, reliability, and authorship, to wit: "early modern printing was not joined by any obvious or necessary bond to enhanced fidelity, reliability, and truth."[78] As Fernando Bouza has noted, the continued instability of printed texts, and the still-important world of manuscript culture, meant that public consumption of texts often gave rise to the creation of new texts. Reading led to writing, in the form of marginal commentary, glosses, and responses. In this period, interaction with previous texts remained the fundamental form of intellectual production, and "skillful redeployment of already well-known and well-established ideas and thematic material" was still valued over and above "texts' innovativeness."[79]

Although Bouza's analysis was based on literary and political texts, the cronicones were also read, rewritten, and redeployed in a variety of ways by an active audience. As we have seen, early modern readers did not accept the cronicones—whether in manuscript or print—as stable "authorities" to be either cited or rejected. Rather, for both skeptics and proponents, the texts remained to be fixed, in both senses of the word. For skeptics, the medium of print had done little to remove fundamental doubts, or to confer greater authority upon what they regarded as essentially apocryphal texts. For proponents, the mere fact of print was likewise relatively insignificant: thanks to unreliable manuscripts, sloppy editors, and incompetent publishers, print alone had not created determinacy in what remained essentially indeterminate, unsteady, and labile texts. For this reason, new texts, such as commentary and polemics, were necessary. At the same time, the historian of the sacred would also need to be a detective, continually on the prowl for *señales* of the truth, and ideally, would remain alert to recent scholarly and archaeological discoveries. As an active and informed reader, the historian would also engage in dialogue and debate among peers to resolve doubts, identify obscure references, and, finally, determine the relevance of the texts to local communities so that they could help foment further scholarship, as well as devotion.

This context, in which the texts themselves were almost less important than the acts of interpretation that made them real, helps make the length and elaborateness of Bivar's commentary intelligible (if not particularly readable). It also explains Martín de Roa's characterization of Dexter-doubters as pusillanimous readers:

> It is truly a property of cowardly minds to turn their faces away from any difficulty that presents itself by denying everything: like turning their backs on the enemy, acting like they don't know they've been challenged, in order to avoid coming up against [the enemy]. It would be a greater glory to confront the difficulty than to refuse to undertake the work necessary to vanquish it. Even the ignorant can contradict, but only the wise know how to back up [their objec-

tions] with proof [. . .] Since they don't know how to support some passages from Dexter, they condemn the whole thing as invented.[80]

As the heuristic and historical difficulties posed by manuscript editions persisted in printed editions, early modern readers of the cronicones had to become co-authors in order to render them useable. In this sense, the history of the reading of the cronicones not only provides additional confirmation of the continued vitality of manuscript culture in the age of print (if any more was needed), but it also helps underline the importance of the next step of the process, whereby these new readings, in turn, became subject to debate in the realm of local sacred history.[81] As we have seen, the dialogue between the false chronicles and their readers remained peculiarly productive well into the seventeenth century. How and why the generous hermeneutic of pious affection receded, and was replaced by a more starkly skeptical stance by the nineteenth century, is the topic to which we now turn.

10

From Apocrypha to Forgery

> In Mariana's *History*
> Virgil relates the tale
> of one of Diana's nymphs
> who, because she was a bad Christian
> was put into a convent.
>
> Scipio Africanus came out against this opinion
> and published, in Castilian, a long dissertation
> on the Trojan Horse
> in which he convinced himself that,
> due to natural reason and anatomy,
> the Paschal Candle should not burn on Epiphany.

Thus did Tomás de Iriarte y Oropesa (1750–1791), an irreverent poet, playwright, and literary polemicist, lampoon some of the more outlandish patriotic and religious anachronisms that, in the view of many late eighteenth-century critics, marked a previous generation of Spanish historical scholarship.[1] While the wryly hyperbolic perspective of Iriarte's *Preposterous Stanzas* (*Quintillas disparatadas*) is, from our vantage point, a recognizable step along the transition from premodern superstition and credulity to Enlightenment rationality, this teleology was not at all clear to many of Iriarte's contemporaries, who did not regard the poet's taunts about the deficiencies of Spanish scholarship with sanguinity. Plenty of well-read and patriotic Spaniards resented the mocking, and the skepticism that seemed to motivate it. This disconnect may have contributed to the fact that, in 1786, Iriarte, like several other thinkers sympathetic to the ideas of the French *philosophes*, was compelled by the Holy Office of the Inquisition to abjure several apparent "errors."[2]

The example of Iriarte helps remind us of the difficult and complex relationship between reason and religion in the Spanish Enlightenment, which would, among other things, shape the evolving fortunes of the false chronicles. During this transitional period, learned opinion would shift, such that by the end of the eighteenth century, the cronicones were no longer regarded by most scholars as useful albeit flawed apocrypha—but, rather, as forgeries: unacceptable, spurious specimens that needed to be quarantined from authentic histories. This development had been set in motion a century earlier, in the 1660s and 1670s, as the principle of pious affection began to lose ground and a small number of readers brought an unprecedented level of skepticism to the texts. These learned gentlemen included Gaspar Ibáñez de Segovia y Peralta, the Marquis of Mondéjar, and his contemporary, Nicolás Antonio, the learned jurisconsult from Seville, both of whom, in private correspondence and polemical treatises, developed serious critiques of the cronicones.

Yet the movement from "apocrypha" to "forgery" was uneven and contested, and eloquent and forceful rebuttals of the chronicles by these so-called *novatores* did not prevent many readers from continuing to embrace them.[3] Nicolás Antonio (1617–1684) completed the manuscript of his *Censure of Fabulous Histories* in the 1670s. Yet its immediate impact was blunted due to its not having been published until the middle of the following century. In the meantime, the cronicones continued to inform the works of historians of the sacred although perhaps not quite as much as in the first half of the century. Indeed, authors did evince a greater sense of caution around the texts than had the earlier generation of Bivar, Caro, and Tamayo de Vargas. For example, in 1674, one Pablo de la Peña drew on Dexter's testimony to affirm that the first bishop of Toledo had been Saint Elpidius, and not, as tradition had it, Saint Eugenius. Peña anticipated critiques, and so he also pointed out that even if Elpidius were not really from Toledo, no harm would be done by venerating him, so long as Toledo did not inadvertently steal him away from another diocese.[4] In his 1696 history of the diocese of Guadix, Pedro Suárez evinced a similar sensitivity when he professed that due to the texts' having been attacked recently by a number of "serious authors," he had opted to disregard a significant amount of material from the cronicones that would have been very favorable to his native region. Yet Suárez's protestation becomes, upon further examination, just another iteration of the topos of critical rejection, that favorite technique of authors trying to seem more discerning than they actually could bring themselves to be.[5] For, notwithstanding his earlier pledge to abstain from drawing upon the chronicles, Suárez cited them repeatedly throughout the text, in order to enhance his portrait of Guadix's sacred history.[6]

This apparent contradiction points to an important dimension in the waxing and waning fortunes of the false chronicles. Debates about the nature of historical truth—and about the relationship between reason and religion—were conducted in the seventeenth and eighteenth centuries, as always, within a broader cultural and political context. While modern critics would eventually conclude that the spurious nature of the texts meant that they should be jettisoned, the older notion of apocrypha as flawed yet useful texts would endure. Indeed, the hermeneutic of pious affection would remain a lodestar for historians of the sacred well into the nineteenth and twentieth centuries. In other words, for many, the authenticity of the chronicles per se continued to be less important than the profound truths, such as the importance of the cult of saints, that they seemed to reinforce. This helps explain why critics were to meet with strong resistance in the mid-eighteenth century, and, moreover, why it took much longer for sustained critique of the chronicles to find widespread acceptance among Spanish scholars.

SHIFTING FORTUNES: SEPARATING TRUTH AND FICTION IN THE SEVENTEENTH CENTURY

In their published treatises, manuscripts, and private correspondence, the scholars in the Castilian learned circles frequented by Ibáñez and Antonio began to develop serious critiques of the cronicones in the middle decades of the seventeenth century. In retrospect, it seems clear that they thus helped change the nature of learned discussions about the texts while also participating in broader European debates about the reliability of historical sources in general. Yet this was not a unidirectional or steady movement. In fact, Ibáñez, Antonio, and their peers might not have decided to raise the hue and cry against Dexter, Maximus, and the other chronicles were it not for the emergence of several new additions to the Dexter family of universal chronicles, as well as a flurry of new historical texts deeply informed by the chronicles in the 1640s, 1650s, and 1660s. This was thanks in large part to the accession of cardinal Moscoso y Sandoval to the primatial see of Toledo in 1646, following the fall of Olivares and the rise of Luis de Haro as the new *valido*.[7] Moscoso, fervent supporter of the false chronicles, was also, as we have seen, a generous patron of historical and hagiographical scholarship. Under his auspices, a newly discovered text emerged that helped complement and bolster the cronicones. This collection of the lost hymns in praise of Santiago by "Aulo Halo," a minor character mentioned in the cronicón of Julián Pérez, was compiled by Juan Tamayo Salazar (1602–1662) and published with Moscoso's approval in 1648.[8] In addition to supporting Santiago's Iberia apostolate, Aulo Halo weighed in on another ongoing debate, that of the antiquity of Zaragoza's two principal churches. Like the cronicones, Aulo Halo supported the claims of the church of El Pilar over Zaragoza's cathedral. The edition also included endorsements by Lorenzo Ramírez de Prado, José Pellicer de Osau, the royal chronicler who would later become a harsh critic of the poems, and Gil González Dávila, yet another royal chronicler.[9]

Three years later, an even more ostentatious monument to ecclesiastical antiquarianism made its debut with the archbishop's sponsorship: this was the posthumous publication of Francisco de Bivar's edition of Marcus Maximus's chronicle. The lavishly produced text—nearly nine hundred pages long, and printed on thick folio stock—was dedicated to Moscoso and the martyrs of Arjona.[10] The same year also saw the publication of Antonio de Quintanadueñas's *Saints of the Imperial City of Toledo and of Its Archbishopric*, which presented Toledan saints, new and old, informed heavily by the cronicones, as well as by Quintanadueñas's own correspondence with local religious houses and parishes regarding their lesser-known cults. The Jesuit's labors had been carefully supervised by Moscoso, who was so solicitous of the book's progress that during the 1649 outbreak of the plague in Seville, he asked Quintanadueñas's superiors to keep him out of the field, lest in ministering to the moribund he fall ill and fail to complete the work.[11] In 1654, the Count of Mora, Pedro de Rojas, published the first part of his *History of the Imperial, Most Noble, Illustrious, and Eminent City of Toledo* with the license of the cardinal-archbishop, as well as a theological endorsement by his old advisor from Jaén, Martín de Ximena Jurado. Rojas drew extensively upon Higuera's *History of Toledo* to write the book, which included a twenty-page defense of Higuera's chronicles and manuscripts, as well as of Annius's pseudo-Berosus.[12]

Yet the most comprehensive use of Higuera's cronicones to write hagiography was commissioned not by Moscoso, but by the bishop of Plasencia, Diego de Arce y Reinoso, whose secretary happened to be the same Juan Tamayo Salazar who had "discovered" Aulo Halo's hymns.[13] As Tamayo Salazar explained, his six-volume folio *Recollection or Commemoration of All the Saints of Spain* (1651–1659), also known as the *Martyrologium hispanum*, was modeled on the Roman Martyrology, but it consisted entirely of "Spanish" saints, many of whom, it turned out, were attested solely by the various authors of the cronicones.[14] In attempting to compile a definitive collection of the lives of saints on a national scale, Tamayo Salazar's texts joined others, such as Ferdinando Ughelli's *Italia sacra* (1643–1662), as well as Jorge Cardoso's *Agiológio lusitano* (1651–1666), which made extensive use of the cronicones.[15]

Still more post-Higueran cronicones emerged shortly thereafter. From 1667 to 1669, these new texts were published by Gregorio Argaíz (ca. 1598–1678), a Benedictine chronicler from Valladolid, in a two-volume compilation entitled *Población eclesiástica de España*, which included post-Higueran chronicles attributed to Hauberto, Walabonso Merio, and Liberato. Among other things, the texts supported the claims by the Benedictines to be the oldest monastic order in Spain, and that Isidore of Seville himself had been a "black monk."[16] Naturally, this irritated those whose vision of the past differed, such as the Madrid Hieronymite Fray Hermenegildo de San Pablo, who countered with a history of the greater antiquity of his own order, which he claimed originated in the fourth-century eremitical practices of Saint Jerome.[17]

LATE SEVENTEENTH-CENTURY CIRCLES OF LEARNING IN MADRID AND SEVILLE

As it happened, Friar Hermenegildo was among a group of learned gentlemen in Madrid, including Nicolás Antonio and Martín de Vázquez Siruela, who gathered regularly to discuss the favorite topics of amateur enthusiasts: history, hagiography, antiquities, genealogy, and curiosities in general. An image of the intellectual communities to which Antonio belonged emerges in an eighteenth-century source, which described how Vázquez Siruela, along with Antonio, the *oídor* Juan Suárez de Mendoza, the Hellenist Manuel Martí, Cardinal José Sáenz de Aguirre, and "many other erudite men," used to frequent the house of Don Juan Lucas Cortés, the legal scholar who had "put together a select library" in his home in Seville.[18] When the men were not collecting manuscripts and books, writing to their learned interlocutors elsewhere in Spain and Europe, or attending to their day jobs at the royal court, they gathered for *tertulias* in Fray Hermenegildo's cell in the Madrid Hieronymite house, or, even better, in the Marquis of Mondéjar's sumptuous library. There they imbibed drinking chocolate while consulting the marquis's thousands of tomes.[19]

In this remarkable moment of transition for the fate of the false chronicles, it is perhaps appropriate that this erudite circle included both skeptics and proponents, as well as some who, remarkably, occupied both ends of this spectrum at the same time. At times, the false chronicles, lead books, and other pious frauds seem to have provided fodder for humor. In the last decades of the century, the royal chronicler of the Indies and cathedral canon of Palencia, Don Pedro Fernández de Pulgar (1621–1698) penned a satirical attack on the cronicones with an ostentatious and purposefully ridiculous title. "The Sigalion or Chiton of the Fabulous and False Chronicles that have been published in Spain . . . Fantasy in a Joco-Serious Dialogue . . . Before Sigalion, Severe Critic of Athens" was dedicated to the Bollandists, and included a purported response from Daniel Papebroeck himself. With its nonsensical and ostentatious allusions to antiquity—Sigalion was the Egyptian god of silence, and the chiton was the long tunic worn by Greek men and women, simply a basic part of any Athenian's daily outfit—the manuscript bears the hallmarks of a learned joke among friends.[20]

At the same time, lettered circles at the royal court could include rather more equivocal figures, such as José Pellicer, the royal chronicler and habitué of the Toledo cathedral archives, who, in addition to having consulted Higuera's manuscripts, also uncovered a spurious chronicle of his own, the *Chronicon de Don Servando*, whose author was supposed to have been the bishop of Orense, confessor to the last Visigoths, Rodrigo and Pelayo.[21] This, in turn, sparked a new chain of polemical exchanges between Pellicer and his foes, such as Diego Antonio de Barrientos, an Augustinian chronicler who, under a pseudonym, attacked these more recent forgeries, as well as those of Higuera and Annius of Viterbo.[22]

In this group, Vázquez Siruela (1600–1664) stood out for his relatively advanced age—he was about two decades older than his peers—and, it seems, for his somewhat more slipshod manner of evaluating historical evidence. This makes sense for a man whose career bridged a previous generation of ecclesiastical historians, many of whom were born in the 1560s and 1570s, with the next, which included acerbic critics such as Nicolás Antonio. During his time as a canon of Granada's Sacromonte and then as a cathedral canon in Seville, Vázquez Siruela worked under men of a previous generation, including Archbishop Castro and the cardinal-archbishop of Jaén. During that time, he drafted dozens of manuscripts on a variety of historical and hagiographical themes, including a history of the Sacromonte itself, a treatise on Roman coins and inscriptions, and a projected defense of the relics of Arjona.[23] Yet in these relatively more modern circles, Vázquez Siruela was apparently considered an object of ridicule; his credulity made him the object of a practical joke on at least one ignominious occasion, when his friends presented a fake inscription and asked him to decipher it. He did so, dutifully, and in a completely invented fashion.[24] Nonetheless, Vázquez Siruela was no dullard, at least when it came to the cronicones and the new saints they had underwritten in places like Seville and Segovia, all of which he defended at length in a manuscript treatise.[25]

If playful teasing was the order of the day for some members of this circle, the joco-serious tone had its limits, particularly when the cronicones seemed to jeopardize a beloved devotion. This is one way to understand the determined efforts of the Marquis of Mondéjar (also of Agrópoli) (1628–1708) to defend Segovia's traditional patron, Saint Fructuosus (or San Fructos, or Frutos). After all, Ibáñez might have been a learned man of the court, but he was just as sensitive about religious traditions as any other early modern Spaniard. As a Segovia native, the marquis was irritated by efforts undertaken by the city's bishops to replace Saint Fructuosus with Hierotheo. As we have seen, Dexter's text converted this legendary disciple of Dionysius the Areopagite into the first bishop of Segovia and a native of Andalusia (either Ecija or Arjona, depending on how one interpreted the text). In 1666, Bishop Diego Escolano y Ledesma of Segovia received Roman approval to introduce an officium proprium in honor of Hierotheo, and the following year, he published an eight-hundred-page *Chronicle of Saint Hierotheus, First of Athens, then Bishop of Segovia*, a heterogeneous text consisting of historical annals, hagiographic polemic, sermons, liturgical readings, an episcopal catalogue, and everything else that Escolano could summon in order to debunk the Marquis of Mondéjar's arguments against the new saint.[26] Escolano's successor in the see, Don Jerónimo Mascareñas, continued to support Hierotheo by searching for the rest of his relics; his head, we will recall, had already been discovered in 1625. Spurred by these alarming developments, the marquis leapt into action with a 1666 diatribe, a *Historical Discourse in Favor of the Patronage of Saint Frutos against the Supposed See of Saint Hierotheo and the Authority Claimed for Dexter*, followed five years later by a more broad-ranging critique of the chronicles' influence on the writing of Spanish history, *Ecclesiastical Dissertations in Favor of the Ancient Office-Holders against Modern Fictions*.[27]

These more serious critiques were being developed in conversation with scholars beyond Spain. The marquis was in correspondence with Étienne Baluze, librarian of Jean-Baptiste Colbert, Louis XIV's *contrôleur général*; Nicolás Antonio exchanged letters with Jean Bolland and Daniel Papebroeck (1628–1714), Bolland's successor in the project of collecting, correcting, and publishing the lives of the saints.[28] Since its inception in the early seventeenth century, the Bollandist project had been one of publishing hagiographic sources purged of their apocryphal and legendary elements. As Bolland explained in the preface to the first volume of the *Acta sanctorum* (1643), this might even involve challenging sources that were otherwise exemplary in morals and religion, for "falsehood should never be used as an incentive to piety."[29] This makes it somewhat surprising that at first he danced around the question of the authenticity of the cronicones. In a section on "Certain Matters Purposefully Avoided," he explained that this was out of fear. Since "most Spaniards tenaciously hold to the opinion" that the text "is [Dexter's] genuine offspring," Bolland wrote, he would prefer not to "descend into a contest with that bellicose race" by voicing his reservations. He nonetheless intimated that there were serious problems with the chronicles attributed to Dexter and Maximus, such that in the *Acta*, he would not rely upon them himself, particularly when they were in disagreement with other authors of greater authority.³⁰

Bolland's reticence was deeply displeasing to Antonio. He noted that "from the books of ours that [Bolland] has seen, he has judged that there is nobody in Spain who does not prostrate himself, and kneel before this false idol."³¹ Already in 1657, Antonio had endeavored to disabuse the hagiographer of this notion and to take a stronger stand. This he did the following year, in the first volume of February saints, attacking all four of the Higueran chronicles clearly and decisively. Like Antonio, he concluded that their authority was "weak and unfounded" (*fluxam & inanem*), since it was unclear whether they were recent inventions or elaborations upon an older manuscript. Like many previous critics, Bolland attacked the texts' unpolished style, anachronisms, and historical errors, asking how it was possible that the same Dexter who Jerome had praised for his assiduous study of Cicero could have written the *Omnimodae historiae* in its current state: "Really, the diction of that Chronicle, how little learnéd! How little it corresponds to the dignity of the author! How little it tastes of the frequent reading of Cicero!" If the real Dexter had written like this, Jerome's praise surely must have been in jest. The three other cronicones simply multiplied the indignities. Their actual author was evidently so "ignorant" that he could not even understand the plain sense of Martial's epigrams. For, as Julián Pérez blithely informed readers, the epigram "To Linus" was about "Pope Linus's practice of kissing in the Christian manner"—in other words, the kiss of peace—when, in fact, as Bolland retorted, it was not about Christianity at all. Rather, Martial had been writing in lighthearted rebuke of the pope for wanting to greet people with a "freezing kiss" during a December so punishingly cold that his beard was "stiffer than that of a Cinyphian he-goat" and an icicle hung from his nose. Such ignominious misreadings and other flaws marked this text, like the others, "not [as] the true and actual offspring of an ancient writer," but rather as a later fabrication, "elaborated for the purpose of supporting the authority of the Chronicle of Dexter."³²

By the time Papebroeck assumed leadership of the Bollandist initiative in the last decades of the century, he cast an even more jaundiced eye upon the cronicones; in a 1671 letter to the Marquis of Mondéjar, he agreed that Higuera's "name and memory" should be expunged, and said he would instruct the Jesuit general in Rome to do so forthwith.³³ Yet Papebroeck overplayed his hand when he began to extend his skepticism to much less controversial texts. In so doing, he sparked the so-called *bella diplomatica* of the seventeenth century. The battles began when Papebroeck demonstrated in the preface to the second volume of April's *Acta sanctorum* (1675) that a certain early medieval monastic privilege was a forgery, based on its formal characteristics—including script, appearance, paper, and format. He then extended this critique to all pre-seventh-century diplomatic charters. By this calculus, nearly all extant Merovingian notarial documents were false, and as one scholar describes, "the older the document claimed to be, the more likely it was to be false."[34] The Jesuit Jean Hardouin (1646–1729) followed this line of thought to its logical conclusion and asserted that all Greek and Latin writers, with the exception of Homer, Herodotus, Cicero, Horace's satires, Virgil's *Georgics*, and Pliny's *Natural History*, were "falsifications undertaken by thirteenth-century friars."[35]

This radical skepticism was countered by the French Benedictine scholar Jean de Mabillon, with whom the Marquis of Mondéjar also corresponded. Mabillon's congregation of Saint Maur had embarked on a Benedictine counterpart to the efforts of the Jesuit Bollandists. The Maurists' collected lives of Benedictine saints and other documents were published in the *Acta sanctorum ordinis S. Benedicti* starting in 1668.[36] Mabillon eventually formulated a comprehensive methodology for what would eventually become the science of diplomatics, as in his *De re diplomatica* (1681). Here he argued against Papebroeck and others: although it was inevitable that interpolations and forgeries would occur, many documents that skeptics would reject could, in fact, be salvaged. Mabillon contended that by scrutinizing the physical and stylistic characteristics of documents, one could not only detect forgery, but also separate false passages from authentic sections of the same text. Although it was true that many medieval documents had been altered or fabricated, with enough knowledge and experience, a skilled critic could quarantine the infected section of a text, rather than rejecting it wholesale, as Papebroeck had seemed to advocate. Moreover, Mabillon also shifted the burden of proof from the documents onto the doubters, and granted the benefit of the doubt to the former: "It is specified by law, and all intelligent judges of these documents agree that a document which cannot be proved spurious by any certain and invincible argument must be considered authentic and genuine."[37] In this effort, it would be especially important to rely on objective criteria, even if the document itself contradicted one's own historical or polemical interests.

Yet this relatively moderate attitude toward measuring truth was to stumble upon that enduring obstacle, the principle of pious affection. As Mabillon would soon discover, many of his peers in late seventeenth-century Catholic circles were perfectly capable of reading and evaluating evidence critically, except when it came to their own interests (even as some scholars took the opposite tack, and argued that Mabillon's criteria were too weak).[38] When he engaged in what has been characterized as "unflinching scrutiny of [the] venerable traditions" of his own religious order—as when he argued that certain saints did not really belong to Benedictine history—Mabillon irked his coreligionists, who countered that it was always better to take the side of the order, even in doubtful matters.[39] For similar reasons, both Mabillon and Papebroeck found themselves attacked by Spanish Carmelites; Francisco de Santa María and other apologists had become determined advocates of the cronicones, which endorsed their order's claims to have been founded by the prophet Elijah in the pre-Christian era.[40] In the last three decades of the century, the Carmelites unleashed a shower of polemical treatises against the Bollandists and lobbied to have Mabillon's texts placed on the Index of Prohibited Books, since both identified these claims as implausible.[41]

NICOLÁS ANTONIO AND THE CENSURE OF FABULOUS HISTORIES

When Nicolás Antonio attacked the cronicones he drew on the standards of textual critique and evolving discourses of forgery that the Bollandists, Maurists, and others were developing. And if the Marquis of Mondéjar aspired to be a Papebroeckian rigorist, Antonio was a Mabillonist, in that he was willing to engage in the laborious task of separating the wheat from the chaff, to salvage a truthful core from an otherwise spurious text. Although the *Censure* was not published until the 1740s, in the long run, Antonio's comprehensive deconstruction of the cronicones would inform nearly every subsequent evaluation of Dexter-Maximus into the twentieth century (figure 10.1). Antonio was trained as a legal scholar, and spent most of his life in the service of various powerful patrons, but he is best known to historians (and bibliographers) for his massive biobibliographic collections, the *Bibliotheca hispana vetus* (1696) and *Bibliotheca hispana nova* (1672), which together catalogued Spanish writers from the Roman era to the late seventeenth century (with a gap from 1000 to 1500).[42] Antonio had spent nearly twenty years early in his career serving as an agent (*procurador*) of Philip IV in Rome, where he was able to consult important collections, such as the famous library of Cardinal Francesco Barberini, and to build his own significant stock, which according to one estimate numbered thirty thousand volumes.[43]

In an early version, the *Censure* bore a working title of *An Apology for the Truth and Integrity of the Ecclesiastical History of Spain against Recent Authors*, which points to Antonio's strategy to protect the authentic historical narrative from Higuera's adulterations.[44] For Antonio, Higuera's forgery was not the shocking maneuver of a pathological personality, as it would become for many subsequent scholars. Nor was it Antonio's intent to debunk the text in toto and thus remove it from scholarly consideration. Rather, Antonio forwarded two theses: as he

CENSURA
DE HISTORIAS FABULOSAS,

OBRA POSTHUMA
DE
DON NICOLAS ANTONIO,
CAVALLERO DE LA ORDEN DE SAN-
Tiago, Canonigo de la Santa Iglesia de Sevilla, del
Consejo del Señor Don Carlos Segundo, i su
Fiscal en el Real Consejo
de la Cruzada.

VAN AÑADIDAS ALGUNAS CARTAS DEL MISMO
Autor, i de otros Eruditos.

Publica estas Obras
DON GREGORIO MAYANS I SISCAR,
Autor de la Vida de Don Nicolas Antonio.

CON LICENCIA.

En Valencia, por Antonio Bordazàr de Artàzu, Impressor del S. Oficio, i de la Il. Ciudad.
Año de MDCCXLII.

Figure 10.1. Nicolás Antonio, *Censura de historias fabulosas* (Valencia, 1742)
© Reproducción, Real Academia de la Historia, 4/273.

explained to Vázquez Siruela, "Father Geronimo Roman de la Higuera, from whose hands all of these histories were revealed for the first time, is either the sole author of them, or he added the greater part of their material, forming them newly according to his whims."[45]

In his treatise, Antonio oscillated between these two alternatives, between what we might call the accusation of "forgery" and the discourse of "apocrypha." In the latter, the texts were hybrids, like so many medieval charters, where those much-maligned monastic scribes were wont to introduce passages of their own invention to what were essentially authentic texts. From this perspective, the "false Dexter" would be an adulterated product, but not necessarily a fake. In that case, Antonio's task would be to disentangle the threads of genuine late antique details from Higueran interpolations; he hoped he might recover a usable core of true chronicle, closely resembling the authentic text that Higuera may have received from Fulda. As he explained to Vázquez Siruela, these efforts would enable Antonio to "show the true and legitimate Dexter to those readers who are enamored of, and who relish, the name of Dexter," and, as a result, rescue the text for serious historians.[46]

In order to identify and eliminate the rotten apples of Higuera's interpolations before they spoiled the barrel, Antonio needed to separate out the innovations so that the *true* chronicles could emerge relatively unscathed. Higuera's texts, like so many other apocrypha, could prove useful if read carefully, closely, and critically. This is why the *Censure* consists entirely of a systematic, point-by-point comparison of three texts: an early draft manuscript of Dexter-Maximus that Vázquez Siruela found among the papers of the deceased Marquis of Estepa; Higuera's *History of Toledo*, passed to Antonio by the courtier Lorenzo Ramírez de Prado; and, finally, the printed editions of the cronicones.[47] Antonio noted that the *"Dextro primitivo"* was much shorter than the later, printed versions. It lacked many of the unique and more extravagant details of later versions, and quite closely followed the genuine late antique chronicles of Prosper of Aquitaine, John of Biclarum, and Hydatius. This led him to suspect that Higuera had indeed received a pure, "primitive" version of Dexter-Maximus from a colleague in Germany, but then, while he composed his history of Toledo, he supplemented that text with passages that suited his fancies.

Antonio walked the reader through the painstaking process of collating these three texts in order to recreate Higuera's working method. By noting every detail upon which the texts agreed and disagreed, Antonio hoped to establish beyond a doubt that Higuera had adulterated the cronicones in order to support the arguments he was simultaneously developing in the *Toledo*. And, indeed, he found that the cronicones had evolved considerably over time: as Higuera revised his history of Toledo, he added material to Dexter-Maximus. This is why the passages Higuera cited in the history of Toledo, and the "primitive" Dexter-Maximus itself, both varied significantly from the cronicones as they appeared in print.

For Antonio, peeling away Higuera's additions was a task made all the more urgent due to the damage the texts had already visited upon venerable and beloved religious traditions. As Antonio complained to Vázquez Siruela, Higuera threatened to discredit the Santiago traditions in the eyes of foreigners by mixing falsehoods in with a text that otherwise did so much to support them, making these and other pious truths guilty by association. Even if Antonio could undo some of this damage by segregating the spurious from the genuine passages of the cronicones, he fretted that this would never be enough to satisfy the hypercritical, who, like Mariana and Baronio, had been so severely skeptical about Santiago. "With my argument," Antonio mused, the tradition "can be repaired." Yet "for foreigners and the scrupulous, it will always be irreparable."[48]

When Antonio's text was finally published, nearly sixty years after his death, it was framed by its editor as an outright rejection of the cronicones as forgeries, rather than as reflecting this more latitudinarian attitude. It is true that Antonio, like many in his circle, was impatient with those, such as Tamayo Salazar, who trod rather incautiously on the delicate territory where pious traditions, the cronicones, and non-Spanish critics converged. It was bad enough, Antonio complained, that Tamayo Salazar had drawn uncritically on Higuera's texts to write his Spanish martyrology. Even worse was that he had gone so far as to slander Bolland, simply because the hagiographer rejected Dexter's opinion that a particular martyr had perished in Galicia. Instead of heeding this venerable arbiter's counsel, Antonio noted, Tamayo Salazar had, shockingly, accused him of "detestable perversity" in his scholarly judgment, as well as many other things. Yet, as Antonio remarked icily, "I do not know what else he says, since I do not understand: so wretched is his Latin."[49]

Yet like many other late seventeenth-century critics, Antonio's skepticism had clear and rather conventional limits. He was not an unsentimental debunker of pious traditions. For while he also harbored serious doubts about the lead books, these compunctions did not prevent him from entering the employ of their defenders and erstwhile custodians, the canons of Granada's Sacromonte. During his stint in Rome, Antonio advised the canons on how to recover the books from Rome and have them declared authentic; a consummate jurist, he also counseled them on how to legitimate the claims to the parcels of land on which Castro erected the abbey.[50] In 1678, Antonio offered another strategy, namely, to commission a new treatise describing the discoveries from the beginning, including the premonitory lights and miracles, in order to "prove juridically" that the relics, which had already been approved, were inseparable from the texts, which had not: "For when the [Roman] judges become convinced that the discovery was miraculous, they will be justly obliged to find a solution to the books' difficulties, and to the interpretations of the propositions or words that sounded bad to them, and not to condemn them . . . [A]nd it would not be a bad idea to draw up a summary of the life of the founding archbishop . . . since vouching for the character of the witness is what gives the most strength to a statement."[51]

THE EIGHTEENTH-CENTURY *BELLA HISTORIAE*

The *Censure of Fabulous Histories* was first published in 1742 in an edition prepared by Gregorio Mayans i Siscar (1699–1781), a self-styled reformer at the royal court and in his native Valencia, for whom the prevalence of the false chronicles in early modern Spanish historiography was an embarrassment, one of many obstacles that impeded the country's intellectual advancement. In the polarized context of eighteenth-century scholarship, Mayans became a combatant in the *bella historiae*, which were waged over how to write the history of Iberia and its overseas possessions. These hinged not only on matters of scholarly principle, but, since debates were inextricably connected to notions of patriotism and progress, they also turned on questions of national pride and, above all, prevailing political winds.[52]

At first, Mayans found favor at court. After having been named royal librarian in the 1730s, he lobbied Philip V's minister José de Carvajal, the Marquis of Patiño, to appoint him to the post of royal chronicler so that he could spearhead a comprehensive reform of the sorry state of Spanish scholarship.[53] This ambitious project would have involved compiling comprehensive dictionaries of literature, fine arts, sciences, and civil and canon law. Above all, it would have meant collecting, collating, and publishing every source of ecclesiastical history, purged of any forged elements. In this plan, Antonio's treatise would have been the first in a long line of voluminous publications of the sources of Spanish history, part of Mayans's project to bring Spain to the level of other countries such as France and Italy in terms of scholarship—but on its own terms and drawing on strengths and traditions specific to Spain.

In this undertaking, which came to naught, it would have seemed logical for Mayans to draw on the resources of the Royal Academy of History, which was established in 1736 under Philip V. After all, like the Bollandists in Flanders, the Maurists in France, and Ludovico Muratori in Italy, eighteenth-century Spanish historians sought to recover the original sources of ecclesiastical history through critical historical and philological study, and to "write a critical ecclesiastical history based on the careful scrutiny of archives."[54] The Spanish Bourbon monarchy took a special interest in this effort, sponsoring research into tracing Spanish "ecclesiastical independence" from Rome back to pre-Islamic times. The work of the learned Benedictine Benito Jerónimo Feijóo y Montenegro developed along these lines; his empirically minded critical essays on a range of topics, including science, religion, literature, medicine, and philosophy, were published in a nine-volume *Teatro crítico universal* (1726–1740) and five volumes of *Erudite Letters* (1742–1760). In one essay entitled "Reflections on History," Feijóo attacked a series of historical legends, such as the notion that Romulus and Remus had established Rome, or that Muhammad was of low birth. Almost as an afterthought, he also denounced the "falsified and supposed histories by various authors," including the Dexter corpus as well as the Annian texts, as "impostures" that he compared to the "devil's doubloons, that first seem like gold, and then turn out to be made of charcoal."[55]

On the face of it, Feijóo would seem like a natural ally for Mayans. Yet, like much else in the sinuous story of the cronicones, matters in mid-eighteenth-century Spanish erudite circles were not so simple. Mayans failed to make common cause with his fellow scholars due to a variety of circumstances. First, he refused a 1737 invitation to join the Royal Academy of History. In so doing, he alienated its members, as well as the powerful Aragonese faction at court; as a result, he became persona non grata in the royal library. To make matters worse, it came to light that Mayans had published a frank and harsh assessment of his peers in a Leipzig periodical, in which he deplored "shallow, derivative, and unpatriotic scholarship" such as the Cartesian and Newtonian empiricism introduced to Spain by Feijóo, whom he accused of "passively and uncritically aping French fashions." Instead, he encouraged his compatriots to look back to their own tradition and to emulate the "rigor and erudition" of luminaries of the sixteenth-century Spanish Golden Age such as Juan Luis Vives, Antonio de Nebrija, Antonio Agustín, and Benito Arias Montano, among others.

While anxiety about the supposed gap between Spanish intellectual achievements and those of her foreign rivals was not new, and an enduring sense of Spanish inferiority, particularly vis-à-vis the French, was one of many persistent tropes among Spanish Enlightenment authors, it was nonetheless impolitic of Mayans to single out his peers by name.[56] When the community in orbit around the royal library, including the members of the Academy of History, learned of the Leipzig article, Mayans's courtly position became untenable. Shortly thereafter, he resigned his post in the royal library and quit Madrid for his native city of Oliva, in the Valencia region. There he continued to prepare his edition of

Antonio's manuscript and established his own rival learned society, the Academia Valenciana.[57]

Mayans was not the only scholar whose efforts foundered on the shoals of courtly factionalism. The Royal Academy's plans to write a new comprehensive history of the Spanish Americas that would answer foreign critics, and also organize information in a manner befitting an enlightened age, were doomed to oblivion due to these same conflicts among courtly factions.[58] Nor was Mayans the only scholar to fret about foreign perceptions of Spain. Ambrosio Morales had earlier professed to have written his *Antiquities* in order to repair the havoc wreaked on the Spanish reputation by the mid-fifteenth-century antiquarian Cyriac of Ancona, who had recorded many seemingly false inscriptions from the Iberian Peninsula. As the text's late eighteenth-century editor Benito Cano explained, by drawing up his own authentic and comprehensive survey of Spanish antiquities, Morales was offering a riposte to Italian critics of Spanish scholarship. In so doing, Morales would, as Cano said, "make Italy know, and indeed, all of learned Europe, that Spain did not need faked or begged glories, and that she could present herself in a dignified manner, with her own clothing in the literary theater of Europe."[59] Since Morales's time, the perceived rivalries had shifted geographically, such that by the middle decades of the eighteenth century, it was the France of the *philosophes*, of Voltaire, Diderot, and Rousseau, and not Renaissance Italy, that attracted Iberian academic envy. For all of these reasons, Mayans's critiques struck a tender nerve.

The poignant hope that foreign critics would realize that Spain did not need forged glories to stand tall on the European stage was to become particularly strong by the end of Mayans's century, with the publication of works such as Juan Francisco Masdeu's *Critical History of Spain* (1783), which contested French criticisms (albeit not in Castilian, but in Italian).[60] Yet in the middle decades of the century, pitched disagreement about the proper sources of religious history continued to divide the Spanish intellectual community. Mayans must have felt vindicated in his refusal to join the Royal Academy when, a year later, a new cronicón was indirectly endorsed by its members. In 1738, *Primitive Spain, a History of Her Kings and Monarchs from Settlement to Christ* was published with the joint approval of the Royal Academy of History and the Real Academia Española. The volume, written by Francisco Javier Manuel de la Huerta y Vega, was a work of Annian proportions and ambitions that outlined Spanish history for the three thousand years preceding the Crucifixion. Remarkably, however, Huerta did not draw on Annius, but on another account of impossibly ancient monarchical lines, a cronicón attributed to one "Pedro of Zaragoza," which he claimed to have encountered in the Royal Library.[61]

Mayans responded with a scathing critique, but not of Huerta's naïveté in relying on forged texts, which Mayans identified as the handiwork of José de Pellicer; rather, he focused his ire on the two royal institutions which, as he fulminated, had embarrassed themselves, and Spain, by sanctioning such fundamentally specious scholarship. It was deplorable enough that many within Spain's republic of letters seemed intent upon merely "aping" French intellectual fashions. Unbelievably, the members of the Royal Academy of History could not even mimic competently: they were unable to discern true from false texts and, in this, they seemed to have failed to absorb any of the new spirit of skepticism and rationalism.[62]

The perceived flaccidity of Spanish intellectual muscle, not to mention the fact that Mayans had few friends in Madrid, contributed to his decision to seek sponsorship for his publications elsewhere. Thanks to the relationships he had cultivated with Lisbon erudites, Mayans had secured the sponsorship of the Portuguese crown for a 1738 reprint of the Marquis of Mondéjar's *Ecclesiastical Dissertations*.[63] In 1742, Mayans's edition of Antonio's *Censure of Fabulous Histories* appeared in Lisbon (although the expensive edition did not sell well).[64] In his dedicatory preface, the Valencian scholar celebrated what he perceived as Antonio's disinterested commitment to the truth, which he likened to that of the reigning Portuguese monarch. Mayans praised João V "The Magnanimous" for the fact that upon its establishment in 1721, *his* Royal Academy of History had stipulated in its founding charters that members were to reject all spurious monuments and apocryphal authors. Mayans was alluding to the "Agreement on the Authority that Should be Given to Some Authors, and a Catalogue of the Condemned" in which Higuera and his latter-day defenders and continuators—as well as the Annian texts—were rejected by the Portuguese academics as unreliable.[65] The charge stung. As part of the ongoing war between Mayans and Madrid, in 1743, his enemies at court persuaded Philip's Council of Castile to seize the printed copies of Antonio's *Censura*, as well as all of Mayans's manuscripts. The council's order specified that Mayans had been accused of fomenting anti-Spanish sentiment, and of giving ammunition to foreign critics of Spanish intellectual life and achievements.[66] Yet it should be noted that not all interpreters were motivated by factional politics. For example, Fray Martín de Sarmiento, one of Mayans's foes, nonetheless shared his disdain for the recent forgeries, as well as for Higuera, whom he called an "archimposter."[67]

Slowly, in the following decades, the Bourbon-era interest in antiquities and history began to yield some significant results, such as in the massive collection of antiquities assembled by the Royal Academy of History's midcentury director, Luis José Velázquez de Velasco, the Marqués de Valdeflores (1722–1772). This was the same era in which other scholars, including the Jesuit Andrés Marcos Burriel and the jurist Don Francisco Pérez Bayer, were sounding the depths of Toledo's rich cathedral archive and coming up with documentary sources for Spain's liturgical and sacred history.[68] Most of these midcentury ecclesiastical historians were treading carefully; the most comprehensive project was that of the Augustinian Enrique de Flórez (1702–1773) who, in 1747, published the first of what, thanks to his posthumous continuators, eventually would become the fifty-six-volume *España sagrada*. With royal sponsorship, Flórez canvassed archives, churches, and local eruditos throughout the Iberian Peninsula to write a comprehensive, critical history of Christianity; for Flórez, collecting sources of ecclesiastical history involved balancing the demands of critical scholarship with enduring respect for local patriotisms and pious tradition.[69] As he explained in volume three:

> The particular traditions of [individual] Churches should not be scorned due to the fact that they are not generalized, nor, on the other hand, should traditions be authorized if they are only known orally, or due to the efforts of some or other recent person. My intent is to support those that I am able to, as long as . . . it does not have greater things in its disfavor. For this reason, I let some things pass where I would rather have found more solidity, but since they are sacred, and since I have not found anything certain against them, I would rather expose myself to the censure of the critics, than abase the reputation of piety.[70]

In light of the enduring appeal of the invented past, even among the courtly elite, this was wise on the part of the Augustinian historian, and it is probably what helped him maintain and secure royal patronage. His caution may have been as pragmatic as it was patriotic, as much about self-preservation as it was piety. We can witness the alternative in the contrasting example of the Catalan scholar Jaume Caresmar who, in the 1770s, defended Saint Severus, Barcelona's legendary bishop, from a series of critiques articulated by Mayans. In thanks, the cathedral chapter of Barcelona allowed him access to its archive. Yet Caresmar was to discover the risks that skepticism entailed a few years later, when he critiqued an apocryphal source from the seventeenth century on the life of Saint Eulalia, a patron saint of Barcelona. His access to the archive was suddenly discontinued, and he found himself the victim of physical assault on the streets of Barcelona.[71]

As new and more unstinting critiques were posed by critics, the cronicones were defended not only by those with vested interest, but also by new forgeries. It took one particularly egregious series of frauds to pierce the protective wall of pious affection surrounding sacred traditions. In 1754, a new set of plomos was discovered in Granada. A cathedral prebend-holder named Juan de Flores was the lucky *inventor* of the texts, which contained proceedings of the early fourth-century council of Elvira, confirmed the Immaculate Conception, and, most importantly, provided corroborating evidence for the original plomos.[72] Flores worked with Cristóbal de Medina Conde, a Malaga cathedral canon and theological consultant (*calificador*) for the Inquisition, to draft a number of new cronicones, including an account of Spanish history written by a descendant of Muhammad, as well as a letter from one of the Moors run over by Santiago's horse during the ninth-century Battle of Clavijo. Aside from providing picturesque detail, the texts also confirmed the long-contested financial levy on Spanish churches claimed by the cathedral of Santiago (known as the *voto de Santiago*). Finally, the pair also invented genealogies for themselves, which they introduced surreptitiously into Granada's notarial records.[73]

In the process, Canon Medina Conde soon became worried that the ill repute of Higuera's cronicones might redound upon his name, as well as upon the lead books, both new and old. Thus, in 1772, the canon published a refutation of Dexter-Maximus, *The Forged Dexter*, whose subtitle reveals what he believed was at stake: *A Critical Dissertation in Which the Fiction of the Chronicones is Demonstrated, as is the Erroneous Opinion That the Lead Books Were Forged in Order to Support the Chronicones; The Differences and Opposition between the Former and the Latter*. Medina Conde tried to disentangle the two sets of texts in order to rebut the persistent accusation that Higuera had written the cronicones in conjunction with, or at least as a textual alibi for, the plomos, or vice versa.[74]

In other words, Medina Conde was not writing as a disinterested observer. He had a specific polemical purpose in mind: namely, to prove the authenticity of one set of forgeries by debunking another. For this reason, his text, like all of those produced in connection with the chronicles, must be used with caution. For example, Medina Conde soon found a significant stumbling block in the correspondence between Higuera and Archbishop Castro, which demonstrated that the histories of these forgeries were, in fact, intertwined, and that Higuera had been intimately involved in defending and promoting the lead books thanks to information Castro sent to him. In order to explain away this significant overlap between the topics, methods, and individuals involved in the production of the texts, Medina Conde attempted to demonstrate that the archbishop had been prescient enough to sense the danger that an association with Higuera would pose. To this end, Medina Conde published a sample of their correspondence, and made special note of one particular passage in a 1600 letter from Higuera addressed to fellow Jesuit Ignacio de las Casas (a translator of the plomos who would later fall out with the archbishop due to his conviction that they were forged). Higuera complained that in spite of Castro's promise to help him with a treatise on Santiago that Higuera was about to send to Rome, the archbishop "has not given me anything."[75] In a footnote, Medina characterized this as evidence that Castro was distancing himself from Higuera; later scholars have extended the logic by interpreting this as a reference to a failed bid by Higuera for financial sponsorship. Yet, in context, it seems much more likely that here Higuera was complaining about his disappointment that Castro had failed to come through with the promised material from the plomos regarding Santiago.

If Mayans's spirit of skepticism was not shared by the Royal Academy in the 1740s, a shift occurred by the 1780s. In this new régime of truth, forgery posed a direct threat to public order. For, if official documents could be falsified, public faith in the guardians of order—including the royal administration—could be undermined. Under Carlos III's vigilant ministers, the new plomos were disproved and, in 1781, the artifacts were burned publicly. Medina Conde and Flores were punished by the royal court (*chancillería*) of Granada, who deemed the falsification of official documents (*escrituras públicas*) to be "contrary to public faith and prejudicial to the State."[76] By the late eighteenth century, this spirit of extirpation even caught on among a number of regional erudites, such as José Martínez de Mazas (1731–1805), dean of the cathedral of Jaén. This aficionado of antiquities traveled throughout the region collecting inscriptions and information about the material traces of Jaén's ancient history. Martínez hoped to draw on this research in order to correct previous accounts of Jaén's history, including pre-cronicones texts by Gonzalo Argote de Molina and Ambrosio de Morales, and, naturally, seventeenth- and eighteenth-century accounts by Francisco de Rus Puerta, Ximena Jurado, Francisco Bilches, and Enrique Flórez. In this effort, Martínez was confronted with the dilemma of what to do about the new saints authorized by little more than the cronicones. Here Martínez emulated Flórez. In his *Memorial to the . . . Diocese of Jaén regarding the Undue Cult Given to Many Uncanonized Saints*, which would remain unpublished until this century, Martínez retained the new devotions in Arjona, Baeza, and elsewhere in the diocese by trying to identify historical evidence for these devotions that *preceded* the discovery of the false chronicles, and thus disentangle an older, authentic history from the more recent forgery that threatened to corrupt it by association.[77]

The intertwining of the cronicones with mainstream Spanish historical inquiry has long been a source of consternation and embarrassment for chroniclers of Iberian historiography. Why, scholars after Antonio wondered, did Spanish readers give credence to texts that, in retrospect, seem like blatant forgeries? One response has been to simply deny that the texts were popular among educated readers at all. This may be why the formidable Benito Sánchez Alonso, author of the still-definitive guide to Spanish historical literature, affirmed in a bit of wishful thinking that "it is most likely that only the body of the common people gave [the texts] any credit."[78] The collective acceptance of the false chronicles among members of Higuera's generation seems puzzling, particularly when we recall that many of them, like Higuera himself, had been trained by scholars, such as Gómez de Castro in Toledo, well-versed in the literary and historical heritage of the classical world, and whose formidable linguistic, philological, and historical knowledge would have enabled them to distinguish genuine material from inauthentic interpolations. The consternation increases when we move to the early seventeenth century and behold luminaries such as Bernardo de Aldrete—a pioneering scholar of linguistics—and Rodrigo Caro—a well-respected antiquary—not only citing the false chronicles, but writing in their defense.

Aside from denial, another explanation has been, until very recently, that these men, like the rest of Counter-Reformation Spain, were gripped by religious fervor—the same irrational fixation that, according to some scholars, contributed to the economic and political decline of the Hapsburgs in the seventeenth century.[79] For those modern scholars convinced of the supposed backwardness of nineteenth- and twentieth-century Spain in relation to the rest of Europe, the false chronicles have been a case in point, an irritating example of Spain's obstinate refusal to move out of medieval obscurantism when the rest of Europe was marching toward modern rationality. From this perspective, the influence of the chronicles in seventeenth-century historical writing was a virulent religious affliction, which, like a pandemic, would go on to recur intermittently over the course of several generations. These outbreaks, multiplying like a many-headed Hydra, weakened the body of Spanish historical scholarship and hobbled Spanish intellectual life in general, well into modernity.[80]

In assuming that the audience was effectively blinded by religious fanaticism into giving credit to the false chronicles, critics have neglected a rich body of evidence that, as we have seen, suggests that neither the author nor the readers of the cronicones approached them naively. And if we set aside the need to rescue or rehabilitate the Spanish national character, we can look more clearly at a phenomenon that was, in some ways, distinctively Catholic and Spanish, and yet that also reveals much about broader discussions about the nature of historical and religious truth in early modern Europe. In the Spanish Enlightenment, the realm of religion was not divorced from the realm of the scholarly. And, as recent scholarship on the Enlightenment has demonstrated, this intertwining of religion and reason was not merely a Catholic, or Spanish, phenomenon, but also characterized the struggle to redefine the nature of truth across Europe.[81] The advent of the new ideas of the *philosophes* did not displace religious narratives, and "pious affection" remained an important hermeneutic principle well into the nineteenth and twentieth centuries, although in Spain it became increasingly limited to apologists for ultramontane Catholicism, particularly during the devastating civil wars of the nineteenth and twentieth centuries.

This productive tension between piety and science is exemplified in a singular moment in 1803, when the Dominican friar and scholar Jaime Villanueva confronted a bind as he attempted to complete the catalogue of documents, relics, and other treasures in the churches in and around his native Valencia that his brother, the also-Dominican Joaquín Lorenzo de Villanueva, had begun. The series would be published under Joaquín's name in twenty-two volumes between 1803 and 1852, as the *Literary Voyage to the Churches of Spain* (although Jaime penned the latter seventeen volumes of the series). As a conscientious and scientifically minded scholar, Jaime was forced to reckon with items of rather dubious provenance. This included the supposed relic of Saint Anglina, which ever since its *inventio* in 1588 had remained in the treasury of the Valencian Dominicans. In the text, Villanueva echoed a critique first forwarded by Antonio: he suggested plausibly that the small slip of paper found with the relics was meant to read "Anglia," indicating the relics' English provenance, rather than the saint's name, "Anglina."[82] Yet he could scarcely bring himself to reject the relic altogether, and so he prayed:

> May the Lord give us the spirit of true devotion in order to separate, with the light of the Church, the true from the false, and not to expose the truths of our sacred religion to the jeers and satires of her enemies. There were times of ignorance in which the intimate harmony between truth and piety was not known, and due to a poorly conceived zeal, things were pretended [*se fingieron*] that enlightened zeal has since had to clarify with science, which is the true zeal.[83]

While the entreaty to preserve the Church from untruth and ridicule would have resonated with Morales, Higuera, and historians of the sacred of the seventeenth century, Villanueva's notion that science should prevail over zeal would have seemed very strange to them indeed. It was the type of prayer that perhaps only could have been offered by a man living during the transition to modernity. And indeed, Jaime himself was in flux. Only a few years later, he would leave the Dominican order outright, and after the abolition of the first Constitution of Cádiz and the return of absolute Catholic monarchy under Ferdinand VII, he would flee with Joaquín to London, where the brothers would remain in exile.[84] Partisans of sacred affection and radical skepticism—and everything in between—would continue to fight over these and other questions into the foreseeable future.

Conclusion: New Saints, New Histories in Modern Spain

If the death knell for the cronicones tolled in academic circles during the late eighteenth and early nineteenth centuries, its last and definitive peal was sounded in 1870 within the halls of the Royal Academy of History by a journalist named José Godoy Alcántara (1825–1875). It had been roughly 130 years since Gregorio de Mayans y Siscar had refused the institution's invitation and prepared the *Censure of Fabulous Histories* himself in Valencia. Godoy Alcántara presented an address on the topic of "Ideas and Opinions . . . about the Manner of Writing History" on the occasion of his induction as a member of the distinguished institution. By now, the topic of the false chronicles had lost its ability to divide serious scholars. This was thanks in part to the emergence of a new "scientific" approach to the study of history, first popularized by Leopold von Ranke, in which documentary sources were privileged over literary accounts. In this spirit, the Academy had gradually picked up where the disenchanted Valencian had stopped in his desultory effort to publish Spanish historical sources, and began to sponsor several landmark collections of sources that appeared in the middle decades of the nineteenth century. These included the *Memorial histórico español*, a forty-eight-volume anthology of letters, treaties, and other historical documents; *Cartas de algunos padres de la Compañía de Jesús*, a seven-volume compilation of seventeenth-century Jesuit letters from the rich collections seized from the Society upon its expulsion in 1767; and a critical and comprehensive account of the Spanish Church that aspired to purge its apocryphal and legendary elements, Vicente Fuente's *Historia eclesiástica de España*.[1]

In this context, we can presume that it came as little shock to the assembled gentlemen-scholars when Godoy Alcántara submitted his manuscript *Critical History of the False Chronicles* for the Academy's consideration. When it was published by the Academy in 1868, it became the first comprehensive history of the various plomos and cronicones and of their authors and promoters; two years later, Godoy Alcántara was inducted into the Academy.[2] Yet while the *Critical History* advanced the rational critique of religious enthusiasm and credulity typical of most post-Enlightenment social science, Godoy Alcántara's text is hardly just polemic. It is also a tour de force of archival research, in which the historian forwarded a twin narrative consisting of the body of text, which argued, and the footnotes, which proved the arguments—a hallmark of modern historical method continued in the early twentieth century by the most famous exponents of "rational" Spanish history, such as Henry Charles Lea and Ramón Menéndez Pidal.[3] Thereafter, Godoy Alcántara's arguments were incorporated into most successive ecclesiastical histories of Spain, and they have been reprised by all subsequent historians.[4]

Godoy Alcántara drew heavily on the works of his predecessors—including the Marquis of Mondéjar, Antonio, and Mayans—but he also examined these authors as historical actors who were themselves part of the story. Unlike previous critics, Godoy Alcántara also placed the texts and their readers within a historical context. In this effort, he drew on a wealth of manuscript material, much of which must have come from those deep Jesuit fonts that had become state property after the Society's dissolution, as had the holdings of so many other ecclesiastical libraries and archives in the various waves of expropriations (*desamortizaciones*) over the course of the nineteenth century. Thus did the manuscripts and correspondence of Baltasar de Moscoso y Sandoval, Martín Vázquez de Siruela, Tomás Tamayo de Vargas, and Nicolás Antonio, as well as of eighteenth-century collectors such as Andrés Marcos Burriel, come into the possession of the Spanish state, eventually to become available to modern researchers.

Yet while this ultimate fate of the cronicones seems to suggest a familiar story about the end of the medieval and beginning of the modern—the end of credulity and the triumph of Truth—the resolution of the tale becomes significantly less neat when we turn from the small circle of intellectuals connected with official and academic channels of history-writing, such as the members of the Royal Academy of History. Although Godoy Alcántara's opus marked the definitive end of academic respectability for the cronicones, it was not the end of these popular texts in other realms of history and memory. Even as Godoy Alcántara was inducted into the Royal Academy, the texts were reenshrined in the realm of scholarship, as when the Abbé Jacques Paul Migne included the chronicles of Dexter, Maximus, and Luitprand in his massive, deeply flawed, yet unprecedented collection of Greek and Latin ecclesiastical texts, the *Patrologiae cursus completus* (1844–1866).[5]

In contemporary times, regional historians—modern successors to Martínez de Mazas of Jaén—have sought evidence to enable them to salvage local traditions, such as the Arjona saints or Sigüenza's cult to Santa Liberata, while circumventing the false chronicles. In this search, the more critically minded and forthright have simply admitted that the task is impossible, and that local sacred history has been tainted indelibly by association.[6] In other cases, the attempt to reconcile the historical record with Higuera's texts continues, as in the case of one Murcian scholar who has identified details in the chronicles that seem plausible, based on his own archaeological research.[7] One late twentieth-century scholar drew upon Martín de Roa's cronicón-inspired history from 1629 to argue that Saint Paul not only really *had* come to Ecija, but, just as the chronicles reported, he had thereupon converted a Roman named Probus who later became Ecija's first bishop.[8]

In Arjona, a public cult flourished in spite of the fact that the cardinal-bishop of Jaén never issued an official decision about the relics' authenticity; his departure for Toledo left the relics in a legal and jurisdictional limbo. In a 1661 report to Rome on the state of the diocese (*visitatio liminis*), then-bishop Fernando Andrade Castro gently nudged the pope, reminding him that Arjona was a "very known and celebrated" place "due to the marvels that had occurred there from 1629 [*sic*—1628] to 1630," about which, he informed the papal secretaries, there is information in the archives "for making the case when it is convenient for the Apostolic See."[9] Yet Rome declined to act, and in the end, scholarship was not kind to the Arjona saints. In 1689, the Benedictine hagiographer Theodore Ruinart concluded that Bonosus and Maximianus were martyred not in Spain, but in Antioch, and the Bollandists concurred.[10]

As in many matters of local pride and religion, the disapproval of foreign hagiographers never quite trickled down to the ground. Negative assessments notwithstanding, there was no direct intervention from Rome, and so the Arjona martyrs endured as symbols of civic pride, as part of the imagined legacy of heroic Christianity that has also, incidentally, helped efface the town's significant Islamic past.[11] This should not be misunderstood as having been due to merely "popular" initiative; elite civic and religious institutions were instrumental in shaping the sanctuary into a compelling visual and devotional spectacle in the mid-seventeenth century, and in supporting the cult ever since. Thanks to the cardinal-bishop's continued patronage, the shrine was completed in 1652; the relics were displayed in an extravagant monstrance donated by the Marquis de Estepa and his son Felipe, and Bonosus and Maximianus themselves were represented as two dashing and angelic soldiers, fashioned from statues originally of the archangels Michael and Raphael.[12] By the twentieth century, the annual *Fiestasantos* had become a massive, two-week festival encompassing basketball and tennis tournaments, bullfights, and flamenco competitions. A number of multigenerational events commemorate the martyrs, including a children's lantern procession, in memory of the lights that heralded the 1628 discovery of the relics, and a "burning of Dacian," in which *arjoneros* exact their own posthumous justice on the Roman persecutor of their saints. The celebration concludes with a procession of the saints and their relics, carried on great platforms by the members of the brotherhood (*hermandad*) of Bonosus and Maximianus. If the authenticity of the relics was an unresolved question for Cardinal-Bishop Moscoso, these long-ago doubts were written out of the story over the course of the intervening three and a half centuries, with a generous dose of pious affection and civic pride.[13]

In this sense, the rise and fall of the cronicones is unequivocal and complete only from a distance. Moreover, even as the cronicones endure as integral elements of local memory and identity, they have also moved into the realm of what might be dubbed "paranormal history." In 2007, the lights and apparitions that heralded the Arjona discoveries were featured on the television program "Cuarto Milenio." The sensationalistic program examines mysterious and unexplainable phenomena, such as extraterrestrials, ghosts, and supernatural events, in what could charitably be called a loosely journalistic style.[14] Arjona appeared in an episode that originally broadcast Sunday, February 11, 2007, which also examined visions of life after death as well as the "mysterious" 1978 death of Pope John Paul I (around which many conspiracy theories swirl). The Arjona segment incorporated information from the seventeenth-century published sources, the talking heads of devotees and local experts, such as the parish priest of Arjona, and dramatic reenactments. The net effect was to give an image of the events in Arjona as an admixture of the paranormal, the religious, and the scientific, in a manner completely characteristic of modern interest in the supernatural. Moreover, just as Martínez de Mazas would have hoped, the story was conveyed without any mention of the false chronicles whatsoever. According to this version of the story, a ghost appeared to a young boy in 1616, presaging the discovery of the relics. The ghost told the frightened boy, "Not yet. All in good time" (*No es tiempo. Todo llega*). This was a reference to the testimony of Juan Múñoz, a resident of Andújar, who, in 1628, told the cardinal-bishop's investigators that a boy in a friar's habit had appeared to him one night a dozen years earlier. In light of subsequent events, Múñoz concluded that this "prodigious vision" must have been an omen.[15] At one point in the segment a guest referred to a "certain document" discovered in 1628 that enabled residents to confirm that saints were buried there, a somewhat incomplete characterization of Bivar's (possibly forged) *Passio Bonosi et Maximiani*.

In light of the devotional import of the saints to modern *arjoneros*, not to mention the tone of the show and the fact that the segment was produced with the assistance of Arjona's municipal government, it is understandable that the producers of "Cuarto Milenio" circumvented the problematic question of the forgeries. The program is one meant to sensationalize myths and legends. It terrifies, mystifies, and tantalizes: it does not debunk. Yet, in this light, it is remarkable that even as the hosts celebrated the events as mysterious and unconfirmable, they also went to pains to emphasize that the cardinal-bishop's investigation of the events was rigorous: this was, to wit, one of the first "scientific processes" in Spain, in which skeptical Church authorities applied the "maximum of scientific rigor" in order to get to the truth of the matter.[16]

This remarkable convergence of "pious affection" with a distinctively modern fetishization of forensic science gives the lie to the notion that the false chronicles were somehow extirpated by proponents of rational historiography after the Enlightenment. Just as Annius's pseudo-Berosus continued to be cited in historical narratives in Spain, France, Germany, England, and, of course, Italy, long after they were debunked on numerous occasions by an international coterie of scholars, so, too, do the false chronicles continue to form the basis for many local and regional histories, two and a half centuries after Mayans published the *Censure* as the opening salvo in his *bella historiae*.[17] If scholarly opinion gradually turned against the false chronicles, and if it was only in the realm of local antiquarianism and "popular" devotion that the texts continued to be tolerated, even this trend is not quite what it seems. For, within the past decades, a handful of scholars of antiquities have begun to revisit some of Higuera's much-maligned manuscripts. Archaeologists, classicists, and numismatists, among others, have noticed that among the many fabricated details that Higuera introduced in the texts he wrote under his own name, including the manuscript histories of Toledo and Spain, he preserved many genuine inscriptions and documents that have not survived elsewhere. This was also the case with many of Higuera's heirs, those regional antiquaries like Jaén's Ximena Jurado, who diligently collected information from the cronicones to write the first modern history of his diocese. Among the coins Ximena Jurado included in his unpublished collection of coins and inscriptions were a number of sketches that contemporary scholars consider to have been faithful reproductions of authentic Punic and Iberic specimens.[18] And while the Arjona martyrdoms have yet to be authenticated by Rome, modern scholars agree that the site was home to a Roman-era municipality from the late imperial period, just as the scholars in the service of the cardinal-bishop of Jaén had suggested.[19]

In the end, perhaps the forger's game was more complicated than scholars have hitherto suspected. Higuera promoted a vision of the Iberian sacred past that was, paradoxically, as deeply steeped in tradition as it was idiosyncratic. Central to his efforts was a concern with specifically Toledan interests. Yet at the same time, Higuera attempted to counter what he perceived as a Roman assault on a shared Iberian religious tradition and identity. Still, it is possible that Higuera did not merely hope that his work would result in the magnification of religious pride in all of those obscure places, such as Arjona, for which he had provided the foundations of a truly modern religious history. Higuera was not just shielding would-be Spanish saints from Rome's early modern revisions of history and liturgy. By interweaving authentic documentary, numismatic, and epigraphic evidence with pious legend, and sifting the resulting product through his own imaginative filter, Higuera created a complex set of texts and traditions that would withstand eradication, as well as easy generalizations, for centuries.

It is for this reason that we simply cannot understand Spanish history without accounting for his enduring legacy, as in the local sacred histories, liturgical observances, and modern popular devotions that Higuera did so much to shape. His influence is visible also in less obvious places, and in ways that the sixteenth-century Jesuit never could have foreseen. As we have seen, his histories were productive on several levels. They engendered several generations and types of texts, including those new cronicones (forgeries of the forgeries) that emerged in subsequent centuries. They also gave birth to new histories, when readers applied what they had learned from Higuera in their own particular historical circumstances. Finally, Higuera's chronicles helped generate a broader discourse in which early modern and contemporary critics debated the criteria by which Spanish sacred history should be written and measured, as well as an ongoing debate at the heart of Spanish intellectual circles about how, exactly, to determine truth. These polemics ultimately contributed to the evolution of critical historical method in Spain. Ironically, the same centuries that saw the emergence of "scientific" history also witnessed a parallel development that would have made Higuera proud, namely, the study of folklore, which brought serious scholarly interest to vox populi for the first time. In these pages we have seen how, in Higuera's manuscripts, and in the historical, hagiographical, liturgical, and practical uses to which they were put, both official and unofficial knowledge—as well as universal and local norms, and elite and popular culture—twisted around and around each others' stalks like so many disparate tendrils, such that they had to be pried apart by determined critics and reformers. For this we have Higuera and his readers to thank, for better or worse. In confusing facts with fictions so completely that scholars into the twenty-first century were still attempting to sort them out, the Jesuit and his acolytes ultimately succeeded in reshaping the past, present, and future.

Abbreviations

AHDJ   Archivo Histórico Diocesano de Jaén
AHN   Archivo Histórico Nacional—Madrid
AHPJ   Archivo Histórico Provincial de Jaén
ARSI   Archivum Romanum Societatis Iesu—Rome
ASV   Archivio Segreto Vaticano—Rome
BAV   Bibliotheca Apostolica Vaticana—Rome
BCS   Biblioteca Capitular Sevillana—Seville
BN   Biblioteca Nacional—Madrid
BUS   Biblioteca Universitaria de Salamanca
CSIC   Consejo Superior de Investigaciones Científicas—Madrid
PL   *Patrologiae cursus completus. Series Latina.* J. P. Migne, ed.
RAH   Real Academia de la Historia—Madrid
VE   (Biblioteca Nacional—Madrid) Varios Especiales

NOTES

In notes, bibliography, and captions, author names and titles for period works retain their original spelling, including lack of diacritics.

AN INTRODUCTION TO HISTORY AND MYTH IN EARLY MODERN SPAIN

1. Godoy Alcántara, *Historia crítica*, 130.
2. Ibid.
3. Quoted in Cirot, "Documents sur le faussaire Higuera," 94.
4. Caro Baroja, *Las falsificaciones*, 16.
5. Ibid., 164; Haft, "Odysseus, Idomeneus and Meriones: The Cretan Lies of *Odyssey* 13–19"; with thanks to J. F. García.
6. *The Geography of Strabo*, 5: 247 (11.6.3); Dueck, *Strabo of Amasia*, 72–74.
7. *The Geography of Strabo*, 5: 157–9 (1.2.35).
8. Quoted in Dueck, *Strabo of Amasia*, 73–74.
9. Printed in Antonio, *Censura*, 529.
10. Ehlers, "Juan Bautista Pérez and the *Plomos*."
11. Cf. Godoy Alcántara, *Historia crítica*, 36.
12. Carrillo, *Historia del glorioso San Valero*, n.p.
13. Ibid., 168.
14. Martínez de la Escalera, "Jerónimo de la Higuera ... culto de San Tirso."
15. Antonio, *Censura*; Córdoba, "Leyendas en la historiografía del Siglo de Oro."
16. Rojas, *Historia de ... Toledo ... Parte primera*.
17. Covarrubias Orozco, *Parte segunda del tesoro de la lengva castellana o española*.
18. Summers, *Michelangelo and the Language of Art*. For *inventio* in the less contentious pre-Reformation context, Atkinson, *Inventing Inventors*.
19. Dávila Toledo, *De la veneración*, 299; and, for an overview of sixteenth-century *inventiones*, Harris, *From Muslim to Christian Granada*, 38–39.

20. Hiatt, *Making of Medieval Forgeries*, 9; see also Grafton, *Forgers and Critics*; Ligota, "Annius of Viterbo and Historical Method."
21. Rivera Recio, *Los arzobispos de Toledo*, xv.
22. Quoted in Mayer Olivé, "Ciriaco de Ancona, Annio da Viterbo y la historiografía hispánica," 354; and see Crawford, ed., *Antonio Agustín between Renaissance and Counter-Reform*.
23. Constable, "Forgery and Plagiarism"; Grafton, *Forgers and Critics*; Hiatt, *Making of Medieval Forgeries*; Ligota, "Annius of Viterbo and Historical Method"; Rowland, *Scarith of Scornello*; Stenhouse, *Reading Inscriptions and Writing Ancient History*.
24. Barrios Aguilera and García-Arenal, eds., *Los plomos del Sacromonte*; García-Arenal, "En torno a los plomos del Sacromonte (I)"; García-Arenal and Barrios Aguilera, eds., *¿La historia inventada?*; García-Arenal and Rodríguez Mediano, *Un oriente español*; Harris, *From Muslim to Christian Granada*; Martínez Gil, "Religión e identidad urbana"; Río Barredo, *Madrid, urbs regia*.
25. Collins, "Renaissance Epigraphy and Its Legitimizing Potential"; Grafton, "Invention of Traditions and Traditions of Invention"; Stephens, *Giants in Those Days*.
26. Stephens, "Complex Pseudonymity," 689.
27. Tate, "Mythology in Spanish Historiography."
28. Cano, *L'autorità*, 164. Vives's critique, from his commentary on Augustine's *City of God*, is cited by Caro Baroja, *Las falsificaciones*, 54. For Annius's enduring appeal in Spain, Caro Baroja, *Las falsificaciones*, 47–78; Lupher, *Romans in a New World*, 203–220; Pérez Vilatela, "La onomástica de los apócrifos reyes." For elsewhere in Europe, Asher, *National Myths in Renaissance France*; Borchardt, *German Antiquity in Renaissance Myth*, 89–91, 111–14; Nice, *Sacred History and National Identity*; Rowland, *Scarith of Scornello*; Stephens, "When Pope Noah Ruled the Etruscans"; Walker, *The Ancient Theology: Studies in Christian Platonism from the Fifteenth to the Eighteenth Century*, 63–131.
29. Borchardt, *German Antiquity in Renaissance Myth*, 128.
30. Brann, *The Abbot Trithemius*; Grafton, *Worlds Made by Words*.
31. Goffart, *The Le Mans Forgeries*; and, more generally, *Fälschungen im Mittelalter: Internationaler Kongress der Monumenta Germaniae Historica, München, 16–19 September 1986*.
32. Gil Egea, "Víctor de Cartena, Tomás Tamayo de Vargas y las falsificaciones"; Ward, *History and Chronicles*.
33. Constable, "Forgery and Plagiarism," 11. For one Spanish example, Cantera Montenegro, "Falsificación de documentación monástica."
34. Wood and Nagel, "Interventions," 408.
35. For the critique, Brown, "*Falsitas pia sive reprehensibilis*."
36. Stephens, "Complex Pseudonymity," 691.
37. Grafton, *Forgers and Critics*, 43–48; Jardine, *Erasmus, Man of Letters*; Rice, *Saint Jerome in the Renaissance*.
38. Cirot, *Études sur l'historiographie espagnole II: Mariana historien* (hereafter *Mariana historien*), 47; Grafton, "Invention of Traditions and Traditions of Invention."

39. Stenhouse, *Reading Inscriptions and Writing Ancient History*, 82.
40. Haskell, *History and Its Images*, 26–36.
41. Momigliano, "Note sulla leggenda del Cristianesimo di Seneca," reprinted in ———, *Contributo alla storia degli studi classici*; for late examples of the tradition, 30 n. 46.
42. Van Liere, "The Missionary and the Moorslayer"; ———, "Renaissance Chroniclers and the Apostolic Origins of Spanish Christianity."
43. Rodríguez de Montalvo, *Amadis of Gaul*, 19–20; and on this trope more broadly, Delpech, "El hallazgo del escrito oculto en la literatura."
44. Sabbadini, *Le scoperte dei codici*.
45. Luna, *Historia verdadera del Rey Don Rodrigo*; Drayson, *The King and the Whore*; García-Arenal and Rodríguez Mediano, "Miguel de Luna, cristiano arábigo de Granada"; Grieve, *Eve of Spain*; Márquez Villanueva, *El problema morisco*, 45–97.
46. Cervantes Saavedra, *El ingenioso hidalgo Don Quijote de la Mancha*, 101–2 (Book 1, ch. 9).
47. Johnson, "Phantom Pre-texts and Fictional Authors," 189.
48. Grafton, "Invention of Traditions and Traditions of Invention," 21.
49. Pastor Bodmer, *The Armature of Conquest*. For similar assertions by thirteenth-century historians in Old French, Spiegel, "Forging the Past"; ———, *Romancing the Past*.
50. Cochrane, *Historians and Historiography*, 425, 433.
51. Ginzburg, *History, Rhetoric, and Proof*; ———, *Threads and Traces*; Grafton, *Forgers and Critics*.
52. Discussed by Grafton, *Bring Out Your Dead*, 136.
53. Burke, *The Renaissance Sense of the Past*; Momigliano, "Ancient History and the Antiquarian"; Weiss, *The Renaissance Discovery of Classical Antiquity*.
54. Quoted in Momigliano, "Ancient History and the Antiquarian," 292.
55. Grafton, *What Was History?*; ———, "The Identities of History in Early Modern Europe"; Herklotz, "Arnaldo Momigliano's 'Ancient History and the Antiquarian': A Critical Review."
56. Cooley, ed., *The Afterlife of Inscriptions*; Cunnally, *Images of the Illustrious*; Haskell, *History and Its Images*; Stenhouse, *Reading Inscriptions and Writing Ancient History*.
57. Collins, *Reforming Saints*; Frazier, *Possible Lives*; Webb, "Sanctity and History."
58. Ditchfield, *Liturgy, Sanctity and History*; ———, "Giving Tridentine Worship Back Its History"; ———, "Thinking with Saints." And see Nice, *Sacred History and National Identity*; Sawilla, *Antiquarianismus, Hagiographie und Historie*; Van Liere, Ditchfield, and Louthan, eds., *Sacred History*; Vélez, "Resolved to Fly."
59. Stenhouse, "Thomas Dempster, Royal Historian," 407.
60. Cameron, "Primitivism, Patristics, and Polemic," 49.
61. Quantin, "Reason and Reasonableness."
62. Kendrick, *British Antiquity*; Sweet, *Antiquaries*; Walsham, *The Reformation of the Landscape*; Woolf, "From Hystories to the Historical"; ———, *Social Circulation of the Past*.
63. Important recent contributions include Beltrán, Gascó La Calle, and Saracho Villa-lobos, eds., *La antigüedad como argumento*; Beltrán and Gascó La Calle, eds., *La an-*

tigüedad como argumento II; Morán Turina, *La memoria de las piedras*; Noble Wood, Roe, and Lawrance, eds., *Poder y saber*.
64. Woolf, *Social Circulation of the Past*.
65. Martínez, *Genealogical Fictions*; Wunder, "Classical, Christian, and Muslim Remains"; ———, "Search for Sanctity."
66. Tate, "The Rewriting of the Historical Past"; Van Liere, "Renaissance Chroniclers and the Apostolic Origins of Spanish Christianity."
67. Ocampo, *Los çinco libros primeros de La Corónica de España*; Cirot, *Études sur l'historiographie espagnole I . . . Les histoires générales*; Lupher, *Romans in a New World*, 50–56; Samson, "Florián de Ocampo."
68. Morales, *La coronica general*, unpaginated *prólogo*. The incident may have been apocryphal, according to Kagan, *Clio and the Crown*, 109.
69. J.-P. Migne, ed., *Patrologiae cursus completus. Series Latina* (hereafter PL), 31, col. 303.
70. Godoy Alcántara, *Historia crítica*, 147.
71. PL 31, col. 49.
72. Constable, "Forgery and Plagiarism," 10.

CHAPTER 1. THE FORGER BETWEEN FRIENDS
AND ENEMIES IN TOLEDO

Epigraph. Kempshall, *Rhetoric and the Writing of History*, 111.
1. Pisa, *Descripcion de la imperial ciudad de Toledo*, 17r–18r; and see Kagan, "The Toledo of El Greco"; Lorente Toledo and Vázquez González, "La ciudad de Toledo en la época del *Quijote*."
2. Bosch, *Art, Liturgy, and Legend*, 43; Gil Calvo, *La Compañía de Jesús en . . . Toledo*, 60–61; Rivera Recio, *San Eugenio de Toledo*; Tausiet, *El dedo robado*.
3. Pisa, *Descripcion de la imperial ciudad de Toledo*, 17v; Cámara Muñoz, "La pintura de El Greco."
4. Mitchell, "Archaeology and Romance in Renaissance Italy."
5. Candelaria, "Hercules and Albrecht Dürer's *Das Meerwunder*"; Moraleda y Esteban, "El Monasterio Agaliense de Toledo."
6. Rivera Recio, *Los arzobispos de Toledo*, 157–58.
7. Cárcamo, *Traslado de la carta*, 4r.
8. Ibid., 4r.
9. Ibid., 3r–4v.
10. Note that Jerónimo gives his birthdate as 1537, but all other sources indicate 1538. Higuera's parents, María Álvarez Romano y Cuellar and Alonso Fernández de la Higuera, had three other children who died in infancy. His brother Hernando died sometime in the 1590s near Marequita, Peru, according to Román de la Higuera, "Tratado del linage," 53r, 66r, and see the autobiographical paragraph in ———, "Historia del Colegio de Plasencia de la Compañía de Jesús," ARSI Bibliotheca, 6-G-15, 38. Other sources for Higuera's biography include Cirot, *Mariana historien*, 246–47; Escalera, "Higuera, Jerónimo (Romano, Román) de la,"; Gil Calvo, *La Compañía de*

Notes to Pages 38–41   321

   Jesús en . . . Toledo, 56–57; Ribadeneira and Alegambe, *Bibliotheca scriptorum Societatis Iesu*, 187.
11. Beltrán de Heredía, "La Facultad de Teología en la Universidad de Toledo"; Kagan, *Students and Society*, 260.
12. The doctorate in theology is according to Antonio, *Censura*, 8. Higuera later served as prefect of studies in the humanities in Plasencia (1603); Escalera asserts that he served in a sacerdotal capacity in Murcia and Toledo, and, according to Caro Baroja, as a lecturer of Philosophy in Alcalá de Henares. Caro Baroja, *Las falsificaciones*, 164, 176; Escalera, "Higuera, Jerónimo (Romano, Román) de la."
13. García Villoslada, *Manual de historia de la Compañía de Jesús*, I, 97–167.
14. Espinosa de Santayana, *Arte de retorica*, according to Simón Díaz, *Jesuitas de los siglos XVI y XVII*, 126.
15. In Higuera's own recollection, this was actually in 1590: Román de la Higuera, "Historia del Colegio de Plasencia de la Compañía de Jesús," 38; and see Cirot, "Mariana jésuite," 348–49. The treatise was López de Montoya, *Los quatro libros del Mysterio de la Missa*; and see Simón Díaz, *Jesuitas de los siglos XVI y XVII*, 126.
16. John W. O'Malley, *The First Jesuits* (Cambridge: Harvard University Press, 1993).
17. ARSI, Hispan., 138, 329r.
18. Kagan, "The Toledo of El Greco," 37, 44; Martz and Porres Martín-Cleto, *Toledo y los toledanos en 1561*.
19. Kagan, "The Toledo of El Greco," 44; Sánchez González, "La cultura de las letras."
20. For "spaces of knowledge," see Lazure, "To Dare Fame."
21. Bataillon, *Erasmo y España*; Camillo, "Interpretations of Humanism in Recent Spanish Renaissance Studies"; Ehlers, "Juan Bautista Pérez and the *Plomos*"; Homza, *Religious Authority in the Spanish Renaissance*; Shalev, *Sacred Words and Worlds*; Van Liere, "Humanism and Scholasticism."
22. For an engaging introduction to these circles, Van Liere, "Shared Studies Foster Friendship."
23. For Higuera's letter, dated July 1576, and Agustín's response, RAH 9/740, 161r–166v; and see Carbonell i Manils, "Quatre cartes desconegudes de l'arquebisbe de Tarragona Antonio Agustín Albanell."
24. Fernández Collado, *Guía del archivo y biblioteca capitulares de la catedral de Toledo*, 73–77; Martínez Gil, "Historia y cohesión urbana."
25. Andrés, "El helenismo de . . . Covarrubias."
26. BN Ms. 1641, 106v–119r.
27. It is not clear whether Schott had joined the Society by the time he came to Spain. Canfora, *Il Fozio ritrovato*; J. Kluyskens, "Schott, André," in Domínguez and O'Neill, eds., *Diccionario histórico*; Nelles, "Historia magistra antiquitatis."
28. He should not be confused with Sebastián de Covarrubias Orozco (d. 1613), author of the *Tesoro de la lengua castellana*, who was Antonio's cousin, nor with Antonio's nephew, also named Antonio de Covarrubias, a canon of the cathedral of Seville under Archbishop Pedro de Castro who wrote in defense of the lead books of Granada. On the latter Antonio, Harris, *From Muslim to Christian Granada*, 41; on the former, Andrés, "El helenismo de . . . Covarrubias"; Aldea Vaquero, Marín Martínez,

and Vives Gatell, *Diccionario de historia eclesiástica de España*, I: 638; Van Liere, "Humanism and Scholasticism."
29. Andrés, "El helenismo de . . . Covarrubias," 255, 277; Kagan, "The Toledo of El Greco."
30. Pisa, *Descripcion de la imperial ciudad de Toledo*, 23r.
31. Lorente Toledo and Vázquez González, "La ciudad de Toledo en la época del *Quijote*," 102.
32. Kagan, "The Toledo of El Greco," 43.
33. "Te martyr, vernule, poscimus . . . ," Cárcamo, *Traslado de la carta*, 2r. Modern scholars agree that a Spanish cult to Tirso—a Greek or Anatolian martyr—did exist in the time of Cixila, and that he may indeed have built a church in Tirso's honor: Christys, *Christians in Al-Andalus*, 23; Fábrega Grau, *Pasionario hispánico*, 2: 205–6, Pérez de Urbel, "Origen de los himnos mozárabes (continuación)," 131–32.
34. Cárcamo, *Traslado de la carta*, 1r–v, 24r–v.
35. This according to Higuera's "Discurso sobre si San Tirso mártir fue español y natural de Toledo, con ocasión de haber la ciudad establecida cofradía a este santo," transcribed and excerpted by Martínez de la Escalera, who consulted the manuscript in a private collection: Martínez de la Escalera, "Jerónimo de la Higuera . . . culto de San Tirso," 85. The manuscript has since been located and partially transcribed by Madroñal, "San Tirso de Toledo, tragedia perdida."
36. In print, the text included the initial letter to the king, supporting testimony from Esteban de Garibay and Alonso de Villegas, an anonymous rebuttal (later attributed to Pedro Salazar de Mendoza), as well as Cárcamo-Higuera's responses.
37. Morales, *La coronica general*, 214r–v; Rivera Recio, "La iglesia mozárabe," 32.
38. Rivera Recio, *Los arzobispos de Toledo*, 140–41.
39. Boynton, *Silent Music*; Hitchcock, *Mozarabs*, 109–10.
40. Martínez de la Escalera, "La circunstancia toledana," 634.
41. Further research will be necessary to determine what stance was adopted by Toledo's municipal cabildo—staffed by jurados—on the San Tirso affair. Aranda Pérez, *Poder municipal*.
42. Martínez de la Escalera, "La circunstancia toledana," 636. For the canons' attempts to prevent the play from being staged, Madroñal, "San Tirso de Toledo, tragedia perdida," 37.
43. Fernández Collado, "Grupos de poder en el cabildo toledano del siglo XVI"; Kagan, "The Toledo of El Greco," 43–44; Pizarro Llorente, "Los miembros del cabildo de la catedral de Toledo."
44. Fernández Collado, "Grupos de poder en el cabildo toledano del siglo XVI."
45. Salazar y Castro, *Historia genealógica de la casa de Lara*, III: 462. On the understudied Loaysa Girón, Henriet, "Political Struggle and the Legitimation of the Toledan Primacy"; Saéz, "Contribution a l'histoire religieuse de l'Espagne."
46. Sánchez González, "Cabildo catedralicio y cabildo municipal en el Toledo moderno"; the article does not mention which tribunal heard this case.
47. On Narbona, Aranda Pérez, *Poder y poderes en la ciudad de Toledo*, 277; Kagan, "The Toledo of El Greco," 69.

48. "Para dar, como dicen, una higa," from Higuera's "Discurso sobre si San Tirso mártir fue español . . . ," transcribed in Martínez de la Escalera, "Jerónimo de la Higuera . . . culto de San Tirso," 92.
49. According to Cirot, *Mariana historien*, 138–39, it was the archbishop's *consejo* that had him imprisoned.
50. Cárcamo, *Traslado de la carta*, 2v.
51. Kagan, "Pedro de Salazar de Mendoza."
52. Martínez de la Escalera, "La circunstancia toledana," 633.
53. Kagan, "The Toledo of El Greco," 63; Sánchez González, "La cultura de las letras," 174–76.
54. This separate pamphlet was later included in the compendium of materials in Cárcamo, *Traslado de la carta*, 7r–13v; see handwritten note on 7r in BN Ms 6184 copy. Salazar was later identified as its author by Pisa, *Descripcion de la imperial ciudad de Toledo*, 136v.
55. Cárcamo, *Traslado de la carta*, 9v.
56. Ibid., 11r.
57. The matter is complicated somewhat by the fact that Spain was using a distinct chronological system at the time, known as the Spanish era. Rivera Recio, *Los arzobispos de Toledo*, 157. For the difficulties of determining historical chronology with precision in the early modern period, Grafton, *Joseph Scaliger*, II.
58. Cárcamo, *Traslado de la carta*, 11v; Freidberg, ed., *Corpus iuris canonici*, II, 344 (liber II, titulus XXII, capitulum I).
59. Cárcamo, *Traslado de la carta*, 23v.
60. Ibid., 21v, 23v.
61. Ibid., 18v.
62. For Garibay's endorsement, ibid., 5r–6v; and for the retraction, identified as his thanks to internal references, R/8499, 1r–5r. For Garibay's time in Toledo, during which he hobnobbed with many of Higuera's peers and also accepted the appointment in 1594 as royal chronicler, Garibay y Zamalloa and Moya, *Discurso de mi vida*. On his work as a historian, Kagan, *Clio and the Crown*, 115–17.
63. Cárcamo, *Traslado de la carta*, 26v.
64. Augustine of Hippo, *The Retractions*. On Villegas, Sánchez Romeralo, "Alonso de Villegas"; Martín Fernández and Sánchez Romeralo, "El maestro Alonso de Villegas."
65. Cárcamo, *Traslado de la carta*.
66. See the July 1595 response from one Licenciado Espinosa of Oviedo, R/8499, 9r–11v.
67. Printed in Antonio, *Censura*, 528–30.
68. Rivera Recio, *Los arzobispos de Toledo*, 160–61.
69. Ibid.
70. Martínez de la Escalera, "La circunstancia toledana," 94.
71. Valdés to Acquaviva, October 3, 1595, ARSI, Hispan., 139, 79r.
72. Ibid.
73. "Porres, Francisco de," in Domínguez and O'Neill, eds., *Diccionario histórico*, 3194; Olavide, "La Inquisición."

74. "Discurso," in Martínez de la Escalera, "Jerónimo de la Higuera ... culto de San Tirso," 92–94; ———, "La circunstancia toledana," 633.
75. ARSI, Hispan., 139, 104r–106v.
76. Cirot, "La famille de Juan de Mariana"; Saéz, "Contribution a l'histoire religieuse de l'Espagne," 236.
77. It is indeed found in his manuscript history of Spain, BN Ms. 1638, 137r–v.
78. "Esta carta vio el doctor Alonso de Narbona, y me dijo convenía remedialla con algún modo de sacar las manchas, porque el maestro Palomares, que de suyo es muy melancólico lo había de llevar mal." Martínez de la Escalera, "Jerónimo de la Higuera ... culto de San Tirso," 85.
79. Ibid.
80. ARSI, Hisp., 139, 105r.
81. Gil, "Judíos y conversos."
82. The debate has not ended; modern scholars disagree about the cultural identity of the Mozarabs: Aillet, "La question 'mozárabe.'"
83. Pisa, Descripcion de la imperial ciudad de Toledo, 277; Hitchcock, Mozarabs, 112, 117.
84. Hitchcock, Mozarabs, 111, who implies that these doubts reflect a broader "crisis" for Mozarabs in sixteenth-century Toledo, which, in light of the fact that only five individuals identified themselves as Mozarabs in the 1561 census of the city, seems overstated.
85. Ibid., 114–16; Ingram, "Historiography, Historicity, and the Conversos"; López Estrada, "Dos tratados de los siglos XVI y XVII sobre los mozárabes."
86. Román de la Higuera, "Tratado del linage," 11r.
87. Ibid., 12r.
88. Bizzocchi, Genealogie incredibili; ———, "Culture généalogique dans l'Italie du seizième siècle"; Redondo, "Légendes généalogiques et parentés fictives en Espagne, au Siècle d'Or"; Tanner, The Last Descendant of Aeneas.
89. Ladero Quesada, "El pasado histórico-fabuloso de España"; Rábade Obradó, "La invención como necesidad."
90. Salazar de Mendoza, El origen, xxxv. Although Salazar's history did not survive, a description of his treatment of Tubal's foundation of Toledo does survive in Irving, The Works of Washington Irving, 316–17.
91. On the lost history of the archbishops of Toledo, Múñoz y Romero, Diccionario bibliográfico-histórico, 262.
92. Martz, A Network of Converso Families; ———, "Converso Families"; Salazar de Mendoza, Cronica, "Al lector," especially 5–13, 19–20; Salazar de Mendoza, El origen, xx–xxi. See also Kagan, "Pedro de Salazar de Mendoza," 86; Sánchez Alonso, Historia de la historiografía española, II: 234–35.
93. Salazar de Mendoza, El origen, xxi.
94. Román de la Higuera, "Tratado del linage," 14v.
95. Ibid., 73r.
96. Gil, "Judíos y conversos," 38–39; Hitchcock, "The falsos chronicones and the Mozarabs."
97. Román de la Higuera, "Tratado del linage," 38–45r, 58r, 113–14.

98. Martínez de la Escalera, "Jerónimo de la Higuera . . . culto de San Tirso," 88. A corroborating version of this story is found in Higuera's marginal note in RAH, 9/1013, 369r.
99. Several individuals with one of Higuera's last names—including Pedro, Teresa, and Ysabel de la Higuera, and one "Doctor de la Higuera," who may be our protagonist—appeared in the 1561 census, Martz and Porres Martín-Cleto, *Toledo y los toledanos en 1561*. Higuera's twin brother Hernando married a woman whose mother's surname was Requera; it seems that Higuera's sister Ysabel also married into this family, as siblings married siblings. One of Ysabel's grandchildren, Alonso, married into the Fernández de Toledo family, some of whom had become members of the nobility (hidalgos) by the 1590s. Román de la Higuera, "Tratado del linage." For conjectures about other relatives of Higuera's, including Juan Fernández de la Higuera, a Toledan notary active at the end of the century, see Martz, "Converso Families," 334–35, citing RAH 9/229, 236r-v.
100. Gil, "*Berenjeneros*"; Rábade Obradó, "La invención como necesidad."
101. Román de la Higuera, "Tratado del linage," 57v.
102. For Pedro, ibid., 66r; and for Hierónimo, 115r. For examples of this confusion, which is understandable in light of the sometimes unclear details of Higuera's family tree, Caro Baroja, *Las falsificaciones*, 173; García-Arenal and Rodríguez Mediano, "Jerónimo Román de la Higuera and the Lead Books of Sacromonte," 259.
103. Román de la Higuera, "Tratado del linage," 51v, 115r–140v. Probanzas were taken over by the Inquisition in the 1570s. Martínez, *Genealogical Fictions*, 63–65; Sicroff, *Les controverses des statuts de "pureté de sang."*
104. Román de la Higuera, "Tratado del linage," 66v–67r, 71r–79r.
105. Ibid.
106. Pike, *Linajudos and Conversos in Seville*.
107. Martínez, *Genealogical Fictions*, 70–87; and see Caro Baroja's concession that pinning down genealogical truth at this distance in time is well-nigh impossible due to the highly charged nature of such accusations, then and now. Caro Baroja, *Las falsificaciones*, 173–74.

CHAPTER 2. THE JESUITS, THE INQUISITION, AND HISTORY

1. Aranda Pérez, *Poder municipal*; Fernández Collado, "Grupos de poder."
2. See Caro Baroja, *Las falsificaciones*, 178; García-Arenal and Rodríguez Mediano, "Jerónimo Román de la Higuera and the Lead Books of Sacromonte," 250. For the misleading and debatable assertion that Higuera requested and was denied Jesuit permission to publish the false chronicles, Kagan, *Clio and the Crown*, 260.
3. Letter to Bartolomé Morlanes, June 4, 1616, cited in Cirot, *Mariana historien*, 428.
4. Acera, "Notas críticas."
5. Porreño, "Historia de los Arzobispos de Toledo" I, 78, BN Ms. 13025.
6. RAH 9/740; and for another example, RAH 9/741, cited by Caro Baroja, *Las falsificaciones*, 172.

7. Cirot, "Documents sur le faussaire Higuera."
8. Respectively: BN Ms. 3249; RAH 9/229 and 9/300; ARSI Bibliotheca, 6-G-15; RAH 9/749; RAH 9/750; and BN Ms. 5556. Higuera's papers survive in significant clusters in these two Madrid repositories. There is no comprehensive index of *Higueriana*, and additional autographs have been located in a number of other places; see Lilao Franca and Castrillo González, *Catálogo de manuscritos de la Biblioteca Universitaria de Salamanca*, 158, 271. However, it should be noted that Higuera is often conflated, in bibliographic catalogues and elsewhere, with a near-contemporary Augustinian named Fray Jerónimo Román, for whom, see Adorno, "Sobre la censura y su evasión."
9. The notes for the martyrology are in RAH 9/1013; and for the *Primado de Toledo*, which contains treatments of a variety of other matters, such as the origin of the term *mozárabe*; the various expulsions of the Jews from Spain; where Christians hid the relics when the Arabs invaded; and whether Latin was used during the Visigothic era, RAH L-7.
10. Antonio, *Biblioteca hispana nueva*, I, 630–31.
11. It is perhaps not a surprise that the text awaits a critical, modern study. The only complete copy is from the seventeenth century, BN Mss. 1285–1293, which totals 2,544 folios, according to Biblioteca Nacional (Spain). *Inventario general* IV, 148–52. *Toledo* has survived in a number of copies, only one of which is complete, which makes cross-referencing difficult. The partial copies are (1) Higuera's autograph manuscript, BN Mss. 1639–1642; (2) a copy from the Jesuit *casa profesa* in Toledo, BN Mss. 1643–1647; (3) a portion of the text from the time of Christ to the early eighth century, in a copy made for Jerónimo de Mascareñas, bishop of Segovia (1668–1671), BN Mss. 2343–2345; (4) a portion of the earliest books, in an eighteenth-century copy, BN Ms. 6939; (5) a nearly complete rendition, missing only about a dozen chapters, which belonged to the Duque de Uceda, BN Mss. 8192–8198; (6) additional fragments in BN Mss. 2000 and 12916; (7) another partial copy, BUS Mss. 1830–1837.
12. Future research may enable us to trace Higuera's itinerant existence in Castilian *colegios* with more precision. For now, Escalera, "Higuera, Jerónimo (Romano, Román) de la."
13. Letter of November 1594 quoted, without citation, in Martínez de la Escalera, "Jerónimo de la Higuera . . . culto de San Tirso," 88.
14. Cirot, "Mariana jésuite. La jeunesse," 349.
15. Porres to Acquaviva, July 8, 1595, ARSI, Hisp., 138, 329r. The first scholar to look for traces of Higuera in the Jesuit archives seems to have been Martínez de la Escalera, "Jerónimo de la Higuera . . . culto de San Tirso."
16. Porres to Acquaviva, July 8, 1595, ARSI, Hisp., 138, 329r.
17. Valdés to Acquaviva, October 3, 1595, ARSI, Hispan., 139, 79r.
18. Kagan, *Clio and the Crown*, 259–60, cites a vote by the jurados on the municipal council to write a letter to the Toledan provincial urging him to allow work to be completed and published by Higuera in November, 1595; they wrote again in 1598, judging from a reference in a letter from Acquaviva to Guzmán, March 1598, ARSI, Tolet., 5-II, 488v.
19. ARSI, Tolet., 5-II, 399r.

20. Although it is often asserted that the Jesuits opposed the publication of Mariana's book, this is contradicted by the fact that the first edition was funded by the Society and printed in its Toledan residence. Rodríguez de Gracia, "Contratos de impresión suscritos por Juan de Mariana, Alonso de Villegas y Francisco de Pisa." For the editions and their varying fortunes, Cirot, *Mariana historien*.
21. Keniston, *Francisco de los Cobos*.
22. Mariana, *Historiae de rebvs Hispaniae libri XXV*, 602.
23. Acquaviva to Camarasa, January 17, 1594, ARSI, Tolet., 5-II, 327v; and see ———, *Historia general de España* I, 727.
24. Mariana and Miñana, *Historia general de España* I, 268.
25. ARSI, Hispan., 139, 79r; also quoted in Martínez de la Escalera, "Jerónimo de la Higuera . . . culto de San Tirso," 77.
26. Porres Martín-Cleto, "La calle de Esteban Illán."
27. Alcocer, *Hystoria*, liij verso; Pisa, *Descripcion de . . . Toledo*, 29–30v, 151r, 172v–173r.
28. Porres Martín-Cleto, "La calle de Esteban Illán," 68, 83–85; and see ———, "Nuevos datos sobre Don Esteban Illán."
29. Pisa, *Descripcion de . . . Toledo*, 151r.
30. BN Ms. 1288, 310v.
31. Draft letter from Higuera, without place or date, to Hernando de Ávila, RAH 9/1013, 369r–370v.
32. ARSI, Tolet., 5-II, 428r.
33. Ibid., 489v–490r.
34. Ibid., 488r.
35. Ibid., 469r: "algunos padres que sean a proposito para eso."
36. Ibid., 507v.
37. Ibid., 511r.
38. Ibid., 557v.
39. Ibid., 566r.
40. Escalera, "Higuera, Jerónimo (Romano, Román) de la."
41. Antonio, *Censura*, 65–66.
42. Quoted in Gil, "Berenjeneros," 139.
43. On Alcocer and Pisa, Kagan, "Clio and the Crown." Scholars have now proven beyond a doubt that, contrary to the assertions of some seventeenth-century critics, Alcocer actually existed, and was not merely a pseudonym for the Toledan humanist Juan de Vergara. Hitchcock, *Mozarabs*, 112.
44. Cf. García-Arenal and Rodríguez Mediano, "Jerónimo Román de la Higuera and the Lead Books of Sacromonte," 250, who refer to this as a "fraudulent history of Toledo."
45. Kagan, "Clio and the Crown," 89.
46. Hyde, "Medieval Descriptions of Cities"; Sot, "*Gesta episcoporum*," "*gesta abbatum*"; Tate, "*Laus Urbium*."
47. For Greek, see Ms. 6939, 179v; and for Hebrew, 54v. Higuera did not know Arabic, and relied upon "those who know the language" to copy and translate inscriptions; see BN Ms. 1639, 202v and Diego de Urrea's assistance in BN Ms. 8194, 399r.
48. Hernando Sobrino, "Cuando la fama"; ———, "De parroquia en parroquia"; ———,

"Higuera y la epigrafía de Ibahernando." Other scholars who have noted that the work contains some value include Benito Ruano, "La "sentencia-estatuto" de Pero Sarmiento"; Márquez Villanueva, *Investigaciones sobre Juan Álvarez Gato*; Pastore, *Il Vangelo e la spada*, 50–51.

49. Alcocer, *Hystoria*, xxxvij. The cave of Hercules remained fertile terrain for mythmaking even after twentieth-century studies concluded that it had served as a deposit for a Roman aqueduct; see García-Diego, "La cueva de Hercules."
50. Pisa, *Descripcion de . . . Toledo*, 14r–v.
51. BN Ms. 6939, 131v.
52. On Tavera, ibid., 138r–v, citing Alfonso Madrigal (el Tostado); and see 139v–140r, 30r–v, 124r–v, respectively.
53. Ibid., 142r–143r.
54. Salazar de Mendoza, *Cronica*, 2–4.
55. BN Ms. 6939, 14r.
56. Alcocer, *Hystoria*, iii verso–iiii verso, xj recto-verso.
57. Cirot, *Mariana historien*, 280–97.
58. Pisa, *Descripcion de . . . Toledo*, 1v–3r.
59. Ibid., 76r.
60. BN Ms. 6939, 25v–26v; and cf. Alcocer, *Hystoria*, ch. 3; Pisa, *Descripcion de . . . Toledo*, 2v.
61. BN Ms. 6939, 1v–2r; and for this trope in *The Book of Good Love*, Dagenais, *The Ethics of Reading*, 83.
62. For the influential critiques of Agustín and Barreiros, Stephens, "When Pope Noah Ruled the Etruscans."
63. BN Ms. 6939, 8r.
64. BN Ms. 6939, 5r, 7v–8r, 13v; and for the tradition of Ham as necromancer, Whitford, *The Curse of Ham*, 43–66.
65. Borchardt, "The Topos of Critical Rejection."
66. BN Ms. 1638, 2v. Note that *Spain* is a separate book, but it is often cited as if it were part of *Toledo*; this is an understandable error, since the autograph volumes of *Toledo* (BN Mss. 1639, 1640, 1641) are mislabeled as *Spain*.
67. BN Ms. 1638, 2r–v.
68. McKitterick, *The Carolingians and the Written Word*, 202–5; Rose, *Ritual Memory*, 25–26.
69. Luna and Bernabé Pons, *Historia verdadera del Rey Don Rodrigo*, 23; Pisa, *Descripcion de . . . Toledo*, 14v.
70. BN Ms. 8194, 139r, 366r–v; and for the legend pre- and post-Luna, Drayson, *The King and the Whore*, 53–57; and see Grieve, *Eve of Spain*, 40, 168.
71. Frazier, *Possible Lives*; Huppert, *The Idea of Perfect History*; Woolf, "Erudition and the Idea of History."
72. ARSI, Hisp., 90, II, 318r–v.
73. Jerónimo Román de la Higuera, "Historia del Colegio de Plasencia de la Compañía de Jesús," ARSI Bibliotheca, 6-G-15, 38.
74. Excerpted in Cirot, "Documents sur le faussaire Higuera," 92–93.

75. According to Maryks, *Jesuit Order as a Synagogue*, 123–25.
76. For the most clearheaded account, Martínez Millán, "Transformación y crisis"; the most exhaustive, Astraín, *Historia* III, 347–420, 475–531.
77. Mariana, *Discurso de las enfermedades de la compañía*; and see García Cárcel, "La crisis de la Compañía de Jesús."
78. Astraín, *Historia* III, 410–17; Lewy, "The Struggle for Constitutional Governance."
79. Pastore, "A proposito di Matteo 18,15."
80. Astraín, *Historia* III, 403, 317–67.
81. Pavone, *The Wily Jesuits and the "Monita Secreta."*
82. Maryks, *Jesuit Order as a Synagogue*, 159–213. One did not need to be a converso to be a dissident, nor is it clear, *pace* Maryks, that the promulgation of limpieza regulations was solely in response to the perceived challenge of the memorialistas.
83. ARSI, Hisp., 90, II, 316r–318v; Astraín, *Historia* III, 499–503.
84. Echarte, I., "Abreo, Francisco de," in Domínguez and O'Neill, eds., *Diccionario histórico*, I: 7.
85. ARSI, Hisp., 90, II, 317v; Astraín, *Historia* III, 364.
86. Quoted in Domínguez, "Historical Polemic: Pedro de Ribadeneyra and the Launching of the Armada."
87. ARSI, *Censurae librorum* 652, I, 235r; the volume contains items from 1578 to 1604.
88. Ibid., 233r.
89. García Cárcel, "La crisis de la Compañía de Jesús," 398; and see Nelson, *The Jesuits and the Monarchy*, 48.
90. Mariana, *De rege et regis institutione libri tres*; and see Braun, *Juan de Mariana*; Höpfl, *Jesuit Political Thought*, 318–21.
91. ARSI, Tolet., 5–11, 416r.
92. Leturia, "Contribuzioni."
93. See 1599 request that Spanish provincials identify suitable candidates: ARSI, Tolet., 5-II, 576r.
94. Astraín, *Historia* V, 93.
95. Leturia, "Contribuzioni," 172–73.
96. ARSI, Tolet., 5-II, 486v.
97. Ibid., 538v.
98. Ibid., 551v.
99. Johnson, "Politics and Sanctity," 86. For more on Rader, see chapter 9.
100. Brouwer, *Antiquitates annalium trevirensium*; and for Acquaviva's assessment, see Duhr, *Geschichte der Jesuiten*, II: 416–30.
101. For an extensive excerpt, Olavide, "La Inquisición."
102. AHN Inq., Lib. 2708, 1r.
103. Ibid.
104. AHN Inq. Leg. 116, no. 10, 2v.
105. Pastore, "A proposito di Matteo 18,15"; ———, *Il Vangelo e la spada*; Pérez, *The Spanish Inquisition*, 89; Perry, *Gender and Disorder*, 120–21.
106. AHN Inq., Leg. 116, no. 10, 3v. Higuera's connections to Toledo continued in exile, judging from the fact that he was asked to contribute an elegiac poem to a 1604

volume composed by Eugenio de Robles, chaplain of the Mozarabic rite in Toledo. Robles, *Compendio de la vida y hazañas del Cardenal don fray Francisco Ximenez de Cisneros*.
107. Ibid., 6r.
108. Ibid., 4r.
109. Ibid., 4r–v.
110. In fact, somebody must have denounced Benavides, since he was called to testify before the Valladolid inquisitorial tribunal, but to no ill effect. He went on to become rector of the Madrid colegio and, in 1608, Toledan provincial. Astraín, *Historia* III, 206, 657.
111. AHN Inq., Leg. 116, no. 10, 4v–5r.
112. Ibid., 6r.
113. Ibid., 3v.
114. Ibid., 5v, 6v. Here my transcription differs from that of Martínez de la Escalera, "Jerónimo de la Higuera . . . culto de San Tirso."
115. Ibid., 5r.
116. Bangert, *A History of the Society of Jesus*, 118; and, for a tendentious yet detailed account, Astraín, *Historia* III, 307–46.
117. For this valuable point, Martínez de la Escalera, "Jerónimo de la Higuera . . . culto de San Tirso," 78.
118. AHN Inq., Leg. 116, no. 10, 5v.
119. Martínez de la Escalera, "Jerónimo de la Higuera . . . culto de San Tirso," 72, 78.
120. ARSI Bibliotheca, 6-G-15, 165.
121. García Cárcel, "La crisis de la Compañía de Jesús."
122. Ribadeneira and Alegambe, *Bibliotheca scriptorum Societatis Iesu*, 187.
123. Bataillon, "Sur Florian Docampo"; Tate, "Mythology in Spanish Historiography."
124. Mariana, *Historiae de rebvs hispaniae libri XXV*, 36; and ———, *Historia general de España*, 47 (book I, chapter 19 in both editions); and see Cirot, *Mariana historien*, 296, 354.
125. Curtius Rufus, *History of Alexander* II, 375; and see Baynham, *Alexander the Great*, 86; Grafton, *What Was History?*, 58–59.
126. For the hypothesis that the interpolator was Francisco de Portocarrero, Cirot, *Mariana historien*, 236–53; for more recent dissenting opinions that in fact Mariana himself drew on the cronicones, Acera, "Notas críticas"; Gómez Martos, "Juan de Mariana y la historiografía ilustrada," 10.

CHAPTER 3. HOW TO FORGE A HISTORY

1. Constable, "Forgery and Plagiarism"; Grafton, *Forgers and Critics*.
2. Stephens, "Complex Pseudonymity," 697.
3. Cited by Martínez de la Escalera, "Jerónimo de la Higuera . . . culto de San Tirso," 72–73, who consulted the document at the monastery of Montserrat.
4. Krebs, *A Most Dangerous Book*; Sabbadini, *Le scoperte dei codici*.

5. Jerome, *On Illustrious Men*, 1, 165; also mentioned in ———, *Apologie contre Rufin*, 164–67 (Book II, para. 23).
6. On Trithemius, Brann, *The Abbot Trithemius*; Grafton, *Worlds Made by Words*, 56–78.
7. PL 31, col. 49.
8. Codoñer Merino, *El "De viris illustribus" de Isidoro de Sevilla*, 153.
9. PL 136, cols. 971A, 977; Godoy Alcántara, *Historia crítica*, 156–57.
10. Grafton, *Forgers and Critics*, 62.
11. For various theories, Collins, "Isidore, Maximus, and the *Historia Gothorum*."
12. Cf. Godoy Alcántara, *Historia crítica*, 19–21, 29.
13. Cirot, "Lorenzo de Padilla et la Pseudo-Histoire"; Ruíz Vega, *Los hijos de Túbal*.
14. Braulio of Saragossa and Fructuosus of Braga, *Writings of Braulio of Saragossa and Fructuosus of Braga*, 163–65; Collins, *Visigothic Spain, 409–711*; Godoy Alcántara, *Historia crítica*, 165–68.
15. See preface in Ramírez de Prado, ed., *Luitprandi subdiaconi toletani*, xlvij; and for his authentic works, Squatriti, ed., *The Complete Works of Liudprand of Cremona*.
16. PL 136, cols. 971A-B, letter from Luitprand to Tractemundus. For Higuera's explanation, Ramírez de Prado, ed., *Luitprandi subdiaconi toletani*, 287.
17. PL 136, cols. 1063, 1071.
18. Ibid., cols. 977, 978B; González Muñoz, "Leyenda de Mahoma."
19. PL 136, col. 987.
20. Ibid., col. 1087.
21. Regimund was also called Tractemund, not to be confused with the eighth-century Christian king of the Lombards by the same name. On *adversaria*, Blair, "Note Taking," 20, 99; Chatelain, "Les recueils d'*adversaria*."
22. Ramírez de Prado, ed., *Luitprandi subdiaconi toletani*, 291–94.
23. Hernández, *Vida, martirio y traslación de la virgen y mártir Santa Leocadia*.
24. PL 136, cols. 1138B, 1155B.
25. Hitchcock, "The *falsos chronicones* and the Mozarabs."
26. Many subsequent authors refer to the author as "Julián Pedro," as did Higuera himself on at least one occasion. For theories about his possible existence, Hitchcock, *Mozarabs*, 120–23.
27. Hitchcock, "The *falsos chronicones* and the Mozarabs," 92; and see the demythologization by Fletcher, *The Quest for El Cid*.
28. Gonzálvez, "Persistence of the Mozarabic Liturgy"; O'Callaghan, *A History of Medieval Spain*, 202–4.
29. Hitchcock, "The *falsos chronicones* and the Mozarabs," 95; Rubio Sadia, "Que de ambos oficios era Dios servido."
30. Hitchcock, "The *falsos chronicones* and the Mozarabs," 203–4.
31. Ramírez de Prado, ed., *Iuliani Petri . . . Chronicon*, 7–9.
32. Ibid.
33. Eusebius and Jerome, *Eusebii Pamphili Chronici canones*; Guenée, *Histoire et culture historique*, 203.

34. Momigliano, "Pagan and Christian Historiography"; and see Grafton and Williams, *Christianity and the Transformation of the Book*.
35. Ditchfield, "What Was Sacred History?"; and, in the same volume, Guazzelli, "Cesare Baronio and the Roman Catholic Vision of the Early Church," 52–71; Orella y Unzue, *Respuestas católicas a las Centurias de Magdeburgo*.
36. Polman, *L'élément historique*, 529.
37. Quoted in Pullapilly, *Caesar Baronius*, 153–54. I have corrected an error in his translation.
38. Morales, *La coronica general*, unpaginated *prólogo*; and for the longer history of this professed "tension between religion and rhetoric," Ginzburg, *Threads and Traces*, 20–21.
39. Ditchfield, *Liturgy, Sanctity and History*, 283.
40. ———, "Reading Rome as a Sacred Landscape"; Haskell, *History and Its Images*, 102–6.
41. Godoy Alcántara, *Historia crítica*, 154–55; Kendrick, *St. James in Spain*.
42. PL 31, cols. 91–147. For the evolution of this tradition, Kendrick, *St. James in Spain*; Van Liere, "The Missionary and the Moorslayer."
43. Escolano, *Decada primera*, col. 216.
44. PL 31, col. 129. For the importance of bishops, Wright, "The Borromean Ideal and the Spanish Church." Modern scholars have concluded that, in reality, the episcopal presence was quite light in fourth- and fifth-century Iberia. Bowes, "'Un coterie espagnole pieuse.'"
45. Johnson, "'That in Her the Seed of the Serpent May Have No Part'"; Kendrick, *St. James in Spain*, 86–103; Stratton, *The Immaculate Conception in Spanish Art*.
46. Vives, "Tradición y leyenda."
47. Baronio, *Annales ecclesiastici* I (AD 66), 641–42; Brady and Olin, eds., *The Edition of St. Jerome*, 72; and see Momigliano, "Note sulla leggenda del Cristianesimo di Seneca."
48. PL 31, col. 189.
49. Ibid., col. 425.
50. For Jerome's letter 52, see appendix in Fuente, *Historia eclesiástica*, 403–4.
51. Baronio, *Martyrologium Romanum* (1597), 66.
52. PL 31, cols. 73, 85, 93, 97, 135, 169, 193, 233; Kendrick, *St. James in Spain*, 120.
53. PL 31, col. 79; Godoy Alcántara, *Historia crítica*, 156. For Peter's daughter, Elliott, *The Apocryphal New Testament*, 397–98.
54. "Messina's Buried Palladium."
55. PL 31, cols. 253, 569.
56. Elliott, *The Apocryphal New Testament*, 164–225; Fradejas Lebrero, *Los evangelios apócrifos*, 289–90, 454–56; Reinhardt and Santiago-Otero, *Biblioteca bíblica ibérica medieval*, 48.
57. Baronio, *Annales ecclesiastici* I (AD 34, no. 228), 215–16.
58. PL 31, cols. 77, 133.
59. Ibid., col. 187, where he imprecisely refers to epigrams 7 and 8 (regarding the cruci-

fixion of Laureolus and the death of Daedulus, mangled by a bear) as evidence for early Christian practice.
60. Burke, "How to Be a Counter-Reformation Saint." Cf. Ditchfield, "Thinking with Saints."
61. PL 31, col. 321.
62. Quoted in Kagan, "The Toledo of El Greco," 57.
63. Quoted in Guenée, "L'historien et la compilation," 126.
64. Hathaway, "Compilatio: From Plagiarism to Compiling"; Minnis, "'Nolens auctor sed compilator.'"
65. Richardson, "Plagiarism and Imitation," 111; and see Constable, "Forgery and Plagiarism."
66. Burgess, ed., *The Chronicle of Hydatius*, 23.
67. Cardelle de Hartmann and Collins, eds., *Victoris Tunnunensis Chronicon*, 11, 78.
68. Dagenais, *The Ethics of Reading*.
69. Cardelle de Hartmann and Collins, eds., *Victoris Tunnunensis Chronicon*, 77ff; Mommsen, *Chronica minora saec. IV. V. VI. VII.* I, 368–69.
70. Burgess, ed., *The Chronicle of Hydatius*, 5–6; Wolf, *Conquerors and Chroniclers*, 3–6; 12–15.
71. Tunnuna is often erroneously rendered as "Tunis." Cardelle de Hartmann and Collins, eds., *Victoris Tunnunensis Chronicon*; Collins, *Visigothic Spain*, 409–711, 50–51.
72. Collins, *Visigothic Spain*, 409–711, 52, 56; Wolf, *Conquerors and Chroniclers*, 8–11.
73. For this moment of relative openness and communication on the part of the inhabitants of Visigothic Hispania with the Mediterranean cultural heartlands, Collins, *Visigothic Spain*, 409–711, 147–61.
74. Martín, ed., *Isidori Hispalensis Chronica*; Orosius, *The Seven Books of History*.
75. Fernández de Malpartida, *Historia y anales de . . . Plasencia*, 76. For a revisionist take on the "Gothic" roots of Isidore and his kin, Collins, *Visigothic Spain*, 409–711, 154.
76. In the entire chronicle, the non-Prosper material is only 21 percent, not all of which is of Higuera's confection. Antonio, *Bibliotheca hispana vetus* II, 409–19; Godoy Alcántara, *Historia crítica*, 30–32, 36.
77. Bivar, ed., *Chronicon*.
78. Reilly, "Bishop Lucas of Túy."
79. Henriet, "Collection hagiographique et forgeries," 61.
80. Reilly, "Bishop Lucas of Túy."
81. Chazan, "Le méthode critique," 233.
82. Quantin, "Reason and Reasonableness," 410.
83. PL 31, col. 69; Elliott, *The Apocryphal New Testament*, 210.
84. Fuente, *Historia eclesiástica*, 65.
85. For this debate, Le Gall, *Le mythe de Saint Denis*; Wilberding, "A Defense of Dionysius the Areopagite by Rubens."
86. Morales, *La coronica general de España* I, 261 ff. Paul's visit to Spain was accepted more widely than that of Santiago, since it had some biblical basis (Romans 15:24 and 15:28); Fuente, *Historia eclesiástica* I, 45–46, 67.

87. Godoy Alcántara, *Historia crítica*, 279–80.
88. PL 31, cols. 239–41, 269–71, 293. On Eugenius, Linehan, *History and the Historians of Medieval Spain*, 275–78; Rivera Recio, *San Eugenio de Toledo*.
89. Extrabiblical traditions about Jesus, the apostles, the Virgin Mary, and the saints proliferated in various media and genres in late antiquity and the Middle Ages, and did not exist as a distinct genre known as "hagiography" until the nineteenth century, when scholars attempted to define and critique it as a genre. Lifshitz, "Beyond Positivism and Genre: 'Hagiographical' Texts as Historical Narrative." Recent scholarship has also demonstrated that hagiographic motifs did not remain cloistered, and moved into literary sources as well; Giles, *The Laughter of the Saints*; Gómez Moreno, *Claves hagiográficas*.
90. Ribadeneira et al., *Flos sanctorum*; Villegas, *Flos sanctorum*. For the evolution of hagiographical critique, Collins, *Reforming Saints*; Frazier, *Possible Lives*; Reames, *The Legenda Aurea: A Reexamination*.
91. Frend, *The Rise of Christianity*, 461; García Villada, *Historia eclesiástica* III, 68–77; Menéndez y Pelayo, *Historia de los heterodoxos españoles* (1956) I: 54.
92. Allard, "Rome au IVe siècle"; Palmer, *Prudentius on the Martyrs*; Roberts, *Poetry and the Cult of the Martyrs*.
93. Fábrega Grau, *Pasionario hispánico*.
94. Ditchfield, "An Early Christian School of Sanctity"; Gaston, "Prudentius and Sixteenth-Century Antiquarian Scholarship."
95. Morales, *La coronica general*, 211v. On the perceived usefulness of poetry for history-writing in antiquity and the Middle Ages, Kempshall, *Rhetoric and the Writing of History*, 360–66.
96. Van Liere, "Renaissance Chroniclers and the Apostolic Origins of Spanish Christianity," and cf. the more optimistic evaluation of Binotti, "Coins, Jewelry and Stone Inscriptions."
97. Castillo Maldonado, "*Angelorum Participes*," 162–65.
98. Palmer, *Prudentius on the Martyrs*, 224.
99. PL 31, cols. 415–73.
100. Bivar, ed., *Marci Maximi* ("S. Braulionis et Hellecanis . . . Additiones"), 52–58; Ramírez de Prado, ed., *Iuliani Petri . . . Chronicon*, 143–58.
101. Tausiet, "Zaragoza celeste y subterránea," 164.
102. Malamud, *A Poetics of Transformation*, 79.
103. Aristotle, *Poetics*, 59 (I: 9); Bartky, "Aristotle and the Politics of Herodotus's *History*."
104. Halliwell, *Aristotle's Poetics*.
105. Kempshall, *Rhetoric and the Writing of History*, 412.
106. Rose, *Ritual Memory*, 23–78.
107. Boruchoff, "The Poetry of History"; Kempshall, *Rhetoric and the Writing of History*.

CHAPTER 4. JEWS, ARABIC-SPEAKERS, AND NEW SAINTS

1. Cabanelas, "Un intento de sincretismo islámico-cristiano"; Hagerty, *Los libros plúmbeos del Sacromonte*.

Notes to Pages 127–134

2. On moriscos, Coleman, *Creating Christian Granada*; Perry, *The Handless Maiden*.
3. Harris, *From Muslim to Christian Granada*; ———, "The Sacromonte and the Geography of the Sacred in Early Modern Granada."
4. Hagerty, *Los libros plúmbeos del Sacromonte*, 41; Kendrick, *St. James in Spain*, 108.
5. Harris, *From Muslim to Christian Granada*, 37–46, 149; Scaramella, "'Una materia gravissima.'"
6. Andrés, "El helenismo de . . . Covarrubias," 312–13.
7. Printed in Villanueva, *Viage literario* III, 278–80.
8. Ibid., 259–78; and see Laursen, "Skepticism and Cynicism in the Work of Pedro de Valencia"; Magnier, *Pedro de Valencia and the Catholic Apologists of the Expulsion*, 199–221.
9. Villanueva, *Viage literario* III, 273; Ehlers, "Juan Bautista Pérez and the *Plomos*."
10. Medina Conde, *El fingido Dextro*, xvi.
11. Ochoa y Ronna, ed., *Epistolario español* II, 46–47.
12. Ibid.
13. Medina Conde, *El fingido Dextro*, xlviii.
14. See, for example, Higuera's advice to discuss the critiques of the cult of relics by Claudius of Turin and the challenges faced by Ambrose of Milan, in ibid., v; on his advice, these examples were incorporated into Antolínez de Burgos, *Historia eclesiástica de Granada*, 644–45.
15. For the "embarrassing ally," Kendrick, *St. James in Spain*, 118; echoed by García-Arenal and Rodríguez Mediano, "Jerónimo Román de la Higuera and the Lead Books of Sacromonte," 264; Harris, *From Muslim to Christian Granada*, 176, n. 21.
16. Medina Conde, *El fingido Dextro*, v.
17. Ibid., iii.
18. Martínez de la Escalera, "Jerónimo de la Higuera . . . culto de San Tirso," 80.
19. Medina Conde, *El fingido Dextro*, iv.
20. Ibid., xiii.
21. Ibid.
22. Ochoa y Ronna, ed., *Epistolario español* II, 46; and see García-Arenal and Rodríguez Mediano, "Jerónimo Román de la Higuera and the Lead Books of Sacromonte."
23. Ochoa y Ronna, ed., *Epistolario español* II, 47.
24. On the manifold dangers of prophetic speech, Kagan, *Lucrecia's Dreams*.
25. Harris, *From Muslim to Christian Granada*; Martínez Medina, "El Sacromonte de Granada y los discursos inmaculistas postridentinas."
26. For this hypothesis, García-Arenal, "El entorno de los plomos: Historiografía y linaje," 57, who considers it plausible that the conversos might have funded Higuera's efforts, as does Gil, "Judíos y conversos"; ———, "*Berenjeneros*."
27. Alcocer, *Hystoria*, xiiij. These attempts to link Spain to ancient Israel were part of a broader desire to imagine Spain as a new Jerusalem; see Beaver, "From Jerusalem to Toledo."
28. Ramírez de Prado, ed., *Iuliani Petri . . . Chronicon*, 8, 211, 428 and *Adversaria*, 8, 134, 424, 431.
29. Arias Montano, *Commentaria in duodecim prophetas*, 463–64. Montano was key in

diffusing these and other notions, but he was not their originator, as many authors mistakenly assert. Ayaso Martínez, "Antigüedad y excelencia de la diáspora"; Gil, "Berenjeneros," 136–38. For the relative absence of Jews in actual late antique hagiographic sources, Castillo Maldonado, "Judíos, conversos y relapsos."

30. Ibid., *Adversaria*, 14–16; and Gil, "Judíos y conversos," 22–24, who provides a useful overview of Higuera's treatment of the Jews, but commits a number of factual errors. For another example, see the spurious epitaph from the Valencian city of Murviedo, which seemed to confirm that an agent of King Solomon had come to the western edge of the Mediterranean to collect tribute from his Iberian subjects, cited by both Alcocer and Higuera, which, it seems certain, had its origins in late fifteenth-century rabbinical writings. Alcocer, *Hystoria*, xv; Martínez Marina, "Antigüedades hispano-hebreas," 379–418.
31. Martínez Marina, "Antigüedades hispano-hebreas," 443–44.
32. Nirenberg, "Mass Conversion and Genealogical Mentalities," 28–29.
33. Alcocer, *Hystoria*, xiiij (verso).
34. Ramírez de Prado, ed., *Iuliani Petri . . . Chronicon*, 555 and *Adversaria*, 111, 434, 474–75.
35. Ibid., 11; and, for a Spanish translation of the letter, Gil, "Judíos y conversos," 28–29.
36. BN Ms. 2343, 6r–7r; and Borchardt, "The Topos of Critical Rejection."
37. BN Ms. 2343, 6r–7r.
38. Medina Conde, *El fingido Dextro*, xxix.
39. PL 31, col. 71; for an earlier articulation of this tradition, Turner, "Jews and Judaism in Peter Auriol's *Sentences* Commentary."
40. Ramírez de Prado, ed., *Iuliani Petri . . . Chronicon*, 86–89, and see 39, 50; and discussion in Gil, "Judíos y conversos," 33–34.
41. Román de la Higuera, "Epistola"; Olds, "The 'False Chronicles,' Cardinal Baronio, and Sacred History in Counter-Reformation Spain." On the trial and cult, Grieve, *Eve of Spain*, 98–104, 227; Haliczer, "The Jew as Witch"; Longhurst, *The Age of Torquemada*, 142–54. Cf. Gil's erroneous assertion that Higuera purposefully silenced the long history of blood libel in order to avoid reminding Toledans "of the events of the Niño de la Guardia" due to his larger aim to rehabilitate Jews and conversos in the eye of most Spaniards. Gil, "Judíos y conversos," 32.
42. BN Ms. 6149, 204.
43. Caro Baroja, *Las falsificaciones*, 166.
44. Brunel, "Versions espagnole, provençale et française de la lettre du Christ tombée du ciel"; Reinhardt and Santiago-Otero, *Biblioteca bíblica ibérica medieval*, 47–48; *Repertorio de historia de las ciencias eclesiásticas en España* I: 72–73.
45. Ramírez de Prado, ed., *Luitprandi subdiaconi toletani*, 529–30. This appendix does not appear in the 1635 edition. On Licinianus, Aldea Vaquero, Marín Martínez, and Vives Gatell, *Diccionario de historia eclesiástica de España* II, 1296–97.
46. Cited by Madoz, *Liciniano de Cartagena*, 71. The other letters considered genuine include a letter in which Aurasius, a seventh-century archbishop of Toledo, excommunicated Fraga, governor (*comes*) of Toledo, for having protected the city's Jews,

and another from Fructuosus, bishop of Braga, to the Visigothic king Reccesvinth, in which the prelate urged the king to pardon rebellious nobles in spite of his father's vow never to do so. The three false letters are between Archaricus and Elipandus; see Gil Fernández, *Miscellanea Wisigothica*, 49; Gil, "Judíos y conversos," 32; and, for the letter from Fructuosus, Vega, "Una carta auténtica de San Fructuoso."

47. Cf. Blair, "Note Taking."
48. PL 31, cols. 239–41 (Segovia), 469–71 (Osuna and Utrera).
49. Baronio, *Martyrologium Romanum (1597)*, 567–68, which was nearly identical to the entry in Usuard and Molanus, *Vsvardi Martyrologivm (1583)*, 181r.
50. PL 136, cols. 1149C-D. To retrace Higuera's steps in arriving at this identification, see notes on Victoria compiled from various historical martyrologies in RAH 9/749, 24v–25r.
51. Román de la Higuera, *Memorial . . . a la villa de Touarra*.
52. PL 163, col. 1154B; and see BN Ms. 1638, 206r–211r, to which Portocarrero also added marginal notes.
53. Quoted in Cirot, *Mariana historien*, 60–61.
54. Baronio, *Martyrologium Romanum (1587)*, 374.
55. PL 31, cols. 337 (Blanes), 461–62 (Urgabonae).
56. Pancorbo, *Relacion*.
57. Bilches, *Santos y santuarios*; Rus Puerta, *Historia eclesiastica*.
58. Francisco de Rus Puerta, "Obispos de Jaen, y segunda parte de la historia eclesiastica deste reino y obispado," BN Ms. 5737, 250r, 313r; and Olds, "Visions of the Holy"; ———, "The Ambiguities of the Holy"; Sabalete Moya, "El Sacromonte de Arjona"; Vincent-Cassy, "Los santos re-fundadores."
59. See collected testimony in Adarve de Acuña and Saro, *Relacion y memorial*.
60. For the reinterpretation of Roman Hispania through the prism of emerging nation-states by Spanish chroniclers of the Indies, Lupher, *Romans in a New World*; on the rise of French national histories in roughly the same period, Huppert, *The Idea of Perfect History*.

CHAPTER 5. THE DEBUT OF THE CHRONICLES

1. The passage, from the manuscript third volume of Alcázar, *Chrono-historia de la Compañia de Jesus en la provincia de Toledo*, is cited by Cirot, *Mariana historien*, 227, n. 3.
2. Gil, "Judíos y conversos"; Hitchcock, "The *falsos chronicones* and the Mozarabs"; Martínez de la Escalera, "Jerónimo de la Higuera . . . culto de San Tirso."
3. Grafton, *Forgers and Critics*, 59.
4. Calderón, ed., *Fragmentum Chronici*, n.p.
5. Lukács, *Catalogi personarum provinciae Austriae Societatis Iesu* I: 800; Schmidl, *Historiae Societatis Jesu Provinciae Bohemiae* I, 357.
6. Grafton, *Forgers and Critics*, 59.
7. Portocarrero, *Libro de la descencion*, "Al lector," n.p.

8. Antonio, *Censura*, 9; Caro, ed., *Flavi Luci Dextri*, unpaginated preface.
9. Broggio, *I gesuiti ai tempi di Claudio Acquaviva*; O'Malley, *The First Jesuits*; Thomas, *A House Divided*, 121–22.
10. Loaysa Girón, ed., *Chronicon . . . Isidori*.
11. Ehlers, "Juan Bautista Pérez and the *Plomos*"; Fernández Collado, *La catedral de Toledo en el siglo XVI*, 93.
12. The manuscript was lost in 1938 during the Spanish Civil War; an inventory was made in the eighteenth century by Villanueva, *Viage literario* III, 196–220, 309–13.
13. Cardelle de Hartmann and Collins, eds., *Victoris Tunnunensis Chronicon*, 60–65, 93.
14. Villanueva, *Viage literario* III, 198.
15. Grafton, *Joseph Scaliger*.
16. Cardelle de Hartmann and Collins, eds., *Victoris Tunnunensis Chronicon*, 40.
17. Schottus, ed., *Hispaniae illustratae* IV, 117, 152, 212. Fragments of these texts had appeared in pre-Schott editions; see Russell, "Chronicles of Medieval Spain."
18. Grafton, *The Footnote*, 148–89; ———, "Church History in Early Modern Europe."
19. Van Liere, "Renaissance Chroniclers," 139–41.
20. Morales, *Antigüedades* I, lxxviii.
21. Ibid., 2.
22. Ibid., 4–73.
23. Stenhouse, *Reading Inscriptions and Writing Ancient History*, 124–28; and, for a similar shift for coins, Cunnally, *Images of the Illustrious*.
24. Morales, *Antigüedades* I: 2; and for similar reflections, ibid., lxxix–lxxx.
25. For the implications of the debate over Hebrew origins and place-names, Beaver, "A Holy Land for the Catholic Monarchy"; Reyre, "Topónimos hebreos y memoria."
26. BN Ms. 1639, 2r; and, for Agustín on coins and inscriptions as more trustworthy, Mitchell, "Archaeology and Romance in Renaissance Italy," 457.
27. BN Ms. 1639, 2r.
28. These forged *fueros* were later cited by defenders of the kingdom of Aragon's legal immunities: Sánchez Alonso, *Historia de la historiografía española* II, 38.
29. Antonio, *Censura*, 686.
30. Ibid., 687.
31. Fuente and Alzog, eds., *Historia eclesiástica de España* III, 76–77.
32. Hernando Sobrino, "Cuando la fama"; and see ———, "De parroquia en parroquia."
33. Mayer Olivé, "Ciriaco de Ancona, Annio da Viterbo y la historiografía hispánica," 354.
34. Hernando Sobrino, "Higuera y la epigrafía de Ibahernando," 189.
35. Ibid.
36. Andrés Escapa, "Historia de unos papeles," 31.
37. Ramírez de Prado, ed., *Luitprandi subdiaconi toletani*, 515–32; the letters did not appear in the chronicle's 1635 edition.
38. Martz, *A Network of Converso Families*, 74.
39. Antonio, *Censura*, 529.
40. For a contrary opinion, Godoy Alcántara, *Historia crítica*, 17–18, n. 1.
41. Kendrick, *St. James in Spain*, 117.
42. Godoy Alcántara, *Historia crítica*, 36, 130–31.

43. Andrés, "El helenismo de . . . Covarrubias," 267.
44. Carlos Villamarín, *Las antigüedades de Hispania*, 154–59; Linehan, *History and the Historians of Medieval Spain*, 357–77.
45. Villanueva, *Viage literario* III, 219, 322–26. For comparison, see Erasmus's method in preparing his editions of the works of Augustine, Visser, *Reading Augustine in the Reformation*, 29–45.
46. Villanueva, *Viage literario* III, 295.
47. Goldgar, *Impolite Learning*, 12–33; for a Spanish example, Lazure, "To Dare Fame."
48. Antonio, *Censura*, 686–92; and see Andrés, "El helenismo de . . . Covarrubias," 267, 282.
49. RAH 9/1013, 247r, and 9/744, 100r–108r.
50. Hunter, *John Aubrey and the Realm of Learning*; Woolf, *Social Circulation of the Past*.
51. Inasmuch as Higuera and his peers were not overtly influenced by Erasmus—whose works had been banned by the Spanish Inquisition in the mid-sixteenth century—nor given to contemplating the nature of friendship, this is not the "religious republic of letters" described by Furey, *Erasmus, Contarini, and the Religious Republic of Letters*.
52. Grafton, "A Sketch Map of a Lost Continent"; ———, *The Footnote*, 148–89.
53. "Lugares santos de Toledo con algunas circunstancias de las muchas que ay en cada uno en y[g]l[esi]a mayor," RAH 9/1013, 364r–368v.
54. For Álvares's letter to Higuera, RAH 9/1013, 313r–328v, and a letter from Higuera to the archbishop of Braga (RAH 9/1013, 41r–42v); for Olivenza, Sandoval, *Tuy*, 11. For Antist, BN Ms. 1638, 193v; for Castilla, BN Ms. 6939, 128v; for Acevedo, Hernando Sobrino, "Higuera y la epigrafía de Ibahernando."
55. RAH 9/1017, 109r–110v.
56. RAH 9/1013, 279r–285v.
57. Ibid., 287r–88v.
58. See, respectively, RAH 9/744, 52r–88r, ibid., 109r–112v, RAH 9/751, 58r–61v, and RAH 9/749, 25r–26v.
59. Hernando Sobrino, "Higuera y la epigrafía de Ibahernando."
60. BN Ms. 6939, 129v.
61. For Cádiz, which is almost definitely Higuera's, RAH 9/1013, 55r–56v. Where the name and addressee is missing, as here, I have tentatively identified the recipient as Higuera based on internal clues and proximity to other *Higueriana* in the collection at hand. For Valencia, BN Ms. 1638, 193v; for Canaries, RAH 9/744, 27r–36v. Additional letters concerned the history of the Order of the Hospitalliers (9/1013, 75r–76v); the history of the Templars in Valencia (ibid., 277r–278v); the monastery of San Pedro de Cardeña, the burial place of El Cid (ibid., 354r–357v); the opening of the sepulcher of King Wamba (ibid., 362–63); and, finally, San Pedro de Baeza, in a letter from a physician named Juan de Almaçan (RAH 9/744, 152ff).
62. For his rendition of Greek, BN Ms. 6939, 179v; for Hebrew, ibid., 54v.
63. The mention of Las Casas is in a letter of October 1600 in Medina Conde, *El fingido Dextro*, xlv; for Urrea, BN Ms. 8194, 399r. On Las Casas, Benítez Sánchez-Blanco, "De Pablo a Saulo"; Rodríguez Mediano and García-Arenal, "De Diego de Urrea a Marcos Dobelio." Further research is likely to illuminate more connections between

Higuera and the Andalusian scholars in the service of Archbishop Castro; for an important start, García-Arenal and Rodríguez Mediano, "Jerónimo Román de la Higuera and the Lead Books of Sacromonte."

64. Backus, *Historical Method and Confessional Identity*, 253–325; ———, "Renaissance Attitudes to New Testament Apocryphal Writings." For the particularly critical stance of Scaliger, Grafton, *Joseph Scaliger* II, 685–702.

CHAPTER 6. IN DEFENSE OF LOCAL SAINTS

1. Usuard and Molanus, *Vsvardi Martyrologivm* (1583); *Martyrologium Romanum, ad novam Kalendarij rationem . . . restitutum*; Baronio, *Martyrologium Romanum* (1597).
2. Antist, *De inventione sacri corporis . . . Anglinae*, n.p. On Antist, Smoller, "From Authentic Miracles to a Rhetoric of Authenticity"; "Vicente Justiniano Antist," at *Biblioteca Virtual del Humanismo Español*, compiled by the Institute of Classical Studies at the Universidad Carlos III de Madrid, http://portal.uc3m.es/portal/page/portal/inst_lucio_anneo_seneca/bases_datos/bvhe/biblioteca/a_b/vicente_justiniano_antist (accessed November 24, 2014).
3. Higuera mentioned the correspondence in the *Ecclesiastical History of Spain*, BN Ms. 1638, 193v.
4. Ramírez de Prado, ed., *Iuliani Petri . . . Chronicon*, 26 (n. 85); Tamayo de Vargas, ed., *Luitprandi . . . Chronicon* (year 960), 79–80; this passage does not appear in the 1640 edition.
5. San Cecilio, *Historia de la vida y martyrio de Don Fray Pedro de Valencia*, vii–viii.
6. Argaíz, *Población eclesiástica de España [. . .] tomo primero, parte segunda*; Haubert (paginated separately) 212; ———, *Población eclesiástica de España . . . Continuada*; Liberatus (paginated separately), 139.
7. Villanueva, *Viage literario* II, 48–49; Torrents and Andrés, *Glorias del Carmelo* II, 81.
8. Guazzelli, "Sacred History"; Sawilla, *Antiquarianismus, Hagiographie und Historie*.
9. Ditchfield, *Liturgy, Sanctity and History*; Van Liere, Ditchfield, and Louthan, eds., *Sacred History*.
10. Backus, *Historical Method and Confessional Identity*; Polman, *L'élément historique*.
11. Ditchfield, *Liturgy, Sanctity and History*, 23–67; Guazzelli, "Cesare Baronio e il *Martyrologium Romanum*," 47–89.
12. Ditchfield, "Tridentine Worship and the Cult of Saints"; ———, "Historia Magistra Sanctitatis."
13. ———, *Liturgy, Sanctity and History*, 60–66, 111–12; Grafton, *Bring Out Your Dead*, 56–57.
14. Joassart, "Un lettre inédite d'Aubert Le Mire à Héribert Rosweyde."
15. Baronio, *Martyrologium Romanum* (1597), 456–58 (October 9).
16. Borromeo, "Il Cardinale Cesare Baronio e la corona spagnola"; Pérez Villanueva, "Baronio y la Inquisición española."
17. Baronio, *Annales ecclesiastici* I (year 51, no. 54) 395, quoted in Cochrane, *Historians and Historiography*, 460–61.

18. Ibáñez de Segovia, *Discurso histórico por el patronato de San Frutos*, iii–v.
19. Ditchfield, *Liturgy, Sanctity and History*, 57; Godoy Alcántara, *Historia crítica*, 38–40; Rowe, *Saint and Nation*, 43. For Gallican irritation with Baronio, Davidson, "Divine Guidance and the Use of Sources."
20. Quoted in Ditchfield, *Liturgy, Sanctity and History*, 59.
21. Portions of Santa María's lost history of Arjona, written sometime between 1628 and 1649, survive in copies made by Martín de Ximena Jurado in the mid-1600s in RAH, 9/3572, 5356v. On Santa María, who also weighed in on the copatronage controversy, Rowe, *Saint and Nation*, 157.
22. Santa María, *Historia general profética*, 235. For the long history of polemic around the Carmelites' claims, Kendrick, *St. James in Spain*; and, beyond Spain, Jotischky, *The Carmelites and Antiquity*.
23. Santa María, *Historia*.
24. ———, *Apologia del tomo primero*.
25. RAH, 9/3572, 5356v.
26. Santa María, *Apologia del tomo primero*, 310.
27. Internal clues identify the author as Antist; RAH 9/751, 19v–20r.
28. On Soria (1560–1600), Sommervogel, Backer, and Carayon, *Bibliothèque de la Compagnie de Jésus* VII, 1391.
29. Baronio, *Epistolae et opuscula* I: 346; for the rest of Soria's correspondence with Baronio, see ibid., I: 243–54, 320–54, 366–67.
30. Van Liere, "The Missionary and the Moorslayer"; ———, "Renaissance Chroniclers and the Apostolic Origins of Spanish Christianity."
31. Ditchfield, "Tridentine Worship and the Cult of Saints."
32. Printed at the beginning of *Proprium sanctorum hispanorum, qui generaliter in Hispania celebrantur, ad formam officij novi redactu[m]*.
33. According to Mazurek, the brief was issued in order to resolve confusions caused by earlier exceptions granted to Spain by Pius V under pressure from Philip II; see Mazurek, "Réforme tridentine et culte des saints en Espagne"; Borromeo, "Gregorio XIII"; Dandelet, *Spanish Rome*.
34. Gélis, "Le culte de Santa Librada."
35. Díaz Tena, "*La vida de Santa Librada* y su fuente medieval."
36. *La vida y martirio de la bienaventurada Sancta Librada virgen y martyr*, n.p. For the other eight sister-virgin-martyrs, Poska, *Women and Authority in Early Modern Spain*, 208–10; Vincent-Cassy, *Les saintes vierges et martyres*, 256–62, 503–8.
37. In the printed edition of the letter, the phrases regarding Wilgefort and Liberata are separated by a period: "Adde, quod D. Vvilgefortis Lusitana Virgo, & Martyr est. S. Liberata soror SS. Quiteriae, Basilicae, & aliarum, quas genuit C. Attilius Lusitaniae Regulus (in vulgatis Codicis perperam ponitur Cattilius, conjunctis litteris, quae debuissent alias esse separatae)." Yet the awkward syntax, combined with the fact that Higuera equated Liberata with Wilgefort elsewhere, suggests that the two sentences originally may have read as one: "Add that Lady Wilgefort, a Portuguese virgin and martyr, is Saint Liberata . . . " This remains a hypothesis, since Higuera's original letter,

which Albericius would have consulted in Rome's Biblioteca Vallicelliana, has not been located. For a translation of the letter, Olds, "The 'False Chronicles,' Cardinal Baronio, and Sacred History in Counter-Reformation Spain," appendix A.
38. Baronio, *Martyrologium Romanum* (1597), 34 (Liberata), 321–22 (Wilgefort).
39. Friesen, *The Female Crucifix*; Gessler, *La légende de sainte Wilgeforte ou Ontcommer*; Nightlinger, "The Female *Imitatio Christi*."
40. Román de la Higuera, "Epistola."
41. PL 31, col. 321; Ramírez de Prado, ed., *Iuliani Petri . . . Chronicon*, 21, 25, 113 and *Adversaria*, 54, 84, 125, and "Varia carmina" in her honor, 157–58; see Nightlinger, "The Female *Imitatio Christi*," 310.
42. Usuard and Molanus, *Vsvardi Martyrologivm* (1583) (July 20), n.p.
43. Quoted in González Chantos y Ullauri, *Santa Librada . . . vindicada*, 85.
44. Ibid., 91–93.
45. Sandoval, *Tuy*, 35r–44v.
46. González Chantos y Ullauri, *Santa Librada . . . vindicada*, 101; Vincent-Cassy, *Les saintes vierges et martyres*, 192–94.
47. González Chantos y Ullauri, *Santa Librada . . . vindicada*, 98.
48. Martínez Gómez-Gordo, *Leyendas*, 13–15, 21.
49. This image is printed in Olds, "The 'False Chronicles,' Cardinal Baronio, and Sacred History."
50. González Chantos y Ullauri, *Santa Librada . . . vindicada*.
51. Martínez Gómez-Gordo, *Leyendas*, 7–8.
52. Vázquez (1549–1604) studied at the Jesuit collegium in Belmonte, and entered the Society of Jesus in 1569, seven years after Higuera. He taught theology for the Jesuits in Alcalá, Rome, Ocaña, and Madrid. Domínguez and O'Neill, eds., *Diccionario histórico* IV, 3912–13; Sommervogel, *Bibliothèque de la Compagnie de Jésus* III, 737–40.
53. Cavadini, *The Last Christology of the West*; Chandler, "Heresy and Empire."
54. Boynton, *Silent Music*, 74–77, 90–98; O'Callaghan, *A History of Medieval Spain*, 186–87.
55. Mariana and Miñana, *Historia general de España*, 216–17 (book 7, ch. 8).
56. Vázquez, *De cultu adorationis*, 271r–v.
57. Hitchcock, *Mozarabs*, 111.
58. PL 136, col. 1091; and, for another version of the story, Cirot, "Documents sur le faussaire Higuera," 93.
59. PL 136, cols. 971C–D, 1088B, and 1093A.
60. For their correspondence, Sandoval, *Primera parte de las fundaciones*, 11r, 18r, 43r.
61. "Prudencio de Sandoval," in Aldea Vaquero, Marín Martínez, and Vives Gatell, *Diccionario de historia eclesiástica de España* IV, 2174–79; Kagan, *Clio and the Crown*, 93, 192.
62. Sandoval, *Tuy*, 11v; also 26r, 34r–v, discussed by Godoy Alcántara, *Historia crítica*, 166–69.
63. Sandoval, *Historias de Idacio Obispo*, 108–11.

64. Candel Crespo, *Un obispo postridentino*, 75 ff.
65. Dávila Toledo, *La vida de San Vidal*. A manuscript of the vita is among Higuera's papers in RAH 9/751, 228r–231.
66. On converting Vitalis and other anonymous relics into actual saints, Harris, "A known holy body, with an inscription and a name."
67. Fuente, *Historia eclesiástica* I, 51.
68. PL 31, col. 111.
69. Burriel Rodrigo, *Un bibliotecario del siglo XVI*; Godoy Alcántara, *Historia crítica*, 170–71; Solís de Santos, "En torno al 'Epistolario de Justo Lipsio y los españoles.'"
70. Burriel Rodrigo, *Un bibliotecario del siglo XVI*, 23–30; Martínez de la Escalera, "Jerónimo de la Higuera... culto de San Tirso," 73.
71. *Dubitavi: An constet Ecclesiam Beatae Mariae Virginis de Columna, seu (ut vulgo dicitur) de Pilari fuisse antiquitus Cathedralem?*, BN Ms. 6712, 15–16. Over the following decades a number of decisions trickled out of the Rota, mostly favorable to El Pilar's claims, including a 1630 decision in which the tribunal acknowledged Pilar's "signs of cathedralicity." For La Seo, this did not resolve the matter. See Burriel Rodrigo, *Un bibliotecario del siglo XVI*, 40–41; Fuente, *Historia eclesiástica*, 51; Godoy Alcántara, *Historia crítica*, 305.
72. Murillo, *Fundación milagrosa... del Pilar*.
73. On Álvares de Lousada, Bouza Álvarez, *Imagen y propaganda*, 36, 52–53; Deswarte-Rosa, "Le voyage épigraphique."
74. On these saints, Vincent-Cassy, *Les saintes vierges et martyres*.
75. Pennotto, *Historia tripartita*, 169, citing a now-lost *Defensorio lectionarij antiqui seguntinae ecclesiae pro officio proprio Sanctae Liberatae* by Álvares de Lousada.
76. RAH 9/1013, 37r ff.
77. Quoted in Sandoval, *Antigüedad... de Tuy*, 41v; Antonio, *Censura*, 68.
78. PL 31, cols. 110, 127; Godoy Alcántara, *Historia crítica*, 177–79.
79. Fuente, *Historia eclesiástica* I, 56–57; III, 161; Van Liere, "Renaissance Chroniclers and the Apostolic Origins of Spanish Christianity," 134, 139.
80. For Álvares to Higuera, RAH 9/1013, 313r–328v.
81. Robles Corvalán, *Historia... Cruz de Carabaca*.
82. Ibid., discussed by García-Arenal and Rodríguez Mediano, "Jerónimo Román de la Higuera and the Lead Books of Sacromonte." For medieval traditions of the cross, González Blanco, "La leyenda de la Cruz de Caravaca."
83. "Tratado del linage de Higuera" RAH, 9/5566, 16r.
84. Román de la Higuera, *Memorial... a la villa de Touarra*, BN, VE 135–32; and see Baronio, *Martyrologium Romanum* (1597), 305–6 (July 9), 567–68 (December 23).
85. Román de la Higuera, *Memorial... a la villa de Touarra*. For Cascales's history, Vicent y Portillo, ed., *Biblioteca histórica de Cartagena* I: 7–242.
86. Causino, *La corte divina, ó palacio celestial*, 280.
87. Quintanadueñas, *Santos... de Toledo*, 407–10; Martín Vázquez Siruela, "Juizio que hizo... del Chronicón de Flavio Dextro" (Marquette University, Raynor Archives, Ms. BR1025.V39 1700z), 12–15.

88. "Reliquias que ay en la villa de Torrejon," RAH 9/1013, 290r–291v; "Relacion verdadera de algunas cosas notables y dignas de consideracion y quenta de las islas Canarias," RAH 9/744, 27r–36v.
89. RAH, 9/744, 342ff and RAH 9/1013, 267–70, respectively.
90. Both the information on the *beaterio* of Santo Espiritu "al torno de las carretas de Toledo," and the response regarding Santa María del Prado, in Pozuelo, are tentatively Higuera's (RAH 9/1013, 45r, and 77r, respectively); the Plasencia material is Higuera's (RAH 9/751, 332–47), as are other letters regarding Palencia benefices (RAH 9/744); questions about the Templars in Spain, with Higuera's annotations at the end, appear in RAH 9/1013, 277r–278v.
91. Griggs, "The Changing Face of Erudition."
92. Christian, *Apparitions*; ———, *Local Religion in Sixteenth-Century Spain*; Mundy, *The Mapping of New Spain*.
93. "Ynstituyçion y memoria de las grandezas y cosas señaladas de la villa de Tendilla," RAH 9/1013, 53r–54v.
94. RAH 9/1013, 337r–338r.
95. For the former, ibid., 279–85; and for the latter, which is tentatively Higuera's, ibid., 306–12.
96. Morán Turina and Rodríguez Ruiz, *El legado de la antigüedad*, 33–36.
97. PL 136, col. 1079.
98. Cited by Antonio, *Censura*, 66–67.
99. RAH 9/1013, 301v.
100. I would like to thank William A. Christian Jr. for directing my attention to this source, "Historia de Nra Sra del monasterio de San Pablo de los Montes," RAH 9/1013 (formerly N-7), 294–301. For an excerpt, Christian, *Religiosidad local en la España de Felipe II*, 277–98, 340, n. 2; and see a parallel passage on the nuns, as well as a hymn in their honor, in Higuera's *santoral*, RAH 9/1013, 177v.
101. Antonio, *Censura*, 66–67.
102. Ibid., 66–67. On Ajofrín and Marjaliza, Jiménez de Gregorio, *Diccionario de los pueblos de la Provincia de Toledo* I, 432; Madoz, *Diccionario geográfico-estadístico-histórico*, XI, 238–39. For a more recent account, see Redondo, "Leyendas, creencias y ritos en torno a Santa Quiteria."
103. "Yo tube una abuela que ha que murio 20 a[ñ]os y murio de 105 que o bien 125 al presente la qual me dijo que aver oydo a sus padres y abuelos, que Sant Ilefonso nacio en esa casa que testifican de mas de 200 a[ñ]os. Y no como de cosa nueva sino vieja y que de muy atras fue son corriente. Esto he dicho para que se entienda como no es la tradiçion de 30 o 40 a[ñ]os sino de tiempo immemorial y semejantes tradiçiones son de mas auctoridad en lo que tratan que algunos historiadores. Por que es opinion de muchos que dicen una cosa misma no en un tiempo sino en differentes tiempos y por eso tiene mas auctoridad que el dicho de 4 o çinco historiadoradores [sic]. Los quales aunque sean muy auctorizados no son dichos de mas que 4 o de seis testigos. Mas en la tradiçion ay dichos de una çiudad que de comun consentim[iment]o sin replica ni contradiçion ni variedad de pareçeres dice lo mismo y por esto se dijo que vox populi vox dei." RAH 9/1013, 369r (emphases in the original).

104. Ibid., 369r–v.
105. Ditchfield, "Tridentine Worship and the Cult of Saints"; Veraja, *La beatificazione*.
106. "Nec audiendi qui volent dicere, vox populi, vox Dei, cum tumultuositas vulgi semper insaniae proxima sit." Gallacher, "Vox Populi, Vox Dei."
107. Boas, *Vox Populi*; and see Boureau, "L'adage," 1072–73.
108. Gallacher, "Vox Populi, Vox Dei," 19.
109. Montaigne, in his essay "Of Glory," cited by Boas, *Vox Populi*, 31–32.
110. Green, "On the Attitude Toward the *Vulgo* in the Spanish *Siglo de Oro*."
111. Norelli, "The Authority Attributed to the Early Church"; Polman, *L'élément historique*, 284–309, 516–17.
112. Cano, *L'autorità*, xiv and 21–22.
113. Ibid., 65–66.
114. Ibid., 164; for a cogent contextualization of these and other critiques of De Voragine, Reames, *The Legenda Aurea: A Reexamination*, 44–69.
115. Cano, *L'autorità*, 166.
116. Ibid., 111–12.
117. Morales, *La coronica general*, unpaginated prologue.
118. Ibid., 208r; and see Van Liere, "Renaissance Chroniclers and the Apostolic Origins of Spanish Christianity."
119. Morales, *La coronica general*, 212v.
120. Ibid., 215r.
121. Aldrete, *Del origen y principio de la lengva castellana*, quoted in Woolard, "Bernardo de Aldrete, Humanist and *laminario*," 454.
122. For similar sentiments from the Spanish-Flemish Jesuit Martín del Río and his teacher, Heribert Rosweyde, see Machielsen, "Heretical Saints and Textual Discernment," 131.
123. Constable, "Forgery and Plagiarism," 25. For patristic sources on the "medicinal" or strategic lie, see Ehrman, *Forgery and Counterforgery*, 542-48.
124. Ibid., 26. See also Jotischky, *The Carmelites and Antiquity*, 320.
125. Southern, *Western Society and the Church in the Middle Ages*, 93, cited by Constable, "Forgery and Plagiarism," 20.
126. Constable, "Forgery and Plagiarism," 20.
127. Jotischky, *The Carmelites and Antiquity*, 6–7; Quantin, "Reason and Reasonableness."
128. Pullapilly, *Caesar Baronius*, 41.
129. Baronio, *Martyrologium Romanum* (1597), 395 (August 31). See Ditchfield, *Liturgy, Sanctity and History*, 98; Mezzazappa, "Cesidio e Rufino 'martiri.'"
130. Baronio, *Annales ecclesiastici* IV (year 324, n. cxviii), cited by Pullapilly, *Caesar Baronius*, 167–68. Baronio's stance on the *Donation* is often misunderstood or misstated, as noted by Bowersock, "Peter and Constantine," 13–14, notes 6, 7, 36, 38. A similar desire to defend the papacy seems to have motivated Baronio's attack on the papal bull known as *Monarchia Siciliae*, which granted the Hapsburgs dominion over Sicily, but which is, in fact, considered authentic. Pullapilly, *Caesar Baronius*, 169.
131. Quantin, "Reason and Reasonableness," 414.

132. BN Ms. 6939, 132r; and see Boon, "Clement of Alexandria, Wookey Hole, and the Corycian Cave."
133. For "counter-history," Funkenstein, *Perceptions of Jewish History*, 22–49.
134. For the celebration of the birth of the future Philip IV in 1605, which refers to Toledo as New Rome, *Relaciones de las fiestas que la imperial ciudad de Toledo hizo al nacimiento del príncipe N.S. Felipe IIII de este nombre*, Madrid, 1605, cited by Kagan, in "The Toledo of El Greco," 61. For examples in art and architecture, see Lleó Cañal, *Nueva Roma, mitología y humanismo en el Renacimiento sevillano*; Wunder, "Classical, Christian, and Muslim Remains."

CHAPTER 7. FLAWED TEXTS AND THE NEGOTIATION OF AUTHENTICITY

Epigraph. Jerome, *The Principal Works of St. Jerome*, 194 (Epist. 107:12).
1. Tamayo de Vargas, *Novedades antiguas*, "A los bien intencionados i doctos," n.p. For the relative value of the *ducado*, Fink de Backer, "Constructing Convents in Sixteenth-Century Castile."
2. Tamayo de Vargas, *Novedades antiguas*, prólogo.
3. Rodrigo Caro, "Defensa de los escritos de Flavio Lucio Dextro i Marco Maximo," BN Ms. 6712, 115r. On the duke, Brown and Kagan, "The Duke of Alcalá." For Pedro de Castro's copy, see Calero Palacios, *Abadía del Sacromonte*.
4. Cited by Martínez de la Escalera, "Jerónimo de la Higuera . . . culto de San Tirso," 73, 96.
5. Quoted in Antonio, *Censura de historias fabulosas*, 28–30; for Brouwer's 1608 inquiry to Jesuits in Spain and Germany, Martínez de la Escalera, "Jerónimo de la Higuera . . . culto de San Tirso," 96; Lapide, *Commentaria in acta apostolorum*, "Chronotaxis actuum apostolorum," 11. The search continued into the late seventeenth century; Godoy Alcántara, *Historia crítica*, 21–29.
6. Antonio, *Censura de historias fabulosas*, 529.
7. This remark has also survived only as hearsay from Daniel Papebroeck, who, in a 1671 letter, quoted Mariana's 1614 letter to Rosweyde. See Vilaplana, "Correspondencia de Papebroch," 331.
8. According to a 1668 letter from the Jesuit Tomás de León. Antonio, *Censura de historias fabulosas*, 672.
9. Escolano, *Decada primera de la historia de . . . Valencia*, col. 216.
10. "De Adventu B. Jacobi Apostoli in Hispaniam," in Mariana, *Joannis Marianae e Societate Jesu Tractatus VII*, 1–32.
11. Chaparro Gómez, "Notas sobre el 'De ortu et obitu patrum' seudoisidoriano"; Pérez González, "Juan de Mariana y su valoración de las crónicas medievales."
12. Escolano, *Decada primera de la historia de . . . Valencia*, col. 217.
13. Ibid., col. 222.
14. Ibid., cols. 220–21. For *defloratio* as part of the process of *compilatio*, Chazan, "Le méthode critique"; Guenée, "L'historien et la compilation." This particular *defloratio* was the same "primitive Dexter" Juan Bautista Pérez read in 1594, which later passed

to Nicolás Antonio and was printed as an appendix to his *Censura de historias fabulosas*, according to Godoy Alcántara, *Historia crítica*, 36.
15. Escolano, *Decada primera de la historia de . . . Valencia*, col. 224.
16. Ibid., col. 225. Charles V had been unhappy with Giovio's depictions of his campaigns: Kagan, *Clio and the Crown*, 86.
17. Quoted in Martínez Gil, "Religión e identidad urbana," 48–49.
18. Roa, *Santos Honorio, Eutichio, Estevan*, 1r–2r.
19. Bovon, "Beyond the Book of Acts."
20. Hiatt, *Making of Medieval Forgeries*, 14.
21. Fubini, "Humanism and Truth."
22. Hiatt, *Making of Medieval Forgeries*, 167. See also Black, "The Donation of Constantine"; Grafton, "Church History in Early Modern Europe," 6–7.
23. Rowe, *Saint and Nation*, 42–43.
24. For the conflagration that resulted, Quevedo Villegas, "Vida de San Pablo Apóstol," 461; Rowe, *Saint and Nation*, 162–63.
25. Murillo, *Fundación milagrosa . . . del Pilar*, quoted in Martínez Gil, "Religión e identidad urbana," 52.
26. Escolano, *Decada primera de la historia de . . . Valencia*, col. 220.
27. Ibid., col. 219; and, for Enoch's apocalyptic significance, Stephens, *Giants in Those Days*, 77–78.
28. Carrillo, *Historia del glorioso San Valero*, 169–70.
29. Ibid., 168.
30. "Advertencias, y respuestas a las obiecciones," in ibid., 3–16.
31. Maldonado, *Chronica universal*, 99r–v.
32. Ibid., 104r.
33. PL 31, col. 101.
34. Maldonado, *Chronica universal*, 101v.
35. Ibid., 99v.
36. Ibid., 92r–98r.
37. Stephens, "When Pope Noah Ruled the Etruscans," 216.
38. Genette, *Paratexts*; and see Smith and Wilson, eds., *Renaissance Paratexts*.
39. Calderón, ed., *Fragmentum chronici*, "Candido et aequo lectori," n.p. An alternate 1619 edition was instead dedicated to the city and *conselleres* of Barcelona, according to Palau y Dulcet, *Manual del librero hispanoamericano* II, 201.
40. Grafton, *Joseph Scaliger* II, 565.
41. Machielsen, "Heretical Saints and Textual Discernment: The Polemical Origins of the *Acta Sanctorum* (1643–1940)."
42. Pedro Díaz de Ribas, "Patronazgo de Sanct Hiscio por la Villa de Tariffa," BN Ms. 1686, 11v.
43. Tamayo de Vargas, *Novedades antiguas*, 2r–v; and for his other works, Menéndez y Pelayo, *Biblioteca de traductores españoles* IV: 276–83.
44. Tamayo de Vargas, *Novedades antiguas*, n.p.
45. Ibid., n.p. On Zúñiga, Elliott, *Count-Duke of Olivares*, 38.
46. Caro, *Antigüedades y principado de la ciudad de Sevilla*; ———, *La canción a las*

ruinas de Itálica; for biographical details, Gómez Canseco, "Rodrigo Caro: Entre libros y amigos."

47. Caro, ed., *Flavi Luci Dextri*, n.p. On the importance of commentary as a bridge between the reader and the text, Enenkel and Nellen, eds., *Neo-Latin Commentaries*, 3–14.
48. Calderón, ed., *Fragmentum chronici*, 20–21.
49. Caro, ed., *Flavi Luci Dextri*, 57r–v ("Hunc locum misere foedatum ex Plinio, Tacito, & Martyr. Romano in suum pristinum decorem restituo"). Erasmus quoted in Brady and Olin, eds., *The Edition of St. Jerome*, xvii.
50. Bivar entered the Cistercian order in 1599, and was abbot of the Leonese monastery of San Esteban de Nogales until his Roman sojourn. Antonio, *Biblioteca hispana nueva*, v. I, 409–10; Bivar, ed., *Marci Maximi*, "Autoris vita," n.p.; Muñiz, *Biblioteca cisterciense española*, 49.
51. Stephens, "Complex Pseudonymity," 696.
52. Grafton, "Church History in Early Modern Europe."
53. "Denys L'Aréopagite (Le Pseudo-)," in Viller et al., *Dictionnaire de spiritualité* III, 244–64; Cochrane, *Historians and Historiography*, 460.
54. PL 31, col. 305C.
55. Ibid., cols. 112C–115C, 253C.
56. Bivar, ed., *Fl. Lucii Dextri . . . Chronicon*, xxviij. On this trope, Pabel, *Herculean Labours*; Rice, *Saint Jerome in the Renaissance*.
57. Bivar, ed., *Fl. Lucii Dextri . . . Chronicon*, xxix–xxxi.
58. Márquez, *Origen de los frayles ermitaños de la Orden de San Augustin*, 171–87, citing PL 31, col. 539; and see Jotischky, *The Carmelites and Antiquity*, 263–73.
59. Pennotto, *Historia tripartita*, 170; and see Quantin, "Reason and Reasonableness."
60. Pennotto, *Historia tripartita*, 171. Álvares was responding to doubts about Dexter's chronicle in a text called *Convenientia monacharum dominicarum*, which I have been unable to identify.
61. Bivar, ed., *Fl. Lucii Dextri . . . Chronicon*, 468–94.
62. PL 31, col. 239; Bravo de Mendoça, *Invencion felissima*.
63. Muñiz, *Biblioteca cisterciense española*, 49.
64. Baronio, *Martyrologium Romanum* (1587), 374–75; and see Olds, "The Ambiguities of the Holy."
65. See the 1628 letter from Moscoso to Francisco Santa María (BN Ms. 4033, 170r), and from Bernardo de Aldrete to Moscoso's agent in Rome (ibid, 20v). These authors do not seem to have recognized the late antique distinction between *acta* and *passiones*, for which see Delehaye, *L'œuvre des bollandistes*.
66. PL 31, col. 337C, "sed dabit Deus ipsis actis aliquando lucem, ut confidimus."
67. BN Ms. 4033, 170r; on Santa María, Rowe, *Saint and Nation*, 157.
68. BN Ms. 4033, 170v.
69. Ibid.
70. "Verdad de las actas del Martyrio de SS. Bonoso, y Moximiano [sic]," in Tamayo, *Discursos apologeticos*.
71. BN Ms. 4033, 204r.

72. According to Michael, "King James VI and I and the Count of Gondomar," 433. See also López-Vidriero, "Asiento de coronas y distinción de reino"; Manso Porto, *Don Diego Sarmiento de Acuña, conde de Gondomar (1567–1626)*; Redworth, *The Prince and the Infanta*, 13.
73. BN Ms. 4033, 204r–v.
74. Ibid., 204v.
75. Adarve de Acuña and Saro, *Relacion y memorial*, 266.
76. BN Ms. 4033, 57r–v.
77. Ibid., 205r, and, for the earlier miracle at Nogales, 172v.
78. Ibid., 205r, "y desde luego digo que V[uestra] P[aternidad] no me toque alli mis reliquias las estimo yo en mucho y aun en mas que tocadas." Vide "no me toque los huevos" in modern Castilian.
79. Aguilar, *Al doctor*.
80. ———, *Carta*; and see Manchón Gómez, "Dos poemas latinos de Juan de Aguilar." The other two texts are *Verdadera relación de los Santos que se van descubriendo al pie de las torres de la Villa de Arjona . . . compuesto por un devoto suyo*, and Pancorbo, *Relacion*.
81. In Spanish, *panecicos de los martires*, for which see Olds, "Visions of the Holy."
82. Rus Puerta, *Historia eclesiastica*, 143v–144r.
83. Pancorbo, *Disquisición de los Santos Martires de Arjona*, 2v–3v.
84. AHPJ, 3733, 139r.
85. AHPJ, 3734: 27v–30v, and 3733: 148r, respectively. For other bequests to the martyrs between 1629 and 1636, see AHPJ, 3733: 269v, 418v, 442r; AHPJ, 3734: 231r–233v, 282v–285v; AHPJ, 3749: 514r–515v.
86. Cirot, "Documents sur le faussaire Higuera."

CHAPTER 8. THE *CRONICONES* IN LOCAL RELIGION

Epigraph. Antonio, *Censura*, 4.
1. Antonio, *Censura*, 4.
2. Gómez Canseco, *Rodrigo Caro*, 49, referring to Caro, *Santuario*.
3. PL 31, cols. 469–71.
4. Caro, *Santuario*, 17v.
5. Ibid., 14v–15r; and see Brown and Kagan, "The Duke of Alcalá."
6. Caro, *Santuario*, 11r–v, a rendition of PL 31, col. 347; for additional examples, ———, *Santuario*, 14v, 18r.
7. Berenberg, "Patrons and Petitioners," 124–26; on Añaya, see Rowe, *Saint and Nation*, 161.
8. Gómez Canseco, "Rodrigo Caro: Entre libros y amigos," 25.
9. Quintanadueñas, *Gloriosos martyres de Osuna*, 7.
10. Alonso de la Serna, "Por la Potestad Pontificia en aprovar nuevos Rezados," RAH 9/3679(13). For Serna, Godoy Alcántara, *Historia crítica*, 257, who mistranscribed his name as "Melchor" de la Serna, as had Nicolás Antonio; for his role in the co-patronage controversy, Rowe, *Saint and Nation*, 92, 161.

11. Olds, "Visions of the Holy"; Sabalete Moya, "El Sacromonte de Arjona."
12. Sacra Congregationis Propaganda Fide, *Decreta authenticata* I, 123–24.
13. Alonso de la Serna, "Borrador de notas al crónico de . . . Dextro," BN Ms. 1491.
14. Rodrigo Caro, "Dubios que se an de resolver acerca de los santos que el . . . Arçobispo de Sevilla recibio al culto y reço deste Arçobispado," BN Ms. 18692.
15. "derribar a Dextro," letter of July 13, 1628. BCS, Ms. 58-1-99, f.254.2.
16. Caro, "Dubios," 1r–v.
17. Quintanadueñas, *Gloriosos martyres de Osuna*, 7, 41–42.
18. ———, *Santos . . . de Sevilla*.
19. Rodrigo Caro, "Respuesta a Don Martin de Anaia Maldonado," BN Ms. 9693.
20. Rowe, *Saint and Nation*, 159–66.
21. Ibid., 165–66.
22. On this type, see Momigliano, *The Classical Foundations*, 54.
23. Ditchfield, *Liturgy, Sanctity and History*; ———, "'In Search of Local Knowledge.'"
24. Rus Puerta, *Historia eclesiastica*.
25. Quintana, *A la . . . Villa de Madrid*; Quintanadueñas, *Gloriosos martyres de Osuna*.
26. Caro, *Santuario*.
27. Cárcel Ortí, *Visitas pastorales y relaciones Ad Limina*.
28. Francisco de Rus Puerta, "Obispos de Jaen, y segunda parte de la historia eclesiastica," BN Ms. 5737. A recent anthology provides a selection of these texts: Rallo Gruss, ed., *Libros de antigüedades*.
29. Roa, *Ecija*, 2r. On Roa, Cañal y Migolla, "Apuntes biobibliográficos"; Pradas and Carrasco Gómez, "Datos biográficos."
30. Roa, *Ecija*, 134v.
31. Ibid., 70r; PL 31, cols. 90–91, 197.
32. Weiss, *The Renaissance Discovery of Classical Antiquity*.
33. Roa, *Ecija*, 73v–74r.
34. Woolf, *Social Circulation of the Past*.
35. Cañal y Migolla, "Apuntes biobibliográficos"; Lazure, "To Dare Fame"; Rodríguez Marín, "Cervantes y la Universidad de Osuna"; Wunder, "Search for Sanctity."
36. June 2, 1628 letter, BCS Ms. 58-1-99, 251.2. Also included on this list was canon Juan Francisco Centeno, who had written against copatronage. Rowe, *Saint and Nation*, 87.
37. On the former, Antonio, *Biblioteca hispana nueva* I: 207–8; López Molina, "Curiosa protesta del maestro . . . Rus Puerta"; Parejo Delgado, "Rus Puerta, Francisco," Suplemento I. On the latter, ———, "Don Martín de Ximena Jurado."
38. Pineda to Moscoso, BN Ms. 4033, 81v. On Pineda, who should not be confused with the Franciscan of the same name, "Pineda, Juan de," Domínguez and O'Neill, eds., *Diccionario histórico*. On Pancorbo, Rowe, *Saint and Nation*, 161–62.
39. Moscoso to Mariner, BN Ms. 6184, 49r–v; Villegas, *Memorial*.
40. Becerra, *Memorial . . . de la decensión de la Virgen*. There was a similar legend in Toledo: Christian, *Apparitions*, 40–57.
41. Notwithstanding the rival claims of Baza in the diocese of Guadix, Eufrasio's cult

was revived in Andújar, thanks to the patronage of the Caño family, although not without local opposition. See the surprisingly unsparing account in Bilches, *Santos y santuarios*, 204. For more, Terrones de Robles, *Vida, martirio, traslación y milagros de San Euphrasio*; Gómez Martínez, *Fé y Religiosidad popular en . . . Andújar*; López Arandia, *La Compañía de Jesús en la ciudad de Jaén*.

42. Acuña del Adarve, *Discursos de las efigies, y verdaderos retratos . . . de Christo*; Moscoso y Sandoval, *Traslado bien y fielme[n]te sacado del Auto . . . sobre . . . fray Pedro Pascual de Valencia*, RAH 9/3589; and see ASV Congr. Riti, Processus 950 and 952. For the *casus exceptus*, Sacra Congregatio Pro Causis Sanctorum, *Index ac Status Causarum*, 341; Veraja, *La beatificazione*, 74. On Acuña del Adarve, see Vincent-Cassy, *L'inventaire des empreintes sacrées*.

43. Rus Puerta, *Historia eclesiastica*, 226v–227r, BN Ms. 5737, 254v.

44. These were Thesiphon, "The Apostle Andreas," and Gregory of Baeza. Ambrosio de Camara, et al., "Memorial de . . . los stos. . . . martyres naturales de la misma ciudad," BN Ms. 4033, 23r–27v; Moscoso y Sandoval, *Officia propria sanctorum giennensis*; ———, *A los nuestros . . . hermanos el Dean y Cabildo . . . Notorio es . . . quan preciosas sean a los ojos de Dios . . . sus Santos Martires*.

45. Juan Acuña del Adarve, "Informe de la causa de . . . Santa Potenciana," (1639), BN Ms. 6184, 24r–26v; Moscoso y Sandoval, *Constituciones synodales del Obispado de Iaen*.

46. BN Ms. 6184, 46r–v; Moral de la Vega, "Comentarios a dos cartas inéditas."

47. Pedro Díaz de Ribas, "Antiapología. Disputa acerca del rezo de Santa Potenciana," Biblioteca de Castilla–La Mancha, Toledo, Ms. 293. Ribas was attacked in two anonymous treatises: *Alegacion apologetica por Santa Potenciana*, and *Un autor que parece mas devoto de los Santos, que noticioso de sus historias [. . .]*, BN R/24563. See also Pancorbo, *Disquisición de Santa Potenciana*.

48. Letter of April 1639 from Moscoso to Vázquez Siruela in BN Ms. 6184, 100r. For other details, Ximena Jurado, *Catálogo*, 549. In the following century her cult seems to have been forgotten, if we are to believe the anonymous annotator of the *Alegacion apologetica por Santa Potenciana* in the copy held by Jaén's Biblioteca Pública (N-2.154), who noted in 1790 that "no public cult" to Potenciana had been celebrated since 1640 (42r). However, Potenciana is the patron of Villanueva de Andújar, now known as Villanueva de la Reina.

49. BN Ms. 5737, 4v–7v; and see PL 31, col. 239.

50. PL 31, col. 455.

51. Adán de Centurión, "Memorial, en que . . . suplica al Señor Obispo de Guadix que . . . mande celebrar en Abla como santos martires de aquel lugar," RAH, 9/3572, 5428r–5431r.

52. Moscoso y Sandoval, *Officia propria sanctorum giennensis*.

53. Ditchfield, "Text Before Trowel"; Stenhouse, *Reading Inscriptions and Writing Ancient History*; Woolf, *Social Circulation of the Past*.

54. Martín de Ximena Jurado, "Explicacion de un antiguo numisma de Arjona," BN Ms. 1180, 306r–v; Ximena Jurado, *Historia o anales . . . de Arjona*, 88, 95.

55. BN Ms. 1180, 307r.

56. Parejo Delgado, "Don Martín de Ximena Jurado, historiador del reino de Jaén."

57. Sánchez González, "La cultura de las letras."
58. Kagan, "Clio and the Crown," 98–99.
59. ASV Congr. Riti, Processus 950, 123v–126r.
60. BN Ms. 6712, 122v.
61. Requena Aragón, *Venida del apostol S. Pablo a España, y predicacion en . . . Libisosa (oi Lezuza)*.
62. AHN, Sección Nobleza, Osuna, C. 2040, D. 9.
63. Varona, *Epitome del glorioso martirio de Santa Caliopa de Lerma*.
64. Gómez Bravo, *Advertencias a la istoria de Merida*; Moya y Munguia, *Tratado Apologetico en favor de . . . San Hierotheo*; Peña y Lezcano, *Memorial por la Primacía del Glorioso Mártir San Elpidio*; Rojas, *Historia de . . . Toledo . . . Parte primera*; ———, *Historia de . . . Toledo . . . Parte segunda*.
65. Pedro Díaz de Ribas, "Patronazgo de Sanct Hiscio por la Villa de Tariffa," BN Ms 1686; for the rival claim by Gibraltar, BN Ms. 4469, 36r–49v.
66. Quintana, *A la . . . Villa de Madrid*; Cordero de Ciria, "Huellas de los 'falsos cronicones'"; Río Barredo, *Madrid, urbs regia*, 106–7.
67. In addition to those cited in previous chapters, add Andrés de Uztárroz, *Monumento de los santos martyres*; Sandoval, *San Antonino español*.
68. Cordón, *Apologia sobre la cabeza de San Sacerdote*.
69. Zaragoza and Huesca, *Teatro historico de las iglesias . . . de Aragón* I: 1–93.
70. Sainz de Baranda, *Clave de la España sagrada*.
71. Múñoz y Romero, *Diccionario bibliográfico-histórico*, iii.
72. This is a working total, since future research into this potentially wide-ranging topic will doubtless reveal many more examples.
73. On orientalism, see the pioneering scholarship of García-Arenal and Rodríguez Mediano, *The Orient in Spain*; and see Kimmel, "Writing Religion." For the contrary opinion, which holds that the relevance of the cronicones was much more circumscribed than that of the plomos, García-Arenal, "Orígenes sagrados y memoria del Islam," 51; García-Arenal and Rodríguez Mediano, "Jerónimo Román de la Higuera and the Lead Books of Sacromonte," 266.

CHAPTER 9. THE POLITICS OF THE
CRONICONES IN MADRID AND ROME

1. For collections that included the cronicones: Andrés, "Historia de la biblioteca del Conde-Duque de Olivares . . . II"; ———, "Los códices del Conde de Miranda en la Biblioteca Nacional"; Mascareñas, "Cartas do historiador D. Jerónimo Mascareñas"; Entrambasaguas, *La biblioteca de Ramírez de Prado*.
2. For scholarly activity in Olivares's circles, Elliott, *Count-Duke of Olivares*, 174–78, 347. On literary controversies at court, Lawrance, "Las *Obras de don Luis de Góngora* y el conde-duque."
3. Kagan, *Clio and the Crown*, 218–19, 261–62.
4. Letter of February 9, 1627, BCS Ms. 58-1-99, 246.1–248.1.

5. For a useful analysis, see Lazure, "Rodrigo Caro y la corte de Felipe IV," 125; see also BN Ms. 8954, 83r-v.
6. February 16, 1629 letter to Fray Francisco de Cabrera, BCS Ms. 58-1-99, 205.1.
7. Tamayo de Vargas, ed., *Luitprandi . . . Chronicon*.
8. See Elliott, *Count-Duke of Olivares*, 279, n. 7, and plate 14.
9. Ibid., 165–66, 616–17.
10. Lazure, "Rodrigo Caro y la corte de Felipe IV," 128.
11. This was probably Los Palacios y Villafranca, a town in the area of Seville. BCS Ms. 58-1-99, 255.2.
12. Caro, *Relación de las inscripciones y antigüedad de . . . Utrera*, 10v.
13. According to Tamayo de Vargas, *Novedades antiguas*, 93v.
14. Lazure, "Rodrigo Caro y la corte de Felipe IV."
15. BCS Ms. 58-1-99, 254.2.
16. Gabriel Trejo y Paniagua (1562–1630) died shortly after being deposed from this post in 1629. Elliott, *Count-Duke of Olivares*, 305, 393–94.
17. Ramírez de Prado, ed., *Luitprandi subdiaconi toletani*.
18. Bivar, ed., *Marci Maximi*.
19. Blackwell, *Behind the Scenes*. Many scholars refer to Inchofer as Hungarian, but he was born in Vienna: Ribadeneira, Alegambe, and Sotuello, *Bibliotheca scriptorum Societatis Iesu*, 608–9.
20. Preto, "Una lunga storia di falsi e falsari," 19.
21. Inchofer, *Epistolae . . . Veritas Vindicata*; ———, *De epistolae B. Virginis Mariae . . . coniectatio*. For the possible importance of the Galileo affair in this incident, Moscheo, "Melchior Inchofer . . . ed un suo inedito." See also Backus, "The Letter of the Virgin Mary to . . . Messina"; Cerbu, "Melchior Inchofer."
22. García-Arenal and Rodríguez Mediano, "Jerónimo Román de la Higuera and the Lead Books of Sacromonte"; Prosperi, "L'Immacolata a Siviglia"; Scaramella, "'Una materia gravissima.'" For French power, Dandelet, *Spanish Rome*, 188–206.
23. PL 31, cols. 253 and 569, respectively.
24. Inchofer, *Epistolae . . . Veritas Vindicata*, 260–85.
25. "Sommario di tutto quello, che si hà nel Santo Offitio intorno alle Lamine . . . di Granata," BAV Barb. lat. 6451, 45r-v, referring to PL 31, col. 173c.
26. Aldrete, *Fainomena*; ———, *Beatorum Martryum Albensium Vrgavonensium Bonosi, Maximiani*. For the possible location of this monument, Kendrick, *St. James in Spain*, 108.
27. "Sommario," 46r; and on Scaglia, Tedeschi, "The Roman Inquisition and Witchcraft."
28. There the artifacts would languish for another eleven years, until the nuncio was finally successful in wrangling them for Rome. Harris, *From Muslim to Christian Granada*, 37–46; Kendrick, *St. James in Spain*, 108.
29. PL 31, col. 1777a.
30. Bivar, *Pro Fl. L. Dextro*.
31. Reames, *The Legenda Aurea: A Reexamination*, 30.
32. Bivar, *Pro Fl. L. Dextro*, 6r.

33. Ibid., 6r.
34. Ibid., 7r.
35. Ibid., 11r.
36. Rader, *Analecta*, 4v, bound with ———, *Ad M. Valerii Martialis*. On Rader, Johnson, "Politics and Sanctity"; ———, "Defining the Confessional Frontier"; Louthan, "Imagining Christian Origins."
37. Rader, *Analecta*, 7.
38. Bivar, *Pro Fl. L. Dextro*, 18r.
39. Dümmerth, "Les combats et la tragédie."
40. Pennotto, *Defensio Censurae . . . Baronii et Bellarmini*, 27–28.
41. Ibid., 11.
42. BN Ms. 4033, 33r.
43. *Dubitavi: An constet Ecclesiam Beatae Mariae Virginis de Columna, seu (ut vulgo dicitur) de Pilari fuisse antiquitus Cathedralem?*, printed pamphlet, BN Ms. 6712.
44. Adarve de Acuña and Saro, *Relacion y memorial*; Aldrete, *Fainomena*.
45. Villegas, *Memorial*, 5v, par. 28. For an analysis of how Moscoso proceeded thereafter, Olds, "The Ambiguities of the Holy."
46. Adarve de Acuña and Saro, *Relacion y memorial*, 491–92; Rus Puerta, *Historia eclesiastica*, 142–43. On the Monja's trial for false sanctity, from which she was absolved posthumously, Haliczer, *Between Exaltation and Infamy*, 55, 131–33, 269; Ochoa, *Epistolario español* II, 371 ff. For an example of the further dissemination of news about Arjona ca. 1629, "Memorial de cossas diferentes curiossas recopiladas por don Juan de Çisneros, y Tagle Corregidor de la villa de Francisca y regidor perpetuo de la de Carrion . . . Cartorçena parte," RAH, 9/431, 61v–65v.
47. Adarve de Acuña and Saro, *Relacion y memorial*, 415.
48. Lazure, "Rodrigo Caro y la corte de Felipe IV," 130.
49. The author was Gaspar Sala Berart. *Proclamacion catolica a la magestad piadosa de Felipe El Grande . . . Los conselleres, y consejo de ciento de la ciudad de Barcelona*, 16, 18; and for Dexter, PL 31, col. 529.
50. On these and other reactions to the revolt, Kagan, *Clio and the Crown*, 239–41; Villanueva López, *Política y discurso histórico*, 110–19, 125–55.
51. Rioja, *Aristarco o censura*, 8v–10r, 32r–v; and see Lazure, "Rodrigo Caro y la corte de Felipe IV," 131–33. On Rioja, Coste, "Datos útiles"; Kagan, *Clio and the Crown*, 223, 260–61.
52. Rodrigo Caro, "Defensa de los escritos de Flavio Lucio Dextro i Marco Maximo," BN Ms. 6712, 117v.
53. Ibid., 118r; and see 122r.
54. Ibid., 117r–120v.
55. Quintanadueñas, *Gloriosos martyres de Osuna*.
56. See, for instance, Quintana, *A la . . . Villa de Madrid*.
57. BN Ms. 8954, 83v–84r.
58. Ibid., 83r.

59. Nieremberg, *Historia naturae maxime peregrinae*, 393–97, 413–18. On Nieremberg, Pimentel, "Baroque Natures."
60. Lapide, *Commentaria in acta apostolorum*, "Chronotaxis actuum apostolorum," 6, 11.
61. Ramírez de Prado, *Adversaria*, 54, and the plate on the following page, BUS Ms. BG/23186.
62. This copy has been digitized by Google; it was formerly held by the Jesuit casa profesa of Madrid, but where it is currently held is not discernible. On López Madera, Harris, *From Muslim to Christian Granada*, 18, 41. For the image of the bearded saint, Olds, "The 'False Chronicles,' Cardinal Baronio, and Sacred History."
63. RAH 5/460, 1.
64. For the gift, Antonio, *Censura*, 12–13.
65. RAH 5/460, 142.
66. For the notion of active reading, Dagenais, *The Ethics of Reading*; Sherman, *Used Books*.
67. RAH 5/1639; *Chronicon*, 28.
68. Ibid., 87, 120, 121.
69. Ibid., 41.
70. Ibid., 47.
71. Ibid., 44.
72. RAH 5/1639; *Chronicon*, 123. Another possible annotator is León Tapia, author of *Examen y refutacion de los fundamentos con que impugnauan el Licenciado Pedro de Losada y otros, el Patronato de la gloriosa Virgen Santa Teresa* (Barcelona: en la imprenta de Sebastian de Cormellas, 1628).
73. Rowe, *Saint and Nation*, 162–63.
74. AHN Bib. Auxiliar, 2203, 93.
75. Ibid., "Heremitiis," 139; "esso parece para bobos y no mas."
76. BN R/3570, 83.
77. Ibid., 9, 63, and 13, respectively.
78. Johns, *The Nature of the Book*, 5.
79. Bouza Álvarez, *Communication, Knowledge, and Memory*, 50.
80. Roa, *Ecija*, 88r.
81. For example, see the many sixteenth-century antiquarians whose works were never published. Stenhouse, *Reading Inscriptions and Writing Ancient History*, 20.

CHAPTER 10. FROM APOCRYPHA TO FORGERY

Epigraph. Iriarte, *Coleccion de obras en verso y prosa*.
1. Iriarte, *Coleccion de obras en verso y prosa*, 288–94.
2. Herr, *The Eighteenth-Century Revolution*, 211.
3. Kagan, *Clio and the Crown*, 256–65; Mestre Sanchís, "Crítica y apología."
4. Peña y Lezcano, *Memorial por la Primacía del Glorioso Mártir San Elpidio*; and see Martínez Gil, "Religión e identidad urbana."
5. Borchardt, "The Topos of Critical Rejection."

6. Suárez, *Historia de el Obispado de Guadix y Baza*, as on 113. For another late example of reliance upon the cronicones, see Gándara, *El cisne occidental*.
7. For these and other details of his career, Olds, "How to Be a Counter-Reformation Bishop."
8. Tamayo de Salazar, *Auli Hali poétae*.
9. Caro Baroja, *Las falsificaciones*, 104–5; Godoy Alcántara, *Historia crítica*, 237–45, 281–89; Jammes and Gorsse, "Nicolás Antonio et le combat."
10. Bivar, ed., *Marci Maximi*.
11. Quintanadueñas, *Santos . . . de Toledo*; and, for the correspondence, RAH 9/3589.
12. Rojas, *Historia de . . . Toledo . . . Parte primera*; ———, *Historia de . . . Toledo . . . Parte segunda*.
13. Andrés, "Los manuscritos del Inquisidor General."
14. Tamayo de Salazar, *Anamnesis sive commemoratio omnium sanctorum hispanorum*; and see Godoy Alcántara, *Historia crítica*, 237–38; Henriet, "Collection hagiographique et forgeries."
15. Cardoso, *Agiológio lusitano*; and see Correia Fernandes, "Historia, santidade e identidade"; ———, *A biblioteca de Jorge Cardoso*. On Ughelli, Ditchfield, *Liturgy, Sanctity and History*, 328–60.
16. The texts were revealed by Antonio de Nobis, also known as Antonio de Lupián Zapata, who claimed to have found them in the Burgos cathedral archive. Argaíz, *Corona real de España . . . y vida de San Hierotheo*; ———, *La verdad . . . y aueriguacion de la que ay en la Segunda parte de Marco Maximo*; and see Caro Baroja, *Las falsificaciones*, 99–102; Godoy Alcántara, *Historia crítica*, 266–75.
17. San Pablo, *Defensa por la religion Geronyma*.
18. Luis Germán Germán y Ribón, "Extracto de los Anales de Sevilla de D. Diego Ortiz de Zúñiga," quoted in Gallego Morell, "Algunas noticias sobre Don Martín Vázquez Siruela."
19. Andrés, "La bibliofilia del Marqués de Mondéjar."
20. Pedro Fernández Pulgar, "El Sigalion, o Chiton de los Chronicones fabulosos, y supuestos, que se han publicado en España . . . Fantasi en un Dialogo jocoserio, divido en dos partes, ante Sigalion Critico severo de Athenas. Publicole Candido Philaleto Hispano, principal interlocutor, por orden de Sigalion. Imprimiose en el Prelo Athensiense del Buho nocturno. Publicase de nuevo por Cephalon Pollicense Ferrantino, en la Prensa Antuerpiense de Iuan Meursio," RAH, 9/560.
21. Andrés, "La bibliofilia del Marqués de Mondéjar," 587; Boynton, *Silent Music*; Kagan, *Clio and the Crown*, 235–44, 261.
22. Barrientos, *Censura a las distinciones entre Marco y Maximo, el Beroso de Caldea y Viterbo*.
23. "Diseño de lo que se puede escribir de los santos i reliquias de Arjona," BN Ms. 6156, 43r–46v; "Varios escritos de Martín Vázquez Siruela," BN Ms. 34; and Vázquez Siruela, *Apologia por los baños de . . . Alhama*.
24. Gallego Morell, "Algunas noticias sobre Don Martín Vázquez Siruela," 8. Athanasius

Kircher would also become the butt of a similar prank: see Findlen, *Athanasius Kircher: The Last Man Who Knew Everything*, 7.
25. Vázquez Siruela, "Juizio que hizo . . . del Chronicón de Flavio Dextro," Marquette University, Raynor Archives, BR1025.V39 1700z, 37.
26. Escolano y Ledesma, *Chronicon Sancti Hierothei*.
27. Ibáñez de Segovia, *Dissertaciones eclesiasticas*; ———, *Discurso histórico por el patronato de San Frutos*; Cueto, *Pánfilos y "cucos"*; Godoy Alcántara, *Historia crítica*, 278–81, 301–2.
28. Morel Fatio, "Cartas eruditas del Marqués de Mondéjar"; Vilaplana, "Correspondencia de Papebroch."
29. Collis, "The Preface of the 'Acta Sanctorum,'" 301; and, more generally, Delehaye, *L'œuvre des bollandistes*; Godding et al., eds., *Bollandistes. Saints et légendes*; Gordini, "L'opera dei bollandisti."
30. "Et genuinum illius foetum esse Hispani plerique mordicus pugnant . . . Nolo ego in certamen huius Scriptoris gratia cum bellicosa gente descendere." Bolland and Henschen, *Acta sanctorum . . . Ianuarius*, xxxj. For another author reluctant to offend, see the mild doubts about Dexter expressed by a prolific Lutheran professor of history in the German university town of Jena: Bosius, *De prudentia*, 168.
31. Antonio, *Censura*, 139–40; Godoy Alcántara, *Historia crítica*, 159.
32. Bolland and Henschen, *Acta sanctorum . . . Februarius*, xvij–xx.
33. Vilaplana, "Correspondencia de Papebroch," 329; and, more broadly, Machielsen, "Heretical Saints and Textual Discernment."
34. Caro Baroja, *Las falsificaciones*, 26–27; 32; Hiatt, *Making of Medieval Forgeries*, 181.
35. Grafton, "Jean Hardouin: The Antiquary as Pariah"; Kelley, *Faces of History*, 208; and for the classical formulation of these "historical Pyrrhonists," Momigliano, "Ancient History and the Antiquarian."
36. Knowles, *Great Historical Enterprises*.
37. Quoted in Kelley, *Faces of History*, 417; and see Hiatt, *Making of Medieval Forgeries*, 184.
38. Hiatt, "Diplomatic Arts."
39. Quantin, "Reason and Reasonableness," 417.
40. Vilaplana, "Correspondencia de Papebroch," 304–10.
41. Critics of the new hagiographers were not only found among Carmelites; for example, a fellow Jesuit in Seville denounced Papebroeck to the Inquisition in 1696 for "false, injurious, scandalous, reckless, erroneous, blasphemous . . . heretical propositions." AHN Inq., Leg. 4462, nos. 18, 22.
42. Antonio, *Bibliotheca hispana vetus*; ———, *Bibliotheca hispana nova*.
43. Jones, *Hispanic Manuscripts and Printed Books* I: 14.
44. Jammes and Gorsse, "Nicolás Antonio et le combat," 421.
45. Quoted in ibid., 424.
46. Ibid., 422.
47. Antonio, *Censura*, xvi. He also possessed other Higuera manuscripts; see his annotation in RAH 9/1013, 398v.

48. Jammes and Gorsse, "Nicolás Antonio et le combat," 425.
49. Antonio, *Censura*, 139.
50. Cirot, *Mariana historien*, 48.
51. Quoted in Godoy Alcántara, *Historia crítica*, 314–15.
52. Cañizares-Esguerra, *How to Write the History*, 143.
53. Mestre Sanchís, *Ilustración y reforma*, 110–23.
54. Cañizares-Esguerra, *How to Write the History*, 142.
55. Feijóo, *Teatro crítico universal* V: 185; and see Herr, *The Eighteenth-Century Revolution*, 37–41; Tausiet, "De la ilusión al desencanto." For another critical voice in the early 1700s, see Interián de Ayala, *El pintor christiano*, I, 458-59, which was originally published in Latin in 1730.
56. Jammes and Gorsse, "Nicolás Antonio et le combat," 418.
57. Mestre Sanchís, *Ilustración y reforma*, 133. For a recent analysis see Benítez Sánchez-Blanco, "Gregorio Mayans y las láminas y libros de plomo de Granada."
58. Cañizares-Esguerra, *How to Write the History*, 135, 143–44.
59. Cano, ed., "Discurso del editor," in Morales, *Antigüedades* I (1792), xxiii.
60. Masdeu, *Historia crítica de España*. For parallel discussions in literary circles, Torrecilla, *Guerras literarias del XVIII español*.
61. Huerta y Vega, *España Primitiva*; Godoy Alcántara, *Historia crítica*, 306.
62. Godoy Alcántara, *Historia crítica*, 305–11; Mestre Sanchís, *Ilustración y reforma*, 125, 129.
63. Godoy Alcántara, *Historia crítica*, 313.
64. García Cuadrado, "Un proceso de impresión."
65. "Assento, que se tomou sobre a autoridade, que se devia dar a alguns Escritores, e Catalogo dos reprovados," *Collecçam dos documentos, estatutos e memorias da Academia Real da Historia portugueza*, between items 20 and 21 (volume unpaginated).
66. Mestre Sanchís, *Ilustración y reforma*, 143–51, who believes that the denunciation originated from Sacromonte. In 1744, the bishop of Malaga also objected that Mayans's works "destruía muchas leyendas de santos, prelados y capillas," and banned his preface to the *Censura de historias falsas*, according to Fernández Ubiña, "Clasicismo y fin del mundo antiguo," 198, n. 23.
67. Santos Puerto, "La censura de la *España primitiva*"; and see Sarmiento's note in BN Ms. 1643, 1r.
68. Abascal Palazón and Cebrián Fernández, eds., *Manuscritos sobre antigüedades*; Boynton, *Silent Music*.
69. Flórez, *España sagrada*. See Henriet, "La dignité de la religion chrétienne." For an earlier attempt along similar lines to cleanse Spanish history of its errors while also venerating the saints, see San Nicolás, *Antiguedades eclesiasticas de España*, 359–60. For parallel efforts among French Catholic scholars, Quantin, *Le catholicisme classique*.
70. Flórez, *España sagrada* III: 37–38.
71. Antón Pelayo, "La historiografía catalana del siglo XVIII."

72. Álvarez Barrientos, "Historia y religiosidad popular"; Harris, *From Muslim to Christian Granada*, 150–51. For sketches of the finds, see BN Ms. 6180.
73. Godoy Alcántara, *Historia crítica*, 324.
74. Medina Conde, *El fingido Dextro*.
75. Ibid., xlv.
76. Quoted in Godoy Alcántara, *Historia crítica*, 325.
77. Martínez de Mazas, *Memorial . . . sobre el indebido culto*. More recently, this task has been taken up with great thoughtfulness by Castillo Maldonado, *La primera cristianización de Jaén*.
78. Sánchez Alonso, *Historia de la historiografía española* II, 160.
79. For example, Nalle, *God in La Mancha*.
80. Menéndez y Pelayo, *Historia de los heterodoxos españoles* (1881) III, 69. For the chronicles as an infection, ———, *Historia de las ideas estéticas en España* III, 318.
81. Lehner, "What is 'Catholic Enlightenment'?"; Sandberg, "Religion and the Enlightenment(s)"; Schaefer, "True and False Enlightenment."
82. Antonio, *Censura*, 322; Villanueva, *Viage literario* II, 48–49.
83. Villanueva, *Viage literario* II, 60.
84. Galmés, "Villanueva, Jaime"; Haliczer, *Inquisition and Society*, 344–45. For context, Herr, *The Eighteenth-Century Revolution*, 368, 411–13.

CONCLUSION: NEW SAINTS, NEW HISTORIES IN MODERN SPAIN

1. Real Academia de la Historia, *Memorial histórico español*; Gayangos, ed., *Cartas de algunos padres de la Compañía de Jesús*; Fuente, *Historia eclesiástica de España*, first published in Barcelona in 1855.
2. Godoy Alcántara, "Ideas y opiniones . . . sobre la manera de escribir la Historia."
3. For this formulation, Grafton, *The Footnote*.
4. Caro Baroja, *Las falsificaciones*, drawing on additional evidence that Godoy Alcántara could not have consulted; and, with dry humor, Kendrick, *St. James in Spain*.
5. On Migne's slipshod editorial practices, Bloch, *God's Plagiarist*.
6. Cueto, *Pánfilos y "cucos"*; Segura González, "Patronazgo de Sanct Hiscio por la Villa de Tarifa"; ———, "La reliquia de San Hiscio"; Yelo Templado, "La Rioja en los falsos cronicones"; ———, "Inautenticidad de la historia fulgentina."
7. González Blanco, "Begastri en los cronicones apócrifos (II)." For examples of nineteenth-century texts influenced by the false chronicles, see Rey Castelao, "La *Historia crítica* de los falsos cronicones de José Godoy Alcántara."
8. Noguera Rosado, "Cristianización de Astigi."
9. ASV, Congr. Concilio, Relat. Dioec., 364.
10. Ruinart, *Acta primorum martyrum*, 664–68; Bollandistes, ed., *Bibliotheca hagiographica*, 213.
11. For another instance in which a pre-Islamic Christian landscape was miraculously discovered, but in the early twentieth-century Balkans, see Valtchinova, "'Unconscious Historicization'?"

12. Morales Talero, *Los santos de Arjona*, 187; for an alternate theory, Domínguez Cubero, "Sobre la iconografía de los santos."
13. News of the annual festivities, as well as images of the shrine and the various representations of Bonosus and Maximianus, can be found at www.portalarjonero.com.
14. I am greatly indebted to William Christian Jr. for this information. The show has been broadcasting on the channel known as Cuatro since 2005: http://www.cuatro.com/cuarto-milenio, accessed February 22, 2013.
15. Adarve de Acuña and Saro, *Relacion y memorial*, 32; 425.
16. At one point a host described Moscoso's investigation as "un verdadero CSI de la Iglesia."
17. For proponents of Annian history in modern Italy, Stephens, "When Pope Noah Ruled the Etruscans."
18. Mozas Moreno, "Un catálogo numismático inédito," 86.
19. Salas Álvarez, "Excavaciones arqueológicas."

Bibliography

In notes, bibliography, and captions, author names and titles for period works retain their original spelling, including lack of diacritics.

MANUSCRIPT SOURCES

ARCHIVO HISTÓRICO DIOCESANO DE JAÉN (AHDJ)

Actas capitulares, 1620, 1628
Cartas, 1627–32
Criminal, 56–59

ARCHIVO HISTÓRICO NACIONAL — MADRID (AHN)

Biblioteca Auxiliar 2203 and 2644
Inquisición, legajos 116 and 4462; libro 2708(1)
Sección Nobleza, Osuna, C. 2040, D. 9

ARCHIVO HISTÓRICO PROVINCIAL DE JAÉN (AHPJ)

Escribanos, Legajos 3732–34, 3749–50

ARCHIVUM ROMANUM SOCIETATIS IESU — ROME (ARSI)

Baet., 19, II, and 20, I
Bibliotheca, 6-G-15: "Historia del Colegio de Plasencia de la Compañía de Jesús."
Censurae librorum, 652, I
Hisp., 90, II, Hispan. Ordinat.
Hispan. 138–39
Tolet., 5-II and 6-I

ARCHIVIO SEGRETO VATICANO — ROME (ASV)

Congr. Concilio, Relat. Dioec., 364
Congr. Riti, Processus 950 and 952.
Segr. Stato, Cardinali, 9 and 15

BIBLIOTHECA APOSTOLICA VATICANA — ROME (BAV)

Barb. lat. 6451
Urb. lat. 1101

BIBLIOTECA CAPITULAR SEVILLANA — SEVILLE (BCS)

Ms. 58-1-99

BIBLIOTECA DE CASTILLA–LA MANCHA — TOLEDO

Ms. 293

BIBLIOTECA NACIONAL — MADRID (BN)

Mss. 34, 897, 1180, 1285–96, 1317, 1334, 1443, 1491, 1538, 1638–47, 1686, 2000, 2343–45, 3249, 3302, 4033, 4161, 4469, 5556, 5732, 5737 (Francisco de Rus Puerta, "Obispos de Jaen, y segunda parte de la historia eclesiastica"), 6149, 6156, 6184, 6437, 6712, 6939, 7364–65, 8192–98, 8389, 8809, 8954, 9140, 9693, 9752–53, 9880–81, 12916, 13025, 18692

BIBLIOTECA UNIVERSITARIA DE SALAMANCA (BUS)

Mss. 1830–1837

RAYNOR ARCHIVES, MARQUETTE UNIVERSITY — MILWAUKEE

BR1025.V39 1700z (Martín Vázquez Siruela, "Juizio que hizo . . . del Chronicón de Flavio Dextro")

REAL ACADEMIA DE LA HISTORIA — MADRID (RAH)

9/229, 9/300, 9/431, 9/560, 9/653, 9/740–1, 9/744, 9/749–51, 9/998, 9/1013, 9/1017, 9/1024, 9/3572, 9/3589, 9/3679, 9/5566 ("Tratado del linage de los de la Higuera como tambien de los apellidos Peña, Romano, y otros y juntamente una relacion de los mozarabes de Toledo")

PUBLISHED PRIMARY SOURCES

THE FALSE CHRONICLES: SEVENTEENTH- AND EIGHTEENTH-CENTURY EDITIONS

Antonio, Nicolás. *Bibliotheca hispana vetus: sive, Hispani scriptores qui ab Octaviani Augusti aevo ad annum Christi MD floruerunt* (1696). 2nd ed., 2 vols. II: 409–19 (Antonio's "Dextro primitivo"). Madrid: Visor, 1996.

Bivar, Francisco de, ed. *Fl. Lucii Dextri . . . Chronicon omnimodae historiae . . . nunc demum opera et studio Fr. Francisci Bivarii . . . commentariis apodictis illustratum . . .* Lyons: Claude Landry, 1627.

———. *Marci Maximi episcopi Caesaraugustani . . . Continuatio chronici omnimodae historiae ab anno Christi 430 (ubi Flav. L. Dexter desiit) usque ad 612, accuratissimis opera et studio Francisci Bivarij.* Madrid: Didaci Diaz de la Carrera, 1651.

Calderón, Juan de, ed. *Fragmentum chronici, siue omnimodae historiae Flavii Lucii Dextri [. . .] cum Chronico Marci Maximi et additionibus Sancti Braulionis [. . .].* Zaragoza: Apud Ioannem à Lanaja, & Quartanet, Regni Aragonū, & Universitatis Typographum, 1619.

Caro, Rodrigo, ed. *Flavi Luci Dextri V.C. omnimodae historiae quae extant fragmenta cum chronico M. Maximi et Helecae ac S. Braulionis caesaraugustanorum episcoporum.* Seville: Apud Mathiam Clavigium, 1627.

Ramírez de Prado, Lorenzo, ed. *Luitprandi subdiaconi toletani [. . .] Opera quae extant. Chronicon et adversaria . . . D. Laurenti Ramirez de Prado consiliarii regii notis illustrata.* Antwerp: Ex officina plantinuana Balthasaris Moreti, 1640.

———. *Iuliani Petri archipresbyteri Santae Iustae chronicon cum eiusdem adversariis, et de eremiteriis hispanis brevis descriptio, atque ab eodem variorum carminum collectio ex bibliotheca olivarensi.* Paris: Laurentium Sonnium via Iacobaea sub Circino aureo, 1628.

Tamayo de Vargas, Tomás, ed. *Luitprandi, sive Eutrandi e subdiacono toletano, & ticinensi diacono, episcopi cremonensis [. . .] Chronicon ad Tractemundum illiberritanum in Hispania episcopum: a multis hactenus desideratum, nunquam editum, ex bibliotheca D. Thomae Tamaio de Vargas [. . .] regis historiographi [. . .] notae, & fragmenta Luitprando attributa.* Madrid: Ex typographia Francisci Martinez, 1635.

THE FALSE CHRONICLES: NINETEENTH-CENTURY REPRINTS IN MIGNE'S PATROLOGIA LATINA COLLECTION

Bivar, Francisco de. "Chronicon omnimodae historiae, una cum commentariis Fr. Francisci Bivarii, Quibus universa ecclesiastica historia, a Christo nato, per annos 430, adamussim expenditur." In *F. L. Dextri necnon Pauli Orosii hispanorum chronologorum opera omnia, juxta memoratissimas Bivarii et Havercampi editiones accurate recognita . . . Accedunt post Leporii presbyteri libellum, scriptorum quorumdam S. Augustino Aequalium opuscula varia.* In *Patrologiae cursus completus. Series Latina* (PL) 31, edited by J.-P. Migne. Turnholt: Typographi Brepols Editores Pontificii, 1968. (Based on Bivar's 1627 edition.)

"Maximi Caesaraugustani Episcopi, scripta quae exstant omnia." In *Saeculum VII. Anni*

601–646. *Scriptorum ecclesiasticorum qui in VII saeculi prima parte floruerunt opera omnia, ordine chronologico digeste* [. . .] *Collectio, si qua alia, insignia nec minus quam duo et triginta numero auctores comprehendens.* In *Patrologiae cursus completus. Series Latina* (PL) 80, edited by J.-P. Migne. Paris: Apud J.-P. Migne, 1863. (Based on a manuscript from the collection of Nicolás Antonio.)

Ramírez de Prado, Lorenzo and Jerónimo Román de la Higuera, eds. "Chronicon Liutprandi Ticinensis Diaconi, Toletani Vero Subdiaconi, Ad Tractemundum Episcopum Illiberitanum." In *Ratherii Veronensis episcopi, opera omnia* [. . .] *accedunt Liutprandi Cremonensis necnon Folquini S. Bertini monachi, Gunzonis diaconi novarienesis, Richardi Abbatis floriacensis, Adalberti Metensis scholastici. Scripta vel scriptorum fragmenta quae exstant.* In *Patrologiae cursus completus. Series Latina* (PL) 136, edited by J.-P. Migne. Paris: Apud Garnier Fratres, 1881. (Based on Ramírez de Prado's 1640 edition.)

OTHER PUBLISHED PRIMARY SOURCES

Acuña del Adarve, Juan. *Discursos de las efigies, y verdaderos retratos non manufactos, del Santo Rostro, y Cuerpo de Christo Nuestro Señor, desde el principio del mundo.* Villanueva de Andújar: Juan Fargolla de la Cuesta en las casas del autor, 1637.

Adarve de Acuña, Nicolás, and Gabriel de Saro. *Relacion y memorial . . . acerca de los prodigios y marauillas que se an visto al pie de la muralla y torres del Alcaçar de la villa de Arjona.* Jaén: Pedro de la Cuesta, 1630.

Aguilar, Juan de. *Al doctor don Alonso de Chincoya y Cardenas, Canonigo de la Santa Iglesia de Antequera.* N.p., ca. 1629.

———. *Carta escrita al señor D. Luys Manuel de Cordova . . . en que se toca la invencion de los Santos Martyres de Arjona, y algunas curiosas Poesias acerca della.* Antequera: Manuel Botello de Payva, 1629.

Agustín, Antonio. *Diálogos de medallas.* Tarragona: F. Mey, 1587.

Alcázar, Bartolomé. *Chrono-historia de la Compañia de Jesus en la provincia de Toledo: y elogios de sus varones illustres.* 2 vols. Madrid: Juan Garcia Infançon, 1710.

Alcocer, Pedro de. *Hystoria, o descripcion de la Imperial cibdad de Toledo.* Toledo: Iuan Ferrer, 1554.

Aldrete, Bernardo de. *Beatorum martryum Albensium Vrgavonensium Bonosi, Maximiani, & aliorum ruditèr inventionem . . . conabur.* Cordoba, 1631.

———. *Del origen y principio de la lengva castellana ò romance que oi se usa en España.* Rome: C. Willietto, 1606.

———. *Fainomena sive coruscantia lumina, triumphalisque crucis, signa sanctorum martyrum Albensium Urgavonensium Bonosi et Maximiani et aliorum sanguine purpurata.* Cordoba, 1631.

Alegacion apologetica por Santa Potenciana. Dispuesta por un devoto suyo. Contra una consulta invectiva hecha por un Religioso grave y docto al Ldo. Pedro Diaz de Ribas Presbitero de Cordova, bien conocido por su erudicion y letras en ella y su comarca. Jaén: Francisco Perez de Castilla, ca. 1641.

Andrés de Uztárroz, Juan Francisco. *Monumento de los santos martyres Iusto i Pastor en la ciudad de Huesca*. Huesca: Ian Nogues, 1644.

Antist, Vicente Justiniano. *De inventione sacri corporis divae Anglinae martyris*. Valencia: Apud Petrum Patricium Mey, 1588.

Antolínez de Burgos, Justino. *Historia eclesiástica de Granada*. Edited by Manuel Sotomayor. Granada: Universidad de Granada, 1996.

Antonio, Nicolás. *Biblioteca hispana nueva*. Translated by Miguel Matilla Martínez. Translation of 1788 Madrid ed., 2 vols. Madrid: Fundación Universitaria Española, 1999.

———. *Bibliotheca hispana nova: sive, Hispanorum scriptorum qui ab anno MD ad MDCLXXXIV floruere notitia*. 2 vols. Madrid: Visor, 1996.

———. *Bibliotheca hispana vetus: sive, Hispani scriptores qui ab Octaviani Augusti aevo ad annum Christi MD floruerunt*. 2nd ed., 2 vols. Madrid: Visor, 1996.

———. *Censura de historias fabulosas*. Reprint of 1742 ed. Madrid: Visor Libros, 1999.

Argaíz, Gregorio. *Corona real de España, fundamentada en el crédito de los muertos y vida de San Hierotheo*. Madrid: Apud Melchor Alegre, 1668.

———. *La verdad en su punto y aueriguacion de la que ay en la Segunda parte de Marco Maximo, Obispo de Zaragoça, que ha sacada impressa don Ioseph Pellicer*. Madrid: Melchor Alvarez: vendese en casa de Bartolome Rugido y Sardeneta, 1676.

———. *Poblacion eclesiastica de España y noticia de sus primeras honras: continuada en los escritos, y Chronicon de Hauberto, monge de San Benito [. . .] tomo primero, parte segunda*. Madrid: en la imprenta Real: a costa de Mateo Fernandez, 1668.

———. *Población eclesiástica de España . . . Continuada en los escritos de Marco Maximo obispo de Zaragoza, y defendida de la vulgar embidia el Beroso Aniano, Flavio Lucio Dextro, Auberto Hispalense, y Walabonso: con el cronicon de Liberato Abad, no impresso antes*. Madrid: Francisco Nieto: a costa de Gabriel de Leon, 1669.

Arias Montano, Benito. *Commentaria in duodecim prophetas*. Antwerp: Christopher Plantin, 1571.

Aristotle. *Poetics*. Translated by Stephen Halliwell. Loeb Classical Library. Cambridge: Harvard University Press, 1995.

Astraín, Antonio. *Historia de la Compañía de Jesús en la asistencia de España*. 7 vols. Madrid: Razón y Fe, 1912.

Augustine of Hippo. *The Retractions*. Translated by Mary Inez Bogan, Washington, D.C.: Catholic University of America, 1999.

Un autor que parece mas devoto de los Santos, que noticioso de sus historias [. . .]. N.p., ca. 1628.

Baronio, Cesare. *Annales ecclesiastici*. Vol. 1. Rome: Ex typographia Congregationis Oratorij apud S. Mariam in Vallicella, 1593.

Baronio, Cesare, ed. *Martyrologium Romanum ad novam kalendarii rationem & ecclesiasticae historiae veritatem restitutum*. Venice: Apud Petrum Dusinellum, 1587.

———. *Martyrologium Romanum ad novam kalendarii rationem & ecclesiasticae historiae veritatem restitutum*. Venice: Apud Marcum Antonium Zalterium, 1597.

Baronio, Cesare. *Venerabilis Caesaris Baronii S. R. E. Cardinalis Bibliothecarii Epistolae et opuscula pleraque nunc primum ex archetypis in lucem eruta: novam eiusdem Baronii vitam operi*. 3 vols. Edited by Raymundus Albericius. Rome: Ex typographia Komarek, 1759–70.

Barrientos, Diego Antonio de. *Censura a las distinciones entre Marco y Maximo, el Beroso de Caldea y Viterbo, y á la poblacion y lengua primitiua de España que ha publicado don Ieseph [sic] Pellicer de Touar y Osaú . . . por don Luis Ioseph de Aguilar y Losada*. Toledo, 1674.

Becerra, Antonio. *Memorial en que se hace relazión de la decensión de la Virgen Santissima Nuestra Señora. Y de la visita que hizo a la Iglesia de San Ildefonso de la ciudad de Jaén, el año de 1430*. Jaén: Francisco Pérez de Castilla, 1639.

Bilches, Francisco. *Santos y santuarios del Obispado de Iaén y Baeza*. Madrid: Domingo García y Morràs, 1653.

Bivar, Francisco de. *Pro Fl. L. Dextro libellus supplex, & apologeticus*. N.p., 1630.

Bolland, Jean, and Godefroy Henschen. *Acta sanctorum . . . Februarius*. Vol. I. Antwerp: Johannes Meursius, 1658.

———. *Acta sanctorum . . . Ianuarius*. Vol. I. Antwerp: Johannes Meursius, 1643.

Bollandistes, Société des, ed. *Bibliotheca hagiographica latina antiquae et mediae aetatis*. Subsidia hagiographica. Brussels: Socii Bollandiani, 1898.

Bosius, Johannes Andreas. *De prudentia et eloquentia civili comparanda Diatribae Isagogicae quarum haec prodit auctior sub titulo de Ratione legendi tractandique historicos*. Jena: Apud Ioannem Bielkium, 1669.

Brady, James F., and John C. Olin, eds. *The Edition of St. Jerome: Collected Works of Erasmus*. Vol. 61. Toronto: University of Toronto Press, 1992.

Braulio of Saragossa and Fructuosus of Braga. *Writings of Braulio of Saragossa and Fructuosus of Braga. Iberian Fathers*, vol. 2. Translated by Claude W. Barlow. Fathers of the Church Series, vol. 63. Washington, D.C.: Catholic University of America, 1969.

Bravo de Mendoça, Tomás. *Invencion felicissima de la Cabeça del divino Hierotheo*. Valladolid: Iuan Lasso de las Peñas, 1625.

Brouwer, Christoph. *Antiquitates annalium trevirensium, et episcoporum trevirensis ecclesiae*. Cologne: Bern. Gualtherus, 1626.

Burgess, Richard W., ed. *The Chronicle of Hydatius and the Consularia Constantinopolitana: Two Contemporary Accounts of the Final Years of the Roman Empire*. Oxford: Clarendon, 1993.

Cano, Melchor. *L'autorità della storia profana (De humanae historiae auctoritate)*. Edited and translated by Albano Biondi. Turin: Giappichelli, 1973.

———. *De locis theologicis*. Translated by Juan Belda Plans. Madrid: Biblioteca de Autores Cristianos, 2006.

Cárcamo, Alonso de. *Traslado de la carta y relacion qve embio a sv Magestad . . . a cerca del Templo que en ella se ha hallado del señor San Tyrso*. Toledo: Pedro Rodriguez, 1595.

Cardelle de Hartmann, Carmen, and Roger Collins, eds. *Victoris tunnunensis Chronicon: cum reliquiis ex Consularibus Caesaraugustanis et Iohnannis Biclarensis Chronicon*, Corpus Christianorum. Series Latina. Turnholt: Brepols, 2001.

Cardoso, Jorge. *Agiológio lusitano*. Fascimile ed., 4 vols. Edited by António Caetano de Sousa and Maria de Lurdes Correia Fernandes. Porto: Faculdade de Letras da Universidade do Porto, 2002.

Caro, Rodrigo. *Antigüedades y principado de la ciudad de Sevilla*. Seville, 1982.

———. *La canción a las ruinas de Itálica*. Bogotá: Voluntad, 1947.

———. *Relacion de las inscripciones y antigüedad de la Villa de Utrera*. Osuna: Juan Serrano de Vargas, Impresor de la Universidad, 1622.

———. *Santuario de Nuestra Señora de la Consolacion y Antigüedad de la Villa de Utrera*. Osuna: Juan Serrano de Vargas, Impresor de la Universidad, 1622.

———. *Varones insignes en letras naturales de la ilustrísima ciudad de Sevilla*. Edited by Luís Gómez Canseco. Seville: Exma. Diputación Provincial de Sevilla, 1992.

Carrillo, Martín. *Historia del glorioso San Valero obispo de la ciudad de Çaragoça*. Zaragoza: Iuan de Lanaja y Quartanet Impressor del Reyno de Aragon y de la Vniversidad, 1615.

Causino, Nicolas. *La corte divina, ó palacio celestial*. Barcelona: Juan Piferrer, 1718.

Cervantes Saavedra, Miguel de. *El ingenioso hidalgo Don Quijote de la Mancha*. Barcelona: Planeta, 1998.

Codoñer Merino, Carmen. *El "De viris illustribus" de Isidoro de Sevilla: Estudio y edición crítica*. Salamanca: Consejo Superior de Investigaciones Científicas (CSIC), 1964.

Collecçam dos documentos, estatutos e memorias da Academia Real da Historia portugueza que neste anno de 1721 se compuzeraõ, e se imprimiraõ por orden dos seus censores. Lisbon: Pascoal da Sylva, 1721.

Cordón, Constantino. *Apologia sobre la cabeza de San Sacerdote, obispo de Siguenza, contra Don Juan Tamayo de Salazar, presbytero ilipense*. N.p., 1720.

Covarrubias Orozco, Sebastián de. *Parte segunda del tesoro de la lengva castellana o española*. Madrid: Melchor Sanchez, a costa de Gabriel de Leon, Mercader de libros, vendese enfrente de la calle de la Paz, 1673.

Curtius Rufus, Quintus. *History of Alexander*. Translated by John Carew Rolfe. 2 vols. Loeb Classical Library. Cambridge: Harvard University Press, 1946.

Dávila Toledo, Sancho. *De la veneracion que se deve a los cuerpos de los Sanctos y a sus Reliquias, y de la singular con que se a de adorar el cuerpo de Iesu Christo nuestro Señor en el Sanctissimo Sacramento*. Madrid: Luis Sánchez, 1611.

———. *La vida de San Vidal martyr que fue en Athenas convertido por San Pablo*. Baeça: por Fernando Diaz de Montoya, 1601.

Dubitavi: An constet Ecclesiam Beatae Mariae Virginis de Columna, seu (ut vulgo dicitur) de Pilari fuisse antiquitus Cathedralem? N.p.

Elliott, J. K. *The Apocryphal New Testament: A Collection of Apocryphal Christian Literature in an English Translation*. Reprinted and corrected ed. Oxford: Oxford University Press, 2005.

Entrambasaguas, Joaquín de. *La biblioteca de Ramírez de Prado*. Fascimile ed., 2 vols. Madrid: CSIC, 1943.

Escolano, Gaspar. *Decada primera de la historia de la insigne, y Coronada ciudad y Reyno de Valencia*. 2 vols. Valencia: Pedro Patricio Mey, 1610–11.

Escolano y Ledesma, Diego. *Chronicon Sancti Hierothei, Athenarum primum, postea segoviensis Ecclesiae Episcopi*. Madrid: In officina Dominici Garcia Morras, 1667.

Espinosa de Santayana, Rodrigo de. *Arte de retorica*. Madrid: en casa de Guillermo Drouy, 1578.

Eusebius, and Jerome. *Eusebii Pamphili Chronici canones*. Edited by John Knight Fotheringham. London: apud Humphredum Milford, 1923.

Fábrega Grau, Ángel. *Pasionario hispánico*. 2 vols. Madrid and Barcelona: CSIC; Instituto Padre Enrique Flórez, 1953–55.

Feijóo, Benito Jerónimo. *Teatro crítico universal, o, Discursos varios en todo genero de materias, para desengaño de errores comunes*. Nueva ed., 9 vols. Madrid: En la imprenta de Blas Román, 1778.

Fernández de Malpartida, Alonso. *Historia y anales de la ciudad y obispado de Plasencia*. Madrid: Juan Gonçalez, 1627.

Flórez, Enrique. Edited by Rafael Lazcano González. *España sagrada*. 57 vols. Madrid: Editorial Revista Agustiniana, 2000–2012.

Freidberg, Emil Albert, ed. *Corpus iuris canonici. Editio lipsiensis secunda: post Aemilii Ludouici Richteri curas ad librorum manu scriptorum et editionis romanae*. Reprint ed., 2 vols. Graz: Akademische Druck-U. Verlagsanstalt, 1959.

Gándara, Felipe de la. *El cisne occidental canta palmas y triunfos eclesiásticos de Galicia, ganados por sus hijos insignes, Santos y varones ilustres y ilustrissimos martires, pontifices, virgenes, confesores, doctores, y escritores que los han merecido en la iglesia militante para reinar con Dios en la triunfante*. Madrid: Julian Paredes, 1678.

Garibay y Zamalloa, Esteban de. *Discurso de mi vida*. Edited by Jesús Moya. Bilbao: Universidad del País Vasco, 1999.

Gayangos, Pascual de, ed. *Cartas de algunos padres de la Compañía de Jesús sobre los sucesos de le monarquía entre los años de 1634 y 1648*. 7 vols. Madrid: Imprenta nacional, 1861.

The Geography of Strabo. 8 vols. Loeb Classical Library. Cambridge: Harvard University Press, 1923.

Gil Fernández, Juan. *Miscellanea Wisigothica*. Ed. altera lucis ope impressa. Seville: Publicaciones de la Universidad de Sevilla, 1992.

Gómez Bravo, Juan. *Advertencias a la istoria de Merida*. Florence, 1638.

González Chantos y Ullauri, Diego Eugenio. *Santa Librada, vírgen y mártir, patrona de la Santa Iglesia, ciudad, y obispado de Sigüenza, vindicada*. Madrid: Imprenta de la Administración del Real Arbitrio, 1806.

Halliwell, Stephen. *Aristotle's Poetics*. London: Duckworth, 1986.

Hernández, Miguel. *Vida, martirio y traslación de la virgen y mártir Santa Leocadia*. Toledo: Pedro Rodríguez, 1591.

Huerta y Vega, Francisco Javier Manuel de la. *España Primitiva, Historia de sus Reyes y Monarcas desde su población hasta Cristo*. Madrid, 1738.

Ibáñez de Segovia, Gaspar. *Discurso histórico por el patronato de San Frutos contra la supuesta cathedra de San Hierotheo en Segovia y pretendida authoridad de Dextro*. Zaragoza: Juan de Ibar, 1666.

———. *Dissertaciones eclesiasticas por el honor de los antiguos tutelares contra las ficciones modernas*. Zaragoza: Diego Dormer, 1671.

Inchofer, Melchior. *De epistolae B. Virginis Mariae ad messanenses coniectatio plurimis rationibus et verisimilitudinibus locuples*. Viterbo: ex typographia Ludouici Grignani, 1632.

---. *Epistolae B. Virginis Mariae ad Messanenses Veritas Vindicata ac Plurimis Gravissimorum scriptorum testimoniis et rationibus erudite illustrata*. Messina: Ex typographia Petri Brede sumptibus Iosephi Matarozij, 1629.

Interián de Ayala, Juan. *El pintor christiano, y erudito, ó Tratado de los errores que suelen cometerse freqüentemente en pintar, y esculpir las Imágenes Sagradas*. Translated by Don Luis de Durán y de Bastéro. Madrid: D. Joachin Ibarra, 1782.

Iriarte, Tomás de. *Coleccion de obras en verso y prosa*. 8 vols. Vol. II: *Varias poesías*. Madrid: Imprenta Real, 1805.

Jerome. *Apologie contre Rufin*. Translated by Pierre Lardet. Paris: Éditions du Cerf, 1983.

---. *On Illustrious Men*. Translated by Thomas P. Halton. Washington, D.C.: Catholic University of America, 1999.

---. *The Principal Works of St. Jerome*. Edited by Philip Schaff and Henry Wace. Vol. VI: *Letters and Select Works*. Grand Rapids: Wm. B. Eerdmans, 1960.

Jiménez de Gregorio, Fernando. *Diccionario de los pueblos de la Provincia de Toledo hasta finalizar el siglo XVIII*. Toledo: Editorial Católica Toledana, 1848.

Lapide, Cornelio a. *Commentaria in acta apostolorum, epistolas canonicas, et apocalypsin*. Antwerp: Apud Ioan et Iacob Meursios, 1647.

Loaysa Girón, García, ed. *Chronicon D. Isidori Archiep. Hisp. emendatum, scholiisq[ue] illustratum*. Turin: Io. Baptistam Beuilaquam, 1593.

López de Montoya, Pedro. *Los quatro libros del mysterio de la Missa: Con unas annotaciones en lengua latina sobre el sagrado Canon*. Madrid: en casa de Guillermo Druy, 1591.

Lukács, Ladislaus. *Catalogi personarum provinciae Austriae Societatis Iesu*. 2 vols. Rome: Institutum Historicum Societatis Iesu, 1978.

Luna, Miguel de. *Historia verdadera del Rey Don Rodrigo*. Edited by Luis Fernando Bernabé Pons. Granada: Universidad de Granada, 2001.

Madoz, José. *Liciniano de Cartagena y sus cartas: edición crítica y estudio histórico*. Madrid: Facultades de Teología y de Filosofía del Colegio Máximo de Oña, 1948.

Madoz, Pascual. *Diccionario geográfico-estadístico-histórico de España y sus posesiones de ultramar*. 16 vols. Madrid: P. Madoz y L. Sagasti, 1845–50.

Maldonado, Alonso. *Chronica universal de todas las naciones y tiempos . . . con diez y seis tratados de los puntos mas importantes de la chronologia*. Madrid: Luis Sánchez inpressor del Rey, 1624.

Mariana, Juan de. *De rege et regis institutione libri tres*. Toledo: Pedro Rodriguez, 1599.

---. *Discurso de las enfermedades de la compañia*. Madrid: Imprenta de D. Gabriel Ramirez, 1768.

---. *Historia general de España*. 2 vols. Madrid: Joachin de Ibarra, 1780.

---. *Historiae de rebvs Hispaniae libri XXV*. Toledo: Petri Roderici, 1592.

---. *Joannis Marianae e Societate Jesu Tractatus VII*. Cologne: Sumptibus Antonii Hiera, sub Monocerote, 1609.

Mariana, Juan de, and José Manuel Miñana. *Historia general de España*. 10 vols. Barcelona: Francisco Oliva, 1839.

---. *Historia general de España, la compuesta, enmendada y añadida por el Padre Mariana con la continuación de Miñana*. Madrid: Gaspar y Roig, 1855.

Márquez, Ioan. *Origen de los frayles ermitaños de la Orden de San Augustin y su verdadera institucion antes del gran Concilio Lateranense.* Salamanca: en la imprenta de Antonia Ramirez viuda, 1618.

Martín, José Carlos, ed. *Isidori Hispalensis Chronica,* Corpus Christianorum. Series Latina. Turnhout: Brepols, 2003.

Martínez de Mazas, José. *Memorial al Yllmo. y mui Venerable estado eclesiástico de el obispado de Jaén sobre el indebido culto que se da a muchos santos no canonizados, o que no le pertenecen por otro título que el de los falsos chronicones.* Edited by Manuel Urbano Pérez Ortega and José Rodríguez Molina. Jaén: Diputación Provincial de Jaén, 2001.

Martryologium Romanum, ad novam Kalendarij rationem . . . restitutum. Antwerp: Ex officina C. Plantini, 1586.

Martz, Linda, and Julio Porres Martín-Cleto. *Toledo y los toledanos en 1561.* Toledo: Diputación Provincial, 1974.

Masdeu, Juan Francisco. *Historia crítica de España, y de la cultura española por Juan Francisco de Masdeu.* 20 vols. Madrid: Antonio de Sancha, 1783.

Medina Conde, Cristóbal de. *El fingido Dextro, convencido de tal por su pluma, ó descubierta con su misma mano.* Malaga: [Imprenta] de la Plaza, 1772.

Memorial del pleito sobre el reconocimiento, aprouacion y calificacion de los milagros, veneracion y colocacion de las reliquias [. . .] que se descubrieron en la villa de Arjona [. . .]. N.p., ca. 1646.

Morales, Ambrosio. *Las antigüedades de las ciudades de España.* Reprint of 1792 Madrid ed., 2 vols. Edited by Benito Cano. Valencia: Librerías "Paris-Valencia," 2001.

———. *La coronica general de España.* Alcalá de Henares: Casa de Iuan Iñiguez de Lequerica, 1574–1577.

Moscoso y Sandoval, Baltasar. *Constituciones synodales del Obispado de Iaen.* Baeza: Pedro de la Cuesta, 1626.

———. *A los nuestros muy venerables y amados hermanos el Dean y Cabildo de nuestra Santa Iglesia de Iaen [. . .] Notorio es, por testimonio del Real Profeta, quan preciosas sean a los ojos de Dios las gloriosas muertes de sus Santos Martires.* N.p., 1640.

———. *Officia propria sanctorum giennensis ecclesiae, et diocesis.* Jaén: Imprenta de Don Narciso de Guindos, 1871.

———. *Traslado bien y fielme[n]te sacado del Auto proveydo [. . .] sobre y en razo[n] de que se renueve con rayos y Diadema la efigie del Santo Martir Don fray Pedro Pascual de Valencia [. . .] y que se pinte con el Abito della,* 1640.

Moya y Munguia, Christoval. *Tratado apologetico en favor de la Cathedra de San Hierotheo en Segovia . . . contra el discurso histórico que sacó a luz D. Gaspar Ibañez de Segovia y Peralta.* Madrid: Domingo Garcia Morrás, 1666.

Muñiz, Roberto. *Biblioteca cisterciense española.* Burgos: D. Joseph de Navas, 1793.

Múñoz y Romero, Tomás. *Diccionario bibliográfico-histórico de los antiguos reinos, provincias, ciudades, villas, iglesias y santuarios de España.* Madrid: M. Rivadeneyra, 1858.

Murillo, Diego. *Fundación milagrosa de la capilla . . . de la Madre de Dios del Pilar, y Excellencias de . . . Zaragoza.* Barcelona: Sebastian Mateuad, 1616.

Nieremberg, Juan Eusebio. *Historia naturae maxime peregrinae, libris XVI distincta.* Antwerp: Ex officina Plantiniana Balthasaris Moreti, 1635.

Ocampo, Florián de. *Los çinco libros primeros de La Corónica de España que recopilava el Maestro Florián de Ocampo.* Fascimile of 1553 Medina del Campo ed. Madrid: Dirección de Estudios y Documentación, Departamento de Publicaciones, Secretaría General del Senado, 1997.

Ochoa y Ronna, Eugenio de, ed. *Epistolario español.* 2 vols. Madrid: M. Rivadeneyra, 1850–70.

Orosius, Paulus. *The Seven Books of History against the Pagans.* Edited by Roy J. Deferrari. Washington: Catholic University of America, 1964.

Pancorbo, Jerónimo. *Disquisición de los Santos Martires de Arjona.* Seville: Simon Faxardo, 1634.

———. *Disquisición de Santa Potenciana virgen.* Seville: Imprenta de Simón Faxardo, 1643.

———. *Relacion escrita al Doctor Ioan Santoyo de Palma . . . dase quenta de las reliquias, y cuerpos santos, que se hallaron . . . en la Villa de Arjona.* Seville: Manuel de Sandè, 1629.

Peña y Lezcano, Pablo de la. *Memorial por la Primacía del Glorioso Mártir San Elpidio; probando que se debe admitir, y nombrar primero Arçobispo de Toledo, y instituirle Rezo, y fiesta especial, en la muy Santa Iglesia Primada de las Españas.* Zaragoza: Agustín Verges, 1674.

Pennotto, Gabriele. *Defensio Censurae . . . Baronii et Bellarmini . . . in sermones ad eremitas Divo Augustino suppositos.* Venice: Apud Evangelistam Deuchinum, 1630.

———. *Generalis totivs sacri ordinis clericorvm canonicrvm historia tripartita.* Rome: ex typographia Camerae apostolicae, 1624.

Pisa, Francisco de. *Descripción de la imperial ciudad de Toledo.* Facsimile of 1605 ed. Toledo: Diputación Provincial de Toledo, 1974.

———. *Descripcion de la imperial ciudad de Toledo . . . Primera parte.* Toledo: Diego Rodriguez, 1617.

Portocarrero, Francisco. *Libro de la descencion de nuestra señora a la santa yglesia de Toledo, y vida de San Ilefonso Arçobispo della.* Madrid: Luis Sánchez, 1616.

Proclamacion catolica a la magestad piadosa de Felipe El Grande . . . Los conselleres, y consejo de ciento de la ciudad de Barcelona. N.p., 1640.

Proprium sanctorum hispanorum, qui generaliter in Hispania celebrantur, ad formam officij novi redactu[m]. Salamanca: Guillermo Foquel, 1591.

Quevedo Villegas, Francisco de. "Vida de San Pablo Apostol." In *Obras de don Francisco de Quevedo Villegas,* edited by Aureliano Fernández-Guerra y Orbe. Madrid: M. Rivadeneyra, 1876.

Quintana, Jerónimo de. *A la muy antigua, noble y coronada Villa de Madrid. Historia de su antiguedad, nobleza y grandeza.* Madrid: La Imprenta del Reyno, 1629.

Quintanadueñas, Antonio de. *Gloriosos martyres de Osuna, Arcadio, Leon, Donato, Nicephoro, Abundancio, y nueve compañeros suyos.* Seville: Francisco de Lyra, 1632.

———. *Santos de la ciudad de Sevilla, y su arçobispado: Fiestas, que su santa iglesia metropolitana celebra.* Seville: Francisco de Lyra, 1637.

———. *Santos de la imperial ciudad de Toledo y su arçobispado.* Madrid: Pablo de Val, 1651.

Rader, Matthäus. *Ad M. Valerii Martialis Epigrammaton libros omnes plenis commenta-*

riis novo studio confectis. Moguntiae: Sumptibus Ioannis Kinckii, Bibliop. Colon. Excudebat Hermannus Maresius, 1627.

———. *Analecta, tertiis commentariorum curis, ad Martialem iam editis, addenda*. Coloniae Agrippinae: Apud Ioannem Kinckium, ad intersigne Monocerotis, 1628.

Rallo Gruss, Asunción, ed. *Libros de antigüedades de Andalucía*. Seville: Fundación José Manuel Lara, 2009.

Real Academia de la Historia. *Memorial histórico español: colección de documentos, opúsculos y antigüedades*. Madrid: Imprenta de la Real Academia de la Historia, 1851.

Requena Aragón, Alonso de. *Venida del apostol S. Pablo a España, y predicacion en ella, y como estuvo en Libisosa (oi Lezuza), su fundacion, y antigüedad: y martirio de S. Vicente, y Leto, hermanos, Patrones de ella, y naturales de Toledo*. Madrid: en la Imprenta de Maria de Quiñones, 1647.

Ribadeneira, Pedro de, Juan Eusebio Nieremberg, Francisco García, and Andrés Lopez Guerrero. *Flos sanctorum de las vidas de los santos*. 3 vols. Barcelona: En la imprenta de los consortes Sierra, Olivér, y Martí, 1790 (first edition 1599).

Ribadeneira, Pedro, and Philippo Alegambe. *Bibliotheca scriptorum Societatis Iesu*. Antwerp: Apud Ioannem Meursium, 1643.

Ribadeneira, Pedro, Philippo Alegambe, and Nathanaele Sotuello. *Bibliotheca scriptorum Societatis Iesu*. Rome: Ex Typographia Iacobi Antonij de Lazzaris Varesij, 1676.

Rioja, Francisco de. *Aristarco o censura de la proclamacion catolica de los catalanes*. N.p., ca. 1640.

Roa, Martín de. *Ecija. Sus santos, su antigüedad eclesiastica i seglar*. Seville, 1629.

———. *Santos Honorio, Eutichio, Estevan, patronos de Xerez de la Frontera*. Seville: Alonso Rodriguez Gamarra, 1617.

Robles, Eugenio de. *Compendio de la vida y hazañas del Cardenal don fray Francisco Ximenez de Cisneros, y del Oficio y Missa muzarabe*. Toledo: Pedro Rodriguez, 1604

Robles Corvalán, Juan de. *Historia del mysterioso aparecimiento de la Santissima Cruz de Carabaca e inumerables milagros, que Dios N.S. ha obrado, y obra por su devocio[n]*. Madrid: Casa de la Biuda de Alonso Martín, 1615.

Rodríguez de Montalvo, Garci. *Amadis of Gaul: A Novel of Chivalry of the 14th Century Presumably First Written in Spanish*. Translated by Edwin Bray Place and Herbert C. Behm. 2 vols. Lexington: University Press of Kentucky, 1974.

Rojas, Pedro de. *Historia de la imperial, nobilissima, inclita, y esclarecida ciudad de Toledo . . . Parte primera*. Facsimile of 1654 ed. Toledo: Zocodover, 1984.

———. *Historia de la imperial, nobilissima, inclita, y esclarecida ciudad de Toledo . . . Parte segunda*. Facsimile of 1663 ed. Toledo: Zocodover, 1984.

Román de la Higuera, Jerónimo. "Epistola XVI. Caesari Baronio Hieronymus Higueras." In *Venerabilis Caesaris Baronii [. . .] Epistolae et Opuscula, Tomus Tertius*, edited by Raymundus Albericius, 163–64. Rome: Ex Typographia Pauli Junchi Haeredis Komarek, 1770.

———. *Memorial que . . . embió a la villa de Touarra de la diocesis de Cartagena al Doctor Gines Gomez Cura de la parroquial de la dicha villa: por el qual consta, que santa Victoria Romana virgen padecio martirio en el termino de la dicha villa, que oy dizen Touarra la vieja*. N.p., ca. 1600.

Ruinart, Thierry. *Acta primorum martyrum sincera et selecta . . . notisque & observationibus illustrata*. Paris: F. Muguet, 1689.

Rus Puerta, Francisco de. *Historia eclesiastica del reino y obispado de Iaen*. Jaén: Francisco Pérez de Castilla, 1634.

Sacra Congregatio Pro Causis Sanctorum. *Index ac Status Causarum*, Editione peculiaris cura Petri Galavotti IV° exeunte saeculo ipsius Congregationis. Vatican City: Congregatio de Causis Sanctorum, 1998.

Sacra Congregationis Propaganda Fide. *Decreta Authenticata Congregationis Sacrorum Rituum ex actis eiusdem collecta eiusque auctoritate promulgata*. Vol. I [1588–1705]. Rome: Typographia Polyglotta, 1898.

Sainz de Baranda, Pedro. *Clave de la España sagrada*. Madrid: Imprenta de la viuda de Calero, 1853.

Salazar de Mendoza, Pedro. *Cronica de el gran cardenal de España, don Pedro Gonçalez de Mendoça*. Toledo: En la emprenta de doña María Ortiz de Sarauia, Impressora de el Rey Catholico nuestro Señor, 1625.

———. *El origen de las dignidades seglares de Castilla y León*. Facsimile of 1794 ed. Edited by Enrique Soria Mesa. Granada: Universidad de Granada, 1998.

Salazar y Castro, Luís. *Historia genealógica de la casa de Lara*. 3 vols., Madrid: Imprenta Real, 1697–98.

San Cecilio, Pedro de. *Historia de la vida y martyrio de Don Fray Pedro de Valencia*. Granada: Bartolome de Lorençana, 1629.

San Nicolás, Pablo de. *Antiguedades eclesiasticas de España en los quatro primeros siglos de la Iglesia*. Madrid: Juan de Ariztia, 1725.

San Pablo, Hermenegildo de. *Defensa por la religion Geronyma de España y su antiguedad*. Zaragoza: Diego Dormer, 1672.

Sandoval, Francisco de. *San Antonino español. Discurso apologetico. Pruevase que el Patron de la Santa Iglesia, ciudad, y Obispado de Palencia, no es el santo frances Antonino, sino es el ANTONINO español, que hasta oy se ha ignorado*. Valladolid: Viuda de Cordova, 1633.

Sandoval, Prudencio de. *Antigüedad de la ciudad y iglesia cathedral de Tuy*. Braga: Em casa de Fructuoso Lorenço de Basto, 1610, and printed in facsimile ed. Barcelona: El Albir, 1974.

———. *Historias de Idacio Obispo: que escribio poco antes que España se perdiesse. De Isidoro Obispo de Badajoz . . . De Sebastiano Obispo de Salamanca . . . De Sampiro Obispo de Astorga . . . De Pelagio Obispo de Oviedo . . . Nunca hasta agora impressas, con otras notas tocantes a estas historias, y reyes dellas*. Pamplona: Nicolás Assiayn, 1615.

———. *Primera parte de las fundaciones de los monesterios [sic] del glorioso Padre San Benito*. Madrid: Luis Sánchez, 1601.

Santa María, Francisco de. *Apologia del tomo primero de la historia general profetica . . . En defensa i apoyo de las proposiciones aprovadas i autorizadas por el Supremo Consejo de la Santa General Inquisicion*. Valencia: Casa de los herederos de Crisostomo Garriz, por Bernardo Noques, junto al Molino de Revella, 1643.

———. *Historia general profética de la Orden de Nuestra Señora del Carmen*. Madrid: Francisco Martínez, 1630.

———. *Historia general profética de la Orden de Nuestra Señora del Carmen*. Madrid: Diego Diaz de la Carrera, 1641.

Schmidl, Joanne. *Historiae Societatis Jesu Provinciae Bohemiae*. 2 vols. Prague: Typis Universitatis Carolo Ferdinandeae in Collegio S. J. ad S. Clementem, per Jacobum Schweiger Factorem, 1747.

Schottus, Andreas, ed. *Hispaniae illustratae seu rerum, urbiumque Hispaniae, Lusitanae, Aethiopiae, et Indiae scriptores varii*. 4 vols. Frankfurt, 1603–8.

Squatriti, Paolo, ed. *The Complete Works of Liudprand of Cremona*. Washington, D.C.: Catholic University of America, 2007.

Suárez, Pedro. Edited by Vicente Castañeda. *Historia de el Obispado de Guadix y Baza*. Madrid: Artes Gráficas ARGES, 1948.

Tamayo, Manuel. *Discursos apologeticos de las reliquias de S. Bonoso y Maximiano y de los demas mas martires que se hallaron en Arjona*. Ba[e]ça: Pedro dela questa [sic], 1635.

Tamayo de Salazar, Juan. *Anamnesis sive commemoratio omnium sanctorum hispanorum*. Lyons: sumpt. Philippi Borde. Laurent. Arnaud, et Claudii Rigaud, 1651–59.

———. *Auli Hali poétae . . . ex M. S. Gothico Codice erutum, correctum, & notis brevibus illustratum*. Madrid: Ex officina Didaci Diaz de la Carrera, 1648.

Tamayo de Vargas, Tomás. *Novedades antiguas de España. Flavio Lucio Dextro . . . Defendido*. Madrid: Pedro Tazo, 1624.

Terrones de Robles, Antonio. Edited by Manuel Urbano. *Vida, martirio, traslación y milagros de San Euphrasio*. Facsimile of 1657 ed. Jaén: Diputación Provincial de Jaén, 1996.

Torrents, Juan Ángelo. *Glorias del Carmelo*. 4 vols. Palma: V. de Villalonga, 1860.

Usuard, and Johannes Molanus. *Usuardi Martyrologium*. Louvain: Apud Hieronymum Vvellaeum sub signo Diamantis, 1568.

———. *Vsvardi Martyrologivm, qvo Romana Ecclesia, ac per mvltae aliae vtuntur*. Antwerp: Apud Philippum Nutium, 1583.

Varona, José. *Epitome del glorioso martirio de Santa Caliopa de Lerma, natural de Lerma, donde le padecio*. N.p. [1716].

Vázquez, Gabriel. *De cultu adorationis libri tres . . . accesserunt disputationes duae contra errores Foelicis & Elipandi de adoptione & seruitute Christi in concilio francofordiensi damnatos*. Alcalá de Henares: Ex officina Ioannis Gratiani, apud Viduam, 1594.

Vázquez Siruela, Martín. *Apologia por los baños de la muy noble y leal ciudad de Alhama: contra el desengaño que de ellos escrivió Francisco Fregoso*. Granada: Blas Martinez, 1636.

Verdadera relación de los Santos que se van descubriendo al pie de las torres de la Villa de Arjona . . . compuesto por un devoto suyo. Jaén: Casa de Pedro Madrigal, 1629.

Vergara, Juan de. *Tratado de las ocho cuestiones del Templo*. Toledo: Casa de Iuan Ferrer, 1552.

Vicent y Portillo, Gregorio, ed. *Biblioteca histórica de Cartagena*. 2 vols. Madrid: Montegrifo, 1889.

La vida y martirio de la bienaventurada Sancta Librada virgen y martyr hija del rey Cathelo y de la reyna Calsia reyes de una ciudad llamada Balcagia la qual nascio juntamente con otras ocho hermanas todas de un parto: cuya maravillosa criança y sancta vida la presente obra recuenta. N.p.

Villanueva, Joaquín, and Jaime Villanueva. *Viage literario á las iglesias de España.* 22 vols. Madrid: Imprenta Real, 1803–52.

Villegas, Alonso de. *Flos sanctorum.* Barcelona: Isidro Aguasvivas, Librero, 1794 (first ed. Zaragoza, 1585).

Villegas, Bernardino de. *Memorial sobre la calificacion de las reliquias de los Santos Martyres de Arjona.* Baeça: Iuan de la Cuesta, 1639.

Wolf, Kenneth Baxter. *Conquerors and Chroniclers of Early Medieval Spain.* Liverpool: Liverpool University Press, 1990.

Ximena Jurado, Martín de. *Catálogo de los obispos de las iglesias catedrales de Jaén y anales eclesiásticos de este obispado.* Reprint of 1654 edition; foreword and indices by José Rodríguez Molina and María José Osorio Pérez. Granada: Universidad de Granada and Ayuntamiento de Jaén, 1991.

———. *Historia o anales del municipio Albense Urgavonense o villa de Arjona.* Edited by Rafael Frías Marín. Arjona: Excmo. Ayuntamiento de Arjona; Caja Provincial de Jaén, 1996.

Zaragoza, Lamberto de, and Ramón de Huesca. *Teatro histórico de las iglesias del reyno de Aragón.* 9 vols. Pamplona: J. M. Ezguerro, 1780–1807.

SECONDARY SOURCES

Abascal Palazón, Juan Manuel, and Rosario Cebrián Fernández, eds. *Manuscritos sobre antigüedades de la Real Academia de la Historia.* Madrid: Real Academia de la Historia, 2005.

Acera, Fernando Martín. "Notas críticas a la obra histórica latino-castellana del P. Mariana (Estudio bio-bibliográfico)." *Durius* 2 (1974), 9–42.

Adorno, Rolena. "Sobre la censura y su evasión: Un caso transatlántico del siglo XVI." In *Grafías del imaginario: Representaciones culturales en España y América (siglos XVI–XVIII)*, edited by Carlos Alberto González Sánchez and Enriqueta Vila Vilar, 13–52. Mexico City: Fondo de Cultura Económica, 2003.

Aillet, Cyrille. "La question 'mozarabe.' Bilan historiographique et nouvelles approches." In *Al-Andalus/España: Historiografías en contraste, siglos XVII–XXI*, edited by Manuela Marín, 295–323. Madrid: Casa de Velázquez, 2009.

Aldea Vaquero, Quintín, Tomás Marín Martínez, and José Vives Gatell. *Diccionario de historia eclesiástica de España.* Madrid: Instituto Enrique Flórez, 1972–87.

Alder, Ken. "History's Greatest Forger: Science, Fiction, and Fraud along the Seine." *Critical Inquiry* 30, Summer (2004), 702–16.

Allard, Paul. "Rome au IVe siècle d'après les poèmes de Prudence." *Revue des questions historiques* 36 (1884), 5–61.

Álvarez Barrientos, Joaquín. "Historia y religiosidad popular en las falsificaciones granadinas del siglo XVIII." In *La religiosidad popular. I. Antropología e historia*, edited by Carlos Álvarez Santaló, et al., 348–56. Barcelona: Anthropos, 1989.

Andrés Escapa, Pablo. "Historia de unos papeles: El legado manuscrito de Guardiola en la librería de Gondomar. Nuevas aportaciones a su biografía y a la escritura de la *Historia de San Benito el Real de Sahagún*." In *De libros, librerías, imprentas y lectores*, edited by Pedro M. Cátedra and María Luisa López-Vidriero, 13–36. Salamanca: Ediciones Universidad de Salamanca, 2002.

Andrés, Gregorio de. "El helenismo del canónigo toledano Antonio de Covarrubias: Un capítulo del humanismo en Toledo en el s. XVI." *Hispania Sacra* 40 (1988), 237–313.

———. "Historia de la biblioteca del Conde-Duque de Olivares y descripción de sus códices, I: Formación." *Cuadernos bibliográficos* 28 (1972), 1–12.

———. "Historia de la biblioteca del Conde-Duque de Olivares y descripción de sus códices, II." *Cuadernos bibliográficos* 30 (1973), 5–73.

———. "La bibliofilia del Marqués de Mondéjar y su biblioteca manuscrita." In *Primeras Jornadas de Bibliografía*, 583–602. Madrid: Fundación Universitaria Española, 1977.

———. "Los códices del Conde de Miranda en la Biblioteca Nacional." *Revista de archivos, bibliotecas y museos* 82 (1979), 611–27.

———. "Los manuscritos del Inquisidor General, Diego de Arce y Reinoso, Obispo de Plasencia." *Hispania Sacra* 33 (1981), 491–507.

Antón Pelayo, Javier. "La historiografía catalana del siglo XVIII. Luces y sombras de un proyecto ilustrado y nacional." *Revista de historia moderna* 18 (2000), 289–310.

Aranda Pérez, Francisco José. *Poder municipal y cabildo de jurados en Toledo en la edad moderna (siglos XV–XVIII)*. Toledo: Ayuntamiento de Toledo, 1992.

———. *Poder y poderes en la ciudad de Toledo: Gobierno, sociedad y oligarquías urbanas en la Edad Moderna*. Cuenca: Ediciones de la Universidad de Castilla–La Mancha, 1999.

Asher, R. E. *National Myths in Renaissance France: Francus, Samothes, and the Druids*. Edinburgh: Edinburgh University Press, 1993.

Atkinson, Catherine. *Inventing Inventors in Renaissance Europe: Polydore Vergil's "De inventoribus rerum."* Tübingen: Mohr Siebeck, 2007.

Ayaso Martínez, José Ramón. "Antigüedad y excelencia de la diáspora judía en la península ibérica." *Miscelánea de estudios árabes y hebraicos. Sección de hebreo* 49 (2000), 233–259.

Backus, Irena D. *Historical Method and Confessional Identity in the Era of the Reformation (1378–1615)*. Leiden: Brill, 2003.

———. "The Letter of the Virgin Mary to the Inhabitants of Messina: Construction of a Historical Event." *Reformation & Renaissance Review: Journal of the Society for Reformation Studies* 2 (1999), 72–93.

———. "Renaissance Attitudes to New Testament Apocryphal Writings: Jacques Lefèvre d'Étaples and His Epigones." *Renaissance Quarterly* 51 (1998), 1169–98.

Bangert, William V. *A History of the Society of Jesus*. Revised ed. St. Louis: Institute of Jesuit Sources, 1986.

Barrios Aguilera, Manuel, and Mercedes García-Arenal, eds. *Los plomos del Sacromonte: Invención y tesoro*. Valencia: Universidad de Valencia, 2006.

Bartky, Elliot. "Aristotle and the Politics of Herodotus's *History*." *The Review of Politics* 64, no. 3 (2002), 445–68.

Bataillon, Marcel. *Erasmo y España: estudios sobre la historia espiritual del siglo XVI.* Translated by Antonio Alatorre. 2nd ed. Mexico City: Fondo de Cultura Económica, 1996.

———. "Sur Florian Docampo." *Bulletin hispanique* XXV, no. 1 (1923), 33–58.

Baynham, Elizabeth. *Alexander the Great: The Unique History of Quintus Curtius.* Ann Arbor: University of Michigan, 1998.

Beaver, Adam. "From Jerusalem to Toledo: Replica, Landscape, and the Nation in Renaissance Iberia." *Past and Present* 218, no. 1 (2013), 55–90.

———. "A Holy Land for the Catholic Monarchy: Palestine in the Making of Modern Spain, 1469–1598." Ph.D. diss., Harvard University, 2008.

Beltrán, José, and Fernando Gascó La Calle, eds. *La antigüedad como argumento II: historiografía de arqueología e historia antigua en Andalucía.* Seville: Junta de Andalucía, 1995.

Beltrán, José Luis, Fernando Gascó La Calle, and José Tomás Saracho Villalobos, eds. *La antigüedad como argumento: historiografía de arqueología e historia antigua en Andalucía.* Seville: Junta de Andalucía, 1993.

Beltrán de Heredía, Vicente, O.P. "La Facultad de Teología en la Universidad de Toledo." *Revista española de teología* 3 (1943), 201–47.

Benítez Sánchez-Blanco, Rafael. "De Pablo a Saulo: Traducción, crítica y denuncia de los Libros plúmbeos por el P. Ignacio de las Casas, S.J." In *Los plomos del Sacromonte: Invención y tesoro*, edited by Barrios Aguilera and García-Arenal, 217–51. Valencia, 2006.

———. "Gregorio Mayans y las láminas y libros de plomo de Granada. Los límites de la crítica ilustrada." In *¿La historia inventada?*, edited by García-Arenal and Barrios Aguilera, 375–93. Granada, 2008.

Benito Ruano, Eloy. "La "sentencia-estatuto" de Pero Sarmiento contra los conversos toledanos." *Revista de la Universidad de Madrid* 6 (1957), 277–306.

Berenberg, Daniel. "Patrons and Petitioners: Evolution of Saint Cults and the Formation of a Local Religious Culture in Early Modern Seville." Ph.D. diss., University of California–San Diego, 2005.

Biblioteca Nacional (Spain). *Inventario general de manuscritos de la Biblioteca Nacional*, Madrid: Ministerio de Educación Nacional, 1953.

Bietenholz, Peter G. *Historia and Fabula: Myths and Legends in Historical Thought from Antiquity to the Modern Age.* Leiden: Brill, 1994.

Binotti, Lucia. "Coins, Jewelry and Stone Inscriptions: Ambrosio de Morales and the Re-Writing of Spanish History." *Hispanófila* 157 (2009), 5–24.

Bizzocchi, Roberto. "Culture généalogique dans l'Italie du seizième siècle." *Annales* 46 (1991), 789–805.

———. *Genealogie incredibili: Scritti di storia nell'Europa moderna.* Nuova ed. Bologna: Il mulino, 2009.

Black, Robert. "The Donation of Constantine: A New Source for the Concept of the Renaissance." In *Language and Images of Renaissance Italy*, edited by Alison Brown, 51–85. Oxford: Clarendon, 1995.

Blackwell, Richard J. *Behind the Scenes at Galileo's Trial: Including the First English Translation of Melchior Inchofer's Tractatus syllepticus.* Notre Dame: University of Notre Dame, 2006.

Blair, Ann. "Note Taking as an Art of Transmission." *Critical Inquiry* 31, no. 1 (2004), 85–107.
Bloch, R. Howard. *God's Plagiarist: Being an Account of the Fabulous Industry and Irregular Commerce of the Abbé Migne*. Chicago: University of Chicago Press, 1994.
Boas, George. *Vox Populi: Essays in the History of an Idea*. Baltimore: Johns Hopkins University Press, 1969.
Boon, George C. "Clement of Alexandria, Wookey Hole, and the Corycian Cave." *Proceedings of the University of Bristol Spelaeological Society* 14, no. 2 (1976), 131–40.
Borchardt, Frank L. *German Antiquity in Renaissance Myth*. Baltimore: Johns Hopkins University Press, 1971.
———. "The Topos of Critical Rejection in the Renaissance." *Modern Language Notes* 81, no. 4 (1966), 476–88.
Borromeo, Agostino. "Il Cardinale Cesare Baronio e la corona spagnola." In *Baronio storico e la controriforma: Atti del Convegno internazionale di studi Sora, 6–10 ottobre 1979*, edited by Romeo De Maio, Luigi Gulia, and Aldo Mazzacane. Sora, Italy: Centro dei Studi Sorani "Vincenzo Patriarca," 1982, 56–166.
———. "Gregorio XIII." In *Enciclopedia dei Papi*, edited by Antonio Menniti Ippolito, et al. Rome: Istituto della Enciclopedia italiana, 2000.
Boruchoff, David A. "The Poetry of History." *Colonial Latin American Review* 13, no. 2 (2004), 275–82.
Bosch, Lynette M. F. *Art, Liturgy, and Legend in Renaissance Toledo: The Mendoza and the Iglesia Primada*. University Park: Pennsylvania State University Press, 2000.
Boureau, Alain. "L'adage *vox populi, vox dei* et l'invention de la nation anglaise (VIIIe–XIIe siècle)." *Annales* 47, no. 4–5 (1992), 1071–89.
Bouza Álvarez, Fernando J. *Communication, Knowledge, and Memory in Early Modern Spain*. Translated by Sonia López and Michael Agnew. Philadelphia: University of Pennsylvania, 2004.
———. *Imagen y propaganda: capítulos de historia cultural del reinado de Felipe II*, Madrid: Akal, 1998.
Bovon, François. "Beyond the Book of Acts: Stephen, the First Christian Martyr, in Traditions Outside the New Testament Canon of Scripture." *Perspectives in Religious Studies* 32, no. 2 (2005), 93–107.
Bowersock, Glen W. "Peter and Constantine." In *St. Peter's in the Vatican*, edited by William Tronzo. Cambridge: Cambridge University Press, 2005, 5–15.
Bowes, Kimberly Diane. "'*Un coterie espagnole pieuse*': Christian Archaeology and Christian Communities in Theodosian Hispania." In *Hispania in Late Antiquity: Current Perspectives*, edited by Kimberly Diane Bowes and Michael Kulikowski. Boston: Brill, 2005, 188–258.
Boynton, Susan. *Silent Music: Medieval Song and the Construction of History in Eighteenth-Century Spain*. Oxford: Oxford University Press, 2011.
Brann, Noel L. *The Abbot Trithemius (1462–1516): The Renaissance of Monastic Humanism*. Leiden: Brill, 1981.
Braun, Harald. *Juan de Mariana and Early Modern Spanish Political Thought*. Aldershot, England: Ashgate, 2007.

Brizzi, Gian Paolo, ed. *La "Ratio studiorum": modelli culturali e pratiche educative dei Gesuiti in Italia tra cinque e seicento*. Rome: Bulzoni, 1981.
Broggio, Paolo. *I gesuiti ai tempi di Claudio Acquaviva: Strategie politiche, religiose e culturali tra Cinque e Seicento*. Brescia: Morcelliana, 2007.
Brown, Elizabeth A. R. "*Falsitas pia sive reprehensibilis*: Medieval Forgers and Their Intentions." In *Kongressdaten und Festvorträge: Fälschungen im Mittelalter*. Hanover: Hansche, 1988, 101–19.
Brown, Jonathan, and Richard Kagan. "The Duke of Alcalá: His Collection and Its Evolution." *Art Bulletin* 69, no. 2 (1987), 231–55.
Brunel, C. "Versions espagnole, provençale et française de la lettre du Christ tombée du ciel." *Analecta Bollandiana* 68 (1950), 383–93.
Burke, Peter. "How to Be a Counter-Reformation Saint." In *The Historical Anthropology of Early Modern Italy*. Cambridge: Cambridge University Press, 1987, 48–62.
———. *The Renaissance Sense of the Past*. New York: St. Martin's, 1970.
Burriel Rodrigo, Mariano. *Un bibliotecario del siglo XVI, defensor de las preeminencias del Pilar: El canónigo Llorente*. Zaragoza, 1956.
Cabanelas, Darío. "Un intento de sincretismo islámico-cristiano: Los libros plúmbeos de Granada." In *Segundo congreso internacional de estudios sobre las culturas del Mediterráneo occidental*. Barcelona: Universidad Autónoma de Barcelona, 1975, 131–42.
Calero Palacios, María del Carmen. *La Abadía del Sacromonte. Catálogo de manuscritos*. Granada: Universidad de Granada, 1999.
Cámara Muñoz, Alicia. "La pintura de El Greco y la construcción de la historia de Toledo en el Renacimiento." *Espacio, Tiempo y Forma. Serie VII, Historia del Arte* 7 (1994), 37–55.
Cameron, Euan. "Primitivism, Patristics, and Polemic in Protestant Visions of Early Christianity." In *Sacred History*, edited by Van Liere, Ditchfield, and Louthan. Oxford, 2012, 27–51.
Camillo, Ottavio di. "Interpretations of Humanism in Recent Spanish Renaissance Studies." *Renaissance Quarterly* 50, no. 4 (1997), 1190–1201.
Cañal y Migolla, Carlos. "Apuntes biobibliográficos acerca del P. Martín de Roa." In *Homenaje a Menéndez y Pelayo*, 525–39. Madrid: Librería General de Victoriana Suárez, 1899.
Candel Crespo, Francisco. *Un obispo postridentino: Don Sancho Dávila y Toledo (1546–1625)*. Ávila: Excma. Diputación Provincial de Ávila, 1968.
Candelaria, Lorenzo F. "Hercules and Albrecht Dürer's *Das Meerwunder* in a Chantbook from Renaissance Spain." *Renaissance Quarterly* 58, no. 1 (2005).
Canfora, Luciano. *Il Fozio ritrovato: Juan de Mariana e André Schott*. Bari: Dedalo, 2001.
Cañizares-Esguerra, Jorge. *How to Write the History of the New World: Histories, Epistemologies, and Identities in the Eighteenth-Century Atlantic World*. Stanford: Stanford University Press, 2001.
Cantera Montenegro, Margarita. "Falsificación de documentación monástica en la Edad Media: Santa María de Nájera." *Espacio, Tiempo y Forma. Serie III, Historia medieval* 26 (2013), 59–76.
Carbonell i Manils, Joan. "Quatre cartes desconegudes de l'arquebisbe de Tarragona Antonio Agustín Albanell." *Faventia* 12–13 (1990–91), 337–52.

Cárcel Ortí, María Milagros. *Visitas pastorales y relaciones Ad Limina: Fuentes para la geografía eclesiástica*. Oviedo: Asociación de Archiveros de Iglesia en España, 2007.

Carlos Villamarín, Helena. *Las antigüedades de Hispania*. Spoleto: Centro Italiano di Studi sull'Alto Medioevo, 1996.

Caro Baroja, Julio. *Las falsificaciones de la historia (en relación con la de España)*. Barcelona: Seix Barral, 1991.

Castillo Maldonado, Pedro. "*Angelorum Participes:* The Cult of the Saints in Late Antique Spain." In *Hispania in Late Antiquity: Current Perspectives*, edited by Kimberly Diane Bowes and Michael Kulikowski, 151–88. Boston: Brill, 2005.

———. "Judíos, conversos y relapsos en la hagiografía narrativa tardoantigua hispana." *Studia historica: Historia antigua* 24 (2006), 185–203.

———. *La primera cristianización de Jaén: historia eclesiástica (ss. IV–IX)*. Jaén: Universidad de Jaén, 2005.

Cátedra, Pedro M. *Imprenta y lecturas en la Baeza del siglo XVI*. Salamanca: Gráficas Cervantes, 2001.

Cavadini, John C. *The Last Christology of the West: Adoptionism in Spain and Gaul, 785–820*. Philadelphia: University of Pennsylvania, 1993.

Cerbu, Thomas. "Melchior Inchofer, 'Un homme fin & rusé.'" In *Largo Campo de Filosofare, Eurosymposium Galileo 2001*, edited by José Montesinos and Carlos Solís, 587–611. Las Palmas de Gran Canaria: Fundación Canaria Orotava de Historia de la Ciencia, 2001.

Chandler, Cullen. "Heresy and Empire: The Role of the Adoptionist Controversy in Charlemagne's Conquest of the Spanish March." *The International History Review* 24 (2002), 505–27.

Chaparro Gómez, César. "Notas sobre el 'De ortu et obitu patrum' seudoisidoriano." *Los visigodos. Historia y civilización* 3 (1986), 397–404.

Chatelain, Jean-François. "Les recueils d'*adversaria* aux XVIe et XVIIe siècles: Des pratiques de la lecture savante au style de l'érudition." In *La livre et l'historien: Études offertes en l'honneur du Professeur Henri-Jean Martin*, edited by Frédéric Barbier, 169–86. Geneva: Droz, 1997.

Chazan, Mireille. "Le méthode critique des historiens dans les chroniques universelles médiévales." In *La méthode critique au Moyen Âges*, edited by Mireille Chazan and Gilbert Dahan, 223–56. Turnhout: Brepols, 2006.

Christian, William A., Jr. *Apparitions in Late Medieval and Renaissance Spain*. Princeton: Princeton University Press, 1981.

———. *Local Religion in Sixteenth-Century Spain*. Princeton: Princeton University Press, 1981.

———. *Religiosidad local en la España de Felipe II*. Translated by Javier Calzada and José Luis Gil Aristu. Madrid: Nerea, 1991.

Christys, Ann. *Christians in Al-Andalus (711–1000)*. Richmond, England: Curzon, 2002.

Cirot, Georges. "Documents sur le faussaire Higuera." *Bulletin hispanique* 8, no. 1 (1906), 87–95.

———. *Études sur l'historiographie espagnole I: Les histoires générales d'Espagne entre*

Alphonse et Philippe II (1284–1556) and *Études sur l'historiographie espagnole II: Mariana historien*. Bordeaux: Feret, 1905.

———. "La famille de Juan de Mariana." *Bulletin hispanique* 6, no. 4 (1904), 309–31.

———. "Lorenzo de Padilla et la Pseudo-Histoire." *Bulletin hispanique* 16 (1914), 405–47.

———. "Mariana jésuite. La jeunesse." *Bulletin hispanique* 38, no. 3 (1936), 259–352.

Cochrane, Eric. *Historians and Historiography in the Italian Renaissance*. Chicago: University of Chicago Press, 1981.

Coleman, David. *Creating Christian Granada: Society and Religious Culture in an Old-World Frontier City, 1492–1600*. Ithaca: Cornell University Press, 2003.

Collins, Amanda. "Renaissance Epigraphy and Its Legitimizing Potential: Annius of Viterbo, Etruscan Inscriptions, and the Origins of Civilization." In *The Afterlife of Inscriptions*, edited by Alison Cooley, 57–76. London: Institute of Classical Studies School of Advanced Study, University of London, 2000.

Collins, David J. *Reforming Saints: Saints' Lives and Their Authors in Germany, 1470–1530*. Oxford: Oxford University Press, 2008.

Collins, Roger. "Isidore, Maximus, and the *Historia Gothorum*." In *Historiographie im frühen Mittelalter*, edited by Anton Scharer and Georg Scheibelreiter, 345–58. Vienna: Oldenbourg München, 1994.

———. *Visigothic Spain, 409–711*. Oxford: Blackwell, 2004.

Collis, Patrick A. "The Preface of the 'Acta Sanctorum.'" *The Catholic Historical Review* 6 (1920–21), 294–307.

Constable, Giles. "Forgery and Plagiarism in the Middle Ages." *Archiv für Diplomatik* 29 (1983), 1–41.

Cooley, Alison, ed. *The Afterlife of Inscriptions: Reusing, Rediscovering, Reinventing, and Revitalizing Ancient Inscriptions*. London: Institute of Classical Studies School of Advanced Study, University of London, 2000.

Cordero de Ciria, Enrique. "Huellas de los 'falsos cronicones' en la iconografía religiosa madrileña." *Villa de Madrid* 26, no. 95 (1988), 59–79.

Córdoba, Pedro. "Las leyendas en la historiografía del Siglo de Oro: el caso de los 'falsos cronicones.'" *Criticón* 30 (1985), 235–53.

Coronas Tejada, Luís. *Jaén, siglo XVII*. Jaén: Diputación Provincial de Jaén, IEG, 1994.

Correia Fernandes, Maria de Lurdes. *A biblioteca de Jorge Cardoso (†1669), autor do Agiólogio Lusitano; cultura, erudição, e sentimento religioso no Portugal Moderno*. Porto: Faculdade de Letras da Universidade do Porto, 2000.

———. "Historia, santidade e identidade. O *Agiologio Lusitano* de Jorge Cardoso e o seu contexto." *Via spiritus* 3 (1996), 25–68.

Coste, Jean. "Datos útiles para la biografía de Francisco de Rioja." In *Mélanges à la mémoire d'André Joucla-Ruau*, 577–93. Aix-en-Provence: Éditions de l'Université de Provence, 1978.

Crawford, Michael H., ed. *Antonio Agustín between Renaissance and Counter-Reform*. London: Warburg Institute University of London, 1993.

Cueto, Ronald. *Pánfilos y "cucos": historia de una polémica segoviana*. Madrid: Fundación Universitaria Española, 1984.

Cunnally, John. *Images of the Illustrious: The Numismatic Presence in the Renaissance.* Princeton: Princeton University Press, 1999.

Dagenais, John. *The Ethics of Reading in Manuscript Culture: Glossing the* Libro de buen amor. Princeton: Princeton University Press, 1994.

Dandelet, Thomas J. *Spanish Rome, 1500–1700.* New Haven: Yale University Press, 2001.

Davidson, Georgiana. "Divine Guidance and the Use of Sources: A Case from the *Annales* of Caesar Baronius." In *Culture, Society, and Religion in Early Modern Europe: Essays by the Students and Colleagues of William J. Bouwsma,* edited by Ellery Schalk. Special issue of *Historical Reflections/Réflexions Historiques* (1988), 114–29.

Delehaye, Hippolyte. *L'œuvre des bollandistes à travers trois siècles, 1615–1915.* Second ed. Brussels: Société des Bollandistes, 1959.

Delpech, François. "El hallazgo del escrito oculto en la literatura española del Siglo de Oro: elementos para una mitología del libro." *Revista de dialectología y tradiciones populares* 53 (1998), 5–38.

Deswarte-Rosa, Sylvie. "Le voyage épigraphique de Mariangelo Accursio au Portugal, printemps 1527." In *Portuguese Humanism and the Republic of Letters,* edited by Maria Louro Berbara and K. A. E. Enenkel, 19–111. Leiden: Brill, 2012.

Díaz Tena, María Eugenia. "*La vida de Santa Librada* y su fuente medieval." *Culturas populares. Revista electrónica* 8, enero–junio (2009), 1–22.

Ditchfield, Simon R. "An Early Christian School of Sanctity in Tridentine Rome." In *Christianity and Community in the West. Essays for John Bossy,* edited by Simon Ditchfield, 183–205. Hampshire, England: Ashgate, 2001.

———. "Giving Tridentine Worship Back Its History." In *Continuity and Change in Christian Worship: Papers Read at the 1997 Summer Meeting and the 1998 Winter Meeting of the Ecclesiastical History Society,* edited by R. N. Swanson, 199–226. Suffolk: Boydell, 1999.

———. "*Historia Magistra Sanctitatis*: The Relationship between Historiography and Hagiography in Italy after the Council of Trent." *Studies in Medieval and Renaissance History* 3rd series, no. 3 (2006), 158–84.

———. "'In Search of Local Knowledge': Rewriting Early Modern Italian Religious History." *Cristianesimo nella storia* 19, no. 2 (1998), 255–96.

———. *Liturgy, Sanctity and History in Tridentine Italy: Pietro Maria Campi and the Preservation of the Particular.* Cambridge: Cambridge University Press, 1995.

———. "Reading Rome as a Sacred Landscape, c. 1586–1635." In *Sacred Space in Early Modern Europe,* edited by Will Costner and Andrew Spicer, 167–92. Cambridge: Cambridge University Press, 2005.

———. "Text Before Trowel: Antonio Bosio's *Roma Sotterranea* Revisited." *Studies in Church History* 33 (1997), 343–60.

———. "Thinking with Saints: Sanctity and Society in the Early Modern World." *Critical Inquiry* 35, no. 3 (2009), 552–84.

———. "Tridentine Worship and the Cult of Saints." In *Reform and Expansion 1500–1660,* edited by R. Po-Chia Hsia, 201–24. Cambridge: Cambridge University Press, 2007.

———. "What Was Sacred History? (Mostly Roman) Catholic Uses of the Christian Past after Trent." In *Sacred History*, edited by Van Liere, Ditchfield, and Louthand, 72–97. Oxford, 2012.

Domínguez Cobero, José. "Sobre la iconografía de los santos Bonoso y Maximiano, patronos de Arjona." In *Homenaje a Luis Coronas Tejada*, 119–30. Jaén: Universidad de Jaén, 2001.

Domínguez, F. C. "Historical Polemic: Pedro de Ribadeneyra and the Launching of the Armada." Presented at the Early Modern History Workshop. Princeton University, March 20, 2010.

Domínguez, Joaquín María, and Charles E. O'Neill, eds. *Diccionario histórico de la Compañía de Jesús: biográfico-temático*. 4 vols. Rome and Casillas: Institutum Historicum, Universidad Pontificia Comillas, 2001.

Drayson, Elizabeth. *The King and the Whore: King Roderick and La Cava*. New York: Palgrave Macmillan, 2007.

Dubois, Claude-Gilbert. *Celtes et Gaulois au XVIe siècle: Le developpement littéraire d'un mythe nationaliste*. Paris: Vrin, 1972.

Dueck, Daniela. *Strabo of Amasia: A Greek Man of Letters in Augustan Rome*. London: Routledge, 2000.

Duhr, Bernhard. *Geschichte der Jesuiten in den Ländern deutscher Zunge in der ersten hälfte des XVII Jahrhunderts*. 4 vols. Vol. 2. Freiburg: Herdersche, 1913.

Dümmerth, Dezsö. "Les combats et la tragédie du Père Melchior Inchofer S.I. à Rome (1641–1648)." *Annales Universitatis scientiarum Budapestinensis, Sectio historica* 17 (1976), 81–112.

Ehlers, Benjamin Alan. "Juan Bautista Pérez and the *Plomos* de Granada: Spanish Humanism in the Late Sixteenth Century." *Al-Qantara: Revista de estudios árabes* 24, no. 2 (2003), 427–47.

Ehrman, Bart D. *Forgery and Counterforgery: The Use of Literary Deceit in Early Christian Polemics*. New York: Oxford University Press, 2013.

Elliott, John H. *The Count-Duke of Olivares: The Statesman in an Age of Decline*. New Haven: Yale University Press, 1986.

Enenkel, K. A. E., and Henk J. M. Nellen, eds. *Neo-Latin Commentaries and the Management of Knowledge in the Late Middle Ages and the Early Modern Period (1400–1700)*. Leuven: Leuven University Press, 2013.

Escalera, J. "Higuera, Jerónimo (Romano, Román) de la." In *Diccionario histórico de la Compañía de Jesús*, edited by Domínguez and O'Neill, 1923–24. Rome and Casillas, Institutum Historicum, Universidad Pontificia Comillas, 2001.

Eslava Galán, Juan. "Las defensas de Arjona." *Boletín del Instituto de Estudios Giennenses* 125 (1986), 26–91.

Fälschungen im Mittelalter: Internationaler Kongress der Monumenta Germaniae Historica, München, 16–19 September 1986. 6 vols. Hanover: Hahnsche, 1988.

Fernández Collado, Ángel. "Grupos de poder en el cabildo toledano del siglo XVI." In *Sociedad y élites eclesiásticas en la España moderna*, edited by Francisco José Aranda Pérez, 149–62. Cuenca: Ediciones de la Universidad de Castilla–La Mancha, 2000.

———. *Guía del archivo y biblioteca capitulares de la catedral de Toledo*. Toledo: Instituto Teológico San Ildefonso, 2007.

———. *La catedral de Toledo en el siglo XVI: Vida, arte y personas*. Toledo: Imprenta Provincial, 1999.
Fernández Ubiña, José. "Clasicismo y fin del mundo antiguo en la historiografía española moderna y contemporánea." In *"Romanización" y "reconquista" en la península ibérica: nuevas perspectivas*, edited by Maria José Hidalgo, Dionisio Pérez and Manuel J. R. Gervá, 191–213. Salamanca: Ediciones Universidad de Salamanca, 1998.
Findlen, Paula, ed. *Athanasius Kircher: The Last Man Who Knew Everything*. New York: Routledge, 2004.
Fink de Backer, Stephanie. "Constructing Convents in Sixteenth-Century Castile: Toledan Widows and Patterns of Patronage." In *Widowhood and Visual Culture in Early Modern Europe*, edited by Allison M. Levy, 177–94. Aldershot, England: Ashgate, 2003.
Fletcher, Richard A. *The Quest for El Cid*. London: Hutchinson, 1989.
Fradejas Lebrero, José. *Los evangelios apócrifos en la literatura española*. Madrid: Biblioteca de autores cristianos, 2005.
Frazier, Alison Knowles. *Possible Lives: Authors and Saints in Renaissance Italy*. New York: Columbia University Press, 2005.
Frend, W. H. C. *The Rise of Christianity*. Philadelphia: Fortress, 1984.
Friesen, Ilse E. *The Female Crucifix: Images of St. Wilgefortis Since the Middle Ages*. Waterloo, Ont.: Wilfrid Laurier University Press, 2001.
Fubini, Riccardo. "Humanism and Truth: Valla Writes against the Donation of Constantine." *Journal of the History of Ideas* 57, no. 1 (1996), 79–86.
Fuente, Vicente de la, and Johannes Baptist Alzog, eds. *Historia eclesiástica de España*. 2nd ed., 6 vols. Madrid: Compañía de Impresores y Libreros del Reino, 1873.
Funkenstein, Amos. *Perceptions of Jewish History*. Berkeley: University of California Press, 1993.
Furey, Constance M. *Erasmus, Contarini, and the Religious Republic of Letters*. New York: Cambridge University Press, 2006.
Gallacher, S. A. "Vox Populi, Vox Dei." *Philological Quarterly* 24, no. 1 (1945), 12–19.
Gallego Morell, Antonio. "Algunas noticias sobre Don Martín Vázquez Siruela." In *Estudios dedicados a Menéndez Pidal*, 404–24. Madrid: CSIC, 1962.
Galmés, L. "Villanueva, Jaime." In *Diccionario de historia eclesiástica de España*, edited by Aldea Vaquero, Marín Martínez and José Vives Gatell, 2762. Madrid: 1972–87.
García-Arenal, Mercedes. "El entorno de los plomos: Historiografía y linaje." In *Los plomos del Sacromonte*, edited by Barrios Aguilera and García-Arenal, 51–78. Valencia, 2006.
———. "En torno a los plomos del Sacromonte (I)." *Al-Qantara: Revista de estudios árabes* 23 (2002), 343–45.
———. "Orígenes sagrados y memoria del Islam: El caso de Granada." In *Europa, América y el mundo: Tiempos históricos*, edited by Roger Chartier and Antonio Feros, 41–66. Madrid: Marcial Pons, 2006.
García-Arenal, Mercedes, and Manuel Barrios Aguilera, eds. *¿La historia inventada? Los libros plúmbeos y el legado sacromontano*. Granada: Universidad de Granada, 2008.
García-Arenal, Mercedes, and Fernando Rodríguez Mediano. "Jerónimo Román de la Higuera and the Lead Books of Sacromonte." In *Conversos and Moriscos in Late Medieval Spain and Beyond*, edited by Kevin Ingram, 243–68. Leiden: Brill, 2009.

———. "Miguel de Luna, cristiano arábigo de Granada." In ¿La historia inventada?, edited by García-Arenal and Barrios Aguilera, 83–176. Granada, 2008.

———. *The Orient in Spain: Converted Muslims, the Forged Lead Books of Granada, and the Rise of Orientalism*. Translated by Consuelo López-Morillas. Leiden: Brill, 2013. A translation of ———. *Un oriente español: Los moriscos y el Sacromonte en tiempos de contrarreforma*. Madrid: Marcial Pons, 2010.

García-Diego, José Antonio. "La cueva de Hercules." *Revista de obras públicas* 121, no. 3114 (1974), 683–700.

García Cárcel, Ricardo. "La crisis de la Compañía de Jesús en los últimos años del reinado de Felipe II (1585–1598)." In *La monarquía de Felipe II a debate*, edited by Luis Antonio Ribot García, 383–404. Madrid: Sociedad Estatal para la Conmemoración de los Centenarios de Felipe II y Carlos V, 2000.

García Cuadrado, Amparo. "Un proceso de impresión: La 'Censura de historias fabulosas' de Nicolás Antonio." *Boletín de la Asociación Andaluza de Bibliotecarios* 64, September (2001), 89–122.

García Villada, Zacarías. *Historia eclesiástica de España*. 4 vols. Madrid, 1929.

García Villoslada, Ricardo. *Manual de historia de la Compañía de Jesús*. 2nd ed. Madrid: Companía Bibliográfica Española, 1954.

Gaston, Robert. "Prudentius and Sixteenth-Century Antiquarian Scholarship." *Medievalia et Humanistica* 4 (1977), 161–76.

Gélis, Jacques. "Le culte de Santa Librada à Sigüenza: Patronage urbain et emblématique impériale." *Revista de dialectología y tradiciones populares* 51, cuaderno primero (1996), 221–40.

Genette, Gérard. *Paratexts: Thresholds of Interpretation*. Cambridge: Cambridge University Press, 1997.

Gessler, Jean. *La légende de sainte Wilgeforte ou Ontcommer, la Vierge miraculeusement barbue*. Brussels: L'Édition Universelle, 1938.

Gil Calvo, Joaquín. *La Compañía de Jesús en la historia de Toledo: 1558 a 1767 y 1903 a 1940*. Madrid: Caja de Ahorro Provincial de Toledo, 1979.

Gil Egea, María Elvira. "Víctor de Cartena, Tomás Tamayo de Vargas y las falsificaciones del siglo XVII." In *Actas del X Congreso Español de Estudios Clásicos (21–25 de septiembre de 1999)*. 3 vols., edited by Emilio Crespo and María José Barrios Castro, III: 97–109. Madrid: Sociedad Española de Estudios Clásicos, 2001.

Gil, Juan. "Berenjeneros: The Aubergine Eaters." In *Conversos and Moriscos in Late Medieval Spain and Beyond*, edited by Kevin Ingram, 121–42. Leiden: Brill, 2009.

———. "Judíos y conversos en los falsos cronicones." In *Inquisition d'Espagne*, edited by Annie Molinié-Bertrand and Jean-Paul Duviols, 21–43. Paris: l'Université de Paris–Sorbonne, 2003.

Giles, Ryan D. *The Laughter of the Saints: Parodies of Holiness in Late Medieval and Renaissance Spain*. Toronto: University of Toronto, 2009.

Ginzburg, Carlo. *History, Rhetoric, and Proof*. Hanover: University Press of New England, 1999.

———. *Threads and Traces: True, False, Fictive*. Berkeley: University of California Press, 2012.

Godding, Robert, Bernard Joassart, Xavier Lequeux, et al., eds. *Bollandistes. Saints et légendes: Quatre siècles de recherche.* Brussels: Société de Bollandistes, 2007.

Godoy Alcántara, José. *Historia crítica de los falsos cronicones.* Reprint of 1868 ed. Granada: Universidad de Granada, 1999.

———. "Ideas y opiniones de nuestros escritores en diversos tiempos sobre la manera de escribir la Historia." In *Discursos leídos en la Academia de la Historia en la recepción pública . . . el día 30 de enero de 1870.* Madrid, 1870.

Goffart, Walter. *The Le Mans Forgeries: A Chapter from the History of Church Property in the Ninth Century.* Cambridge: Harvard University Press, 1966.

Goldgar, Anne. *Impolite Learning: Conduct and Community in the Republic of Letters, 1680–1750.* New Haven: Yale University Press, 1995.

Gómez Canseco, Luís. *Rodrigo Caro. Un humanista en la Sevilla del Seiscientos.* Seville: Diputación Provincial, 1986.

———. "Rodrigo Caro: Entre libros y amigos." In Caro, *Varones insignes . . . de . . . Sevilla,* 25–40. Seville: Exma. Diputación Provincial de Sevilla, 1992.

Gómez Martínez, Enrique. *Fé y Religiosidad popular en las fiestas de Andújar durante el siglo XVII. Discurso de Ingreso . . . en el Instituto de Estudios Giennenses. Andújar, marzo de 2002.* Jaén: Diputación Provincial de Jaén and IEG, 2002.

Gómez Martos, Francisco. "Juan de Mariana y la historiografía ilustrada. Un debate a propósito de los falsos cronicones." *Cabeza encantada: Humanism e-review* (2014), 1–22.

Gómez Moreno, Ángel. *Claves hagiográficas de la literatura española del Cantar de mio Cid a Cervantes.* Madrid; Frankfurt am Main: Iberoamericana; Vervuert, 2008.

González Blanco, Antonino. "Begastri en los cronicones apócrifos (II)." *Alquipir. Revista de historia* 7 (1997), 13–25.

———. "La leyenda de la Cruz de Caravaca y la historia de la villa al filo del comienzo de la reconquista." *Anales murcianos* 9–10 (1993–94), 293–300.

González Muñoz, Fernando. "La leyenda de Mahoma en Lucas de Tuy." In *Actas [del] III Congreso Hispánico de Latín Medieval: León, 26–29 de septiembre de 2001,* edited by Maurilio Pérez González, 347–58. León: Universidad de León, 2002.

Gonzálvez, Ramón. "The Persistence of the Mozarabic Liturgy in Toledo after AD 1080." In *Santiago, Saint-Denis, and Saint Peter: The Reception of the Roman Liturgy in León-Castile in 1080,* edited by Bernard F. Reilly, 157–85. New York: Fordham University Press, 1985.

Gordini, Gian Domenico. "L'opera dei bollandisti e la loro metodologia." In *Santità e agiografia: Atti del VII Congresso di Terni,* edited by G. D. Gordini, 49–73. Genoa: Marietti, 1991.

Grafton, Anthony. *Bring Out Your Dead: The Past as Revelation.* Cambridge: Harvard University Press, 2001.

———. "Church History in Early Modern Europe: Tradition and Innovation." In *Sacred History,* edited by Van Liere, Ditchfield, and Louthan, 3–26. Oxford, 2012.

———. *The Footnote: A Curious History.* Cambridge: Harvard University Press, 1997.

———. *Forgers and Critics: Creativity and Duplicity in Western Scholarship.* Princeton: Princeton University Press, 1990.

———. "The Identities of History in Early Modern Europe: Prelude to a Study of the *Artes*

Historicae." In *Historia: Empiricism and Erudition in Early Modern Europe*, edited by Gianna Pomata and Nancy Siraisi. Cambridge: Massachusetts Institute of Technology Press, 2005.

———. "Invention of Traditions and Traditions of Invention in Renaissance Europe: The Strange Case of Annius of Viterbo." In *The Transmission of Culture in Early Modern Europe*, edited by Ann Blair and Anthony Grafton, 8–38. Philadelphia: University of Pennsylvania, 1990.

———. "Jean Hardouin: The Antiquary as Pariah." *Journal of the Warburg and Courtauld Institutes* 62 (1999), 241–67.

———. *Joseph Scaliger: A Study in the History of Classical Scholarship*. 2 vols. Oxford: Clarendon, 1983–93.

———. "A Sketch Map of a Lost Continent: The Republic of Letters." *Republics of Letters: A Journal for the Study of Knowledge, Politics, and the Arts* 1 (2009), 1–18.

———. *What Was History? The Art of History in Early Modern Europe.* Cambridge: Cambridge University Press, 2007.

———. *Worlds Made by Words: Scholarship and Community in the Modern West.* Cambridge: Harvard University Press, 2009.

Grafton, Anthony, and Megan Williams. *Christianity and the Transformation of the Book: Origen, Eusebius, and the Library of Caesarea.* Cambridge: Belknap, 2006.

Green, Otis H. "On the Attitude Toward the *Vulgo* in the Spanish *Siglo de Oro.*" *Studies in the Renaissance* 4 (1957), 190–200.

Grieve, Patricia E. *The Eve of Spain: Myths of Origins in the History of Christian, Muslim, and Jewish Conflict.* Baltimore: Johns Hopkins University Press, 2009.

Griggs, Tamara Anne. "The Changing Face of Erudition: Antiquaries in the Age of the Grand Tour." Ph.D. diss., Princeton University, 2003.

Guazzelli, Giuseppe Antonio. "Cesare Baronio and the Roman Catholic Vision of the Early Church." In *Sacred History*, edited by Van Liere, Ditchfield, and Louthan, 52–71. Oxford, 2012.

———. "Cesare Baronio e il *Martyrologium Romanum*: Problemi interpretativi e linee evolutive di un rapporto diacronico." In *Nunc alia tempora, alii mores: Storici e storia in età postridentina*, edited by Massimo Firpo, 47–89. Florence: Leo S. Olschki, 2005.

Guenée, Bernard. *Histoire et culture historique dans l'occident médiéval.* Paris: Aubier-Montaigne, 1980.

———. "L'historien et la compilation au XIIIe siècle." *Journal des savants* 1, no. 1–3 (1985), 119–35.

Haft, Adele J. "Odysseus, Idomeneus and Meriones: The Cretan Lies of *Odyssey* 13–19." *The Classical Journal* 79, no. 4 (1984), 289–306.

Hagerty, Miguel José. *Los libros plúmbeos del Sacromonte.* Madrid: Editora Nacional, 1980.

Haliczer, Stephen. *Between Exaltation and Infamy: Female Mystics in the Golden Age of Spain.* Oxford: Oxford University Press, 2002.

———. *Inquisition and Society in the Kingdom of Valencia, 1478–1834.* Berkeley: University of California Press, 1990.

———. "The Jew as Witch: Displaced Aggression and the Myth of the Santo Niño de La Guardia." In *Cultural Encounters: The Impact of the Inquisition in Spain and the New*

World, edited by Mary Elizabeth Perry and Anne J. Cruz, 146–55. Berkeley: University of California Press, 1991.

Harris, A. Katie. "'A known holy body, with an inscription and a name': Bishop Sancho Dávila y Toledo and the Creation of St. Vitalis." *Archiv für Reformationsgeschichte* 104 (2013), 245–71.

———. "Forging History: The Plomos of the Sacromonte of Granada in Francisco Bermúdez de Pedraza's Historia Eclesiástica." *Sixteenth Century Journal* 30, no. 4 (1999), 945–66.

———. *From Muslim to Christian Granada: Inventing a City's Past in Early Modern Spain*. Baltimore: Johns Hopkins University Press, 2007.

———. "The Sacromonte and the Geography of the Sacred in Early Modern Granada." *Al-Qantara: Revista de estudios árabes* 23, no. 2 (2002), 517–43.

Haskell, Francis. *History and Its Images: Art and the Interpretation of the Past*. New Haven: Yale University Press, 1993.

Hathaway, Neil. "*Compilatio*: From Plagiarism to Compiling." *Viator* 20 (1989), 19–44.

Henriet, Patrick. "Collection hagiographique et forgeries. La *Commemoratio omnium sanctorum hispanorum* de Tamayo Salazar (1651–1659) et son arrière-plan de fausse érudition." In *Europa sacra. Raccolte agiographiche e identità politiche in Europa fra Medioevo ed Età moderna*, edited by Sofia Boesch Gajano and Raimondo Michetti, 57–82. Rome: Carocci, 2002.

———. "La dignité de la religion chrétienne et de la nation hispanique, ou Enrique Flórez et l'*España sagrada*. À propos d'une réédition." *Revue Mabillon* 73, no. 12 (2001), 296–306.

———. "Political Struggle and the Legitimation of the Toledan Primacy: The *Pars Lateranii Concilii*." In *Building Legitimacy: Political Discourses and Forms of Legitimacy in Medieval Societies*, edited by Isabel Alfonso Antón, Hugh Kennedy and Julio Escalona, 291–318. Leiden: Brill, 2004.

Herklotz, Ingo. "Arnaldo Momigliano's 'Ancient History and the Antiquarian': A Critical Review." In *Momigliano and Antiquarianism: Foundations of the Modern Cultural Sciences*, edited by Peter N. Miller, 127–53. Toronto: University of Toronto Press in association with the UCLA Center for Seventeenth- and Eighteenth-Century Studies and the William Andrew Clark Memorial Library, 2007.

Hernando Sobrino, María del Rosario. "Cuando la fama te precede: Jerónimo Román de la Higuera y la epigrafía hispana." In *Scripta antiqua: in honorem Ángel Montenegro Duque et José María Blázquez Martínez*, edited by Ángeles Alonso Ávila and Santos Crespo Ortiz de Zárate, 501–15. Valladolid: Universidad de Valladolid, 2002.

———. "De parroquia en parroquia. Notas de epigrafía orensana de Jerónimo Román de la Higuera." In *La filología latina. Mil años más. Actas del IV Congreso de la SELAT (Medina del Campo, 2003)*, edited by P. P. Conde Parrado and I. Velázquez, 2013–30. Madrid, 2005.

———. "Jerónimo Román de la Higuera y la epigrafía de Ibahernando (Cáceres)." *Zephyrus* 63, enero-junio (2009), 185–203.

Herr, Richard. *The Eighteenth-Century Revolution in Spain*. Princeton: Princeton University Press, 1958.

Hiatt, Alfred. "Diplomatic Arts: Hickes against Mabillon in the Republic of Letters." *Journal of the History of Ideas* 70 (2009), 351–73.

———. *The Making of Medieval Forgeries: False Documents in Fifteenth-Century England*. London and Toronto: The British Library and the University of Toronto, 2004.

Higueras Maldonado, Juan. *Humanistas giennenses (s. XIV–XVIII)*. Jaén, Cordoba: Universidad de Jaén; Publicaciones Obra Social y Cultural CajaSur, 1998.

Hitchcock, Richard. "The *falsos chronicones* and the Mozarabs." *Journal of the Institute of Romance Studies* 3 (1994–95), 87–96.

———. *Mozarabs in Medieval and Early Modern Spain: Identities and Influences*. Aldershot, England: Ashgate, 2008.

Homza, Lu Ann. *Religious Authority in the Spanish Renaissance*. Baltimore: Johns Hopkins University Press, 2000.

Höpfl, Harro. *Jesuit Political Thought: The Society of Jesus and the State, c. 1540–1630*. Cambridge: Cambridge University Press, 2004.

Hunter, Michael. *John Aubrey and the Realm of Learning*. New York: Science History Publications, 1975.

Huppert, George. *The Idea of Perfect History: Historical Erudition and Historical Philosophy in Renaissance France*. Urbana: University of Illinois Press, 1970.

Hyde, John Kenneth. "Medieval Descriptions of Cities." In *Literacy and Its Uses: Studies on Late Medieval Italy*, 1–32. Oxford: Manchester University Press, 1993.

Ingram, Kevin. "Historiography, Historicity, and the Conversos." In *The Conversos and Moriscos in Late Medieval Spain and Beyond*. Vol. I: *Departures and Change*, 335–56. Leiden: Brill, 2009.

Jammes, Robert, and Odette Gorsse. "Nicolás Antonio et le combat pour la verité (31 lettres de Nicolás Antonio à Vázquez Siruela)." In *Hommage des hispanistes français à Noël Salomon*, 411–30. Barcelona: Laia, 1979.

Jardine, Lisa. *Erasmus, Man of Letters: The Construction of Charisma in Print*. Princeton: Princeton University Press, 1993.

Joassart, Bernard. "Un lettre inédite d'Aubert Le Mire à Héribert Rosweyde." *Analecta Bollandiana* 124, no. 1 (2006), 44.

Johns, Adrian. *The Nature of the Book: Print and Knowledge in the Making*. Chicago: University of Chicago Press, 1998.

Johnson, Carroll. "Phantom Pre-texts and Fictional Authors: Sidi Hamid Benengeli, *Don Quijote* and the Metafictional Conventions of Chivalric Romances." *Cervantes: Bulletin of the Cervantes Society of America* 27, no. 1 (2007), 179–200.

Johnson, Trevor. "Defining the Confessional Frontier: Bavaria, the Upper Palatinate and Counter-Reformation 'Historia Sacra.'" In *Frontiers and the Writing of History, 1500–1850*, edited by Steven G. Ellis and Raingard Esser, 151–66. Hanover-Laatzen: Wehrhahn, 2006.

———. "Politics and Sanctity in Matthaeus Rader's *Bavaria Sancta*." In *Europa sacra. Raccolte agiographiche e identità politiche in Europa fra Medioevo ed Età moderna*, edited by Sofia Boesch Gajano and Raimondo Michetti, 83–100. Rome: Carocci, 2002.

———. "'That in Her the Seed of the Serpent May Have No Part': The Agredan Visions and the Immaculate Conception of the Virgin in Early Modern Spain and Germany."

In *The Church and Mary: Papers Read at the 2001 Summer Meeting and the 2002 Winter Meeting of the Ecclesiastical History Society*, edited by R. N. Swanson, 259–70. Woodbridge: Boydell, 2004.

Jones, Harold G. *Hispanic Manuscripts and Printed Books in the Barberini Collection*. 2 vols., Vatican City: Bibliotheca Apostolica Vaticana, 1978.

Jotischky, Andrew. *The Carmelites and Antiquity: Mendicants and Their Pasts in the Middle Ages*. Oxford: Oxford University Press, 2002.

Kagan, Richard L. *Clio and the Crown: The Politics of History in Medieval and Early Modern Spain*. Baltimore: Johns Hopkins University Press, 2009.

———. "Clio and the Crown: Writing History in Habsburg Spain." In *Spain, Europe and the Atlantic World: Essays in Honour of John H. Elliott*, 73–99. Cambridge: Cambridge University Press, 1995.

———. *Lucrecia's Dreams: Politics and Prophecy in Sixteenth-Century Spain*. Berkeley: University of California Press, 1990.

———. "Pedro de Salazar de Mendoza as Collector, Scholar, and Patron of El Greco." In *El Greco: Italy and Spain*, edited by Jonathan Brown and José Manuel Pita Andrade, 85–93. Hanover and London: National Gallery of Art, University Press of New England, 1984.

———. *Students and Society in Early Modern Spain*. Baltimore: Johns Hopkins University Press, 1974.

———. "The Toledo of El Greco." In *El Greco of Toledo: Exhibition Organized by the Toledo Museum of Art, with Museo del Prado, National Gallery of Art, Dallas Museum of Fine Arts*, edited by Jonathan Brown, 35–73. Boston: Little, Brown, 1982.

Kelley, Donald R. *Faces of History: Historical Inquiry from Herodotus to Herder*. New Haven: Yale University Press, 1998.

Kempshall, Matthew S. *Rhetoric and the Writing of History, 400–1500*. Manchester: Manchester University Press, 2011.

Kendrick, Thomas D. *British Antiquity*. London: Methuen, 1970.

———. *St. James in Spain*. London: Methuen, 1960.

Keniston, Hayward. *Francisco de los Cobos, Secretary of the Emperor Charles V*. Pittsburgh: University of Pittsburgh, 1960.

Kimmel, Seth. "Writing Religion: Sacromonte and the Literary Conventions of Orthodoxy." In *Poiesis and Modernity in the Old and New Worlds*, edited by Anthony J. Cascardi and Leah Middlebrook, 117–38. Nashville: Vanderbilt University Press, 2012.

Knowles, David. *Great Historical Enterprises: Problems in Monastic History*. London: Thomas Nelson, 1963.

Krebs, Christopher B. *A Most Dangerous Book: Tacitus's* Germania *from the Roman Empire to the Third Reich*. New York: W. W. Norton, 2011.

Ladero Quesada, Miguel Ángel. "El pasado histórico-fabuloso de España en los nobilarios castellanos a comienzos del siglo XVI." *Estudios de historia y de arqueología medievales* 9 (1993), 55–80.

Laursen, John Christian. "Skepticism and Cynicism in the Work of Pedro de Valencia." In *Skepticism in the Modern Age: Building on the Work of Richard Popkin*, edited by José

Raimundo Maia Neto, Gianni Paganini, and John Christian Laursen, 139–58. Leiden: Brill, 2009.

Lawrance, Jeremy. "Las *Obras de don Luis de Góngora* y el conde-duque: mecenazgo, polémica literaria y publicidad en la España barroca." In *Poder y saber: bibliotecas y bibliofilia en la época del conde-duque de Olivares*, edited by Noble Wood, Roe, and Lawrance, 157–81. Madrid, 2011.

Lazure, Guy. "Rodrigo Caro y la corte de Felipe IV: Itinerario de unas ambiciones frustradas." In *Poder y saber: bibliotecas y bibliofilia en la época del conde-duque de Olivares*, edited by Noble Wood, Roe, and Lawrance, 121–40. Madrid, 2011.

———. "To Dare Fame: Constructing a Cultural Elite in Sixteenth-Century Seville." Ph.D. diss., Johns Hopkins University, 2003.

Le Gall, Jean-Marie. *Le mythe de Saint Denis: Entre renaissance et révolution*. Paris: Champ Vallon, 2007.

Lehner, Ulrich L. "What is 'Catholic Enlightenment'?" *History Compass* 8, no. 2 (2010), 166–78.

Leturia, Pietro. "Contribuzioni della Compagnia di Gesù alla formazione delle scienze storiche." *Analecta Gregoriana* 29 (1942).

Levy, Evonne Anita, and Kenneth Mills, eds. *Lexikon of the Hispanic Baroque: Transatlantic Exchange and Transformation*. Austin: University of Texas, 2013.

Lewy, Guenter. "The Struggle for Constitutional Governance in the Early Years of the Society of Jesus." *Church History* 29, no. 2 (1960), 141–60.

Lifshitz, Felice. "Beyond Positivism and Genre: 'Hagiographical' Texts as Historical Narrative." *Viator* 25 (1994), 95–113.

Ligota, Christopher. "Annius of Viterbo and Historical Method." *Journal of the Warburg and Courtauld Institutes* 50 (1987), 44–56.

Lilao Franca, Oscar, and Carmen Castrillo González. *Catálogo de manuscritos de la Biblioteca Universitaria de Salamanca*. 2 vols. Salamanca: Ediciones Universidad de Salamanca, 1997.

Linehan, Peter. *History and the Historians of Medieval Spain*. Oxford: Oxford University Press, 1993.

Lleó Cañal, Vicente. *Nueva Roma, mitología y humanismo en el Renacimiento sevillano*. Seville: Diputación Provincial, 1979.

Longhurst, John E. *The Age of Torquemada*. 2nd ed. Lawrence, Kansas: Coronado, 1964.

López Arandia, María Amparo. *La Compañía de Jesús en la ciudad de Jaén: El Colegio de San Eufrasio (1611–1767)*. Jaén: Ayuntamiento de Jaén, 2007.

López Estrada, Francisco. "Dos tratados de los siglos XVI y XVII sobre los mozárabes." *Al-Andalus* 16 (1951), 331–61.

López Molina, Manuel. "Curiosa protesta del maestro Juan [sic] de Rus Puerta contra el Obispo de Jaén en 1624." *Boletín del Instituto de Estudios Giennenses* 176 (2000).

López-Vidriero, María Luisa. "Asiento de coronas y distinción de reinos: librerías y aprendizaje nobilario." In *Poder y saber: bibliotecas y bibliofilia en la época del conde-duque de Olivares*, edited by Noble Wood, Roe and Lawrance, 223–47. Madrid, 2011.

Lorente Toledo, Enrique, and Alfonso Vázquez González. "La ciudad de Toledo en la época del *Quijote*." In *El espacio geográfico del Quijote en Castilla–La Mancha*, edited by Félix Pillet and Julio Plaza, 107–38. Cuenca: Ediciones de la Universidad de Castilla–La Mancha, 2006.

Louthan, Howard. "Imagining Christian Origins: Catholic Visions of a Holy Past in Central Europe." In *Sacred History*, edited by Van Liere, Ditchfield, and Louthan, 145–64. Oxford, 2012.

Lupher, David. *Romans in a New World: Classical Models in Sixteenth-Century Spanish America*. Ann Arbor: University of Michigan, 2003.

Machielsen, Jan. "Heretical Saints and Textual Discernment: The Polemical Origins of the Acta Sanctorum (1643–1940)." In *Angels of Light? Sanctity and Discernment in the Early Modern Period*, edited by Jan Machielsen and Clare Copeland, 103–41. Leiden: Brill, 2012.

Madroñal, Abraham. "San Tirso de Toledo, tragedia perdida de Lope de Vega." *Hipogrifo* 2.1 (2014), 23–54.

Magnier, Grace. *Pedro de Valencia and the Catholic Apologists of the Expulsion of the Moriscos: Visions of Christianity and Kingship*. Leiden: Brill, 2010.

Malamud, Martha A. *A Poetics of Transformation: Prudentius and Classical Mythology*. Ithaca: Cornell University Press, 1989.

Manchón Gómez, Raúl. "Dos poemas latinos de Juan de Aguilar dedicados a los municipios de Arjona y Andújar (Jaén) con un apéndice de otros textos latinos del autor." *Boletín del Instituto de Estudios Giennenses* 184 (2003), 313–62.

Manso Porto, Carmen. *Don Diego Sarmiento de Acuña, conde de Gondomar (1567–1626): erudito, mecenas y bibliófilo*. Santiago de Compostela: Xunta de Galicia, 1996.

Márquez Villanueva, Francisco. *El problema morisco (Desde otras laderas)*. Madrid: Ediciones Libertarias-Prodhufi, 1991.

———. *Investigaciones sobre Juan Álvarez Gato: contribución al conocimiento de la literatura castellana del siglo XV*. Madrid: S. Aguirre Torre, 1960.

Martín Fernández, Julio, and Jaime Sánchez Romeralo. "El maestro Alonso de Villegas: postrimerías de su vida." *Anales toledanos* 36 (1998), 63–90.

Martínez de la Escalera, José. "Jerónimo de la Higuera, S.J., Falsos cronicones, historia de Toledo, culto de San Tirso." In *Tolède et l'expansion urbaine en Espagne. Rencontres de la Casa Velázquez*, 69–97. Casa de Velázquez: Madrid, 1991.

———. "La circunstancia toledana de una 'tragedia' de Lope de Vega y el nombre Tirso." *Revista de literatura* 53 (1991), 631–40.

Martínez, María Elena. *Genealogical Fictions: Limpieza de Sangre, Religion, and Gender in Colonial Mexico*. Stanford: Stanford University Press, 2008.

Martínez Gil, Fernando. "Historia y cohesión urbana. La escuela historiográfica toledana del Siglo de Oro." In *Ensayos humanísticos. Homenaje al profesor Luis Lorente Toledo*, edited by Rafael Villena Espinosa, 303–18. Cuenca: Ediciones de la Universidad de Castilla–La Mancha, 1997.

———. "Religión e identidad urbana en el Arzobispado de Toledo (siglos XVI–XVII)." In *Religiosidad popular y modelos de identidad en España y América*, edited by J. Carlos Vizuete Mendoza and Palma Martínez-Burgos García, 15–57. Cuenca: Ediciones de la Universidad de Castilla–La Mancha, 2000.

Martínez Gómez-Gordo, Juan Antonio. *Leyendas de tres personajes históricos de Sigüenza: Santa Librada, Virgen y Mártir, Doña Blanca de Borbón, Reina de Castilla y el Doncel de Sigüenza.* Sigüenza: Centro de Iniciativas y Turismo, 1971.

Martínez Marina, Francisco. "Antigüedades hispano-hebreas, convencidas de supuestas y fabulosas. Discurso histórico-crítico sobre la primera venida de los judíos a España." *Memorias de la Real Academia de la Historia* 3 (1799), 317–468.

Martínez Medina, Francisco Javier. "El Sacromonte de Granada y los discursos inmaculistas postridentinas." *Archivo Teológico Granadino* 59 (1996), 5–57.

Martínez Millán, José. "Transformación y crisis de la Compañía de Jesús (1578–1594)." In *I religiosi a corte: teologia, politica e diplomazia in antico regime*, edited by Flavio Rurale, 101–26. Rome: Bulzoni, 1998.

Martz, Linda. "Converso Families in Fifteenth- and Sixteenth-Century Toledo: The Significance of Lineage." *Sefarad* 48 (1988), 117–96.

———. *A Network of Converso Families in Early Modern Toledo: Assimilating a Minority.* Ann Arbor: University of Michigan, 2003.

Maryks, Robert A. *The Jesuit Order as a Synagogue of Jews: Jesuits of Jewish Ancestry and Purity-of-Blood Laws in the Early Society of Jesus.* Leiden: Brill, 2010.

Mascareñas, Carlos Eugenio. "Cartas do historiador D. Jerónimo Mascareñas ao cronista Francisco Andrés de Uztarroz." *Broteria. Revista de cultura* 48 (1949), 43–57.

Mayer Olivé, Marc. "Ciriaco de Ancona, Annio da Viterbo y la historiografía hispánica." In *Ciriaco d'Ancona e la cultura antiquaria dell'Umanesimo: Atti del convegno internazionale di studio (Ancona, 6–9 febbraio 1992)*, edited by Gianfranco Paci and Sergio Sconocchia. Reggio Emilia: Diabasis, 1998.

Mazurek, Antoine. "Réforme tridentine et culte des saints en Espagne: liturgie romaine et saints ibériques." In *The Council of Trent: Reform and Controversy in Europe and Beyond (1545–1700).* Göttingen: Vandenhoeck & Ruprecht, forthcoming.

McKitterick, Rosamond. *The Carolingians and the Written Word.* Cambridge: Cambridge University Press, 1989.

Menéndez y Pelayo, Marcelino. *Biblioteca de traductores españoles.* 4 vols. Santander: CSIC, 1952–53.

———. *Historia de las ideas estéticas en España.* 4th ed., 5 vols. Madrid: Hernando, 1930.

———. *Historia de los heterodoxos españoles.* 2nd ed., 3 vols. Madrid: Librería Católica de San José, 1881.

———. *Historia de los heterodoxos españoles.* 2 vols. Madrid: Biblioteca de Autores Cristianos, 1956.

"Messina's Buried Palladium." *The Catholic Fortnightly Review* 16, no. 19 (1909), 554–58.

Mestre Sanchís, Antonio. "Crítica y apología en la historiografía de los novatores." *Studia Historica. Historia Moderna* 14 (1996), 45–62.

———. *Ilustración y reforma de la Iglesia: Pensamiento político-religioso de Don Gregorio Mayáns y Siscar (1699–1781).* Valencia: Publicaciones del Ayuntamiento de Oliva, 1, 1968.

Mezzazappa, Stefania. "Cesidio e Rufino 'martiri': tracce archeologiche del culto." In *Baronio e le sue fonti*, edited by Luigi Gulia, 341–76. Sora, Italy: Centro dei Studi Sorani "Vincenzo Patriarca," 2009.

Michael, Ian. "King James VI and I and the Count of Gondomar: Two London Bibliophiles, 1613–18 and 1620–22." In *"Never-Ending Adventure": Studies in Medieval and Early Modern Spanish Literature in Honor of Peter N. Dunn*, edited by Edward H. Friedman and Harlan Sturm, 421–35. Newark, Delaware: Juan de la Cuesta, 2002.

Minnis, Alastair. "'Nolens auctor sed compilator reputari': The Late-Medieval Discourse of Compilation." In *La méthode critique au Moyen Âges*, edited by Mireille Chazan and Gilbert Dahan, 47–63. Turnhout: Brepols, 2006.

Mitchell, Charles. "Archaeology and Romance in Renaissance Italy." In *Italian Renaissance Studies: A Tribute to the Late Cecilia M. Ady*, edited by E. F. Jacob, 455–83. London: Faber and Faber, 1960.

Momigliano, Arnaldo. "Ancient History and the Antiquarian." *Journal of the Warburg and Courtauld Institutes* 13, no. 3/4 (1950), 285–315.

———. *The Classical Foundations of Modern Historiography*. Berkeley: University of California Press, 1990.

———. *Contributo alla storia degli studi classici*. Rome: Edizioni di Storia e letteratura, 1955.

———. "Note sulla leggenda del Cristianesimo di Seneca." *Rivista storica italiana* 62 (1950), 325–44.

———. "Pagan and Christian Historiography in the Fourth Century A.D." In *Essays in Ancient and Modern Historiography*, 107–26. Oxford: Blackwell, 1977.

Moral de la Vega, José. "Comentarios a dos cartas inéditas del Prior de Villanueva de Andúxar, Doctor don Juan Acuña del Adarve, referentes a la causa de Santa Potenciana." *Boletín del Instituto de Estudios Giennenses* 147 (1993), 61–71.

Moraleda y Esteban, Juan de. "El Monasterio Agaliense de Toledo." *Boletín de la Real Academia de Ciencias Históricas de Toledo* 35 (1928), 130–38.

Morales Talero, Santiago de. *Los santos de Arjona*. Madrid, 1957.

Morán Turina, José Miguel. *La memoria de las piedras: anticuarios, arqueólogos y coleccionistas de antigüedades en la España de los Austrias*. Madrid: Centro de Estudios Europa Hispánica, 2010.

Morán Turina, José Miguel, and Delfín Rodríguez Ruiz. *El legado de la antigüedad: arte, arquitectura y arqueología en la España moderna*. Madrid: Istmo, 2001.

Morel Fatio, Alfredo. "Cartas eruditas del Marqués de Mondéjar y de Étienne Baluze (1679–1690)." In *Homenaje a Menéndez Pelayo. Estudios de erudición española*, 1–39. Madrid: Librería General de Victoriana Suárez, 1899.

Moscheo, Rosario. "Melchior Inchofer (1585–1648) ed un suo inedito corso messinese di logica dell'anno 1617." *Quaderni dell'Istituto Galvano della Volpe* 3 (1980–81), 181–94.

Mozas Moreno, María de los Santos. "Un catálogo numismático inédito en un manuscrito del siglo XVII." In *XIII Congreso Internacional de Numismática, Madrid, 2003: Actas*, edited by Carmen Alfaro, Carmen Marcos, and Paloma Otero, 85–93. Madrid, 2005.

Mundy, Barbara E. *The Mapping of New Spain: Indigenous Cartography and the Maps of the Relaciones Geográficas*. Chicago: University of Chicago Press, 1996.

Nalle, Sara Tilghman. *God in La Mancha: Religious Reform and the People of Cuenca, 1500–1650*. Baltimore: Johns Hopkins University Press, 1992.

Nelles, Paul. "*Historia magistra antiquitatis*: Cicero and Jesuit History Teaching." *Renaissance Studies* 13, no. 2 (1999), 130–72.

Nelson, Eric. *The Jesuits and the Monarchy: Catholic Reform and Political Authority in France (1590–1615)*. Aldershot: Ashgate; Institutum Historicum Societatis Iesu, 2005.

Nice, Jason. *Sacred History and National Identity: Comparisons between Early Modern Wales and Brittany*. London: Pickering and Chatto, 2009.

Nightlinger, Elizabeth. "The Female *Imitatio Christi* and Medieval Popular Religion: The Case of St. Wilgefortis." In *Representations of the Feminine in the Middle Ages*, edited by Bonnie Wheeler, 291–328. Dallas: Academia, 1993.

Nirenberg, David. "Mass Conversion and Genealogical Mentalities: Jews and Christians in Fifteenth-Century Spain." *Past and Present* 174 (2002), 2–41.

Noble Wood, Oliver J., Jeremy Roe, and Jeremy Lawrance, eds. *Poder y saber: bibliotecas y bibliofilia en la época del conde-duque de Olivares*. Madrid: Centro de Estudios Europa Hispánica, 2011.

Noguera Rosado, Joaquín J. "Cristianización de Astigi: San Pablo. Diócesis Astigitana." In *Actas del I Congreso sobre historia de Ecija: Celebrado en Ecija (Sevilla) entre los días 26 y 29 de noviembre de 1986*, edited by Genaro Chic García, 281–87. Ecija, 1988.

Norelli, Enrico. "The Authority Attributed to the Early Church in the *Centuries of Magdeburg* and the *Ecclesiastical Annals* of Caesar Baronius." In *The Reception of the Church Fathers in the West: From the Carolingians to the Maurists*, edited by Irena Backus, 745–74. Brill: Leiden, 2001.

O'Callaghan, Joseph F. *A History of Medieval Spain*. Ithaca: Cornell University Press, 1975.

O'Malley, John W. *The First Jesuits*. Cambridge: Harvard University Press, 1993.

Olavide, Ignacio. "La Inquisición, la Compañía de Jesús y el Padre Román de la Higuera." *Boletín de la Real Academia de la Historia* 42 (1903), 107–19.

Olds, Katrina B. "The Ambiguities of the Holy: Authenticating Relics in Seventeenth-Century Spain." *Renaissance Quarterly* 65, no. 1 (2012), 135–84.

———. "The 'False Chronicles,' Cardinal Baronio, and Sacred History in Counter-Reformation Spain." *Catholic Historical Review* 100, no. 1 (2014), 1–26.

———. "How to Be a Counter-Reformation Bishop: Cardinal Baltasar de Moscoso y Sandoval in the Diocese of Jaén, 1618–1646." *Sierra Mágina: Revista universitaria* 12 (2009), 197–213.

———. "Visions of the Holy in Counter-Reformation Spain: The Discovery and Creation of Relics in Arjona, c. 1628." In *The "Vision Thing": Studying Divine Intervention*, edited by William A. Christian Jr. and Gábor Klaniczay, 135–56. Budapest: Collegium Budapest Institute for Advanced Study, 2009.

Orella y Unzue, José. *Respuestas católicas a las Centurias de Magdeburgo*. Madrid: Fundación Universitaria Española, Seminario "Suarez," 1976.

Pabel, Hilmar M. *Herculean Labours: Erasmus and the Editing of St. Jerome's Letters in the Renaissance*. Leiden: Brill, 2008.

Palau y Dulcet, Antonio. *Manual del librero hispanoamericano*. 2nd ed., 28 vols. Barcelona: Librería Palau, 1948–77.

Palmer, Anne-Marie. *Prudentius on the Martyrs*. Oxford: Clarendon, 1989.

Parejo Delgado, María Josefa. "Don Martín de Ximena Jurado, historiador del reino de Jaén." In *Actas del I Congreso de Historia de Andalucía (diciembre de 1976): Andalucía medieval*. 2 vols. I: 275–85. Cordoba: Monte de Piedad y Caja de Ahorros de Córdoba, 1982.

Pastor Bodmer, Beatriz. *The Armature of Conquest: Spanish Accounts of the Discovery of America, 1492–1589*. Stanford: Stanford University Press, 1992.

Pastore, Stefania. *Il Vangelo e la spada: L'inquisizione di Castiglia e i suoi critici (1460–1598)*. Rome: Edizioni di storia e letteratura, 2003.

———. "A proposito di Matteo 18,15: *Correctio fraterna* e inquisizione nella Spagna del Cinquecento." *Rivista storica italiana* 113 (2001), 323–68.

Pavone, Sabina. *The Wily Jesuits and the "Monita Secreta." The Forged Secret Instructions of the Jesuits: Myth and Reality*. Translated by John P. Murphy. Saint Louis: Institute of Jesuit Sources, 2005.

Pérez, Joseph. *The Spanish Inquisition: A History*. New Haven: Yale University Press, 2005.

Pérez González, Carlos. "Juan de Mariana y su valoración de las crónicas medievales, en lo relativo a la venida de Santiago a España, en el *De adventu beati Iacobi Apostoli in Hispaniam*." In *Congreso internacional sobre Humanismo y Renacimiento* I, 537–47. León: Universidad de León, 1998.

Pérez de Urbel, Justo. "Origen de los himnos mozárabes (continuación)." *Bulletin hispanique* 28, no. 2 (1926), 113–39.

Pérez Vilatela, Luciano. "La onomástica de los apócrifos reyes de España en Annio de Viterbo y su influencia." In *Humanismo y pervivencia del mundo clásico. Actas del Primer Simposio sobre humanismo y pervivencia del mundo clásico (Alcañiz, 8 al 11 de mayo de 1990)*, edited by José María Maestre Maestre and Joaquín Pascual Barea, 807–20. Cadiz: Exma. Diputación Provincial de Teruel; Servicio de Publicaciones de la Universidad de Cádiz, 1993.

Pérez Villanueva, Joaquín. "Baronio y la Inquisición española." In *Baronio storico e la controriforma: Atti del Convegno internazionale di studi Sora, 6–10 ottobre 1979*, edited by Romeo De Maio, Luigi Gulia and Aldo Mazzacane, 5–53. Sora, Italy: Centro di Studi Sorani "Vincenzo Patriarca," 1982.

Perry, Mary Elizabeth. *Gender and Disorder in Early Modern Seville*. Princeton: Princeton University Press, 1990.

———. *The Handless Maiden: Moriscos and the Politics of Religion in Early Modern Spain*. Princeton: Princeton University Press, 2005.

Pike, Ruth. *Linajudos and Conversos in Seville: Greed and Prejudice in Sixteenth- and Seventeenth-Century Spain*. New York: Peter Lang, 2000.

Pimentel, Juan. "Baroque Natures: Juan E. Nieremberg, American Wonders, and Preterimperial Natural History." In *Science in the Spanish and Portuguese Empires, 1500–1800*, edited by Daniela Bleichmar, 93–114. Stanford: Stanford University Press, 2009.

Pizarro Llorente, Henar. "Los miembros del cabildo de la catedral de Toledo durante el arzobispado de Gaspar de Quiroga (1577–1594)." *Hispania Sacra* 62, no. 126 (2010), 563–619.

Polman, Pontien. *L'élément historique dans la controverse religieuse du XVIe siècle*. Gembloux: Imprimerie J. Duculot, 1932.

Porres Martín-Cleto, Julio. "La calle de Esteban Illán" and "Nuevos datos sobre Don Esteban Illán." *Revista Toletum. Boletín de la Real Academia de Bellas Artes y Ciencias Históricas de Toledo* 5, 2a época (1972), 63–95, 155–63.

Poska, Allyson M. *Women and Authority in Early Modern Spain: The Peasants of Galicia.* Oxford: Oxford University Press, 2005.

Pradas, Antonio Martín, and Inmaculada Carrasco Gómez. "Datos biográficos inéditos sobre el Martín de Roa." In *Luis Vélez de Guevara y su época*, edited by Piedad Bolaños Donoso and Marina Martín Ojeda, 379–83. Seville: Fundación El Monte, 1996.

Preto, Paolo. "Una lunga storia di falsi e falsari." *Mediterranea: Ricerche storiche* 3, Aprile (2006), 11–38.

Prosperi, Adriano. "L'Immacolata a Siviglia e la fondazione sacra della monarchia spagnola." *Studi storici: rivista trimestrale dell'Istituto Gramsci* 47, no. 2 (2006), 481–510.

Pullapilly, Cyriac K. *Caesar Baronius, Counter-Reformation Historian*. Notre Dame: University of Notre Dame, 1975.

Quantin, Jean-Louis. "Reason and Reasonableness in French Ecclesiastical Scholarship." *Huntington Library Quarterly* 74, no. 3 (2011), 401–36.

Rábade Obradó, María del Pilar. "La invención como necesidad: Genealogía y judeoconversos." In *Estudios de genealogía, heráldica y nobiliaria*, edited by Miguel Ángel Ladero Quesada, 183–201. Madrid: Universidad Complutense, 2006.

Reames, Sherry L. *The Legenda Aurea: A Reexamination of its Paradoxical History*. Madison: University of Wisconsin, 1985.

Redondo, Augustin. "Légendes généalogiques et parentés fictives en Espagne, au Siècle d'Or." In *Les parentés fictives en Espagne, XVIe–XVIIe siècles: Colloque international, Sorbonne, 15, 16 et 17 mai 1986*, edited by Augustin Redondo, 15–35. Paris: La Sorbonne, 1988.

———. "Leyendas, creencias y ritos en torno a Santa Quiteria en la Castilla del siglo XVI." In *Folclore y leyendas en la península Ibérica. En torno a la obra de François Delpech*, edited by Helene Trope and María Tausiet, 37–56. Madrid: CSIC, 2014.

Redworth, Glyn. *The Prince and the Infanta: The Cultural Politics of the Spanish Match*. New Haven: Yale University Press, 2003.

Reilly, Bernard F. "Bishop Lucas of Túy and the Latin Chronicle Tradition in Iberia." *The Catholic Historical Review* 93, no. 4 (2007), 767–88.

Reinhardt, Klaus, and Horacio Santiago-Otero. *Biblioteca bíblica ibérica medieval*. Madrid: CSIC, 1986.

Repertorio de historia de las ciencias eclesiásticas en España. 4 vols. Salamanca: Universidad Pontificia, 1967–79.

Rey Castelao, Ofelia. "La *Historia crítica de los falsos cronicones* de José Godoy Alcántara." In *¿La historia inventada?*, edited by García-Arenal and Barrios Aguilera, 395–435. Granada, 2008.

Reyre, Dominique. "Topónimos hebreos y memoria de la España judía en el Siglo de Oro." *Criticón* 65 (1995), 31–53.

Rice, Eugene F. *Saint Jerome in the Renaissance*. Baltimore: Johns Hopkins University Press, 1985.

Richardson, Lisa. "Plagiarism and Imitation in Renaissance Historiography." In *Plagiarism in Early Modern England*, edited by Paulina Kewes, 106–18. Houndmills: Palgrave Macmillan, 2003.

Río Barredo, María José del. *Madrid, urbs regia. La capital ceremonial de la Monarquía Católica*. Madrid: Marcial Pons, 2000.

Rivera Recio, Juan Francisco. "La iglesia mozárabe." In *Historia de la Iglesia en España*, edited by Javier Fernández Conde. Madrid: Biblioteca de Autores Cristianos, 1982.

———. *Los arzobispos de Toledo: Desde sus orígenes hasta fines del siglo XI*. Toledo: Diputación Provincial, 1973.

———. *San Eugenio de Toledo y su culto*. Toledo: Diputación Provincial, 1963.

Roberts, Michael John. *Poetry and the Cult of the Martyrs: The* Liber Peristephanon *of Prudentius*. Ann Arbor: University of Michigan, 1993.

Rodríguez-Moñino Soriano, Rafael. *Aproximación a la historia eclesiástica de la ciudad de Baeza (Jaén). (Del esplendor renacentista y barroco a la crisis liberal del XIX)*. Jaén: Instituto de Etudios Giennenses and Diputación Provincial de Jaén, 2000.

Rodríguez de Gracia, Hilario. "Contratos de impresión suscritos por Juan de Mariana, Alonso de Villegas y Francisco de Pisa." *Hispania Sacra* 55 (2003), 51–84.

Rodríguez Marín, Francisco. "Cervantes y la Universidad de Osuna." In *Homenaje a Menéndez Pelayo. Estudios de erudición española*, 757–99. Madrid: Librería General de Victoriana Suárez, 1899.

Rodríguez Mediano, Fernando, and Mercedes García-Arenal. "De Diego de Urrea a Marcos Dobelio, intérpretes y traductores de los plomos." In *Los plomos del Sacromonte: Invención y tesoro*, edited by Barrios Aguilera and García-Arenal, 297–333. Valencia, 2006.

Rose, Els. *Ritual Memory: The Apocryphal Acts and Liturgical Commemoration in the Early Medieval West (c. 500–1215)*. Leiden: Brill, 2009.

Roth, Norman. *Jews, Visigoths, and Muslims in Medieval Spain: Cooperation and Conflict*. Leiden: Brill, 1994.

Rowe, Erin K. *Saint and Nation: Santiago, Teresa of Avila, and Plural Identities in Early Modern Spain*. University Park: Pennsylvania State University Press, 2011.

Rowland, Ingrid D. *The Scarith of Scornello: A Tale of Renaissance Forgery*. Chicago: University of Chicago Press, 2004.

Rubio Sadia, Juan Pablo. "'Que de ambos oficios era Dios servido.' El origen de la dualidad litúrgica toledana en la historiografía renacentista." *Hispania Sacra* 59, no. 119 (2007), 141–62.

Ruíz Vega, Antonio. *Los hijos de Túbal: mitología hispánica, dioses y héroes de la España antigua*. Madrid: Esfera, 2002.

Russell, J. C. "Chronicles of Medieval Spain." *Hispanic Review* 6, no. 3 (1938), 218–35.

Sabalete Moya, José Ignacio. "El Sacromonte de Arjona." In *Religión y cultura* II, edited by Salvador Rodríguez Becerra, 201–13. Seville: Junta de Andalucía and Fundación Machado, 1999.

Sabbadini, Remigio. *Le scoperte dei codici latini e greci ne' secoli XIV e XV*. 2 vols. Florence: Sansoni, 1914.

Saéz, Ricardo. "Contribution à l'histoire religieuse de l'Espagne. Étude introductive à l'édition du synode tenu à Tolède en 1596, sous la présidence de García de Loaysa, gouverneur de l'archevêché." *Mélanges de la Casa de Velázquez* 22 (1986), 223–68.

Samson, Alexander. "Florián de Ocampo, Castilian Chronicler and Hapsburg Propagandist: Rhetoric, Myth and Genealogy in the Historiography of Early Modern Spain." *Forum for Modern Language Studies* 42, no. 4 (2006), 339–54.

Sánchez Alonso, Benito. *Historia de la historiografía española.* 3 vols. Madrid: CSIC, 1941–50.

Sánchez González, Ramón. "Cabildo catedralicio y cabildo municipal en el Toledo moderno." In *V Reunión Científica Asociación Española de Historia Moderna,* edited by José Luis Pereira Iglesias, José Manuel de Bernardo Ares, and Jesús Manuel González Beltrán, 137–46. Cadiz: Universidad de Cádiz, 1999.

———. "La cultura de las letras en el clero capitular de la catedral toledana." In *Sociedad y élites eclesiásticas en la España moderna,* edited by Francisco José Aranda Pérez, 163–235. Cuenca: Ediciones de la Universidad de Castilla–La Mancha, 2000.

Sánchez Romeralo, Jaime. "Alonso de Villegas: Semblanza del autor de la *Selvagia.*" In *Actas del quinto congreso internacional de hispanistas, celebrado en Bordeaux del 2 al 8 de septiembre de 1974,* edited by Maxime Chevalier, François López, Joseph Pérez, and Noël Salomon, 783–93. Bordeaux: Université de Bordeaux III, 1977.

Sandberg, John M. "Religion and the Enlightenment(s)." *History Compass* 8, no. 11 (2010), 1291–98.

Santos Puerto, José. "La censura de la *España primitiva*: una aclaración historiográfica." *Hispania: Revista española de historia* 59, no. 202 (1999), 547–64.

Sawilla, Jan Marco. *Antiquarianismus, Hagiographie und Historie im 17. Jahrhundert: Zum Werk der Bollandisten. Ein wissenschaftshistorischer Versuch.* Tübingen: Max Niemeyer, 2009.

Scaramella, Pierroberto. "'Una materia gravissima, una enorme heresia': Granada, Roma e la controversia sugli apocrifi del Sacromonte." *Rivista storica italiana* 120, no. 3 (2008), 1003–44.

Schaefer, Richard. "True and False Enlightenment: German Scholars and the Discourse of Catholicism in the Nineteenth Century." *Catholic Historical Review* 97, no. 1 (2011), 24–45.

Segura González, Wenceslao. "La reliquia de San Hiscio." *Aljaranda: Revista de estudios tarifeños* 47 (2002), 16–17.

———. "Patronazgo de Sanct Hiscio por la Villa de Tariffa." *Aljaranda: Revista de estudios tarifeños* 16 (1995), 12–14.

Shalev, Zur. *Sacred Words and Worlds: Geography, Religion, and Scholarship, 1550–1700.* Leiden: Brill, 2011.

Sherman, William H. *Used Books: Marking Readers in Renaissance England.* Philadelphia: University of Pennsylvania Press, 2008.

Sicroff, Albert A. *Les controverses des statuts de "pureté de sang" en Espagne du XVe au XVIIe siècle.* Paris: Didier, 1960.

Simón Díaz, José. *Jesuitas de los siglos XVI y XVII: Escritos localizados.* Madrid: Universidad Pontificia de Salamanca; Fundación Universitaria Española, 1975.

Smith, Helen, and Louise Wilson, eds. *Renaissance Paratexts.* Cambridge: Cambridge University Press, 2011.

Smoller, Laura Ackerman. "From Authentic Miracles to a Rhetoric of Authenticity: Examples from the Canonization and Cult of St. Vincent Ferrer." *Church History* 80, no. 4 (2011), 773–97.

Solís de Santos, José. "En torno al 'Epistolario de Justo Lipsio y los españoles': el aragonés Bartolomé Morlanes y Malo (1576–1649)." *Humanismo y pervivencia del mundo clásico: homenaje al profesor Antonio Fontán* 3, no. 3, edited by José María Maestre Maestre, Luis Charlo Brea, and Joaquín Pascual Bareum, 1331–1345. Madrid: Alcañiz, 2002.

Sommervogel, Carlos, et al. *Bibliothèque de la Compagnie de Jésus*. 11 vols. Brussels and Paris: Oscar Schepens, Alphonse Picard, 1890–1932.

Sot, Michel. "*Gesta episcoporum,*" "*gesta abbatum.*" Turnhout, Belgium: Brepols, 1981.

Southern, R. W. *Western Society and the Church in the Middle Ages*. Harmondsworth, England: Penguin Books, 1970.

Spiegel, Gabrielle M. "Forging the Past: The Language of Historical Truth in the Middle Ages." *The History Teacher* 17, no. 2 (1984), 267–83.

———. *Romancing the Past: The Rise of Vernacular Prose Historiography in Thirteenth-Century France*. Berkeley: University of California Press, 1993.

Stenhouse, William. *Reading Inscriptions and Writing Ancient History: Historical Scholarship in the Late Renaissance*. London: Institute of Classical Studies, University of London School of Advanced Study, 2005.

———. "Thomas Dempster, Royal Historian to James I, and Classical Scholarship in Early Stuart England." *The Sixteenth Century Journal* 35, no. 2 (2004), 395–410.

Stephens, Walter. "Complex Pseudonymity: Annius of Viterbo's Multiple Persona Disorder." *Modern Language Notes* 126 (2011), 689–708.

———. *Giants in Those Days: Folklore, Ancient History, and Nationalism*. Lincoln: University of Nebraska Press, 1989.

———. "When Pope Noah Ruled the Etruscans: Annius of Viterbo and his Forged Antiquities." *Modern Language Notes* 119 (Supplement) (2004), 201–23.

Stratton, Suzanne L. *The Immaculate Conception in Spanish Art*. Cambridge: Cambridge University Press, 1994.

Summers, David. *Michelangelo and the Language of Art*. Princeton: Princeton University Press, 1980.

Sweet, Rosemary. *Antiquaries: The Discovery of the Past in Eighteenth-Century Britain*. London: Hambledon, 2004.

Tanner, Marie. *The Last Descendant of Aeneas: The Hapsburgs and the Mythic Image of the Emperor*. New Haven: Yale University Press, 1993.

Tate, Robert Brian. "Mythology in Spanish Historiography of the Middle Ages and the Renaissance." *Hispanic Review* XXII, no. 1 (1954), 1–18.

———. "The Rewriting of the Historical Past: *Hispania et Europa*." In *Historical Literature in Medieval Iberia*, edited by Alan Deyermond, 85–103. London: Queen Mary and Westfield College, 1996.

———. "*Laus Urbium*: Praise of Two Andalusian Cities in the Mid-Fifteenth Century." In *Medieval Spain: Culture, Conflict, and Coexistence. Studies in Honour of Angus MacKay*, edited by Roger Collins and Anthony Goodman, 148–59. New York: Palgrave Macmillan, 2002.

Tausiet, María. "De la ilusión al desencanto: Feijóo y los 'falsos posesos' en la España del siglo XVIII." *Historia social* 54 (2006), 3–18.

———. *El dedo robado: Reliquias imaginarias en la España moderna*. Madrid: Abada, 2013.

———. "Zaragoza celeste y subterránea. Geografía mítica de una ciudad (siglos XV–XVIII)." In *L'imaginaire du territoire en Espagne et au Portugal, XVIe–XVIIe siècles*, edited by François Delpech, 141–70. Madrid: Casa de Velázquez, 2008.

Tedeschi, John. "The Roman Inquisition and Witchcraft: An Early Seventeenth-Century 'Instruction' on Correct Trial Procedure." *Revue de l'histoire des religions* 200, no. 2 (1983), 163–88.

Thomas, Andrew L. *A House Divided: Wittelsbach Confessional Court Cultures in the Holy Roman Empire, c. 1550–1650*. Leiden: Brill, 2010.

Torrecilla, Jesús. *Guerras literarias del XVIII español: la modernidad como invasión*. Salamanca: Universidad de Salamanca, 2008.

Turner, Nancy L. "Jews and Judaism in Peter Auriol's *Sentences* Commentary." In *Friars and Jews in the Middle Ages and Renaissance*, edited by Susan E. Myers and Steven J. McMichael, 81–98. Leiden: Brill, 2004.

Valtchinova, Galia. "'Unconscious Historicization'? History and Politics in Interwar Bulgaria Through the Eyes of Local Visionaries." *Anamnesis* 2 (2006), 90–114.

Van Liere, Katherine Elliot. "Humanism and Scholasticism in Sixteenth-Century Academe: Five Student Orations from the University of Salamanca." *Renaissance Quarterly* 53, no. 1 (2000), 57–107.

———. "The Missionary and the Moorslayer: James the Apostle in Spanish Historiography from Isidore of Seville to Ambrosio de Morales." *Viator* 37 (2006), 519–43.

———. "Renaissance Chroniclers and the Apostolic Origins of Spanish Christianity." In *Sacred History*, edited by Van Liere, Ditchfield, and Louthan, 121–44. Oxford, 2012.

———. "Shared Studies Foster Friendship: Humanism and History in Spain." In *The Renaissance World*, edited by John Jeffries Martin, 242–61. New York: Routledge, 2007.

Van Liere, Katherine Elliot, Simon R. Ditchfield, and Howard Louthan, eds. *Sacred History: Uses of the Christian Past in the Renaissance World*. Oxford: Oxford University Press, 2012.

Vega, P. A. C. "Una carta auténtica de San Fructuoso incluída por Román de la Higuera en su Luitprando." *La Ciudad de Dios* 153 (1941), 335–44.

Vélez, Karin. "Resolved to Fly: The Virgin of Loreto, the Jesuits and the Miracle of Portable Catholicism in the Seventeenth-Century Atlantic World." Ph.D. diss., Princeton University, 2008.

Veraja, Fabijan. *La beatificazione: Storia, problemi, prospettive*. Rome: Santa Congregazione per le Cause dei Santi, 1983.

Vilaplana, María Asunción. "Correspondencia de Papebroch con el Marqués de Mondéjar." *Hispania Sacra* 25, no. 50 (1972), 293–349.

Villanueva López, Jesús. *Política y discurso histórico en la España del siglo XVII: las polémicas sobre los orígenes medievales de Cataluña*. Alicante: Universidad de Alicante, 2004.

Viller, Marcel, Ferdinand Cavallera, J. de Guibert, and Charles Baumgartner. *Dictionnaire de spiritualité ascétique et mystique, doctrine et histoire*. Paris: Beauchesne, 1957.

Vincent-Cassy, Cécile. "L'inventaire des empreintes sacrées. Le discours de Juan Acuña de Adarve sur les Saintes Faces (Jaén, 1637)." In *Folclore y leyendas en la península ibérica: en torno a la obra de François Delpech*, edited by María Tausiet and Hélène Tropé. Madrid: CSIC, 2014.

———. *Les saintes vierges et martyres dans l'Espagne du XVIIe siècle: Culte et image*. Madrid: Casa de Velázquez, 2011.

———. "Los santos re-fundadores. El caso de Arjona (Jaén) en el siglo XVII." In *L'imaginaire du territoire en Espagne et au Portugal, XVIe–XVIIe siècles*, edited by François Delpech, 193–214. Madrid: Casa de Velázquez, 2008.

Visser, A. S. Q. *Reading Augustine in the Reformation: The Flexibility of Intellectual Authority in Europe, 1500–1620*. New York: Oxford University Press, 2011.

Vives, José. "Tradición y leyenda en la hagiografía hispánica." *Hispania Sacra* 17, no. 33–34 (1964), 495–508.

Walker, D. P. *The Ancient Theology: Studies in Christian Platonism from the Fifteenth to the Eighteenth Century*. London: Duckworth, 1972.

Walsham, Alexandra. *The Reformation of the Landscape: Religion, Identity, and Memory in Early Modern Britain and Ireland*. Oxford: Oxford University Press, 2011.

Ward, Aengus. *History and Chronicles in Late Medieval Iberia: Representations of Wamba in Late Medieval Narrative Histories*. Leiden: Brill, 2011.

Webb, Diana. "Sanctity and History: Antonio degli Agli and Humanist Hagiography." In *Florence and Italy: Renaissance Studies in Honour of Nicolai Rubinstein*, edited by P. Denley and C. Elam, 297–308. London: Committee for Medieval Studies, Westfield College, 1988.

Weiss, Roberto. *The Renaissance Discovery of Classical Antiquity*. 2nd ed. Oxford: Blackwell, 1988.

Whitford, David M. *The Curse of Ham in the Early Modern Era: The Bible and the Justifications for Slavery*. Farnham, England: Ashgate, 2009.

Wilberding, Erick. "A Defense of Dionysius the Areopagite by Rubens." *Journal of the History of Ideas* 52, no. 1 (1991), 19–34.

Wood, Christopher S., and Alexander Nagel. "Interventions: Toward a New Model of Renaissance Anachronism." *Art Bulletin* 87, no. 3 (2005), 403–15.

Woolard, Kathryn A. "Bernardo de Aldrete, Humanist and *laminario*." *Al-Qantara: Revista de estudios árabes* XXIV, no. 2 (2003), 449–75.

Woolf, Daniel R. "Erudition and the Idea of History in Renaissance England." *Renaissance Quarterly* 40 (1997), 11–48.

———. "From Hystories to the Historical: Five Transitions in Thinking about the Past, 1500–1700." *The Huntington Library Quarterly* 68, no. 1/2 (2005), 33–70.

———. *The Social Circulation of the Past: English Historical Culture, 1500–1730*. Oxford: Oxford University Press, 2003.

Wright, A. D. "The Borromean Ideal and the Spanish Church." In *San Carlo Borromeo. Catholic Reform and Ecclesiastical Politics in the Second Half of the Sixteenth Century*, edited by J. M. Headley and J. B. Tomaro, 188–207. Washington, D.C.: Folger Books, 1988.

Wunder, Amanda. "Classical, Christian, and Muslim Remains in the Construction of Imperial Seville (1520–1635)." *Journal of the History of Ideas* 64, no. 2 (2003), 195–212.

———. "Search for Sanctity in Baroque Seville: The Canonization of San Fernando and the Making of Golden-Age Culture, 1624–1729." Ph.D. diss., Princeton University, 2002.

Yelo Templado, Antonio. "Inautenticidad de la historia fulgentina." *Antigüedad y cristianismo: Monografías históricas sobre la Antigüedad tardía* 2 (1985), 45–52.

———. "La Rioja en los falsos cronicones." *Cuadernos de investigación: Historia* 10, no. 1 (1984), 287–94.

INDEX

Note: Page numbers in italics indicate figures.

Abundius (martyr), 142, 248–49
Acevedo, Pedro González de (bishop of Plasencia), 160–61
Acquaviva, Claudio (Jesuit general): censorship by, 91–92; Higuera and, 68–69, 70–74, 84–85; Mariana and, 69–70; memorialistas and, 85–88, 92; promises and pitfalls of historical scholarship for, 88–91; tension with Spanish royal court and, 86–88, 94–96; Tirso controversy and, 30–31, 52–54
Acta sanctorum. *See* Bolland, Jean; Bollandists
Acuña del Adarve, Juan, 248, 251
adoptionist heresy, 176–77
adversaria, 104, 107, 264
Afán de Ribera, Fernando Enríquez (Duke of Alcalá), 202, 237, 255
Agali monastery, 36, 104
Agostinho de Jesus (archbishop of Braga), 160, 180, 202
Aguilar, Juan de, 231
Agustín, Antonio, 10, 13, 17, 22, 39–41, 57–58, 148–49, 154, 220; Higuera's correspondence with, 40
Ajofrín, 186–87, 196
Alcalá de Henares, 255
Alcocer, Pedro de: biographical information about, 327n43; history of Jews in Spain and, 134–35; *History . . . of Toledo* compared to Higuera's, 71, 75–80, 134; Mozarabs and, 56; use of sources, 79–80
Alcuin of York, 189–90
Aldrete, Bernardo de, 193, 247–48, 270, 274, 306, 348n65
Alexander (martyr), 142, 248–49
Álvares de Lousada Machado, Gaspar, 160, 180–81, 225–26, 343n75, 348n60
Añaya Maldonado, Martín de (canon), 239, 241–42
Andalusia, xv, 22. *See also specific locations*
Anglina (martyr), 139, 163–65, 170, 307
Annius da Viterbo (Nanni, Giovanni): citations and defenses of, 11, 19, 58, 79–81, 151, 211–22, 289, 313; critics and critiques of, 11, 80–81, 157, 204–5, 271, 291, 300, 302; forgeries of, 11, 16, 79–82, 102, 112, 151, 204–5; Higuera on texts by, 81–82; Higuera's chronicles compared to, 204–5; Higuera's use of, 112; historical method and, 16; layout and print rhetoric of, 213, 222; paratextual materials and, 222

antiquarianism: Baronio and, 109–10, 195; Bollandists and, 235; ecclesiastical history and, 17–18; epigraphic evidence and, 36, 152–54; forgeries and, 13, 15, 195; Higuera and, 20, 84, 150; *historia sacra* and, 235–36; historical method and, 17–18, 84, 150–54; numismatic evidence and, 152–54, 250. *See also* epigraphic evidence; *historia sacra*; Morales, Ambrosio de; numismatic evidence

Antist, Vicente Justiniano (Dominican), 160, 163–65, 170, 341n27

Antonio, Nicolás: biographical information about, 295; *Censura de historias fabulosas* and, 234, 287, 295, 296, 299, 301–2, 346n14, 358n66; correspondence with Bollandists, 292–93; Higuera's texts and, 7, 75, 117, 234, 287–88, 291–93, 295, 296, 297–99, 301–2, 346n14, 358n66; intellectual community of, 290; manuscripts and letters of, 310; philological method and, 295, 297–99, 307; "primitive Dexter" and, 346n14; value of pious traditions for, 298

apocryphal texts and traditions: active reading and, 208–9; Baronio and, 167–68; biblical, 118–19, 125, 161, 201, 271; Bivar and, 224, 271–72; definition of, 118, 240, 271; early modern attitudes toward, 120–21, 125, 166–68, 212–23, 240; eighteenth-century critiques of, 303, 308; forgeries versus, 4, 13, 287, 292–93, 297; Higuera and, 2, 25, 51–52, 82–84, 111–13, 118–19, 137, 145–46, 150, 161–62, 167–68, 176, 240, 271, 292–93; Higuera's chronicles as, 161, 207–12, 269, 271–72, 284, 288; Mariana and, 98; Mayans and, 302; medieval uses of, 118–19, 125, 208; Renaissance humanists and, 13–14, 167–68, 208; Toribius of Astorga and, 160; as useful albeit flawed, 206, 208–9, 212, 288, 297, 303. *See also* Gelasian Decree

Arceo, Manuel de (Jesuit), 94–95

Arce y Reinoso, Diego de (bishop), 289

Argaíz, Gregorio (Benedictine), 164, 289–90, 356n16

Arias Montano, Benito, 75, 128–29, 134, 154, 300, 335n29

Aristotle, 118, 124

Arjona, *xv*, 140–42; the paranormal and, 312–13, 360n16; saints and relics of, 227, 249, 251–52, 253; Santa María's lost history of, 168. *See also* Bonosus and Maximianus; Moscoso y Sandoval, Baltasar

Athanasius (bishop of Zaragoza), 178, 258

Augustinian Canons, Order of. *See* Pennotto, Gabriele

Augustinian Hermits, Order of. *See* Márquez, Joan

Aulo Halo, 288–89

Baeza, *xv*, 142, 227–28, 237, 248–49, 251–52, 255. *See also* Moscoso y Sandoval, Baltasar

Barbata (saint), 174, 280. *See also* Paula of Ávila

Barberini, Francesco (cardinal), 272, 295

Barcelona, *xv*, 117, 141, 157, 206, 275–76, 303, 347n39

Baronio, Cesare (cardinal): *Annales ecclesiastici* and, 108–10, 121–22; antiquarianism and, 18, 67, 110, 235; apocryphal material and, 111–13, 167–68; Dionysius the Areopagite and, 167–68; Donation of Constantine and, 195–95; Hapsburg claims to Sicily and, 168, 345n130; Higuera's chronicles and, 110–14, 165–66, 209, 220, 272; Higuera's 1589 letter to, 165–66, 173–75; pious affection and, 193–95; Prudentius and, 121–22; reform of Roman liturgy and, 165–75; Santiago and, 130, 168, 170, 205, 298; Spain and, 169–72, 345n130; *vox populi* and, 193–95. *See also* liturgical sources; Roman Breviary; Roman Martyrology

Barrientos, Diego Antonio de (Augustinian), 291
Bellarmine, Robert (cardinal), 108, 130, 166, 168, 171, 174–75, 270, 273
Belmonte. *See under* Higuera (Román de la Higuera, Jerónimo)
Benavides, Francisco de (Jesuit), 95–96, 330n114
Beuter, Antoni, 19, 81, 135, 171
Bilches, Francisco (Jesuit), 248, 305
Bivar, Francisco: Arjona saints and, 227–31, 312; biographical information about, 227, 348n50; Congregation of Index and, 270–74; Dexter-Maximus chronicle 1627 edition by, 180, 215, 217, 222–26, 223, 227, 230–31, 267–74, 276, 278–79, 284, 289; Hierotheo and, 226–27; lead books and, 269–70; Maximus chronicle 1651 edition by, 268, 289; Moscoso y Sandoval and, 227–31, 289; nature of truth and, 233; patrons and, 229, 261, 267–68, 270; pious affection and, 271–72; Sacra Rota and, 180
Blancas, Jerónimo, 41–42, 154–55, 338n28
Bolland, Jean (Jesuit), 292. *See also* Bollandists
Bollandists, 165, 187, 235, 290–95, 298–300, 311
Bonosus and Maximianus (saints): archaeological evidence and, 141–42, 227; relics of, 140–42, 227, 311–12; sources regarding, 141, 227–32; veneration of, 142, 231–32, 239, 251–52, 274–75, 279, 311–12. *See also* Arjona; Bivar, Francisco; Moscoso y Sandoval, Baltasar
Bouza, Fernando, 284
Bovon, François, 208
Bowersock, Glen, 195, 345n130
Bracciolini, Poggio, 14
Braga, *xv*, 59, 67, 117, 151, 160, 180–81, 202, 224, 281, 283, 336n46, 339n54
Braulio chronicle, 103, 213
Breviary, Roman. *See* Roman Breviary
Brouwer, Christopher (Jesuit), 92, 204, 329n100

Burriel, Andrés Marcos (Jesuit), 302–3, 310

Calderón, Juan de, 147, 213–16, 214, 215, 217, 218, 224–26, 233, 277, 283
Caliopa (martyr), 255
Cameron, Euan, 18
Campi, Pietro Maria, 171, 243
Canisius, Henry, 150, 264
Cano, Benito, 301
Cano, Melchor, 11, 190–91
Caravaca, 182
Caravaca, Cross of, 181–82, 279
Cárcamo, Alonso de (corregidor), 32, 33, 43–47, 49, 63, 73. *See also* Tirso controversy
Cardoso, Jorge, 289
Caresmar, Jaume, 303
Carmelite order, 165, 169, 295. *See also* Pancorbo, Jerónimo; Santa María, Francisco de
Carmona, 255
Caro, Rodrigo: Andalusian learned community and, 235–36, 242, 247–48; *Defense of the Writings of . . . Dexter* by, 276–78; Dexter-Maximus 1627 edition by, 217, 219, 220, 221, 222, 237, 238, 261–62, 264, 276–79; epigraphic evidence and, 220, 222, 237, 238; historical texts as ghostwritten for, 267; idea of truth and, 233; Julián Pérez chronicle draft and, 264; new saints in Seville and, 235–37, 255; search for patronage and, 237, 261–62, 264, 267, 279. *See also* Castro y Quiñones, Pedro de; Osuna; Rioja, Francisco de; Seville; Utrera
Caro Baroja, Julio, 3–4, 9, 137, 325n107
Carrillo, Martín, 6, 210–11
Carvajal, Álvaro de, 46
Carvajal Girón de Loaysa, Pedro, 32, 34, 46–48, 51–52
Casas, Ignacio de las (Jesuit), 161, 304
Casaubon, Isaac, 41, 167
Cascales, Francisco de, 184

Castillo, Alonso de, 14, 161
Castro y Quiñones, Pedro de (archbishop): correspondence with Higuera and, 129–32, 138–39, 160, 168; Higuera's chronicles and, 202; lead books and, 127, 129–32, 210, 304; new saints in Seville and, 139, 236, 239, 255; Tirso controversy and, 132, 139. See also lead books (plomos) of Granada; Sacromonte
Casus exceptus, 251, 254
Catalan Revolt (1640–52), 275–76
Catholic Church. See individual clerics, congregations, and religious orders
Cecilio (saint), 127
Centurión, Adán de, Marquis of Estepa, 251, 264, 275, 297, 311
Centurión, Felipe de, 275, 311
Cervantes, Miguel de, 14–15
Charlemagne, 66, 104, 107, 138, 176–77, 189, 213
Chirinos, 181–82
Christian, William, Jr., 196, 344n100, 360n14
chronicles, false. See Higuera, chronicles of
chronicles, false, post-Higuera, 288–91, 301, 304–5, 356n16. See also Argaíz, Gregorio
chronicles, late antique and medieval, 107–9, 116–19, 224. See also Eusebius of Caesarea; Hydatius of Galicia; Isidore of Seville; Jerome; John of Biclarum; Lucas de Tuy; Orosius, Paulus; Prosper of Aquitaine; Victor of Tunnuna; Ximénez de Rada, Rodrigo
Chronicon omnimodae historiae [The Chronicle of Universal History] (Dexter). See Dexter chronicle
Cirot, Georges, 98
Cixila of Toledo (archbishop), 35, 37, 48–49, 104, 178, 184, 322n33. See also Tirso controversy
Claudius of Turin, 107, 335n14
Cobos, Francisco de, 70
Cochrane, Eric, 15

commentary (ilustraciones), importance of. See paratext
Congregation of Rites, Roman, 166, 171, 174–75, 239–40
Congregation of the Index of Prohibited Books, Roman, 268–70, 272–73, 295
Constable, Giles, 10, 12, 25, 193
conversos. See La Guardia, child-martyr of; Higuera (Román de la Higuera, Jerónimo); Higuera, chronicles of; Jesuit order; Jews and conversos; limpieza de sangre (purity of blood) statutes
copatronage debate. See Santiago
Cordoba, xv, 104, 121, 170, 247
Cortés, Juan Lucas, 290
Council of Trent, 2, 15, 18, 41, 111, 190–91, 243, 273
Covarrubias, Antonio de (Seville canon), 321n28
Covarrubias, Diego de, 40–42
Covarrubias, Sebastián de, 8, 321n28
Covarrubias y Leyvas, Antonio de (Toledo maestrescuela), 41–42, 128, 154, 321n28
Crispinus (saint), 246
cronicones of Higuera. See Higuera, chronicles of
Cusa, Nicholas of, 208
Cyriac of Ancona, 17, 156, 301

Dacian (Roman governor), 122, 139, 312
Dávila Toledo, Sancho (bishop), 8, 117, 146–47, 178–79, 201–2
Dempster, Thomas, 18
Dexter, Flavius Lucius, 1, 101. See also Dexter chronicle
Dexter chronicle (Higuera): authentic sources of, 24, 117–18; Bollandists and, 292–93; creation and composition of, 117–19; dissemination of manuscript copies of, 146–47, 202; early adopters of, 146–47, 179–80; early manuscripts of ("primitive" Dexter), 297–98, 346n14; errors in, 157, 179, 212, 215; Eusebius-Jerome chronicle tradition and, 107;

hagiography and, 120–24; Higuera's failed attempt to print and, 202–3; Immaculate Conception and, 203, 212; imperfect state of manuscripts of, 203–4, 206, 216–17, 276–77; imputed author of, 101, 157; Jerome and, 1, 24, 101–2, 276, 293; Jews and conversos in, 56; as medieval chronicle, 23–24, 107, 117–19, 133, 211–12; Mozarabs and, 56; "old" christians in, 56; origin story and "rediscovery" of, 1, 5–6, 101–4, 107, 147–48, 210, 229–30; patristic references to, 24, 101; philological scholarship and, 158, 213–15; El Pilar and, 6–7, 147, 179, 203, 206, 210, 224; pre-Higuera versions of, 101–2; Santiago and, 1, 6–7, 56, 110–11, 117–18, 203, 206–7, 209, 283, 305; Seven Apostles and, 209; Toledo and, 56, 75. *See also* Higuera, chronicles of

Dextro, Flavio Lucio. *See* Dexter, Flavius Lucius

Díaz de Ribas, Pedro, 216, 251, 255, 351n47

Diocletian (Roman emperor): Great Persecution of Christians under, 121–23, 139, 164, 232, 236–37, 252. *See also* Dacian

Dionysius the Areopagite: Baronio and, 167–68; Higuera and, 119–20, 179; historical figure of, 119–20; Pérez chronicle and, 107. *See also* Hierotheo

Ditchfield, Simon R., 18, 122, 168, 171, 243

Dominicans. *See* Annius da Viterbo; Antist, Vicente Justiniano; Cano, Melchor; Maldonado, Alonso de; Villanueva, Jaime; Villanueva, Joaquín Lorenzo de; Voragine, Jacobus de

Donation of Constantine, 194–95, 208, 345n130

Ecclesiastical History of Toledo [*Toledo*] (Higuera): overview of, 67, 76–77; Annian texts and, 81–82; Antonio and, 297–98; forgery vs., 64, 72–75; historical and critical method in, 64, 67, 74–78, 80–84; Jesuit order and, 64, 67–68, 70–74, 88–89, 97; Jews and conversos in, 133–35, 336n30; legendary material and, 80–84, 328n49, 336n30; local controversy regarding, 63–64, 70–72; manuscripts of, 326n11, 328n66; Mozarabs and, 133; peer texts and, 75–84; Quiteria in, 188; Toledan municipal patrons of, 63, 72–73, 326n18; use of sources in, 67, 76–77, 79–80, 83–84, 161, 313, 327n47; *vox populi* and, 188

Ecija, *xv*, 245–46, 255, 292, 311

Elipandus of Toledo, 104, 176–78, 180, 336n46

Elpidius (saint), 287

Enlightenment, 7, 286–87, 300, 306–7

Enríquez Afán de Ribera, Fernando, Marquis of Tarifa, 255

epigraphic evidence: Agustín and, 10; antiquarian method and, 17–18, 36, 84, 152–54, 156, 252; Bivar and, 222; Caro and, 220, 237, 238; forgery of, 13, 15; Higuera and, 17–18, 36, 66–67, 76, 84, 154–56, 160–61, 182–85; Higuera's chronicle used as, 237, 238; lead books and, 269–70; local sacred historians and, 242–46, 250; Vázquez Siruela and, 291

Erasmus of Rotterdam, 13, 111, 150, 222, 339n45, 339n51

Escalona, 154

Escolano, Gaspar de, 111, 157, 205–7, 209

Escolano y Ledesma, Diego (bishop), 292

Eufrasio (saint), 248–49, 251–52, 350n41

Eugenius of Toledo (bishop), 34, 45, 120, 287

Eulalia (saint), 121, 303

Eusebius of Caesarea, 83, 107–8, 110, 113, 116, 119, 145, 224. *See also* chronicles, late antique and medieval

Eutrand (author), 103, 176, 264. *See also* Luitprand chronicle

false chronicles (*falsos cronicones*): definition of, 7. *See also* Higuera, chronicles of

Faustus (martyr), 142, 249

Feijóo y Montenegro, Benito Jerónimo (Benedictine), 300
Fernández de Pulgar, Pedro, 290–91
Flores, Juan de, 304–5
Flórez, Enrique, 258, 303, 305
Flos sanctorum, 50, 120–21
Fonseca i Figueroa, Juan de (royal librarian), 217
forgeries: aims and techniques of, 8–16, 21, 24–25, 37, 98, 99–107, 138–39, 146–47, 165–66, 193–95, 208, 283; apocrypha vs., 4, 287, 297; evolution of historical criticism and, 16, 288, 290–307; historiography of, 10; Le Mans texts and, 12; medieval, 12–13, 193; Renaissance, 13–14; Spanish reputation for, 10–11, 301–2, 306–7; Wamba, *hitación de* and, 12. *See also* Annius da Viterbo; Higuera, chronicles of; lead books (*plomos*) of Granada
Forstman y Medina, Gregorio, 256–57
Frías de Albornoz, Bartolomé, 183
Fructuosus (saint *also called* Fructos *or* Frutos), 120–21, 139, 227, 258, 291–92
Fructuosus of Braga, 336n46
Fulda, abbey of, 2, 5–6, 25, 100–101, 103–5, 107, 146–48, 178, 204, 210. *See also* Luitprand chronicle

Galicia, 356n6
Galilei, Galileo, 22, 269–70, 353n21
Garibay y Zamalloa, Esteban de (chronicler), 50, 75, 97, 134, 154, 322n36, 323n62
Gelasian Decree, 82–83, 271
Genette, Gérard, 213
Gibraltar, 255
Gil de Zamora, Juan, 148
Ginés Gómez, Doctor (parish priest), 183–84
Giovio, Paolo (historian), 206, 347n16
Godoy Alcántara, José, 2, 9, 24, 157, 309–10
Golden Legend. See Voragine, Jacobus de

Goldgar, Anne, 159
Gómez de Castro, Álvar, 40–41, 189, 306
González Chantos y Ullauri, Diego Eugenio, 175
González Dávila, Gil (Jesuit), 54, 84, 87–88
González Dávila, Gil (royal chronicler), 289
González de Acevedo, Pedro (bishop of Plasencia), 160–61
González de Mendoza, Pedro (archbishop of Toledo), 58
González de Mendoza, Pedro (Granada canon), 213
Grafton, Anthony, 10, 16, 147
Granada, xv, 128, 139, 247–48. *See also* Castro y Quiñones, Pedro de; lead books (*plomos*) of Granada; Sacromonte
Gregory IX (pope), 49
Guadalajara, 233
Guadix, xv, 249, 251, 287, 350n41
La Guardia, child-martyr of, 136, 170–73, 336n41
Guenée, Bernard, 107–8
Guevara, Antonio, 13
Guzmán, Ana Félix de, Marchioness of Camarasa, 69–70
Guzmán, Diego de (archbishop), 241–42, 247

hagiography: defined, 120, 334n89; Higuera's chronicles and, 2, 112–14, 120, 122–24, 139, 182–84, 203, 208, 289; humanist revisions of, 18, 84; post-Tridentine revision of, 18, 166–68, 235. *See also* Baronio, Cesare; Bollandists; liturgical sources; Mabillon, Jean de; Voragine, Jacobus de; *specific saints*
Háñez de Herrera, Francisco de, 141, 227, 242
Hardouin, Jean, 294
Harris, A. Katie, 10, 128
Hauberto chronicle, 290, 356n16
Heleca chronicle, 3, 103, 213, 219

Henry of Susa (Hostienses), 193
Hercules, 11, 35–36, 77, 81; cave of (Toledo), 77–79, 83, 196, 328n49
Hermenegild (saint), 160–61, 213
Hermits, Augustinian. *See* Márquez, Joan
Hernández, Miguel (Jesuit), 34
Hiatt, Alfred, 8, 10, 208
Hierotheo, 107, 120, 139, 170, 151, 226–27, 251, 258, 272, 291–92. *See also* Dionysius the Areopagite
Higuera (Román de la Higuera, Jerónimo): Agustín and, 40; ancestors of, 57–61; antiquarianism and, 20, 84, 150–51; Antist and, 163–64; Arabic and, 76, 327n47; authentic sources preserved by, 76, 137–38, 155–57, 313, 327n48, 336n46; Baronio and, 165–66, 173–75; Belmonte Jesuit house and, 73–74; biographical information about, 38–42, 59–61, 144, 320n10, 321n12, 321n15, 324n90, 325n99, 344n103; Blancas and, 41–41, 154–55; Castro and, 129–32, 138–39, 335n14; converso ancestry and, 59–61, 133–34; correspondents and, 146, 154–55, 159–61, 164–66, 185–88; critical acumen of, 150, 153–55; devotion to the saints and, 144–45; education of, 38–41; Garibay and, 50, 322n36; Greek language and, 76, 327n47; Hebrew language and, 76, 327n47; historical method and, 20–21, 84, 105, 148–51, 157–58, 203–4; history of Jews and conversos and, 133–37, 335n25, 336n30, 336n41; Jesuit order and, 38–39, 52, 68–69, 84–86, 88, 92–97, 144–45; lead books and, 128–32; legacy of, 3–4, 25, 65–66, 97, 110, 142–43, 156, 313–14, 327n48; letter to Baronio and, 165–66, 173–75; Lope de Vega and, 85; Madrid Jesuit house and, 38, 74; Mariana and, 65–66; Mozarabic ancestors and, 55–56, 58, 181–82; Ocaña Jesuit house and, 38–39, 48, 53, 69, 74, 84–85, 88, 93–96, 140, 147; philological method and, 105, 148, 150, 157–58; Plasencia Jesuit house and, 38, 66, 74, 93–97, 321n12; Portocarrero and, 88, 140, 148, 217, 330n126; Quevedo and, 85; Quijote and, 9; research by, 9, 29, 34–36, 40, 42, 66–68, 105–6, 138–39, 156–57, 176, 196–97; Soria and, 160, 170; Toledan allies of, 31, 45, 63, 68, 88, 326n18, 329n106; Toledan intellectual community and, 34–36, 39–42, 130–31, 149; Toledo Jesuit house and, 38, 54–55, 68, 73–74; Villegas and, 50–51, 102, 180–81, 322n36; *vox populi* and, 193–94. *See also* Higuera, chronicles of; Jesuit order; Tirso controversy

Higuera, chronicles of: overview of, 1–2, 23–25; active reading and, 279–81, 282, 283–84; authentic sources of, 101–2, 106–7, 112, 117–19, 145, 155–57, 165, 172–75, 181–84; Baronio and, 110–14, 165–66; Bollandists and, 290–91; chronicler's working method and, 107–8, 114–15, 117–18, 138; chronicles of Braulio and Heleca and, 103, 213; dissemination of manuscripts of, 5, 146–47, 178, 202; ecclesiastical chronicle style and, 23–24, 99–100, 109–10; errors in, 6, 9, 21, 129, 146, 157, 179, 201, 203–6, 211–13, 215, 218, 220, 224–25, 240, 276–77, 283, 293; evolution of historical method and debates about, 288, 290–307; hagiographic and liturgical texts and, 2, 112–14, 120–25, 139, 182–84, 289; Hierotheo and, 107, 120, 139, 226–27, 251, 258, 292; *historia sacra* and, 234–36, 245–46, 255, 258–59, 287–88, 311; as history and poetry, 124–25; Immaculate Conception and, 110–11, 128, 203, 212, 267, 269; intertwined with reception of lead books and, 5, 133, 259, 269–70, 272, 304–5; Jews and conversos and, 56, 132–38, 336n41; legacy of, 234–36, 255, 258–59, 286–88, 311, 313–14; Mozarabs and, 133–34; origin story and "rediscovery" of, 2, 5–6, 25, 100–107, 146–48, 204, 210; patristic and medi-

Higuera, chronicles of (continued)
eval textual alibis for, 24, 102, 106, 112;
Royal Academy of History (Portuguese)
and, 302; Royal Academy of History
(Spanish) and, 309–10; saints and local
saints' cults and, 2, 114, 139–42, 164–65,
167, 172–76, 178–84, 186–88, 196, 209–
10, 226–34, 239–41, 246, 248, 252, 255,
258–59, 269, 287–89, 305, 313–14; Santiago and, 1, 6–7, 110–11, 117–18, 147, 151,
157, 171, 179, 181, 203, 205, 209, 281, 283,
298; Seven Apostles and, 111, 151, 209,
255; success and influence of, 2, 7–10,
22–23, 56, 58, 67, 84, 135–36, 138–42,
161–65, 171–72, 181, 184–88, 196–97,
226–27, 231–32, 236, 240, 243, 251, 255,
258–59, 275–76, 287, 311–14, 352n72;
as verisimilar, 122–25. *See also* Dexter
chronicle; Julián Pérez chronicle; Luitprand chronicle; Maximus chronicle;
*individual critics, editors, patrons, and
readers*

Higuera, chronicles of—adopters, patrons,
and proponents of: 6–7, 21–22, 203;
Aldrete, 274, 306; Barcelona city councilors, 275–76, 278; Cardoso, 289; Carillo, 6, 210–11; Dávila, 146–47; Díaz
de Ribas, 255, 352n65; Escolano, 111,
157, 205–7, 209; Escolano y Ledesma,
292; Gómez Bravo, 352n64; Háñez de
Herrera, 141, 227, 242; Ibáñez, 291–95,
302, 310; Inchofer, 204, 268–69, 272–
74, 353n19; a Lapide, 280; Llorente y
García, 179–80; Maldonado, 211–12;
Mariana, 98; Márquez, 225; modern,
311; Morlanes y Malo, 179, 202; Morovelli de Puebla, 209, 281, 283; Murillo,
206–7, 209; Nieremberg, 264, 279; Pancorbo, 232, 277–78, 349n80; Peña y Lezcano, 352n64; Porreño, 65–66; Portocarrero, 140, 148, 217, 330n126; Quintana,
350n25, 352n66; Quintanadueñas, 236,
241, 243, 245, 247–48, 254–55, 278, 289;
Roa, 207, 245–46, 254, 285–85; Robles

Corvalán, 181–82; Rojas, 226, 280, 289;
Salazar, 146–47; Salazar de Mendoza,
58, 217, 247; San Cecilio, 164; Sandoval,
146–47, 160, 175, 178, 180, 201–2; Santa
María, 217, 295; Suárez, 287; Tamayo
Salazar, 289; Vázquez, 146–47, 176–77,
201; Vázquez Siruela, 248, 291, 296–98,
343n87. *See also* Moscoso y Sandoval,
Baltasar; Olivares, Count-Duke of; El
Pilar; *the editors of each of the chronicles'
print editions by name*

Higuera, chronicles of—critics and opponents of: 21–22, 203; Antonio, 7, 75, 117,
234, 287–88, 291–93, 295, 296, 299, 301–
2, 346n14, 358n66; Bollandists, 290–91;
Bosius (German Lutheran), 357n30;
Feijóo, 300; Fernández de Pulgar, 290–
91; Godoy Alcántara, 2, 9, 24, 157, 309–
10; Mariana, 97–98, 204–5, 209; Martínez de Mazas, 305, 311–12; Medina
Conde, 304–5; modern, 311; Pennotto,
180, 225–26, 273, 279; Pérez, 5, 157–59;
Rader, 91, 272–73, 278–79; Rioja, 240,
247, 261, 267, 275–76, 278–79; Salazar
de Mendoza, 247, 322n36, 323n54;
Serna, 240, 267; Suárez, 287. *See also*
Mayans i Siscar, Gregorio

Higuera, chronicles of—print editions of:
about, 4, 202–3, 212, 215; emendation of,
203–4, 213–15, 217–26, 219, 221, 223, 224,
237, 238, 261–62, 263, 264, 270–74, 276–
81, 282, 283–85; marginalia and active
reading of, 218, 263, 278–81, 282, 283–85,
355n72; nineteenth-century *Patrologia
latina* editions of, 310, 363–64; paratext
and learned commentary as necessary
for, 24, 103–5, 107, 137–38, 213, 217–26,
218, 219, 220, 221, 223, 264, 269, 277–79,
284; preparation of texts by would-be
courtiers and, 261, 264, 267; surviving
copies of, 215. *See also* Bivar, Francisco;
Calderón, Juan de; Caro, Rodrigo;
Ramírez de Prado, Lorenzo; Tamayo
de Vargas, Tomás

Higuera, manuscripts of: overview of, 65–68, 98, 326n8, 326n9, 328n66, 339n61, 344n90, 344n100; *Discurso sobre si San Tirso mártir fue español y natural de Toledo*, 322n35; *Ecclesiastical History of Spain*, 53, 66, 76, 82–83, 96–97, 156, 160, 313, 324n77, 328n66, 340n3; *Epistola Jesu de die dominica*, 136–39; failed attempts to print, 63–68, 72–74, 96–97, 202–3; *Historia del Colegio de Plasencia de la Compania de Jesus*, 66, 97, 320n10; *Itinerary of Antoninus Pius* and, 42, 73–74, 96–97, 105, 140, 154–55; *Treatise of the Lineage of the Higueras and also of the Last Names Peña, Romano, and others, and also an Account of the Mozarabs of Toledo*, 57–60, 66, 182, 320n10, 325n99. See also *Ecclesiastical History of Toledo [Toledo]* (Higuera)

historia sacra (sacred history): Andalusian authors of, 242–43, 244, 245–46, 248, 256, 257; Andalusian learned networks and, 247; audience for, 254–55; Baronio and, 243; genre defined, 18, 243–46; Higuera's chronicles and, 234–36, 245–46, 255, 258, 311; "local Baronios" and, 243; local memory and, 254–56, 257; local religion and, 234–37, 238, 239–42

historical method: eighteenth-century evolution of vis-à-vis Higuera's chronicles, 288, 290–307. See also antiquarianism; forgeries; *historia sacra*; philological method

Huerta y Vega, Francisco Javier Manuel de la, 301–2

Huesca, 258

humanism, Renaissance, 8, 13–14, 17–18, 39–40, 45, 51, 76, 84, 108–11, 114, 121, 129, 148, 150–53, 179, 203, 208, 236, 272. *See also individual scholars by name*

Hurtado, Geronymo (friar), 186

Hydatius of Galicia, 108, 115–17, 146, 149, 297

Ibáñez de Segovia y Peralta, Gaspar, Marquis of Mondéjar, 287–88, 290–95, 302, 310

Ignatius of Antioch, 23, 113, 224

Ildefonso of Toledo (saint), 36, 72, 148, 188–89, 248

Illán, Esteban, 71–72, 188

Immaculate Conception, 110–11, 128, 203, 212–13, 227–28, 267, 269, 304

Inchofer, Melchior (Jesuit), 204, 268–69, 272–74, 353n19

Innocent XI (pope), 128, 133

Inquisition: Roman, 96, 128, 169, 269, 274; Spanish, 50, 52, 59–60, 86–88, 92, 128, 270, 286, 329n82, 353n28

inscriptions. See epigraphic evidence

Iriarte y Oropesa, Tomás de, 286–87

Isidore of Beja, 67

Isidore of Madrid, 255

Isidore of Seville, 24, 44, 53, 102, 104, 108, 115–18, 149, 158–59, 192, 205, 290

Itinerary of Antoninus Pius: Blancas and, 154–55; Caro and, 237; Higuera's chronicles and, 141, 184; Higuera's manuscript of, 42, 66, 73–74, 96–97, 105, 140, 154–55; Morales and, 152

Jaén, xv, 22, 59, 70, 140–42, 148, 160, 227, 235, 247–48, 254–55, 256–57, 258, 305. *See also* Arjona; Baeza; Marmolejo; Moscoso y Sandoval, Baltasar; Rus Puerta, Francisco de; Ximena Jurado, Martín de

James the Greater (Santiago). *See* Santiago

Jerome: apocryphal material and, 201; Dexter chronicle and, 1, 24, 101–2, 104, 112, 145, 157, 206, 213, 224, 276, 293; Erasmus's edition of, 13, 222; Hieronymites and, 290; medieval chronicle tradition and, 107–10, 115–19, 145, 224

Jesuit order: censorship and, 91–92; conversos and, 87, 329n82; Dominicans and, 53, 86, 96; expulsion from Spain and, 309–10; France and, 89–90;

Jesuit order (continued)
  Higuera's *Toledo* and, 63–64, 72–73, 88, 96–97; informal correction of heretical propositions and, 86–87, 93; politics and, 88–92; Spanish Inquisition and, 64, 85–88, 92; Spanish monarchy and, 64, 86; Tirso controversy and, 30–31, 52–54, 88. See also *memorialistas*; *individual Jesuits by name*
Jews and conversos: as ancestors of Toledo's Mozarabs, 56, 133–34; blood libel and, 136, 336n41; as early Christians, 107, 111, 135–36; *Epistola Jesu de die dominica* and, 137–38; as first settlers of Toledo, 75, 133–34, 335n29; Higuera and, 55–61, 133–36, 329n82, 335n26, 336n30, 336n41; Jesuit order and, 87, 329n82; Paul's Epistle and, 132, 134–35; Spanish vs. Jerusalem, 56, 107, 135. See also La Guardia, child-martyr of; Higuera, chronicles of; *limpieza de sangre* (purity of blood) statutes
João V (king), 302
John of Biclarum, 108, 115–16, 149–50, 297
Julián Pérez chronicle: authentic medieval chronicles and, 99–101, 106–7; Benedictine order in, 283; El Cid and, 105; errors in, 281, 283; imputed author of, 3, 105, 280–81, 331n26; Jews and conversos and, 56, 75, 107, 134–36; manuscripts of, 148; Mozarabs and, 56, 105, 182; origin story and "rediscovery" of, 2, 5–6, 100–101, 107, 148; print edition of, 107, 175, 262, 263, 282; Reconquest and, 105–6. See also Higuera, chronicles of; Ramírez de Prado, Lorenzo
Justus (martyr), 142, 248–49

Kagan, Richard, 254

Lapide, Cornelio a (Jesuit), 204, 279–80
Laureano (saint), 239
lead books (*plomos*) of Granada c. 1595: overview and discovery of, 5, 10, 14–15, 127; Arabic and, 14, 127–28, 134; Cervantes and, 14–15; contrasted with Higuera's chronicles, 133, 259, 304–5; critics and opponents of, 97, 128–31, 133, 269–70, 304–5; dissemination of, 133; genre of, 133; as heretical, 128, 133; Higuera's interest in, 129–33; *historia sacra* and, 243, 255; Immaculate Conception and, 128, 269, 304; influence of, 259; Inquisition and, 128; intertwined with history of Higuera's chronicles, 5, 304–5; moriscos and, 10, 14–15, 127; Philip IV and, 128, 270, 353n28; proponents and patrons of, 30, 127–33, 210, 264, 269–70, 272, 298–99, 304–5; relics found with, 127, 272, 298–99; Roman condemnation of, 128, 133, 269–70, 353n28; "Salomonic" script and, 127–29, 133; Santiago and, 127–28, 130, 305; Seven Apostles and, 127–28, 255
lead books (*plomos*) of Granada of 1754, 303–5
Leocadia (saint), 34, 41, 44–45, 51, 104, 121, 131
León de Zamora, Pablo, 187–88
Lerma, 255
Lerma, Duke of (Francisco Gómez Sandoval y Rojas), 95, 160, 178, 247–48, 267
Leto (saint), 184, 255
Lezuza, 184, 255
Liberata (saint), 113–14, 173–76, 178, 180–81, 279–80, 341n37
Liberato chronicle, 290, 356n16
Licinianus (bishop), 137–38
Ligorio, Pirro, 13
limpieza de sangre (purity of blood) statutes, 55, 57, 60–61, 132, 136, 138, 325n103, 325n107, 329n82
liturgical sources: Baronio and, 18, 166, 171, 194; Bivar and, 224; Higuera's composition of new versions of, 66; Higuera's texts as resembling, 123, 124, 203, 208; Higuera's use of, 31, 36, 62, 67, 112–13,

120–25, 172–74, 180, 184; Morales and, 106, 152, 192; Mozarabic, 44–45, 48, 50, 106, 192; Roman vs. historical, 166–67. See also *Casus exceptus*; hagiography; Mozarabic rite; *officium proprium*; *Pastoralis officii*; Roman Breviary; Roman Martyrology

liturgy, Mozarabic. *See* Mozarabic rite

Liutprand (*also* Liudprand) of Cremona, 103, 264. *See also* Luitprand chronicle

Llorente y García, Bartolomé (El Pilar canon), 179–80

Loaysa Girón, García, 46, 53–55, 131, 149

local and regional scholars. See *historia sacra*

local history. See *historia sacra*

local religion: Ajofrín, 195–96; Higuera's chronicles and, 5, 8–9, 139–42, 165, 171–72, 184, 196–97, 258; Higuera's defense of, 171–76, 196–97; Higuera's influence on, 255–59, 352n72; Higuera's survey of, 185–86. See also *historia sacra*; saints and local saints' cults

local sacred history (*historia sacra*). *See historia sacra*

local saints' cults. *See* local religion; saints and local saints' cults; *specific saints*

Lope de Vega (Lope Félix de Vega Carpio), 45, 85, 179, 190

López de Madera, Gregorio (jurist), 280

Lucas de Tuy, 106, 118–19, 145

Luisa de la Ascensión (La Monja de Carrión), 275, 354n46

Luitprand chronicle: Anglina (saint) in, 164; authentic sources published with, 137–38, 156, 336n46; citations of, 176–77, 183, 310; Higuera's commentary in, 104; imputed author of, 103, 105; Jews and conversos in, 107, 137–38; medieval references to, 24, 103; Mozarabs and, 103–6; origin story and "rediscovery" of, 2, 5–6, 25, 100–101, 103–5, 107; Percellius (saint) in, 140; print editions of, 215, 264, 265, 266; tale of buried Benedictine convent in, 195–96; Tamayo de Vargas's critique of, 233; Tirso controversy and, 104; Victoria (saint) in, 139–40, 183–84. See also Higuera, chronicles of; Ramírez de Prado, Lorenzo; Tamayo de Vargas, Tomás

Luna, Miguel de, 14–15, 83, 182

Mabillon, Jean de, 294–95

Madrid, *xv*; Arjona relics at, 275; Higuera in Jesuit house of, 38, 74; Higuera's chronicles and local religion of, 255, 258, 260–61, 350n25, 352n66; Jesuit order's tensions with, 64, 86–87; learned community of, 290–92; politics of Higuera's texts at royal court of, 260–68, 275; readers of Higuera's chronicles at royal court of, 279–80. See also *specific rulers, courtiers, chroniclers, and institutions*

Maldonado, Alonso de (Dominican), 211–12

Le Mans forgeries, 12

Mantuano, Pedro de, 70, 98

Marcén, Antonio, 86–87

marginalia. *See also* Higuera, chronicles of

Maria de Campi, Pietro, 171, 243

Mariana, Juan de: Annian forgeries and, 97–98, 204–5; critique of Higuera's chronicles by, 97–98, 204–5, 209; *Discourse of the Ailments of the Society* and, 86; Higuera contrasted with, 65, 97–98; *Historiae de rebus Hispaniae* (*General History of Spain*), 65, 69–70, 80, 89, 98, 327n20; historical and critical method and, 65, 70, 80, 97–98, 106, 149, 177; lead books and, 97, 128, 130; regicide and, 89–90; Santiago and, 70, 209, 298; Tirso controversy and, 54, 65; *transcribo plus quam credo* and, 97–98, 138; use of Higuera's chronicles by, 98; *vox populi* and, 189

Marianus (martyr), 142, 248–49

Mariner, Vicente, 248, 264

Marmolejo, *xv*, 230–32

Márquez, Joan (Augustinian Hermit), 225–56
Martí, Manuel, 290
Martial, 66, 113, 152, 272, 293
Martínez de Mazas, José, 305, 311–12
martyrologies, historical. *See* hagiography; liturgical sources; Mozarabic rite
Martyrology, Roman. *See* Roman Martyrology
Maryks, Robert, 87, 329n82
Mascareñas, Jerónimo (bishop), 292, 326n11
Maximianus (saint). *See* Bonosus and Maximianus
Maximus chronicle (Maximus, Marcus): authentic sources of, 117–18; content of, 103; imputed author of, 12, 102, 213, 283; Isidore of Seville's reference to, 102; origin story and "rediscovery" of, 2, 5–6, 25, 100–104, 107, 147; print editions of, 180, 213, 214, 215, 216, 218, 219, 220, 221, 222, 223, 224, 268; textual alibis for, 102. *See also* Bivar, Francisco; Calderón, Juan de; Caro, Rodrigo; Dexter chronicle; Higuera, chronicles of
Maximus of Zaragoza (bishop), 102, 283. *See also* Maximus chronicle
Mayans i Siscar, Gregorio, 299–303, 305, 358n66
Medina Conde, Cristóbal de (canon), 304–5
memorialistas, 86–88, 92–97, 329n82. *See also* Higuera (Román de la Higuera, Jerónimo); Jesuit order
Mendoza, Fernando de, 160
Menology, Greek, 48, 50–51, 236–37
Mérida, 66, 121, 255
Merio chronicle, 290, 356n16. *See also* chronicles, false, post-Higuera
Messina. *See* Inchofer, Melchior; Virgin Mary: letter to Messina of
Metaphrastes, Simeon, 48, 50–51
Migne, Jacques-Paul, 310, 363–64
Molanus, Johannes, 174

Momigliano, Arnaldo, 17–18
monarchy, Bourbon. *See* Philip V
monarchy, Hapsburg. *See* Madrid; *individual rulers*
Monegro, Juan Bautista (*maestro de obras*), 34, 36, 43, 53
Morales, Ambrosio de: antiquarianism and, 150–53; *Antiquities of*, 20, 150–55, 301; on Dionysius the Areopagite, 119–20; epigraphic evidence and, 152–53, 220; *General Chronicle*, 19–20, 151; historical method and aims of and, 19–20, 109, 122, 191–92, 207, 301, 307; influence of, 20, 120, 122, 170–71, 181, 220, 242–43, 245; Santiago and, 122; Seven Apostles and, 14; *vox populi* and, 189, 191–93
Moreno Vilches, Antonio, 247, 264, 267, 279
moriscos, 10, 14–15, 127. *See also* Casas, Ignacio de las; Castillo, Alonso de; lead books (*plomos*) of Granada; Luna, Miguel de
Morlanes y Malo, Bartolomé (El Pilar canon), 179, 202
Morovelli de Puebla, Francisco (Seville canon), 209, 267, 281, 283
Moscoso y Ossorio, Lope de, Count of Altamira, 275
Moscoso y Sandoval, Baltasar (cardinal and bishop of Jaén): addition of new saints to Jaén liturgical calendar and, 239–40, 249, 251–52; as archbishop of Toledo, 268; Arjona saints and, 141–42, 227–33, 239–40, 251–52, 274–75, 313, 348n65, 360n16; Baeza saints and, 248–49; biographical information about, 247–48, 275; Bivar and, 227–31; Eufrasio cult and, 249; Higuera's chronicles and, 268, 273–74, 288–89; manuscripts and letters of, 310; reform of local religion and, 247–49; religious and scholarly patronage of, 247–48, 268, 270, 288–89; Rome and, 239–40, 268–69, 273–74

Moscoso y Sandoval, Melchor de (bishop), 227
Mozarabic rite: defined, 44–45; Elipandus and, 177; as heretical, 177; Isidore as author of, 192; Morales and, 192; Prudentius and, 121; significance in Toledo of, 44–45; texts of, 329n106; Tirso and, 44–45, 48, 50; trial by fire of, 106. *See also* hagiography; liturgical sources
Mozarabs: defined, 56–57, 324n82; heresy and, 177; Higuera's ancestors and, 55, 58, 181–82; Higuera's chronicles and, 25, 56, 103–5, 177–78; Islamic Toledo and, 37–38, 133, 178; Jews and, 56, 58, 133–34; limpieza and, 56–57, 177; Old Christians and, 56–57; sixteenth-century Toledo and, 324n84; Visigoths and, 57. *See also under* Higuera, chronicles of; Julián Pérez chronicle; Mozarabic rite; Tirso controversy
Múñoz y Romero, Tomás, 258
Murillo, Diego (Franciscan), 206–7, 209

Nanni, Giovanni (Annius da Viterbo). *See* Annius da Viterbo
Narbona, Alonso de, 47, 54
nationalism: ecclesiastical history of Spain and, 170, 303, 305; Spanish historical scholarship and, 286, 299–302, 305
Niebla, 255
Nieremberg, Juan Eusebio (Jesuit), 264, 279
numismatic evidence: antiquarian method and, 152–54, 235, 242, 250, 291; forgeries and, 10, 13; Higuera and authentic specimens of, 313; *historia sacra* and, 235, 242, 252, 253, 277–78

Obdulia (martyr; *also known as* Oddilia *or* Ottilia), 173, 175
Ocampo, Florián de, 19, 40–41, 81, 97, 151, 155
Ocaña. *See under* Higuera (Román de la Higuera, Jerónimo)

officium proprium (*officia propria*, pl.), 130, 167, 172–75, 239–40, 247, 258, 292
Olivares, Count-Duke of (Gaspar de Guzmán), 217, 260–62, 263, 264, 266, 267, 275–76, 280, 288
Olivenza, Bartolomé Andrés de (Jesuit), 94, 160
Origen of Alexandria, 51, 83
Orosius, Paulus, 24, 101, 108, 113, 116
Osuna, 23, 139, 239–41, 243, 247, 278

Padilla, Lorenzo de (chronicler), 102
Palencia, 202, 258, 290, 344n90
Paleologus, Pedro, 71
Palermo, 268
Palma del Río, Count of, 275
Palomares, Cristóbal, 5, 32, 47, 51–52, 54, 159
Pancorbo, Jerónimo (Discalced Carmelite), 232, 248, 277–78
papacy. *See* Congregation of Rites, Roman; Congregation of the Index of Prohibited Books, Roman; Gregory IX; Inquisition: Roman; Rota, Sacra; Urban VIII
Papebroeck, Daniel, 290–95, 346n7, 357n41. *See also* Bollandists
paratext: as argument for texts' authenticity, 24, 213, 284; Bivar and, 217, 222, 269, 284; Calderón and, 213, 277; Caro and, 217, 220, 221; defined, 213; Higuera and, 104–5, 107. *See also* Higuera, chronicles of—print editions of
Pascual, Pedro (martyr), 248, 251–52, 254
Pastoralis officii, 172, 197, 240, 341n33
Paul (apostle), 13, 82, 111–12, 119–20, 132, 134–35, 242, 311, 333n86
Paula de Ávila (saint), 174. *See also* Barbata (saint)
Pecha, Hernando de (Jesuit), 3
"Pedro, Julián," 3, 280–81, 331n26. *See also* Julián Pérez chronicle
Pelayo (bishop), 12
Pellicer de Osau, José, 276, 289, 291, 302

Pennotto, Gabriele (Augustinian Canon), 180, 225–26, 273, 279
Percellius (saint), 140
Pérez, Juan Bautista: friendship with Higuera and, 157, 159; Higuera's chronicles and, 5, 157–59, 205–6, 346n14; lead books and, 128–29, 131; Segorbe Codex and, 149–50, 158–59, 338n12, 338n17; Tirso controversy and, 51, 53. *See also* philological method
Pérez, Julián. *See* Julián Pérez chronicle
Peter (apostle), 36, 82, 112–13, 135, 195, 243
Petri, Suffridus, 16
Philip II (king), 34, 41, 44, 50, 86, 104, 117, 151, 185–86. *See also* Tirso controversy
Philip III (king), 82, 86, 160, 168, 178. *See also* Lerma, Duke of
Philip IV (king), 128, 261, 270, 280, 295. *See also* Olivares, Count-Duke of
Philip V (king), 299–303. *See also* Royal Academy of History (Spanish)
philological method, 114–15, 117–18, 149–50, 203–4, 213–16, 220–22; Higuera and, 105, 148–50, 157–58. *See also* Pérez, Juan Bautista
Pico della Mirandola, Giovanni, 51
El Pilar (Santa María del Pilar church), 6–7, 110, 147, 179–80, 203, 206–7, 209–13, 214, 242, 254, 274, 283, 289, 343n71
Pilate, Pontius, 113, 119
Pineda, Juan de (Franciscan), 248, 350n38
Pineda, Juan de (Jesuit), 81, 350n38
pious affection, hermeneutic of, 22, 51, 131, 139, 193–95, 233, 285–88, 271–72, 294–95, 303–4, 307, 312–14; Baronio and, 195
Pisa, Francisco de: *Description of . . . Toledo* and, 71, 75–80; historical and critical method and, 75–76, 106; on "Moorish streets," 43; on Mozarabs, 56
Plasencia, xv; Higuera in Jesuit house of, 38, 74, 93–97, 321n12; Higuera's chronicles and, 202; Higuera's manuscript history of, 66, 97, 360; Higuera's papers and, 185, 344n90; manuscript martyrology from, 183–84. *See also* Arce y Reinoso, Diego de; González de Acevedo, Pedro
plomos. *See* Castro y Quiñones, Pedro de; lead books (plomos) of Granada
Porreño, Baltasar, 65–66
Porres, Francisco de (Jesuit), 53–54, 68–69, 72, 87–88, 90
Portocarrero, Francisco (Jesuit), 88, 140, 148, 217, 330n126, 337n52
Portugal: Higuera's chronicles and, 119, 142, 302. *See also* Agostinho de Jesus; Álvares de Lousada Machado, Gaspar; Braga; João V; Royal Academy of History (Portuguese)
Potenciana (saint), 249, 251–52, 351n47–48
Prester John, 137
Prosper of Aquitaine, 108, 115–17, 121, 145–46, 297, 333n76
Prudentius, Aurelius Clemens, 121–25, 152, 155, 192
Ptolemy, Claudius, 152, 183–84
purity of blood statutes. *See limpieza de sangre* (purity of blood) statutes

Quevedo, Francisco Gómez de, 85, 179
Quintanadueñas, Antonio de (Jesuit), 236, 241, 243, 245, 247–48, 254–55, 278, 289
Quiroga y Vela, Gaspar de (archbishop), 41, 149
Quiteria (saint), 186–88, 281

Rader, Matthäus (Jesuit), 91, 272–73, 278–79
Ramírez de Prado, Lorenzo (courtier), 175, 215, 261–62, 263, 264, 265, 266, 267–68, 280–81, 282, 283, 289, 297. *See also* Julián Pérez chronicle; Maximus chronicle; Olivares, Count-Duke of
Rates, Pedro de (saint), 181
reading, active. *See* apocryphal texts and traditions; pious affection, hermeneutic of

reading, history of. *See under* Higuera, chronicles of
Regimund (bishop of Iliberis), 104, 331n21
Relaciones geográficas, 185–86
relics: authentication of, 130, 274, 311; Counter-Reformation veneration of, 44, 110, 128, 177; of Crispinus, 246; of Eufrasio, 248; of Hierotheo, 272, 292; Higuera's research and, 181, 185–86; "innumerable" of Zaragoza, 123; of Laureano, 239; of Nunilo and Alodia, 155; *Pastoralis officii* and, 172, 240; from Roman catacombs, 140; of Sacromonte, 127–31, 272, 298–99; of Santiago, 209; sixteenth-century discoveries and recoveries of, 8, 33, 41, 104, 117, 170, 229. *See also* Anglina (martyr); Arjona; Baeza; Leocadia (saint); Liberata (saint); Obdulia (martyr); Potenciana (saint); Vitalis (saint); *other individual saints*
Republic of Letters, 21–22, 159, 165, 185, 236, 339n51. *See also* Higuera (Román de la Higuera, Jerónimo); *historia sacra*
Ribadeneira, Pedro de (Jesuit), 54, 86–87, 89–90, 97, 120–21
Ricla, Count of, 275
Rihuerga, Juan de, 102
Río, Martín del (Jesuit), 345n122
Rioja, Francisco de (courtier), 240, 247, 261, 267, 275–76, 278–79
Roa, Martín de (Jesuit), 90, 207, 236, 245–47, 251, 254, 284–85, 311
Robles, Eugenio (rhetorician), 329n106
Robles, Juan (Seville author), 247
Robles Corvalán, Juan, 181–82
Rojas, Pedro de, Count of Mora, 226, 280, 289
Rojas y Sandoval, Bernardo (archbishop), 184
Román, Jerónimo (Augustinian), vs. Higuera (Jesuit), 326n8
Roman Breviary, 152, 166–68, 170–72, 240, 251
Román de la Higuera, Jerónimo (Higuera).

See Higuera (Román de la Higuera, Jerónimo); Higuera, chronicles of; Higuera, manuscripts of
Roman Martyrology, 111, 121–22, 139–41, 163, 167, 170–73, 183–84, 194, 227, 249–51, 289
Rome. *See* Acquaviva, Claudio; Jesuit order; Urban VIII; *individual papal congregations*
Rosweyde, Heribert, 165, 204, 215, 345n122. *See also* Bollandists
Rota, Sacra (papal tribunal), 179–80, 274, 343n71
Rowe, Erin, 242
Royal Academy of History (Portuguese), 302
Royal Academy of History (Spanish), 153, 299–303, 305, 309–10
royal court in Madrid. *See* Madrid; *specific rulers*
Rubens, Peter Paul, 264, 266
Rufinianus (martyr), 142, 236–37, 249
Rufinus (ecclesiastical historian), 116
Rufinus (martyr), 142, 236–37, 249
Ruinart, Theodore, 311
Rus Puerta, Francisco de, 242–43, 244, 245, 248, 251–52, 254–55, 256–57, 260, 305. *See also* Arjona; Baeza; Jaén; Moscoso y Sandoval, Baltasar

sacred history. *See historia sacra*; local religion
Sacromonte (Granada), 66, 127–28, 130, 139, 269–70, 291, 298, 358n66. *See also* Castro y Quiñones, Pedro de; lead books (*plomos*) of Granada; Vázquez Siruela, Martín
Sáenz de Aguirre, José (cardinal), 290
saints. *See* hagiography; liturgical sources; Roman Breviary; Roman Martyrology; saints and local saints' cults; *specific saints*
saints and local saints' cults. *See* Ajofrín; Alcalá de Henares; Arjona; Baeza; Barce-

saints and local saints' cults (continued)
Iona; Braga; Caravaca; Carmona; Cordoba; Ecija; Galicia; Gibraltar; Granada; Guadalajara; Guadix; La Guardia; hagiography; *historia sacra*; Huesca; Jaén; Lerma; Lezuza; liturgical sources; Madrid; Marmolejo; Mérida; Messina; Niebla; *officium proprium*; Osuna; Palencia; Palermo; *Pastoralis officii*; Segovia; Seville; Sigüenza; Tarifa; Tobarra; Tocina; Toledo; Tuy; Utrera; Valencia; Villanueva de Andújar; Xérez de la Frontera; Yepes; Zaragoza

Sainz de Baranda, Pedro, 258

Salazar, Juan (cardinal), 146

Salazar de Mendoza, Pedro: Annian forgeries and, 58; El Greco and, 48; Higuera's chronicles and, 58, 146–47, 217, 247; as Higuera's pupil, 85; Higuera's *Toledo* and, 79; limpieza and, 55, 58, 61–62; Tirso controversy and, 48–50, 52, 62, 322n36, 323n54; University of Osuna and, 247

Salucio, Agustín, 57

San Cecilio, Pedro de (Mercedarian), 164

Sánchez Alonso, Benito, 306

Sandoval, Prudencio (chronicler), 146–47, 160, 175, 178, 180, 201–2

San Pablo, Hermenegildo de (Hieronymite), 290

Santa María, Francisco de (Discalced Carmelite), 168–71, 217, 228–31, 295, 341n21, 348n65

Santiago (James the Greater): Aulo Halo and, 288–89; Baronio and, 130, 168, 171, 205; copatronage debate regarding, 203, 209; defense of, 66, 70, 110, 130, 160, 168, 205, 209, 305; evangelization of Spain by, 1, 14, 110–11, 117–18, 127, 171, 209; Higuera's chronicles and, 1, 6–7, 110–11, 117–18, 147, 151, 157, 171, 179, 181, 203, 205, 209; humanists and legend of, 14, 122, 151, 171; lead books and, 127–28, 130, 305; Mariana and, 205; El Pilar and, 6–7, 179, 203, 209–11; post-Higuera false chronicles and, 304; relics of, 110–11, 209; Seven Apostles and, 14, 127, 151, 171, 209; Spanish Jews and, 56, 111

Sarmiento, Martín de, 302

Sarmiento, Pedro, 136

Sarmiento de Acuña, Diego, Count of Gondomar, 229

Scaglia, Desiderio, Cardinal of Cremona, 269–70

Scaliger, Joseph Justus, 120, 150, 167

Schott, André (Jesuit), 41, 149–50, 321n27

Segorbe Codex, 149–50, 158, 338n12. See also Pérez, Juan Bautista

Segovia, xv, 81, 139, 226–27, 255, 258, 291–92

Seneca the Younger, 13, 111–12, 272

La Seo (Zaragoza cathedral), 6–7, 179–80, 209–11, 274, 289, 343n71. See also El Pilar

Serna, Alonso de la (canon), 239–42, 247, 267, 349n10

Seven Apostles (*los siete varones apostólicos*), 14, 111, 127–28, 149, 151, 170–71, 209, 255

Severus (saint), 206, 303

Seville, xv; Higuera's chronicles and, 139, 202, 207, 234, 236–42, 238; learned community of, 247–48, 290; saints and local saints' cults of, 139, 234, 236–42, 291. See also Caro, Rodrigo; Castro y Quiñones, Pedro de; Osuna; Quintanadueñas, Antonio de; Utrera; Vázquez Siruela, Martín

Siculus, Lucius Marineus, 19, 171

Sigüenza, xv, 172–75, 181, 202, 255, 258, 311

Silo, King of Asturias. See Tirso controversy

La Sisla, Santa María de (monastery), 53, 148, 225

skepticism: dangers of, 205–10, 303; eighteenth-century historical scholarship and, 286–87, 293–94, 302, 305; pious affection and, 97–98, 211–12, 298–99

Society of Jesus. *See* Jesuit order; *individual Jesuits*
Soria, Juan de (Jesuit), 160, 170–71
Stephens, Walter, 13, 100
Straton (martyr), 142, 236–37, 249
Suárez, Pedro, 287
Suárez de Mendoza, Juan, 290

Tamayo de Vargas, Tomás, 251; *Ancient Novelties of Spain . . . and Defense*, 202, 216–17, 261–62, 278; Higuera's chronicles and, 202–3, 216–17, 233, 247; manuscripts of, 310; print edition of Luitprand, 215, 262, 264, 336n45; search for patronage by, 261–62, 264
Tamayo Salazar, Juan, 288–89, 298
Tarifa, 255
Teresa of Ávila (saint). *See* Santiago: copatronage debate regarding
Thesiphon (saint), 127, 351n44
Tirso (martyr): Mozarabic cult to, 322n33; Portuguese veneration of, 180–81
Tirso controversy: overview of, 29–31, 61–62; accusations of forgery during, 46, 51–52, 61–62; Castro and, 132; "C S" medal and, 34, 35, 37–38, 47, 49; debate about Higuera's chronicles and, 30; discovery of ruins and, 29–30, 33, 34, 48–49; hermeneutic of pious affection and, 50–51; Higuera's allies during, 31, 43–47, 49–51, 63, 178, 180–81, 322n36; Higuera's chronicles and, 104; Higuera's opponents during, 30, 45, 47–53, 58, 61–62, 322n36, 323n49, 323n54; historical chronology and, 49, 323n57; Jesuit order and, 52–55, 69, 88; Lope de Vega and, 45; Mozarabic hymnal as proof text in, 44, 48, 50; Mozarabs and, 29–30; religious and political implications of, 30–31, 43, 45–47, 57; renewed cult to Tirso and, 38, 45, 61; Silo of Asturias's letter and, 29–31, 32, 35, 36–37, 43–44, 46–54, 57, 104, 184, 324n77; Spanish Inquisition and, 50, 52; Toledo intellectual community and, 30, 36, 61–62; Toledo's urban renewal and, 30, 42–43. *See also* Cárcamo, Alonso de; Garibay y Zamalloa, Esteban de; Palomares, Cristóbal; Philip II; Salazar de Mendoza, Pedro; Villegas, Alonso de
Tobarra. *See* Victoria of Tobarra
Tocina, 255
Toledo, *xv*; cathedral manuscript collection of, 281, 291; Higuera in Jesuit house of, 38, 54–55, 68, 73–74; Higuera's chronicles and, 117–18, 254–55; University of, 38–39, 47, 50, 85. *See also Ecclesiastical History of Toledo [Toledo]* (Higuera); Higuera (Román de la Higuera, Jerónimo); Jews and conversos; Moscoso y Sandoval, Baltasar; Mozarabs; Quintanadueñas, Antonio de; Tirso controversy
topos of critical rejection, 82, 135, 287
Torralba, Thomas (Jesuit), 6, 147–48, 204
Tractemund. *See* Regimund
Trejo Paniagua, Gabriel (cardinal), 267, 353n16
Tribaldo, Luis de, 264
Trithemius, Johannes, 11–12, 101
Tubal, 11, 76–77, 79–80, 102, 134
Tuy, 178
Tuy, Lucas de (chronicler), 106, 118–19, 145

Urban VIII (pope), 251, 269, 274
Usuard, 167, 174, 192, 227–28
Utrera, 139, 235–37, 238, 240–41, 245, 255, 276

Valdés, Francisco (Jesuit), 52–54, 69, 71–72
Valencia, 258. *See also* Anglina (martyr)
Valencia, Pedro de, 128–29
Valla, Lorenzo, 17, 150, 167, 194, 208
Vasaeus, Johannes, 19, 171, 181
Vatican library, 224, 228–31
Vázquez, Dionisio (Jesuit), 87
Vázquez, Gabriel (Jesuit), 146–47, 176–77, 201, 342n52

Vázquez Siruela, Martín (canon), 248, 251, 290–91, 296–98, 310
Vergara, Juan de, 40–41, 81, 148, 327n43
Vicente (saint), 184, 255
Victor (martyr), 142, 248–49, 283
Victoria of Cordoba (saint), 121, 170
Victoria of Tobarra (saint), 139–40, 182–84, 337n50
Victor of Tunnuna, 108, 115–16, 149–50, 333n71
Villanueva, Jaime, 307–8, 338n12
Villanueva, Joaquín Lorenzo de, 307–8
Villanueva de Andújar, *xv*, 249, 351n58. *See also* Potenciana (saint)
Villegas, Alonso de, 50–51, 102, 120–21, 180–81, 322n36
Villegas, Bernardino de (Jesuit), 248
Virgin Mary: appearance in Jaén by, 248; appearance in Toledo by, 148, 350n40; lead books of Granada and, 127–28; letter to Ignatius of Antioch of, 23, 113, 224; letter to Messina of, 113, 224, 268–69; various images and miracles of, 175, 185, 187, 235, 237. *See also* Immaculate Conception; El Pilar
Vitalis (saint), 178–79
Vives, Juan Luis, 12, 81, 191, 300

Voragine, Jacobus de, 121, 190–91
vox populi, 21, 94, 188–93, 196, 254–55, 258, 314

Walabonso chronicle, 290, 356n16
Wilgefort (saint), 113–14, 173–76, 279–80, 341n37. *See also* Liberata (saint)
Woolf, Daniel R., 19, 247

Xérez de la Frontera, 255
Ximena Jurado, Martín de, 248–49, 250, 252, 253, 254, 256–57, 263, 280–81, 283, 289, 305, 313, 341n21
Ximénez Cisneros, Francisco (archbishop), 45
Ximénez de Rada, Rodrigo, 11, 106, 118, 145

Yepes, 140

Zaragoza, *xv*; Braulio and Heleca chronicles and, 103, 213; Higuera's chronicles and, 210, 213, 258; local history and, 6, 117, 154, 210–11. *See also* Maximus of Zaragoza; El Pilar; La Seo
Zúñiga, Balthasar, 217
Zurita, Jerónimo de, 22, 40, 154–55